I shot the President's verse:

selected literary journalism

Kevin Kiely

Author: Kevin Kiely PhD., University College
Dublin; MPhil., Trinity College (Dublin); W. J.
Fulbright Scholar in Poetry Washington (DC); Hon.
Fellow in Writing, University of Iowa.

www.KevinKiely.net *kevin kiely (poet) wiki*

With thanks and due acknowledgement to the Editors
for publishing my Reviews/Essays in *Hibernia, Irish
Examiner, The Democrat Arts Page, Irish Studies
Review, Honest Ulsterman, Fortnight, Books Ireland,
The London Magazine, MAKE IT NEW, The Irish
Book Review, Poetry Ireland Review, Irish Times,
The Irish Independent, Irish Arts Review, Inis, Irish
Literary Review, The Irish Literary Supplement,
Idaho Arts Quarterly, Humanities (DC), Village
Magazine, The Journal of the E. E. Cummings
Society, The Wallace Stevens Journal, The Robert
Frost Review*

books by the same author:

Quintesse (St Martin's Press)

Mere Mortals (Poolbeg)

A Horse Called El Dorado (O'Brien Press)

SOS Lusitania (O'Brien Press)

Francis Stuart: Artist and Outcast (Liffey Press/Areopagitica)

Breakfast with Sylvia (Lagan Press)

Plainchant for a Sundering (Lapwing Press)

The Welkinn Complex (Number One Son Publishing, Co., Florida)

UCD Belfield Metaphysical: A Retrospective (Lapwing Press)

UCD Belfield Metaphysical: New and Selected Poems (Areopagitica)

Harvard's Patron: Jack of all Poets (Areopagitica)

Seamus Heaney and the Great Poetry Hoax (Areopagitica)

Arts Council Immortals (Areopagitica)

Cromwell Milton Collins Carson (CLIII-CLXIV; CLXXXII-CXCVII):

from *Yrland Regained: Central Cantos* (Cyber Wit, India)

Endgames: Good Friday Agreement Cantos (CXCVIII-CCXXVII) & *Mrs Windsor's Hitmen Cantos* (CXIX-CXXXIII):

from *Yrland Regained: Central Cantos* (Cyber Wit, India)

Yrland Regained: Central Cantos I & II (Complete I-CCXL) (Areopagitica)

Contents

INTRO: THE CRITIC AS ARTIST 1

YOUTHFULNESS 22

WHY ARE THE CRITICS NOT WEEPING: president must be a poet, insists President Higgins 28

THE IRISH PRESIDENCY: EXPOSING THE FEEBLENESS OF OFFICE 33

FANNING THE FLAMES 38

SATIRE, GRIEF AND LESSER TIGHT-LIPPED EXPRESSIVENESS 43

THE ROAD TO LIMBERLOST 51

THE IT GANG 58

FAILING AGAIN TO FIND CARAVAGGIO: RHA 63

AOS DÁNA: where self-selection meets self-praise, in a faux Gaelic, Haugheyesque arts beano 68

ALONENESS 73

NOT ALL EXALTED 79

CONFUSION 84

KEEPING IT SIMPLE 89

A GREAT LYRICIST BUT A THREADBARE POET? 94

OF LOVE, DEATH AND THE MUSE 97

SONGS FROM THE STREET 102

AMBIGUOUS GREEN 108

TUPPENCE COLOURED 111

POETRY, VOICES AND ECHOES 116

READERS' FRIENDS 124

COME INTO THE PARLOUR 128

SURGEON'S DOZEN 134

HAUNTINGS 143

CRITICS AT WORK 149

BOTH ENDS 155

SOMETHING WORTH SAYING 162

DESERT OF DOWNTOWN 169

AND THEN NO MORE 175

GOTHIC POET 180

FORMAL, SLAM, INFORMAL 186

LONG LIFTED NOTES 191

EXPLAINING POETS 199

A HIGH-POWERED EXPLORATION OF THE 'IRISH' POUND 205

BEYOND THE POLITICS? 211

POSTHUMOUS CANTOS 217

LITERCHOOR IS MY BEAT 221

POETS' MANIFESTATIONS 231

MEANING? 238

HOW IT LOOKED 243

OF BLIGHT AND BLISS 248

OF CONCEPT AND IDEA 254

TIME IS THE CLASS 263

BEATNIKS, POST-ANGSTIANS, WITS AND NOSTALGICS 272

SIMPLE IS SACRED 279

FRANKENSTEINS OR DRACULAS? 287

MAKING THINGS HAPPEN 294

THAT SIMPLE? 299

FREE THINKER SUPERTHINKER 303

A SHAVIAN GUIDE FOR BEGINNERS 308

LUNCH WITH SHAW.. 313

BATTLER OF THE BOOKS.. 319

IMMORTAL EXILES 325

LITERARY CONSORTS 331

A COLD EYE 337

KING OF THE CATS 342

WILLIE DESPAIRS... 347

HORSEMAN GO SEEK 355

DOMESTICITY... 363

'I HEAR AMERICA SINGING' 368

DOWN THE MINE, UP AMONG THE STARS: [...] A CULT OF CELEBRITY 373

MEN OF LETTERS 378

TO THE GALLERY OR TO THE GODS 385

FLANELLESS FLANN 393

CAN A CATHOLIC BE A MODERNIST?.................................. 400

DISGRACING OURSELVES AGAIN 406

RUSTIC BARDS 413

HEANEY AND OTHER NOBLEMEN....................................... 419

THE HEAT OF THE DAY BEFORE 426

DONE YOUR THIRD HAIKU YET? 434

SHADOWLANDS.. 440

IN CAMERA 447

PRENTICE POETS.. 451

PUNISHMENT 457

IN DEEP 463

WRITER TO WRITER 470

PSYCHE'S SWINGS 475

BROADCASTING 481

SAME STORY 484

SLIPPERY SLOPES OF PARNASSUS 489

KENNELLY: FATHER AND DAUGHTER 495

OF MONEY, SEX AND POLITICS 499

CENTENNIAL CASH-IN 505

ALL ABOUT EVERYTHING 511

STREET ANGEL 519

PROSPECTOR'S LUCK 526

SHEMITE 533

A BIZARRE THEORY THAT MAPS AND LETTERS FROM THE 1830s–40s
MIGHT HAVE INSPIRED Joyce, Beckett, Synge and Mangan 539

UNCROWNED 545

CULTURAL CHATTELS 550

BENEFACTOR 556

FADÓ 559

JOURNEYS INTO A BALKAN HEART OF DARKNESS 563

BLACKLISTED 568

HUSH HUSH 574

DEVIL ÉIRE 580

THE LIFE AND CRIMES OF CJH 586

HISTORY HURTS 591

HOMO HERO 596

A VIVID, PACY ACCOUNT OF A BLOODY EPISODE IN IRISH HISTORY.... 605

AN UNEVEN WORK, MISSING OUT ITS SUBJECTS' COMPLEXITIES 610

REJECTED, DISOWNED AND BANNED.. 615

FROM MARCHING TO MILITARISM 620

TRUE NORTH... 625

GAEL FORCE... 631

RAGING AGAINST THE DYING NATION'S LIGHT 637

CRITIC AND CELT... 642

COSMOMICRON 648

THE LIES THAT LAST 655

TELLERS OF TALES 663

HOT PROPERTY 668

TINSELTOWN 674

SUFFICIENT UNTO THE DAY... 676

ONCE AGAIN
TO
PAMELA MARY BROWN

INTRO: THE CRITIC AS ARTIST

I am informed by 'enemies' that my 'getting into controversy' and 'trouble' over criticising certain writers and their published books, is not wholly desirable, especially with regard to President Michael D. Higgins and that minor verse-man, Seamus Heaney. 'Controversy' is a matter of scale, definition, perspective and may be wholly desirable. My literary criticism of Heaney and Higgins became mainstream news which I will outline, briefly. However, there were reactions regarding many of the reviews and essays in this selection, besides the outraged coat-tail coteries of H & H. All these reactions, resulted in criticism of the critic in question, namely myself which is wholly desirable. The label 'controversial critic' came my way long before writing 'Explaining Poets' about the Brearton/Gillis *Oxford Handbook* and commentary about establishment poetry cabals. Infallibility is not axiomatic with literary criticism.

I want to avoid vanity and bombast at the outset, and yet not sound disingenuous. To bring in 'controversy' (here) about my own poetry that equally resounded with varying reactions will seem like paralleling, self-promoting, self-exalting. Therefore I am only going to address some remarks concerning the reviews and essays presented in *I Shot the President's Verse: Selected Literary Journalism.*

I assert the autonomy of the reader, fundamentally as to knowing both like and dislike. It is that simple. My experience is that dogmatic critical mass is the preserve of collectives, not the individual who has critical conviction to put into print autonomous criticism. From my first published 'reviewing' work for *Hibernia* in the 1970s, I found 'reaction' thrust upon me. Autonomous criticism is not dogma but asserts a critical perspective of taste, hierarchy, scale and comparison.

1

A critic can be 'wrong' but the best criticism 'sticks', is taken forwards and other critics concur over time. This 'Introduction' does not need to enlarge into a manifesto. I have already embedded critical apparatus, comparisons and aesthetics in my essays/reviews.

These 'pieces of writing' classifiable in *genre* as book reviews, essays, literary criticism are located in the stylistics and artistic form of the essay. The Montaigne *essai*, the encyclopedia tradition of the French Revolutionary period, the Enlightenment Era, and eventually riding into Modernist and Post-Modernist approaches to Literary Criticism.

The poet writing criticism is the ideal critic of poetry. The innate sensibility surveying poetry and other varieties of critic so as to produce valid criticism. Poets as critics are the normal critical acumen reflected here; and if mentioning Montaigne sounds remote, well not to me. I demand from the Critic as Artist, a vast sweep of literature that echoes within such 'pieces' compacted and succinct, and adhering to necessary form within the content, and 'fixed' by the book or books one has to 'write up'. Vast knowledge of literature does not necessarily create the critic of merit. Ideally, the critic of sensibility reacts not only to a vast knowledge of literature but more importantly within the intense quality of comparative reactions.

I would never denigrate Montaigne or *his* work as 'pieces of writing', or indeed 'reviews'. What I explicitly mean is that the 'essay' as a form holds an expansive gamut of material artfully written. There never can be laws (except in totalitarian propaganda) as to the essay. Practicality is where Editors' demarcations of 'word count', dependent on print space is a binding part of the commission to write a review. I never write beyond commissioned word counts, unless invited as is often the case.

Editors are circumscribed by space, and were especially so, in the days before online-ezines. To write beyond the word count is unprofessional, to fall below word count the lesser infringement.

Writing for print publications is conceptually like fitting the word count into the pattern of a jigsaw, and means inches and centimetres of words added or subtracted to meet the Editor's requirements. Layout remains a geometric situation which I learnt principally while being a Literary Editor of *Books Ireland*.

Imagine a book of 400 pages that is reviewed in 1,500 hundred words. This cannot be a precis. There is the incumbency, the imperative of deliberating about the practice and performance of literature, the signposts of achievement, merit, standard, style, language, engagement, and a rocketing list of criteria. Many can be reckoned with by instinct in making a critique of any book that is worthy of serious report and review.

In my experience, many writers 'cannot' review books. They find it impossible to see beyond their vanity and ego. Such writers are irked by other writers, dismayed that the world hosts so many books. They are 'crushed' by the vast catalogues in libraries, defeated by the colossus of literature. Whereas in my world, I demand the infinity of literature.

My anxiety is that there may not be enough books, but there is, and this largesse is beyond description; therefore criticism 'supports' the universal in literature. Literature is not only miraculous in its execution and reception but survives miraculously, just as Ovid's lamentation poetry from Pontus, sent to Rome pleading for the end of his exile while maintaining some good humour under the circumstances. This is one image of the poet with the poems leaving the place of writing, and not least, Emily Dickinson's lament, despite her spiritual sublimity, accusing the world 'That never wrote to me'. Well, the world did get back to Emily. I am ranking criticism extensively coeval with literature and paratextual to poetry as written by a genuine poet.

I can achieve artistic pleasure writing criticism, my only hesitation is when writing about a book which ends up with 'a bad review'.

However, a bad review is good for literature, and any great 'bad review' is a triumph for criticism. I far prefer the enigma of exposing the experience of good literature which is one of the most difficult forms of critical writing. To criticise is the specialty demanded according to my connection with poetry and literature. To find fault is simple and instinctual; contrarily to writing about the greatness of literature (I repeat) which requires abilities often beyond the critic. It is not original to state that the greatest criticism of literature is to write the next best work.

Poetry and literature are perfectly secure and have been, long before Confucius, Li Po and David the Psalmist. The necessity of criticism is to exclude, so as to exalt and praise the real arts. This is not a chore but an excitement, a stimulus so as to continue the eternal discussion.

A dear friend insisted I might extrapolate about the 'Critic as Artist' where my intention was to simply acknowledge the list of Editors and Publications. Am I being self-effacing, adopting 'reverse psychology' as perhaps she might say, in referring to my selected writing as 'pieces'. However, she has given me my title for the Introduction. Besides, I am being self-effacing in using the word 'Journalism'. Anyone who delves into the process of criticism is confronted with creating an artefact, a separate entity based upon 'the book(s)'. I do not 'like' the phrase 'reviewing a book'. The exercise is exacting beyond 'reviewing' to the ethical and artistic limits.

It is never mechanical; each book brings forth the Critic's scales, the Anubian rite of assessment. Mayakovsky's poem to the Tax Inspector is acerbic. The tax man presumes that writing must be easy: 'some poems are barely a page in length and don't use many words.' The Russian poet, tartly replies 'Here, you try it?' Indeed. The work of a critic similarly rebuffs the cynic. A 'book review' is not cobbled together easily. It is, of course reductionism requiring conviction that the extraction performs crucible magic and presents the synthetical essence of the book, or books.

My claims are based in being a poet, writer, and author over many genres and one who writes critical essays and reviews. Also to 'combattre' because I recognise genuine literature is infiltrated by cliques who hate literature, poetry, and art. What is presented in my *Selected Literary Journalism* is far from a crusade or polemic of 'attack' which would give assailants more merit than they ever deserve from a literary artist.

These essays and reviews in word count, demanded energy and the writer's blast-forge to flame, burn, and spark them into life within the invigorating universe of the artistic self. Criticism of a book may well be at the end of the queue with regard to other writing, however, it is the same writer at work. Criticism is not 'dashed off' as mere exercise, or what were once known as holiday-postcards. Criticism involves solving the gamut of aesthetic issues to be resolved, whatever length the written statement occupies. Book criticism is not something 'hacked out' in a throwaway manner. Not by me, in forty years of this art form during a peculiar period in my country, despite some prevalence of academic hackery promoting itself as the real deal, the imprimatur, doxology, the orthodox one true church of critical values. Literature as propaganda and 'everyone' muzzled by it? I refuse to be muzzled in language and there is plenty of this from advertising, newspapers, media and some university campuses, and many 'poets'.

The peculiarity of the era enters my discussion within these pages. When I use the term critic and poet, I am referring to myself. The predominance of poetry criticism in this volume including praise, echoes what Celan called 'noems' trying to supplant poems during a definitive bronze age, if not leaden one for poetry. The real poetry was underground, yet to be discovered. However, writing criticism presented opportunities to create commentary. I always prefer the personal reader as critic than critics in academic circles engulfed in closed curricula imposing critical values, especially upon students. I am passionate that students must be given free access to all literature, not the myopia of some professors whose critical taste is lazy, unformed and narrow.

I was a reluctant critic in my twenties not willing to write criticism. In England at that time as a food factory worker in Quality Control, I read Gibran but soon realised Tagore was better. Reading Fitzgerald's translation of Omar Khayyám along the Cam, some students with their boats, picnic baskets and pukka voiced girlfriends, informed me that the Rubaiyat included the translator's improvisations of additional stanzas. Cambridge led me to find Rumi and Kabir. Does literature through criticism involve comparisons? Essentially it does but without wishing to evoke disharmonies from whence arrive the controversies of criticism.

John Mulcahy's *Hibernia* was a singular fortnightly newspaper. I wrote to Mulcahy, forgot to sign my name with the poetry and prose writing samples. He invited me to review, addressing the envelope: 'The Anonymous Writer-in-Residence' followed by the flat number, street and location. I got into 'trouble' reviewing for *Hibernia*. Mulcahy supported me but not his Literary Editor who showed me the door. Being 'fired' over a reviewing 'scandal' would recur. Meanwhile, my reluctance about writing criticism, equalised the experience, and I had my own work to build up.

In Galway, I was living in a caravan, and having been given Patrick Kavanagh's 'By Night Unstarred' which the poet seemed uninspired himself to complete, I muddled through reading, wavered, fumbled a review on my portable Remington typewriter, and abandoned the work. I could have done with the fee but I erased my pencil marks on the book and handed it back to the *Galway Advertiser*. Later, when writing for the literary editor of the *Donegal Democrat*, my motives were really only to push whatever poems of mine the newspaper would print. Same with the *Mayo News*. I wrote very little criticism then with little belief in the process.

The reluctance had nothing to do with my capabilities to write. The real crux was writing unbiased criticism, non-partisan content, honestly and truly, rather than the provincially primed majority of reviews, including the provincial *Irish Times* Books Pages 'steamrolled' by insider intrigues, writers interconnected within 'Napoleonic' hysteria for puffed up gloating reviews of their books by trading-post friends. The first and only time I published with Co-Op Books, my volume received every possible review (I boast not!) and favourable ones which pleased, but puzzled me.

I had knocked no doors, made no clandestine phone calls, sent no 'reminders', bought no lunches (not possible!). My book *Quintesse* mysteriously slid past the cliques, garnering 'rave' reviews 'everywhere', plus Radio and RTÉ's *Folio The World of Books*. Was I actually feared as 'the viscous loud-mouth born again Rimbaud' which Sydney Bernard Smith labelled me in his Bohemian novel *Flannery*?

I had witnessed book-promotion and 'the clicking of the cliques' like automatic weapons when the literary scene in 1980 was 'militarised'. The *Belfast Telegraph, Irish Independent, Irish Examiner, Irish News* and *Irish Times* placed their corporals on parade; definite controls became martial law. I kid you not. The *Times* with the lowest circulation of any broadsheet newspapers (the great unkept secret) held a frowsy 'unionist' bygone ethos which meant nothing to me. Unionism is tyrannous, elitist, the 'Afrikaans' element known as Anglo-Irish that hates Ireland's Independence.

All the major Anglo-Irish literati whose works are reflected in my criticism (here) accepted Ireland as one country, devoid of foreign rule. I abhor imperialism and do not conceal this abhorrence. I accept fully that British academics write about Irish poetry, literature, history and politics but such books are treated by me *cum grano salis*. In reviewing such books as an Irishman, I have had to correct their cultural bias just as they would correct mine in writing about England. I have written England into my political poetry of exposure in *Yrland Regained: Central Cantos*. I utterly disapprove the puffing of London's monarchs and British culture fused into Irish Media. London's pretence that Irish Nationalism ended in 1921, is propaganda sold to pro-British Irish, not to me. Cultural Nationalism, unfortunately will remain until London fully removes itself from Ireland.

As a poet about his business, I 'saw through' the reviewing structures because I was ubiquitous on the scene for company, converse, festivity, high jinks, revelry, as well as what Hemingway in describing Bohemianism, called 'a wasting of time in bad air'. There was some bad air, factions, arguments amidst the ravages and excesses of Bohemianism. However, for someone unwilling to concede to the consensus there were further prospects, as I discovered. Later on, the offer of a Literary Editorship came on the horizon which increased my insider's knowledge of the Satanic Mills of the Publishing Promotion Circus.

To backtrack a moment, from childhood I 'found' myself a poet and book reader. I've no idea which book showed me the immortal phrase of Horace 'poeta nascitur non fit'. I always read to completion, and cross-read which if slightly maniacal, is intoxicating. But obviously more than Horace's tag line, words were a universe for me, long before reading Criticism, Gematria, Epistemology, Linguistics and Aesthetics. Vowels and consonants—stars and comets of language are a cosmos parallel to the cosmos. No metaphor will explain language, it being a metaphor itself, mirroring off into infinity towards the Ain Soph of the *Kabbalah*. I could barely recognise this essential reality when I was very young but knew I was a poet, and went, or was rather sent to London to my aunt Esther, seasonally. Travel can intensify the reading of literature and writing.

Godmothers, that Irish phenomenon is more than a myth. She was my generous Godmother and subsequently, I was amidst a Cistercian Boarding School from thirteen to sixteen, thereafter a day school, and thence in and out of University, then a wanderer, independent scholar, divided as to ultimate direction other than poetry and literature. Within the few hundred books, collected by my father, I began, after his death when I was nine years old, to inhabit a critical sensibility. It might sound prodigious. It is true of my life.

I realised pretty quickly that poems by Browning, Tennyson, Hardy, and Yeats were vastly different to those by Kipling, Bridges, De La Mare and Service. A random choice from memory. My father's books were an eclectic library with English and Irish poetry anthologies. My aunt Eleanor across the Atlantic had sent him many *New Yorker* selections and other disparate books such as Francis Parkman's *The Oregon Trail*. Ogden Nash was flippant compared to Poe, Longfellow, Whitman, Jeffers, Sandburg and the other poets who led me into modern twentieth century American Literature. Critical taste develops early, intricately modified through intense conversancy with literature.

Psychologically, it became an imperative to read my father's books which 're-appear' at certain times, the same editions gleaming along a shelf in a second-hand book shop, library, or other locations, as if these volumes belong on the shelves of my childhood. In Boarding School at the age of thirteen, was I writing criticism? Engagement with literature and writing does not have an age limit. The 'school essays' that any of us wrote, were pedagogical despite the aura of Latin, French, English and Gaelic texts on desks, window-ledges and shelves. There was a library in every study hall, a monastery library of three tiers with spiral stairs, and a library in the Guest House. We were read to during meals (sometimes) and in Chapel. The Bible, Liturgy, Church History and selections from Theology. The Benedictine-Cistercian ethos was not strictly orthodox and doctrinaire. We were shown that Bernard of Clairvaux was not only a poet, scholar, and theologian but a wine maker. Irreverence and opinionated questioning were encouraged. We studied the mystical writings of the Saints, were told to 'put away childish things' so as to look into a polished glass, not a clouded mirror.

None of us were classicists but we were reading classic literature, critical discourse, and many of us emerged as serious readers. Class debates were pretentious, in retrospect. I was asked to address the theme 'Wordsworth and Coleridge: Romantic poets of excessive language and imagery'. At fourteen! There was a hauteur in class. Books were subjected to Q&A resembling academic discussion. Shakespeare's *Julius Caesar* is a political drama? Does Mark Twain idealise life on the Mississippi? Is *Paidín Mhaire* a great short story or a great yarn? In my first year, *The Tempest* was the Middle Year play, we were reading *Julius Caesar* and *The Merchant of Venice*. The Sixth Year students were indulgently spreading *Hamlet* like a hermetic doctrine along corridors and class rooms.

Sixth Years wanted to 'get their honours in English'. The 'play' was being 'declaimed' at one improvised class reading on a rainy afternoon when no sports or recreation were possible. I heard Hamlet and the Ghost recited, preceding the rudimentary student discussion. The 'Ghost' stood on a desk. 'Hamlet' walked into the classroom on queue, 'surprised' to finally meet the spirit of his father. I was rapt in attention. I found a battered library copy of the play, glancing at the glossary where necessary. I suddenly realised that whoever wasn't already Hamlet, would become Hamlet. Lines of poetry expanded like the horizon of freedom beyond the College that had a golden eagle on each gate pillar. Far off in perspective, the eagles seemed to be twins. It was my first symbol of Gemini. My luggage to and from Boarding School (once a year) included the book box with dictionaries and books for eight separate subjects. Literature was closest to freedom during term time.

Boarding School had to contain the student for the long school year, the long hours of classes, the long study hours, each week utilising copious sources, days and nights of ink (biro pens forbidden). The amount of 'writing up' was extensive. Study halls resembled scriptoria, laden book shelves, dull desks, the glaring ceiling lights. Our bent heads, vibrating hands over books and copies, writing for hours until yawns and sighs coincided with the day closing. Days moved slowly. There was no idleness. The inculcated benefits of discipline were reiterated and did not confer understanding upon me as to the regime. We dated our written work, beginning a new month, reminded of how lengthy the month that had just passed.

Silence more atmospheric than would ever prevail in any public or college campus library. There was the transcendental relief of literature and what I discovered the 'Heimat' that is literature. However, the institution also felt like penal sentencing to scholarship, knowledge, and the pursuit of learning. We sampled many poets, playwrights, novelists and essayists in English and Gaelic with French and Latin adding ballast. I had never before in scholarly manner interconnected texts to other books and texts. The French Poetry Anthology, edited by Yvonne Servais; Latin Anthologies, there was no shortage of cross referencing.

I'm suggesting that the 'scholarship' in Boarding School was formative in my becoming a writer able to sail through seas of literature. No other form of travel was available until the 'explosive' nights and days before the holidays. Then books and other items were turned into missiles, book-box 'bombs' flung over railings, through windows and the occasional revenge burnings outdoors of Hall and Knights *Algebra* or Lipschutz *Set Theory*.

Summer holiday re-unions from Boarding School were 'London months', and seaside sojourns in the South of England. My mother was recovering from breakdown and grief supported by my aunt. I transferred to a Day School for my two final years, thereafter became a university student. Literary converse became more developed in university, and the relationships between students were best as co-faculty. These 'couples' and friendly gangs were the ethos in the debating societies, the social scene and college clubs. Essays with references and bibliography became part of the norm.

Annie Murphy was 'doing pure English', her shoulder bag laden with some battered and pristine books. She discoursed through a fog of *Silk Cut* cigarettes with cups of coffee, reading out passages from Beckett's essay on 'Proust'. 'He's good,' she exclaimed, 'compared to George Steiner. Cornflakes. Roland Barthes. Ineffectual.'

Catriona Murphy (no relation) was 'so brilliant at French' she should have been a maverick professor, not a student. She was 'mainlining twentieth century French poets'. During our first conversation, we found common ideological ground about academe and 'books about Books'. She recommended 'real critics' including Lukács, Benjamin and Julia 'Mordant' Kristeva. By the age of 19, I had had a good ten years of 'devouring' books. Problematically for others in my circle, I learnt not to trust the majority, the minority, institutions large or small, political parties, logic, rationalism, superiority, inferiority, commonality, societies, groups, affiliates, curricula, consensus. In other words, the poet's obtuse individuality, capable of changing the emotional weather with white heat postulates and arguments, casting a shadow, unable to avoid contention, actually attempting harmony, but I had become highly problematical even for myself.

While University was, for a few seasons Utopia, I dropped out for dreaded England but quickly discovered far better countries: France and Spain. I could live, work, read and write. I shall never know whether University College Dublin ran out of patience over me, or I ran out of patience over UCD? Another bad marriage that eventually concluded in mediation and their inviting me in for a research PhD which I achieved, and produced the far safer text based on the PhD, *Harvard's Patron: Jack of all Poets* (2018).

&&&&&

Books Ireland owned by an Englishman, Jeremy Cecil Addis offered me the Literary Editor position in 1995 which I held for ten years. Before taking on the Editorship, I had written reviews for *Books Ireland* with its circulation, besides in shops, in Libraries, Embassies, and Cultural Outlets worldwide. As a 'monthly' publication, operations were suspended during the Summer, and the month of January. 2026 sees the publication of it, in some shape or form celebrating 50 years.

During my first week with *Books Ireland*, Addis confided in me as to the publishing scene referring to 'State Sponsored Books'. The Features Editor, Shirley Kelly knew the saga first hand and had to write copy with occasional hints that commented on the toxicity. The conspiracies and collusions, I would later outline in a book *Arts Council Immortals* (2020).

Long before I joined the staff on *Books Ireland* there existed a time of literary siege. Addis had many 'mad letters and communications' preserved in what he called the *Books Ireland* Archives. He wanted evidence about his dealings with the State Publishers: Lilliput, Gallery, Salmon, Dedalus and others. He had resentment against the 'State Publishers'. They constantly demanded that only recommended reviewers be given their books to review; especially demanding was Fallon of Gallery Press. All of them were demanding, as I discovered.

Addis had become an Irish citizen, a Catholic, made a home in Dublin for his wife and family. He was, in fact of Jewish origin. His grandfather was a Russian exile who'd found 'safety' in of all places, we used to laugh, Norfolk; and by coincidence I had worked there in my twenties for three years.

The *Irish Times* particularly fired its sallies of objections, mistrusted

Books Ireland for being independent and not joining in the consensus of the collectives. Their 'book people' disliked *Books Ireland* for the amount of reviews we published of Irish books and Books of Irish Interest, mainly from the American University Presses. Addis had pioneered wide circulation of *Books Ireland* in the US from which came a steady 'chute', as he called it, of books about Shaw, Wilde, Synge, O'Casey, Yeats, Gregory, George (AE) Russell, and Beckett but few if any about living contemporaries.

This was the dilemma of Ireland post 1970s—the intense anxiety of achievement and performance. The deafening non-echo of local talent amidst the 'State Sponsored Publishing Boom' principally engineered by the *Irish Times*, the Arts Council and *RTÉ*. Basically, an incestuous triplicate. The latter two institutions didn't care much about American academic approval, however the *Irish Times* 'writers' courted, cajoled and propositioned any academics, especially local academics like you know what, in any Dockland port on any given weekend. The 'nervous kittens' abhorred *Books Ireland* when Wake Forest Press, Syracuse among other US University Presses, and the Irish University Presses unleashed their list of critical studies for review. The 'avalanche of Lit Crit', Addis called these books.

The *Irish Times* fawned with hyperbole upon American professors when reviewing their 'select fawns'. *Books Ireland* reviewers had no vested interest; 'we' reviewed these tomes without fit or favour, and at least objectively. Many such reviews of American professors are here in my *Selected*. I found the America professors admirable folk, fully open to fair reviewing as the individual critic's response, but locals begged and campaigned for hyperbole-ridden-reviews. I never yielded to such corruption.

Out on the literary scene, at far too many launches and events, I heard comments that Addis was 'old fashioned in adherence to wanting principle, honesty, integrity and such bullshit'. Addis stolidly never edited reviewers' content, unless matter entered libel which was rare. His reviewers/critics occasionally veered into what he called 'clatter and chatter' outside the book's content. This superfluous embellishment was the main feature of newspaper critics who saw reviewing as involving the necessity of personal memoir/reminiscence, completely away from the book under review. Reviewers of this sort were favour seeking both on the scene and from other reviewers for the future. They dare not receive an adverse critical review. Paranoia and factions were obvious the minute one strolled into any event or book launch. To us in *Books Ireland* it was generally 'comedy' but to the nervous kittens it meant 'tragedy'. Their well laid plans were not fully secure.

When other directions as poet, critic, and author propelled me forwards, I quit the Literary Editorship. I travelled various paths, various adventures, and reverses, and always within the central focus of writing. On returning from the United States, I was contacted by Addis offering me to work once again with *Books Ireland*. He gave me President Michael D. Higgins *Selected Poems* along with other poetry collections. The review entitled 'Youthfulness' caused a media furore. Professionally, he phoned a week later addressing me (jokingly) 'Professor of All Professors' and commissioned further reviews.

I'm not bothering to relate the full President Higgins debacle from my perspective. The Press, Radio and the media 'fall out', if one delves into the coverage, was really for those few who took Higgins's side, as if it had been an assassination attempt on the President by me. My tag line stated that President Higgins's verses were nothing less than 'crimes against literature' for his dull, misshapen 'bad poems'. Whatever about the stylistics of my book review it became news and stayed news.

When you examine the names defending *Il Presidente* as some Shakespearean genius, they were predictably arts council state sponsored writers who had Presidential ambitions among their crazy sights. The real perplexity was why the media Establishment found a way to hang President Higgins out to dry with his embarrassing 'farce-verse'. The reasons for this I could not possibly know but my review was the first shot fired. Never again would Higgins inject his 'poetical genius' into public events or speeches, and the Media for a while quoted me as the professor-critic who had copper fastened the President as poetaster.

I was supposed to feel like a dissident along the boulevards having opposed the literary tyranny which showed the regime did hold, or tried to impose dogmatic consensus. Any poet and critic who questioned it was suspect, irrational, suffering from 'insanity' as the *Sunday Independent* stated. The *New York Post* went further, I was 'inhuman' and the newspaper added, 'Cruelty thy name is Kevin Kiely.' O'Dowd, the Editor of the *Irish Voice* joined in disapproval of 'cruel Kiely'. An Irish academic colleague, among others, felt I had 'committed unpatriotic cultural treason' insulting the President's poetry. Legally, he was incorrect, the Statute Books erased Treason after we gunned the British out of the Republic of Ireland.

My own reaction to the 'reactions' could not meet their level of opprobrium. My critical writing had caused a few debacles before and I was hardly going to become a trading post swopping hyperbole. My own poetry had never been given bad reviews by the Press and Media. The President Higgins's supporters were on the side of consensus. They reflected their own 'product' supporting his verse which in any event they had only done for publicity. If they really thought Higgins was the Ó Rathaille *de nos jours* then they were critically inept. I had written a review. That was my part. I had hardly, like Giordano Bruno, pointed out that the Sun was a single star, one of an infinite number of stars in the infinitely expanding Cosmos and that official cosmology was a hoax. I was, after all on the side of literature and more certain that they hated literature, especially real poetry.

There were emails from professors who agreed with my critique of President Higgins, and emails from professors who disagreed. My replies were almost the same to everyone. Addis and myself on meeting in his office over coffee, shook our heads and laughed, not with any conversational swipes at the 'errant knaves' but we knew what went on behind the circus, and what was allowed to appear as 'news' in as much as they had some control. Many of the disaffected thought I must have connections to the Media. How else could much publicity have been given to a review? I'm not a poet with international media connections, except for my poems making their way through the usual outlets. Besides, I believe that a real poet has a destiny not a career.

Addis had been around the scene from the 1960s. His parents had both been successful novelists in London. Addis himself had dropped out of Cambridge University after losing interest in 'Reading English' and founded, first a print shop in London, thereafter he 'went to the country' where at one time or another, set up local newspapers. We drank our coffee, talked of other matters. He reverted to the Higgins's debacle and those who were outraged. 'So, they really are "they". Like all collectives. Did you know how vulnerable they would appear?' He had another edition of *Books Ireland* to get to the printers. I had more books to review.

Addis was like a lighthouse keeper, on his own as publisher, everyone else were treating reviewing as enabling careers, reviewing as pay back and favour calling. Addis, accurately referred to many newspaper reviews as extended blurb, puffing 'the home fried product'. The levels of dishonesty made one wonder about the 'criminal' element on the literary scene, posers as well-wishers. It was Iago. It was Brutus and Cassius. There were no ethics: the game plan was: you fix me a wow-review, I fix you a wow-review.

I had overstepped the rules (to my shame!) but two years later the

Irish Independent wanted the 'Collected Seamus Heaney' in two dull winter volumes to be reviewed by me. John Spain, the Literary Editor couriered the books North where I was in domicile. His copy day was perched and ready. The *Irish Independent* extended me two pages in the Saturday edition for the Heaney review. I had never met Spain, the Literary Editor. This time, the furore was similar with the *Guardian* and *The Sunday Times* who both pose as Liberal but uphold flagrantly establishment positions in the arts. Thereafter, at launches and along the streets of Dublin, the arts council gang would shake their heads, wag fingers, U-turn, sneer and 'throw' remarks. I decided to write a book *Seamus Heaney and the Great Poetry Hoax* about the farce-verse hoax of the era.

My 'reputation' through *Books Ireland* and other reviewing venues, however, did alert the sort of Editor who want impartial non-partisan appraisal from me. Michael Smith of *Village Magazine* not only favoured the President Higgins' review, but also the Heaney book and commissioned many articles, including 'The President Must Be a Poet'; 'Digging for the real worth of Heaney'; 'Going Through the Poetic Motions'.

Book reviews are not meant to be a long advertisement of obvious hyperbole. Egger's *A Heartbreaking Work of Staggering Genius* in part, concerns the San Francisco literary scene as he outs 'carpetbaggers' of their 'literature product'. Addis and I repeatedly 'suffered' authors demanding reviews of their books which *had to be* considered nothing less than heartbreaking works of staggering genius. Thus they implied by pathetic pleading. They wanted these demands met because the arts council had approved them and so should *Books Ireland*.

Our yearly, or bi-yearly visit to one of our sponsors, The Arts Council, greatly amused us. We'd be summoned by the director and always kept waiting. We knew 'how to say little', the only necessity to know if the grant application form was undergoing revision, so as to prepare for its twenty pages of gobbledygook and jabberwocky and ensure some chance of next year's grant. Addis had a dislike of the process. His riposte was 'who else reviews most of their hand-picked writers other than *Books Ireland.*'

Addis uttered the immortal words: 'Arts Council State Sponsored Books do not have to sell more than a handful of copies on launch night to friends since the publishing costs are covered. They are vanity publishers without a farthing to be paid by the author. Arts Council State Sponsored 'poetry' publishers don't have to sell more than five copies, launch or no launch.'

There were, what Addis called 'the complainants of *Books Ireland*' when 'a book had been independently assessed' and reviewed not to their liking. Addis was courteous on the phone, affable, and talkative. However, incursions from 'complainants' elicited different responses. He was the first I heard, saying 'this publication is not controlled by the Arts Council. We do get a small annual grant from them. Our largest revenue comes from Advertisers, Subscriptions, Sales and other patrons. *Books Ireland* is an independent publication. Our reviewers are uncensored. We copyedit reviews, and check for libel, obscenity etc., Don't tell me how to run my business. Good Day!' 'Complainants' who arrived in person, met with the same reception. I was happy to deliver similar phraseology to 'complainants' who hankered to the Office Door with stuttering pallid faces.

I have gone on at some length as to *Books Ireland* but could cite editorial professionalism, decency and fair play. Michael Smith of *Village*, Tina Neylon at the *Irish Examiner*, John Spain of *The Irish Independent,* Tony Bailie of *The Irish News*, Katy Dang of the *Boise Weekly,* Rick Ardinger for the *Library of Congress Journal* among others but this would rehash the list of publishing venues already mentioned in the *Acknowledgements*.

Since the 1970s, I have written essays and a lot more reviews concerning poetry, biography, literary criticism, memoir, psychology, mysticism, history and politics. My advantage is in dealing with Editors who permit me the freedom to write. While I have reviewed fiction, I generally avoid the 'establishment' whose novels I find antiseptic. The most promoted fiction of the era came from once-budding journalists turned novelists: Binchy, Banville, Tóibín and Company who engineered their heavily-traded publicity. I chose deliberately to review none of these, unable like others in my circle to read them with any interest. I preferred being paid reviewing books of my choice; criticism is also gainful employment.

Comparative literature is critical writing. The critic as artist is the obvious solution to criticism. Homer's 'lost' work on aesthetics is mentioned by Plato and referred to by Alexander Pope in *The Dunciad*. Literature within its structure contains the ghost of critical values, the apparatus of critique embedded within the dynamics. Criticism becomes more exacting than 'reading for pleasure'. My critical faculty never sleeps during critical reading. As a critic I am on the side of literature, a representative for it, by the very act of being a poet and critic. I cannot give in to collusions, propagandas, agendas, conspiracies, log-rolling.

I do not like the word 'expert' in an era of too many 'bought' experts. When I am reading poems, the directions in which to locate their achievement or otherwise, is instantaneous. Catchphrases about writing such as 'everything is editing', 'a good first draft...', 'deconstruction is the same as construction', 'writing is re-writing' these mean nothing to me. With any writer whom I can trust in conversation, there is useful discussion but it is often distracting 'club talk'.

Let me conclude in repeating that literature contains critical apparatus, and true literary criticism is an artistic artefact that can approach literature itself. Such expertise is not only instinctual but requires vast reading, therefore instinct is not the sole requirement for the critic. These statements are cursory. I am not giving in to prefacing this selection of my critical work to embark on paradigms of aesthetics already alluded to, where space and structure permitted such explorations in the essays and reviews that follow.

I have no notion how I write anything. In writing prose, I have to have the energy and let it flow. Reviewing a book ignites response to its value as literature, or else it falls below into mediocrity. How could I praise what is not poetry or literature? A poet cannot do this and remain a poet. The poet is pledged never to break what Beethoven calls the artist's vow: 'never to kneel, especially before any worldly throne.'

—KK

Textual Note: This copy-edited version of the reviews, essays and articles is taken from online resources. Year of publication is given with the name of the newspaper, journal, magazine or other print source. There has been no rewriting of any texts. That would counterfeit my critical acumen. Various house-styles are reproduced; italicization is sporadic, some reviews give page numbers in brackets for quotes referring to the book(s). Importantly, overall critical assessment can be taken as final, whatever about my initial probes into poets, writers, academics, historians, journalists and others. What follows originally appeared in print publications and represents a selection of my total critical output in this genre.

YOUTHFULNESS

An Paróiste Míorúilteach/The Miraculous Parish Selected Poems
Máire Mhac an tSaoi (O'Brien Press)

Speech Lessons John Montague (Gallery Press)

New and Selected Poems Michael D. Higgins (Liberties Press)

The Smile and the Tear ed. Sean McMahon (Londubh)

A Tour of the Lattice Maurice Scully (Veerbooks)

Louis de Paor provides an extensive introduction which firmly locates Mhac an tSaoi writing in Munster Irish. It is cogent to quote her in this influential dialect despite many able translators of her work into plain English by de Paor, Biddy Jenkinson, Douglas Sealy, Celia de Fréine and others. Mhac an tSaoi writes the traditional lyric as in 'Codhladh an ghaiscígh' and 'Dán próis do Inigo'. The elegiac is sustained in 'Adhlacadh iníon an fhile': "Baineann seanaois le coiteann;/Roghnaigh sise a mhalairt". Her use of elegy and love-poem pushes the form only slightly towards being modern since she is cadenced from a remote past and to contemporary native speakers must seem antiquarian. Mhac an tSaoi's achievement is the gentle and fluid emotion effectively filtered in Gaelic that lives apart from its broken heritage. Epigrammatic poems do well such as 'Ceann bliana':

Tá sneachta fós ar ithir na cille,

Sínim le hais an choirp ar mo leabaidh

While 'Cad is bean' might rank as a feminist poem it also lends itself to be read as ironic making it post-feminist. Her top lovelost method is in 'Ceangal do cheol pop': "Beagáinín os chionn an ghabhaill—/San áit a neadód an páiste/Dá mbeadh aon pháiste ann!' This is an example of her eroticism rooted in a wide context. Others in somewhat similar mood are 'An dá thráigh' with sustained exposition of misery (the great Irish standby): "Is mé tobar searbh ar shliabh/Is mé foinse an usice is goirt" while 'Cian á thógaint díom' has some finesse, "Bheith beo in éineacht, fiú gan cnaipe 'scaoileadh." 'Ceathrúinti Mháire Ní Ógáin' is perhaps her best long poem concluding: "Luí chun suilt/Is éirí chun aoibhneas/Siúd ba chleachtadh dhúinn—/Dá bhfaighinn dul siar air."

The quarrel with the gunman father is less convincing in 'Fód an imris: Ard-Oifig an Phoist 1986' as is her political poetry in 'An fuath (1967)' and 'Cam reilige 1916-1966'. Mhac an tSaoi's hallmark is a youthful spirit as espoused in 'Maireann an tseanamhuintir' where a girl in school delivers wisdom at will when the word "bé" (muse) comes up in class. The child replies: "Bean gan aon éadach uirthi!"…/Do gháir Eoghan Rua." Yes, the muse is naked and poetry is never dominated by laughter.

A slim volume that centres on Montague's ancestors (including a photograph of them) particularly his grandfather and grandaunt Winifred in 'Patience and Time' about the card game, then onto milking cows and farm work in "rounding up the strays:/a heifer calving/sheltered by the lime kiln" ('Home Coming'). Strays is more appropriate to the American prairies than locked fields in Tyrone. Besides, these rural themes are well worn post-Kavanaghesque as in 'Devotions' and 'The Long Hangar' which gives a full treatise on "three kinds of turf" and does not use Derry but "Londonderry". One is tired of turf in Irish poetry. Grandfather Montague occupies the sequence 'In My Grandfather's Mansion' which daringly and somewhat failingly takes the form of a dialogue between Montague and his forebear. It is short on discourse while embalmed in memory about heirlooms including "Bibles massive as flagstones" and on reading "The Apocalypse, God's Horror Comic!/Like the scary film, with Boris Karloff". "A Resigned President" is a belated elegy, belated in feel and in performance for Cearbhall Ó Dálaigh. Perhaps, the neatest piece of all is 'Leap' for John Berryman, belated too yet riper; news of the poet's death was conveyed by telegram as "Death by Ice". Montague is staggering but still producing after a fashion. His attempt to topple Thomas Hardy in 'A Hit at Hardy' reveals his own position and the one Irish poet is exalted: "between proud Yeats/and your so humble craft/there is an arrogance—yours, alas!"

The foreword from Mark Patrick Hederman claims that "[President Michael D. Higgins] exercises the ambigious dexterity of being both poet and politician." Higgins's 'The truth of poetry' is dedicated to Hederman while John O'Donoghue is dedicatee 'Of possibility'—all three make up a school of the bland, the imprecise and the ultimately incomprehensible along with John Moriarty. Higgins provides between the verses, interlinking prose vignettes beginning with his birth in 1941. This is a shocking book because of the profusion of lame, stale and stilted lines (examples to follow).

In 'The betrayal' his father is portrayed as hard pressed to buy glasses after the optical benefit "was rejected by de Valera for poorer classes". Meanwhile, Dev got his spectacles in Zurich! Further token political comment and trite observation are present in 'The Master' who "was/very cold". In 'Requiem for a parish priest' the padre "took to writing verse". "Dark memories" and other pieces 'discuss' the Civil War but the subject comes across as remote. He is over fond of using "dark" and "light" and their usage is vague as in "brothers all,/in the light,/out of the dark" ('Brothers'). This might seem like quoting Higgins at his worst but there is little choice. In 'Of sons and mothers' he declares: "I am becoming my mother" and proceeds to enumerate womanly traits. 'Stargazer' has the absurd line: "There is nobody to ask now for the stars". "The collecting" finds him in a school yard: "As my eyes peel the playground" which is syntactically awkward and physically impossible. "The man who never had a visitor" is obviously about loneliness but merely anecdotal, melodramatic and inherently from the Ireland's Own School of Verse.

His quasi-philosophical verse not even humble fireside or armchair philosophy is similarly cringe worthy as in "Questions without answers" and 'Take care' which concludes: "Hold firm./Take care./Come home/together." "And the trees wept" as far as one can make out is about Jesus while Higgins attempts comedy with 'Jesus appears in Dublin in 1990 at the Port & Docks Board site'. He is also a lame duck in comedy with 'Bank manager faints at the mayor's ball'. 'Of utopias' baldly states: "Old utopias never die/nor do they fade away" which is illogical. His final statement of philosophy presumably comes in the last line of 'The ebbing tide' "And tomorrow is another day"—this is basically Scarlett O'Hara's closing line in the movie Gone with the Wind. Higgins must be addressing his notebook and pencil solely otherwise he can be accused of crimes against literature.

MacMahon revels in being eclectic with Synge's 'The Curse' and Cecil Frances Alexander's hymn 'All Things Bright and Beautiful'. Kettle's famous sonnet to his daughter is amidst songs that dominate while many of the finest are from nineteenth century Anglo-Irish such as Ferguson's 'The Lark in the Clear Air', Lady Dufferin 'The Irish Emigrant' while the oft sung Macushla is (not often remembered) the work of Josephine V. Rowe. Thackeray wrote 'Peg of Limavaddy' proving that many Irish songs and ballads are not home grown with the exception of Percy French whose 'Abdul Abulbul Ameer' marks the lack of national boundaries for subject matter.

This evergreen cornucopia (backward looking) includes Dion Boucicault's 'The Wearing of the Green' among a plethora of rollicking nationalist ballads 'God Save Ireland', 'The Rising of the Moon', 'Bold Robert Emmet', 'Kevin Barry' and Pearse's 'Mise Éire'. Moore's symbolic nationalism 'Rich and Rare' fits well alongside Katherine Tynan's 'The Wind that Shakes the Barley' while songs of emigration abound (and topically) 'The Shores of Amerikay'. MacMahon does not forget Teresa Brayton's occult classic, 'The Old Bog Road' nor the author 'Anon' with such as

'Coortin' in the Kitchen' and its perfect rhyming: "Come single belle and beau, to me now pay attention,/And love I'll plainly show is the devil's own invention." The most famous songs are anonymous according to this anthology, 'Cockels and Mussels' and 'My Own Lovely Lee' but not 'The Rose of Tralee' (William Mulchinock). His Gaelic section (left to last) is rich with 'Anon': 'Fáinne Gael an Lae', 'Trasna na dTonnta', 'Lannigan's Ball' and 'Finnegan's Wake' while Patrick Pearse's 'Óró 'Sé do Bheatha 'Bhaile' must be in the mix which is the method here. Therefore you also have Swift's 'The Description of an Irish Feast'. This sort of mixture is his fixture.

Selected poems [of Scully] based on former schools of poetry. Beckett is echoed in 'Stone': "Suddenness of/the end of/things//of the end of things…". Bygone modernism ingests the untitled Cummings-look-alike piece "happy art fluid art/who are so/serious//happy art a cow/in experience/daisies//buttercup grass happy". Carlos Williams is responsible for most of the typography and content in Scully as with 'or:' "a/song/is/a//a/song/ is/a//a/song/is/a//sh/ap/e." Typographical shape and print layout are also taken from Dadaism and other earlier movements which Scully reproduces a century and more later. This self-regarding makes him pour his content into old moulds while claiming new forms as in Sonnet-Ode. The results are a menagerie of disconnected language, not L-A-N-G-U-A-G-E poetry but a belated response to Brian Coffey whose better work is in the Missouri Sequence and his translations which privilege sentience and communication.

The following in Scully is merely playful (yet unrewarding) as the dog barks in an expletive: "at the Rhadsody & Squash a tankard yes & a/dog at the door: fuck! [space] fuck-fuck!/fuck-fuck-fuck!" 'Sonnet'. His repetitious method is to patch together detail upon random detail in imitation of reality with the presumption of being identifier of reality but the level of communication is far too low. The results are pre-communication childish patter as if learning language by using it lamely to signify what is perceived and seen. Ultimately fake-profundity purports to be lost in meaning within this solipsistic love-affair with imprecise language. 'Variations' begins: "Once upon a time there were three/billion bears. Ling. Dab./Who studies happiness." A prose piece from 'Sonata' includes: "If the Seamstresses of steel become home-makers/or widows at their windows at home in chrome &/leatherette". This is post-Gertrude Stein. Scully seems unaware of dressing an old emperor in old clothes.

—*Books Ireland* 2012

WHY ARE THE CRITICS NOT WEEPING: president must be a poet, insists President Higgins

Michael D. Higgins, the ninth president of Ireland, according to BBC News Europe is claiming that 'the demands of the presidential role have slowed his literary output' and he is 'unlikely to release another [collection of poetry] due to the demands on his time as head of state.' Higgins, as poet lacks substance with regard to standards of literary credibility. Indeed, the purveying of himself as a poet suggests dissatisfaction with the role of president. In his foreword to *The Irish Presidency* (2014) he disputes with one of its contributors, Michael Gallagher that 'the president of Ireland cannot be identified as a significant actor'. Higgins's tone is apologetic and hesitant when he concludes that the office of president is 'an institution of state, which, it is generally accepted, has served our citizens well'. There has been no incumbent of Áras an Uachtaráin to compare with the first president Douglas Hyde's eminence in literature. His *Literary History of Ireland* is a classic. As folklorist and translator from Gaelic poetry, he produced abiding works such as *Love Songs of Connaught*. W.B. Yeats praised him as a poet 'that noble blade the Muses buckled on'.

Meanwhile, the BBC had a note of hope about the president's writing since Higgins intends 'to publish a volume of his speeches.' The announcement was provoked by his poem entitled 'The Prophets Are Weeping', reverently hailed by Sam Griffin in the *Irish Independent*. Griffin lamented the fact that Higgins 'was putting his career as a poet and writer on hold'. The poem (full text below) had already been excerpted in the president's annual Christmas card and was only made available to the general public as late as February. Griffin 'believed [it] to be a commentary on the social and political upheaval in the Middle East, including Syria and Iraq.' Commentary on the poem is further confounded in more geography since the BBC stated that it was completed in November after 'his three-week visit to Ethiopia, Malawi and South Africa.' In point of fact the poem has no known location or place-name in its make-up.

The expense of spirit or time in its actual production of 27 lines comprising five short irregular stanzas that include repetitions easily suggests that it was knocked off in a few minutes. The immediate conundrum is categorizing it as a 'poem' at all. The whole exercise is a media gratuity to Higgins as president implying that if he writes poetry it must be significant and newsworthy. The typography at a glance gives it the shape of a poem but on reading the lines, anyone who claims it as poetry are being merely polite like Ronan McGreevy in the *Irish Times* who located its point of reference as 'northern Iraq and those in flight from the Syrian conflict'. The relevance of the poem to Iraq and Syria is highly problematic simply because there is no reference to either country. The lines, McGreevy pointed out were completed before the massacre in the offices of *Charlie Hebdo*. This sort of spin was meant to lend some sort of parallelism with the *Charlie Hebdo* murders but in truth the poem cannot be said to reflect this atrocity.

'The Prophets are Weeping' is utterly vague despite newspaper commentators and the media heralding it unequivocally. It is not clear who the prophets are meant to represent. Why they are weeping is not stated with enough poetry or prose to engage one's attention. To examine the lines closely is not difficult. Poetry doesn't necessarily have an ultimate meaning but this plays into Higgins method. For instance, in the opening stanza it states that the prophets are weeping because of the abuse of their 'words' scattered 'to sow an evil seed'. The phraseology does not achieve any depth or stature. There is the confusing use of 'words' while the use of 'evil seed' is not qualified, developed or given any context whatsoever.

After telling the reader that 'it is reported...', the meaning changes in lines 6 & 7 to: 'Rumour has it that,/The Prophets are weeping'.

So what are the prophets weeping at with 'their texts distorted,/The death and destruction,/Imposed in their name'? One never finds out. The lines go on to make obvious statements about refugees in terms of parents and children. 'Mothers and Fathers hide their faces' in line 15. There is no mention of the Middle East.

What are the texts that he refers to? Mohamed wrote the *Quran* that was revealed and inspired by Allah. Higgins uses the word 'texts' (plural), whereas the *Quran* admittedly has many verses but is one text. And those who kill in the Prophet's name presumably kill for the *Quran*? Whether the 'texts' referred to in Higgins's lines are other than the *Quran* is never revealed. However, there is certainly no reference to the *Quran* or any other sacred text, or even texts.

Basically, the 27 lines are blithe, if not bland as in the conclusion which repeats the line about 'The Prophets are weeping' for the third time. Apparently their words 'have been stolen'. These words 'once offered/A shared space,/Of love and care,/Above all for the stranger'. The aspiration to some utopia in the latter lines cannot approximate to the complexity of Israel, Palestine, Syria and Iraq. But how is one to know if Higgins refers to such places?

The President insists he must poeticise, as in his most recent Arts Council funded *New and Selected Poems* from Liberties Press in 2011. 'The Prophets are Weeping' as his latest effusion is an appalling piece of confused mystification in keeping with his low literary standards. His lines, by no stretch of the imagination could be said to measure up to a poem. There is no statement or evocation of anything that is either recognisable or comprehensible according to the praise lavished on the lines by the media. The lines are merely posing as poetry with pretence to an emotive theme in attempting to cite the Middle East. It would be better for the president to honour his office by making explicit statements about the Middle East. Now that he has sidelined his so called poetical labours, allegedly, because of the constraints of public life, perhaps he can give full time to his speeches.

The Prophets are Weeping:

To those on the road it is reported that

The Prophets are weeping,

At the abuse

Of their words,

Scattered to sow an evil seed. (5)

Rumour has it that,

The prophets are weeping.

At their texts distorted,

The death and destruction,

Imposed in their name. (10)

The sun burns down,

On the children who are crying,

On the long journeys repeated,

Their questions not answered.

Mothers and Fathers hide their faces, (15)

Unable to explain,

Why they must endlessly,

No end in sight,

Move for shelter,

for food, for safety, for hope. (20)

The Prophets are weeping,

For the words that have been stolen,

From texts that once offered,

To reveal in ancient times,

A shared space, (25)

Of love and care,

Above all for the stranger.

—*VILLAGE: politics and culture* 2015

THE IRISH PRESIDENCY: EXPOSING THE FEEBLENESS OF OFFICE

The Irish Presidency: power, ceremony and politics
John Coakley and Kevin Rafter (Irish Academic Press)

President Michael D. Higgins's foreword to these analytical essays by nine contributors takes Michael Gallagher to task for stating that the president of Ireland 'cannot be identified as a significant political actor'. In every respect, from Douglas Hyde to Higgins, this remains the delicate pivot: *significant actor or not?* De Valera enshrined the values of the presidency in the Dail in 1937 as possessing 'strictly limited areas of responsibility'. On taking office in 1959 he jested about having written into the 1937 Constitution 'a nice, quiet job without too much work for his old age'. There is also truth in the 'cynical description of Aras an Uachtarain as a retirement home'. Past presidents have suffered the laxity of public profile. Only three—de Valera, Robinson and McAleese—have 'addressed a meeting of the Houses of the Oireachtas'. No president has 'issued a message or address to the nation, other than their inaugural address'. Robert Elgie's incisive commentary focuses on referral and veto by Irish presidents, who have referred (only) '15 bills to the Supreme Court since 1938'. In terms of *realpolitik* the president has no role in the formation of the government: 'can neither initiate nor veto legislation, has no power over the budget, does not select or have veto power over any appointees to any public positions, and has no role in foreign policy'. The only tangible power is that of refusal 'to grant a dissolution of the Dail (and hence an election) to a Taoiseach in certain circumstances', especially if the Taoiseach had lost a confidence vote in the Dail or during a crisis in the government. Elgie also broaches an extreme situation whereby a president can be impeached for 'misbehaviour', which requires two-thirds of both Houses of the Oireachtas 'declaring that the charge has been sustained'. Michael Gallagher compounds the impotence of the Aras in that it 'has rarely had direct impact upon political life'. He thoroughly investigates Ó Dalaigh's resignation in 1976 and 'Robinson's handshake with Sinn Fein leader Gerry Adams in 1993'. John Coakley, amidst an academic dirge of detail, claims that the Viceregal Lodge as residence of the lord lieutenant from 1781 to 1922 haunts the twentieth-century location for Irish presidents.

Ciara Meehan, while repeating the central thesis of the book, outlines the presidencies of Hyde, O'Kelly and de Valera and shows that Hyde, as political appointee, was deliberately chosen for his 'Irish sovereignty' profile to champion the 'two national ideals of Ireland free and Ireland Gaelic'. Hyde possessed safe non-militant credentials because of his resignation from the IRB in 1915 as Gaelic League founding-father. Still, his position as presidential eunuch became obvious on consulting with the Council of State in January 1940 over the Offences Against the State (Amendment) Bill. What happened behind the scenes is unknown. Hyde duly signed the bill into law. Nevertheless, his referral of the School Attendance Bill (1942) to the Supreme Court resulted in its being deemed unconstitutional.

During O'Kelly's term of office 'the international role emerged', with foreign visits, notably to Rome and the United States, representing the tactic of 'selling Ireland'. This American visit induced, if not inspired, JFK's Irish visit in 1963 during de Valera's presidency (1959-73). Historically, de Valera's falling star was signalled in the 1966 election, when he scraped through to a second term by a margin of 10,000 votes. The JFK visit and subsequent assassination prompted de Valera's visit to the US in 1964. Dev's version of republicanism was blanked by American legislators in the House of Representatives, when its speaker, John McCormack, reiterated 'that the American government could do nothing to influence Britain's position on Northern Ireland'. Meehan fails to point out that the pecking order concerning Northern Ireland affairs has always been London, Washington and Belfast, with Dublin unjustly last and least. Kevin Rafter shows President Childers in office supporting government policy *contra* the IRA. Childers stated: 'the IRA can only destroy any reputation we have and discourage unity in the Six Counties'. This statement is the definitive Dail position on the North from Bloody Sunday to the Arms Trial and onwards.

Rafter keenly records how Ó Dálaigh's two years in office were destroyed by Donegan's 'thundering disgrace' remark (history records that he actually used the F-word). Indeed, Ó Dálaigh's sense of ethics and responsibility, exemplary in Irish public life, meant that he felt himself to be insufficient as 'agreed candidate' and merely 'a substitute for an elected president'. He would have preferred to be tested by the rigours of a campaign and the ballot box. Ó Dálaigh was 'awkward' with the media but had a strong international profile' and became 'the first head of state to visit the European institutions'.

Rafter authoritatively denounces the disgraceful government conduct towards Ó Dálaigh, who had invoked the Council of State in March 1976 over the Criminal Law (Jurisdiction) Bill, and later in the same year over the Emergency Powers Bill. It was the era of the Dublin bombings and the seven days' detention without charge—hysterical political terrain—yet the bill was signed into law in October 1976. Donegan's destructive remark ultimately compounds the weakness of the Irish presidency, while Cosgrave's 'excessive loyalty' to Donegan easily brought about the fall of Ó Dálaigh.

Rafter correctly dwells on the weakness of the office in general, and Hillery (1976-90) in particular, in the aftermath of Ó

Dálaigh's being hounded out of office. During the government crisis of February 1982, Hillery would have been able to 'exercise new powers but [he] was unwilling to consider constitutional intervention to prevent a general election'. Hillery's inauguration had met with 'international indifference'. He faced the political aggression of Haughey in 1982 over the loss-of-confidence vote in Fitzgerald's government. In point of fact, 'the President's staff had been verbally threatened' by Haughey, who wished to form a government without an election.

Yvonne Galligan champions the struggles of Robinson on the campaign trail for the Aras and under sexist attack from Minister Padraig Flynn, and, while in office, Haughey's intermittent threats, such as attempting 'to deter her from meeting the Dalai Lama' (1991). Robinson would proceed to visit Queen Elizabeth II in London in 1993, and a month later would effect the famous 'Adams handshake' during her epoch-making Northern visit. The liberal agenda of Robinson was fully redeployed throughout the McAleese years. Brilliantly, McAleese steered onwards despite her stand-offs with RTE's *Today Tonight* in the guise of Joe Mulholland, who refused to cover the Sands funeral, and she was staunch in opposition to Haughey's 'acceptance of the Anglo-Irish Agreement and [his] support for the extradition of Irish republican terrorist suspects to Britain'. McAleese would see off many critics—including Eoghan Harris, who slighted her as 'a tribal time bomb'—on her path to all-Ireland reconciliation and her hosting of 'the UK monarch' in 2011. Eoin O'Malley discusses the boisterous 2011 campaign under the dictate that voters ultimately 'choose the candidate whose ideological profile fits their own'.

The inaugural addresses are given in full in a separate appendix and unfortunately are not satisfactorily analysed, which is the collective flaw. Textually, they provide crucial, if crucible-sized, data. Hyde's address comprises three and a half lines! Sean

T. O'Kelly, brief on both occasions, occupies less than a page. De Valera's first address is mere gratitude for the office. His second address, on the cusp of the 1916 commemorations, stresses all-Ireland unity and the preservation of Gaelic. The most mellifluous and lengthy address is by Ó Dálaigh ('Carball'), as he quotes the constitution alongside Flann O'Brien, Maud Gonne, Douglas Hyde, Lincoln, Chekov, John Drinkwater, Thoreau, Standish O'Grady and even Cromwell. Patrick Hillery's two addresses are conservatively neutral. Mary Robinson is as flagrantly cultural as Ó Dálaigh, referencing ancient Tara, Yeats, the Irish diaspora and communal identities of Ireland: the provincial amidst the national.

Mary McAleese stressed her nationalism as Ireland's 'first President from Ulster', quoting Yeats, MacNeice and—for some reason—the English poet Christopher Logue in invoking the theme of building bridges. Her second address celebrates the Northern peace process, casually finding in Heaney a link to unity (latterly disavowed by the poet). Higgins evokes an Irish citizenry proactive, alongside constitutional review, 'to be the arrow not the target' in his no-frills, no-poetry speech, while quoting James Connolly and anticipating the 'decade of centenaries that lies ahead'.

There is a threat to democracy in the manipulation of the presidency from its genesis as serving of the government while being fully under the control of the government. Decisively, the Dáil and Constitution have actively diminished every Irish president in office. This legacy of de Valera has damaged and lowered the role, not only in the eyes of the public but in that of the present incumbent, whose foreword to the book is sadly defensive. It is an alarming book that exposes the feebleness of the office of the Irish presidency.

—*Books Ireland* 2014

FANNING THE FLAMES

The Cambridge Introduction to Modern Irish Poetry, 1800-2000
ed. Justin Quinn (Cambridge University Press)

Overall for most of the nineteenth and early twentieth century the socio-cultural paradigm that Quinn holds to is Leland Lyons's theory in Culture and Anarchy in Ireland pertinent to this era where the central precept is that the Irish Catholics made all the anarchy while the settlers, Anglo, or otherwise created the culture. From the outset this agenda delineated with many prognostications, restricted by space is what makes this provoking book. Many critics may not approve of the debunking of nineteenth century geniuses such as Thomas Moore, J.J. Callanan, J.C. Mangan, Samuel Ferguson, and William Allingham in favour of the exaltation of the poet James Henry; solid Trinity College, Dublin alumni and Trans Alpine classical scholar. "Tennyson's Ireland" as classification for nineteenth century references the formidable Victorian poet laureate to implicate Irish poetry as closely intertwined with England and the tendency to omit the Gaelic past and heritage as if Irish poets wrote solely for the purpose of becoming English.

Hence the Gaelic past, indicative to many as the "leaf, blossom and bole" of Irish poetry is marginalized by Quinn despite the fact that epic Gaelic themes inspired Samuel Ferguson's "Congal," Denis Florence MacCarthy's "The Voyage of St Brendan," Aubrey de Vere's "Inisfail," and W. B. Yeats's "The Wanderings of Oisin." The Gaelic tradition comes right up to Austin Clarke, Seamus Heaney, John Montague, and beyond to the postmodern-Gaelic revival headed by Nuala Ní Dhomhnaill and others. These poets among a glittering constellation cropped together for his purposes showcase the caravan of poetry over the two centuries. Where the inherent Gaelic past was involved in poetic artifice the very landscape and people defied Allingham's "Laurence Bloomfield in Ireland" as literature, and this heralded the Anglo-Irish Literary revival, the revolutionary period, and beyond to the Irish Free State. Irish literature of anarchy reached out towards cultural synthesis of many traditions that are still substantial focus and not just ghost in the machine. Quinn's introductory dictate on twentieth century Irish poetry is slightly at odds with this where its practitioners are "poets of the English language, and that they are Irish is only of secondary importance" (2).

The chapter on Yeats heralded by preceding one on Douglas Hyde, Katharine Tynan, Ethna Carbery, and Emily Lawless supports the dualism of poets writing in English metamorphosed through and by the Gaelic legacy that he usefully outlines as "the diverse uses to which Irish mythological material was put to by Revival writers" (52). His classifications reveal a critic willing to speak his mind and radically reorder the canonical terrain, thus Padraic Colum is dismissed as peasant-poet, and Francis Ledwidge's work is "essentially an ornamental poetry that is never cathected by any larger forces, whether of nature, politics, or human emotion" (55). Synge's verse is highly praised while "The Ballad of Reading Gaol" given short shrift is "a terse, pathetic complaint" (58). Yeats is granted his laurels satisfactorily amidst occasional mawkish handling of the historical background as in the following on 1916: "There followed bloody week of fighting in Dublin, and the unconditional surrender of the revolutionaries" (67). As lyric poet, Yeats follows the destined trajectory towards fascism, and nationalist poet and Anglo-Irish poet, merging both of these necessary traditions placed in the background as mere causality: which is an interesting gloss by Quinn.

MacNeice has "limiting perspective and there is not sufficient imaginative pressure exerted against the pressure of events." Autumn Journal by MacNeice does not make the grade. This is all refreshingly anarchic and may find ripostes from scholars. Modernists are sufficiently praised, such as Denis Devlin and Brian Coffey, along with Thomas Kinsella, all of whom arouse his enthusiasm with contemporaries such as Randolph Healy, solely because of the "mordantly satirical in his treatment of nationalism"(109). Quinn's dictate is call for Irish literary history without nationalism: daring revisionism. While strictly follower of languages poets, he ultimately favors poetry that reaches "a poetics of chaos and conflict, texts which aim to reproduce the randomness of the world" (109). He is most revealing of his personal tastes in tone of manifesto positing modernism as the supreme poetry—a critic nailing his colors to the mast.

Poets are grouped together in grid framework outlining his delineation of schools and movements which some may approve as useful. "Mahon and Longley have especially proved hugely influential on the succeeding generation of Irish poets, with Murphy's work somewhat sidelined by the fact that he was not part of the Northern Irish Renaissance" (128). He gives Heaney an American status with the international dimensions appropriate to his audience "Lowell's example confirmed Heaney in his use of poetic autobiography" (136). Heaney's Irishness and/or Britishness is erased as bygone and useless debate with the resolution "that Heaney writes in native language of Ireland" suggestive of the principle of "Anglophone poets in Ireland' enmeshed 'in political identity on the island, that between Irish and English." (142). Furthermore, he elaborates succinctly while evolving the theory that "Heaney is first and foremost an English poet, by which means that he is poet of the English language and not the Irish language." Again, the ability of this text to provoke is perhaps significant of necessity to redefine these two centuries. There is much balance when investigating Irish poets as translators with notable examples from Beckett and Derek Mahon; however, Denis Devlin and Brian Coffey might have been included. His pronouncements on Gaelic show it as marginal to the first three volumes of The Field Day Anthology while with justice An Duanaire: 1600-1900, Poems of the Dispossessed, is discussed as "one of the finest bilingual anthologies of Irish poetry," yet its co-editor, Thomas Kinsella, is castigated as purveying an "interpretation of Irish literary history... is so plainly wrong" (147). He is not afraid to question modern poetry in Gaelic having no significant audience and the anxiety over its possible extinction. Michael Hartnett's return to his roots in writing poetry in Gaelic is shown as heroic while Gaelic poets question modern poetry in Gaelic having no significant audience and the anxiety over its possible extinction. Gaelic poets such as Nuala Ní Dhomhnaill are quoted on marginalization, not in reference to writing in their native tongue but for being a woman. Otherwise, feminism is the hallmark of Eavan Boland with Éilean Ní Chuilléanain among her peers whose "feminism branches out into other issues."

Sifting through post-Heaneyites he locates Paul Muldoon as an emigre, based on the poet's grappling with "hybridity" which is explained as writing about America veiled as Northern Ireland, or writing about Northern Ireland veiled as America: on this factor rests "the major achievements and major failures of Muldoon's poetry since the 19905" (185). Quinn ranks him among the inner-emigres defined as "poets who were born and raised in one part of the island and have settled in another" (177). This somewhat unfortunate demarcation covers multitudes: perhaps he means mainly the Northern Poets who came south or went west of west, generally. Eamon Grennan is placed in this pigeonhole of emigre beyond Irish-American, and as Irish living long term in the U.S. where "his loss of public world leaves him with the personal as his main theme" (189). Quinn skims through many contemporaries: there are of course many omissions: to list them would add symmetrical partisanship to his chosen constellation of poets. He closes with Catriona O'Reilly having reached back to Kennelly and Durcan who is ranked as therapoetic since "his work found wide audiences at the very time that practices such as group therapy, psychoanalysis and support groups were taking root in the country"

(195) Kennelly's satire in his second phase beyond erstwhile lyricism is not discussed but Quinn has had a vast area of scholarship to cover and this will challenge both student and teacher as text book that does not pretend to be conservative since his heart is clearly with the abstractions of language poetry. Deep down one gets the feeling that mainstream Irish poetry does not greatly hold his attention and this viewpoint steers his critical assessment.

If it is subversive "to read him" as counter-cultural anarchist against traditional and popular poetry, one of the contradictions is that his pleas for social poetry is against an aesthetic embodied in abstraction and language poetry. Ireland of course has social poetry, political poetry, and every kind of poetry: these are a legacy to the literature of the world. Quinn seems to have sectional interest in the form and flagrantly mistakes the extra factor of the non-abstract nature of some of his masters, such as Devlin and Coffey. He comes across as someone who can only appreciate one type of poetry as normal: the high versus low art debate with tendencies to the alleged cultural fascism of Yeats. However, one assumes he is above snobbery in literature no matter how it is pronounced. Alternatively, to give him the benefit of the doubt: if there is no contention between poets, critics and others there can be no literary tradition with life in it. Quinn may well be jousting with his readers in order to keep the debate going towards what is beyond the riches of these two hundred years of Irish poetry as it ripples infinitely outwards in the fragility and fortitude of the literary world.

—*Irish Literary Supplement* 2010

SATIRE, GRIEF AND LESSER TIGHT-LIPPED EXPRESSIVENESS

The Immodest Proposal: a satire Sydney Bernard Smith (Lapwing)

Selected and New Poems Robert Greacen (Salmon Poetry)

Sundial Colette Nic Aodha (Arlen House)

The Bowsprit Janice Fitzpatrick Simmons (Lagan Press)

Satire? Yes, and this is the bard well-dressed. One does not want to enter into hyperbole but sincerely dear reader this is Sydney at his brilliant best as wordSmith. Don't take this hack's opinion on this long, neatly-rhyming feat, none other than Ted Hughes of poetic infamy is facsimilated inside the front cover with a letter he wrote to SBS (if there was a GBS why not SBS?). Hughes is succinct in his epistle from Devon of 5 February 1997: 'thanks for the enlivening read and surprising lines.' Hence this long poem must have been around a while yet still keeps its Spring fever fervent.

What is most to admire is the intellect at work. Satire is fencing with a reaping hook to this gentle reader. It is not quite the thing for a holy day, but the obligation to imbibe it is a pleasurable duty. Smith, not unlike Orwell's Winston Smith, is contra mundum. This is the convention of the satirist who must be ever cavilling despite Mr Kavanagh's harangue that satire bears 'shoots of wild pity'. Smith is not a conformist Pope. The poet is a church of one and so with this city poet Sydney. Who are the targets here? Many. Women. The yin and yang of the abortion debate. Professors (the likes of Barthes, eponymous cartoon philosopher).

The media — 'gutter-press-power!', 'news is mere commodity'. All this is clean air to inhale after — let's face it — the Daily Bilge. America too gets it hot and heavy: When is a war crime not a war crime? When the winning side suppresses all report.

Lying quantum physicists take Smith on an exposition of his own theology. Freud is 'two-dimensional and pallid'. Not forgetting to mention a real bunch of airy fairies, whom no one will complain at their having their backsides pummelled by SBS:

...what drives these self-referential smirking prats through canons of cant

(it can't be truly vital) from Althusser to [actin-Foucault-shite-all?]

He does not tug the forelock to many writers except Plato, while Jung —'shuts nothing out' — and Vonnegut are considered of high merit.

The satirist is of course 'on the boiler', as Yeats described the dubiously-placed public podium of his childhood days in Sligo, where any drunk or public-minded splenetic could vent his spleen, and so it is with SBS. He keeps his dunce's cap on and is never too wise and all-knowing:

I sound exasperated and irascible: my job nowadays is plain impossible.

The best poets know they are redundant, unemployable misfits, and SBS never places himself above the exalted status of his office of poethood. Because Ezra Pound boxed our ears into free verse and gave the two fingers to militaristic rhyming poetry, a certain reckless nerve is called for to drag form back formally to Dryden, Swift and Pope. Hence, Mr Smith makes this performance in deliberate ill-mannered rhyme zing, and it's a good old delight for its use of the bell clapper:

Free Will! — derided by Behaviourologists & other pseudo-academic bolloxists...

You will never find here a Daniel O'Donnell mammy's boy butterscotch mealy-mouthed satirist, so hurray for SBS frothing at the mouth. It would be merciless not to quote from his formal performance stanzas, especially since he does perform to the Platonic dictate as best a poet can, and stares directly at the sun:

Flow can you school a fourteen year old boy Whose AK 47 is his toy?

This poet is worth his salt and hopefully the nation can pay him his weight in salt since he is worth it, whether one might agree or disagree with him as he blubbers like a whale come ashore:

All text is equal. Hence: no high no low art, no classical, no thoroughbred no runty,

no opera worth more than Broadway Show-art -- the norm is inside-outed back-to-fronty...

But why then study — Why Genet? Why Homer? Austen?! Why not Beano? Why not Bunty?

If no one text's more worthy than another & thinking hurts the mind so much — why bother?

There is a hoard of Greacen here, and while not being the full-kit Collected for plotting his trajectory as poet, this is a handy hold-all and friendly read with occasional hints of menace. Throughout there is, behind the poems, the tales of three cities: Belfast, Dublin, London. One Recent Evening (1944) is a confident beginning with freer rein than the later tightlipped distinctly NI poetry, which is worth a comment to pin it down:

We were the Northmen, hard with hoarded words on tongue,
Driven down by home disgust to the broad lands and rich talk,

To the country of poets and pubs and cow-dung

Spouting and shouting from every stalk...

O hurry to Dublin, to Dublin's fair city..

- 'CYCLING TO DUBLIN'

This along with another early poem 'Ulster' expresses much of every Northman's delicate pact with Dublin, and one might claim that poets are and have been trying to breach the divide, obliterate the divide, cross the divide or whatever it is that one has to do to bridge or get beyond the divide.

With The Undying Day (1948) there is a slight falling off, albeit with the valuable chance to read Greacen from that time. Then the long hiatus until A Garland For Captain Fox (1975), a successful persona, part Zelig, part surrealistic surrogate non-self, part Le Carreesque creation with the necessary hint of menace (already mentioned), and decidedly more London than Dublin or Belfast. It is as if a necessary exile both geographic and /or psychological releases the poetry while he is left coping with the clipped tight-lipped NI muse. Fox and his milieu, part real, part imaginary, part Simenon, wheedles his way into the poems in Young Mr. Gibbon (1979). London and literary London and beyond fill out the lines, many poems about poets provide the impetus for the only kind of poem available, and always in the background is the nigh-audible struggle to get any poems at all written, and the dearth of inspiration with the gaping unfilled, if not unfulfilled, page ("Oh, this compulsion to make marks on paper when awake", from 'Words').

Often family snapshots can be his best stuff, such as 'Uncle Jack' from Carnival at the River (1990), and again it is an English scene-poem of an Irishman in exile. The imaginary persons too are usually fruitful:

A week before his flight he and I lunched

With Carrington-Smythe at the Athenaeum,

Heard how our Foreign Office friend

Mislaid some papers, nearly caused a minor war.

—Kinsky

Even in *Lunch at the Ivy* (2002) and *Shelley Plain* (2003) other poets help him write his poems. This vampiric method holds him in good stead since Greacen while in exile remains NI like all NIers — this reviewer being an NIer himself is entitled to make this point. It is as if Nlers can only be in exile, must be in exile, must wake from the nightmare or dream that is NI, and remain tight-lipped whether in NI or out of NI. Whether Foyleside or Laganside, such sons of Ulster are always nervous of utterance and struggling to come to full utterance, tight-lipped poets of the tongue-tied tribe:

And what he said was roughly this

—If indeed Lao-Tsu really knew

Why did he write a book about his knowledge?

Nobody spoke for ages.

- 'KNOWING AND NOT KNOWING'

Colette Nic Aodha in Sundial trades with much endeavour in rural subject matter, keeping place foremost. Still, the village tailor in 'According To His Cloth', the shearer in 'Yarn', and 'Haymaking' can also exercise her. The pastoral for her is apparently pervasive and really even suffusing:

Clouds hover overhead,

their black shapes compliment bare trees,

a cow stands near a leafless trunk...

- 'VISION'

But sometimes it just sounds awkward,

as in the unfortunate use of the word 'suss':

Wasps and bees suss out sweetness...

- 'AFTERNOON'

Far more successful are those occasions when she escapes her native parishes, but this is not to disparage the rurality which is obviously a furrow for her to plough. Surprisingly, Annaghmakerrig produces a good poem, 'It Rained Pavlova'. One often wonders about that hallowed spot outside Newbliss. Is it the ghosts of the Guthries, the

47

house and grounds, the hanky-panky or the food that warms up the muse? ('They think they are clever, / they know the 'classics', god-alecs. / I'd like to tell them that Oedipus / was a cousin of my mother...'). Overall this collection suggests many directions, various strivings, various engagements, various defeats with the form plus the surprise of the trans-Rural in 'The Mob', which is a frontal attack on modernism. Her most effective use of place other than the nostalgic is 'Uneasy in Castlebar' drained my thoughts by drinking / fifteen pots of tea'), which avoids adoration of the local — which in any event requires major attenuations of hate and love for balance. No one really adores their native landscape and such poetry can risk moving too close to the greeting card. The sense here is of work in progress, there is work and there is progress, it is often just tentative without the delicacy of tentativeness.

Fitzpatrick Simmons strides with simplicity and grace across difficult terrain, goes deep and manages to make her disaffliction convincing in the end, if there can ever be an end to loss. Of course, the collection is affecting, and of course the poetry community knows about her lost poet-husband, he is Simmons and to many 'Jimmy Simmons', but she still has to endure, and presumably had to write this out. It is a horrible slur to suggest 'therapoetics' here as dignity battles with aesthetic sensibility. Some people yawn at confessional poetry, and those who have gone down the confessional road perhaps engage with the notion that poetry itself is inherently confessional and not confessional at all, also. The whole matter is murkily theoretical, yet reading these affecting poems all theory sounds bunk as it should when faced with the prime material: poetry. The invasion of her private grief is her public work, and in the instant otherness of grief as portrayed, this reader was both shielded and kept from the totality of her plight but not from the poet's conveyance: language, which pitches her grief at full force. So her transmutation is the first thing to admire. Were it a thematic, dirgeful collection it might be acceptable, but for those who cavil at the confessional mode (excluding this reviewer), here under the exposition of the metatexuality (to use an abominable academic term), her artistic problems are confronted. This is her achievement.

Grief enlarges these poems, justifying her descent into such an inferno. It is not one's task to comment on her private trials. You can pick up the thread of this grief in any poem, such as 'A Thing With Feathers', 'The Ladder Road', 'Faith', 'Green Fire': these need to be read aloud. Grief is of course catching, cloying, engulfing, all-embracing with a universality that can easily test the person to the limits: war, pestilence, grief — the latter figures high in human misery. In this respect Fitzpatrick Simmons has passed through the fire, at least one puts this down in a review under this assumption, one based strictly on the final poem. Of which, a few thoughts in a moment.

There is the atmosphere of Juliet's tomb within this book, as in the famous play's closure, the dark plaintive music of woe in excelsis: 'I mean a chair, a single chair,/the ghost of your chair beside me, a ghost whiskey, a ghost hand running fingers/through my hair. Your death has blurred/my boundaries. You are in the corner of my eye, a rib in the fabric of what I know, the shadow/of love and not love itself'—'THE CHERRY TREE'. To quote these lines is some kind of injustice, they require to be seen in the entirety of the poem on the page.

Since your death I would like to shout

into the broad cavern of your grave and ask you why.

But then, I have asked God too,

His answer always: to endure.

— 'THE GLENVEAGH PASS'

The rendition of grief suddenly abates in the final and longest poem 'Indwelling', in which Fitzpatrick Simmons calls out her dead

49

finally beyond fear, and of course the dead will not harm her, for those among them whom she loves, love on. Her husband is there 'guitar across his chest'. Elysium is not for the living, it is for the dead: 'into the waters of time he faded', once he has admonished her. The dead cannot be summoned at will; is this her resolve? The chimerical elsewhere is difficult to contact, no appointments can be made on demand. The dead are in control of the living. Never the other way around.

—*The Poetry Ireland Review* 2006

THE ROAD TO LIMBERLOST: the dream and reality of a small poetry press

The map that shows the road to Limberlost Press indicates Idaho City far beyond the house of Rick Ardinger and Rosemary Powers Ardinger, who have distinguished themselves among small press poetry publishers for over 30 years. A drive on a torrid summer's day goes outside Boise, past Lucky Peak Lake and Reservoir towards the turn off for More's Creek. Sequestered among trees, a dirt road brings you to a halt where welcoming dogs leap and bark. Rick calls them to heel, a quiet spoken seraphic man with trifocal spectacles and long beard. Rosemary, who was born in Brighton, Massachusetts, and Rick from Homestead (near Pittsburgh), PA, become more talkative after the initial moments, then cut to the chase and put you at your ease. Food and drink abounds, as guests are entertained: Chuck Guildford, the poet, along with Johnny Thompson, a wood carver, musician, and firewatcher. Thompson's wife Linda, a teacher, is talking with Rosemary and others. Rick sips a beer slowly, considers before replying to initial questions, then launches forth with a winning smile. "Oh yea: Limberlost," he says, as if half-forgetful, "well you've come to the right place!" He occasionally checks a fact or a date with Rosemary, whom he calls Rosie.

Rick founded Limberlost when he was 23. At 22, he had set out from Lawrence, Massachusetts to a small press publishers' convention at Harvard University. This initial glimpse into the process of printing proved to be a day of destiny. Coincidentally what also arrived through small press publishing was the High Noon of the Beat poets that had their genesis at the Six Gallery, San Francisco, as recounted in Timothy Gray's *Gary Snyder and the Pacific Rim: Creating Counter-Cultural Community*: "The audience was treated to the first performance of Ginsberg's "Howl" and introduced to a cadre of young writers (Philip Whalen, Philip Lamantia, Michael McClure, and Gary Snyder) whose work would forever be linked with the Beat

Movement." Donald Allen's anthology *The New American Poetry* captured this era, heralding the post-modernists Olson, Creeley, Duncan, Dorn, Levertov and Zukofsky, as well as the New York poets, Ashberry, Koch and O'Hara with the West Coast Renaissance including Corso, Ferlinghetti, Ginsberg, Snyder. Looming mystically in the wings was Kerouac.

Rick would meet and publish many of these literary luminaries finding the realization of his dreams through *Limberlost Review,* a photocopied, hand-folded, stapled magazine with issues in the low hundreds. In one issue, he published an interview with wife of Neal Cassady, Carolyn Cassady, who wrote *Off the Road. Limberlost Review* demanded unceasing ardor, as well as a distribution network and soldiered on through 16 issues over 10 years until 1986, notably, and latterly producing *Gone in October: Last Reflections on Jack Kerouac* exclusively written by John Clellon Holmes, a great friend of the Ardingers. One of Limberlost's finest books is Holmes's *Death Drag: Selected Poems.* The Kerouac issue is non-mainstream and gives an account of the Ginsberg Boulder Conference of 1982 with classic photographs, especially, the frieze of Orlovsky, Ferlinghetti, Burroughs, Corso, Holmes, Ginsberg, Carl Soloman and Robert Frank.

Dining with Rick and Rosemary gives a sense of their privileged contact with the fire and brimstone of these poets. Rick's conviction-- like that of the Beats through the ghostly figure of Whitman-- emanates the glory of many poets as he talks of Limberlost Phase Two: the road to Pocatello. There are echoes of Kerouac and Ken Kesey, when in 1986 Rick and Rosemary drove west in a 1966 VW Bus. Rick was a published poet by then, *One Place For Another* had appeared from the Confluence Press in 1983. Their destination was Idaho State University. Rosemary graduated and became a teacher while Rick worked on a Master's thesis, making him an adept of Ezra Pound's *Cantos*: the essential 'education through provocation.' The final *Limberlost Review* celebrated the Pound Centennial, coinciding with a conference which Rick organized in Hailey, centered at the Liberty Theater. Distinguished guests were Olga Rudge, who Rick describes as "the love of the poet's life and very defensive of any criticism of him," and his daughter, Mary de Rachewiltz. Hailey retains an occult redolence for Poundians such as Rick, who is proud of the Pound-Hemingway connections, or what he called "those odd and startling coincidences that fuels Idaho's literary mythology."

Limberlost Review recounted the debacle over a special Pound postage stamp which was cancelled and the die destroyed by the US Postal Service. The happier outcome was the glittering contributors to the volume: Pound's publisher, James Laughlin, as well as locally resident Idaho poets, Robert Wrigley and Norman Weinstein alongside seasoned Poundians, Hayden Carruth, Peter Dale Scott, William Stafford, William Studebaker, John Tytell and notably, an essay by Charles Bukowski. The Centennial Pound *Limberlost Review* is as rare as gold and silver in Idaho City.

We linger around the library as sunset causes us to squint. Rick leads off towards the *poetarium*—his word. This is a sanctuary, off limits to the dogs, fondly shoed away while I am invited in, and the conversation turns to time-honored publishing mavericks *City Lights Press*, *Copper Canyon Press*, *Black Sparrow Press* and *Three Mountains Press* whom Rick admits are key influences. There is a distinct levity in his introduction to the Chandler and Price letterpress, the contraption redolent of the early eras of printing: a type cabinet, racks of lead letters and strange looking tools. The printing machine has a large fan belt and moving parts that could easily injure muscle and limb. Rick tightens a screw with a wrench, and declares, "This weighs well over a ton, and we had to winch it into the garage with help from friends." He says 'garage' without any frills: at one level this is the *poetarium* and at another the garage. "There was a Baptist minister in New Plymouth, Idaho, who was selling up and moving to New York City," begins Rick, "and, of course, we haggled and I bought the whole lot off him: press, tools, type, and all for 500 dollars borrowed from my brother in Ohio. The minister didn't say much, just that he used it for his church and community printing needs. I badly wanted the whole caboose but had no clue about how to print on it. Rosie and I, had by then, stopped the *Limberlost Review*. So at last we had a printing device and needed to get know-how."

Undaunted, he set about becoming an apprentice letterpress printer through an Idaho Commission of the Arts grant of $3,500, and a month's training in Story, Wyo., under the tutelage of Tom and Barb Rea of Dooryard Press who were publishing Richard Hugo's *Sea Lanes Out*—his final chapbook. They also published a chapbook of Rick's, *Report From More's Creek*, and one by Sam Hazo. "Two former Pittsburghers are printing a book by Pittsburgh's poet laureate!" recalls Rick. "We kept our name Limberlost; not based on Gene Stratton Porter's novel *Girl of the Limberlost*. There was a cabin by that name where Rosie and I stayed during our time in Slippery Rock State College."

The letterpress, with menacing jaws, crashes out a dummy print run with some lines from a poem on a test sheet of paper for demonstration purposes. The explanation of how the Chandler and Price platen press prints a chapbook is easy to understand as you watch the monster doing its thing. As a sample, he hands over a copy of a recent chapbook: Edward Sanders' *This Morning's Joy*. A 32 page chapbook contains eight sheets of paper, printed back and front. To have the titles of poems in color, the printing process is repeated. Each page has to be handset with the type backwards: proof reading requires elements in one's make-up of Leonardo Da Vinci, noted for his ability to read 'mirrored words.' Imagine Mark Twain as 'niawT kraM' and you roughly have the task before Rick. Try this in a sentence backwards and then in a whole poem? Hence, each book is a labor of love and much labor, besides.

"Is small-press publishing counter-cultural? A counter-flow to publisher conglomerates like Time Warner, Random House?" I ask, opening the clean white cover of *This Morning's Joy*. "I guess in the digital age the printed book is again revolutionary," answers Rick, looking like some medieval magician or alchemist who turns empty sheets of vellum, ink and colored ink into a fully stitched readable book. Their first titles were *Death Drag* by John Clellon Holmes, and *No Wild Dog Howled* by another close friend and poet Bruce Embree. Later in the 1990s, Embree's *Beneath the Chickenshit Mormon Sun* became the most conflicted print run at Limberlost due to the poet's suicide.

Limberlost made literary history when Ardinger brought Allen Ginsberg to Idaho for readings in 1994, and the poet 'did' a Limberlost book, *Mind Writing Slogans,* soon followed by Ferlinghetti's *The Canticle of Jack Kerouac* and *The Street's Kiss*. Limberlost is not only distinctive in its stable of poets who are chosen and magically choose the press, it also has memorable titles as well as memorable covers. For instance, *Pale Blue Wings* by Nancy Takacs, *The Rat Lady at the Company Dump* by William Studebaker, *Not Cancelled Yet* by John Updike, *Winter Horses* by Chris Dempsey, or one of their proudest and, by their standards, most successful titles, *Three on Community* by Gary Snyder, Wendell Berry and Carole Koda. This title had a printing run of 800. Most of the books reach less than half that number. In keeping with small presses, there are no contracts between publisher and poet, royalties are in copies, and there is the happy requirement of a proportion of signed copies. Limberlost titles total over sixty titles, so far, as well as poetry postcards and broadsides that become framed wall hangings by their owners. Rick's position as executive director of the Idaho Humanities Council means that Limberlost is pushed back to the nighshift: he lives in a merry conflict betwixt being Arts supremo and obeying the lure of Centaur, Benedictine

Book, and Lydian (his favorite typefaces).

Rick concludes his tour of the *poetarium*. We return to the house as Limberlost seems to remain outside and their guests sit around talking in clusters. Rosemary corrects the impression that their publishing is confined outside the home, explaining cloth binding, board-editions, wrappers, and sewing: work for the domestic hearth! One of the poems in Sanders's book *The Question of Self-Publishing* is very appropriate:

For 25 years William Blake

>> kept the copper plates for

>>>> the *Songs of Innocence*

to print a copy or two on a need

& then he hand-painted the colors

>>>> with Catherine's help

Walt Whitman helped set & print

>>> his own *Leaves of Grass*

>> in the Brooklyn vastness

Woody Guthrie

a mimeographed edition of his songs in '39

& Ginsberg mimeo'd some "Howl's"

>>> in '55

& so it goes

& goes so well

Rick quotes Pound: "It doesn't matter who writes the great poems as long as they get written." He bites his lip and begins to chuckle "That old guy Pound was really what he claimed to be, the Ezuversity," he says. Gildner chimes in, "There's a huge difference between the English faculty and the English faculty of the spirit," and tries to recall who used the phrase, eventually remembering it was Jack Spicer. Rosemary mentioned the Limberlost Weekend in Salt Lake City in 2003: a tribute to all their poets including Rosalie Sorrels and Greg Keeler, among others.

It was time to thank the Ardingers for their hospitality, looking forward to the next occasion, realizing that here was another department of the Ezuversity with its alternative curriculum. Rick bade me wait when I mentioned Robert Creeley. "There is an image of a poem written by Creeley in the Sander's book," he says. This was our closing recitation for the night. Sure enough, the lines scrawled on a napkin were photo-reproduced in the book. "Things/come and go,/Then/let them." Yes, it doesn't matter who writes the great poems as long as they get written. It very much matters that the small presses assert their own hegemony, independence, and valor. Throughout my visit, neither Rick nor Rosemary Ardinger claimed any special position in small press publishing, but that, as they say, is integrity.

—*Idaho Arts Quarterly* Winter 2008

THE IT GANG

Fintan O'Toole, Colm Tóibín, Roy Foster, Diarmaid Ferriter & Joseph O'Connor can always rely on fellow *blurberistas* with O'Toole as Literary Editor at the *Irish Times* making the group a queasy quintet and their publishers on tow. Superlatives and praise are easily concocted. Blurbs a part of product placement. However O'Toole, Tóibín, Foster, Ferriter & O'Connor bring to their blurbs in-house shameless double-dealing that utilises every possible media outlet especially the *Irish Times*.

O'Toole in turn for his books ensures snippy quotes of adulation with Ferriter and Foster as pulp historians alongside Tóibín and O'Connor as pulp-historical novelists, all playing this blurb-amigos game. The gang are in bed together as *fawnatisti* blurbing away the front and back covers of books. Tóibín is master of the art and would presumably also endorse Ferriter, Foster and the others if they turned out books on travel, cookery or gardening.

For instance take two books: *The Irish Story* and *Modern Ireland 1600-1972* both according to Tóibín, rank Foster as 'the most brilliant and courageous Irish historian of his generation'. The same blurb appears on the back of both books. Tóibín puffing Foster can equal his assessment of Ferriter's *The Transformation of Ireland 1900-2000* (front cover) deemed 'a landmark book' while on the back cover there is space for more fulsome praise: 'a timely and masterful new survey'…'a transformation in historical methodology'. Tóibín's sycophancy must be so alluring that Profile Books re-used this block-quote on Ferriter's book on Ireland in the 1970s, *Ambiguous Republic*. However, there is nothing ambiguous about the thick carpet of blurb.

Catastrophically, Ferriter has revised the modern perception of both John Charles McQuaid and De Valera. McQuaid in *The Transformation of Ireland* is defended from every attack by other commentators since 'this does scant justice to the multitude of tasks that he performed'. He is praised as educationalist, administrator, reformer as well as 'pioneer of social services and theologian, and [he] facilitated the construction of schools and hospitals'. In the light of institutional evils visited upon the innocent and the poor during McQuaids's reign this is dangerously incorrect.

Foster puffs fellow historian Ferriter's *The Transformation of Ireland: 1900-2000* 'it will be an influential book, and is a remarkable achievement' while O'Toole does his bit blurbing Ferriter's *Occasions of Sin: Sex and Society in Modern Ireland* '[the] superbly researched narrative is a powerful prophylactic.' As a gang they pass out mutual prophylactics regularly and cannot publish without the assistance of hand-holding blurbs.

O'Toole as their leader is reliably shoddy when you examine the zany appendix to *Enough Is Enough: How to Build a New Republic*. The appendix lists *50 Key Actions* which are actually altruistic slogans. Behind his manifesto is the veiled spiel of someone toying with the decision to run for public office or not. O'Toole dreams of various changes to taxation and political structures such as 'reduce the size of the Dáil to 100 members.' 'Adopt a long-term national goal of pegging house prices in Ireland to Western European averages.' And the winning slogan, No. 50. 'Declare a Republic'. Crackbrained stuff, worthy of an apprentice Mussolini.

O'Toole recently edited a collection of essays from various contributors '*Up the Republic: Towards a New Ireland*'. Unfortunately, his own 54 page essay is of the knee-jerk variety as vintage champagne socialist and parlour pink. His starting point is Alphonse de Lamartine, French romantic poet in 1848 but O'Toole's approach is thin postgraduate analysis. Lamartine asked the question 'Do you know what a republic is?' and O'Toole sets out to explore the 'deep and resonant republican tradition that stretches back over thousands of years'. Thankfully, he doesn't stretch back to *republican* Normans, Vikings, to St Patrick and the

Druids.

He is eclectic on reference with asides from Haughey and Ahern. Typical of his analysis is the following: 'The vague, incomplete half-republic that existed between 1922 and 2008 is gone for good.' Mealy-mouthed rhetoric is the norm: 'A republic is not something people are given but something they choose to become'. The conclusions are dull: 'the real Irish national anthem is not "Amhrán na BhFiann", it is Gloria Gaynor's "I Will Survive"'. His final sentence lacks meaning, especially as the conclusion to a polemical essay. 'Injustice and inequality are now starkly visible. They are the governing principles of the new polity. The choice is either to learn to live with them by forgetting the republic again—this time for good—or to cease to have either to remember or to forget the republic because it has become a reality'. This phraseology is obscure, contradictory and does not make sense.

Roy Foster is entrenched and close to xenophobia in historical reportage. As O'Toole looks to his one-man utopian revolution, Foster's historical perspectives remain revisionist and repressive. His companions such as Tóibín obviously support this approach to Cromwell, the Famine and the 1916 revolutionary tradition. Foster exclusively celebrates 'the Ascendency mind' in *Modern Ireland 1600-1972*. Cromwell's 'footprints have been so deeply imprinted upon Irish history'…'[they are] still inextricably identified with massacre and expropriation'. The massacres are footnoted merely. During the Famine, landlordism was 'seen as to blame for the catastrophe by many — illogically, but understandably'. The Young Ireland Movement had 'an insurrectionary ethic founded in an almost psychotic Anglophobia'. The revolutionaries of 1916 are rebels with 'atavistic Anglophobia'. Foster's history is exclusively for reading in Oxford with tea and cake overlooking the river Isis. His revisionist position according to Brendan Bradshaw has 'a natural anti-Irish bias' and his personal psychology castigates the Irish as part of 'a competitive victimhood in the history of colonised nations'. This is wilfully cruel.

Diarmaid Ferriter disavows any labels of being a coffee-table book historian and lashed out at fellow De Valera biographers, Tim Pat Coogan and Anthony Jordan when his own pictorial book (not a biography) *Judging Dev* was questioned by them. Jordan exposed the commercial vested interest of RTÉ as co-publisher giving much favourable exposure to *Judging Dev*. Ryan Tubridy, of course, found it 'a watershed in the telling of Irish history…every Irish home should have one'. Education Minister, Mary Hannafin plonked it onto the curriculum—making the book official history.

Ferriter tenaciously defends his feelgood friendly '*Judging Dev* [was] deemed to be suitable for schools because of original documents, the study of which forms part of the Leaving Certificate history curriculum'. Ferriter complained of Coogan's 'personal antipathy to de Valera [and] because my book dared challenge the conclusions of his biography'. This plays along with De Valera's well laid plans for posterity as Ferriter promotes this caption version of history while Foster promotes his Oxonian version.

Coogan wrote of Ferriter's *Judging Dev* proving that the De Valera Papers have circumstantial value only, 'I also consulted [the archive] while writing my de Valera biography. I can say with certainty that, though they are of interest, those well-winnowed papers do not contain any great insights into de Valera's mind and motivations.'

Meanwhile, Tóibín and O'Connor praise each other endlessly. Tóibín praised O'Connor's *Ghost Light* another historical fiction, the favoured metier of this duo. *Ghost Light* had 'an astonishing command of voice, using tones that are both tender and powerfully emotional, with a brilliant command of the period.' O'Connor cites a 'masterful' touch from Toibin's *The Master* a bowdlerized history of the novelist, Henry James who awakens from a dream 'like an old door.' Hardly, mind-blowing style! Nor does O'Connor refrain from a gushing-blurb for Tóibín's *The Testament of Mary*. 'I cannot praise this book highly enough; the voice of Mary is so clear'. Tóibín cannot be bested in return over O'Connor's story collection *The Thrill of It All* 'playful but also at times sorrowful; it allows in great quantities of life'. And so on. Tóibín and O'Connor have stolid pals in Foster and Ferriter of course who in turn praise their use of history in fiction while O'Toole is Godfather in the wings. Basically O'Toole, Tóibín, Foster, Ferriter & O'Connor blurb away—conspicuously crooning each other's praises. The mutual blurbing reflects on the value of their work, ultimately and highlights their cowardice in the republic of letters.

—*VILLAGE: politics and culture* 2014

FAILING AGAIN TO FIND CARAVAGGIO: RHA 185th Annual Exhibition

The current president, Mick O'Dea, designated PRHA highlights the Academy as 'exhibiting work that is innovative and representative of the broad spectrum of best practice from here and abroad'. Well, if you bother to inspect the present show this is a fiction. Meanwhile, hyper-inflated self-praise is a hallmark of RHA writing just as the exhibition prides itself on catchy titles for the artworks and some claim to postmodernity.

O'Dea noted that 2014 saw a '28% increase in sales' as he proclaims that 'Ireland's art investment has clearly turned a corner'. He sees the gallery as 'the perfect spotting ground for the aspiring and discerning collector.' RHA's sponsors include AXA Insurance, the ESB, and vested interest galleries such as Adams, De Veres and Whytes, as well as the Ireland-US Council and the *Irish Arts Review,* edited and presided over by the elsewhere discerning cultural stalwart, John Mulcahy.

Amongst the sponsors are the gullible buyers or dealers. However, art markets are financially created for finance, and rarely subject to viable critical faculty, certainly, if one considers this year's show. The Academy niftily gleans a six-figure annual grant from the Arts Council and dispenses in-house prize money (not a lot) to the tune of €45,000 donated by the sponsors. The prizes in the main go to members in a definitive rotation scheme.

Many RHA members are coincidentally also members of Aosdána. Most of these receive the Arts Council annual cnuas of €17,180 to top up their takings which explains the *raison d'être* behind the annual show. Members mixed up in Aosdána include James Hanley, Veronica Bolay, Diana Copperwhite, Gary Coyle, Michael Cullen, Imogen Stuart (recently given a Saoi by Aosdána gang members), Martin Gale, Richard Gorman, Charles Harper, Gene Lambert, Alice Maher, Stephen McKenna, Carolyn Mulholland, Patrick Pye, and Barbara Warren. Eithne Jordan RHA is brother of the movie maker genius. Her *Underpass II* is probably the best of a bad lot in the show with its Orson Wellsian bleak modernity, however, an artist collectivised among self-elevated boffins pays a price to personal integrity and in the scheme of things: ultimate validity, performance and worth. The Aosdána ethos of collectivisation and cosy caucus prevails at the RHA.

O'Dea is sanctimonious about open submissions from non-members who are permitted to present a maximum of three works and try their luck for inclusion at the annual exhibition. These artists totalled over 1,000 in 2015 while RHA members can, and do exhibit up to seven works without any pre-selection process. Director, Patrick T. Murphy emphasised with great praise the 8 Academy members giving 5 full days of their time inspecting the open submissions 'not once but twice to select about 10% of the artworks that have been submitted.' Surely they can give the submissions a second glance. Murphy added 'it is a rigorous and concentrated exercise'.

Their high point according to the press release, the exhibition catalogue, and the newsletter is Tracy Emin's *Wanting You*—a neon florescent light. Basically a snow white heart and the text in pink. Limited edition at €110,000 per unit. Emin, except for those afraid to admit it, is a joke on the art scene, a loud Cassandra and purveyor of kitsch. But her offering to the distinctly provincial RHA is taken seriously as some sort of coup. Aidan Dunne stated that her work 'seems quite at home' in Dublin. Wow! You can get neon lights to order in better condition and a lot cheaper at any hardware supplier. Behind Dunne's tired praise in the *Irish Times* is hyperbole upon hyperbole which does not reflect the realities of the Royal Hibernian Academy or its dinosaurs, its council, board, benefactors and staff. Dunne's lazy approach is no more than blurb with his praise for Martin Gale's *Talking at Doonfeeny* putting 'people in the picture...struggling in some way with the reality of living in the country'. It is actually Gale's usual oiled-up photorealism, basically a pier wall, high tide, two windswept figures and a collie dog. Gale's daughter is a staffer at the RHA which illustrates the inner landscape of protocol and in-house preferences demonstrably felt in the number of solo shows that the gallery hosts throughout each year for members.

Overall, the exhibition beggars description with the members prancing about in robes on opening night, wine at exorbitant prices per glass, and the sculpture room with pieces that look as if they were rough hewn using crowbars and sledge hammers rather than more effective tools. Eileen MacDonagh is sister sledge using limestone if you consider her *Archimedes Gate*. Marie Smith's swollen bronzes are unpleasant and their purported realism vague. Janet Mullarney's *Giotto's Circle* of papier-mâché and wire, at the other end of the scale is kindergarten art for the school windowsill. John Behan peddles his stock in trade *Famine Ship* with a price tag of €21,000 making it an expensive bathroom display. Remco De Fouw's triptych of stone and glass is barely souvenir shop standard.

Dunne believes that in the academy 'portrait painting has survived the advent of the selfie'. He could not be more wrong. Ever since the pervasive influence of Robert Ballagh, incidentally a staunch Aosdánaí himself, the RHA purveys an incipient school of photorealism in oils. The group includes Thomas Ryan. *High Mass, St Kevin's* in his perennial 'out of focus' oil-style. Carey Clarke, another dinosaur follows the standard selfie-digital portrait from RHA practitioners. Work that makes Homer and Marge Simpson look more accomplished. Clarke presents Professor Lonergan of TCD in this mode along with O'Dea's *Christina and Michael* typical of the crinkly portrait school of photorealism. Another doyenne of this mode is Anita Shelbourne with a morbid collage and acrylic of Maud Gonne and Robin Buick's *Print 1*.

There is a definite suspicion that RHA members who do portraits adopt the fraudulent Giclée method or similar methods. In other words: photographing the subject, then resorting to the use of inkjet printing directly onto a roll of canvas and making reproductions of the original two-dimensional artwork, photographs or computer-generated art. Hey presto the result ends up on the gallery wall as a canvas framed or unframed. This Giclée method and ancillary methods are all used. Whether the majority of members can actually draw, paint or sculpt to any high standard is the great No-No of the academy. It is not permitted to ask whether the emperor wears clothes.

Landscapes predominate under the influence of Sean McSweeney who is part of the show. This Itchy and Scratchy School of art has been adopted by those who constantly cruise rural Ireland with stop-offs at centres such as Ballinglen in Co. Mayo which explains Pat Harris's presence with *From Stonefield*. Basically the sea with a sliver of blurred green landscape and a big sky. Veronica Bolay, Joe Dunne, Charles Harper, and Donald Teskey follow suit. One could easily interchange the names and mass-produce these landscapes for Tesco for less, or Euro Store. But there are other RHA members lured into easy subject-matter landscapes depicting night or day. There is also the pretty dead still life school reflected by RHA dinosaurs, particularly Stephen McKenna *Four Donegal Cloths*, David Hone *Still Life*, and John Long *Two Peaches*.

Photography at the RHA has always been monopolised by Amelia Stein whose *Sheep Wire* is post-Warhol. How brilliant to think of photographing sheep wire for a print edition of 10, framed or unframed. Abigail O'Brien's *Paper Trail* is a print showing shelves of dusty files which of course Dunne finds 'compelling...evocative of endlessly circuitous legal bureaucracy as Dickens's *Bleak House*'. It is easier to associate *Paper Trail*, if with anything, the RHA itself. Overall, the photography hits an all time low, especially Mella Travers *Stealth* mawkish, morbid, pseudo-Gothic in yet another limited edition, framed or unframed.

The novelty act besides Emin's neon is Martin & Henri Gibbins 'recycled' *Filthy Robot* looking like a Dr Who relic in a junk shop, or the Tin Man gone wrong from *The Wizard of Oz* but it certainly wouldn't make the Late Late Toy Show.

Coming up to the revolutionary centenary, the RHA promises an early annual show in March to cash in on 2016. They should convene a board meeting and drop the 'Royal' to The Hibernian Academy. At least, in homage to our patriots but then members would have HA after their name and associate members would give the game away by being AHA. Anyway, expect more from the Daub-Daub, Dab-Dab and Drab-Drab schools in their 2016 exhibition, unless original submissions can be sneaked past the RHA's assessors who see themselves as born again Caravaggios.

—*VILLAGE: culture and politics* 2015

AOS DÁNA: where self-selection meets self-praise, in a faux Gaelic, Haugheyesque arts beano

Cosy cartel if not secret society, Aosdána is an independent group who serve themselves from within the bursary system administered by the Arts Council. Since its founding in the 1980s the central function of Aosdána has been to ensure its membership continues siphoning off the *cnuas*—a Gaelic term—for the yearly hand-out of €17,180 to the self-elected members. Their central agenda as a collective is access to this annual handout. Other arts practitioners seeking Arts Council funding must formally apply for a bursary in competition with fellow artists. Bursaries are far less in monetary value than a *cnuas*. Gaining a bursary means disbarment for succeeding future years. Aosdána is therefore a protectorate that has unjustly placed itself above the democratic system of bursary application. Smart move, eh! Last year, the Arts Council had its budget slashed by a quarter to (*circa*) €61 million from (*circa*) €80 million. Yet Aosdana's150+ members in receipt of the annual €17,180 suffered no reduction in their hand-out. Many groups had to soldier on despite the Arts Council cuts but not the Aosdanaí.

The Arts Council Report (2011) reveals that 152 individual creative practitioners received bursaries amounting to €1.5 million. In the same year, 156 Aosdána members drew down their self-appointed, self-designed *cnuas* totalling €2.7 million—almost twice as much in funding compared to the amount in bursaries granted to individuals. In other words, bursary applicants had a funding pool of approximately half that of the secured allotment to Aosdána.

Anthony Cronin, founder member of Aosdána receives his *cnuas* along with his partner, Anne Haverty as there are many couples who have nominated and voted each other in, so as to corner the €17,180 each. Others in this couples-category includes Theo Dorgan and Paula Meehan, Dermot Seymour and Maud Cotter, and in the past, Deirdre Madden and Harry Clifton, Shelley McNamara and Michael

Kane, John Arden and Margaretta D'Arcy to name but a few. Stalwarts of the *cnuas* since its set-up include Leland Bardwell, Ulick O'Connor, Paul Durcan, Patrick Hall, John Montague and Richard Murphy persons who obviously see themselves above the bursary application process.

Another issue of injustice concerning the 156 Aosdanaí drawing down their Merrion Square arts-dole is that it exceeds the welfare benefit. Also the 156 names are meant to represent persons devoted full-time to their so-called art as judged by themselves in the first place. As one reads the list of Aosdanaí on arts-dole bafflement sets in as to who among tax-paying citizens would recognise even a minority of those on the list. Then there are insider-trading elements detectable when certain *cnuas* recipients such as Pat Boran also operates a publishing venture *Dedalus* subsidised by yet again, the Arts Council. *Dedalus* has published many books by Boran himself. Similarly, Peter Fallon's *Gallery Press* is heavily subsidised by (can you guess?) the Arts Council and he publishes many fellow-members of Aosdána just as *Dedalus* does. Fallon has also published himself on many occasions using his own *Gallery Press*—how very convenient!

The wheeling and double-dealing of this collective within the Arts Council is ultimately inspired by C. J. Haughey, the instigator who rubber-stamped Aosdána. The Haughey stigma resonates throughout their crooked practices. In the early 1980s, only fifty members received a *cnuas* worth IR£5,000 per annum but with much conniving and their insider-voting-in system more than thirty years later members tenaciously hold onto their annual stipend which they have puffed to its current level of €17,180. Aosdána's hallmark is members voting in family or friends as originally with Louis le Brocquy, his sister Melanie le Brocquy, and his wife Anne Madden since nepotism is pervasive among the group.

Aosdána is from the Old Irish meaning 'people of the arts' and was named by Máire de Paor of the Arts Council Board in the 1980s that choose the smokescreen term *Aosdána* instead of *An Torc* which was the initial and equally ridiculous suggestion for its name. The torc based on the ancient Irish gold necklace remains in Aosdána as an honour conferred on certain members by a vote of all members. It comes as no surprise that founder-member, Anthony Cronin was voted to receive a torc himself which makes him a 'High-Saoi' or 'wise one' according to Aosdána's terminology. Wise one indeed, since with Haughey's assistance, Cronin secured an arts-advisor job coincidentally at the time of Aosdána's being founded. Cronin has been a board member of Aosdána for years, or in their parlance, one of the *toscairí*.

Cronin's holding the highest award given by members to a member is laughable amongst other ridicule about Aosdána. For instance, its wildgoose chase in trying to bestow a torc on Samuel Beckett at a proposed ceremony in Áras an Uachtaráin to be presided over by President Patrick Hillery. Year after year, Aosdána implored Beckett to come home from Paris for his torc, so much so that by 1985 the Arts Council announced: 'The Beckett Saoi Torc presentation [is] still unresolved.' Finally, without Beckett present, a dinner was held in Dublin by the toscairí and the torc conferred in his absence on the writer's 80th birthday. What a farce!

Originally, Aosdána came into being through Cronin and a clique of unknowns surrounding themselves with writers and artists of repute. These involuntary members included Samuel Beckett, Seán Ó'Faolain, Benedict Kiely, Francis Stuart, Denis Johnston, Anne Yeats, and Charles Brady among others. Not only Beckett but to the present writer's knowledge these invited members felt bullied into joining Aosdána by an ogre such as Cronin at the time who was wielding Arts Council power through Haughey. The bullying of Beckett into accepting a torc by Aosdána's registrar, Adrian Munnelly (a native of Haughey's birthplace, Castlebar) as Director of the Arts Council who had supplanted Colm Ó'Briain with Cronin in the background is less hilarious and ultimately sinister.

The darker side of Aosdána includes its close relationship with the university system through mutual cultural collusion as well as its harbouring and granting *cnuas* support to payroll academics such as Nigel Rolfe, and for instance Maeve McGuckian of QUB. Aosdána consistently has had members on the board of the Arts Council including Colm Tóibín. The Arts Council have often been pushed into using adjudicators from among Aosdána's ranks while such members of course grant favours to their associates. An even darker side of Aosdána is its continuing support for Cathal Ó'Searcaigh's sex-tourism in Nepal and funding this as he is a *cnuas* recipient himself. Neasa Ní Chianain's documentary *Fairytale of Kathmandu* revealed Ó'Searcaigh as opportunistic predator grooming innocent impoverished Nepalese youths of sixteen and buying them bicycles and ice cream in return for sex. An art auction held in Letterkenny raised €50,000 for Ó'Searcaigh's visits to Nepal enabled by establishment figures including Gay Byrne and a full coterie of Aosdána members.

Meanwhile the earth shattering achievement of Aosdána in 2013 was to finally organise their in-house voting procedures after thirty years! 'All returned ballot papers (including blank papers) will count towards the calculation of the quota.' This motion was carried at the meeting of the Toscaireacht on 3 February 2013 and signed into *Aosdána Law* by those present: Anthony Cronin, Theo Dorgan, Mary FitzGerald, Alice Hanratty, Brian Maguire, Shelley McNamara, Jane O'Leary. Two other members Mary O'Malley and Colm Tóibín had sent their apologies for being absent during this monumental debate. After thirty years you might think that members could organise a voting system among themselves.

Aosdána must be abolished, primarily because of the membership who receive the *cnuas* and have a finger in so many other cash-cushy arts pies. Space prohibits the names that one could out in this matter especially various RHA members, as well as in-house RTÉ folk such as Jerome de Bromhead. The membership of Aosdána should collectively sign a public apology for their arrogance that is if the public would recognise the majority of their names. Most culpable is their lack of any ethics in wilfully taking large sums of Arts Council funds for the past thirty years which by now amounts to considerable millions. Those who need arts council funding have the option of filling in the bursary application form and entering competitively to gain an award under the democratic process not like the shameless collective of Aosdanaí.

In the end in the arts as in all other endeavours, self-selection, like self-praise is nothing.

All *cnuas* recipients are listed at
http://aosdana.artscouncil.ie/Cnuas.aspx

—*VILLAGE: politics and culture* 2014

ALONENESS

Painting the Vestibule Betty Thompson (Scalltamedia)

Miracle Fruit Moyra Donaldson (Lagan Press)

The Truth in Mustard Terry McDonagh (Arlen House)

The Green Crown Roderick Ford (Bradshaw Books)

Curve of the Moon Noel Monahan (Salmon Poetry)

Encountering Zoe : new and selected poetry Tom MacIntyre (New Island)

What catches most attention are the poems inspired by Ana Maria Pacheco, sculptors Barbara Hepworth, Louise Bourgeois, and the artist Duncan Grant but not "Curlew At Bull Island" where the speaker is a bird watched by birdwatchers. Just as "Leaves after Rain" and "Golden Ash" are archaic. "Louise Bourgeois at the Serpentine" needs more structure for disparate images such as 'Here, clothes-hangers are bones/whose knuckled ends trap shoulder straps' "Ludwig's Gifts" begins awkwardly: 'I bring gloves to guard your fingers'. "Life Swell" is 'about' the flotsam and jetsam in a river but little else: 'Years ago a piano, no longer upright, /its walnut casing bobbing on the waves, /was sighted near the bridge at Church Street/and hauled up with ropes. /' "Piano shop, Manchester" invokes Edward Hopper's art of shut stores: 'to gaze at grand pianos, parallelograms/of dull walnut or watery white casing'. This is her finest piece. "Sound" is too wordy: 'brushing against a jelly mould, /sent it hopping and spinning on the tiles below/where its tinny hollows resonate.' "Seeing Angels" is 'painterly' in a visionary mode. These are her two parameters: light and the chaos of random images as in "Lunchtime at Nussbaum & Wu": 'Ceiling fans whir like birds who have flown absentmindedly/into a garden room'.

Ghoulish gothic eclectic collection referencing the seventeenth century Scottish surgeon John Hunter in 'What John Hunter Said To Me': 'I could stand for hours in the cold,/my only company the opened stinking corpse/before me, and I myself almost motionless,/a pair of forceps and my own open fingers/picking asunder the connecting fibres/of structure, the heart, the lactating breast,/'. The implication is that the surgeon and the poet have a facility for exploration that makes others shudder. The omission of explanatory notes is a flaw when faced with "The Skeleton of the Great Irish Giant" about Charles Byrne whom London body snatchers waited for 'like harpooners/round a whale'. His skeleton is in the Hunter a Museum in London. Hunter himself is dissected in "The First Hunter an Oration 1814—John Abernethy": 'He came to the conclusions that blood/held the secret of Vitality and I like to believe/he also came to see God in the blood'. "How To Make A Pig-Faced Woman" is about Gisela Steevans, benefactor of the hospital that bears her name and who endured derision in Dublin: 'Everyone knew Madame Steevans had the face of a pig.' In "Mrs Frame" a phantom pregnancy proves to be real when at the autopsy 'they found therein the skeleton of a child'. Focus on the dissection room is alleviated in "How To Feed Your Lover", "How to Become A Buddha Through Self-Mummification" and solitude is explored in "Dunluce Avenue". Donaldson explores pitiful life stories in order to test the anatomy of her work.

More yarns than poems as in "Three Nuns in a Pickup", "A Gypsy Woman in Ireland", "The Pit Bull" and "About Albert" that ramble on quite a bit. "Seven Arabian Days and Nights" has scenes of life in Kuwait but his metaphors are overloaded: 'I see myriads of water tanks fixed to rooftops/like curlers to a drinking woman's head.' McDonagh's metaphors like darts hit the dartboard but end up on the floor. Morbid nostalgia for radio is in "An Address Somewhere in PYE": 'Luxemburg was new. We didn't say cool,/brilliant or super./I had no words for Dante's darkness either.' No connection for the last line can be discerned from those that precede it. Otherwise vagueness abounds as in "A Writers' Festival on Bali": 'I try to visualise what I see/but only see/what I sense in the percolating dark.' The title poem is equally flawed: "The Truth in Mustard" replete with childhood nostalgia repeats a recipe using mustard for bacon. His short poems are squibs [//=double spacing]: "Lovely Women": 'Rubens' women were/round and fat.//Beckham's wife/is very thin.//Rubens' women/are alive and well./With Beckham's wife/you cannot tell.' McDonagh's closing poem should gain the award for bizarre poem of the decade "Let Everything Have an End": 'Make the most of it cow, roared bull…won't/be back this way for another year, dear.'

This kind of 'poetry' used to fill *The Messenger* and *The Far East* written by idle clerics or precocious townsfolk with spare time, notepaper and pencils. Ford is devotional but quite obviously not in the manner of T.S. Eliot, St John of the Cross or Rilke. This is chocolate box spirituality that is eerily spooky and disconcerting while the result is to trivialise profound experience: 'With heaven in my eyes I walk these roads/and though I'm shunned none will do me harm,/for all must take the sacrament of death,/' ("The Dinner Guest"). "The Carpenter's House" based on the life of Christ is spiritually bland: 'till there's a whisper of a gently opening door/and Christ walks down the stairs with wooden feet.' Also "The Spinner": 'I cast my nets in Galilee and drew forth men/whose souls were winged like angels'. The chances of anyone finding such utterances original is impossible. "Room of Red" might just about make it onto a Valentine's Day Card: 'I went to bed with a wandering girl,/her dark hair shone with glints of moon'. Ford's fake luxury and the faux-naif is more faux than naïf. "A Plate of Holes" concludes with 'those pearls still lie below the sea/and dream forever in their shells'. Pearls do not dream. "Auntie" is anecdotal about a woman who liked to cook and to talk: 'We put her in it for her cremation,/she really looked her best just then, she grinned,/as the oven door clicked shut.' This is unreal or surreal. He also has a poem entitled "The Bad Back" simple about a bad back. He doesn't have any poems about bad poems!

A bumper collection, anecdotal and imagist including the lengthy "Diary of a Town" and with sonnets while the truest criticism is in "Summer Holiday": 'We are a possessive people, attached/To small holdings, a view we take on trips./ and 'Holidays homes if we won the lotto,'. In "A Ghostly Letter From Sheridan To Swift" the contemporary is glossed with another era: 'Only Pat the Baker survived the fall/And Dunnes Stores Better Value Beats Them All.'

Dissatisfaction pervades "Catching Each Other By The Tail": 'Politicians in mohair suits,/Grease the wheels of the treadmill,/Bend the Green Greenness of Éire/So the peas can run freely in their pods,/Then pause and listen to themselves.' In Monahan's Ireland the natives wear tight shoes and perhaps never run free. The moon leitmotif as blade of reality is benign in "Curve of the Moon": 'Maiden, mother and moon,/Ladleful of milk in the stars' while "November Moon" is the celestial clock with 'Its drowned face below a sea of stars/Has yesterday's light on its lips.' Nature and Eros are the only constants as in "Sheela Na Gig" which yields a redolent image, 'Gaping vulva in the curve of the moon.' "Diary of a Town" is both dirge and celebration over twelve sections evoking Monahan's townspeople, moving from schooldays to the grave while the conclusion is mildly comic as trousers have to be put on to face another year. Time is not but was: this is the Monahan's vision.

Good production values with cover of couchant female (by Clayton Bastiani) in keeping with the theme of conquest. Mac Intyre is a Bard transposed to modern times yet predominantly rural like his folkloric theatre plays. Translations from Gaelic are either deliberately colloquial or strive after dialect. He maintains a gasping line that end stops to the audible beat of a drum (almost) that can annoy or entertain. "The Yellow Bittern" concludes: 'no, mates, drink it up—an' piss it down,/warm them worms waitin' undergroun'.' There is never any involvement with images except mildly in "Candour of the Well": 'where berry stares/at candle-end,/and candle-end/gives back the stare.' Often, his titles are baffling as to the connection with their content and bafflement reigns go leor as if poetry were a completed crossword puzzle lacking any clues and with inversions 'ambassador mine from the Cliffs of Love.' ("Eagle"). "Ghost At The Feast" has a dense stew of language and makes one move on with a shrug. Anecdotes proliferate occasionally buried in the linguistic register that veils everything. This is solipsistic poetry, soi-disant with personal reference as in "She" where one learns little about her except that 'here the gown ne'er torn' and she is a 'Daughter of The Deep-Dish Leaves'.

Hyperbole occurs a lot as in "The Sea Potato": 'arpeggios, misted, ten/thousand shells chime/in the waves' undertow.' This joy is not felt by the reader because delivered in secondhand narration. "Bonheur d'Esclavage" cites woman's underwear as a flag: 'the panties a pennant,'. There is much of this staccato-braggadocio also exemplified in "Down Ski-Pistes of Gossamer The Goldfinches Came" which is very Hopkinsesque. There is no let up on through the closing clatter of sonnets entitled "The Final Mother-Fuck (Perhaps)". The hesitative use of 'perhaps' reveals the tight space of the sonnet for Mac Intyre amidst further linguistic contortions rather than gymnastics. The conquest of women dominates. "Why Veins Show" recounts a momentary encounter: 'In the hall with this young women/(only just met, but we're about to part.' Feminists would shrug this off as male locker-room badinage where the world of men and women is defined as sexual jousting. Thus, Tóg Bóg Í, in other words "take her easy" is merely that since she is an easy take: 'retreats in disorder, you do that to many,/Love, you there stitching your garments of plenty.' Only in "Cattle, Errislannin" is there personal insight where the conquering hero admits his Don Juanism: 'She looked at me, beloved phantom bride,/looked thru me, listened, heard the music fled.' Mac Intyre invokes Marina Tsvetayeva's truth in "Imagine, One Alone" and that "aloneness is Imagination's loom". Tsvetayeva's philosophy was equally espoused in Eliot's *The Waste Land* and can be clearly stated: the modern ego resides alone in the teeming modern world. Thus Mac Intye finally accepts and bows out with panache: "Death is a waiter" and "What's he do with the crumbs?" Answer: "yours, mine,/in ceaseless flow thru Demeter's mill again". Celtic bards are sent to the Underworld for their transgressions.

—*Books Ireland* 2011

NOT ALL EXALTED

New Collected Poems Derek Mahon (Gallery Press)

In This Life Michael O'Loughlin (New Island)

Close Quarters Justin Quinn (Gallery Press)

Ocean Letters Joseph Woods (Dedalus Press)

The Cotard Dimension Macdara Woods (Dedalus Press)

Capering Moons Anatoly Kudryavitsky (Doghouse)

Tongue-tied poems of exile which also tend to the confessional mode, beginning in Belfast "this desperate city" and onto Kinsale. The MacNeicean sequences originally published as *The Hudson Letter* and *The Yellow Book* appear as individual poems showing the strong influence of *Autumn Journal* and *Autumn Sequel* revealing Mahon's quest for total form. These poems are backward looking and dismissive to contemporary culture. With minor changes from the originals this is his crowning achievement. It is a "collected" which possesses the damning attribute of repetition and is otherwise redolent of a career that is cloistered, constricted and covert. Many dedications to poems make it a sort of club poet's "narrative" inherently lived more in literature as inspiration than in full bodied life. There are weak effusions such as 'After the Titanic' and 'Synge Dying' among others.

'A Disused Shed in Co. Wexford': "There have been deaths, the pale flesh flaking/Into the earth that nourished it" is a companion piece to "A Garage in Co. Cork" and both "confess" him as Ulster runaway towards Sartre's *La Nausée* cited in "Craigvara House" while "Heraclitus on Rivers" plumbs total despair. Runaway is true of this generation of poets. The collective nomenclature "Northern poets" needs rectification to "staunch exiles." For Mahon the North is hell: people and place "The police charge and the stricken home" 'Camus in Ulster'. He admits in 'Afterlives': "Perhaps if I'd stayed behind/And lived it bomb by bomb/I might have grown up at last/And learnt what is meant by home." 'The Sea in Winter': "Portstewart, Portrush, Portballintrae/un beau pays mal habité,/policed by rednecks in dark cloth/and roving gangs of tartan youth." Abandoned homeland shrouds Mahon's work as in 'Axel's Castle' "yet I too toil not neither do I spin, I too/have my carefully constructed artificial paradises". 'Schopenhauer's Day' typically exhibits jaundiced scholarly usage: "life's guilt or the servitude of love and hate"; and this permeates his ancient aesthetic as in 'A Quiet Spot' "'Wrong life,' said Adorno, 'can't be lived rightly.'" This is also reprised in a poem that loses its drapery of literary reference 'Art and Reality' dedicated to James Simmons where he claims "We two/both wanted to help dissipate/the 'guilt and infantile self-hate.'" Simmons comes out better than Mahon whose exile from NI renders his work post-poetry where karmic retribution makes the work devoid of any transcendence which may well be the price for deserting and never finding his true North.

The contents in IV and V are to be avoided: he really falls over, egoism emerges and other repugnance especially in "The Widows' Prayers" however I, II and III are vastly superior as with "And feel the delicious clattering/Of stilletto heels on cobblestones/As girls cross the square with a pink/Flame clenched between their thighs." "The Moscow Suburb" also has a Holocaust poem "It all happened so quickly" and one prescriptive about protest marches: "But we weren't marching, we/Were just hamsters running on a wheel in a cage." The translations from the fictional Mikelis Norgelis upstages its creator as in 'A Latvian Poet Writes an Ode to Capitalism,' 'A Latvian Poet Does the Joycean Pilgrimage' and 'A Latvian Poet Encounters Róisín Dubh' which concludes: "I want to fillet out your spine/and have it mounted in Kildare Street/alongside the Great Irish Elk/just to make the poor extinct fucker quake." O'Loughlin as Dr Frankenstein must nurture Norgelis and abandon himself!

Prague and Blackrock, Dublin with personal life and associates serve no other purpose than filling the contents. Predominance of strict stanza structures and rhyme is fatally observed. Sonnets deliver overtly clanging couplets as with 'Sonnet on Missing a Trip:' "leaving us illumined in the dark,/and hardly there but for the odd remark." The theme is conversation over wine with friends which results in little value from the poem as poem. 'The Months' sonnet sequence is similarly weak though no 2 begins promisingly "The snow turns down the sound on everything." However, the subject matter about witnessing a fight in a public park is banal and defeated by the horrendously poor couplet "After an hour or so the fighting ends/and they shake hands like colleagues or old friends." 'Musílkova'—a staggered narrative reaches the conclusion: "Incredible to think that this would pass." 'Ivory and Gold' "inspired" by Horace declares: "My work is marginal to everything" One cannot but feel that it is subconscious self-exposure. 'Russian Girl on Pařížská' yields his best effort while 'The City Gates' dulls the senses, 'Streetwalker' is a mere exercise constricted as to deployment and execution. In 'Divorce' which is presumably serious matter results in the trivial: "When you wake up I see/the fathoms that you swam,/and your eyes ask of me/who on earth I am." Invariably he destroys with single lines as in 'The Huge House': "a labyrinth of rooms and passageways." In 'For My Brother in Khartoum' there is no evidence as to why hyperbole is being handed out except from overbearing family pride: "to pass the time until your morning flight,/that will take you out of here, Shane, my brother,/best of company in Africa tonight."

Undistinguished collection that reeks of ennui while 'Letting the Cat out of the Bag' is far too reminiscent of Heaney's 'The Early Purges.' In 'Clanbrasil Street' Dublin disappoints and the cherry tree yearns for "its leap over a wall." 'Old Country Awakening' is distinctly anti-pastoral: "Pike stirring in the lakes/of Leitrim and great populations of crows/rising in Roscommon." 'Bedside Locker' has weak phrasing: such as "colour-coded for eternity" and the wardrobe: "whose contents will one day/walk from the charity shop." Childhood isolation is redolent in 'Signal Box' and 'Tinsel Hut' and such material in any event sits uneasily within the structure like 'Handball Alleys.' These are all from the penny dreadful school of Irish poetry. He writes better when "away" from Ireland yet is constantly dragged home: 'Luis Piedra Buena, Patagonia' "had something of Kinnegad." Poems about travel are aimless with somnambulant dreaming in bookstores as in 'Bookshops in Rangoon' and 'A Bookshop in Shimla' that begins "Little of interest here." Such postcard pieces should have been sent by post solely. This mode unfortunately informs Woods in 'Kyoto Revisited, a ghazal diary' "I drink a bowl of freshly whisked and frothy green tea,/look over the pond and consider the civilisation of gardens." In 'Why do the wrong people travel...' the same problematical issues appear: a menu is given in full and other information appropriate to travel diary-notes towards poems, perhaps. The collection makes one question the whole notion of achieved poetry alongside the perplexity that Woods might well be travel writing while travelling.

'Caltagirone' delivers a scene: nothing more or less, otherwise he is confessional in asides that reveal the poet's inner state as in 'Work in Progress': "Would you ever fuck off/I say to truth." In 'The Village Festive:' "Sixty years on the Ranelagh Road/A long long way/From catching pinkeens/In the vanished harbour at Portobello." The confessional impinges amidst anger over aging and the indisposition of being a writer: "And oh to be lying perfect now/in those Dublin underwater gardens/that bloom in Summer/with orchid greenery/in the bed of the Grand Canal." 'Follies'. 'Overview' shows the spirit resilient: "The ghost-train of my life/Rolls on across the steppes." The mid-length poems are better than the longer ones which get bogged down when his resolution is lost in too many words. Ultimately, honesty and humility shines through wistfulness as in the shamelessly Beckettian: 'In May The Park and Me Revisited' "With those delusive ghosts/Of loneliness and failure/All the empty spaces of the years/Left unredeemed/And all the missing people/Myself among them."

The sight of a clatter of haiku may unnerve you with its vacant lots of white space on the page where Kudryavitsky does two main types: the sugary greeting card verse: "after the wedding,/white butterfly clinging/to the ivy." Nuptiality might be said to persist: "snowman/and snowwoman/melting into each other" ; "a robin hiding/in the snow-covered hedge/sunrise" ; "telegraph wires/dawn singing a song/to the nightingale." The latter are twee and too nicely nicely. He is slightly better served by haiku on snails: "heading towards/the twin chimneys,/a two-horned snail" ; "Wicklow mountains/snails climb a lopsided/pillar-box." The former provides some visual certainly in words but the latter is "messy": which Wicklow mountains and supposing you do not know the Wicklow mountains? Lopsided is a notoriously lopsided word therefore the effect is blurred. "Shannon Airport/rushes pin the sky/to lake water" yea, one gets the last two lines but the airport is arbitrary. Just as a little bit of limerick goes a long way: a little bit of haiku goes a long way also. O well, one more in this hit and miss collection: "war musem/two gas masks/staring at each other." Poetry may not be meant to entertain or at least poetry as entertainment may not be its so called exalted equivalent.

—*Books Ireland* 2011

CONFUSION

Before Troy Fergus Allen (CB Editions)

Unsweet Dreams Anne Le Marquand Hartigan (Salmon Poetry)

Of all Places John McAuliffe (Gallery Press)

Before You Leeanne Quinn (Dedalus Press)

Sailing Lake Mareotis Eamonn Wall (Salmon Poetry)

Allen is assured, formal and yields wit at his best, despite archaic usage which occasionally jolts, such as "casement" (instead of window) in "Dying in Naples". He delivers occasional arresting lines with restraint: "the sun has been shot down over Atlanta" ('In Morocco') and prolifically utilises classicism as bygone scaffolding such as Orpheus who uncharacteristically generates a few laughs: "my remains serving to fatten the kites,/while my bare head floats singing down the stream."

'Midnight Tattoo Artist' can't be said to do much more than provide a glimpse into a real situation for the purposes of felicity and entertainment while many-sided irony reveals Allen's claims for the impermanence of his own work as a mere tattoo: "The fools don't realise that art is serious/Here in the House of Tattoo in Yokahama." "New Night-Life" and "The HJ Knife" propound similar aesthetics, the latter more acerbic about a Hitler Jungend knife in an auction room where the subject matter is disavowed and the form barely lifts the verse above a ballad. Allen definitely knows his stature and can seem mechanical, as if he is making to order sometimes but his best quality is readability since often much that goes for "poetry" is unreadable.

'The Woman on the Islands' refers to Homer's Circe and debunks the myth and legend. Allen's Calypso is intentionally broken and witty: "Yes, an old man's unfashionable thoughts—/But I have never been a trendy fellow." "Flying Down to Macroom" is a well wrought product with adherence to rhyming structures, clear exposition of the verbal situation, the right word in place felicitously but the end result leaves one seeking more. The theme is trivialised which is reminiscent of John Arlott's poetry, and about reckless driving that results in a poor unfortunate chicken being topped, or as Allen puts it: "This Chicken Licken had journeyed to the underworld—."

To rank Allen with Gavin Ewart or John Betjeman is spurious, all are different from each other yet similarities collectively pervade their work. Their form suggests an ultimate reticence which is conservative, in other words each of these poets place restrictions that tie them down beyond complete expression. When Allen attempts to encompass humanity within a Swiftian misanthropic structure the results are much less, as is "A Note from the Superman". He is always happier in the land of whimsy and wit which enable his usual performance in comic verse. This sort of performance is, of course, a giveaway since the full charge of poetry is definitely not his aim. Yet his verse is better than many who claim their work is "poetry."

Le Marquand Hartigan's naïve artwork adorns the covers and inside she holds rigidly to her title, gyrating between the minimal in 'The Two Cs'/ "Women's independence/The car and/The condom." and the sentimental in 'The Sheets' of which there are cheekily too many examples. When she gives herself more space, she becomes a sort of Stevie Smith as in dealing with having been jilted in the title poem: "and as I reach the/final verse I've bills/to pay, my zip has burst/I've put on weight/that's not the worst". This is revisited in 'Song to the Unfaithful' less successfully. 'Not a Word' has the mellifluous subtitle: "Poem written on a sick bag on a flight/between Dublin and Heathrow" however, she is slightly better at ground level with 'Viewing the Landscape' which is deliberately feminist: "Either the subject or the object, women/are useful to decorate a frieze or lie in a poem/black skinned or white whichever increases the tension/the sensuousness, the sexuality of the pose or picture."

There is a helping of wisdom in 'Forgive Us Our Trespasses' which is a bit old fashioned, however: "Parents are increasingly obsolete, dumb dinosaurs/Made to be stuffed". In 'Dark Goddess' one wonders whether she longs to be a stand-up comic looking for laughs about her dog: "It is maytime and my black bitch/Is on heat." This sort of fun is bypassed in 'Death and Sex' where the ghost of laughter keeps it well below a serious poem of any depth since death is seen as mere spoiler of hanky panky.

A book replete with lines like this "A dry spell engenders nostalgia for rain." 'The Coming Times'. Such lines alongside many others of the same weight all amount to no-value as poetry. "He looks like America,/ smiling…" this is from 'Grave Goods' about the author's brother. Who can accept that any person looks like America? 'Bringing the Baby to Rossaveal' is similarly banal about the familial: it fills in some facts based on the title in a pedestrian manner and has a refrain: "Goodbye to the first times, goodbye Galway." 'Badgers' is cut from the same jib, meaning in this case, jibberish as with 'The Listowel Arms.' 'Crash' is a hopeless attempt to convey Roger Casement's arrest in 1916 and is absurdly dated from that year as if it were a contemporary account. Meanwhile 'Continuity' renders a special category of metaphor which is pounded into insensibility: "The wind sails leaves around the house like late notices/of the garden's deterioration." Of 'North Korea' he declares "Time is not wasted in your subtle temples" this, even on a postcard to a friend would bring laughter. But every page yields such syntactic disasters as in the following examples: 'Loose Ends' "The sun deceived the open door." Many's a day one sees this epiphenomenon! 'A Likeness' "The wind makes itself known/in the laurel". 'A Game of Li Bo' brings out his wobbly philosophical flair: "each moment a last thought saying its goodbyes." 'A Deaf Ear' "The sun's a no-show"—what a phrase to open a supposed poem. 'Sunrise' "There are nights I snag on a single morning—". 'Black Box' "The stable I called a dungeon is the coal shed". 'The

Territorial Army' "The rain was nobody's business, a surprise." This sort of pallid and dull writing has no merit as poetry.

Despite some difficulties, Quinn manages to give some sort of performance. The difficulties certainly make their presence felt in her hit and miss collection where random images do her a disservice (compared to her strengths) as in 'Graffiti on the Plant Store' where "A woman carrying a tray of coffee like a bomb" is too melodramatic. And also in 'This is Where' "quick as a/guillotine the line goes dead' as well as 'Frequent as the Naked Dream' "I/descend into unconcealed panic". She has a good closing line for 'Eating Out': "reading the menu, like a page-turner". However, a disastrous mode for her is the prose poem, in 'Rubble': "Oh you can hardly make me out" and 'Storms' which descends to random notes, random thoughts, and 'Houses' "Bare walls made bad companions" all too clichéd and obvious.

What is incredulous about her work is not the facts of isolation grappled with but the impassive isolated self that is too much promoted by her within the poems, leaving one to believe that it is a mere pose. This is also narcissism and a pitfall 'In Paint'. Her work is unavoidably self-absorbed yet strives to move beyond the self and fails as poetry since the narcissism is undetected by her. Her pose works better in 'A House in the Ocean' where much is happening through the unified central image of the title and where the imagined inhabitants: "Or do they already lie adrift/on pummelled land, inconsolable//as this rootless house,/still looking like it could keep/the outside out".

The sort of collection one might unwittingly fling at the poor cat. Uncurbed use of language, lines and structure yielding a very turgid read. To begin at the end (and try to recover from the tedium) of 'Actaeon's Return' which is a dialogue with an undisclosed doomsday agenda based on wisps of banality from his native Enniscorthy with (typical) lines such as "Great debts I owe to pike, salmon, trout". Wall reaches a drivel of diction loaded with rhetoric that makes one squeal in agony: "From a great distance, urgent voices call my name:/Each seeks a song of gin, gore, highwaymen profane." 'A Sort of Crusade'. In 'Your Rivers Have Trained You' he employs his much used method of juxtaposing Ireland, or more usually Wexford with the United States (could any two locations be more different): "Hudson, Missouri, Mississippi: your rivers are majestic./The Slaney has assumed your face's fair shape". No, it hasn't.

One is aghast at the cosy cloying lyricism of 'Lakeside Falling, Co. Sligo,' 'The Last Cricket of the Season' (not sport!) and 'The Pilgrims Emerge From the Forest'—a bizarre fantasia about St Senan full of syntactical confusion such as the closing line: "The Slaney rocks on an ancient tide". Similarly with 'The Monastery Bell' ending in the strained rhetoric of: "I have but little time to linger in your lovely home." This would even be difficult to get away with in conversation but in a so-called poem it is awful. His own anti-Republican American slant is obvious and half-baked in 'CBS: One Morning in a Café in Denver Breakfast Hour'. Breakfast usually kicks in during the morning, at least he gets that correct! Remarkably among the surfeit of verbal detritus there is one readable piece 'Bilingual Tripper:' "I joined/youths for coffee—/that's lingua franca/on bright/formica." Apart from this Wall unremittingly wields language as if using a sledgehammer to push in a thumb tack.

—*Books Ireland* 2012

KEEPING IT SIMPLE

Stray Birds/Éanlaith Strae Rabindranath Tagore/Gabriel Rosenstock (Salmon Poetry)

The Parrots of Villa Gruber Discover Lapis Lazuli Julian Stannard (Salmon Poetry)

Pretending to be Dead and other entertainments Ross Hathaway (Seven Towers)

The Fadó House Mary Noonan (Dedalus Press)

The Best of Frances Browne: poems, stories and essays by the blind genius of Stranorlar ed. Raymond Blair (Rathmore Books)

Rosenstock projects poetry as purely the sound of music not via Rodgers and Hammerstein but from Moore's Melodies and onto Tagore (1861-1941) who strayed into the Anglo-Irish Literary Revival through Yeats. Tagore may have been the inspiration for the 1916 Rising taking place primarily in the GPO since his folkloric play The Post Office (1912) significantly resounded with Irish revolutionaries. As poet Tagore is the prompter of this theory: "The movement of life has its rest in its own music" "Glacann gluaiseacht na beatha a scíth ina cuid ceoil féin". Rosenstock transposes Tagore from Bengal to the Hill of Tara with Ian Joyce's sporadic blobs as illustration.

Tagore's mystic-aphoristic phrases usually deliver an acute transcendentalism. He might be said to pre-empt Heidegger in stating "That I exist is a perpetual surprise which is life" rendered by the translator as Iontas síoraí is ea é gur beo dom agus sin é an saol. Rosenstock always keeps it simple: Fan socair, a chroí ionam, is paidreacha iad na crainn mhóra. "Be still, my heart, these great trees are prayers".

Tagore's thought is keen: "A Mind all logic is like a knife all blade. It makes the hand bleed that uses it" which Rosenstock renders in style "Aigne gan aici ach loighic nó scian gan aici ach lamh (beidh fuil ar an lamh dá dheasca)". "Man is worse than an animal when he is an animal". "Is measa ná ainmhí é an duine nuair is ainmhi é".

Straining after comedy is a disadvantage here: "The train is now a mountain goat/and the seats as hard as luck" ('The Blessing of Salami at Sant' Olcese'). 'The Seedy School of English' is meant to depict the typical language school and unfortunately uses a very old joke: "One of the requirements of the job/would be a low level of English". The title piece like all others is fixed to his formulaic grasp of reality beside the Mediterranean and overuses a colloquial postcard style without any edge. He is quite the plodding tourist full of incidental detail as in 'Villa Giovanna': "& there's a white towel, almost a beatitude/& the city's turning into Havana with Scottish castles/& Ruth's on the terrace holding a melon." On a perpetual holiday everything is poetry to him: "Darkness has fallen/upon the Ligurian hills etc." ('Furthest, Fairest Things').

His comparisons are outlandish and melodramatic: "the horizon's schizophrenic eyeball" and "The sea will crack with electrifying voices". In 'Oh' the list of tragic events are pitched in mocking comedy but are not in actuality: "Aunt Lou went in for a lobotomy/but died under the anaesthetic". He finally emerges from the poetry closet in 'Vic Makes Me Lasagna' where a friend makes "lasagna for minor poets". 'Soup' is addressed to his mother who made this "mainstay of hope". He has the Michael Longley pitfall in writing about wars he never fought in or survived, therefore the poem 'Vonnegut's Dresden' is ridiculous since Stannard never was a soldier. The use of a refrain (over a dozen times) "when you could be a dog" is nauseating in 'Dog Talk'. He has three Cole Porteresque/Dorothy Parkeresque lines as highlight: "After she'd gone absolutely/mental in the Continental/I took Gloria to the Astoria" ('Riviera Blues'). Bob Dylan famously said: if he had a good quote he'd be wearing it. Stannard is not very quotable and parades in his poems as if they were a coat of many colours with tassels and all but in fact each poem is uncannily uniform in a fussy style that does not wear well. Similarly his titles appear memorable but are easily forgotten.

Strictly performance poetry with repetitions and seriousness is outlawed. 'Cantankarous' (his spelling) is a series of squibs pretending to be based on the Oriental tanka form. As a sequence they are heavy going and would require a good delivery in performance. The problem with performance poetry is that it often does not perform well in print but this is no excuse. 'Possum' is a typical Perf-poem: "No TV license? Pretend to be dead." "You could pretend/to be well read/or to be dead." Hattaway deals basically in throwaway improv-action-poetry where language is a blunt tool unconcerned with ultimate meaning: "Walking the house/at two in the morning/just to stay alive." 'Aisling'. 'Election Manuscript' goes for the laughs: "We are the Prose Party./Tough on rhyme/and the causes of rhyme." "We would welcome coalition/with the Short Story Party." Surprisingly in 'The Church of the Bad Shepherd' he breaks his own aesthetic (if he ever had one) and gets metaphysical and declares himself "safely beyond/opposing/belief/or non-belief." The illustrations by Paul Hattaway are not in any manner related to the poems and give visual relief from the dirge of language which never seeks to be poetic. This is after all a hybrid of anti-poetry.

Of which the less said the better despite a good Duncan Grant reproduced on the cover "Juggler and Tight Rope Walker". The opening pages are quite a shock especially 'Swallow' with its plaintive bygone fustian style all about a bird. Metaphor is badly handled: "The yellow U-Bahn took us home, its bulbs rocking,/pale petals fluttering in the arc of its lamplights" ('At the Zoo') This type of imagism is tenth rate Arthur Symons and very out of date. Also with the diction of 'Persephone' "What hope/for us, rooted in Hades, unfurling,/forever opening our palms." 'Frida and the Monkeys' about Frieda Kahlo has an irritating solipsistic egoism similar to 'Muse Manqué' (again note the 1890s title). Noonan guarantees banality in 'Household Plant' that begins: "Countless plants, budded under a bad star,/came to terminate their existences here." This mawkish effort to humanise a few potted plants is weak while 'Turnip' comes straight from the Michael D. Higgins school of poetry: "The more you talked about the white spring turnip". She translates a Baudelaire poem and one by de Nerval, however, ego abounds as in 'Mahal': "My letters of love, my spectral songs,/I let them drift on the forest floors of night." Heaneyisms pervade 'Oracle Bone' a pallid description of archaeology from the China room of the British Museum. Such writing is merely for exhibition glass case notices. Her heavy hand is prevalent in 'River in December' "The grey waters lumber/through the river's womb." Rivers do not conceive children.

Blair as editor spells her name Frances Browne (1816-1879) whose father was postmaster in Ballybofey. However, in nearby Stranorlar, County Donegal there is a commemorative plaque to the poet on the house where she was born: 'Frances Brown poetess-novelist-journalist.' She contributed to various newspapers, magazines and journals, came under the spell of Dickens and was critically praised alongside Charlotte Brontë and Elizabeth Barrett Browning. She is as good as Thomas Davis and Arthur O'Shaughnessy, and at her best in poems such as 'Songs of Our Land'. Her essays reflect an eclectic scholar, imaginative in digressions but never dull. The prose narratives are a lesser achievement, at times lugubrious and inherently obsessive on the theme of friendship. The poems are her crowning glory, of their era, embalmed in Thomas Moore many set to music but not quite reaching to Christina Rossetti, Tennyson or Swinburne. However, she has the true melancholy and depth of any of these poets: "of faith found false, of hope grown faint" ('The Poet's Wealth'); "This world is the same dull market,/That wearied its earliest sage"; "The heart that when life was wintry/Found summer in strain and tome" ('Going Home').

Blair has fittingly brought her uncollected writings to light but is none too scholarly with a scanty introduction that fails his legendary poet who was blind like Carolan, Ó'Huiginn and Raftery, and entered the literary scene of Edinburgh and London, received a Civil List pension from Sir Robert Peel and died in penury. Blair should have researched the definitive spelling of the poet's surname. She is buried in Richmond-upon-Thames in an unmarked grave as one of her poems predicted. The Frances Brown Summer School in Stranorlar may not be far off and one of the heavily subsidised poetry presses might bring out her collected poems as something genuine rather than their regular dubious product under the same name.

— *Books Ireland* 2012

A GREAT LYRICIST BUT A THREADBARE POET?

Lit Up Inside Van Morrison (Faber & Faber)

Ian Rankin's foreword saturated in nostalgia claims Van the Man has 'music to warm the soul'. Eamonn Hughes's slightly longer introduction does little also because of his plodding phraseology about Belfast as 'a city mapped by [Morrison's] music'; 'the blues can then roll down Royal Avenue' and 'back streets can turn into mystic avenues'. Hughes misses important subject matter by not exploring 'the music business's sharp practices'. He is way off the mark citing Morrison's musical influences as 'Orange Bands, Salvation Army Bands' that evolved into 'many song styles' and neglects to exemplify the styles or encompass in his introduction a fitting appraisal of the songwriter. Rankin and Hughes deal in lazy nostalgia and hyperbole without the evidence for it.

Morrison's lyrics are either covert or otherwise clear and simple. The pretension with which he is discussed is not part of his image. More than any other designation, he is a soul-gospel bluesman with light emphasis on the blues. Unlike fellow Ulsterman, Rory Gallagher a bluesman with heavy emphasis on the blues. Both began in the Irish showband era which you would never glean from Hughes or Rankin.

The highest pitch that radiates from Morrisons' lyrics is gospel with occasional fundamentalism especially through much usage of 'mystical', 'mystic', 'vision' and so forth. The mystical element is not expressed in the much admired 'Moondance', 'Have I Told You Lately that I Love You', 'Bright Side of the Road', 'Tupelo Honey' and the early 'Gloria'. Nor does it surface in lyrics of humane sympathy to prostitution as in 'Madame George', or in the exoticism of 'Who Drove the Red Sportscar?', 'Snow in San Anselmo' or the more intense 'Madame Joy'.

Unlike Baez, Dylan, Cohen and Lennon, or his namesake Jim Morrison, he was never involved with causes and protests as 'The

Great Deception' proves. 'Well, the plastic revolutionaries take the money and run/Have you ever been down to Love City/Where they rip you off with a smile/And it don't take a gun.' Morrison is a songwriter as outlined in his lyrics 'Pay the Devil', 'Show Business' and 'Songwriter'. He has no bullshit-factor like Bono's pseudo-economic diatribes and no human rights profile like Geldof nor does he dispense phoney wisdom or self-analysis. In fact, he is anti-intellectual in many of the lyrics especially in 'Meaning of Loneliness' where Dante, Sartre, Camus, Nietzsche and Hermann Hesse do not grant him any solace. 'Into the Mystic' is close to Dylan's recent 'Duquesne Whistle' just as both have the content of 'When the Saints Go Marching In'.

While 'Days Like This' became the official anthem of the NI Peace Process, Morrison remains like many from George Best to Joey Dunlop onwards about as apolitical as the polarised NI region permits to celebrities trying to avoid public statements of loyalty. Claims cannot be made for 'Crazy Face' as a Troubles portrait of a gunman or a Shankill butcher. Nor does he bother much with ballads of exile. There is the token 'What Makes the Irish Heart Beat' which is nowhere near as good as Henry McCullough's 'Belfast to Boston'.

As songwriter Morrison has recreated his ascent into joy and his aesthetic of the discovery of such joy from childhood through his parents who were obsessed with music. Morrison's thinly veiled glimpses of autobiography devoid of the crises of a Belfast childhood celebrate music on the radio, the 78 rpm, the 45 rpm and the LP. Songs surpass the present into his version of the mystic. 'Cleaning Windows' is new age Buddhism referencing Christmas Humphries standard text on Zen. The mysticism is effective in songs about ennui, emptiness and angst as with 'Mystic of the East' where County Down is ironically a state of being: 'Deep in the heart of Down'.

The secret of Morrison is in Tir na Nog (his spelling), 'Rolling Hills', 'In the Garden', 'I Forgot that Love Existed', 'These are The Days', 'So Quiet in Here', 'No Religion', 'Hymns to the Silence' and overtly in 'Whenever God Shines his Light' and 'Rave on John Donne/Rave On, Part Two'. Morrison is only as specific as any personal mysticism can be. For instance in 'Beautiful Vision' the vision is rendered thus: 'In the darkest night/You are shining bright/You are my guiding light/Show me wrong from right'. Behind this lack of explicit statement is his orthodoxy. His mis-adulators such as Rankin and Hughes gush on about his early burgeoning career imbrued with nostalgia of place and homeland for instance in 'On Hyndford Street'. As a lyric it has the defining Morrison line as when he 'carried on dreaming in God'. Such statements are his alpha and omega.

This collection is presented in the Faber colours and format with pretence as a poetry title. Calling Morrison a poet is for eulogists whose precision lacks definition. Many of the famous lyrics look threadbare here. A book of song-lyrics shows the shortfall of multitudinous repetitions which are the hallmarks of 'Gypsy', 'I've been workin'', 'Comfort You', 'Wavelength' and many others. A lot of Faber's recent poetry list is dubious as in Lachlan Mackinnon's Small Hours. It's a safer business for them to publish Van Morrison's lyrics—about a third of his output. However, as in his appearance on the poetry reading circuit for the London launch with mawkish Michael Longley and erratic Edna O'Brien is hardly his next career move.

—*Books Ireland* 2015

OF LOVE, DEATH AND THE MUSE

On My Way Desmond O'Grady (Dedalus Press)

Love Life Micheal O'Siadhail (Bloodaxe Books)

Collected Poems Sean Dunne (Gallery Press)

O'Grady's collection is a mixed bag, with the Eliotic credo: 'We shall not cease from exploration'. There is a 'Sailing to Byzantium' tone, even if it is not quite possible to locate his ideal city or ideal Kinsale. 'I've reclaimed my homeland. You're still expatriate', he announces in 'Joseph Brodsky Visits'.

Gisele provides a drawing of the poet and is profiled in return, in two poems. In 'The Painter Gisele', the poet drops his guard to tell it as it is, with a ghost of a quote from Pound's Pisan Cantos thrown in for good measure. He will not bow to timor mortis — 'Death ends or begins all. Either end leaves nothing to mortally fear.' He sings not of summer 'in full-throated ease' but, perhaps, of autumn:

The wise exit life with equanimity and no wish to replay it.
Chant no dirge for death.
Sing joy.

Elsewhere there is humility, 'succumb to sleep as a nomad curls up beside his camel' 'CA Winter Night'). And 'The Poet C.P. Cavafy's Mother' ends:

The reality of experience, imagined or lived, generates the life of what we leave after us.

The lyric is laid to rest as he opts for as full an utterance as the Muse allows, and she of the Parnassian Summit is evoked in the best poem here, 'Makers and Breakers':

I had envisioned your light rose travertine shaded lips, deepwater golden, sunbrown onyx of your flesh; dark velvet in your southern eyes; translucent marble that's your smile.

Such luxuriance is a small luxury since this is doggedly unassuming, self-effacing poetry, and while he is apparent in the background, there is not a tinge of melancholy nor a dirge or lament, not even in a transposition after Leopardi, the master of doom and despair, 'Her Birthday Night'. There is Attic grace in 'Self-Portrait':

That's what matters, all tried or done: live life aware, curious, involved,

die gladly, like an equation solved.

Time casts a long shadow but it is not fearful for him apparently. He is surprised by joy and obedient to custom, in 'May Day':

Last night we erected and dressed up the whitethorn, drank and sang, danced round the roaring bonfire.

Some slunk away to lark in secret bushes. A few heard cuckoos coo love and forgot you must not give anything away May Eve.

Only once does rage break through in the laid-back ballad 'The Battle of Kinsale 1601', where to be Irish reveals how you have to ingest the twist of fate. Yes, it is that time of year for O'Grady, for 'Winter in Sevilla', and with effulgence:

My marshes of memory

fertilize winter flowers

in my garden of imagination,

spout the fountains' leap and fall,

fill and enliven fish pools, duck ponds,

rivers with the gallivant of nature's affairs.

If all this is true, he is gathering himself up into the artifice of eternity with quiet soul singing.

O'Siadhail's collection is not set out as a sequence and might well have been since its close on seventy or so poems are monothematic.

The subject matter is poet and muse. Don't cringe — he may win you over with this decidedly New Male effusion to the beloved:

Think that I might never have happened on you...

- 'HEALING'

Dante, Petrarch, Shakespeare and Herrick are pencilled in lightly or heavily, perhaps as references — but he has nothing bad to say at all.

Pace again battlements Hamlet O'Siadhail

Or say confusion is not an ignoble state

(Imperfectly I rhyme with Brian Friel).

- 'DURATION

Woman is bliss, especially the woman in the house (should there be echoes of Coventry Patmore?), in this case his Brid — redolent perhaps of the saintly Brigid of ancient Ireland. His impetus is from Solomon's 'Song of Solomon', as in 'Long Song', and elsewhere in 'Crimson Thread' the motif of 'the crimson moment' appears.

Here is a testament to decades of a relationship without any chinks, or at least with no such admissions. He keeps poise with understatement. You must not expect emotional detonations. There are none. The climax begins to build up as you read through and without any sequential pointers.

All that weathers us in what we weather.

Still my mistress mariner. And still together.

— 'IOU'

The unknowable factors about the beloved are all bonuses, as in 'Selves' — 'Am I the surprise for you that you're for me?' One might make a glib conclusion from O'Siadhail's 'report': Women are the new men according to the Irish zeitgeist, and the new O'Siadhaileach man is comfortable about it. Otherwise his summation might well be found in 'Mistress':

Flagrante delicto I glimpse your metamorphosis. A flash smile turns to reassure my gaucheness.

Peter Fallon has a caveat in his note on Sean Dunne (1956-1995): 'How good a poet he would have become we can only guess'. There seems to be three phases in this Collected, roughly speaking: the early one which is obsessed with the Irish Lyric (there is a feint echo of Jeremiah J Callanan, his kin in the Munster landscape); this phase giving way to an engagement with Akhmatova in which he seems to have found a commensurate suffering for his own; followed by the final phase. In all three phases is found the far more complicated notion of 'Catholicism' which is this poet's core. Here are his final words on Weil,

When you died starving, waiting on God,

no realm of words could call you back.

— 'SIMONE WEIL, 1909-1943'

and on Merton, in 'Marginal Man':

Wood-gatherer in a snowy field,

you pose on logs in rolled-up sleeves, a Buddha at ease. Your silence spreads.

The raw gales rip yachts from moorings. The morning's thaw is a new page turning.

Merton and Weil might have wagged their fingers at this analysis of their spirituality, but Dunne is nailing his colours to the mast. 'Morning at Mount Melleray' and Anniversary' are not dissimilar. Even in the earlier 'Message Home' there is scepticism:

...I read Mother Julian in her cell: each page a promise that all shall be well.

He is of his time, a Fifties child from the deep south inured to those mainly dark ages and times which revisionists record as spiritually shallow, if not in many instances dangerously fascistic-Catholic. Some vague satire emerges in the deliberately Audenesque 'Letter from Ireland',

I have no time for the view that Ireland's the sum of the scenes at a Munster Final.

He clings to the legendary landscape of Gougane Barra, but such could be the road to Paradise. His grief comes across in the turn of the Nineteenth-century lament rendered here as "Timoleague Abbey'.

Ultimately Dunne gives the hint of Keatsian agony but without the great blasts of poetry, the 'Bright star, would I were steadfast as thou art...' He escapes sometimes in very small poems like 'The Smell of Cake', in the more robust spirituality of 'The Stone Carver', with its envy of the glorious sensualist Eric Gill —

You treated stone with a lover's tact,

edges peeled back like a thick

jumper raised as static sparkled...

and in the dirge of 'The Sheltered Nest', the well-turned lament 'Heading for Crete', and 'The Frail Sprig': "The night is freezing hard. Frost stiffens grass where I walk and watch a full moon rising over our small, lost planet no saviour now can touch. You pose in blue in a photograph set near my table and its waiting reams. The dark floss of your hair enfolds a face where smiles and hurt combine...".

—*The Poetry Ireland Review* 2006

SONGS FROM THE STREET

The Noise of Masonry Settling Leland Bardwell (Dedalus Press)

Neon Baby: new and selected poems Aidan Murphy (New Island)

Leland Bardwell is poised between pity and the confrontation of pain; pain is not her central exploration but is nonetheless conspicuously present. The adoption of pity reminds one of George Moore's credo about pity as the hallmark of literature in Hail and Farewell. Her evocation of the poor and the afflicted is also prevalent; she does not make herself the subject of this, and beyond it she explores the poor in spirit. Meanwhile, the rich in shekels and 'the Boom' are given puritanical treatment in 'The Horse Protestant Joke is Over':

Two grinning

Millionaires

Have bought the Big House

And they will have horses, And they will have jeeps, And maybe ride rough-shod Over the parishioners

Of the little church

Which says

Everyone welcome.

Otherwise, you might see her poems as 'sprinkling my secrets to the mourners / Like the violets of the poor (The Violets of the Poor'). The litany and legion of the poor are everywhere, as in a long-titled poem for her friend a street-trader, Mrs Katherine Dunne:

The bingo of life picks the strangest numbers And drums up tunes in the weirdest disarray.

'We Don't Serve Travelling People' places her among the Irish Beat poets (there is such a grouping):

102

We don't serve travelling people Or prostitutes.

Homage is made to Stevie Smith who also inspires the Smithesque sparsity of 'The Bedbug'. There are two poems for an unnamed friend in Portlaoise Prison — Ireland's Spandau. At Bardwell's Raggy-Trousered Ball others accumulate, such as Michael Hartnett of West Limerick:

His waging, lonesome

As any poet's, playing the poker

Of 'See you, raise you' till its echo tumbled

From the kitty of common sense.

How well he knew

'The act of poetry

Is a rebel act'

— 'THE ACT OF POETRY IS A REBEL ACT'

Also present, in 'Drum Up a Poem', is the gay Aquarian, Sir Eddie Linden:

Drum up a poem

They said, for Eddie's birthday,

And me as empty as An upturned barrel.

Her range is wide within the crucible method alluded to above, and not all via Stevie Smith. The only ease in life for her comes from love and art; however, she would not use such a term as 'art'. Bardwell works with reality: there is no precious and fussy language poetry, poetry itself is given the two fingers, almost. Such is the Beat aesthetic, since that tribe generally doesn't abide the mealy-mouthed 'taking ourselves very seriously as poets' attitude. A poem such as 'Moving House' does its work quietly; there is no formality, one is also light years from Yeats's ceremony and phantasmagoria. Street poetry has a very long tradition and is very true of the streets: for the streets, by the streets and from the streets without declaring any democratic principle — idealistic, pragmatic or otherwise.

A portent pervades some of the poems, as in 'Barnacles':

It is six o'clock, the island calls, And the geese face into the gale, A cardiograph in the sky...

And yet a warm radiance of resolution often shines through, as in 'Love Poem':

The nicest thing

You ever said to me

Was

Do we always have to live

Like Bonnie and Clyde?

Aidan Murphy may well have that affliction which Harold Bloom devoted a polemic to, The Anxiety of Influence. An influence is ever pernicious: the poet's hand requires to be held as it were by the parent poet, and in the best cases of influence it is often difficult to ascertain fully. Auden spoke about the necessity of neurosis for the poet in somewhat similar terms to Rimbaud's gospel of derangement of the senses. Murphy creates his cold turkey out of nothing less or more than Leonard Cohen, except like most imitators of Cohen the results are not as poetically profitable. (Cohen in this reviewer's salad days ever proved a killjoy to high jinks on the party circuit, and was equally dismal for a private session).

Murphy is quite a trudge through, not a gentle skim at all, in order to ascertain his limits, his highs and lows if you like. There isn't rage or nihilism articulated here, not even mania, high, low or manic depressive, enshrined beyond the base metal of the imagination in eclipse; none of this could claim to be 'bare, forked', even allowing for a fool's grace. If Bardwell is attuned to the poetry of the street,

Murphy is little beyond a shout in that same thoroughfare. The other unfortunate attribute is his liking for anecdote, such as Jesus and Iodine', 'Snapshot', or, worst of all, using the presumed significant incident as an impetus for poetry, in 'On L. Cohen's Birthday': anecdote can be poetry but that is subject matter for another time and place.

When he attempts something clear and simple, such as 'Game Boy', it doesn't impact. However, 'On the Demolition of the Arcadia Ballroom, Cork' does yield these images:

A couple float Chagall-like

over the abandoned mills.

The rest dance into the city centre

and foxtrot in the hollow shopping malls or take their shoes off and recline

on the steps of the Capitol Cineplex —all their spirits fading into summer's end.

Equally, 'Friendship' has the ache of a poem within its misshapen form. So here and there an image repays the reader but the following image, from 'A Death in the Family' is clotted, lacking fluidity:

the plough in the sky like a new saucepan.

What he does best is the 'riff' in lines. 'Mere riffs in lines' brings up the continuing academic debate as to what is and what is not poetry; Yeats's exhortation was schoolmasterly, 'Irish poets, learn your trade', T S Eliot's admonition also: 'no *vers* is *libre* for the man who wants to do a good job' (the French form making Eliot's point about the potential free-for-all sloppiness at the hands of a malefactor in free verse).

The problem with the song lyric as poetry when it is not fully sentient is the problem of banality posing as profundity, mutton dressed up as lamb.

She turned her grief to the green star, the only one raining in London.

She picked up the bottle

and smashed the guitar.

The neighbours, perturbed by the music, screamed — Turn It Down, Turn It Down. She took off her crown.

She filled up the bath and then

sleepily drowned.

That's better, they sighed. Classical music.

—'CLASSICAL MUSIC'

This isn't derangement or neurosis, and certainly not the transformation within words that explodes into poetry: 'See, see where Christ's blood streams in the firmament'(from Marlowe's Doctor Faustus). Besides stars do not rain, not even green stars except in special-effects movies.

It's Winter,

Friday the 13th.

No cornflakes in the bowl

and every reason to be blue.

The postman bangs on the door with a fistful of holiday brochures and a final notice from the ESB.

He tells me it's really Friday the 14th, but what the hell.

The human condition, as expressed here in 'Stark Naked Blues', is alas never that simple; or perhaps it's a case of 'what oft was thought but not very well expressed'; there's an abundance of this: Let's rock once more around the block, Mount Pleasant Avenue, Friar's Walk, South Summerhill and Douglas Street. I'll dance the cold from your dead feet.

However, even the reviewer's theory can be overturned: 'Last Night with a Victorian Wardrobe' is a good lyric for singing, reciting or even anthologising, perhaps, by the inner circle of poetry's political courts and enclosures:

My flight leaves at ten.

Give me these final hours. You remind me of someone I tried to know.

One can never have too many good lyrics from the streets.

—*The Poetry Ireland Review* 2007

AMBIGUOUS GREEN

Being Anywhere: new and selected poems Fred Johnston (Lagan Press)

As the Hand the Glove Pat Boran (Dedalus Press)

Contemporary Irish experience, especially Northern Irish experience is uniquely formidable. You might look no further than Johnston's poems for some kind of survival guide? In the introduction, poets are rebuked for their mutual censorship and the poetry scene is said to have emerged into a "green literary carnival" while "criticism becomes politics or peevishness". Johnston's use of 'green' might be intentionally ambiguous, it might mean naive, ubiquitous or not least, unripe. However this self-dissatisfaction works well for his poems that have a real honesty. As a Northern poet in exile he will not keep the local commandment of whatever you say, say nothing and yet has managed to be prolific despite what he calls "the cynic angel".

This selection/collection is from a half dozen previous collections with a bulkhead of new work. As savage self-critic he has not allowed back into print much of his oeuvre confining himself with fine support from Lagan Press, to less than a hundred pages. The immediate impression is of the divided heart of the guilty Belfast exile ("To be two-hearted is no simple island matter"). This comes across in 'For Emma', 'My Grandfather Inspects His Medals' and 'Chopin'. Between the lines of hatred he shows some love for Pearl Street, Bread Street and St Donard's Spire,

"yet in this city of pious bell-ringers and hymns raised up in honour of murder your full clear note sounds loudest and breaks the heart"

For Emma'

Division of selfhood and identity are exposed in 'Crossing the Bann' while in 'Sunday Afternoon' recreating his father's piano playing is doubly disturbing, criss-crossing the bravery of the young men who

fought in Flanders' mud and "the quiet Post Office revolution" —
in other words the twentieth century crossroads of Irish history, The
Great War and the 1916 Rising. He is also honest about the women
elders of his Belfast childhood, "We did not know them. If we say
we did we lie."

Johnston claims that "All poetry owes a debt to folk song; hence he
has love songs that are memorable, one can say without
condescension, tuneful: such as "From The Irish, Perhaps" You
might think that poems to friends: Desmond O'Grady, Robert
Greacen, Norman Dugdale and Breandan Ó hEithir might soften his
roar, but far from it

I follow an old routine

from pillow to pen

from dreaming to imagining and back again

'Poet On An Island'

This is not poetry of negativity, it speaks about survival, coping with
the wound but above all staying loyal as an exile to his community,
even though he admits, "My True North is always shifting".
Whether in London, Paris or amongst the folk musicians of Galway
he sounds close to Belfast and still the ache of exile throbs

You could be anywhere,

But here you are, with the Japanese

Tourists, the red buses and the old despair 'Being Anywhere'

However, you will find among the new poems a fitting resolution to
this ache and that is the real surprise here.

Boran might easily be accused of adopting a casual if not simplistic
method of writing poetry. That said there is a strange hankering after
rhyming which is (hopefully) deliberately naive — 'father' and
'rather', 'bones' and 'stones'. 'Eden' and 'No Man's Land' are good

examples of his poems that rhyme. The subject matter is the casual, the quotidian, in fact anything that comes along. He is decidedly anecdotal as in 'Machine' about a car alarm that is silenced by a passerby wielding a yard brush to smash the offending vehicle.

A problem with Boran is his use of metaphor as in 'Turning' a brief elegy for Michael Hartnett

The desk calendar on its last leaves. In the lampshade a tiny spider weaves a winter shroud.

Another elegy is far better. 'Am' which avoids any forced metaphor and brings into focus what he does best: miniatures such as 'A Natural History of Armed Conflict'

The wood of the yew

made the bow. And the arrow. And the grave-side shade.

He is also on safer ground when he is not trying to be too clever as in some of the shorter pieces. In 'Penknife' the tiny poem is doing fine until he squeezes in a paradox about the treasured memento that severs and connects in memory. In 'Transportation' the metaphor of a clothesline with washing, as a galleon might well be a bit forced but these are matters of personal taste.

When paintings and photographs suggest a subject he allows himself the usual latitude to say anything spontaneous as if the poem were a mere writing exercise, a throw away, perishable item somewhat like Charles Bukowski's poetry.

In the closing pages of what is his fourth collection, he has far better work in 'Lost and Found', and poems about childhood games, 'Driving into History'...

—*Fortnight* 2002

TUPPENCE COLOURED

Shelley Plain: Literary Encounters Robert Greacen (The Happy Dragon Press)

Through Glass Darkly Brian Power (Bayleaf Publications)

God in France: a Paris sequence 1994-1998 Harry Clifton (Metre Editions)

Translations: a selection Michael Hartnett (Gallery Press)

Robert Greacen's poems from previous collections, including *Lunch at the Ivy*, present a thematic parade of seventeen poets met in person or literary encounters. Robert Greacen the imagination—all distilled: a brew of high proof. His title comes from a line in Browning's 'Memorabilia' referring to a meeting with Shelley: "How strange it seems, and new!" What is live about each poet or writer is that beyond their life, work and reputation, tarnished or not, they remain uniquely in focus.

There is no collective noun for poets. One might suggest a haggle, a whirlpool or even a barrage? Whatever it may be, among Greacen's group are some heavyweights: Pound, Eliot, Auden and some damning fellow poets including Kavanagh on Austin Clarke:

Bloody old bags

Not worth twenty fuckin' fags.

Such loud-mouthing is strongly contrasted with John Hewitt's tight-lipped Northern reserve. Similarly, Greacen has an ironic riposte to Behan's remark about horse Protestants, calling himself "a Protestant without a horse".

Greacen hardly makes heroes of his lot; Pound is depicted after his battles with government and incarceration in a loony bin, found to be still living in hell; Eliot is the Anglo-American gent in London with "the features of clerical cut". He might almost be a twin of Noel Coward who is wickedly captured and parodied by the poet as a young man, complimenting him, "You were simply wonderful tonight".

While Heaney is included with overt graciousness, the haunting portraits here are of Spender, Alex Comfort, Fred Urquhart and Clifford Dyment—these are given Greacen's full irony and gentleness while the poet himself, as companion to each, thrusts them back into the limelight. There is not only a ghostly presence, but echoes of speech and often sadness. Triumph would seem too bombastic for Greacen's pen. His poets are all too human.

Power's poems (this is third collection) come from the most fleeting moments, hence the immediacy. The language is plain, simple and mainly unselfconscious. You can almost pinpoint the precise moment of inspiration. He evokes Yeats and perhaps, naturally, Hopkins since he is a priest but otherwise this is not literary material. Neither is it Biblical (as might be expected) except for the occasional poem finding an impetus from that source.

In poems about mortality, there is no theology or mystical quotation—'Snapshot'; 'Singularity', 'After the Plane Crash', 'At the Health Centre', 'In the Hospital Coffee Shop'. The theme continues into meditations on 9/11 such as 'The Shattering' where the globally transmitted event is seen as mere media images for some and something quite different for others. 'Morning at Marchamley' reflects his own response—

Taking a seat in the monastery chapel

I face the fourth station where Jesus

stoops for his mother reaching

to touch his burdened shoulder

It has all been described before.

Power looks into the heart of reality, this is the power here, with a faith expressed from the front lines of life:

All shall be well. I trust. Meanwhile

At times I squat with Jonah on his dunghill

And challenge the Almighty to forgive my spite.

('Signs of Contradiction') Note: it is Jonah not Job. Don't get the impression that this is a poetry of dirges along the lines of 'sic transit gloria mundi'. The unbearable lightness of being of the title poem and such miniatures as 'Word', 'Dawn at Hawkstone' really shine true.

Despite the accomplishment of Clifton's sequence there is a definite discomfort; whether implied or actually felt, is difficult to establish. This is not because of the imprecision of emotion. You cannot really place these poems in the heavy emotional arena. His dis-ease with Paris lurks everywhere. Not for him a Paris long seen as the Irish exile's heaven. Not that it is hell, but it is never quite the Champs Elysees. To be simplistic about it, there is a feeling of his being small, the kind of alienation and ennui sung by French poets from Baudelaire, Verlaine and Rimbaud onwards. 'Matchbox Sculptures' and 'Reductio' prove his point about the Parisian or visitor, dwarfed among the human race and the city.

Of disconnected people, faces, times,

Humanity, dissolving into shapes

At the end of avenues, at the end of rhymes.

('Reductior')

The sequence is loosely threaded together and the better for not bogging itself down in some overall unifying elements. When one reads 'Zone' one thinks of Apollinaire's longer poem. Even the poem based on Descartes muddling through in Stockholm is a rendition of pity for the philosopher. It is only when you get to the title poem that there is some relief from "The Sunday afternoons that run on Michelin tyres" as he lightens up and celebrates

Protected by the nearnesses of women, their sex

Blown sheer through summer dresses, loving my food,

My freedom, as they say a man should.

Hartnett's selection of translations, according to his publisher Peter Fallon, Translations : a selection complements the five other Michael Hartnett 'Gallery' volumes in this genre. There is the reminder that the poet was a transliterator rather than slavish translator, hence he boards many languages outside his immediate ken, rendering the Tao Te Ching (his spelling) apparently written during his curatorship of Joyce's tower in Sandycove. Its companion piece, based on twenty-four poems by Sikong Tu is equally inspiring to read, even if its main obsession is the writing of poetry while the Tao addresses life directly with an intensity that has kept the text in print for centuries.

Catullus is rendered into good plain English that gives into the slack where necessary, where the colloquial and scatological are embraced. Hartnett's empathy and sympathy comes through for poor old Catullus, the pining lover with his woes and tough-woman-muse. The idyllic love-life is shattered before his eyes as she dumps him in search of others, firing his anger and fuelling his verse:

I hate and I love. Why do I do this? Perhaps you will ask me. I don't know. But I feel it. And I am in torment. (LXXXV)

Despite Hartnett's fondness and skill with the foreign—even Heine rising from doom to angelic balm, or Lorca prophesying his own execution—he seems more comfortable with his own race. The lovely, the beautiful, the musical and the brilliant flow from 'On getting up one morning' (Anon). Yet, the subject matter is violent and angry—Saxon conquest in Ireland, and in the same vein Eoghan Rua Ó Suilleabhain's malediction against the invader is more vigorous, naming names and wishing them every ill under the sun.

Hartnett commemorates his Latin teacher David Hayes in name and title with a version of Horace (Odes IV, vii) and a flamboyant closing stanza plus arabesques—

Loyola can't save from darkness

Father Hopkins pure and mild;

Nor can the Sphinx break off the chains
From her beloved Oscar Wilde.

A collection of largesse, not least the concluding, 'Portrait', translated from his own beloved Gaeilge-

a frost-fall is in my hair,

burst blood-vessels in my face,

there is a staff on my forehead,

cacophonous music written by age.

—*Books Ireland* 2004

POETRY, VOICES AND ECHOES

Soundings: poems we did for our leaving cert Augustine Martin;
foreword Joseph O'Connor (Gill & Macmillan)

O'Connor reaches near hysteria and hyperbole in the foreword
because he is awash with nostalgia and praise: 'It was Gus Martin's
genius to know that loving poetry is a marriage' and designates him
'a great educator'. Martin (1935-1995)—nationally known as
'Gus'—gained first place in Ireland in Leaving Certificate English,
and in his early thirties was broadcasting on radio and television.
Out of this background came *Soundings*, and *Exploring English* (1
& 3) which hallmarked his selection from the Irish Short Story
genre. He would go on to a brilliant career in UCD, in the Abbey
Theatre, and in the Irish Senate. His lectures and tutorials in college
were always challenging as well as entertaining and filled with
incident as the time when he exalted Jane Austen above William
Faulkner riling his young audience in approving *The Sound and the
Fury* and *As I Lay Dying* while eloquently defending *Persuasion* and
Emma.

O'Connor's praise is loud: 'In *Soundings* we had been given a gift
that would last a whole lifetime'—he presumably means the gift of
reading poetry. 'Led Zeppelin sang of the Stairway to Heaven, but
poetry was a walk on the wild side'. Lou Reed's "Walk on the Wild
Side" was released a year after *Led Zeppelin IV* that includes
"Stairway to Heaven":

New York City's the place where they say,
Hey babe, take a walk on the wild side

Reed's lyrics of sex, Valium, James Dean and gender bending is
slightly better than the embarrassing and vague "Stairway to
Heaven" which except for the guitar work of Jimmy Page on the
song is as worn out an old chestnut as "Bohemian Rhapsody".

Gus is explicit in his introduction about the high versus low-brow debate: 'A Beethoven symphony comes less easily to the ear and the sensibility than a pop song, but once it has made its impact it endures. So too with a great poem.' This high versus low culture dilemma may have been resolved if one supports the Axelrod-Roman-Travisano [*The*] *New Anthology of American Poetry* (2005) where sections outside of the poetry are headed as follows: 'Parlor Songs and Ballads', 'Blues', 'Jazz and Musical Theater Lyrics', and 'Gospel Music'. *Soundings* was strictly classical and canonical with over 90% of the poems still maintaining their power and glory while the pop songs of youth are a pale memory. This debate began with the Beats in America as to whether ballads, rock and pop could be classified within the poetry tradition. Kenneth Rexroth, founding father of the Beats movement in San Francisco felt that Bob Dylan was a poet along with Leonard Cohen and Jim Morrison. Hendrix's "Angel" that had the line: "Silver wings silhouetted against the child's sunrise" while not being Keats or Shelley was hailed by hippies: this was poetry too. David Shumway asserts that '[b]y the end of the 1960s, the idea of rock poetry was widely accepted by ordinary listeners and many young poets, even if it was mainly pooh-poohed in the academy'.

However, Gus enmeshed in the academy supported the Richard Ellmann-Robert O'Clair agenda which is reflected in *Soundings*. Ellmann and O'Clair produced the *The Norton Anthology of Modern Poetry* (1973) a canonical textbook beginning with Whitman, reaching up to James Tate, and including Irish, British, and Canadian poets. The target readership was students seriously engaged with literature using anthologies as signposts to vaster treasuries and collections of poems. *Soundings* stated imperially in 1969: 'Between the covers of this book there is a splendid body of poetry, some of the finest poems from one of the greatest literatures in the world.' Gus meant the English tradition and headlined Chaucer, Shakespeare, Donne, Milton, Dryden, Pope, Wordsworth, Shelley, Keats, Hopkins and Dylan Thomas. He included

Tennyson's "Choric Song of the Lotus Eaters"—a terrific exposure to an episode from Homer's *Odyssey* with its drug laden atmosphere. Hardy's pagan effusion "Afterwards" must have slipped past the more conservative who vetted the final selection for what was after all the highly regulated late 1960s Ireland. Wordsworth's romantic and philosophical credo looms within "Tintern Abbey" yet there was no Coleridge. However, had Gus interjected Coleridge, Swinburne and Browning, *Soundings* would have been an inclusive survey course in poetry suitable for any fresher in Oxford and Cambridge.

He was stolidly pioneering the classics in order to alert students and inspire them beyond contemporary culture. Dylan's "Desolation Row" was ignored by Gus since it was ubiquitous along with other protest songs. Instead, he was injecting Dylan Thomas's masterpiece "Fern Hill" and the technically skilled elegy "A Refusal to Mourn". Teachers who had to 'use' *Soundings* had the added bait of Gus's notes, glossary and biographical notes. The anthology potentially gave students a powerful art experience that would inform their critical taste alongside the psychedelia of Lennon's "Lucy in the Sky with Diamonds" and the vague rhetoric of Bowie's "Oh You Pretty Things".

One of the deftest touches was the American content: Emily Dickinson with T. S. Eliot—both inherently metaphysical poets—very unfashionable poetry at the time. *Soundings* is startlingly metaphysical in content and commences with Chaucer's Pilgrims gathering in a tavern in Southwark on their way to Canterbury, 15 of Shakespeare's sonnets with meditations on time, decay and despair set in powerful language, ironic and witty just like young people. While 'Poor soul, the centre of my sinful earth' (No. 146) pleads for acceptance, quietism and contemplation: 'Within be fed, without be rich no more'. 'Soul' and 'sin' occur in the poems—deliberately or not—for instance in Herbert's unique poem "Love" and in John Donne's: 'Wilt Thou forgive that sin where I begun' ("A Hymne to God the Father"), also in Kavanagh's "Advent", of course in Hopkins which includes his poems written in despair: "I wake and feel the Fell of Dark" and "No Worst, there is None", as well as in Dickinson's "The Soul selects her own Society". Dickinson is never despairing, quite the opposite: the reclusive poet of Amherst is full of beautiful glee and genius.

The greatest success in *Soundings* was Eliot's "The Love Song of J. Alfred Prufrock" that has become the Mona Lisa of Modernism and is as infamous a poem as Keats "Ode to a Nightingale". 'Prufrock' is a metaphysical ghost. The 'I' of the poem sounds hip, confused and ultramodern (even still) and the bigger questions of existence are to the fore: 'And I have seen the eternal Footman hold my coat, and snicker,/And in short, I was afraid.' One recalls 'Prufrock' being 'performed' aloud in class, quoted in snatches outside class, especially that opening cosmic image of the evening sky 'Like a patient etherised upon a table'. And farfetched as it may sound, 'Prufrock' entered the party culture. It was acceptable in accommodating circles to recite the poem in full (with a stray copy of *Soundings*) after the drinking, dancing and frolicking when sobriety and the dawn chorus of birds arrived. The poem was a balm for post-pleasure, hangover and the blues. 'Prufrock' written in 1910 published in *Poetry* (Chicago) in 1915 was older than "It's a long way to Tipperary", "Alexander's Ragtime Band" , "Star Dust" and much deeper than Pink Floyd's *Dark Side of the Moon.*

Not every *Soundings* generation teenager agreed that 'Prufrock' was artistically superior to Pink Floyd. However, Gus with his hidden agenda was like every gifted teacher wishing to communicate through the best literature. The achievement of his selection is all about the poems. One does not recall the examinations or the handed-in homework except for the poems amidst inked and pencilled notes, as well as pummelled graffiti and the normal maniacal effusions of seventeen, eighteen and nineteen year olds in textbooks. The poems also 'inspired' the owners of *Soundings* to experiment lewdly or otherwise and write lines of joy, doggerel and protest. The poems performed their secret ritual and everyone who found the subject a pleasurable doss were faced with no difficulties except for references to Apollo, Pan, the Maenads, Ozymandias (easily turned into 'Ozzy Osbourne' with a biro), Provençal song, Hippocrene, Eremite, Heraclitus, Lyonesse, Troy, Lydaen, and the initially impenetrable Yeatsian phrase: 'perne in a gyre'. Gus had foreseen this: 'Some of the poems are immediately understandable and enjoyable, others present certain obstacles to the reader.' These obstacles were not just occasional arcane references: and some of the poems *were* difficult but ultimately vital, notably in the Irish Poets Section with Yeats's "Sailing to Byzantium" and "Among School Children".

He was not going to follow the agenda set for editors commissioned by Longmans as well as Browne and Nolan who before *Soundings* produced what now seem archaic compendiums for schools, with English ballads, and poems from Irish Nationalism of the nineteenth century alongside Chesterton's "The Donkey", Kilmer's "Trees", Brooke's "The Soldier" and Masefield's "Sea-Fever". He was not going to launch a folkloric anthology using an out-of-fashion formula. His insistence was for exercising intellect, broadening minds and fructifying imagination. He was bound to a certain extent by including Kavanagh and the surprising element in *Soundings* is his scanty selection from Irish poets while the Yeats poems seem deliberately to show Yeats's superiority to Clarke, Kavanagh and Kinsella. Gus was a devout and fervent Yeatsian.

Since he had been an educational broadcaster, he might have felt pressurised to include RTÉ poets but struck free of being informed by any clique. Clarke was certainly not an RTÉ poet though an occasional broadcaster in Donnybrook. Gus had written him into his TV programmes on poetry. Kavanagh was a self-invented 'peasant' but not really liked in RTÉ and his passing coincided with the preparatory work on *Soundings*. Indeed, the rural element but not necessarily the Gaelic element was steered by Kavanagh in *Soundings* where both Clarke and Kinsella are demarcated as being 'rural' poets through the miniscule selection of their work. The concept of Clarke and Kinsella as 'rural' is far from the case but Gus may have been pandering to the fact that a sizeable number of his students were rural, and he himself was from John McGahern's hometown Ballinamore, County Leitrim. This 'county theme' which is tribal would have been abhorrent to Yeats. However, it is a central part of the Irish psyche even today, and is expressed paradoxically in Kavanagh's "Stony Grey Soil" where the writer as cute-hoor with pretence to loathing his native county makes a ballad of covert myth-making based on his native turf, literally.

The real agenda circulating through *Soundings* is Modernist poetry. Yeats and Eliot are 'visibly' present with Pound and Joyce finding their way into the introduction, notes and glossary: 'the new direction was supplied by Yeats, by Ezra Pound, but above all by Eliot'; Joyce is mentioned in comments about prosody. Gus's anthology takes its breath and scope from the English tradition that ultimately informed the bulk of Modernism, and he could hardly have been expected to include other major modernist practitioners: Wallace Stevens, William Carlos Williams and Conrad Aiken. So the achievement in *Soundings* is the highlighting of Modernism as well as Yeats, whereas previous generations of students were handed out not much more than Yeats's tiny lyric "The Lake Isle of Innisfree". Gus on his own power trip was fighting for what he loved: literature. He was not going to sell himself or the vast numbers of his students short, nor was he forgetting his teacher-readers.

Behind the selection is, of course, solid critical acumen and further back the Modernist greats. There is no obeisance to Dylan, Cohen, Pink Floyd, Led Zeppelin or "Stairway to Heaven" in the introduction. Gus's roots were steeped in the English tradition: why else did he include the entire Book 1 of *Paradise Lost* as well as

Miltonic sonnets and the whole of "Lycidas". He was also being trenchantly European and doing what a teacher does best: mediating what is new for the student. He was importantly facilitating the exposure of Irish students to this newness, essential to an Island people who generally leave the island by necessity or choice. The homespun culture is pervasive and too pejorative but foreign cultures must be encountered as early as possible in life, and education is (or should be) a preparation for life beyond what has been called 'the little school of the family'.

Yes there was Elvis, The Beatles, The Beach Boys, The Stones but students need education in everything despite their excitement, apathy, indolence and innate anarchy. Classical English poetry as a central birthplace of Modernist poetry in English was also the genesis of Joyce and Yeats who made their own version of Modernism ultimately based on their Irishness. *Soundings* which cunningly begins with Chaucer's *Canterbury Tales*—the first novel (albeit) written in verse in English then returns full circle back to Ireland and Yeats.

The legacy of *Soundings* extends to Cian Hogan's *Poems: A New Anthology of Leaving Certificate Poetry* (2008) in maintaining the Yeats-Eliot connection while Keats and Adrienne Rich are companioned which maintains the English and American connection. The Eavan Boland-Michael Longley dominance is somewhat balanced by the 'Unseen Section' with at least one poem from another twenty-three poets, even if the poets are mixed diversely in scope and talent. The Niall MacMonagle *Poetry Now: Leaving Certificate English Poetry* (1999) had some of the same strengths with thirty-nine poets given in single representation in the 'Unseen Section'. MacMonagle's larger representation of poems tended to bond Elizabeth Bishop with Eavan Boland for some reason and with Longley as well which is eclectic to say the least while including the minor though once popular poet of angst, Philip Larkin which was a great misadventure, especially when Yeats was only represented by one short early poem. Such a blinkered choice is comparable to preparing an anthology for English Grammar Schools where Shakespeare would be represented by only one short lyric such as: "Tell Me Where is Fancy Bred?"

In this respect *Soundings* is rich in literary wealth when one considers the limitations of others who were handed on the overpowering responsibility of being cultural arbiters. When it comes to choosing poetry for the student, critical acumen and wide parameters of sensibility are a necessity. *Soundings* earned its laurels justly and honourably because of its authentic editor.

—*Inis: the children's book magazine* 2011

READERS' FRIENDS

Bearing Witness: essays on Anglo-Irish Literature Augustine Martin (University College Dublin Press)

Literature in Ireland: studies Irish and Anglo-Irish Thomas MacDonagh (Relay)

Images of Invention: essays on Irish writing A. Norman Jeffares (Colin Smythe)

Coleridge in Italy Edoardo Zuccato (Cork University Press)

Dr Anthony Roche has written an insightful and affectionate introduction to these essays and reviews by Augustine Martin, whose lifelong enthusiasm for literature "found its expression in a staggering diversity of platforms". Roche eloquently notes the 'utile' and 'dulce' and 'delight' shown by Gus, the people's critic; who without deadening the enduring mystery, made everyone welcome at the banquet of Literature whether in lecture hall, tutorial, radio, TV or the pub. As a literary critic, Martin has revelations about Synge's 'apotheosis of loneliness' and Yeats's apocalyptic vision: "which is Rosicrucian, cosmopolitan, esoteric" moving towards "the birth of a new Dionysiac dispensation involving the return of the old gods". Out of context this is obscure. However, Martin displays an artesian level of understanding about Yeats's visionary stories The Tables of the Law, The Adoration of the Magi and the poems in The Secret Rose. He was dazzled, if not overwhelmed by the works of W. B. Yeats.

Elsewhere, he shows James Stephens as a literary precursor of Flann O'Brien, The Crock of Gold begot The Third Policeman; Austin Clarke's 'erotic frankness' in the epic poems published in the twenties and their 'note of sexual frankness was new in Irish metric of Donald Davies' more formal poems. 'Inherited Dissent: the dilemma of the Irish Writer' is a landmark essay on writers' prejudice, posing, posturing and fixed ideas against creeds, institutions, the State, the public and society in general. The book reviews are good too; he dislikes the form of Francis Stuart's novels, yet still hails Redemption and The Pillar of Cloud; and applauds Aldan Mathews' Lipstick on the Host. Dr Roche's expertise has found an early review by Gus, of Heaney's Death of a Naturalist. In retrospect it is accurate and poignant; and even more poignant are the extracts from an unfinished biography of Patrick Kavanagh. Augustine Martin's vision may well have been in the words of Schiller who is quoted: "I believe that everything the best mind of humanity really wishes for, and formulates the wish, must come to pass".

There are remarkable qualities about the prose in this eighty-year-old book (Thomas McDonagh's), which is a hymn to poetry. The book is an established classic. Ezra Pound liked it. The revolutionary nationalism for which Mac Donagh died is present; but perhaps the text would not offend anyone who claims to be Irish. His true patriotic fervour never overtakes the content. On the contrary it heightened this reader's pleasure. He can be sacred and profane, pagan and mystical; ever the enthusiast, utterly convincing because of the sublime peaks in the prose, which are so infectious that it would be impossible not to read on. Where to place this book in the canon is another matter. It is a general, rather than a specific introduction to literature but a really fabulous one, devoid of any offending theories. Mac Donagh is a grammarian: words should be tested 'by their current value'; a considerable linguist, glossing a chunk of De Quincey into French, Latin, colloquial English and the Gaelic of Geoffrey Keating. In Gaelic poetry 'too much ado has been made of the metres' though he praises O'Curry and the pantheon of translators: Mangan, Meyer, Hyde, Sigerson and O'Grady. Paradoxically, he was openly suspect of the Gaelic League, Connradh na Gaedhilge "an organisation with the official institutions of a political propagandist society". He was more in favour of a living theatre, and that Irish people should want to learn

Gaelic "in order to read and know Irish literature". His translations are interesting but not great.

He very definitely claims that medieval Gaelic verse is in the larger world tradition; so J. J. Callanan is the confrere of Ernest Dowson, and Helen of Troy the literary sister of Deirdre of the Sorrows. He contrasts Irish poets with Horace, Catullus and Virgil. On one page he translates a poem by Pearse and on the next refers to Villon and Verlaine. He is at ease with William Dunbar's 'Lament for the Makaris' or Thomas Campion on the Elizabethan lyric but obsessively dislikes W. E. Henley's poem 'Out of the night that covers me'. His translation of Is Truagh gan Mise i Sasana is very good. The book is certainly a minor masterpiece but otherwise difficult to classify. The critical opinions are acceptable for the simple reason that they make pleasing correspondences. Nothing offends and yet nothing is far-fetched. History records that they shot Thomas Mac Donagh. They shot a poet and a gentleman.

Cork University Press have a lavishly produced book here, including the fine art cover and, among the illustrations, Englehart's The Garden of Boccaccio. Zuccato's notes are a useful mine of information in this scholarly study, which is free from any desire to scene-set or biographise Samuel Taylor Coleridge; who solipsistically revelled in the concept of 'the wandering bard', managing to travel even briefly through Italy after two years in Malta, despite ailments and personal miseries.

Zuccato's sources are vast and wide-ranging; they evoke excitement and best of all make the book very readable. There are good shorthand summations, "Coleridge opposed the clarity of Classical art, in which everything is immediately given in phenomena, with the complexity and depth of Gothic art, in which phenomena have become symbols. Greek art was beautiful, Gothic art sublime." Coleridge presumed that the alchemist Girolamo Cardano 'was a braggard and a quack' like Paracelsus; "his greatest debt was to Boehme as a Trinitarian thinker" and his favourite sculptors were Praxiteles, Thorwaldsen and Flaxman.

Zuccato controversially finds Coleridge's religious disposition when discussing Dante: "Coleridge regarded Dante as a precursor of the Reformation" and "Dante's style above Milton's"; the poem 'Limbo' is Dantescan and Coleridge saw The Divine Comedy as stylistically expressive and Gothic because it can set the reader dreaming. There is good use of the modern scholar, Frances Yates in the chapter on Coleridge and the Renaissance, and a marvellous chapter on Italian sonneteers Petrarch, Giambattista Marino whose 'Alla sua arnica' is a brilliant poem and perhaps the even greater poet, Gabriello Chiabera.

However much unhappiness Coleridge suffered over his unresolved love affair with Sara Hutchinson, he had the consolatory delights of poetry, study, scholarship and speculation; some of these treasures are excellently exhibited by Edoardo Zuccato without a heavy agenda, rather in the Renaissance manner of a delightful thesis writer.

—*Books Ireland* 1997

COME INTO THE PARLOUR

New Guests of the Irish Nation Bryan Fanning (Irish Academic Press)

Landing Places: immigrant poets in Ireland eds. Eva Bourke and Borbála Faragó (Dedalus Press)

One who writes in these contexts is potentially trying to save lives because history records that the road through hatred and racism leads to Dachau and Auschwitz. Fanning, in the Socratic manner outlines his polemical tutelage reaching back to Martin Haverty's The History of Modern Ireland from the Earliest Period to the Present Time (1867) a book acquired through his grandfather 'that promoted the Fenian cause'. He is not a partisan Teague based on such background; nor is it ethically permissible to display partisanship in polemics. His many contributions to this highly contentious and inflammatory topic, as to who are the guests, and whose nation is it anyway, include: Immigration and Social Change in the Republic of Ireland. In the former, claims are made for the intensity of anti-Semitism in Ireland having 'much in common with anti-Semitism in Nazi Germany.' Yes, this sounds alarmist yet reveals with vitality the dangers in society and amongst individuals with the notion of 'foreigner'. One has to admire his engagement with the themes of racism on our doorstep, reminding the reader that he is discussing matters of life and death, freedom and liberty, public truths and private lies. He has to grapple with intense issues that are revelatory of human limitation, especially the degrees of evil within humanity cruelly unleashed upon 'the other'.

Fanning does not resort to art or literature for counsel, and briefly alludes to Synge & Yeats on the Irish psyche. Rather he relies on the watery theology of liberalism; the ultimate yardstick of government legislation, and media exposé. Within these three domains he presents the all too human results when foreigners and 'others' suffer racial affliction in Ireland. Racism as depicted in these pages has ended in bloodshed and death. This is not a jeremiad; he is not Zola, he is not a screaming Cassandra, yet he has to hold the fiery torch of Diogenes albeit with effective restraint on invective.

Fanning points out that notable polemicists of the past were vile as well as racially incendiary: Engels being anti-Irish, John Mitchel advocating slavery 'as the best state of existence for the Negro,' and Fr Creagh of Limerick and Arthur Griffith, both publicly anti-Semitic. One recoils from listing the religious justifications for racism referenced, fearing that context, and quotation can easily be misconstrued as to meaning, stance and viewpoint even from a reviewer. His main thrust is in trying to reclaim justice in the midst of past injustice, with regard to groups and individuals being anti-Semitic, anti-Traveller and anti-Immigrants. The 'political exploitation of anti-Traveller prejudice in Clare' has a close focus on Ennis. This makes for disturbing and compelling exposition, especially in the aftermath of a racial murder. His sourcing of local citizens in the town, proved them dangerously racist with comments such as, 'Oh, you're talking about the knacker who got himself killed.' While the Incitement to Hatred Act and the Department of Justice, Equality and Law are in place, he also cites the sociological parameters of Frank Salter's 'ethnic nepotism' that accurately posits the theory 'that members of an ethnic group tend to favour members of their group over others because they are more related to the former. It emphasizes a disposition to favour kin over outsiders especially where people and groups have to compete for scarce resources.'

His explication from theoretical sources is always satisfying. He does not go in much for statistics except on immigration, and provides evidence of the statistic of one, namely John Ward of the Travellers, shot dead by Pàdraig Nally, 'throughout the trial and appeal Nally received widespread support and was, to a considerable extent, portrayed as the victim of the Travellers.' Fanning substantially hits his stride in dealing with 1995-2000 involving immigrants 'under one quarter million', whom he notes as 'guest workers, asylum seekers, migrants and non-citizen ethnic minorities.' The crux for asylum seekers is how they can 'exercise a right under the 1956 United Nations Convention Relating To The Status of Refugees' and also the 2004 Citizenship Referendum in Ireland 'structured by tensions between domiciliary rights—including the right to vote in local government elections—and citizenship rights.' He is cautionary, 'the republic of Ireland must begin the business of integrating or otherwise coming to terms with the one in ten living in Irish society who were not born here.' The essential fact he posits is that 'human rights depend, as such, upon what states (and their citizens) will or will not do about them'. He includes a polemical war between Seamus Deane and Cruise O'Brien over Edmund Burke, however, the conclusion is that 'Deane identifies two Burkes—one who is a defender of liberty, another of liberty causes—but likes neither.' Deane is accused of 'addressing one side of the story'. Is Fanning a Burkean fellow traveller? Very difficult to say 'yes' or 'no'.

Rotimi Adebari, the Nigerian-Irish mayor of Portlaoise (pictured on the cover) is the softer focus of this polemic while the ever trenchant academic base in citing Kant's Perpetual Peace and claims for world citizenship are about as redolent in meaning as John Lennon's "Imagine" when compared to the realpolitik of Irish immigration policy as practiced in what is a small truncated island republic. There is a spirited grappling with the cocktail-bar economist and soothsayer, David McWilliams who in The Pope's Children and The Generation Game catches attention purely for some leavening sociological demographics. McW can always provide statistics like a circus magician such as 1% 'of Irish people are Lithuanian'. Fanning in his turn can statisticate with nuggets such as Scoil Cholm, whose 83 junior infants in 2007 had parents from 'Nigeria, Colombia, Romania, Poland and Moldova'.

Ireland as insubstantial Ellis Island is perhaps the real message here.

Jurisprudence and the legislator are the control centres behind Fanning's careful, caring, and unflinching realism over many diversities, not least the status of 'the Irish-born non-Irish child' and how it feels on the street and on public transport for our guests. Frank O'Connor's story that gives the book its title, caused the famous Corkman difficulty in finding a conclusion suitable to the material, hence his many versions. Fanning warns that 'citizenship without recognition is not always enough to ensure integration, the absence of both renders integration very difficult indeed. The problem is not too many immigrants seeking Irish nationality but that many of those living here are unlikely to naturalise.' He is devoid of Swiftian and Yeatsian indignation about the Irish. However, acceptable irony comes through when he quotes a popular song, 'If you're Irish come into the parlour/There's a welcome there for you.' One is averse to adding further irony.

Bourke is on the scene longer than Faragó but their joint introduction to 66 immigrant poets is happily not shamrock waving. Faragó's arrival in the mid-nineties is telling of the era: 'after every introduction people would ask, "when are you going home?" The editors suggest that the Irish, inured to emigration are foreign to immigration, and natives imply in any event, 'why would you want to live here?' Despite the acknowledgements about seeking poets through the Irish Times (the voice of God on arts' matters) plus bowing and scraping to Harry Clifton with a lugubrious epigraph from him, it is not surprising that many so-called 'established names' pepper this anthology. Chris Agee, Chuck Kruger, Anatoly Kudryavitsky, Judith Mok, Matthew Geden, Susan Millar DuMars, Mark Roper, Jo Slade, Richard Tillinghast and Ann Zell. Nor is one admitting universal admiration of the latter list.

On the whole, this anthology is not illuminating about, to use Fanning's nomenclature, New Guests of the Nation, what they think of their adopted island retreat or what they think of Ireland; nor should it be their central concern. However, the best of the few swipes at the country comes from Raphael Josef Stachniss "The red cow": 'going out/in the cold/the wind/and the rain/searching for truth/for something/new and unknown/feels like/driving through/the red cow roundabout/in dublin/ireland/the very/first time'. Annie Deppe in "Salt Over the Shoulder" catches the uncertainty of European life but without being a newly fledged 'Eireyann', while Theodore Deppe is uncannily real in "The Singing" but his theme is not, happily, remotely Irish. Paul Grattan is effective as post-surrealist. Kudryavitsky's "Out of Harm's Way" is one of the best poems here. Panchali Mukherji, Tom Myp, Julia Piera are worth reading while Kinga Olszewska catches our rural conniving suspicion in "Site for Sale". 'Are you local? the man behind the desk asks disbelievingly./I have been local for the last ten years./But you are not really Irish?' Eckhardt Schmidt tries to survive the abominable climate. His short poem should be etched on some prominent wall of the town hall. "At Sea in Monaghan" 'Monaghan, the capital of rain;/Kerbs becoming quays/With no ship waiting for me.'

One questions the raison d'être of this anthology, quite obviously a publisher's concept and funded for cross-cultural reasons but Poetry does not have borders, nor gloat about nations—balladeers gloat about nations. Poetry should move beyond territories, surely, hence this publication smacks of the very provinciality that it purports to interrogate and dispel. In this respect, the exercise is conspicuous for its drawing awkward attention to the immigrant factor rather the artistic factor. The introduction highlights immigration, referencing homelands of 'poets from countries as far apart as Japan and Canada, Spain and the US, Poland, India, Germany and South Africa.' There are multiple ways of avoiding lugubriousness with an art project but that did not happen here. The Irish literature establishment, such as it is, is a closeknit homespun nexus of provinciality, and one wonders if among the 'immigrant poets'— what an awful adjective for poets, an adjective that is racially intimidating itself—there must be the usual left out 'outsiders' who could show up the Irish with fragile identities and ultimately racial, tribal, and rural, ever suspicious of every 'other'!

—*Books Ireland* 2010

SURGEON'S DOZEN

The Irish Times Book of Favourite Irish Poems Colum Tóibín
(Irish Times Books)

Modern Irish Poetry: a new alhambra Frank Sewell (Oxford
University Press)

Thomas Kinsella: the peppercanister poems Derval Tubridy
(University College Dublin Press)

The Familiar Thomas Kinsella (Peppercanister)

Godhead Thomas Kinsella (Peppercanister)

Citizen of the World Thomas Kinsella (Peppercanister)

Littlebody Thomas Kinsella (Peppercanister)

Tóibín makes vast claims for poetry in almost religious terms—its
power as chant and ritual—in eloquent introduction and many will
agree. On the other hand there is in actuality only a small sect of
both poets and poetry readers leaving aside the other machinations
of what in the US is called po-biz. It seems that Wordsworth's
injunction about poetry and its survival and finding its true audience
among the people rather than the public is proven true more than a
century later.

Nearly all anthologies repeat the selections made by previous
anthologists, no-one daring enough to make a truly personal
selection without using already over-anthologised work. The present
selection can be only partly blamed since it has a different agenda—
its genesis came from an Irish Times survey of the hundred best-
loved poems and some 3,500 of their readers responded. Originally,
Theo Dorgan of Poetry Ireland spurred on literary editor Caroline
Walsh to assist him, and she in turn called on colleagues in the
newspaper Katie Donovan and Brenda McNiff for help. The
hundred most nominated poems are listed and Tóibín has included
the nominations except in a few instances such as Joyce's 'Ecce

Puer'. A peculiar feature is that the poets have their poems scattered throughout the contents rather than clustered together in their particular allotment of space. Many are represented by a single poem, notably Montague with 'All Legendary Obstacles'.

There is an index of poets which gives you the score as to which poems have been chosen and how many; Wilde and Goldsmith, both of whom were obvious readers' choices, are represented by extracts from The Ballad of Reading Gaol and The Deserted Village, respectively. Yeats weighs in as winner with twenty-five poems from his earlier rather than later work. One presumes that many poetry readers first met Yeats and others in the Leaving Certificate poetry book Soundings compiled by Augustine Martin—their taste reflecting early formation and little change thereafter?

Similarly, Kavanagh who is the second most represented comes through in well-known and well-anthologised pieces either from the Leaving Cert syllabus or elsewhere, but there is nothing from his satirical poems, even though what is here represents some of his best late sonnets. When it comes to Heaney it is interesting that up to now he has not been major syllabus material except at third level for arts students and this is reflected in what's on display here. Of the eight complete poems presented, the best seems to be 'Mid-term Break'.

After this, things do not necessarily go downhill but there is quite a mix from Raifteiri and Ó Rathaille to Pearse and Plunkett and contemporaries like Boland, Kinsella, Durcan and Hartnett. Pearse's poems here would look shallow, were it not for the facts of his life which bear out the claims for his life-sacrifice; 'The Wayfarer' is the best of his lot. Surprisingly, a shining gem or two can almost untopple pages of the familiar and better known, so Kettle's sonnet to his baby daughter can actually break your heart and for a war poem it has none of the ire and angst of Sassoon or Owens. Kettle was a real genius even in prose but one who is woefully neglected.

Colum's 'She Moved Through the Fair' is another great lyric which can often be heard at sing-songs or in the streets at night from a stray drunken voice—and Colum is almost forgotten. Kavanagh's Raglan Road, also here, is a popular song via the Luke Kelly rendition but is not much of a poem.

There are infuriating things such as Mangan's representation by the evergreen 'My Dark Rosaleen' and nothing else; and MacNeice, a considerable figure is represented by almost misrepresenting his output—but this is popular taste. And then there are omissions such as Kennelly, Mahon and others. Does this mean that they and others are not popular? All in all this is a minor treasury not because of what it is but because of what it doesn't have—if you want this as your only store of verse then you are perhaps not obsessed with poetry but with a tiny part of the universal voice of poetry. Still, this alone might be able to unlock the untold riches, the consolation and—one might even suggest—the healing and annealing for the spirit which is another side of poetry's strange power.

Sewell sure sets himself a delightful if difficult task and not least in the selection of four practitioners which represent his chosen corner of poetry. For some reason he sequentially slots Ó Searcaigh between O Riordain and Ó Direáin with Ní Dhomhnaill bringing up the rear. Sewell from the start insists on placing these poets and their work at the centre of life but neither above nor below it since he is never Olympian. With Ó'Riordain's censure of Corkery in the 1970s concerning James Joyce, came a personal statement about the bridging of both traditions and also his poem in homage as Gaeilge naturally further makes the point. But still he remained a poet who saw himself "without roots, torn between two languages". His panegyric to Corkery is double-edged, reflecting his divided mind about an old friend and mentor. When he is seen as finding poetry in common things like Kavanagh this doesn't diminish or hide his confrontation with the darker recesses of his mind and character and yet a mere poet all the while scribhinn bhreacaithe ar phar

Is scribinn eile trasna air.

(writing jotted on a page

and other writing jotted over it.)

Yet, obsessed with "what is poetry? how do you make a poem? what does making poems make of you?" Sewell's depiction of the poet's despair is very keen and he quotes a diary entry of April 1940, "poverty is largely responsible for disease. And people are afraid that Hitler will destroy civilisation! If he does it won't be soon enough. Puffed-up Christianity with no conscience!" Ó Riordain is resurrected as a major linguistic innovator despite Máire Mhac an tSaoi's "earlier attacks on his own ability to use Irish".

Sewell's approach to Ó'Direáin is weighty, taking into account his indulgences with Nietzsche and Spengler. His greatest and lengthy persona-poem 'Ó Morna' is in the voice of the landlord who dominates and not the tenant. The poet is seen as outsider—a loathed and despised authority figure. He is compared to Kavanagh in hating 1950s Ireland and its "victory of mediocrity" at the wake in progress for "the corpse of 1916, the Gaelic Language, the inferiority complex . ." The poet never abandoned his telling of winter—the winter of the spirit according, to Sewell and his 'Comhairle don Fhile Og' (Advice to a Young Poet) remains more scarifying than Yeats's advice in "Under Ben Bulben".

From Sewell's reading Ó'Searcaigh comes across as a kind of Irish Kerouac but one with a love of the rural in conflict with cosmopolitan longings, hence the poem 'If You're Going to San Falcarragh'. However, he sounds like an erstwhile shamrock wearing Hippie at times and happily invoking Buddha more than Christ. One of his gurus is Krisnamurti and the life plan of having "the capacity of meeting everything anew from moment to moment without the conditioning reaction of the past"—this may well require a complete renunciation of quotidian reality rather than achieving it by dedication to writing? The poet may have risen to prominence through his sexual disposition rather than his poems

ach na foscail do bheal, na sceith

uait an sceal; to ar ngra ar an taobh tuathal

den tsoisceal.

(don't open your mouth, don't tell a soul; our love's on the wrong side of the gospel.)

Is it? However, he is not afraid to speak of the love that dare not speak its name but also of other 'shut down' secrecies of his country which Sewell sees as a duty of responsible citizenship and is highly praised for his overt sequence 'Gort na gCnarrih' (Field of Bones) dealing with victims of Irish repression such as Joanne Hayes and Ann Lovet.

Ní Dhomhnaill is shown confronting "the fear and monsters of her unconscious" and also "as a child-bearer and rearer". The debate concerning narrative poetry's place within the canon of poetry is healthily aired since she tends to the narrative and anecdotal but is trenchantly at home with "two linguistic entities in dynamic interaction". Like the other four poets discussed, Ní Dhomhnaill is amply quoted in both languages and all her collections are dealt with while some complete translations are given at the end of this provoking study.

Kinsella's imperial decision of 1972 showed a poet coming into his own with a singular imprint, Peppercanister, heralding all future work and this comes under the sober scrutiny of Derval Tubridy in a study without hyperbole or any grandiose characterisation of her subject. She gets into deep and close confrontation with twenty-one of the Peppercanister books while showing their author's insistence on his autonomy even though they originated from the heady days of Liam Miller and Dolmen Press and are now distributed by

Dedalus. There is some allusion to 47 Percy Lane where the poet and his wife Eleanor set up shop to sell the poems.

She begins with Butcher's Dozen and comes up as far as Godhead. The first volume was a *succés de scandale* as the poet vented his ire about the Widgery Report on Bloody Sunday, finding it scurrilously untrue; he has also been politically labelled because of his truth telling. The elegiac poetry for O'Riada is as deeply felt and ranges on into a subsequent volume, *Vertical Man*, with its Audenesque subtext and homage. In pieces such as 'The Ghost of Sean Ó'Riada Attends a Private Musical Evening in Philadelphia'—the composer comes to play a role in the Kinsella schema somewhat similar to that of Synge with Yeats. The Kennedy Oswald poems may be less fiery but not totally lacking either.

By the time *Notes from the Land of the Dead* and its sequel *A Technical Supplement* appeared, readers knew an epic was under construction and the poet's scalpel would leave nothing unpicked or unscraped until he reached his desired poetical goal. For this purpose a huge scaffolding was unveiled or veiled as the case might be, since the approach was not entirely lyrical, with Diderot and Voltaire in the background and other ghosts. The arrival of volumes seven and eight showcased Jung and Lao Tzu, and others provided elements necessary to the structure, with Celtic Mythology on hand for further piquance. Then the poet's father John Kinsella, James Connolly, Marx, Engels and Larkin filled out a scene as it were.

In *Her Vertical Smile*, Thomas Mann and his Doctor Faustus entered the tableau with an emblazoned theme of lovers using Alma and Gustav Mahler. But such flirtations with Viennese bohemians dissolves in the next volume to a structure based on Eriugena's theology while in St Catherine's Clock the poet's Dublin is considered beginning in 1803 with the horror of Emmet's execution, and Kinsella's terrifying music can startle the ear.

One Fond Embrace began the connection with the Dedalus Press and his rage at the Wood Quay development and a good thrashing for Haughey and Cruise O'Brien. Further volumes never flag with Tubridy's proviso that just as "serial music is composed with a very small degree of redundancy, requiring listeners to attend closely if they are to perceive serial differences, so Kinsella's Peppercanister poetry demands similar attention". One might add that he is a fine example of an Irish metaphysical poet producing this baroque musical verse, eschewing obscurity only where necessary, and all too aware of his literary predecessors.

Tubridy's volume reproduces much of the artwork and covers from all volumes discussed, which somehow keeps her book closer to the original works themselves.

The first of these has a long love poem which is delicate in its execution, artful in the presentation of the erotic and assured in the presence of the m u n d a n e , making it sacrificial and ceremonial. The lovers maintain the sacred throughout: 'I sliced the tomatoes in thin discs/ in damp sequence into their dish;/ scalded the kettle; made the tea.'

The other pieces in this slim volume have intense clarity in places but remain inherently lyrical. With *Godhead* the short title sequence is prefaced by two pieces, one a vast metaphor perhaps for the subconscious—the ocean swell—the other ghostly, a mere jot of lines. The more substantial sequence emerges from some mystical charge, meek and mighty at once. It could easily be interpreted as a prayer to the triune deity? Kinsella achieves the paradox of this type of poetry at once intensely clear above and beyond immediate meaning. As he is undemanding to read so is he rewarding. In conversation he emphasised his credo of plain language poetry.

Of the dozen poems here the title one is longest. There may be no connective fissures between each of these and the entire corpus. Hence it is acceptable not to make tenuous links with the proviso that there may yet be overall unities which have missed the present reviewer at a few sittings. Again, to repeat, there is a keen visual quality which is foremost and the language is clear and nearly every piece is refined and lyrical: 'She is swathed in scarlet,/ descending a curved marble staircase/ into an ocean of music,/ her arms and the tops of her breasts bare.'

One tends to zone in on the title poem which states a personal belief for him as exile within and without—in other words compared to living lives like Goldsmith and Dr Johnson. The darkest thoughts come from the latter and the big themes are: enemies, contemporaries, death and dying. The mood hits with 'Theme and variations' but only just, if the reader is still recovering from the depths of the title piece.

The contents of *Littlebody* are shorter than the previous volume. 'Glenmacnass' and 'Cul de sac' reveal tense scenes from childhood. A good example of his method is in the following lines with their shock of insoluble mystery, the awesome glimpse of reality both for the poet who saw and the reader who sees again through his language:

A man lying in the headlights

in a black soutane at the foot of the steps,

with his arm across his face.

'The Body Brought to the Church' has Kinsella's usual tense fear in the vicinity of death, the numbness and observation aloof as it is accurate yet the experience as conveyed is loaded with discomfort and more than a shiver of negation—if this were a painting of the scene it would have a dark beauty of irredeemable humanity, one feels. Yet he does not falsify his vision which is the poet's duty to art and humanity. The mourners constrained in the ceremony of the religious service for the deceased, once outside the church when the close family drive away:

we mixed again in the same

friendly confusion.

Exchanging numbers. Arranging

to keep in touch.

The poet is with his people in mutual clumsiness and confusion with the tentative gestures towards communality and communion.

—*Books Ireland* 2001

HAUNTINGS

The Haunted Inkwell: art as truth, prophecy and spirituality Mark Patrick Hederman (Columba)

Collected Poems Thomas Kinsella (Carcanet)

In eight mixum-gatherum chapters, a few more passionate than others, the guru-monk tackles some of the frontiers of art as truth and its ability to shape if not predict the future. The overall tone is somewhat triumphalist as if art is the one true church. His bigger agenda is an attempt to find a meeting place for "philosophy, literary criticism, art and truth"—a tall order. Hederman joins other notable clerical critics such as William T. Noon and Thomas Merton as a committed Joycean. It might be said that this text almost fits alongside Merton's The Seven Story Mountain in finding Joyce a rich source—the amazing situation in Merton's case was that he felt that the apostate Joyce had bolstered his vocation as a monk.

Hederman is not so revelatory but certainly art is never less than God's bounty in his opinion and, more than anyone, Joyce is placed at the centre of influence. A stray comment from him about liking "the notion of the Holy Ghost being in the inkbottle" and from Finnegans Wake the house of Shem the Penman is described as 'the haunted inkbottle' easily revealing the chosen title here. Hederman might well be seen as competing for a certain public alongside John O'Donohue (Anam Cara) and John Moriarty in providing accessible feelgood spiritual reading that is non-denominational and outside the imprimaturs of the dark past of censorship and clerical influence. It is worth emphasising the irony that in Hederman's youth such trumpeting of Joyce and others was strictly anathema to churchmen.

He cuts a good jib often enough when he is piling reference, citation and quotation and just about manages to stay waffle-free in an area of esoteric comment where it is all too easy to lose the thread. There is a plea for high-culture and Heaney's many critics of both persuasions are listed but he gives the overall impression of being uncertain about our Laureate's stature, with strong hints of A. N. Wilson's derogatory negative gloss on the poet. The text peaks a little in discussing Rilke and especially Heidegger—"poetry is our only detectable contact with Being". This is placed paradoxically with the notion that "no word that we can invent corresponds to Being as such." If one can sum up Heidegger via Hederman it appears that he may have considered poetry a sore loser in the struggle "to capture the evanescent reality that underpins everything".

The notes give Iris Murdoch's birthplace as Dun Laoghaire (incorrect) and a fast forward through some of her novels, according to Hederman linking philosophy, art, religion and morality. She presented some intense refutations of Heidegger: "The concept of 'Being', used as a substitute for 'God' or 'Absolute', is of dubious value". Murdoch's last novel Jackson's Dilemma displays her rejection of philosophy as being "adequate to the task of capturing the subtle 'stuff' of consciousness"—the central character who is writing a book on Heidegger while being fascinated by the philosopher rejects him ultimately.

The chapter on the poet Leopold Sklar Senghor is an engaging digression with fruitful quotes such as that the act of writing is an "admission of great loneliness". The poet's involvement with political life in West Africa, his negritude and prison life provide a source of useful critical comment. However no one can take from the central concern here and not surprisingly Joyce gets the most space. Ulysses is sidelined, and Joyce as the prose poet is singularised and his earliest critics of Finnegans Wake, Wells and Pound are dismissed. Instead, Sheldon Brivic's Joyce between Freud and Jung is paraded for his purposes. Beckett is only cited as interpreter of Joyce, defining him as an artist involved in the perception of coincidence beyond every other lofty claim for art. Joyce is shown rejecting psychoanalysis but discovering 'the night world' of dream, nightmare and the subconscious; paradoxically because of his mentally ill daughter who was 'seen' by many analysts. Hederman becomes emphatic praising his hero who opened a new frontier, "the unconscious as language itself, not the unconscious described by language". Joyce is quoted about his final novel: "My art is not a mirror held up to nature. Nature mirrors my art." Language was "the father for whom Joyce was searching"— the language found in the Wake.

Finally, Heaney is given an honourable outing, his many translations receive more merit than his other work ("Why was Heaney's post-Nobel masterpiece a translation of Beowulf?") and somehow Helen Vendler, a notable Heaney apologist—"I find her influence too narrow-minded and pedantic"—is given a bit of a critical trashing. Heaney's review of Ted Hughes Birthday Letters is highlighted to good effect. The sequence according to Heaney suggests the origin of all true poems as "the place of ultimate suffering and decision in us".

Ted Hughes is quoted on Birthday Letters and his deep regret about withholding it from earlier publication: "I might have had a more fruitful career—certainly a freer psychological life". This is marvellous material and news of Hughes and his ultimate blockage as a poet and the necessity for him of changing traditions and opting for the confessional mode in his final collection. Hughes' work with Daniel Weissbort on a last poem—a translation of Pushkin's 'The Prophet' quoted in the text—becomes a powerful fugue and closing statement on his life and perhaps, as such fulfils Hederman's purposes as well: There God's voice came to me: 'Stand, Prophet, you are my will. Be my witness. Go/Through all seas and lands./With the Word/Burn the hearts of the people.'

The present reviewer must admit to being a latecomer in Kinsella's work and found his promotion during the turmoil of student days in the early seventies seemingly out of proportion to what was on offer, but there is little need to imply academic contamination. It is often the case that some Irish students are put off by the native brew however potent since youth wants to travel and travel far in the mind. Similarly Kinsella may well not be suitable for young Turks at all, and his poetry is a delight in middle age and most of all the Peppercanister sequence.

The latter occupies two hundred and more pages here and are all the more satisfying for their scope and density. The early work, by no means to be disparaged, ends on page 130 with 'Wyncote, Pennslvania: a gloss'—typical of his solo lyrical flights which are often short insets into the major sequence, usually finding the poet on his own observing. Surprisingly Kinsella has attempted to do something new in nature poetry that is decidedly anti-romantic. Some other generalisations: he is haunted, clairvoyant and hunted by spectres throughout—ghosts are tangible in the way they populate Yeats's opus. However, he is not as such a transcendentalist but more of a metaphysical in that if he accords glimpses of a life beyond this dimension he does not hanker after it; but the ghost ridden landscape of Ireland and Dublin in particular is often palpably real.

When he visits the scenes of Bloody Sunday a month after the events, the ghosts of the slain speak. Here he articulated a definite political colour, critical of the 'sectarian supremacy'; unable to use either Londonderry or Derry, he names it Columcille's town for which some of his critics have shown displeasure, such as Denis Donoghue. The obvious anthem quality of 'Butcher's Dozen' is actually with hindsight restrained and still articulates the majority view of Ireland's population.

Kinsella can be just as harsh on the South from as early on as the ironies of Nightwalker, the poet civil servant turning forty and laying on the irony thick and fast having absorbed Eliot and more so Auden ('ghost of brilliance') to good effect about the government and the Christian Brothers:

Lend me your wealth, your cunning and your drive.

Your arrogant refuse.

Let my people serve them

holy water in new hotels and

That by our studies here they may not lack

Civil Servants in a state of grace.

The better known 'Baggot Street Deserta', 'Downstream' and 'Phoenix Park' all presaged what was to come—his engagement with the mystery which is the poet's real job. The formalism of 'In the Ringwood' and 'The Laundress' did not become the norm in terms of diction or method but were never fully eschewed since he has a love for the metre and rhyme of Swift and Pope. Hallowed places are never forgotten whether they be Inistioge, Inchicore, Irwin Street, Phoenix Street, Westland Row, Ely Place and of course, Mount Street "with the little peppercanister cupola". His visual portraits of the ordinary from such places as opposed to other sources of history are equally rooted in place. Kinsella's strength of vision is asserted early in the opening address of 'Wormwood' but resolution does not come until the twenty-two part sequence Peppercanister.

This sequence (ongoing?), impossible to discuss in a small space, can actually stand alone outside his other work—it is too early to see into all the unities but it is undoubtedly a coherence with a solidly imposed structure containing history, politics, elegy (O'Riada, JFK), lament, satire, vitriol; bitterness and bile in the case of the ironically entitled One Fond Embrace:

Dirty money gives dirty access.

And we were the generation

of positive disgrace.

An office car park sunk deep in history. May their sewers blast under them!

Open Court makes a visit to Circe's layer in the form of an evening among the literati of Patrick Kavanagh's heyday with the old grump himself presiding—the Tourist Board who promote a city of cosy literary doings would be appalled by the realism. Kinsella is decidedly Joycean at times but safely manages to carve out a piece of the city for himself and his myth. Some of the non-national highlights are when he evokes Diderot "the Athenians were never wickeder than in the time of Socrates, and perhaps all they owe to his existence is a crime the more". The cast is impressive—Scotus Eriugena (vide 'Harmonies' and other poems) killed by his students for making them think, Goldsmith depicted on his deathbed, Austin Clarke "his knife-glance curiously amongst us", Jack Yeats—again ghosts are everywhere and some like Auden uncannily present. The metaphysical takes over after the love lyric is regained in a revisit to the Ringwood in *The Familiar* and later the absolute mystery of God is approached, another ghost experienced at San Clemente and the intriguing elf of *Littlebody* provokes in this reader utter astonishment—a bagpipe-playing elfin creature appears to him, where else but in his beloved Glenmacnass and naturally they converse.

The rumour is that Kinsella is in exile—well he must be lonely for his country which is swathed in his steady gaze, page after page but he will not kill the mystery behind reality with any falsifications or by boasting of having achieved a full outline of his vision while he is unyielding in the passion to recreate creation, penetrating down deeply as far as the poet is able. The glimpses of what might be reality transposed into poetry are very accomplished in places. A full achievement by omission through no fault of his own.

—*Books Ireland* 2002

CRITICS AT WORK

Journalism Derek Mahon (Gallery Press)

Austin Clarke Remembered: essays, poems and reminiscences to mark the centenary of his birth R. Dardis Clarke and Austin Clarke (The Bridge Press)

Irish Poetry since Kavanagh ed. Theo Dorgan (Four Courts Press).

'The Distrest Poet' by Hogarth on the cover isn't particularly appropriate because of the contemporary nature of these fifty-seven varieties of Mahon's literary journalism. He dislikes Gore Vidal's phrase 'book-chat' or what W. B. Yeats called the "devil of mere journalism" which Terence Brown's introduction claims "both pays and costs". It is a fantasy for well-heeled academics such as Mahon and Brown to imply they are striplings shivering in their garrets.

At best Mahon can in Auden's phrase "put across the soul in telegrams" but with a typical Belfastian pith and reserve. "Where does the money come from in a society where security has long since replaced textiles and shipbuilding as the largest industry? Presumably from security," he comments. He does a lot of nodding towards the northern family of poets. All are patted on the back obliquely or otherwise including Longley & Longley; and some of the reviews of locals sound like the devil of mere duty to editorial deadline.

Specifically, he knows his Rilke, MacDiarmid and Robert Graves among others, illuminating them in sparky reviews that gutter out leaving nothing behind. He admires Robert Lowell's prose 'Near the Unbalanced Aquarium' about incarceration in the Payne-Whitney Clinic, New York. Interest in Wilde is slight, while Nora Barnacle is shown as the model of a modern Irishwoman. About the author of The Good Soldier "Ford had a good eye but, I suggest, a faulty ear." Better on MacNeice, Beckett and Brian Moore "the best since Joyce, if Joyce was novelist". There is considerable praise for Beckett's tiny poems 'Dieppe' and 'Saint-Lo' but not as much for the original miniaturist and happier poems of Samuel Menashe. He fits in a long speech from Godot, epitomising Beckett's vision and writes well about French writers: Simone Weil has him digging deep. While not being parochial in dealing with the master cynic, Celine, he has no sympathy for Baudelaire.

It's a bit of a thrill knowing he hates certain movies. Death in Venice "so tedious" and the forgivable hash John Huston made of Lowry's Under the Volcano. In that novel Mahon notes: "Of the four main characters only Geoffrey himself rings entirely true" and doesn't relegate it to perdition as a 'drunk book'. The film and the novel are "as different as Coca-Cola from mescal". He is funny about Sartre and Huston in Wicklow co-writing a screenplay on Freud. The cigar smoking film-maker said of the existentialist "he was the ugliest little bastard you ever saw." Also: "Waugh, for example, who, in response to Graham Greene's expressed intention of not writing about God any more, objected that such a move would be like Wodehouse giving up Jeeves" ; and Mahon meeting Beckett in Paris who concludes of age "it's great, I've been looking forward to it all my life".

He subscribes to America's unwritten law concerning long poems; since perhaps they make bad reading tour material. He is colossally unfair to Wyndham Lewis, both his paintings and prose, while praising Donleavy, whose writing is often a dolefully dull diatribe of doubtful diction. Cyril Connolly is panned as a shallow hedonist. A little harsh. Dropping the mask of journalism there are effective and graceful pieces on the cult of J. G. Farrell, and salad days or is it nights, at Trinity College, Dublin. Overall Mahon's eclectic taste is sincere so he cannot be accused of being, in Connolly's phrase "a great armchair snob". He even finds art and life in Raymond Chandler and Jay McInerney's *Bright Lights*.

You get a lot more than the subtitle promises. Poems from Mahon,

Kennelly and translations from Gaelic, amounting to largesse flowing with Montague and Heaney, who introduces this gentle book. The women critics win the cigars. Lucy Collins suggests Clarke's mental breakdown was inherently sexual and, with critical help from Terence Brown, dates his isolation from the post-Civil War imposition of Church as central to Irish identity. Did Clarke wear the black clerical hat and become the other in search of himself? Douglas Sealy mentions Whitman's "every man shall be his own priest".

Lucy Collins attempts to explain why he "concentrated his efforts on verbal rather than physical expression of liberty" and is a healthy contributor to the ongoing battle of the sexes illuminating Clarke grappling with the feminine. Complementing her debate, are perceptions from Mary Thompson, who finds riches in his early Miltonic-sounding long poems and their use of personal trauma— "the disintegration of personality, a metaphoric dying". She implies with huge devotion that he ever after inhabited "the amniotic landscape" and points to Eliot's "the immense panorama of futility and anarchy which is contemporary life".

Gregory A. Schirmer's highly readable piece is too brief, revealing the poet as an isolata who created a more authentic Celtic Twilight than Yeats. These are old battles but Schirmer uses Clarke's huge critical output, including the account of meeting Joyce who was redolent of Jesuitry; both "could not completely exorcise religion" from their lives. Nor should have, he implies. The sensitive ordeal over Gaelic past and present is in Clarke's work and Gus Martin agrees he "found liberty in the Gaelic tradition" using "Gaelic metres and Catholic terminology to dramatise his escape". Gus trumpets international claims for the poet from Donald Davie, Hugh MacDiarmid and Christopher Ricks, implying a search for transcendence through the erotic and pantheistic.

Light and lovely reminiscences come from Michael Hartnett who once hungover visited Clarke accompanied by John Jordan and James Liddy. They brought along a bottle of Advocaat which was put aside for mugs of tea. Aileen Dempsey recalls childhood memories of her Uncle Austin and gives an account of the funeral in Belfast including the poems his son Dardis read that day in nineteen-seventy-four. Mr R. Dardis Clarke is editor of this book and ever faithful keeper of his father's flame. Patricia Boylan has a rare account of earlier days about the poet and Thomas MacCarthy shows his fealty in a goodish essay. Naturally Thomas Kinsella provides a landmark critique, locating antecedents as well as highlighting the unevenness of the total output. All contributors render Clarke canonical without any loud hailing.

These eleven essays derive from RTÉ Radio's Thomas Davis Lectures. The editor doesn't specify where they differ from broadcast text but some do apparently. Gus Martin, Gerard Dawe and naturally Terence Brown deliver satisfactorily. Brown lacks diffidence when discussing a type of lyric from North compared to 'The Settle Bed', a very Heaneyesque title but a poem of wit and less easily noticeable effects. If Brown is a Heaney idolater, and who isn't Anthony Roche is more scrutinous of the Nobel Laureate's path to recognition. Roche's essay is realistic concerning poetry magazines and the poetry publishing scene. He proves Cyphers magazine was vital to Paul Durcan's "development as a poet". John Goodby packages contemporary poetry from the sixties to the present using a particular cultural context slant. Eamon Grennan's "American Relations" quotes Padraic Fallon's acceptable poetics, "each poem is different from any other and demands its own kind of language and approach." Grennan equals the range and depth of Alan Titley and Caoimhín Mac Giolla Leith valuing rightly Maire Mhac an tSaoi and Ó Ríordáin; while coupling Ó Tuairisc with Ó Direáin who took on the atomic bomb poetically. Titley has written what may prove to be a landmark essay on modern Gaelic writers: "that never was so much poetry written by so many for so few". The beginnings of the current continuum of Gaelic poets is traced under his confident title of 'Innti and Onward'.

Hell hath no fury like Nuala Ní Dhomhnaill's attack against marginalisation of the woman poet and relegation of her historic ancestors to mere keeners. Hinting about the thousand-year lineage and the tradition of women through ups and downs, she is not happy with Sean Ó Riordain's line "Ní file ach filiocht i an bhean". Thomas Kinsella is decried for excluding na mna from the New Oxford Book of Irish Verse and Seamus Deane's Field Day Anthology is roasted except for the promise of an all-woman fourth volume. She calls Deane and Valentin Iremonger "minor male talents". Concerning one of her recent collections from the Gaelic into English done mainly by men, she says: "Immediately the critics hailed me in terms of being a kind of Muse. Now let us get one thing quite clear. I was not their Muse: they were my translators". Her essay calls woman to declare total war between the sexes in the polemical arena if not on all fronts.

Theo Dorgan's introduction couldn't compare with his conclusion 'Looking over the Edge', which prophetically envisages a continued boom in literary festivals: "six hundred public readings of poetry in Ireland now each year" and nothing compared to his prognostications for the future. "Poets will publish sell-out editions, travel the world giving readings, transmit new poems or even collections to remote computer terminals". He locates this "sea-change" in poetry to rock'n'roll and warns the reader "we cannot understand our terrible century until we begin to understand Russia." Undaunted, "nevertheless, I am optimistic ... an Irish author giving a series of readings in a particular US region, for example, may find *her* or *his* [italics mine] books being marketed throughout that region by a distributor whose catchment area maps onto the reading circuit". If your daughters or sons inquire about a career in 'poultry' be sure you heard them clearly, they may well not have heard Theo Dorgan's deceitful words: "whole lives in poetry will be carried on with no reference to the strictures or blessings of the literary Mafia."

—*Books Ireland* 1996

BOTH ENDS

Drunken Sailor John Montague (Gallery Press)

The Ship of Birth Greg Delanty (Carcanet Press)

Selected Poems Istvan Baka (Abbey Press)

Selected Poems Fernando Pessoa (Declaim)

Montague as drunken sailor has only one theme and it does not make for a happy drinking song—the collection Drunken Sailor. John lives in the shadow of death. He is no Yeats but whatever roistering is done here lyrically, the tone is of old age; and grumpy and gloomy at that—"The snail progress of a poem" from 'Hermit' gives the correct impression of a recalcitrant muse. These poems may have been wrestled for at the expense of energy and spirit. A translation or two among them suggests a modus operandi for the writing in order to give it a kick-start. He goes back to the ninth-century poem that evokes birdsong and the poet's agony—

After so many years, I cannot translate

a word they are saying, signals they're exchanging.

Long conferences on telephone wires:

twittered alarms, melodious monotony.

—'The Scribe in the Woods'

Adopted County Cork never seems to spark off what the Northern terrain can do for him. He works 'happiest' in the short-line-lyric but often gains more majesty in longer-line poems. One gets beyond elegy to dredge up a family row between himself and Turlough Montague, the poet's brother. This debunking of Ireland's holy family myths is fabulous:

Later, wives and lives came between us, differing codes of conduct and belief

'Demolition Ireland' peddles the liberal agenda of global

consciousness and the dogmas of the eco-Church that is becoming a brand of fundamentalism.

Riverbanks, so slowly, lushly formed, haunt of the otter and waterhen,

bulldozed into a stern, straight line; dark trout pools dredged clean

so that doomed cattle may drink any time

One is almost as jaded from global warning as the planet is from global warming. A return to medieval bliss without oil, cars and pollution is highly unlikely in the capitalist era. The poet longs for death and burial in his Northern spiritual landscape. There is a minor odyssey or journey poem 'The Plain of Blood' too diffuse to unravel in a review, with Carolan, pre-Christian Ireland, the Golden Stone in Tyrone and beyond to Ben Bulben and St Patrick. And there is the surprise and delight of two near-mystical poems, 'The Listeners: Elizabeth's Dream' and 'A Holy Show' "as the thrice blessed Hermes says, and all the sages know the same above as here below, the galaxy a holy show."

Delanty strikes a blow for the sentimental man, the expectant father and gestates with this sequence on the birth of his son Daniel. Focusing on pregnancy and the developing infant in the womb, he reverses his title based on D. H. Lawrence's poem 'The Ship of Death'. It can be read as a sequence, and has the expectation of the pacing father, looking in on motherhood. Mothers might well take note of the sheepish father who is always somewhat redundant at such times, woman the centre of attention and, of course, the arriving child. Delanty is for equal billing of the traditional three players in this primeval human drama.

Many of the poems are pretty much pedestrian; they follow the process in all its mystery and mundanity; occasionally the wait is worth it:

Our plump snowman, whose eyes are still as blind

As buttons, soon we'll show you this and so

much more; how now what is called wind

blows a snow kiss, invisible as they say God is.

- 'Snow and Wind' 'Canticle to an Unborn Child'

The father sees himself as "an obedient chauffeur, a bag-lugging coolie". The little critter is "within the zeppelin,/dirigible, hot air, gas bag and rocketoon". This familiarity and fun is fatherly, watching over the spectacle of pregnancy as outsider. The mother is shown in her glory, mammalian at times, as in, 'The Turtle Mother'

struggling to get up from bed

or couch, flapping her flippers

helpless, bewildered, sad,

The waiting becomes plotlike

Child, even as we complain you're overdue,

We crane to catch our first glimpse of you

The delivery is enacted in 'A Circus' which is "the greatest show on earth" and the child "none other than the cannonball Kid himself".

What adds to the surprise is that the sex of the child was foretold by none other than Seamus Heaney on a visit: "You predicting / a boy, vatic as the woolly bear / forecasting winter".

What will ring true for fathers is the villanelle appropriately entitled 'The Language of Crying'—the best piece here. It puts all the schmaltz into perspective as the bawling little brat assaults the nerves of his parents. The delicacy of the infant babe is fully wrought in 'Fontanelle'. There is a human narrative of a mother developing cancer to balance the arrival of new life, showing life's natural process.

There is plenty of juggling of landscapes, American and Irish. The keynote is of bad weather stateside during the pregnancy. On the whole Delanty passes the test of fatherhood. Maybe poets make better fathers than football coaches who it is said would prefer the boy-child to arrive aged six or seven beyond diapers and tantrums and irregular sleeping patterns, ready for kicking ball in the park with their dad. Delanty is happy with the infant boy.

Baka (1948-1995), self-proclaimed poet laureate of his native Hungary, cannot be mocked at for such boasting. Even in translation there comes across all the fire of the genuine article. He fits into a category largely out of fashion in modern poetry—the work is metaphysical, theological and questioning of existence. Very much in the manner of Heidegger, or one might easily put him in the company of Baudelaire with the irony of Jules Laforgue. It might be insulting to a Hungarian to be classified alongside these French fellows and Heidegger but it is a high rating.

Sooner or later as you read such poetry it becomes a Libran quest as to which side the poet will lean on, in his final assessment of human existence—Thomas Carlisle's dilemma of the everlasting yea or the everlasting nay. There is no room for stoicism in Baka. He beats against the wall, as Yeats said of Blake, till truth obeys his call. It is easy to place him also with Beckett, Camus and Simone de Beauvoir.

The poems are majestic in their form even though one is getting this in the secondhand of translation. In this Baka is, one presumes, well served by Peter Zollman. He generally plumps for tight quatrains and is fully dexterous in execution. Nothing rhymes to make one wince, and best of all is the surprise of the echoing word, and even the amnesiac moment when the rhyming scheme is forgotten and it renders its truest music.

When Pound attacked the Georgians, he only half-believed his own castigation, while revering Thomas Hardy's poetry, and yet adventuring with every fibre and also adopting the tight structures of Gautier and others in 'Hugh Selwyn Mauberley'. Baka also has it every way: modernist, formalist and traditionalist. There are so many good poems in this selection that they outweigh the harvest from all other collections under review.

You cannot level at him that he wore his heart on his chest, but as slavish romantic he writes under the shadow of Liszt, Mahler and Rachmaninov. These help him produce his own brute music, punctuated always with arresting if not shocking images—"while the moon / is dangling on the star's watch-chain— / and in the space between their legs / funeral phalluses toll the bells." Mahler brings this out in him and Liszt: "All Hungary / is sleeping. The horizon pouts her lips for a kiss, / makes smacking noises in her sleep and drools".

Rage at the world and the hidden or absent God provoke great utterance, and especially the art of poetry, or his version with its guttural cursing, mixed with sweetness in 'Yorick's Arse Poetica'. Leaving aside this, how about some of the sweetness even if it is slightly mocking:

and turn my verse into a tender rose

or into herbs of sweet exquisite scents

to tempt a fine aristo's dainty nose

to lakeside walks where scented sentiments ...

There is perfect tone in 'All Soul's Day'—a triumph of a translation, rendering a poem of schooldays but this collection is full of poetry that yields the real art experience and if any critic attempts to explain the process no-one would blame you if you nodded off.

Portuguese Pessoa (1888-1935) is ranked in a pantheon of Dante, Shakespeare, Kafka and Joyce—wow you think reading the blurb, attributed to Harold Bloom. Then you read him and however much Bloom is respected, one disagrees. Pessoa is quite a writer but he is not in their league. He is not a Joycean at all as shown in this collection, nor does he share any of Kafka's incisive insights into mass-institutionalisation, global control from the top or the alienated individual.

In fact, one could make hardly any claims for Pessoa as a modernist; he has hints of irony about the human condition but when you see through him, he remains a fairly old-fashioned poète maudit. As a pose it serves him fairly well:

Excusez un peu ... what a rotten, physical cold. I'm in need of truth and an aspirin.

- Ó Guardador de Rebanhos.

The tragedy for poor old Pessoa is that he ends up with a handful of aspirin and not much more. He does have a perfect abnegation of the self but it does not populate him by way of any personae. He is writing from the empty heart, the cold heart:

I'm not even a poet : I see.

If what I write has value, it is not I who has it: The value is in my verse.

Elsewhere he begs: "Break, heart of painted glass!" – "Blast life and everyone involved in it!" Oh dear he is very cross and grumpy, isn't he?

So many poets pretend to admit this but generally their burgeoning bristling ego and self-importance is all that gets through to the reader. At least Pessoa's misery is genuine; one hears so many claims of humility—not with Pessoa.

Pass, bird, pass, and teach me to pass!

- Ó Guardador de Rebanhos.

Even in the 'Tobacconist's (you get facing page originals) 'Tabacaria', the philosophising and speculation of the poem are set in motion by his peeping out of his window across at a customer

who is going in for smokes while the poet himself smokes—
"metaphysics is a consequence of being out-of-sorts". He can't even
sing a hymn to smoking.

Then out of nowhere he claims:

God gave the sea its dangers and depths, But in it he mirrored the
heavens.

- Portuguese Sea

This kind of revelation is rare in Pessoa's dark night of the soul.

—*Books Ireland* 2005

SOMETHING WORTH SAYING

Ferocious Humanism: an anthology of Irish poetry from before Swift to Yeats and after W. J. McCormack (Dent)

Gubu Roi: poems and satires 1991-1999 Hugh Maxton (Lagan Press)

THIS anthology has an introduction which is intentionally a manifesto with strong attitude under the banner of a definite agenda. Many may find the choice of poets and poems eclectic, over traditional, if not bizarre and confounding. There is no need to whinge at his choices since anthologists are generally despotic, however one might wince at some of what is here and chuckle at what has been left out. Some readers may even smirk at the title and hoot at the cover. The cover follows a fashion, de rigueur in these times, depicting Irishness, in this instance Countess Markievicz, the infamous lieutenant, in her Citizen Army uniform.

This should not be mistaken as a declaration of his true political colours which would contradict the provocative title. He could hardly have meant 'Ferocious Republicanism', nor does the Countess have a speech bubble which might read "When I hear the name Poetry Ireland, I reach for my gun"—she does carry a pistol in her right hand. McCormack is certainly firing off some weapon in the introduction and purposely excluding poets born after 1950; otherwise the scope of the anthology is representative of three hundred years of what he calls 'Ferocious Humanism'.

Instantly he makes himself a protagonist and the present reviewer makes the challenge of a duel in Stephen's Green with either pistol or poem since this critical jousting is more alarmist and sensational than anything else. He includes Swift's well-known tirade on Ireland from a blustery Holyhead, and is himself very much in a Holyhead state of mind, half-way between John Bull's and the troublesome other island. He lambastes Irish self-congratulatoriness and self-contentment. Hurray! Similarly, he is honest enough to state that for some writers, "Hell is other poets". And in common with Conor Cruise O'Brien, is almost prepared for a public hanging of Charles J. Haughey, who however, may in time be viewed as a great unhanged Irish Patriot since the Gaels love rogues, rascals and deviants even financial ones. He even rages, referring to Charlie 'Big House' Haughey and his *eminence merdeuse*. He begs the heavens that Swift be alive this age to lacerate CJH. He can also understand that Humanists are all too human since 'Louis Althusser murdered his wife'.

And in case the feminists should begin boiling enough water to roast him, he brings on the ladies pretty quickly and sincerely, from Maria Edgeworth right up to Medbh McGuckian, of whom he is particularly enthralled, finding in her 'feminist poetry an end to ferocious huMANism'. In other words, as a bright spark, and he is a fairly bright spark in the firmament of critics along with a colleague of his whom he cites, J. C. C. Mays, but is in fact also as Irish as the Irish themselves. However, there is no Shavian logic about McCormack; he is not a ranter or a purveyor of cant and his passionate distress about the state of Ireland comes across as genuine albeit sometimes in academic tones, "The scandals which have rocked church and state in Southern Ireland—episcopal adultery and priestly child-abuse, tax evasion by government ministers, the usurpation of political authority by beef-barons and the cloud of clever unknowing which hangs over the illegal drugs industry—have largely gone unsung."

One might add utterly unsung in poetry; still he is less pessimistic. He doesn't of course state the obvious that the most celebrated Irish poets are all Northern exiles: Heaney, Montague, Mahon while the local Kinsella is given much praise and his 'Night-walker' holds an uncanny contemporary feel with its prophecy about the building boom and its Poundianisms.

Two young Germans I had in

this morning

Wanting to transfer investment income

and 'One Fond Embrace' strikes a Swiftian note of revolt and ferociousness.

Generally, selections from living writers are scanty and often too well-known but representative of his agenda, while the lion's share is given to classics from the great tradition. There is plenty of Swift but he doesn't shirk on the 'mad' Dean's neurotic disposition with regards to female bodily functions, nor his asexual recoil from sensuality; however to give balance, he includes Merriman's erotic masterpiece in Frank O'Connor's translation. Kavanagh's 'Great Hunger' depicting all the horror of the furtive and repressed 1940s is alongside Eugene Watters' 'The Weekend of Dermot and Grace' in extract. Watters' tone is a casualty to that dark repressive era and one fears that Dermot and Grace will have to admit to being off on a dirty weekend since sex could only be dirty in the Ireland of those days. The country never gave birth to a D. H. Lawrence who would in literature take real life sex beyond smuttiness, loathing and dirty jokes. On a grimmer note, Watters' poem announces the arrival of news of the massacre at Hiroshima to Ireland with a lot of help from T. S. Eliot's diction and method.

Wilde's great ballad is alongside Goldsmith's great epic poem in praise of the village of his youth—tourists still long for such Irish villages! Lady Wilde has a poem included. There are two versions of the lament for Timoleague by Ferguson and Mangan, leaving the reader fighting with himself as to which is the best. O'Connor's translation of the powerful Lament for Art O'Leary reminds one of his strengths as translator. Women are, to repeat, made the stars of this showcase with Lady Gregory's 'A Woman's Sonnets'.

A curious choice is the hallmark of this weird anthology but there you have it. There isn't much point in listing all of the contents in ones enthusiasm for most of the selection, just to add that he sticks by his blueprint with an implied rejoinder, that poetry after 1950 should have 'rhyme, stanza-making and metre'. This is McCormack on his boiler expecting the Olympian standards which true poetry can deliver. For those who do not know it, Hugh Maxton is the pen-name of W. J. McCormack and this slim volume of fiery brew has been unleashed mercilessly, and all credit to the Lagan Press for publishing such a shameless collection. If you like post-Kavanagh rural nostalgia with lyrical effusions about Mother peeling potatoes or Father unblocking the pump in the farmyard and paeans to blackberrying and farming, this will not be to your taste; and if there's an overdose of puritanism in your psychological make-up you may well be shocked, since he can be mystifying yet his mysticism may be blasphemous according to fundamentalists. However the dominant mood is satirical. Among his whipping posts are the Irish Prime Minister, An Taoiseach Charles J. Haughey, the Ireland he created and not least Northern Ireland of the big woes and savage endurance.

He lashes out at Haughey, the darling of the 1980s who has been defamed and is allegedly a big time embezzler-cum-robber baron with his short stature and hooded eyes, finally revealing a slimy reptile whom a majority of the Southern public now despises though thousands of the same public could not have enough of their great leader a decade ago. He has become the nation's Charlie Hitler. The GUBU of Maxton's title refers to Conor Cruise O'Brien's famous epithet for Haughey as Gross, Unbelievable, Bizarre and Unprecedented. This is also one of the epigraphs to the book. In the light of recent disclosures about CJH, O'Brien seems a trifle too polite. The ROI of the title can also mean not only the Republic of Ireland, that ever contentious principality, but the French word 'Roi' making it King Gubu, an obvious Swiftian nomenclature. Swift is never far from Maxton's inspiration and the diction is Swiftian, the language Hiberno-English with a smattering of Gaelic.

Kinsealy Spuds. You get what you see. Golden wonders.

And a callus on each, flinty-flinched from the disturbing spade

Out of context, the heat of this is lost and Maxton is too subtle to directly attack Mr Haughey's palatial residence at Kinsealy not to mention his combined assets. The other epigraph reflects the ordinary PAYE citizen through pejorative graffiti, 'Ben There, Dunne That, Bought the Taoiseach'. The millionaire Ben Dunne gets no further mention than this.

For the apolitical and the apathetic there are always targets in the Arts and among these satires are various epigrams well worth pondering, if at times they read like diffuse clues to some intellectual crossword. Aosdana is hardly besmeared but it does get a mention. However, Maxton is not the total satirist, perhaps. Generally the titles and contents of the longer pieces are spot-on, 'Bomb Culture', 'Low Water Howth', 'Six Shots at a Letter' and an elegy for Martin Cahill with a Swiftian title, 'A Satirical Elegy On The Death of a Late Famous General: or a Short and Swift Exchange of Condolence'.

May his mangled soul rest at Mount Anville

Under an epitaph hacked by Banville.

Highly noticeable are his locations of writing, very often Greek islands which also raise the poet's ire:

In Lemnos, Seriphos and Voulis

Young gods display their awesome goolies:

Bogus ikons, girly postcards

Flutter in the breeze for yards,

With calendars of cat and cunt—

A pussy featuring each month.

Otherwise away from nudist beaches, buttocks of various political hues are bared, even beloved buttocks:

I read the two

loaves of your arse

printed on the bath's floor.

But it isn't all Byronic angst, generally the writer is enduring a mere heartburn of the soul:

An exile now of church and state,

In troubled peace I watch and hate.

In fact one can easily like his hates a lot, whether it's Smurfit buying a Jack B. Yeats or the 'Arse Poetica', and elsewhere 'empty torcs' reveal an unspecified disgust with the Republic's Academy of the Arts, Aosdana, its founder Antonio Cronin, the standing army of poets and their Al Capone patron, CJH.

At the reception of Christ J. Herod,

Angels stood guard on Bullies' Acre,

The Great Book held aloft

by Theo (for God)

As prophets bowed before their maker. Some may remember the hullabaloo about 'The Great Book of Ireland' and Maxton's washing of this soiled linen is salutary. In every way it is nothing short of satisfying to see him wielding satire's horsewhip but often the targets are either too hidden or scant of immediate meaning as in *Finnegans Wake*. When his gaze is turned on Northern violence, the effect is very serious.

Before the Seventies exploded

In pubs and under cars. Reloaded

Crosses hoisted thieves,

Good Friday's bloody once again.

The North certainly doesn't lend itself to rollicking satire from Maxton's quivering quill strokes since he is too responsible to get beyond its gravitas. However, we Irish amongst our national attributes are prone to a sneering and cynical wit, not only about the North but also the South and among the arty sarchy community, especially in gossiping about 'the Arts', while the press and media rarely print anything along these lines, and nearly everyone is afraid to scoff and jeer in print or on the media about such matters as the writing Irish, so Maxton's efforts are very welcome.

——*Books Ireland* 2000 and *Honest Ulsterman* 2001

Both reviews (merged) of Maxton's *Gubu Roi* (Lagan Press)

DESERT OF DOWNTOWN

The Inferno of Dante Alighieri Ciaran Carson (Granta)

Lunch at the Ivy Robert Greacen (Lagan Press)

Exemplary Damages Dennis O'Driscoll (Anvil Press)

Birds Saint-John Perse/Derek Mahon (Gallery Press)

If your Italian is restricted to the Berlitz phrasebook, Carson's translation will provide access to Dante's infamous narrative poem. But if you have read previous translations you might be a little disappointed. Carson in the acknowledgements admits that he is "unfamiliar with the Italian language" and gives a list of his sources, including the dreaded D. L. Sayers whose canonisation into Penguin Classics meant that her somewhat abominable Dante was standard for decades. Critical mavericks have long sworn by many others, not least Longfellow, remote as he sounds, while Ezra Pound doggedly supported Laurence Binyon's translation. When the ghoulish and gothic inmates of Hell converse with Dante, as he hikes through that arduous terrain, leaving aside the original, it is somewhat offputting when they patter of their woes with clanging rhymes.

Carson's notes and the introduction are very slight on major details such as the unrest in contemporary Florence and the complicated political situation of Italy. He might well have given a glossary of characters—it is fair to say that you should not produce a translation of the *Inferno* without one. Carson has nothing about Beatrice, the cataclysmic meeting between Beatrice and Dante takes place in the *Purgatorio,* part two of the three-part *Divina Commedia—but* it too requires a comment in any notes on the *Inferno* since she is the poet's muse and mentioned in part one. Of Dante's marriage into the Donati family—unhappily for him, emotionally, politically and socially—there is no mention and the bare modicum about his exile at the age of thirty-seven to the end of his life at fifty-six years of age. In fact, rather disastrously, the introduction gives his year of birth as 1365 and year of death as 1321, even if the correct figures are given on the dust jacket (1265-1321).

There is one clear echo of Carson's Belfast as Dante and his guide, Virgil, in Canto VI discuss the troubles in Florence:

> what holds the future for the citizens
>
> of my divided city? Is there one just man in it? Or are
> they all sectarians?

Carson's devils do not chatter in Belfastese, surprisingly, as they torture the poor souls, though he does include the odd colloquialism. He unrelentingly rhymes along through the thirty-four cantos except for some deliberate lapses. He concisely gives his working method as the Hiberno-English ballad "taking in both formal discourse and the language of the street". However, inversions can seem awkward: 'And he to me: "You know that Hell is round,/and though you've come a long way, anti-clockwise, ever downwards to the pit profound' while modern usage adds a necessary jest to the otherwise grim pilgrimage,

With that, he flung him in, and off he flew

as fast as beagle on a hunting trip,

or exciseman in search of smuggled booze

Still, as you travel deeper and deeper with Dante and Virgil on their daunting journey, at times they converse somewhat like a medieval version of Holmes and Watson on their toughest case.

It needs to be stressed that without sufficient notes (many of the best translations have the benefit of footnotes) this Hell is a lot more bewildering at times. There should be a note on Boccaccio, Dante's first biographer and there is not enough for the first-time reader on Pope Boniface VIII, 'the Prince of modern Pharisees', upon whom Dante rains many a tirade though the mouthpiece of his characters. Similarly, Dante vents his spleen without hesitation on those cities among whose citizens he finds fault with such as the Sienese ("Is there a people quite so silly as the Sienese? Even the French are not so puerile.") Bolognese, Pisans, Genoese—these tirades need explicatory material more than Carson gives.

These quibbles apart, Carson does a good job, often imitating his original in simple speech and simple rhyme:

Get up! breathe with the soul, for it is brave in every battle, and will always win,

unless the heavy body be the grave.

He sticks by this method in his version of Hell from the hideous giants of Malebolge and on to the city of Dis where triple-headed Lucifer or Satan is chained for all eternity for treachery—the most heinous of sins in this habitation of the most evil ones, according to Dante. Satan in the freezing region of Cocytus chews on notable traitors: Judas, Brutus and Cassius. Just as it was said of Milton that he was of the devil's party since he found matter for the unique creation of Lucifer in Paradise Lost—somewhat similarly Dante is said to have put his enemies into hell as personal revenge.

Dante's meeting with Ugolino (Canto XXXIII) and the subsequent narration of his death and that of his sons from starvation in the Famine tower, is one of the most pitiable tableaux in the poem and of such potency that no translation can distort its power and neither does Carson.

There follow three poetry collections that have many unifying elements, though only one, Birds, was intended to be all of a piece. Greacen's poem 'Neighbours', dedicated to Heaney, mentions their sharing the dubious distinction of being 'servants of the craft and the mystery'. Dubious might well describe Greacen's overall tone. He leads you through the London of his salad days from 1936, with a brief foray or two into the tight-lipped Ulster of his boyhood, in one instance an anecdotal throwaway poem about stealing a biscuit and the consequences.

His epigraph from Eliot about old men needing to be explorers, moving into another intensity, opens this collection and it ends with a dirge, 'Following Darkness'. In between is a trawl through the past, the backward look at life as a poet. Fellow poet Clifford Dyment (1914-71) who fell before the Muse and perished, is celebrated. Glittering careers are assessed, including Alex Comfort, poet but more famous as the author of The Joys of Sex. Greacen gives a puritan's glimpse of the joys of sex in 'London, W8' with no kiss or tell and other poems in this vein are also chaste. With Comfort, Greacen edited an anthology under the supervisory hauteur of T. S. Eliot. Many other figures from his London days, including Eliot, get a poem each, such as the old plum voice himself, Noel Coward, Muriel Spark and Kinsky (intriguingly without a footnote) since he was shot moments before Greacen and another friend had arranged to have a reunion.

This retrospect and prospect—there is a poem about blue plaques and 'Fame, that goddess they lusted after'—conceals a savage irony for the writer's life in every respect, a shrug of horror, yet some kind of salutation for the craft. The whole collection bristles with a kind of tongue-in-cheek obituary or notes towards such. However, Greacen at eighty-two has a new collection due out this year.

O'Driscoll has produced a hefty sheaf of work of two strands: the comedie-noire and the world-weary. The title refers to the Irish propensity for suing for as small a lesion as sprained wrist. Modern life is given a thorough trashing and the only trait worth praising is his stolid refusal to produce a feel good product almost as revenge against the evil god of consumerism that will not permit anything sacred. The tone is decidedly of the poète maudit: God is dead, life is dead and O'Driscoll sounds as if he is not feeling very well himself either—"Our one true God has died," and we "are rewarded with chainstore loyalty points".

There is a little relief but only in the romantic's praise of nature—though nature isn't all merry robins and blackbirds. Even visits to England cannot lift his spirits as in a long poem to Albion. In a discreet homage to Carlos Williams he states his terms of reconciliation

Come back, Granma Moses,

lead us from the desert of downtown

to the promised land of the red barn

Shopping is certainly not sexy in O'Driscoll's world, nor sex; there are litanies of the tyranny of getting and spending but you might well find more substance in Naomi Lewis's No Logo on the wider parameters of this subject. There is nothing wrong with unhappy poets doling out the negative vision; the Bible has quite a stock of them. O'Driscoll may have to spend longer out in the storm like King Lear, since the storm seems to be the graduation school, according to Shakespeare, for those who wish to become God's spies—the Bard might have included the poets in this august company.

Mahon is almost petulant about translating the French but perhaps one is the better for his renderings. His contemporary, Montague, is also consistently blasting the Irish scene with fresh poems and iridescent aromas from the French. This is not Perse's best work, his Anabase is too well known among aficionados while Exil is a prose-poem masterpiece, as translated by Denis Devlin. Oiseaux was written to accompany bird lithographs by Georges Braque and, to be honest, at times reads like words setting off a definite series of artworks.

Naturally with a master, there are flashes of genius, that Mahon gives full vent to, as in Perse's gloss on the bird's "interstitial system, designed for swift oxidation, connecting the branching veins to the spine and toes". It might have been too costly for Gallery to have reproductions of Braque's birds with this translation, but it would have given the whole enterprise the completeness missing here, since when you read, "such are the birds of Georges Braque, whether sea-birds or birds of the plain, shore-birds or those of the ocean," the problem is that you can have no sensual connection or precious little with any birds in these programme notes. Perse, in other works, and certainly poetry at its best, can provide a correlative to our sensual experience and all the more miraculous coming through the flawed medium of words.

—*Books Ireland* 2003

AND THEN NO MORE

Poems James Clarence Mangan ed. David Wheatley (Gallery Press)

Selected Poems James Clarence Mangan ed. Jacques Chuto (Irish Academic Press)

The Collected Works of James Clarence Mangan: prose 1832-1839 and 1840-1882 James Clarence Mangan ed. Jacques Chuto (Irish Academic Press)

Wheatley's selection is brief. Chuto's is almost four times greater. Irish Academic Press can boast a collected edition of Mangan (1803-1849) for the first time, in the bicentenary of his birth, and a definitive biography by Ellen Shannon-Mangan in 1996. Both editors' introductions are suitably lachrymose and solemn in their tone but pretty quickly into the poems you cannot deny the incorrigible raucous fun, in 'Where's My Money', 'Song for Coffee-drinkers', 'A Song for Cloud-Blowers', 'Knight of the Kitchen' and others.

Never stroll abroad, night, noon or morning,

Unprovided with a lit cigar,

If you do so after this my warning

Otherwise Mangan dwells on love, lost love and death excessively. Hence, poems such as 'The Grave', 'Rest Only in the Grave', The Funerals', 'The Dying Enthusiast to his Friend', 'Gone in the Wind', 'Hypochondriasis', 'Life and its Illusions', 'Love and Madness', 'A Melancholy History'—there are many in this vein. The swing of mood from the occasional fun and mockery to tragedy is utterly bipolar: "I saw her once, one little while, and then no more: 'Twas Eden's light on Earth awhile, and then no more. Amid the throng she passed along the meadow-floor: Spring seemed to smile on Earth awhile, and then no more."

There is a predominance of the ballad form with the bell-clapper of rhyme. His renderings from the Gaelic including O'Rahilly stand alongside translations from Goethe, Schiller, Ruckert and other European poets. Where Mangan does not cite a source poet, the substance is his work veiled as being a translation. In the domain of translation from the Irish, he comes into his own, setting a standard, a precedent and a tradition. Terence Brown in his introduction states that "the intensity of feeling seems individual, yet raised to national import by a poet who knows the personal can be political". "Oh! there was lightning in my blood,/ Red lightning lightened through my blood,/My Dark Rosaleen!' It does not go far into hyperbole to suggest that Yeats' Cathleen ni Houlihan, a century after Mangan picked up on this lightning.

In Mangan's begging letters that mark his destitution, there is a triumph of the spirit similar to Shakespeare's closing consummation in that lyric of pure joy, "Hark, hark! the lark at heaven's gate sings". One does not want to go overboard in comparisons with Mangan or impose any triumph of the spirit with hints of a beatific ecstasy, based on his writings—the tragic life story would not be surprising had it ended in suicide. But this was not the case, since his resolve in the final days, based on evidence from the letters, adds to the heroic mystery of the man and poet.

In the poems, Mangan has a poetical persona to hide behind and, where most effective, the poetry is utter concealment from the autobiographical. Mangan wrote before the dawning of modern confessional poetry but manages two poems prefiguring this mode, 'The Nameless One' and 'Twenty Golden Years Ago'. A year before his death he writes to a friend, "If you can really obtain me 10s—say by Thursday—you will save me from a doom that I dread to contemplate". He penned many such, in reference to homelessness. To Charles Gavan Duffy, editor of The Nation he sends credentials in lieu of further literary commissions based on a testament proposing abstinence from intoxicating liquor: a claim

176

beyond his will power. His letter to Duffy concerning the afterlife is compelling, based on personal insights from St Paul's letters.

When it comes to enduring poverty there is no bitterness, self-pity or sentimentality. There is exultation on reading in Doctor Johnson the destitute life of Richard Savage. He exults in the vicissitudes of Chatterton's suicide and fulminates against the successful Robert Southey. Carlton is berated for accusing him of being an opium smoker. But there is no acerbic tone in Mangan over his lot, no cynicism of the kind that one finds in George Gissing's New Grub Street or his tales of Victorian poverty in The House of Cobwebs.

Mangan can be said to have triumphed in his beloved poetical labours and in the infamy of a reputation issuing from the gutter. Only once does the heroic tone slip—in the intense commentary on his life and his fiend of a father, broken in poverty, the suffering mother and his blighted siblings. Mangan was one of four children in their dark dire den of a dwelling in Chancery Lane. He was sent out to work as a scrivener at fifteen years of age to support the downcast at home. His brief autobiography makes one a voyeur, delving into a horrific gothic tale of the depravity of being a down-and-out drunk tackling the steep incline of life.

Again, the letters in their asides tell all— "Death, however, came not; but in its place there came something worse than Death— Love." There is an anodyne to love's madness in the short piece, 'My Transformation'. This has a wonderful flow of prose, an ingenious handling of personal circumstance, a distancing from the pain of being betrayed in love until the conclusion—a welling up of wisdom at the folly of it all that breaks into a tide of raucous laughter. Somewhat similar hysterical laughter is achieved in, 'A Treatise on a Pair of Tongs' and 'My Bugle, and How I Blow It'.

The reminiscences of contemporaries written at the close of his life show his adoration for Gerald Griffin whose discovery through literature was that, "we come at last to discover that we have 'no

True Friend but God'.'" However good the short essays on Griffin and Edgeworth are, that on Maturin is sublime. Next to William Godwin's St Leon, Mangan's favourite novel would appear to have been Maturin's, The Milesian Chief. Mangan wore a cloak in homage to Maturin who had also worn such a garment. He never dared approach his hero but once or twice stalked him.

The aphorisms in 'A Sixty-Drop Dose of Laudanum' are entertaining and more than packed with insight. His stories based on Balzac reveal further hero-worship and valid literature wrought from homage. All his short tales are utterly spellbinding in their delivery. It is as if one is in the presence of Coleridge's Ancient Mariner, unable to hear anything, as the busy world is removed and a genuine art experience ensues, leaving one startled and enamoured, if not addicted.

The gleanings of his deepest held opinions and beliefs on the art of poetry take up most of these two volumes of the prose. Those on Spanish poets, and particularly the plentiful pieces on German poets, introduced in his original two-volume anthology, maintain a critical exegesis that is never convoluted. His remarks are exacting, yet general in their intent without mishandling the deeper essence of the poetry under scrutiny. Examples aren't always quoted, often merely cited by title, but one can gloss these translations from his complete poems. He has none of the obsessive prolixity of modern criticism.

Mangan maintains his passionate emotion in the greatest poems whether they are translations or not. His acceptance of his Gaelic mother tongue and its demise meant a confrontation with English and thus he wrote English that even the English might envy. This was the path that Davis, Ferguson, Yeats and Joyce took.

The comedy reverberates after the dirges: "I am grinning night and day like a mountebank through a horse collar;" "If you have invited a gentleman to dinner, it is a piece of suburban vulgarianism to tweak him by the beak with a pair of tongs, merely because his political opinions are not in harmony with yours." Or the yarn about the woman at a dinner party beside a chap with a protruding hooter in the middle of his face. She told herself, that to even allude to it would be utterly unbecoming but in asking for another potato, pointed to the dish out of her reach and said, "I'll trouble you, sir, for a—nose!"

—*Books Ireland* 2003

GOTHIC POET

James Clarence Mangan Ellen Shannon-Mangan (Irish Academic Press)

This dense book should have as subtitle 'a critical biography' because of the additional chunks of poems, prose and letters. Nowhere in the text does Ellen Shannon-Mangan explain her relationship with the poet. Not until the end is there mention by name of her husband Richard Mangan and their requesting the Dublin Cemeteries Committee for two lines extra on James Clarence Mangan's gravestone in Glasnevin Cemetery, sic "Ireland's National Poet / O my Dark Rosaleen, Do not sigh, do not weep!" This was in 1981. In the preface she says that her husband didn't live to see the biography completed. The book's dedication is to Augustine Martin who died last year.

Obsequies aside, there remain problems, a few of which are unresolved here and many unresolvable, because of incomplete information on her biographical subject. She uses Mangan's autobiography effectively, but it contains many exaggerations and is vague about core events. The poet wrote it at the request of Father Charles Meehan and produced what would please, rather than compromise a Catholic priest of the time. It is obvious from the fragment of autobiography that his father lacked basic parenting skills, and became worse after failing "in eight successive establishments" which led to a life of idleness, forcing his children to earn the money. The family lived in Chancery Lane and Peter Street, following a series of moves from the poet's birthplace at No. 3 Fishamble Street, where in better days the father was a shopkeeper.

The suspicious death of one of the Mangan children and evidence of a serious scalding of another child may well have traumatised James Clarence Mangan, who became shy and introverted, and went to work as a scrivener at fifteen in the offices of Thomas Kenrick, No. 6 York Street. He called the work "dull drudgery . . . my heart felt as if it were gradually growing into the inanimate material I wrote on"; copying legal documents for eighteen hours a day, with four months off when the courts were not in session. Though Mrs Shannon-Mangan makes great claims for his handwriting, the samples given in illustrations look rather average. Half way through his apprenticeship he had a nervous breakdown and developed a fever which got him into the Hardwicke Hospital, Cork Street. His own account of having to share a hospital bed with another sick patient may have resulted in sexual contact, but his biographer is certain he was "not homosexual" nor ever "had a full sexual experience". Still Mangan says that as a seventeen-year-old he contracted "a hideous malady, a gangrene of the blood".

A passionate enthusiast and rhymer, he first contributed 'charades, enigmas & riddles' to the almanacs and directories which were plentiful at the beginning of the nineteenth century. "His verses were signed with a variety of pen-names, such as 'An Idler' or XX-XX". Later he contributed poetry to the Comet and Dublin Penny Journal. The latter found him influential friends: John O'Donovan, who married Eugene O'Curry's sister, and George Petrie, who got Mangan a job in the Ordnance Survey. O'Donovan and Mangan avidly read Emanuel Swedenborg's supernatural writings and studied phrenology. Cranial analysis was a fad of the times. There were numerous books and a society founded in Dublin, and a popular farce, The Phrenologist, by Sterling Coyne. One of the appendices at the end of the book, by J. Wilson from 1835, gives a phrenological description of Mangan's head, detecting manic depression and "in religion, he would be more speculative than devotional". He was also the victim of hypochondria, melancholy and 'anomie', a medical name for feelings of hollowness or, in modern psychiatric parlance, depersonalisation. Unremitting neurasthenia compelled him to take laudanum. In his own words, he spent "nights at the round table" in various pubs, such as the Phoenix Tavern on D'Olier Street, nurturing a serious drinking problem.

Many of his poems refer to roses, including "The Hundred-Leafed Rose" which owes something to opium if not hashish or "bang" addiction; and he wrote some funny prose pieces, especially 'A Treatise on a Pair of Tongs', with an aura of opium or alcohol or both to them. The Dublin University Magazine—the 'Maggy', as Mangan and his fellow wags of the Comet and Satirist called it—would publish some of his best poems, beginning with a sonnet 'Love' and translations; these eventually became the only book to reach publication in his lifetime, and that only because of the philanthropy of friends.

As a translator his poetic credo was "to mould the existing materials into new and more beautiful forms". A self-taught linguist, he pilfered German, Persian, Turkish and Arabian poems for translations "as barriers against Insanity". Despite Douglas Hyde's remark, "he did not know Irish"; Mangan removed from the original 'Roisin Dubh' Rosaleen's "round white breasts" and "doing a trick behind the ring fort". His present biographer lavishes praise on this infamous Mangan poem, possibly the Mona Lisa of Irish poetry but equal in stature to Poe's 'Annabel Lee'. Mangan made better translations, for instance of 'Gile na Gile' or Rückert's 'Und dann nicht mehr' under the title 'And Then No More'. The doom of many poets is consolidated by the popularity of a single poem, overshadowing all their other poems. Long forgotten poets would of course be very happy with such doom. He also hacked out the Annals of the Four Masters with O'Donovan and helped a rival translator, Owen Connellan, who was hoping to claim the field, with another version of the Annals.

Among his favourite reading were the Arabian Nights, Faust and anything written by the Gothic novelist Charles Maturin; also William Godwin's St Leon, actually published in Dublin. Morbidly timid, his social self was problematic and the list of notables in the purlieus of the 'Maggy' included Isaac Butt and Charles Lever, who were not even his passing acquaintances. Mangan idolised Maturin from a distance and ever after imitated his wearing of a cloak. William Carleton poured him a glass of whiskey at a party in Summerhill but Mangan scarpered soon after drinking it. Catherine Hayes was an early love and when she died of cholera, his "sorrow was intense ... he literally would not be comforted". A year later he fancied Anna Exshaw, followed by "a somewhat more adult love" for Margaret Stackpoole who got rid of his attentions by claiming she was already married. These passionate longings were largely fantasies.

Ellen Shannon-Mangan gives the necessary historical background on Father Mathew's temperance crusade (which did little to cure the poet's drinking); the founding of The Nation by the editorial trio of Davis, Duffy and Dillon; O'Connell's monster meetings seeking repeal of the Union; the Famine and the Young Ireland movement. However, she fails to recreate the Gothic life-style which remains the greatest myth of this poet. She is also prone to frequent weather reporting: "it was exceptionally cold in Ireland in January 1838", "the weather as the new year opened was memorably violent", "the lovely summer continued to spin out its long, lazy days". There is nothing wrong with this per se. It may represent scholarly zeal and vast research, and indeed Mangan was a victim of awful weather during times of vagrancy and destitution. Still, this biographer who appears flawlessly factual is nearly always fatally unatmospheric.

Approaching the age of forty, Mangan was dumped by the Ordnance Survey, "his Latin not being good enough". Dr George Petrie, the antiquarian author of 'Essay on the Round Towers of Ireland', fixed things up with Dr James Henthorn Todd of Trinity College, and Mangan was employed as library clerk at the same salary of £15 quarterly. He was unable openly to contribute to The Nation because of Dr Todd's anxiety about his nationalist associations and eventually would lose the library job by refusing to shave off his moustache.

After his father's death, Shannon-Mangan claims that he began writings which were "an unprecedented accomplishment in the history of Romantic poetry". The German Anthology in two volumes was published after a tussle over prefaces between the publisher and the poet, who got £25. Both prefaces can be found as appendices in this biography. There were twelve reviews, mainly notices of publication, and considerable praise from the Quarterly Review and naturally so in The Nation. The Dublin Review commented "the writer is a complete literary Proteus". Father Meehan's description of the poet is evocative and not too long for Mrs Ellen Shannon-Mangan. Nothing is too long for her to quote and the vast expanse of her biography easily surpasses D. J. O'Donoghue's little memoir, which was in a class of its own for over a hundred years.

Mangan and his brothers lived on at Peter Street after their mother's death about which the poet has left no word in print or gossip. They became tenants in their former home and not long afterwards he and his elder brother went from lodging to lodging. Mangan began drinking and wore out his nervous system. He endured delirium tremens and horrific visitations from his dead father. Ellen Shannon-Mangan dismisses ghosting clear that people also see ghosts when they are not in a state of torpor or intoxication. By his non-existent standards of travel, he set out on an odyssey two years before his death and visited "his mother's family home near Kiltale in County Meath". A letter from the country during this six-week idyll tells how he regained health through sobriety. There is no weather bulletin from Ellen Shannon-Mangan.

Perhaps it was a glorious summer. However he confirms his own enslavement: "there may be worse intemperance in eating than ever in drinking" and soon he was on "Raw Whiskey" according to Father Meehan. Mangan wrote to a Young Ireland sympathiser, James Haughton, "from a fireless and furnitureless room with a sick brother near me ... I was unable to buy him more than an egg on

Christmas Day". She does a great service bringing in the begging letters, some never in print heretofore, and the biography gains a kind of majesty in the closing chapters. He politely begged from everyone, so whatever about pleas of being "befooled in love", he wasn't betrayed in friendship. Writing to John Anster, he signed by mistake Anster's name instead of his own. A letter to James Hardiman came from lodgings in No. 151 Abbey Street asking for a pound. Later another source saw him being thrown out on to Abbey Street. Father Meehan notes his leaving St Vincent's Hospital in St Stephen's Green and "a few mornings after his exodus he was a patient in the Richmond Surgical Hospital, bruised and disfigured by a fall of nearly fifteen feet into the foundation of a house, then recently sunk". Many people did help and the Freeman's Journal announced a Fund for Relief of James Clarence Mangan. Meanwhile he began, heroically because of his mental and physical condition, a series of nine 'Sketches and Reminiscences of Irish Writers' for The Irishman, including Maturin, Petrie, Anster, and three he'd never met: Maria Edgeworth, Gerald Griffin and William Maginn. Six of the sketches appeared before his death in the Meath hospital with the ever-faithful Father Meehan close by. John McCall's biography states that "the old papers under the patient's pillow" were thrown into the fire; and by chance or luck Frederick Burton made the only portrait of the forty-six-year old poet, laid out in the morgue. True to form, Mangan's life was a Gothic tale from start to finish.

—*Books Ireland* 1996

FORMAL, SLAM, INFORMAL

Throw in the Vowels: New and Selected Poems Rita Ann Higgins
(Bloodaxe Books)

New and Selected Poems James J. McAuley (Dedalus Press)

Familiar Strangers: new and selected poems 1960-2004 Brendan
Kennelly (Bloodaxe Books)

Social commentary is her apotheosis. She rages against social
injustice. 'Return to Sender' lambasts Galway City Council policy
on eviction. Ireland needs a good dose of having its innards
examined and exposed. She also may want to out Ireland and its
remaining die-hard fogies, young and old, from various closets, and
why not? Higgins seems to crave the status of stand-up comic and
lust after the punch line, for instance in 'That Shower':

I can stomach Frank Sumatra for a while but he can't act for nuts.

As poetry, for some, this might be of the fast food variety. Whether
you prefer Rita in a rage or Rita satirical there is much here from
eight collections. Her eye for contemporary detail includes junk
culture and the daily media saturation that spoon-feeds the nation,
from the Lotto to the soporific Eastenders and onto more Lotto. Her
aim is often accurate, as in 'My Face Goes Scarlet', echoing the
voice of a County Meath curate on modern rural Ireland:

They start hanging around the wall in sixes and sevens,

if they're not smoking dope

they're sniffing glue

And if they're not sniffing glue

they're up the backs giving blow-jobs.

Heaney, Joyce, Yeats and Synge get the rap treatment in 'The
Clemson Experience'. Generally, her titles herald what is to come:
'Good Friday in Majorca', 'You'd Know He Had A Lovely Mother',

'Mothercare', 'Trapped Doctor on Cork to Galway Bus', 'He Leaves the Ironing-board Open', 'God Dodgers Anonymous', 'Anything Is Better than Emptying Bins'. She lashes out at the Abominable Irish male and the equally Abominable Irish female. Rita Ann is salutary when you consider that behind some satirists of her cartoon sort there is actually a puritan screaming to get out. One prefers Rita Ann as she is.

James J McAuley is always accessible and what immediately comes into the equation is a CV which includes that most delightful and daunting of professions — director of Creative Writing Programs. Brendan Kennelly has also made this part of his achievement in the academic sphere. Poets inured to being workshop hosts are perhaps always in the shadow of such experience. Many questions can be asked of the 'poetry schools'. Do they instill habitual over-tinkering or even over-wroughtness from apprentice poets, or do they successfully push the art to its limits? However potentially beneficial, is the teaching of creative writing anathema to the creative writing process? Ezra Pound thought it as valid as any other method of earning the rent. Many poets and writers have knocked out a living through workshop employment. It is a phenomenon of the era.

McAuley's selected ranges from *Observations* (1960) on through eight collections up to new poems. The search for God, prevalent in some poems, is leavened by many other themes. His father crashed after takeoff from Tehran at a place, 'called in Persian Desert of Salt'. The bare facts are in 'Map'. The latter might well be the primum mobile of McAuley's life in poetry pitted between the USA and his native Dublin, and at odds with the rural scene as in 'Draft Balance Sheet' — 'Near Aranmore, lit up like a Disney palace'. There is much US influence in 'After the Blizzard'.

He is political, lamenting global greed and wars, in 'Flight':

From the flames of Stalingrad, Dresden, Hiroshima, Nagasaki,

Destroyed in order to save them According to the ancient rites Of Dulce et Decorum.

To die for Oil and Steel,

We need only wait in our houses

In 'The Holy Wars' there is a line, "'Agitate the hornets' nests of Islam". Film footage of a massacre from 1960s Congo causes quite a wrench, vented in 'The Passion' that becomes a squealing howl at the void. The accidental killing of a squirrel sets off a meditation in the appositely titled, 'For the Humanism Class at Fairchild Airforce Base, in Place of a Lecture on the Book of Job'. There are also craftily pleasing performances in 'Cheirons' about a jockey, 'House Burning Down' and 'The Dying Swan' — obviously set off by Tchaikovsky. Yeats gets a trashing in 'Letter to Richard Hugo from Drumcliff' which reveals an attack of the anxiety of influence. The poet's calling is to the forefront in 'A Farewell to His Poems', that touches a delicate nerve of insecurity. 'Persistence' (for Robin Skelton) challenges friendships between poets, the 'Bitch Muse' and 'our despicable trade'.

However, the search for meaning and ultimate truth gives validity here amongst the variety of performance. 'Deposition of Harold Moore, Gardener' and 'The Nun of St Michan's' address the burning questions in this poet's Godsearch.

Kennelly's longer poems Cromwell and The Book of Judas render the reader as blood-thirsty puritan and expose the inner Judas. There are brief extracts from these in his New and Selected, while the The Man Made of Rain, (given in full) is a visionary post-operative plunge into madness, as much as a confrontation with 'many Englishes', and also an adventure journey towards the father, the father eternal:

I'm in my father's grave, the man of rain picks up a bone and hands it to me.

'You love that, don't you,' he says

'It always loved you.'

In 'I See You Dancing, Father' the tone is less visionary, more personal:

Your lips are enjoying themselves Whistling an air.

Whatever happens or cannot happen In the time I have to spare

I see you dancing, father.

Kennelly might be called the Billy Blake of rhyme and bliss. Dialect sonnets such as 'flushed' add to the variety in this mammoth selection that replaces all previous ones:

fifteen pints o' cider a man i never lied

about drink in me life we pick up two

fine tings an screw em crosseyed up in de park

ozzie said tis hard to whack de fukken ride

It's impossible to find the man behind the masks and many personae: Shelley, Islandman and Johnny Gobless. Commemoration poems exalt Kavanagh and Frank O'Connor. There are translations from Pasternak, Mandelstam, Eibhlin Dubh Ni Chonaill, Ovid's 'Actaeon', The Hag of Beare. He is above politics except for occasional satire in 'Points of View':

A neighbour said De Valera was

As straight as Christ, As spiritually strong. The man in the next house said

'Twas a great pity

He wasn't crucified as young.

The Kennelly poem is at once a ferocity of expression, and a thing to make you furious at the liberty of it with a disdain for language almost, because the muse must be obeyed and transcribed in one

189

draft, or so it appears. The speed of execution is palpable even when it runs upon itself to great effect or otherwise, As Yeats said, 'the worst are full of passionate intensity', and so it is here.

What makes him readable as opposed to unreadable is the utter absence of ego, the resignation to the ordinary, the quotidian — any person or facet of life becomes significant. He is refreshingly non-literary, non-solipsistic. He does not bother to be polite, keeps things bare-forked and is never far off the mark, not least in a sonnet about the old lady of Pimlico with her pet rat who may not remain an ally when she dies alone.

There are no pietistic platitudes while reverence and bawdiness vie for sanctity. He muses on Jesus in 'My Mind of Questions':

When he saw the sadness of sex
Did he sit and think

Or slip down a Nazareth laneway

For a happy wank?

The poems are thematically ordered in the Contents which seems an impossibility because of his eclectic oeuvre, including some formal oeuvre, including some formal performances: 'The Singing Girl Is Easy in Her Skill', 'Prayer to Venus (after Lucretius)' , 'Like the Swallow', 'Begin'. Kennelly is likely to remain wild, untamed and linguistically experimental, but unlikely to join the overwrought, the language poets, the overtly anecdotal or the clever lyricists who unravel like a Chinese puzzle. Whether windswept from the Atlantic or under the influence of the Irish Sea he is not for the theme park.

—*The Poetry Ireland Review* 2005

LONG LIFTED NOTES

Sonata Mulattica Rita Dove (W W Norton)

Little Boat Jean Valentine (Wesleyan University Press)

Selected Poems W S Merwin (Bloodaxe Books)

George Augustus Polgreen Bridgetower (1780-1860) cuts a dash as violinist extraordinaire through nineteenth-century Europe amidst Haydn and Beethoven in a five-part sequence by Dove, who is daring in this epic poem made up of poems of varying lengths. Her vast historical paradigm has much to depict: 'God's whip lash straight down / the heaving back of England'. It is also metaphysical: 'proof that each of us bears inside / a ruinous, monumental love.' Bridgetower's concert tour is heralded the way John Lennon wrote 'Being For the Benefit of Mr Kite!', which the Beatle 'found' on a poster; hence she uses contemporary journalism in 'The Seaside Concerts': 'the boy is / a former pupil of Haydn, as well as

the grandson / of an African prince'. And the wunderkind is also exposed in persona poems, where he raps:

So let's scrape the catgut clean, stack

the chords three deep! See, I'm no quack

—though my only house is on my back.

All men are beggars, white or black.

Bridgetower, a mulatto, is post-political, he is not a prototype of W E B Du Bois or Malcolm X, more Nigel Kennedy crossed with the late Michael Jackson, and with no illusions about showbiz ('I am a smudge, / a quenched wick, / a twig shrouded in snow'), where the rise to fame is a never-never land of false promise.

Dove ingeniously manages the required plot: 'Summer ended powerfully — as if God / had snapped a branch from his mightiest oak'. And, protagonists such as Haydn, an establishment figure, is not too happy that the public have a new idol in Bridgetower: 'the daily newspapers thickened / with judgments on the drummed-up duel / between the Maestro and his student of yore.' Shades of Ibsen's Master Builder. There has to be sex: erotica, exotica but subtly non-Kama Sutra, achieved in 'Seduction Against Exterior Pilaster, Waning Gibbous': 'the humpbacked moon / dumped its rapturous froth / over lawn & balustrade.' Things that go hump in the night. Dove is not a costume drama poet, obviously does not believe in it, or strive for the past as in Pound's Cathay or Berryman's 'Homage to Mistress Bradstreet'. This is not literature as museum artifact fakery, instead the dynamic of the silent poetical line as cold as print is musically alive through the language. She does not descend to descriptive passages and deftly brings in European cities:

London surges, Rome bubbles, Paris promenades;

Dresden stands rigid, gazes skyward, afraid.

Vienna canters in a slowly tightening spiral.

Beethoven enters the fray while Bridgetower anticipates a life of glory and profits. Poems such as 'First Contact' and 'Augarten, 7 am' reveal how tough it gets trying to crawl up to the top. The sequence becomes a short drama between sections showing Bridgetower's chat up lines upstaging a romantic like Beethoven. He can score barmaids but it will be short lived. It is only an ageing boffin like Haydn can truly claim, 'I have starved in these streets with nothing / but a splintered voice / and the angels inside my head'.

As with any creative enterprise, Dove has to find an ending, or as poets say 'an abandoning' of the poem. She takes her cue from the maker of Citizen Kane. Welles said, 'If you want a happy ending, that depends, of course, on where your story stops.' Bridgetower is not Paganini, Keats or Modigliani, so a tragic close is not pursued, in that a tragic life in the arts must have a substantial talent or myth behind it. She saves her poem by zooming in on Haydn's head, literally. The lost skull of Haydn makes her point about the artist's immortality. Bridgetower becomes a mere study in contrast and on that reading of this poem, you will have to make up your own mind. Bridgetower is the minor artist through whom the major artists in Dove's tableaux are exposed to their detriment. This is satisfactorily about the arts scene even as Balzac portrayed it, revealed as a shady if not dirty business. She admits, in 'The End, with Map Quest': 'Do I care enough, George Augustus Bridgetower, / to miss you? I don't even know if I really like you.' So Dove as Galatea creates her masculine Pygmalion and wonders if using all that plaster was a waste of studio materials? Yes, and no. Bridgetower is no more than Woody Allen's Zelig, a 'nobody' with a walk-on part in his era, but the irony for Dove seems to be that Haydn's skull is an item of interest, a museum piece, while his art is the immortal part; presumably and in many ways this is the artist's ultimate gamble in life and art. Haydn's skull, incidentally, she tells us, was re-united with its skeleton only in 1954 at Eisenstadt. Come to think of it, Bridgetower too was a much-travelled head in his day. Alas, poor Yorick. Alas, poor Bridgetower. Alas, poor Haydn. One thinks of Robert Emmet, Edmund Burke and Frank Lloyd Wright, who are of unknown final resting place. Bridgetower is buried in Kensal Green, London and has a small plaque to his name. So he made it after all.

A frequent visitor to Ireland, Jean Valentine has, in *Little Boat*, produced a collection reminiscent of Robert Creeley and Cid Corman. There are overt sources in the notes indicating the Gnostic Gospel of Thomas and the insight wisdom of Bhanu Kapil Rider; however, scholarly sources never impinge in these miniaturist, crucible poems. Their effects at best implode gently in the mind like a koan an after a fruitful period of meditation. Her title comes from la chalupa, the drifting boat of the soul, as she implicates Medieval

Theology and goes as far back as Aristotle's De Anima. There is originality of form and content, meta-linguistics, and metaphysicality. Yet accessibility is her primary aesthetic, so revelatory narcosis is the most you will receive. If you are never going to buy this book, at least get it at a library or borrow it just to open the doors of perception and discover Valentine's inscape and epiphany. Leaving aside her traditional source landscapes, this collection is light as thistledown that blooms in mushroom clouds within the psyche. It is a psychedelic reading experience. Buddhism meets mysticism and various other schools of esotericism, the occult and her Gnostic Jesus as in 'The Woman's Poem', where a mother quotes St Thomas's Gospel since mothers are, generally, God to their offspring:

And now you say Split a piece of wood, and I am there.

In Annunciation Poem' an infant is present:

circles dark hair, your fontanel

— since that second you've been the eye of my eye.

Elsewhere, there are vast depths between each word rendering a resplendently spiritual presence through the post-print dreamscape, as in 'The Afterlife Poem', which would have to be quoted in full: perhaps you will read it sometime.

Major life events and changes such as death are calmly transformed: 'Time—you bore it on a green leaf / under the ground.' 'At last' has an epigraph from Blake which is a quiet triumph over death. Quite a claim, eh? In 'The Look' there is a Buddhist affirmation:

Pain took me, but not woke me —

no, years later, your look

woke me…

This is a poetry of immediacy, her language is explicitly new and beyond simple statements: 'All night long I listened to the coal train'. Wisdom gently creeps out from these poems as their titles draw you into serious matter: 'How will you / have you prepare(d) for your death?', which concludes in the dying words to the world declared by Jesus and paraphrased by John of the Cross: 'I know you brokenheart before this world, / and I know you after.'

In 'Eye of Water' the language becomes mere sound not sense. 'Moose and calf' takes it impetus from a memory of being on the highway but soon becomes a complexity about pain:

whose heart in your side is broken in two just by a chance comma of time...

The 'comma' is le mot juste that is everywhere the tenor of this collection, further exemplified from 'To my soul':

And what we had

give way like coffee grains brushed across paper...

It echoes with Lawrence's 'The Ship of Death' and has a depth beyond Eliot's 'I have measured out my life with coffee spoons'. Some may clamour at Valentine that poetry should be like stand-up comedy with jerky jokes about conservative politics, should make us laugh all the time, in awe at its rehearsed cleverness. Whereas she is with Plato and the wisdom tradition: philosophy is a preparation for death, and poetry too. Her poetry comes from the myriad mood swings of solitude, written in solitude and for the times of solitude, be they long or short.

One can't help associating W S Merwin with the arresting line, as in Eliot's infamous one about the sky like 'a patient etherised upon a table'. Both poets are poles apart but not in this effect, which Eliot surpassed, while Merwin adopts a muted and occasional startling simplicity. To choose at random in this fulsome Selected, from 'Departure's Girlfriend':

Loneliness leapt in the mirrors, but all week I kept them covered like cages.

Or, from 'Provision': 'The dead increase their invisible honey'.

He is only a 'mere' New Yorker by birth, a Princeton college boy praised by Auden and something of an émigré in the American tradition linked to Henry James, Pound, Eliot, and Plath. Captain Bloodaxe here presents a copious assessment anthology of Merwin, showing deep meditation on death and intense grief but with a steady gaze, a cold Yeatsian eye devoid of luxuriant song. Within the inferno of his work there is nothing creepy or Gothic, nothing Poe-esque: there is control. One of the elegies — more restrained than Hopkins's 'Felix Randal' — is 'The Dry Stone Mason': a fairly devastating performance but again great control in a post-emotional poetry about a sublime visit to a graveyard where one close to the heart lies buried:

And stones drip where his hands left them
Leaning slightly inwards
His thirst is past

'Avoiding News by the River' has the same Merwinnian qualities — post-grief, post-Pantheist and post-Romantic:
I am not ashamed of the wren's murders
Nor the badger's dinners
On which all worldly good depends
If I were not human I would not be ashamed of anything

In those lines are Merwin's vision: the present poet-reviewer tends to judge poets on their treatment of pain, evil and the sunnier sides of life, amongst other poetic tenets. A typical political poem of the late 1960s is 'Presidents': 'The president of shame has his own flag / the president of lies quotes the voice / of God'. Some retrospective pieces here tend to outshine familiar poems ('The Drunk in the Furnace' and 'For the Anniversary of My Death'), such as 'Berryman', an early mentor of Merwin's, who here is depicted as holding to the tradition and codes of creativity:

he said the great presence
that permitted everything and transmuted it

in poetry was passion

passion was genius and he praised movement and invention

Another piece in this vein is 'Lament for the Makers', a Who's Who
of the poet's life and contacts, from Dylan Thomas to James Merrill
and the dreaded dame of American poetry,

Sylvia Plath then took her own

direction into the unknown

from her last stars and poetry

in the house a few blocks from me

His presence in London as his friend passes away is part of this
tapestry of la vie du poète; the exciting matter for Merwin is that
akin to Eliot: poetry is personally unimportant, which is a quality of
the post-Ego, a non-concern for posterity, poetry as the preparation
for letting go as in 'Cover Note'. Merwin's life voyage can be
charted — if you know his work — through this collection, with its
Giorgione cover painting, 'The Hour Glass' — irony of ironies,
attributed to Giorgione, somewhat like one of those poems attributed
to Shakespeare that can't be proved to be of his authorship.
Merwin's final jettatura here is another irony perhaps, about being
bereft of the muse, in 'The Nomad Flute'. He has been a nomad
himself, a Ulysses (one of his favourite mythological heroes,
mentioned in some poems). Merwin could survive one feels in his
present Hawaiian hermitage even without the muse, as a defiant
ageing Rimbaud, yet he is still publishing — his Pulitzer Prize-
winning The Shadow of Sirius is due later this year from Bloodaxe
— and is currently a vigorous circuit poet in America: they are
rightly proud of him.

THE NOMAD FLUTE

You that sang to me once sing to me now

let me hear your long lifted note

survive with me the star is fading I can think farther than that but I forget

do you hear me

do you still hear me

does your air remember you

oh breath of morning

night song morning song

I have with me

all that I do not know

I have lost none of it

but I know better now

than to ask you

where you learned that music where any of it came from once there were lions in China

I will listen until the flute stops and the light is old again

—*The Poetry Ireland Review* 2009

EXPLAINING POETS

The Oxford Handbook of Modern Irish Poetry eds. Fran Brearton & Alan Gillis (Oxford University Press)

The Irish Novel 1960-2010 George O'Brien (Cork University Press)

Beginning with The Wanderings of Oisin, Matthew Campbell and the editorial team chart a partisan prescriptive manifesto from the academic pulpit: all opinions assured, all conclusions smug. Campbell's agenda asserts a primordial tradition not only from the Gaelic but from 'Homer or Dante for Heaney or Carson, as they had done for Joyce and Beckett before them' while Ní Dhomhnaill 'establishes another version of authenticity turned to fiction for the purposes of poetry'. Warwick Gould manages individuality but the theme of Yeats and Symbolism can hardly offend or upend the Brearton-Gillis fixed agenda: preservation of their favourite contemporary poets. Michael O'Neill with certainty extracts Clarke from Yeats within a definite traditional line. Contributors openly pay obeisance to the commander-in-chief editors, as with O'Neill: 'Gillis has written trenchantly of Austin Clarke.' Jim Haughey considers poets of the Great War era including Ledwidge, Kettle, Dunsany, Patrick MacGill, AE, Katherine Tynan and Eva Gore-Booth but squeezes them into a tradition which is a hoax. Gerard Dawe also sources Gore-Booth balancing her alongside Thomas MacDonagh who always looks good in quotation. Edna Longley (as you might expect) performs well on an easy target: Yeats and Violence while tradition has to be bowed to, and there is no hiding the agenda in Part III: Modernism and Traditionalism.

Edward Larrissy sources 'unity of culture' in Yeats and T.S. Eliot: a discussion cramped into essay space. Susan Schreibman (as usual) hawks about MacGreevy (he is no longer a footnote to Coffey and Devlin). Disastrously, her impetus is the 1934 review of Irish poetry by Beckett which has lost elasticity as academic chewing gum. The wannabe-Beckettian, David Wheatley embalms his idol: Beckett is in all poets Mahon, Carson and Kinsella while 'Beckett's relationship to Muldoon mirrors that of a parasite and its host.' Dillon Johnston negates Joyce as a formal poet. Johnston is a master of illogicality: 'it is very probable that Muldoon shares Stephen Dedalus's belief in the absent author' and Carson's narrative poem-sequence For All We Know is 'a love story, but more precisely a noirish epistemological thriller.' (The use of noirish presumably refers to film noir but may be hurriedly read as an Oirishism).

Kit Fryatt tows the party line for poetry in the South: you must be a Heaneyite or some sort of pretend Durcanite while Kavanagh is definitely sliding in her expert opinion because he 'proved unable, except in a handful of poems, to serve his own potentiality.' Tom Walker snippets MacNeice's brief friendship with F. R. Higgins (why?) and otherwise plays the old chestnut as to whether MacNeice hankered after home while in exile (yawn, yawn). Richard Kirkland tackles the rise and demise of what he terms the Ulster neo-Romantics: Greacen, Rodgers and Hewitt snuffed out by the 1950s and thereafter clambering for re-emergence. John McAuliffe traditionally probes Kinsella-meets-Clarke:

'Clarke insisted that his new work in the 1950s and 1960s partook of the "unbroken" tradition of the Literary Revival, and it may be that this insistence led Kinsella to his famous opposing formula of Ireland's broken and dual traditions...'.

Jonathan Allison rakes through MacNeice's prose memoir *The Strings are False* to locate childhood imagery that later appears in some of the poems: her essay barely manages to avoid the Brearton-Gillis agenda.

Neil Corcorcan 'does' poetry parallel-with-painting as he explains poems that 'enact the opportunities of the ekphrastic'. He is close to hysterical describing Mahon's 'Courtyards in Delft' as 'characteristic poetry of light' and the word 'lambency' in the same poem has him reeling in ecstasy. Damien Keane is beside himself on recorded poems and musical influence and poets who wrote elegies, such as for Ó Riada. Keane is far too cosy with Michael Coady and Greg Delanty but surprisingly useful with Blanaid Salkeld. Rui Carvalho Homem re-covers Corcoran's poets and paintings concept, and startlingly trashes McGuckian via Clair Wills who finds her poetry presents women's experience 'as unknowable and therefore useless'. One says startlingly because this OUP production is cloyingly reverent and persistently singing in praise. Peter Mackay sets a pose pretending to a contention of Heaney versus Carson with Muldoon as mere foil.

Aodán Mac Póilin returns to Hyde, O'Grady, Sigerson and the Anglo-Irish greats as translators focusing on the tiny ninth century poem, Int én bec (the little bird) as translated by many poets up to Carson. Eric Falci does 'translation' also via Muldoon's Ní Dhomhnaill where Muldoon 'reconfigures texts' and ultimately takes and breaks 'creative license'. Justin Quinn treads the translation trail, and Paul Simpson discourses on stylistics with occasional absurdity: 'modern Irish poetry makes an all-embracing stylistic analysis of it impossible' then off he goes in pursuit of 'the flux and flex of language'. Heather Clark plummets into politics (her version) in making mileage out of Montague's nauseous 'The Rough Field'. She presents Kinsella downgrading his own Butcher's Dozen as doggerel while North presumed by Heaney and Faber as catching the moment is ranked as showing 'an affiliation or sympathy with a particular side'. This is at least refreshing. Shane Alcobia-Murphy cites the political cashing-in of poets such as Heaney's bravado when quizzed by a Sinn Féin official: 'When, for fuck's sake, are you going to write/Something for us?' 'If I do write something,/Whatever it is, I'll be writing for myself.'

John Redmond tackles the Durcan-Kennelly contention and disassembles it placing both as Southern media figures under the sway of C. J. Haughey 'managing director of the Culture Industry' according to W. J. MacCormack. Redmond exposes Durcan as sycophant (psychophant!) for Haughey quoting chunks of his palsied praise bestowed on the politician, especially and in actuality when Haughey 'holds the poet's hand' supportive of 'Durcan's wild bias…ineffective in relation to the political sphere.' Redmond finds Kennelly the 'significant literary figure'. In-house trading betwixt contributors is never far from the text as when Leontia Flynn discusses McGuckian. (Flynn is discussed elsewhere as with the Wheatley-Quinn nexus). Flynn finds early McGuckian 'inadequate' and ruminates on that oldest of all chestnuts in Irish criticism 'the question of what a woman poet is'. Gail McConnell discusses God & Catholicism in Kavanagh, Clarke and Heaney. Elmer Kennedy-Andrews discusses Alan Gillis and Sinéad Morrissey while Peter McDonald resurrects the ghost of James Simmons and his attacks on Heaney. Mahon and Longley were also subject to Simmons's penetrating gaze. Maria Johnston finds more acolytes for Kinsella among younger poets than for any other contemporary. Hugh Haughton grapples with the poet as critic jumping from Yeats to Mahon too quickly in a skimmed survey since the chosen terrain is overlarge. Steven Matthews deals with the poet as anthologist and falls into another vast terrain. Jahan Ramazani tackles news, journalism and poetry stating that news discourse 'has been Irish poetry's shadow self'. He neglects to discuss the influence of journalism in shaping Irish poetry. Alan Gillis discusses the Irish sonnet via Yeats, Kavanagh, and Heaney. Stephen Regan on the elegy begins with a MacNeice radio play *He Had a Date* (1944) (for some reason) and Heaney and Co are trumped out. It is left to John Goodby to praise what he calls alternative Irish Poetry. He elevates Eugene Watters' *The Week-End of Dermot and Grace* as he puffs a host of so-called modernists who maintain a coterie and their own festivals with gurus such as Goodby himself and Trevor Joyce, making it morbidly lugubrious as well as ludicrous claiming their forebears in Pound, Olson, Ron Silliman et al. Goodby quotes Catherine Walsh's dictate that you must be within a tradition and acknowledge 'an ongoing linear tradition' which is the crazy clarion of this doorstop of a handbook.

Meanwhile one of the editors in chief, Brearton discusses the TCD trio of Wheatley, Quinn and Caitríona O'Reilly, basically a little cartel playing the cross-channel card as a plea for talent. The former two are Fallon-Gallery published. Irish poetry publishing is not on any agenda in the handbook. Catriona Clutterbuck writes on recent poetry, especially Vona Groarke finding her work divided between the 'likelihood of bad faith... and the possibility of good faith' proving that many critics who find a platform for poetry exude profound sounding, extra referential mystification. The real agenda here is that poetry is a mystery requiring experts to explain it. Miriam Gamble explains NI post-peacetime from Leontia Flynn, Alan Gillis and Sinéad Morrissey to Muldoon—the bugaboo of Irish poetry. Flynn's sonnet 'Washington' a parody of Shelley's 'Ozymandias' is hailed. There you have it, according to the experts.

A novel for each year from O'Brien's *The Country Girls* to Paul Murray's *Skippy Dies* with an overall viewpoint on each of his personal favourites (presumably). *The Country Girls* is shown as a narrative with Cait and Baba as deliberate opposites. Skippy Dies is a routing of the insipidity of the Harry Potter era for a reality check into the school system: sexual abuse leads to a suicide beyond 'mere facile institutional targets.' Besides critical readings at the end of each analysis, other novels published in the same year are listed. His choices are fairly obvious with *The Third Policeman*, *Strumpet City*, *Black List Section H*, *The Butcher Boy*, *Hood* and *Reading in the Dark* except he gets John Broderick wrong with *The Fugitives*, Beckett's *How It Is* (his worst novel) and Trevor's *The Silence in the Garden*. He keeps the door open to much bland albeit popular fiction such as Dermot Healy's *A Goat's Song*, Roddy Doyle's *Paddy Clarke Ha Ha Ha*, Sebastian Barry *A Long, Long Way*, Anne Enright *The Gathering*. O'Brien makes up for this with Eoin MacNamee *The Blue Tango* and Colum McCann Let the *Great*

World Spin. Gerard Dillon's 'The Yellow Bungalow' on the cover is a suitable narrative painting, naïve and dolefully Irish.

—*Books Ireland* 2013

A HIGH-POWERED EXPLORATION OF THE 'IRISH' POUND

Ezra Pound and Modernism: the Irish factor eds. Walter Baumann & William Pratt (Edward Everett Root Publishers)

16 high-powered academic essays on the poet, scholar, critic & musician Ezra Pound (EP), astutely linking him with a coterie of writers: Synge, Yeats, Joyce, Colum, Beckett, Hopkins, McGreevy, and particularly Iseult (Gonne) Stuart. There is nothing of the love-in from these critics amidst the cornucopia of their work since they are also well capable of the lash contra the Idaho-born poet in what is predominantly an exploration of the 'Irish Pound'.

Familial connections are fitfully delineated by Catherine E. Paul and Anne Conover. The latter establishes the extent of the quarter century Irish-American friendship beginning with Pound's 'future mother-in-law, Olivia Shakespear [who] brought him (EP) to one of Yeats's literary gatherings'; her cousin was the 1890s poet, Lionel Johnson. EP was Yeats's secretary, best man at his wedding, and personal editor. Olivia's daughter became (Mrs) Dorothy Pound who in turn became a close friend of (Mrs) Georgie Yeats 'inseparable, in and out of each other's houses'.

Rapallo, EP's adopted Italian town lured Yeats as visitor and who saw it looking like 'Sligo in Heaven'. "Byzantium" 'was first sketched' there representing a 'holy city of the imagination [...] a world of immortality beyond the limits of time and space'. Caterina Ricciardi notes EP as Yeats's inspirational Mediterranean guide. They shared an obsession with Nativity art (not only Botticelli) and maritime Caves. Capri was significantly the location where Yeats completed the "Dove or Swan" section of A Vision.

Catherine E. Paul shows the poets with their gloves off after earlier closeness, 'I ask my friend Mr. Ezra Pound to point out everything in the language of my poems that he thought an abstraction' and he helps 'to punctuate my new poems'. In one draft of Yeats's A Vision the American is 'rude' 'a very violent talker' and with 'no manners'. The older poet to some extent 'understands' The Cantos as 'founded on that of a fugue'. As they fell out, Yeats calls him 'economist, poet, politician, raging at malignants with inexplicable characters and motives'. EP hated this:

'God damn Yeats' bloody paragraph. Done more to prevent people reading the Cantos for what is on the page than any other smoke screen'. Paul shows that 'Yeats reading Pound is a wounded man, and each re-reading re-opens his wounds'.

Walter Baumann states that 'Pound was a very important Synge substitute' because Yeats had 'experienced what he called a "breakdown" [and] was depressed over the death of Synge'. EP praised Synge as 'the only modern dramatist who profoundly moves us […] part of a past and mythical Ireland'. Synge crystallised EP's notions of attacking Whitman's aphorism that 'to have great poets there must be great audiences too'. Pound believed this was Whitman being 'tired' since 'the artist is not dependent upon his audience' except for 'the spirits of irony and of destiny and of humor, sitting within him'. 'Had the savior of the world a great audience […]' Pound said of Jesus.

Desmond Egan discusses Hopkins as pre-modernist Joycean in the Heraclitean Fire poem. EP admired Hopkins's "The Leaden Echo" but 'tended to lump' him together 'with [Robert] Bridges' calling the latter 'Rabbit Britches'. However, writing to American poet, Louis Zukofsky, EP says 'look at G. M. Hopkins, he happened, not IN any current. Insulated and isolated'. Mary de Rachewiltz (Pound's daughter) implies that EP meant 'Zukofsky could learn from G. M. Hopkins'.

William Pratt's essay is a totality of pronouncements as in 'it seems a shame that Pound never asked Eliot to do for The Cantos what Pound had done for The Waste Land' in other words given direct editorial input. EP remains not only the modernist as in the line

'Beer-bottle on the statue's pediment!' but the poet as fundamental critic. However, Pratt boldly displays Eliot's castigations: 'In The Cantos there is an increasing defect in communication'. Pratt presents a general introduction to Pound that includes his phenomenal support for Joyce which activated the serialising of A Portrait of the Artist as a Young Man in The Egoist and the early chapters of Ulysses in The Little Review.

Heinz Ickstadt discusses Eva Hesse, translator of Die Cantos (2013). She categorically absolved EP of any academicism. His work is 'unwissenschaftlich' ('unscholarly') which is fantastic exegesis in a word. Hesse worked with 'her beloved husband and co-researcher Mike O'Donnell' as EP dictated: 'don't translate what I wrote, translate what I meant to write'. Ickstadt with Manfed Pfister concluded her German translation and alludes to glittering fellow scholar-Poundians including Roxana Preda, Marjorie Perloff, Richard Sieburth and Massimo Bacigalupo whose essay focuses on the Stuarts.

EP wrote in Canti postumi 'I remembered Iseult, who was the great love'. The Pound-Iseult Gonne love story is given centrality. The poet placed her 'in a context of enlightenment, of mystical insight'. Her works are quoted and she is invoked in Canto 104: 'have compassion'. Pound's daughter Mary with the musician Olga Rudge was to have been named 'Iseult' and EP 'wanted to leave his wife' for Iseult Gonne. The affair is a terrific episode in Stuart's *Black List, Section H*.

Ira Nadel 'does' EP and Beckett dining at Les Trianons with Joyce in Paris. A raucous evening of food, wine and barrage. Pound forking an artichoke, asks Beckett with sarcasm 'what long poem might he be writing?' Beckett noted 'he inquired cuttingly what epic I was engaged in at the moment?' Precariously their mutual respect and dignity evolved. EP acknowledged Endgame and Happy Days. Beckett read the Irish poets Brian Coffey, Thomas McGreevy and

Denis Devlin as Poundians 'that constitute already the nucleus of a living poetic in Ireland'. Pound's Make It New struck Beckett as 'a galvanic belt of essays, education by provocation'.

The writers coalesced in aesthetics: Beckett's 'see hearer clearer' and EP's 'meaning is all tied up with sound'. Both were in loving relationships 'with musical women' Suzanne Deschevaux-Dumesnil and Olga Rudge. Beckett demanded 'a theatre reduced to its own means, speech and acting […] the setting had to come out of the text without adding to it'. EP 'insisted that the allusions, references and details in The Cantos did not need explanation'. Both were frugal, Beckett's 'big expense was a piano'. Pound late in life generated 'interest for his work in the marketplace but for the wrong reasons: his committal to St Elizabeths. Ironically, for one who wrote extensively about money and its value, Pound had little of it. The economics of Pound's career still remains a question mark'.

There are non-Irish themes. Jonathan Creasy writes on Florence Farr and Arnold Dolmetsch amidst EP's musical poetics where the exactitude of rhythm is 'the inner form of the line […] it is only by mastery of this inner form that the great masters of rhythm—Milton, Yeats, whoever you like—are masters of it'. Canto 75 includes 'Gerhard Munch's violin setting of a lute transcription'. Creasy quotes William Carlos Williams on Pound 'he is a poet, a great one, but a musician—never!'.

Jo Brantley Berryman explores Aubrey Beardsley's erotica and The Yellow Book which led to an artistic scandal. Pound includes him in the lines:

La beauté, "Beauty is difficult, Yeats" said Aubrey Beardsley

when Yeats asked why he drew horrors

or at least not Burne-Jones (200)

Oscar Wilde turned against him but Pound 'understood that ironists like himself, Laforgue, and Beardsley were at odds with popular publications and the conventional views they expressed'.

John Gery discusses lines from Canto 93 extrapolating the poet's forced exile as 'a loss of authority, and an estrangement from one's mother tongue' 'finding himself at odds with his native land and countrymen'. Gery identifies exiles as people being 'at odds with one another [and] must learn not only to co-exist but more fundamentally, to acknowledge the impact they can have on each other'. There are many exiles pervading The Cantos and tested within the epic poem as to their compassion, benevolence and virtue (jên) in Confucian terms. EP looked to Mencius, Confucius, Feng Lan as being 'of greater antiquity'. Gery indicates the Cantos as 'epic poem, neither a philosophic compendium nor a sacred text'.

Giovanni Epifania's scholarly grasp is contradictory discussing translations while asserting EP's preference for Laurence Binyon who 'produced the most interesting English version of Dante that I have seen or expect to see' [...] 'a transparent translation' that 'does not erect a barrier between the reader and the original'. Epifania references the abominable D. L. Sayers version of Dante. One can abide Longfellow's beautified version. Sayers is akin to Clive James's disastrous 'Picador' Dante. However, Epifania states 'Dante may very well have been his (EP's) daimon, the intangible center from which he speaks and operates'. This statement is vital exegesis and criticism.

The Seamus Heaney contribution reveals much 'I swam with pleasure in the opening six, seven, eight Cantos but then allowed my effort to weaken' which openly admits as if he could only read a handful of Shakespeare sonnets, the opening of Berryman's Dream Songs, or a few pages of Robert Lowell.

Pound's sensibility is asserted through these essays as essential modernist illuminating the universal in real poetry. Immersed beyond his own work, signifying other genius-poets while upholding the role of critic 'to see that justice is done and to prevent or put an end to various forms of injustice'.

—*Books Ireland* 2018

BEYOND THE POLITICS?

Ezra Pound in The Present: essays on Pound's contemporaneity
eds. Paul Stasi & Josephine Park (Bloomsbury)

This converges in the PM (Post-Moody) era making it possible to proceed after his biography (Vols.1-3) beyond the usual EP tainting and on to the poetry, literature, and economics-poetics. The editors join six fellow scholars, freely speaking in essays and unbound collectively in a three part compendium, thematically under 'methods', 'worlds' and 'values'. There is however some continued castigation but it is balanced by those who want to avoid the obvious politics unless it informs the totality of comprehension.

Charles Altieri digs out Amy Lowell's "In a Garden", EP's "The Return" and H. D.'s "Doria" to fix the 'Imagist phase' that became continuous within Mauberley (6). His discussion frames the 'essay as a clumsy version of how Kenner might have responded to Sherry's 'Modernism and the Reinvention of Decadence (Sherry) (7). Regardless of decadence, he finds EP's 'certitude' as the principle of poetics in the poems of this phase. Altieri adds the gloss that 'Certitude does not usually produce success in the social world' (19). The footnotes are parallel exhortations intrinsic to the text 'One of the great mysteries of literary history for me is how the author of Mauberley could publish in the same year the draft of the first three cantos' (8).

Josephine Park focuses on Franco Moretti's methods linking him and EP in mutual 'data-driven desires to China, the ultimate storehouse of big data in the Western imagination' (24). She recasts EP's works as '"How to Read Less" and the "ABC of Not Reading" (26) presupposing the poet's necessity for the epigrammatic methodology and 'essentials of the first picture of man, tree or sunrise' (29). Pound's dumping of Aristotle 'mixture of weeds and loose language' (32) for 'the clean boots of Confucius' is highlighted (32). Park is quick to point to the success of Cantos XIII and XLIX and the failure in cantos where 'the drive towards data' (34) and 'immediate need for data' (44) as in the Chinese Cantos which becomes 'a set of reader's notes' (41). Her far from dismissive report grounds itself finally stating that 'Pound's comparative literature was always media studies' (44).

Aaron Jaffe delves into the comic Canto XII, unravelling the trio of 'Baldy Bacon, Dos Santos, and the Honest Sailor' (49) where 'each anecdote provides an economic fable [...] through Pound's burgeoning economic concerns' (62). It is an evocative essay in detective work as to the conversation at Café Dante (1922) with EP and TSE on vacation in Verona. Here's a short movie begging to be made with the missing gaps filled in by the screen play? What did the two poets discuss? Jaffe gives a fabulous peep show of EP berating TSE and the scenario is referred to also in Cantos VIII and LXXVIII. According to Jaffe, EP's scolding was 'for trading in a private poetics composed merely of fragments' [...] the Eliotic citational method [...] shoring up the damaged poetic self with shoddy literary-citational plaster' (53). Pleasurably these essays are free-thinking and robust for avoiding complicity. Jaffe sounds off slating EP as 'an unresolved figure for literary history' (62) and as early as Canto XII for displaying 'toxic racism, homophobia, anti-Semitism, and misogyny' (62). Quinn is fully credited with ownership of the Honest Sailor story. XII is a canto that needs to become popularised since it grounds the economics and the poetry in a highly postmodernist form and is knockabout entertainment for any performance delivery.

Christopher Bush locates the Japan elision 'when the first four cantos are revised as part of A Draft of XVI Cantos in 1925, the Noh references are mostly edited out' (87). The Kitsano friendship is mined as EP 'envisions a kind of spectral league of nations' through the Cantos (90). As Fenollosa led to China, the Noh led to Japan (as it were) and this is made central in Bush's ample discourse. Jean-Michel Rabaté places the poet as having 'had a lasting impact on our disciplines' including English, Comparative Literature, Literary, Cultural Theory and World Literature Today (107). Wide curricula are posited as EP's ideals demanded a global literary scholarly community capable of weighing 'Theocritus and Yeats with one balance' (111). Rabaté re-opens Spirit of Romance to get his bearings and veers off in various directions as far as Tagore showing that EP felt that the Bengali poet was 'superfluous' as a religious teacher (119). Pound's dreams of uniting world cultures holds ironies, he being 'the only graduate student flunked in Penniman's (UP) graduate class on the history of literary criticism [...] also the only student interested in the subject' (131). 'Pound wanted to create a department of Comparative Literature, and was frustrated' at UP (132). Has not EP created various and disparate departments globally.

Rabaté places the poet on his 'quest with an ethical demand insisting on one's unquenchable curiosity and the family values upheld by Greek tragedy. The tragedy was before and after—its arc encloses Pound's works' (132). This is definitely PM, no politics, and on with the forums for global poetics. EP and Nietzsche are postulated as 'both being deviant philologists ready to criticize everything' (133). Rabité permits himself a purple passage conclusion praising the poet's 'East-West fantasmagoria'; '[P] wanted to disturb and function like a cosmopolitan guide to a better sense of life and history' (134).

Christine Froula invokes a what-if history. What if Italy chose Matteotti instead of 'Mussolini's overmastering student Hitler, might The Cantos not have ascended?' (136) She propounds and develops many queries against happenstance and finds that in the Cantos 'history "includes" the poem rather than the other way around, shattering its mind and voice, scattering fragments over the pages' (136) as she preferences Homage to Sextus Propertius. The Pisans are half-praised if argued down as 'an improvisatory voice rising from the enormity of its circumstances, interweaving diaristic, mnemonic, and contemplative strands of time' (136). EP's economic-poetics hold validity based on 'the crisis of human voice and agency escalated by industrialist capitalist warfare from 1914 on' (138) as they grapple 'with the violence intrinsic to the epic' (141). She queues in Simone Weil's essay on Homer. Mussolini is given a lot of space with his 'rape of Ethiopia' and the explosive footnotes in terms of the war-carnage are shocking facts and figures. (142). The Cantos reflects 'the Iliad's tragic knowledge that there's no refuge from fate' (144) as 'the business of the artist is make humanity aware of itself [EP]' (152).

There's an aside prompted by LXXVII when Maukch 'thought he/would do me a favour by getting me onto the commission/to inspect the mass graves at Katin'. Katyn the Russian atrocity visited on 5,000 Polish military is 'a wound that refuses to heal' (157) fully explored and heavily footnoted not least Wajda's film of the events in 2007. EP's guilty admission over the putative Maukch's invitation from 'the German consulate in Florence' (157) is exposed as the Hitler regime wished to exploit the 'propaganda potential' of the massacre. She shows relief in that 'the poem doesn't bury the Katyn massacre. It flags it' (160). Froula wades in deeper showing 'The Pisan cantos moral failures are the world's. Pound's "Katin" passage is an inconsequent reflection of Churchill's and Roosevelt's deliberate burial of the Katyn massacre during—and after—the war' (161). No one is cleared by Froula quoting Sieburth and the Italian cantos as the 'moral nadir' proving the poet's 'absolute loyalty' to Mussolini. (163). She is not beyond the politics.

However, it is left to Stasi to root out the base details of EP's economics involving a reading of Moishe Postone's Time, Labor and Social Domination. Otherwise, Stasi quarrels with The Pisans as 'a capitulation to the very form of capitalist culture he was attempting to overcome' (176). The preference for the Chinese/Adams cantos is clear as well as EP's sublime in 'the aim of state education has been (historically) to prevent people from discovering that the classics are worth reading' (190). This leads to the adoration of Adams as 'ideal Poundian subject' (191) from his letters and as stated in LXVII 'no more agreeable employment/than the study of the best kind of government' (Adams). Stasi points to EP as anti-isolationist American (192) and in the PM era after the concretization of the dirty linen exposures there remains The Pisan Cantos 'lovely, in all their individualistic, unapologetic, fascist glory' (199). PM: it is time for the poetry centre stage.

The book doesn't close in soft focus for C. D. Blanton whose essay on XLII that aspects the Siena Bank 'The Mount of Pity (or Hock Shop)' (202) featuring EP's economic tutors for the epic, Orage, Douglas and Gesell 'eccentric theories of credit and money, respectively, that were to send it spiralling into idiosyncratic petulance' (203). The background is formidably explained from William Paterson's 1694 revolutionary works on the Bank of England onwards. There is much amusement about the 'crudely rendered sketch of six pyramidally stacked boulders' (209) at the end of XLII as well as discussion of the poet's 'affirmative program and design, his prescription of a policy' (216) whereby 'to keep bridle on usury' (XLIV). Blanton fine combs the cantos to suggest that 'the Bank of Siena presides over, but also induces, a radical revision of Malatesta's founding gesture' (217). This will require a reply elsewhere from scholars.

What Blanton thrives on is Douglas and the milestone Macmillan Committee (1930). The smirk is wiped off Blanton's closing pages in a binary of economic theorists such as to 'juxtapose Keynes and Douglas, placing the central figure in modern economic thought alongside one of its more notorious cranks' (222). This evolves to state that 'Keynes was not ready' to 'abandon the bankers for the cranks' but 'the Keynesian revision [...] in which supply and production present secondary effects of demand and consumption' (223) includes K's 'great puzzle of Effective Demand [...] [which] could only live on furtively, below the surface, in the underworlds of Karl Marx, Silvio Gesell or Major Douglas' (224). Here, Keynes should have thrown in EP: Britain off the Gold Standard with Pound and Douglas locating Keynes as 'orthodox economist' (227). However, Blanton treats Pound as a disreputable economist. He quotes Surette 'the Keynesian revolution took place in the midst of Pound's economic evangelism' and adds that this 'rendered it largely obsolete' (228) concluding that 'he divulges a concept for which his poem lacks a knowledge' (230). One has to take sides: surely Blanton is not forgetting the concept and leitmotif-central in XLV 'With Usura'?

—*Make It New* 2016

POSTHUMOUS CANTOS Ezra Pound ed. Massimo Bacigalupo (Carcanet Press)

Bacigalupo plumps for 1922/1923 as EP's pinnacle years 'fixing' The Waste Land and when he 'radically revised the overture' that 'gave quasi-final form to Cantos 1-16 for book publication'. The overture is in the Ur I-IV but Bacigalupo neglects to emphasise the meeting with Olga Rudge that added fire to the poet's product. Pound's vital muses including Spann and Martinelli were essential provokers of creative eruptions that enabled the Cantos. The presence of the Ur-Cantos I-IV will immediately grasp the attention of aficionados. It closes with St Trophime looking ahead to Canto 45.

The fascination remains that the Cantos begin where that portion of Homer is set in the language register of 'The Seafarer'. It remains speculative discourse as to the poet's subconscious choice of this opening having placed it in Ur III surrounded with the John Hayden material leading to Andreas Divus, and initially translated as 'Down to the ships we went, set mast and sail'. Subsequently it becomes the familiar 'And then went down to the ships, set keel to breakers'; the latter phrase more powerful than 'set mast and sail'. There is more than a glimpse of the editorial process in Ur-III amidst the shards of notes dismissing Haydon when Wordsworth is invoked through the mention of 'false pastoral'.

Wordsworth 'appeared' in Ur-I while 'Sordello' enabled the earliest ascent/descent into the Cantos in 'discussion' with Browning: "Give up th' intaglio method'" ; 'you mix your eras' ; 'To set out so much thought, so much emotion'. Browning is credited and revered but he lacks the 'beastly and canterkerous age'. In Ur-I the Dogana steps are mentioned as 'My stone seat was Dogana's curb'. It's quite a paean to Browning but not so Wordsworth and his 'speech figurative' whereas the writer of the Cantos will use 'straight simple phrases'. Then, he launches into the line 'Gods float in the azure air'.

The method can be discerned from these fragments and not merely Ur I-IV as poetry created from material resources primarily. There is so much architecture not only in the language but architecture and place (Tigullio et al) and personages from history. Behind the ghostly paradigms, incomplete as the Posthumous are, they always point to the Cantos. However, it is occasionally a pitch battle of great emotion in the struggle of poetic creation towards final form. In this respect the frozen incomplete architecture of the Posthumous is a work rising upwards, intensely satisfying and not at all fragmentary.

The project admits to the 'Sweet lie! — Was I there truly?' despite 'truth and memory,/Dimmed only by the attritions of long time'(Ur-I). The momentum of this sort of interrogative aesthetic subtext is arresting. It can be said to have more emotion than the finalised version. Towards the close of Ur-I it becomes metaphysical: 'are they the gods behind me?'

Posthumous is in eight sections from 1915 to 1972. The Paris section is brief: one fragment repeated three times 'No ancient glory ever fades from the world'. Canto 49 (in draft) rears up with Usury via Dante's Geryon 'That the state by creating riches/shd. thereby run into debt'. One thinks, here he goes pleading for divine economics on earth, except in these shards and fragments is the resonance of trying to get airborne into his various sublimes and falls and fragments.

EP 'got into trouble' with Eliot who in 1923 had written 'I object strongly on tactical grounds to yr first line. People are inclined to think that we write our verses in collaboration as it is, or else that you write mine and & I write yours. With your permission we begin with line 2' (Letters 2: 141). The problematic usage for Eliot was the opening line of Canto IX (later Canto VIII) 'These fragments I have shelved (shored)'. In The Criterion, Canto IX appeared with line one omitted which Pound was happy to concede.

Posthumous has no Eliotics, just as Eliot has no Poundistics. This volume yields evidence of the creative process through the vast tableaux of history, visionary lines and the terrestrial-visionary such as the 'white swimmers' (Ur-I). The cast list is familiar but the hierarchy is different proving that the Cantos in their gestation had leading characters omitted eventually or otherwise 'survived' through to the final versions. Thus, here in Posthumous Hotep-Hotep and Moses rub shoulders with stalwarts such as Catullus, Kwannon and Confucius—'a man with sky in his heart' author of 300 odes 'their sole injunction: think straight'. Confucius is given equal status with the Buddha who does not rank as high in the final Cantos.

There are five draft-fragments for 51 here (Eliot permitting!) including the compelling assertion that *phallus pharos mentis*. The emotion is in lines like 'Work is not a commodity. No one can eat it'; 'capital is a ravenous danger' and 'a ravenous unsleeping peril. A poison to be watched at all times'. The eloquent lyrical breaks into glee with Erigena who is given lines as a Plastic Paddy-the-Irishman speaking and referring to Dante's letter to Can Grande 'at any rate he cant take a rale intherest/sure but the owld hook nose'. It is not too late to address biography as the lines to Iseult Gonne are substantial and conclusive as to their liaison: 'And I remembered Iseult, who was the great love' plus other details. The poet's women as goddesses (Rudge, Spann and Martinelli) is prevalent whatever feminists might say; 'the more beautiful she is, the greater the peril'. Canto 75 is provisionally 'present' and more visionary in the passage ending 'then again the golden mist closed up' and with a further fragment celebrating motherhood. There is of course no diffidence in any of the Posthumous, the epic of history burgeoning within and eventually beyond these lines but herein he uses the word 'coherence' a lot and holds conviction, visionary and otherwise: 'How is it that I hear the ancient voices/clearer and more frequently than ever before'. 'What thou lovest well' is present if fragmented.

Olga is much quoted and has an entire section 'that she saw the Duce with level eyes'. Did he? One asks.

Bacigalupo as EP family associate, of course renders the job well done with a timeline, introduction, and good notes but one ludicrous comparison cited from his Grotta Byron is Seamus Heaney as 'the fourth towering presence' along with Shelley, Byron, James and Pound linked to Portovenere's plaque or tablet to Byron. Well, it is ludicrous: any comparison of Heaney with Byron. (!) unless you can imagine Byron gaining inspiration from cutting turf, milking a cow, churning butter, or claiming to find ecstasy in the water pump down on the farm.

—*MAKE IT NEW* 2015

LITERCHOOR IS MY BEAT

'Literchoor is my beat': A Life of James Laughlin, publisher of new directions Ian MacNiven (Farrar, Straus and Giroux)

From the start, MacNiven, half-in-love with James (Jas.) Laughlin, demands the same of the reader. He is a sort of Nick Carraway to his subject, not that Laughlin, who is soon self-titled "J" had Gatsby's romantic malady, far from it, though romantic entanglements were profuse in his life, for J the green light across the dock did not bear him back ceaselessly into the past but rather into the future, to his publishing house New Directions (ND). Behind it all, MacNiven (MacN) is endlessly resourceful, even swamped in resources, and pursues his subject as an enigma. It may sound formulaic, but his achievement as a biographer is in kindling huge interest about the publisher whose "decisions shaped English-language modernist poetry." It is a boast met by the evidence from J's unique model as to how modernist poetry got into print via ND. He, of course, scores high, accumulates honours and epaulettes in the end, unlike the antipathetic fictional guy in the mansion on Long Island who ends face down in the pool.

MacN occasionally attempts to explain the psychological profile and occult driving force behind the compulsive publisher's professionalism, but refrains from reaching a definite statement. J is well caught in a Virginia Schendler photograph (1979) with the backdrop of books and the window of many panes sitting in an armchair wearing presumably fawn slacks, T-shirt, and sport jackets smoking a pipe. The face, however, is the giveaway, as if he cannot assume the vanity that he strives towards: the pomp is overshadowed by a deeply wistful even troubled puritan guilt. As Shakespeare puts it, there is no art to find the mind's construction in the face.

Freudian analysis from MacN posits an identity-seeking J amidst his four main passions: poetry, publishing, skiing, and womanising. Where Gatsby "dies" for passion, leaving the reader only half–

sympathetic if at all, J lives and earns as much affection as MacN can bring to the exposition of the enigma in its habitual variations. It is a more active life than a bunch of transatlantic Jamesian characters, yet wholly wistful in the biographer's handling, because of the unresolved and highly evolved immense struggle with poetic identity pitched against human performance.

MacN naturally does not bother with the "lurve" aspect as much as with the poetry, the poets and the publishing. Indeed, there is such a milieu as witnessed in the three page appendix (small font) of every modernist published by ND from Conrad Aiken to Louis Zukofsky. Thus the biography can only attempt the equivalent of a graphic novel's scenic details or Dell comic encounters to encompass J's life and contacts as publishing superhero. The skiing intrudes occasionally as J's perfected if none too dangerous masochism. There are many injuries and various hospital sojourns for fixing broken limbs, but there are nurses abounding on location and the white snowy slopes which, unlike the poems, produced his major mystical experience. You cannot "know" J without acknowledging this, based on his spiritual journey centred on himself and particularly, Thomas Merton. It sounds like the watered down life of a lukewarm transcendentalist and yet, he is quite the conundrum amidst his travels and accumulation of living poets, writers, various arts scenes, and his own quest.

From the outset, sibling rivalry emerges with his five year older brother, Hugh, at odds with "Mam-ah" Marjory (Rea) Laughlin who "wielded the hairbrush, the accepted rod of correction." His father is almost a caricature if real, as the benevolent asylum-bound, bipolar, philanthropic gentleman, family philanderer and outsider to J's mildly disturbed childhood.

The parents' engagement made the society pages in the New York Times which highlighted their wealth and stock. J "resolved" his phobia and neurosis of being well-to do, Presbyterian, and from

Pittsburgh through ND. He remained sang-froid about lineage and overtly puritanical, even Calvinistic in outlook: plagued by inherent self-scrutiny, keeling over into Emersonian and Poundian fervour, and feeling one "had to improve the world." MacN never quite settles the Freudianism of his hero; meanwhile Aunt Leila Laughlin Carlisle and Uncle Dicky "adopted" him from the quietly troubled, domestic scene onto Robin Hill, Norfolk, Conn. (not quite the Xanadu of Charles Foster Kane). After matriculation at Eaglebrook, Mass., Robin Hill became the alternative, less fractious homebase. Still, he emotionally placed Aunt Leila alongside his mother and subconsciously enlarged the generous, hearty, genial woman into the stern "Ogre Aunt." Robin Hill, named after Galsworthy's The Forsyte Saga, boasted a sizable acreage and a "three-storey Neo-Georgian-Palladian mansion designed by Uncle Dicky's cousin the architect Charles Everett in 1927."

MacN imperatively follows the narrative but is never linear since there is too much happening once J settles into his life as publisher, as well as writing problematic epigrammatic poems. Skiing is obsessional: a resort in Alta (Utah) always delighted him: "I take great pride in Alta because it is the one place that's left that's a little bit like the old skiing."

Though his father was a Princeton man, J was sent to Harvard; obviously his mother's decision, while his father literally wept. By 1931, J was hooked into Frances Steloff's Gotham Book Mart in NY "purchasing books regularly with a charge account." Professor Dudley Fitts recommended suitable reading matter: MacLeish, Pound, Joyce, Stein. However, judicious as always, or nearly always, J found Cummings' Tulips and Chimneys "too high at $15." A subscription to transition meant further encounters with hard-core modernism of the Parisian and international variety.

J drove his "Model A Ford to Plattsburgh, New York, to see his father wearing a straitjacket in a small private sanatorium that catered to patients from wealthy families," or otherwise visited the old man maintaining tranquillity under sedation. Such visits "would haunt James for the rest of his life." The Harvard scene of the 1930s is well done: Theodore Spenser, Harry Levin, Robert Fitzgerald, R. P. Blackmur, Lincoln Kirstein, and F. O. Matthiessen who praised him as "one of the coming literati of the Harvard-Yale axis."

Fitts gave him contact details for Pound, 12 via Marsalla, Rapallo to whom he gratuitously introduced himself by letter as "editor of the Harvard Advocate and the Yale Harkness Hoot." Later, he would write of Pound in Byways: "that man is going to save the world if he can…one of the lords of the lyre." Face to face, Pound provided complexity and hectored him: "practically NO poetry satisfies me/not even my own…don't go on in my erroneous vein, by being too damn uncivil." A year on, they had become lifelong friends, Pound addressing him by letter "Dilectus Filius." J's gift for friendship was inestimable and the cast of names unfolds steadily. Stein spoke of how "Joyce and Proust copied their work from my Making of Americans." MacN never spares the lighter comic ambiences as J learnt about writers first hand, including Stein as a dangerous driver. Distinctive ennui pervades the excitement of the European tours and with it, his frugality on $3 a day. "I don't want to come home and kick around and get melancholy," he writes from Paris during the glorious summer of 1934. The next trip to Rapallo is a year before Pound wrote Canto 45. Quickly enough, cultural influence is absorbed and Harvard slated as his ranting mentor tells him that the academy is "usurped by professors bent on killing poetry, subsidized by the mercanti di cannoni who were in unholy alliance with the bankers to kill people."

Pound was not "a replacement for his own father" rather a soul-father. MacN never states the irony of J's life that both patriarchs spent long periods in insane asylums.

Skiing runs parallel and provides contrast to the relentless narrative of the business venture: 1935 finds him "in the Austrian Tyrol, the glorious skiing country west of Innsbruck" in the milieu of the Orient Express. In the same year, at Pound's suggestion, J set about establishing a publishing house. Aunt Leila and Uncle Dicky offered White Cottage on the estate for ND, while Marianne Moore and other notables were consulted. Laughlin Senior handed out the securities for ND's opening gambit "approximately $100,000—not far south of $2 million in 2014 dollars." The first anthology New Directions in Prose and Poetry bore "the imprint NEW DIRECTIONS/NORFOLK, CT./1936."

With ND up and running his resolve is absolute. "I begin to think maybe I have found my vocation. The books are coming along beautifully and are going to be terribly handsome…almost a justification in themselves for some of our accumulated sins as a family." MacN glosses the dynastic family company Jones & Laughlin who had been called "the toughest anti-union company in America." Sins of the fathers would, if not engulf J, certainly keep him progressing as publisher amidst challenges and pitfalls. Carlos Williams' White Mule was a learning curve. The novel in manuscript failed to impress Eliot at Faber, but took off while J had gone skiing in New Zealand. 500 copies sold out. The remaining 600 unbound, languished as "Williams watched in anguish."

Whether he went into publishing to foster his own poetry amidst the milieu of poets is never resolved or addressed. He was possibly influenced by Cummings' typewriter metric, certainly absorbed Pound while Williams made sense declaring the typewriter as "the vehicle of the new age." In 1938, he "found" Dylan Thomas: writing to his mother J said "I feel more or less that God has put him in my care and I must keep him alive." Thomas, like others, came with individual issues and problems. Privately appalled, he confided in Merton how "poor old Dylan Thomas was one ghastly mess." There is a bizarre account (too lengthy to quote) of J identifying Thomas for purposes of the death cert.

It wasn't all skiing. He seriously set up office in a hotel, one fruitful summer in Paris, reeling in Henry Miller and Jean Cocteau. His range grew wide, publishing the founder of the monologue intérieur Edouard Dujardin in translation as We'll to the Woods No More. He faced on-going financing and illustration problems, as well as the contingencies of distribution and sales as full-fledged industrious publisher. After one sales visit, he declared: "nobody in this land gives a hoot in hell about poetry." In terms of illustrators, he hired Alvin Lustig, "who had studied briefly with Frank Lloyd Wright" at Taliesen East and Warhol who produced "four jackets for ND beginning in 1951."

Problematic poets came with the job. His patience with everyone, particularly Pound proved to be exemplary, expert, and professional. As his "main American publisher" and "a convert to Ezra's economic theories, not at all to his politics," J warned him: "keep absolutely mum about money/jews/fascism you will not be liked/If you mention any of them subjects you will have one hell of a time"; "I want to push you hard as poet and writer, but not get tangled up in the political end"; "yr. politics have cooked yr revered goose to a point you wd. not believe."

When J's "lovelife out west had become so active, he solicited the advice of Bill Williams" and married in 1942 ("his family told him that he must go through with it") receiving congratulations from many writers including Nabokov. Marriage inspired "a New York presence" for ND: 67 W 44th. His first meeting with Nabokov at a Lincoln Kirstein party led to Tennessee Williams "looking very nervous." Knock-on networking was a vital asset. Nabokov's ancienne régime politeness withheld a disdain which J felt, remarking: "he would force a smile for me sometimes but it was a long-ways-away smile." He had to orchestrate friends delicately: in spite of Delmore Schwartz' objections to Scott Fitzgerald, Laughlin published The Crack-Up and the out of print The Great Gatsby.

The Pound indictment invades the narrative but MacN renders the array of poets and writers with equal billing. Both Merton and Robert Fitzgerald rank among lifetime friends. Like Cornell, J remained stealthily judicious, not too alarmed about the treason rap and was protective of the Pounds, fearing public sentiment which was strongly in favor of conviction. J's loyalty to literature rode the fall out. MacN goes for the Overholser theory of how Pound found an insightful supporter at St Elizabeths even if it came with state controlled incarceration. Effectively, detention with indefinite release derailed the potential trial for treason. Importantly and strategically J had to keep "his name out of circulation on the Pound issue" while advancing publication of The Pisan Cantos. He published Brecht and moved to new offices at 500 5th in New York.

With the "arrival" of Merton the biography turns volte face away from the EP saga, keeping it just above footnote level on the Bollingen Prize controversy. Bowles' The Sheltering Sky (1949), put out by ND, became a huge success, clearing the three and a half thousand print run and meeting the demand for 45,000 copies three months later. But how was ND faring? Gross sales in 1940 were $6,702 compared to gross sales in 1949 of $232, 831.

J "found" Borges and was recalcitrant about the Beats. He would meddle with Snyder but rejected Kerouac's Dr Sax finding that the Beats lifestyle "offended his sensibilities." He befriended and published Rexroth as both remained above and beyond the Beats and their "ecology motif in American poetry" despite poets like Corso and others combining "a disordered life with a productive commitment to poetry." As Snyder boasted of their "harder-edged politics than the hippies of the 1960s," J left Ginsberg to City Lights and Ferlinghetti. The big coup for ND in fiction was Hesse's Siddharta which became J's record bestseller in 1970 with sales of over three hundred thousand copies.

How he "lost" Merton's classic spiritual primer The Seven Story

Mountain and Beckett's work is fascinating reading; he would not touch Lolita under any circumstances since it "made him uncomfortable." He passed on Tropic of Cancer, finding it and the whole trilogy "anarchic" and against "the bourgeois order."

The Pound exit from America gets the same space as the W. C. Williams party for the fifth volume of Paterson. Politically, he was anti-Kennedy and avoided peace protest movements.

With Kenner's input, he had a cohort to finalise an edition of The Cantos. A casual letter from Charles Tomlinson in 1964, praising J's two poems in Akzente as "marvels of grace, poise, fineness of mind and ear" brought an astonished response, explaining the polarities of being a poet writing for "personal amusement, or vanity" while "accepting responsibility in a public way" if he went along with Ferlinghetti's offer of a collected volume. Indecision ruled. "J's major Selected Poems would not appear from City Lights for another twenty-two years." Meanwhile, he was happier noting that "Ezra had retracted his anti-Semitism." Pound's mental condition almost reflected his own impending era of bipolarity. On visiting him in 1968, he found the poet under "a collapse in spirit." Merton's death by accidental electrocution in a Bangkok hotel room left J the task of editing what would become the Asian Journal. Having depended on Merton as spiritual mentor, he was bereft: "His death really knocked me for a loop." Merton's life had never achieved "a major mystical experience." This also shook him and is given much space. J's own on Mont Blanc is included: "the whole sky above the peak was suffused with a golden radiance. I heard angelic music and my beloved father's voice spoke to me from nowhere, telling me of his love. I did not see him, but it was his voice. The whole event lasted perhaps five minutes."

He became close to Hayden Carruth and relied on "a daily dosage of 300 milligrams of lithium carbonate" and was "fortunate that in Ann he possessed a wife willing to put up with his mood swings" as well as adolescent regression behavior. With invitations to universities and honors, he felt conflicted about accepting his part in enabling culture since "the barrier between the constantly shifting "high-brow" avant-garde and 'mass culture' had fallen." After Pound's passing, his verse often lashed out: "The pedants of deconstruction/ [are] lathering each other's backs"; "the young were uneducated, the junk bond system was bad, the capitalist system itself was 'awful'". When Rexroth's American Poetry in the Twentieth Century appeared in print, J was praised as publisher and poet. In 1971, Neruda's Nobel Prize marked "a triumphant note for ND" (395) and Kenner's The Pound Era (1972) from Faber established the modernist tableaux among first critical works of some length.

After twenty nine years ND moved to 80 8th street: "although somewhat less in total area than at 333…it was only a four-minute walk from his Bank Street apartment." He forged ahead past his son, Robert's suicide and the death of Rexroth battling with mental issues amidst the publishing, writing, and accepting public invitations. "My talk on economics was a failure as no students asked me for plastic explosives to blow up banks." He had addressed the Pound conference in Alabama and later published Pound as Wuz: Essays and Lectures on Ezra Pound. Morbid introspection dominated his notes, some cut from Flaubert: "without the Concept of Happiness existence would be more bearable"; "I make myself drunk with ink as others do with wine." An affair with Vanessa Jackson in Paris involved a manic if "glorious sentimental journey: old memories, new sentiment." He held things together by seeing off Vanessa while adapting to his new "minder" Gertrude Huston, who became his wife in 1990.

"As his body slowed, his mind raced faster and faster than ever, conscious of diminishing time." Guy Davenport was one of his last great "finds." The National Book Foundation's Medal for Distinguished Contribution to American Letters was for "being a lifelong friend of lost literary souls." His poems pinpointed the agonised self: "Could it /Be the unforgiveable sins of the/Fathers sins from which there/Is no escape?" Self-accusations abounded: "I swim in the vanity of/frivolous poetry & torment/myself with imaginings of/profane and forbidden love." By 1994 the Collected Poems of James Laughlin kept him self-accusatory. He found the book far too long and a "monstrous megalomaniad." He wondered if it would have been "better [to] be silent?" Diffidence did not falter in terms of writing epigrammatic poems, but the self-accusation that came with creating them never faltered.

Sensuality plagued and pleasured him. "To need to recapture/The raptures of the past." He continued taking Lithium for mania and Relafen for arthritis. Huston predeceased him. Ginsberg died and he wrote a poem revaluating him. He praised the poets: "and what they wrote/has been my joy" (486). His epitaph on the tombstone in Norfolk says simply "James Laughlin 1914-1997 Poet Publisher" (488). If an epitaph proclaims the life in summation, one must take the poet on his lines

that all I learned in books/
and from the muses I've ta-/
ken with me but my rich pos-/
sessions I have left behind.

James (Jas.) Laughlin, like his co-modernists was a tortured poet, hardly like Poe or Aiken or Plath, yet tortured. MacNiven evokes a Gatsby of sorts, if you can imagine the Long Islander as significant publisher rather than a shady underworld ghoul, bond dealer and romantic.

—*Make It New* 2015

POETS' MANIFESTATIONS

The Art of Brian Coffey Donal Moriarty (University College Dublin Press)

A Broken Line: Denis Devlin and Irish poetic modernism Alex Davis (University College Dublin Press)

Nothing deserves a warmer welcome that this full-length study of Coffey's poetry yet one might spend a whole night if not longer arguing with Moriarty about his findings and critical affirmations. He is not a dogmatist and, far from it, one can understand his being enthralled with his subject and pursuing a microscopic approach in examining lines of poetry, phrases and words according to the time-honoured Empson tradition; so one presumes that he doesn't give two hoots for Wordsworth's dictum that "we murder to dissect" as he chooses a tweezers for his purposes.

This is admirable and not at all irritating since the book is brief; he never pontificates but naturally enough follows a definite line of inquiry in a sleuthlike manner without, if one might cavil, any representation of Coffey's immense erudition and baggage which has been artfully squeezed into the poems. Another quibble is his assertion that Coffey is not "a conventional lyric poet" which he is, of course, except that unlike a host of competent lyric poets he is more than just that kind of writer. For god's sake, surely nothing is more shamelessly lyrical than

the rose the glaucous the amethystine wave work carpeting

Similarly the following is almost dripping in Tennysonian syntax

how slowly-swiftly time does move now as walls crumbling

through centuries

now as lightning out of the east

Moriarty is not beyond stressing Coffey's aesthetic principle as expressed though his poems, if not elsewhere, that:

real words fail darling thought

and in the same vein

seldom clear-sky clear-say

If one wants to play along with hunt-the-source, is the latter not close to G. M. Hopkins?

All his fine point analysis is naturally enough worked out through Coffey—the poet who not only thought about what he would write next but only after having considered what he had last written. His poems remain a challenge to those poets whose works perish beyond brilliance in a final draft. Their effusions are often gushing while his are "all too visibly word vehicles albeit of course, essentially fallacious"

—one can argue that till the cows come home

argue that till the cows come home.

However, Coffey, whom Moriarty makes a strong case for being a valiant intruder into the established poetry scene, remained paradoxically an outsider also, but with a touch of the elitist. Moriarty canonically places him alongside such experimentalists as George Oppen, Lorine Niedecker and David Antin to name those odd species of poet, and of course Coffey was a rare owl himself. There is a definite hint of his obstreperousness against Yeats and Eliot and a genuflection towards the oddest bird of all, Ezra Pound.

Meanwhile, Coffey is never underrated, nor is he found wanting for philosophy since one is told that he "Was more learned than Beckett or Joyce". He is shown as a founding father of a group known under many different names including 'experimentalists', no doubt almost insulting to the practitioners themselves, one of whom, Billy Mills, is reputedly world-weary from "the lyric 'I' voice in Irish poetry". One sympathises, but then again the personal pronoun is often unavoidable and poets complaining about the deadness of language is a pretty old chestnut in itself.

So as it were, Moriarty pours out the Coffey opus, beginning with a rigorous and acceptably lengthy discussion of Third Person linking its meditational backdrop and scaffolding to amongst others, the un-tongue-tied Coleridge who might have found these 'experimentalists' too meek in the flesh for his loquaciousness. There is ample testimony to Coffey's brilliant translations; he is contrasted with Beckett, particularly since both made versions of Rimbaud's 'Le bateau lure'. However, personally speaking, Coffey's finest hour is the treatment of de Nerval's 'Vers dorés' which is mentioned while unmentioned is his poem adapted from de Nerval as 'Christ among the Olives'.

There is intelligent comment on Mallarme's cryptic and infamous poem, which has long been a credo for experimentalists *Un coup de des jamais n'abolira le hazard* done into English by Coffey as 'Dice thrown never will annul chance'. Mallarme's influence, pernicious or otherwise, never let him alone; they remain first cousins poetically and in its turn, Mallarme's Coup de des has strong roots in Coleridge's 'Rime of the Ancient Mariner' except that Mallarme's mariner is a symbol of the poet throwing his lines as a potter might with clay, and the French poet's pessimism is fully explored by both Moriarty and Coffey who translates the penultimate line as

All thought utters dice thrown.

Coffey's version became one of Liam Miller's strangest slim volume productions to hail from the Dolmen Press and at first sight looks like a poem for children with its multi-font changes on each page, and spacing that might lead one to believe that Mallarmé, who rightly insisted on the typographical layout in his own editions of the poem, was a few lines short of a sonnet himself.

While Moriarty insists that Coffey's attunement to language and its infinite variety and effects makes him as unique as Mallarmé, he differed from his chèr maître in being an existentialist Christian and this is exemplified from Advent. The latter can helpfully be linked to his first book Third Person and ominously looks forward to the choice of Hektor as a persona for his long last poem. Advent has the usual Coffeyesque features with hidden layerings from Thomas Aquinas and other thinkers. Its lyricism is effusive at times:

It is here in the passing swan

beauty beauty swan

jade on down a flow going past not nothingness

Meanwhile there is the usual instructive comment on The Death of Hektor comfortably embodying Coffey's sense of the underdog— no Achillean proud hero for his subject matter, ever the jackal, never the tame pet and also human, in that it has one plonker of a line amongst its grandeur:

We can not hold time fast in our sights.

It's impossible not to compare this with the other book above, however Davis's text is more substantial with a wider critical reference but is not necessarily more effective. His introduction travels well-known ground: Austin Clarke's antipathy to the Revival and especially Yeats; Kavanagh's similar stance and Beckett's influential appraisal of 'Recent Irish Poetry' in The Bookman where every phrase of condemnation and praise has become a manifesto. One can agree with much of this, including his tracing of MacGreevy's epic poem *Crón Trath na nDeithe* to The Waste Land. Devlin, heralded by Beckett, is also slotted into an American tradition, especially that of Wallace Stevens.

There is more incisive comment as the book progresses, locating Devlin's 'Communication from the Eiffel Tower' in dream and the poetry of Blaise Cendrars and other experimenters who were influenced by Andre Spire. Meanwhile critical reception of Devlin was mixed, Spender disliking the "enormous inflation of purely verbal values" and Randall Jarrell hailing a new voice. Davis is dogmatic in referring to Devlin:

'Bacchanal' registers the political climate of the 1930s as much as any poem by Auden, MacNeice or Spender.

A lot of time is spent labelling Devlin's pedigree; he is excluded from the Pound-Williams modernist tradition but can sit on the same shelf with George Oppen, Louis Zukofsky and Lorine Niedecker. Leaving all this mad dash into pedigree aside, his work is seen as broadly 'religious' albeit syncretic in that direction, hence the poem 'Ank'hor Vat' echoes Charles Olson's 'The Kingfishers', otherwise it evokes a Buddhist temple of the Khmer empire as a basis for religious searchings which would penetrate deeper into the long poem 'Lough Derg' and his subsequent lengthy detour through "Jansenist stress on the lack of observable divine justice in human affairs". Of course Devlin's efficacy is not a dark agnostic miasma as his sonnet 'Casa Buonaroti' attests.

Davis naturally cannot avoid discussion of Devlin's love poetry, perhaps his highest achievement such as 'The Colours of Love':

When leaves have fallen and

There's nothing left

But plainsong from ascetic bony birds, I say a prayer for all who are bereft

Of love, of leafy summer,

of loving words.

This alone shows Devlin's vulnerability and gentleness. More of which is evident in the longer 'Heavenly Foreigner' where "he constructs a relationship to a deity out of the 'raw material' of the desire for a literal woman". In other words Devlin was a non-pagan Keatsian hybrid pushed into the so-called-real world of international diplomacy, and under the circumstances of living such a dual existence, came up with the likes of this:

At the Bar du Depart drink farewell

And say no word you'll be remembered by;

Nor Prince nor President can ever tell

Where love ends or when it does and why.

There speaks the surly diplomat and the swooning poet.

One can agree with most of Davis's analysis on such poems as 'On the Tomb of Michael Collins', however its icy detached tone is easily disgraced in anecdotes about Devlin's discomfort at giving a reading on a foreign radio network. "I felt a fool broadcasting rimery during a war," while being more comfortable reciting 'Under Ben Bulben' under the influence of British Embassy wine to Mervyn Wall and a few others standing at the Trevi Fountain in Rome as war seemed inevitable. A positive feature of Devlin's professional career meant his meeting a fellow writer on the diplomatic circuit, St-John Perse.

The great flaw of Davis's book is the manifesto-like quality of the last two chapters which eschew Devlin, having done a good job on his works up to that point. However, the book might have ended gracefully here since he then proceeds on a crusade for Michael Smith and Trevor Joyce, founders of the pioneering New Writers Press in the late 1960s. Naturally, Davis is usually interesting as he pitches a sporadic analysis of their work rooted in Irish modernism, but by trumpeting them as foraging members of an underground movement, he may be doing them a disservice, since poetry by its very nature is almost totally underground except for the few names on everyone's tongue. The parading of Geoffrey Squires and Montague's 'The Rough Field' tends to lose buoyancy even with mention of the latter's upbraiding of his fellow workers for being oblivious to Pound, Lawrence and Williams.

This kind of strident aesthetic pigeonholing is largely unhelpful since Irish poetry demands a broad church and even in the purlieus of Poetry Ireland and other sanctioned institutions, many types and varieties are presumed to be represented. Dangerously enough, whenever fascist strongholds of poetry dominate there is injustice, but that is a big subject beyond the present piece. However, Davis is thumping the pulpit for the forgotten, in his phrase 'Irish Neo-Avant-Garde' and diminishes this reviewer's fleeting admiration for them in the process. He lists and discusses these heroes: Randolph Healy, Billy Mills, Maurice Scully and Catherine Walsh while giving the wrong impression of a self-serving elite who purvey "Language poetry through their shared challenge that the avant-garde has died in post modernity, its demise brought about by the supposed collapse of boundaries between pop and high art, and the canonisation of works, like Marcel Duchamp's, once viewed as aesthetically offensive." Huh? To repeat, Davis runs along well and good until these two closing chapters with their dominant hiccups that generally splutter into much ado about nothing. Perilously, he may not bring healthy attention to his commune of poets, neglected or otherwise, and besides Ireland, if not the world, is awash with neglected poets whose claims to being avant-garde geniuses, true or false, are just as trenchant in their own manifestos; either spoken or printed.

—*Books Ireland* 2000

MEANING?

Market Street Damian Smyth (Lagan Press)

A Fool's Errand Dermot Healy (Gallery Press)

Eye of the Hare John F. Deane (Carcanet Press)

Imaginary Menagerie Ailbhe Darcy (Bloodaxe Books)

Island of Shadow: Irish Poetry Across the Centuries ed. Brian Lalor (Gill & Macmillan)

Smyth's is by far the best of these collections. It has plenitude and avoids the self-consciousness of the others and is a cornucopia based on his Downpatrick. From pharmacy to pawnbroker for which he gives an inventory (probably based on window shopping) there is a substantial sampling of his native sod based on literature in the broadest sense from entertainment to history, philosophy and folklore. History is prevalent as in Martin McGuinness who provides the text from an interview sourced in The Belfast Telegraph. "We may not remember this generation showed extraordinary forbearance and forgiveness. We will just wonder if it had a particular fondness for dangerous men." The Belfast Telegraph also serves Smyth well in the McMaster murder where the unarmed brother of the victim challenged the gunmen. In every respect these pieces are found-poems from original or other sources however as he states in the useful notes: "A town writes its own biography, if not always very well." Therefore Smyth allowes himself the liberty of finding his native place as well as including himself in the source notes. It is not just local history and proprietors that catch his gaze but anything in somewhere (Downpatrick); even the 15 Ulsterbus to Belfast and the cinema which he studiously links to Plato's parable of the cave. Occasionally, a note is not a fitting counterpart to its poem yet on closer inspection fits fairly well: "The things that happen here do not seem to mean anything; they mean something somewhere else" (Chesterton). An abandoned rail line at

Ballynoe had the infamy of being without a village where the railway station was located near "a well-preserved prehistoric stone circle." A book such as this is a fairly open-genre since it as readable as an almanac. "A Dip from the Cooneyites" (a five-section piece) may well be his crowning glory on the little known Christian sect whose membership numbers 200, according to the notes.

In Nine parts with each section titled but the titles seem arbitrary. The structure is basically the line breaks imitating the line break structure and nothing more. The title (used twice in the poem) purports to be profound: life is a fool's errand. Shakespeare's fools are not as daft as this in their comic rendering of existence whereas Healy is ponderous with pretence to profundity which is not a hallmark of poetry. Geese provide the main motif or theme but don't expect Hitchcock's *The Birds* or Saint-John Perse's *Oiseaux*. That said there are a few flashes but nothing brilliant in what is actually a bit of a wild goose chase as regards ultimate meaning. Nor can a long poem achieve much on a few mediocre flashes. Vagueness is a feature that stalks the phraseology: "as the orchestra of memory/takes to the air"; "the unsure knowledge"; "the hand of a clock,//comes to rest,/at last, on nought ." There is no zero on a clock. On a digital clock there is, however chronometric time is never zero unless in SciFi or on a military expedition or some such. What does this actually mean in the following (there is also use of internal rhyme) yet: "The bird is a poor excuse for becoming a recluse in some place like heaven." This is meaningless. Elsewhere: "The stars/while away the hours." This usage is awful. The avian atmosphere in his efforts to evoke or depict it greatly lacking: "as the geese wheel in/across the thundering sea". Wheel is badly chosen. Are the geese on roller skates or bicycles? And thundering sea is just about adequate. There is something inept in this image also: "Overhead/an arrowhead of stars//follows after an arrowhead of geese." This is somewhat clear except that stars don't follow birds in the sky. He rhymes 'frantic' with 'Atlantic' but it all flops ultimately: "Oystercatcher, /gull, snipe, curlew/are at it." At what? Otherwise, he cannot but assume sham-music: "they break overhead in thousands/with a marvellous/pouring of song/into the beyond." Marvellous is just not good enough. And unfortunately the use of 'break' which he uses to suggest flight or movement comes across as personal bird damage. Song has never been poured, has it? Flying birds are also placed "in little lots". This is blatant cliché. His plural is "a fleet of ducks". Again clumsy usage and this is meant to be poetry. So where do all the geese go that have made Healy resonate with the profundity that life is a fool's errand, a wild goose chase: "They take their song with them."

Too strong on rhetoric about the Deity as in 'Song of the Suffering Servant,' 'Chewing on Stones,' 'Roots:' "Poets have been asserting, yet again, the demise of God, world-maker." There is a persistent backdrop of nostalgia and anecdotal recollection in 'Bikes' and 'Sheets' with its opening weak line: "When she was through with them, the sheets" washed by his Granny, the sheets are full of "love." Of course they are. Meaning is a problem too among imagery in 'The Garden, Waiting:' "We are written down under the skin of the world/as cloudbones manuscript the skies." As prose whatever about poetry this is fatuous: we are not written down under the skin of the world. The image of cloudbones simply does not emerge. This is solipsism without any communication. The poems on nature strike an awkward pose and all centre around a hare: 'The Hare,' 'Eye of the Hare' and 'Dusk' which has an unintentional Walt Disney/Lewis Carroll sort of image: "It was April, but a late March hare was shadow boxing/with the evening moon" It is usually late when the evening moon appears. How cute that a hare's paws are depicted as boxing and cutesiness of linguistic invention is never far from Deane. Otherwise, he preaches in a diction that is embarrassing for example "World, Flesh and Devil:" "The poem holds within it all sanctity and sin." Meaning what? Other poems focus on words since he must be the poet as with shrive in "Abundance" and "rust-meld"

240

in "More". He is from Achill, so this justifies a sequence over twelve pages combining all of his attributes in 'Achill: The Island'.

Darcy's aesthetic is involved with a fast-food type of poem. One might even suggest that she is none too serious about poethood and her work is throwaway and sporadic. This may be circumscribed in the aesthetic philosophy in "Panopticon:" "I live/as best I can. I do the awful maths" and where Henry James is quoted, "remember that every life is a special problem which is not yours but another's, and content yourself with the terrible algebra of your own." Her poetry reflects this modernist precept and is without personal bonds or boundaries: "Detroit, Chicago, Boston or New York,/along the Amtrak or the South Shore." Such work does not quote well. Whole poems restore no order for her. Poetry is not a call to something beyond the mess and chaos as in "The mornings you turn into a grub." In 'The Hotel' the speaker is with one partner but may as well be with the stranger that catches her attention. Similarly in 'The Art of Losing:' "with all I gather to me, I dwell/so often on the things I've shed." This collection offers no easy solutions and the poems have an inherent almost self-destructive meaning. Nothing is soft-edged. 'Swan Song' ends: "I've lined your throat with feathers." The expression speaks for the poem since poetry is not life. This is her exact departure and she sticks to it.

Since this is not an anthology, quibbling over the poetry, song and ballad selection is superfluous. There is AE's "Germinal," Colum's "She Moved Through the Fair," and WB Yeats represented by four poems including "Red Hanrahan's Song about Ireland" as well as accompanying art works that are a distraction as well as enhancement for the poems. The painters are many and usually whom you would expect such as Francis Bacon, James Barry, Harry Clarke, Patrick Colins, Percy French, Grace Henry, Sarah Purser, Nano Reid, Mary Swanzy and Jack Yeats. Gerard Dillon's "Connemara Lovers" is alongside Moore's "She is Far from the Land" and "The Croppy Boy" alongside Orpen's "Portrait of a

Youth." An eclectic personal mix of text from the Táin Bó Cúailnge (a brief excerpt) to "The Bells of Shandon" from "A Nation Once Again" to Heaney's "Digging" in picture-matching-poem with Paul Henry's "The Potato Diggers." Gogarty's "Ringsend" is barely geographically close to Harry Kernoff's "Murphy's Boat-Yard, Ringsend, Dublin". Elsewhere the concept of picture-matching-poem has to remain as tenuous and colour is welcome beside the words. The agenda is leisure and dreaming. Nothing to shock or arouse since the atmosphere is soporific. Nothing to tax the mind even in the poetry and the intended audience could well be that of the Ireland's Own readership. In any event this is the sort of coffee-table book that is 'never' completely read by any one reader. Coffee table books have a strange forlorn existence. Still this solves the Christmas present problem for Uncle Seamus and Auntie Marie who may have a liking for poetry and art that has no urgency to be used. It is a furniture item as well as potential book to aid conversation or sleep. Coffee table books are for anyone but essentially achieve the potential of neglected reading matter.

—*Books Ireland* 2011

HOW IT LOOKED

Hurting God Part Essay Part Rhyme Rita Ann Higgins (Salmon Poetry)

Selected Poems Kerry Hardie (Gallery Press)

Red Riding Hood's Dilemma Órfhlaith Foyle (Arlen House)

Latch Paul Jeffcutt (Lagan Press)

Drifting Under the Moon Ger Reidy (Dedalus Press)

Dogs Singing: A Tribute Anthology ed. Jessie Lendennie (Salmon Poetry)

Professor Karen Steele's brief introduction encapsulates her subject's appeal as 'iconoclastic poet of the underclass, an unforgettable voice in a nation teeming with literary talent.' The collection has a written-out feel: a re-visiting of well used material. There are a handful of poems accompanying what Steele admits are 'impressionistic vignettes of reminiscence'. The Ireland of repression, priests and poverty of the 50s and 60s is the national dodo explored here. Higgins's retelling of working in Mervue Industrial Estate in the 1970s where 'Sexy was the word made flesh that dwelt amongst us' is weakly Carveresque. She gets vaguely political 'the multinationals ran and took the money with them' but never achieves any commentary on Irish economic experience. "Melancholy in the TB Ward" is followed by "The Priest is Coming we Can Feel It in Our Bones" visits the same terrain: 'A pep talk/ from Sister Mammary—/to put zip in our loins/glucose in our mug.' "Toronto Interlude" is prose alongside her best poem "Ask the Concierge" where naked desire is revealed outside a shop (appropriately) called 'Seduction': 'underwear to raise the Titanic/healthy looking mannequins with brazen breasts/balefuls of Canadian promise./They come hither you but you never come hither them./Their chilling look deceptive, their cherry lips,/kiss me kiss me, but only in your dreams loser.' This admission is redolent of the psyche behind Higgins's controlled rage. Her haven in Spiddal is peaceful with cultural resolution: 'Joyce is the other Ó Cadhain. Ó Cadhain is such a complex and hugely challenging writer.' Her homecoming is also in "Borders": 'warbler boulevard/ meander lane the pace the same/the borders here are invisible'.

Hardie is flagrantly metaphorical, pastoral and buoyantly spiritual but often lacking in the power to convince of her vision. There is too much mention of swallows. The selection picks up as it goes along after the problems of her first collection A Furious Place (1996). Jerky lines with occasional abuse of language as in "May" with 'The birdsong/bouncing back out of the sky'. In "Interlude" her use of 'the fragile blossom of the cherry trees,' is very weak. The discursive poem "At St Laserian's Cathedral, Old Loughlin" is better stuff. "Exiles" is replete with a family tree—often a dangerous departure in poetry unless some extraordinary correlative beyond the family album is gained. Only with "After the Storm" and a line 'like Leonardo's man, describing his full circle' is there any cutting off of the fatty linguistic register. Lyrics made to measure are the achievement in her work as in "After My Father Died" yet it may be too triumphantly post-grief. "On Derry's Walls" is among her best: 'because all we can ever say is/This is how it looked to me—'. "When Maura had Died" is good, still over-triumphant but the writing is non-cloying: 'the drops/ on the crossbar hanging in the light'; 'hanging' works but the poem is full of observation more than image. "The High Pyrenees" is an old fashioned imagist poem maintaining its structure contrasting mountains and 'the ancient sea of the mountains,/only the night coming down on the great dark slide of its waves.' Her lilting is often frustrating somewhat like sub-Synge crossed with Masefield yet the image (thanks to Carlos Williams) in "Genesis" is startlingly good: 'And always a wheelbarrow parked by a flowerbed./And always a rain butt, running black silk.'

The title poem which names the collection is poor stuff yet it may or may not have sparked the stylised cover artwork from Pauline Bewick. Foyle born in Nigeria of Irish parentage unveils her background in "And Where Else?" Despite its failings there is a ripe line 'and Aboriginals must look good for the tourists'. "According to Albert Speer" is an over-ambitious theme in attempting to evoke the Nazi evil. Van Gogh and Emily Bronte inspire her but not as strongly as in "Akhmatova" who 'breathed blood-fingered air'. "I Saw Beckett The Other Day" is the best long poem though steering close to disaster and saved by a final line: 'Beckett used to blow his coffee cool'. Occasionally everything collapses as in "Betrayal": 'You slammed love away into/the cold quarters of your heart'. This is terrible language abuse, lazy and meaningless cliché compared to the latent majesty of "Later In Leningrad" amidst diction that does not offend or lilt: 'And later in Leningrad/—I stood still./I stood still/And I remembered its first name'. The blues ballad "Take It From The Spleen, Baby Doll" is a musical riff that makes its own little fire.

"Evacuation East" is not very effective, transposed as if he arrived on a Nazi train to the gas chambers on a 'Hot July day, no breeze.' Jeffcutt does better rendering visual scenes as in "Pranzo": 'Across huge tapestries/wolves are hunted down/with hounds and spears.' And in "Still": 'he's laid out like a medieval knight,/pale and sunken cheeks scarred/from the nurse's clumsy shaves.' The opening of "Longanizas" is effective as random observed human scenery: 'Tottering her bar-stool,/stylish blonde sucks the lips off/suave caballero groping her arse.' "Abandoned Along La Ruta De Don Quijote" makes randomness an inner technique including a postmodernist internal reference: 'a book on chivalry, whose name/I do not care to recall,/stamped Biblioteca de Toledo.' Attraction to the visual has its downside when it fails in "Scapegoat": 'A black,/white, brown face/with shifty, slitty eyes'. One knows what he refers to but the words for colours merely clash. The same happens in "Twilight Tjukurpa": 'In a lost ocean of terracotta sand'.

Again 'lost ocean' is weak; terracotta sand is fine at the builders' suppliers but Jeffcut makes a mish-mash with an unfortunate choice of words.

These are nature notes dressed us as what? Would they even make Nature Notes in a 1940s or 1950s provincial newspaper? "The Reunion" suggests an impossible phenomenon: 'A single leaf falls from an elegant tree/laden with the sadness of a closed church'. The craw-thumper "Exiles" begins 'Sometimes my little currach/lures me towards the edge/and my poor soul drifts into the depths'. Not even in a Mayo pub when conversation has totally dried up, could anyone come out with such diatribe. In "The Lesson" 'I drove the cow from her dim stall/out into the winter every morning'. As they say in America: like who cares! And in the one entitled "Cows" you've guessed it, he declares: 'From them I'm learning stoic simplicity'. That is why cows were created to give milk, butter, cheese and of course, stoicism. In "Midlife": 'Suddenly he woke to the sound of a bell/tolling beyond history'. Can anyone spare a Panadol? "Spring Snow" presents an impossible occurrence amidst landscape: 'Over the shoulder of a frozen hill/a curtain sweeping in from the north'. Later in the same piece you hear that 'The stars retreated south'. Yea every star in the galaxy! Perhaps, to surrender to the Moon? One never finds out. Finally, another incredible geological spectacle seen only to Reidy in "Flooding Near Lenane". 'All summer the mountains were aloof,/the river turned away to the sea.' Aloof mountains, sulking rivers, elegant trees, his poor soul, tales from the University of Stoic Cattle, and bells tolling beyond history are all in this collection. Enjoy.

The editor is unabashed in saying that this is for 'my beloved Zookie' and 'my gorgeous Zach'. Eileen Battersby chants: 'It is the ultimate joy, the ultimate love, the ultimate sorrow; it's the dog—your dog, my dog, our dogs, all dogs.' Every poet here is brought to their knees hugging their doggies in a verse anthology as infectious as your dog(s). Despite weak efforts from Neil Astley and

Peter Fallon you get a kennel full. Here are a few of the poets in barking form: Fred Johnston's "A Sick Dog": 'My old buddy, I want/a dog/to judge the world: bury it/under its own leprous dung.' Seamus Cashman writes of Tucker 'bright writ today in our family hall of fame'. Michael O'Loughlin's "Elegy For A Basset Hound" that 'settled into an Amsterdam bookshop'. Joseph Woods' "Kerry Blue": 'bundle herding/all the deer/in Phoenix park.' Maxine Kumin's "Xochi's Tale": 'Who dines in style and sleeps the sleep of kings.' Nessa O'Mahony "Circumnavigator": 'your pink-tongued grin tells the truth of it'. Joan I. Siegel's "Dog Outside a Grocery on Broadway": 'how he waited where someone told him to wait'. Andrea Cohen's "Seven Dogs": 'The life of a man/ is measured by seven dogs.' Caroline Lynch's "A Moment of Woof": 'forever chasing bumble bees'. Dogs inspire poetry and that is only one reason why dogs are loved. You can read these out to your four legged friend who may wish to use it as an unsatisfying bone. Dogs have no use for poetry.

—*Books Ireland* 2011

OF BLIGHT AND BLISS

Laments Jan Kochanowski (Gallery Press)

Frightening New Furniture Kevin Higgins (Salmon Poetry)

Uttering Her Name Gabriel Rosenstock (Salmon Poetry)

Where's Katie Elaine Feeney (Salmon Press)

Invitation to a Sacrifice Dave Lordan (Salmon Poetry)

Lamentations Damian Smyth (Lagan)

The Fall Anthony Cronin (New Island)

When Love is Not Enough: New & Selected Poems Maurice Harmon (Salmon Poetry)

Polish poet, Kochanowski (1530-84) depicts losing his daughter Ursula before her third year, 'She'd barely risen above ground when Death/Felled the dear child with his infectious breath'. Heart-wracked he declares: 'Now emptiness reigns here; the house is still;/Nobody ever laughs nor ever will.' Stanislaw Baranczak's rhyming couplets were completed by Heaney as 'fine-tuner' towards 'a more standard or more literary turn of phrase.' The result is full throated and emotionally replete. Kochanowski begs of his departed daughter: 'Comfort me, haunt me; you whom I have lost,/Come back again, be shadow, dream, or ghost.' Pure reason fails the poet: 'This tomb keeps no corpse; this corpse keeps no tomb:/Here the room's tenant is the tenant's room.' He implores 'Time, father of forgetfulness' for a resolution to his distress. The emotional register controlled in the poems up to that point is unleashed in the final divinely structured closing poem of the nineteen Laments achieving a new form and pressure. Instead of the floodgates of lamentation heretofore, in this powerful visionary poem he is told that Ursula 'chose to close/The door early and cut life's sorrows short. 'Tears cannot call back souls who are called home.' He must accept 'time's great remedy' and 'Bear humanly the human lot. There is —/Never forget—one Lord of blight and bliss.' Kochanowski reaches the peace that passeth understanding through credible truths in poetry that cannot be denied when tested on the emotions.

Products, movie stars and such permeate Higgins' work Supervalu, Woolworths, Janet Leigh, Anne Frank, Frosties, Cup-a-Soup and so on. The epigraph from Trotsky is quite gratuitous: this is not 'Trot' material since the aim seems to be verse, wit and whimsy as in "Yesterday's Pinstripe Suit:" 'You wake up one day/and find your whole life mislaid.' "2009" gives the ultimate dire vision: 'The world is a Christmas gift/the shop won't take back.' He cannot deny: 'the complexity of an Israeli bomb/tearing a child's face off.' ("The Lost Years"). In "Stage Left": 'He's a glass of red wine before breakfast/the day he decided/to fall down the stairs' reveals the dichotomy in Higgins: the effort to reduce everything to a laugh yet life is not a series of jokes. In grasping after three pinches of wit, one pinch of surrealism and leaving out reality you end up with a porous formula in each poem. "Nemesis:" 'A down to the last bit of toilet paper type of day.' Come back Ogden Nash all is forgiven!

Orisons or spiritual evocations (110+epilogue) to the Indian goddess Óma with Celtic twilight and a contemporary feel. The use of archaic words such as 'goatherd' and a hint of the exotic East and some boasting: 'I take hallucinogenic snuff/exploring Your honeyed essence/vision after vision after vision.' Not without self-irony and humour as in Dar Óma Lieder which he sung 'like a deranged nightingale.' The spiritual register is: 'You are in the vibrations/of Your name/my name/eternal echoes of OM.' Óma becomes all celestial presences. Rosenstock, Irish language poet is offering balm for the spirit with occasional smiling lines. His debut collection in English.

Ray Glasheen's cover with Markievicz in a miniature photo on a monolithic red silhouette. Some poems are controlled hate: 'The Opus Dei men with their shiny shoes—/with their pretty girl children skipping/to Dev! Dev! Dev!/Vote, Vote, Vote for De Valera!' "Blood" is a protest dedicated 'For survivors of church abuse'. Feeney snapshots Ireland with hints of European sojourns however home is where: 'Yeats you fucking pansy!/The young are dying in one another's arms.' The title poem almost achieves elegance as a paean to mother Ireland: 'Ask for this land again,/go on, dare ye, ye cowardly fucks.'

Her best poem, lugubriously titled: "Reflections in January" delivers airy lines devoid of the endemic Irish lift, and also in "Máire": 'She's a heavy old heap of/Ophelia bubbles in the salty sharp water.' "Red Stiletto" captures a national event, 'Half a bottle of vodka/and your red stillettos are required/for Junior Cert results celebration.' Young folk are drinking far more but one gets the point.

Lordan's angst may cause his defection or election to the Stand-Up Scene. The work is loose, open, raplike. He is not far from being a Dadaist and anti-poet. The worst feature is anecdote "Nightmare Pastoral" and "Bullies". In "Spite Specific" he eschews political correctness for 'that rotting old hypocritical wanker of a nun' on the theme of clerical sexual abuse. Reading him nurtures ones inner anarchist. "Funeral City Passeggiata" is a good rant: 'To us the unbreakable glass of shopfronts/where all the most desirable murderers' names/are on continuous display.' "Gaff" involves Kurds in Palmerstown, their landlord, the Gardaí and the tenants ending up in clink. In "The Heckler" he abolishes the pub-drunk as an unfortunate amidst the city frieze along with 'a trio of drugorexic ghetto teens.' His final trumpet blasts in "A resurrection in Charlesland" howls and screams on a downer: 'jobless insomniacs,/paupers who were affluent a year ago'. This tirade spews forth over eighteen pages. Lordan's real persona is town-crier fond of dirty realism, irony stacked on irony in excelsis amidst longing for disaster.

Lamentations has the expressive cover reproduction of The

Lamentation of the Dead Christ (c. 1520) by Hamburg Master which sets the tone for Smyth's 'brief elegies' relaying 'grief, the simple fuel of heartbreak'. He gives the mystery of personal loss: 'my father's death and my brother's' who 'was at ease in spite of violence/done in the driver's seat.' There are 70 double stanzas in terza rima and many have quiet elegances such as number '38' beginning: 'When two mothers who have lost a child meet,/we take up postures as in the Dutch masters.' Smyth presumably finds some universal sympathy mentioning three doctors all in their twenties who died in a car accident. The absolute here is his private haunting: 'The dead go somewhere else before they enter/dreams. The landscape of grief takes on unnatural features, 'Around the Mournes the clouds are like migraines.' 'I believe/in God as an alternative to fear.' His fear comes from many sources including the touch of coffins 'for a while in these two hands.' There is no blurb on the book which throughout maintains a dignified silence since he knows that 'people hate the grief of others.' These poems register loss and mark the residue of guilt amidst the isolation of mourning. In this respect the book performs a major service as a healing work to the reader.

The berating of God or the lack of God reveals weak theology in the pseudo-ironic, "Christmas Letter to God the Father". The intention seemed to have been a summing up on the author's grasp of the concept: 'if God has a mysterious Grand Design' (he finds none!) which comes from a dull poem about the death of an Auschwitz survivor. Rothenberg and Snodgrass are among the few who have achieved post-Holocaust poetry. The "8 Poems About Women" reach the earth-shattering cliché that women are 'adept/At changing the subject'. The short pieces, "Power", "Death", "Progress", and "Smiles" are mere squibs. The few rhyming poems are strangulated by their rhymes.

"Intimations of a Fall" is very thin sham-philosophical speculation which is grumpy, agnostic, pessimistic, and misanthropic. The fall here is the collapse of poetry since there is no fire, passion or even vigour. These nervously lined poems that are far too prescriptive for their own good. Cronin's viewpoint journalism clashed uneasily if ungainly with his Audenesque poems which basically clamour of leftist-liberal politics. Like some other poets who succumbed to the arts job and committees in pursuit of the role of cultural commissar, he exalts the collective, namely the Abominable Aosdána, and is a torq-bearer of this institution, crowned by its self-regulating hierarchy. Poets are ultimately judged not on how many committees they serve but on their poems alone.

Harmon's octogenarian year is celebrated by Salmon with this New & Selected plus a tribute book Honouring the Word edited by Barbara Brown where Heaney, Kinsella, Montague and Longley line out in his praise. Poems about childhood, school ("Schoolboy") and the Clergy in "O Christ Almighty" traverse terrain that fitted out Clarke in battle stride. In Harmon's overtly crafted work such subject matter is remote from more contemporary concerns. Joyce laid to rest much anguish that may not require further visitation and purgation. Harmon's poems often fixed to an anecdote with the dying fall of the Irish lyric, as in the title poem. Irony does well in "A Politician's Defence" more than in "Lost for Words", the burlesque "Song of Our Time" and the bizarre "Dear Editor". "The Making of a Poet. A Wife's Complaint" has dubious authenticity. The translations are clean enough such as "Créde's Lament", however his strophe and choice of diction had better maintain its own inner aesthetic laws: 'Sad is the cry the thrush makes in Druim Caín,/no less sad the blackbird's voice in Leitir Laíg.' Mallarmé's dictate holds: poems are made of words (that is the measure!) so one questions 'cry', 'voice' and 'no less sad'. He does well with Ana Romaní, rendered as "Because I know You Sometimes Leave": 'I would descend through darkness and pain/to be the limb from the past/that softly trembles against you/when you turn/from silence to be part of me.' Harmon in actual terms with a long career as

252

professor, editor and critic is a 'young' emerging poet.

—*Books Ireland* 2010

OF CONCEPT AND IDEA

Country Music: Uncollected Poems 1974-1989 Gerald Dawe (Starling Press)

The Sun-Fish Eiléan Ní Chuilleanáin (Gallery Press)

At Grattan Road Gerard Hanberry (Salmon Poetry)

The Owl and the Pussycat and other poems Tom Mathews Dedalus Press

When the Air Inhales You Máighréad Medbh (Arlen House)

Next to Nothing Chris Agee (Salt Publishing)

At a distance, this looks substantial. The illustration of Oliver Jeffers Song Writing Machine depicts a guitar with machine heads and strings connected to an Imperial Portable Typewriter, a benign surrealism blending strumming and typing. Hard to see how this connects to Dawe's 'uncollection': a handful of poems from the time span. Cultural historian, Terence Brown provides a perspective on the poet's Northern roots, from the Luftwaffe bombings of Belfast to Coleraine University in 1971 and a loose connection to Ivan Morrison. Alas, everything cultural from the six counties is linked to Van, sooner or later. Browne suggests that this trajectory endows Dawe with 'a war haunted poetry'. His work 'knows the world is a dangerous place'. As a fellow Nordy (Dubliners' name from NI folk) the present reviewer is not privy to such special pleading since Ulster or the North or whatever faction claims to name it, remains a confused landmass vied for by various tribes and allegiances. This gives the location its complex identity as political work-in-progress, a mongrel of two large islands. This debate is not prime in Dawe's poems, except obliquely.

Dawe is not actually dependent on his homeland (if Northerners have such a place?) for subject and theme, though these pieces are locatable to his native hearth with a coda piece (three pages +) in prose: a parody of Joyce's Molly Bloom Soliloquy as cultural adoption, since Joyce and Belfast were never bedfellows. Nor does it sit well here in this hardback that Brown calls 'chapbook' for some reason. Brown rightly asserts that Dawe writes from refuge and shelter, however claiming a European agenda for him is scarcely true. "Late News" is all too Northern, and Northern writing of this species is inadvertently polarized, it literally comes with the territory:

convent girls turn in sleep as the sea

throws itself against DANGEROUS ROCKS

and the students climb home by a locked church

to late news about the weekend's disturbances

Similarly, "Castaways" peeks into 'the spotless guest house foyer' where some play dominoes, the reading matter is Wilkie Collins's The Moonstone, 'and from the hoarding's YE MUST BE BORN AGAIN' glares through in the typography echoing legions of NI slogans. "History Class, 1985" is NI irony par excellence; it might even be explosively overloaded. The warscape that Browne's sepulchral tones suggest is hinted at merely, since you cannot be NI-er and overt about anything, in "On Early Trains" but it is the local war: 'Between the border and here/cows stray over mined fields-/soldiers are farmers, farmers soldiers/and a bread van's upturned in a clammy lane.' Oh aye: clammy all right for both Sammy and Seamus. You cannot have valid nature poetry in NI, the land does not give way to such longing and adoration unless the variety of nature nostalgia poetry. Uladh was always at battle internally and otherwise from ancient times onwards. In NI, it is always the people, places, demarcations and its Nature Poetry only rings nostalgic: Dawe doesn't do nostalgia and rightly so. In "Elocution Day" the cultural parameters evoke Longfellow, Robin Hood and Churchill as Nobel Prize winning historian. Belfast as university of life easily prepares the candidate for Berlin, Beirut, or Kashmir.

As one expects: a tense collection, abstract, don't expect rationality and in a diction where the poet is never visible. This allows her to flaunt with anecdote, a dangerous departure for any poem but Ní Chuilleanáin utilizes the storyline for a wider purpose and does not render comfortable closures. Hence in "On Lacking the Killer Instinct" her father's fleeing a Crossley full of soldiers in 1922 posits life's twists and turns; the result was a happy escape as strangers momentarily make him part of their family pretending he just arrived home for supper. This makes the poet declare that her coursing through life displays caution with less of the hare, less of the revolutionary. It is not a feminist position so much as an artistic position. Kith and kin are subject matter in a piéce d'occasion for her son Niall and his marriage to Xenya in 2009. Such a piece works beyond being token while searching headstones in "Ballinascarthy" gives up various ancestors. She grapples with abtractions in "The Litany": nothing is tidied up, nothing resolved. The experience of reading her demands neither codependency, nor easy solutions:

As every new day waking finds its pitch

Selecting a fresh angle, so the sun

Hangs down veils, so the old verbs

Change their invocation and their mood.

It is a Heraclitean worldview with a hint of the lyrical-transcendental in the title poem of four movements where awe at the existence of sharks in formation builds to a cosmic line, 'the ocean swathing the globe is a snake mask'. Nature as imagined through the eyes of the sharks gives her 'a visitation' 'Like the faces of my two parents looking at me/From the other side, from the outside/of the misty screen of winter.' It is just as well that such is vouchsafed since as a whole this is a tough unstinting collection, not betrayed by title or content, as in 'The Cold', 'In the Desert' and particularly 'The Sister' while in 'The Married Women' complex imagery maintains the mystery: 'The woman turned and under the towel as if/Shrouded by the mantled oxter/Of a heroic bird was a girl's mother-of-pearl sheen,/A girl's hesitant body, sheltered by the bird's broad wing.' "The Copious Dark" maintains the same disparateness, the connections made only in poetry, life being something else or mere raw material. She will not explain because she cannot explain, 'Why the wasps are asleep in the dark in their numbered holes/And the lights shine all night in the hospital corridors?'

Tom makes the transition from cartoonist to cartoonist-in-verse, or it more cartoonist-in-worse. He is no Lear (Edward) or Carroll (Lewis), in point of fact, or pint of fact as Tom might have it, the best thing here is the owl on the cover from Andrew Folan. But look-a-here, Uncle Tom will have his Irish Times coterie to cosset him, survive, and badmouth the reviewer. There is some admiration (grovel, grovel) for "Villon" from which: 'He gives his blessing, for a blessing's free./No wounds of nails are in his well-heeled palms./I'll rest my back against this dying tree/And starve before I'll ask the cunt for alms.' Or you could sing along to "Tomorrow", '"Sit down and I'll get us a couple of beers,/Here, borrow my hanky and dry your tears,/It'll all be the same in a hundred years/And things will be better tomorrow, my darling,/Things will be better tomorrow."' Be-bum!

Overall, though a bit of a travesty, if deliberately on this rhymester's part, the use of Proper Nouns is just eye-candy: Napoleon, Joyce, Beckett, Shaw, T. S. Eliot, Henry James, Queneau, and Li Po. Besides being inherently anti-intellectual, these bits and pieces, flotsam and jetsam reek of the hangover recollected in sobriety. Some of the puns are post-Myles, the jokes undergrad-hashish induced laughter that a day later is unfunny such as "Gogo's Song": 'A tree. The wind. A moon. Ho hum./Don't suppose Godot's going to come.' Marginally worse is "Young Men in Spats": '—You look like Bertie Wooster with that hoe./—What hoe?/—Now you're talking like Bertie Wooster.' In this vein, you can have "False Start": 'I and Pangur Bán my dog.' Ho hum, ho hum. His parodies are not up to much as in the William Carlos Williams one. However, these collected beer mat jottings are ideal reading in the pub but perhaps should end up on the floor with the night's sweepings? Speaking of which "Mengele" reaches regrettable schadenfreude; who would want to write two lines on the Nazis' evil pogroms: 'He sees them sweep the leaves in piles,/Remembers Auschwitz. And he smiles.'

Hanberry has a penchant for the colloquial, and be it admitted the parochial: these are not his strengths. He seems to mistrust his inner critic. One can often find his sense of conclusion leaving the reader with the agony of excision and the work such as it is after his efforts. It is too dangerous leaving the dialect of the tribe unpurified: poetry is not what people say, however extraordinary it sounds and the 'modern thing' has in part stooped very low towards conversational transcription. Modernists instigated this more than the English Romantics, and as T. S. Eliot rightly said 'no vers is libre for the man who wants to do a good job'. The real deal is to make it seem colloquial and conversational but not attempt verisimilitude. Thousands of court testimonies are made to sound funny or quirky by tabloids but even they require careful editing. Poetry is super-journalism, in the least ingredient. Hence, "Speech, After Dinner" transposes a bit of Diogenes' biography and sideswipes capitalism not that capitalism ever gets hurt: instead, it hurts poets of a certain type who ultimately want martyrdom like Baudelaire. 'The Great Alexander once asked him what he wanted-/For you to move, replied the relaxing Cynic,/you're blocking my sun.' Hanberry does not go so far as to implicate capitalism in charging us the sun, moon, and stars but he comes close enough. Social realism peaks in "Francis Bacon at The Tate" with the hard-pressed taxi driver over the hill and the victim of being a charioteer through the urban jungle. As aging novice taken to hackney man for a living, this avoids sentimentality, though the average taxi driver has to be a closet axeman on his rounds. Again, this poem of concept and idea maybe overworked.

Hanberry presents an eclectic collection lurching from dull rurality to Miss Hottie in "The Scene" where the lazy lushes with 'their wolverine eyes ravishing every sweet inch of her' leads up to the conclusion where a mere metaphor of life as movie scene ends with the cry of 'cut'. In the same vein "Fatal Distractions" gives a version of Innisfree with pretense to wishing for a hermit's life: 'spend my days with ink and quill,/never have to pay a bill,/reject the flesh, the pub at night-/and then, perhaps, I'll start to write.' While "Meet the Punctuations" is comic verse where the exclamation mark becomes, 'The sunbathing stud,/the most erotic of the Punctuations. Look at him standing there,/proud, erect, stiff as a poker.' "Ode to a Rejected Cliché" mines the same territory less funnily, and also "Wake Talk". Between rural, colloquial and witty there is a darker thread in Hanberry that requires a sharper technique. This might well be his greatest challenge as tragedy and the void demand nerve and sinew, breakdown and recovery but still the hints in "Lifers" augurs well for his work, 'their past crimes far from glamorous,/no jewel heists, no ripping off Las Vegas./Lifers now, doomed to serve out their time/with bucket and mop'. "Alone" can hardly be said to drip with oozings of cosmic solitude yet it touches some vein: 'It comes when she is standing/at her kitchen sink, evening/tight against the pane, washing/one cup, one plate, one knife, one fork, one spoon.'

Dedicated to the astrologer, counsellor, and healer Pat Griffin, this is strongly familial and marks indelibly major changes in Medbh's life due to the passing of her sister Máire Buckley (d. 2006). Part One entitled "Saturn's Little Colours" has various poems such as to her sons Aonghus and Fionn which manipulate myth for her purposes, and "Caged" that positively postulates 'the bones are inside the skin./We are already part outside our prison.' She is good on the manipulation of children by consumerism in "Little Darling" while the erotic enters "The Photograph". However the real stuff comes through the suffering over her sister's departure which she entitled Eitilt (Flight) the first piece in the sequence controlling the

259

floodgates of emotion: 'who knew all we can see is only a speck/on an infinite canvas, and joining the dots/is the work of a million lifetimes in thought.' It might be expected to pursue this trajectory in finding a language for 'The most profound mystery/ is that she is gone' ("No Happy Returns") but surprisingly this observes a grief through its stemming. 'Through a fall of tears I touch your hair./My hand swims in its silk/and I stroke it goodbye.' ("In the Morgue"). "How dare the world, that promised fun,/ deprive me of my precious one…' ("Rant"). She breaks effectively with the verbal music that is oft too precocious in part one of this collection and finds a diction that disregards such poeticisms: 'You had wanted to move, have a house in the country./You've almost achieved it, but at such a price!' ("Visiting the Grave"). Medbh cannot deny her grief nor transpose it beyond what it is in the sequence: this proves to be a fittingly muted aesthetic: "Your grave is swaddled in a blanket of flowers./It's silly to hope they're keeping you warm./I don't want to leave because, tell the truth,/I'm not coping. I've lost my way." ("Lost").

She has not flinched in recording what is effective diary-poetry, and in "What Happens", she questions the core of life, birth, and death without any conclusion. Then miraculously the sequence shifts to a new perspective that comes across as valid for her: "Guide or not, you had led this sceptic/into the shocking realm of peace." ("Hypnotherapy") The sequence rich in longing finds its conclusion, if such a sequence could ever find closure, yet collections obey banal laws like poetry sequences. The closing poem "Accompanied" is in Amsterdam, the city as human creation, but for Medbh filled with 'everything natural'. She has re-awakened from the dangerous plight of grief and her sister being dead is close. It is a Heideggerean conclusion, the dead are always knocking on our heads, bumping into us, they are noisy and they will never leave us alone, so she is not abandoned: 'You grow from the air in fine cafés,/summoned by art; as the forms of the great/rise from the landscape and re-tell it.'

("Accompanied").

Agee's grief for a lost daughter of tender years, Miriam Aoife Agee (1997-2001) cannot but interrogate the pages of his collection. He spares the reader somewhat with his dignity but behind the poems is the volcanic force of what has impacted. Immediately is the shock of recognition that intense suffering lessens one's ability to connect with art and as Camus asserted takes away the taste for literature. Agee lists war dead including a friend lost in Vietnam: 'Robert Ransom, whose death's single/rippling heartbreak brushed my boyhood/in May of '68.' This is from the five-part "Heartlands" sequence that charts various wars, 'death-soaked Gettysburg,/the kitsch of Korea's, a World War Two/work-in-progress...'. Such acclamations render everything naturally in grief or rather unnaturally upside down, enmeshed in futility and disdain for life. A variety of writing that is difficult since it has a private dimension at odds with the necessary public element involved in publication: quite a dilemma.

Most of all the loss of Miriam seeps, saturates through what is here amidst the more known names of Auschwitz and W.G. Sebald (1944-2001) who not only informs a poem dedicated to him: 'everything/Is happening in a single world-image like tens of millions/Of words in a Babel of thousands of tongues coexisting/In its archive of consciousness'. For Sebald the unremitting evil of the Nazi holocaust haunted his life, and may have like a prime Holocaust victim, Primo Levi hastened his death through symbiotic survivor's guilt. So much cries out for release with grief even the life of the survivor. Such an extreme is beyond the dicta of critics even Adorno's oft quoted remark of poetry impossible after Auschwitz. It is not art; it is life that is at stake for Agee, and paradoxically the death of the poet's daughter. You have to balance this fact and poetry, depending on your aesthetic. From such a de profundis whether it is to your taste as to its quality or not, whether a fit vehicle for grief's moods, while all that holds it from spooling irrationally out of control is its own necessity, its own concrete expression when words alone are all, and not so much certain good, as uncertain. Sebald's Campo Santa is the last item (Agee at this point being speechless as it were): 'Where will they all go, the dead of Buenos Aires and Sao Paulo, of Mexico City, Lagos and Cairo, Toyko, Shanghai and Bombay? Very few of them, probably, into a cool grave.'

Agee makes his poems to Miriam, as if for her eyes: a child's eyes. This innocence is the hallmark of them "Your face": 'Swims/in the window/where I wave/at the childminder's/new child'. Agee goes as gently as he may and as close as he can into that good night, "A whole"/ lifetime/without Dotie/like the rainbow's/adieu/over the Village/bridge/the afternoon/of your death.'

—*Books Ireland* 2010

TIME IS THE CLASS

Painting Rain Paula Meehan

Diversifications: Mayakovsky, Brecht & Me Augustus Young

The Woman Who Lived Her Life Backwards Ann Leahy

Making Music Patrick Cotter

Starting from Anywhere Lex Runciman

'The magpies sound like flying castanets'—No they don't, they do to a Spanish child or a poet fixing a bit of a metaphor that might sound catchy. You don't need special effects 'flying' around in a poem like 'Death of a Field'; in any event a pretty heavy handed piece of Religio-Eco. Meehan is not an eco-preacher or eco-fascist as far as one can make out but may have an inner eco-priestess screaming to be let loose. Maybe the planet can take care of itself without more eco-cults. 'The Wolf Tree' attempts that most dangerous of all pastimes the exposition of some wisdom but here it is sham-metaphysics and in any event lacks sentience.

She is not averse to awful Irish lyrical droning as in 'Tanka': 'This coming winter/he will dream the vast ocean/back into his eyes./The morning he'll rise to leave/his eyes will be deepest blue.' Do you get it: after this somnambulant dive into the oceanic dreamscape, his eyes will be bluer because the sea is blue! Scientists can prove it. 'This coming winter'? Winter is coming, it will come, it will arrive, it always gets here, it is not public transport: it is a season, they tend to come along naturally. Similarly, 'Hagiography' is a 'Michael Hartnett poem'. If Michael Hartnett had a free pint for every elegy that has followed his passing, he would be the director of Guinnesses-in Heaven three times over. She uses an anecdote about a schoolchild who lives in a street named after the poet, hence, 'I Live in Michael Hartnett.' Get it: it should work for every street in the world named after any person.

Her sonnets are best passed over quickly, they reek of cosmopolitan pub talk such as 'cars are stuck in jams or droning home'. What banality. The only readable poem here is a villanelle since the discipline stretches her to achieve something, even if it is not a strict villanelle in 'Quitting the Bars': 'Quitting's hard but staying sober's harder'.

One has to tread very softly, as most of the collection is autobiographical-memoir intentionally; heavily anecdotal, and it must be said, it parades poverty. It is fine parading poverty but this is not exclusive to her: the poverty club is the largest club around, membership ever accessible, the new members' office never closes. This said, there is real pain on show here, the genuine pain of marital disharmony with divided loyalties for siblings as well as warring parents. There is nothing that is not deeply felt in all this travail of human suffering but one wonders at it being chopped up into verse lines when often they impede the reader from getting the grim facts that are really in effect, prose. Prose could have called up a greater logic and narrative flow for her whereas in her narrative poetry there are elisions and stilted forward progressions at vital points: it all seems overworked too. Longfellow's 'Evangeline' and Wordsworths' 'Michael' are harrowing long narrative poems. The form does not work well in this era it requires a formidable energizing aesthetic, metric and a formalism that has become fustian. Meehan admits in her coda that gives the collection its title, 'I am trying to paint rain'. She is quite exigent, to her credit. It is so very difficult to paint the rain that you must implicate rain without using any; art suggests without being specific, resulting in effects that are not present except by accumulation, even in photography. The art of poetry must reach for the sky, must reach for hell or at least create these illusions with maximum intensity of language and find catharsis throughout. Some professors translate Aristotle's word for catharsis as refinement. Meehan struggles with the difficulty of conveying (her italics): 'When trouble comes to your door he/doesn't knock and he doesn't wipe his feet—' One must

264

commend her for trying to paint rain especially when it does not seem to bring mercy.

Young finds himself old. His muse comes from the east and the approaching sunset. He gracefully admits that 'Mayakovsky and Brecht gave me courage'—the tone is set by M&B as Young translates from their work. His stage managed anger is dissipated in felicity and wit as in the poem-sequence of his own work entitled 'The Long Habit of Living'. This might seem extravagant as he fitfully indulges himself, as in 'Swat in the Autumn of Life': 'As you grow older the flies/linger longer on the nose./Why? Because the hand slows.' Daringly he asserts that, 'The cancer on my grave's a cactus'—Doctor Johnson rightly asserted that we admit to the end but the how and the where is less discernible until afterwards.

I owe my corps more than a throw of the dice.

Some analyse écologique would be nice.

One needs to get into Young's crank-angst to find the laughs. He aches with old age and suddenly there is nothing to laugh at, 'No mad arias, only some quiet weeping'—which is the refrain in 'Melancholy Truce'. His language is unobtrusive, there is no droning. He deals in delivery not self-conscious deliberation. One wishes him more mad arias and less weeping, or a bearable blend of both. The main ballast in this collection comes from Mayakovsky's 'A Cloud in Pants'. There is no fuss about fidelity to translation or the usual apologies by poets for content lost in translation which is usually a tedious self-admiring practice as with someone taking ten minutes to describe a simple poem that takes less than a minute to read. You can expect Mayakovsky to arrive with truckloads of nihilism. Young does not sugar the pill. The Tetraptych he leans on comes from 1915 where each section in on the attack, first off contra (romantic) Love that fares badly as you might expect, since who needs 'a red hot coal' for a heart anyway. The art of poetry is derided 'on the omission in/Homer and Ovid of lowlife characters/like us. Sooty skin pocked like the moon.' Society gets it where 'Sunset/bleeds to death'. Those executed should serve a useful purpose

When hanging

from the gallows

to jingle,

'Drink

Van Houten's

Cocoa'

Youngs's use of Brecht is skilful and equally sidesplitting on occasion. Old friends meet in the street and nervously talk of umbrellas, 'and enduring friendship'. This poem entitled 'Friends' concludes, 'More would be unbearable'. 'On Being Important' is dark realism turned into comedy. Brecht's song translated as 'What Keeps Man Alive' (1928) states: 'What keeps mankind alive is keeping humanity repressed.' It is all satisfyingly savage. Things tense up with Brecht's annoyance over Walter Benjamin's suicide, there is, dare one admit, a moral

Your last idea was your worst.

Now if you were here I would

tear it apart, remind you

of your responsibility,

not just to yourself, Comrade.

It sounds like a health and safety poster but this is a serious subject. Brecht did not do any cultural dancing at the crossroads, or drone with cheap consolation not even a glass of vodka is offered, just the intoxication of his work

Starting life in sorrow

I grew up into gloom.

Happiness where are you?

You had better come soon

It's not quite Jem Casey, Flann O'Brien's People's poet but then again the Irish who are experts at galgenhumor do not deliver much of this brew in poetry. Young brings in the goods and the cover itself has an irony with Huib Fens' oil reproduction, 'Tall Writing Table'. There is something else for Arts Council Grant Aid: tall tables for writers' workshops, longer cables for laptops!

The title poem here indicates Leahy's strengths or otherwise. What exalts the poem that seems like a conventional love-poem is the ghostly triumph over adversity. The speaker leaves the personal impasse unstated. The metaphors are 'saved' by her overall production. Do sheep have a 'startled look' after shearing; do cobwebs unravel 'on the breeze'? Metaphors must not have the reader cogitating about their accuracy and goodness of fit: they must simply work. Why does she feel the need to invert the final line: 'I would every day grow young'?

As a shadow unpeels itself

across a mountain, or a red balloon

drifts from it's owner's grasp,

I am in love again. In love

with the startled look

sheep have after shearing,

Her worst features are Alice Taylorisms: poems of rural nostalgia and description that might otherwise adorn a calendar oozing sentimental verse. Nothing wrong with a swoon down memory lane over a cup of a tea and a chocy biscuit, however, Alice Taylor does not deliver prose poetry like Baudelaire and St John Perse. When

Leahy turns in this direction, she is doling out comfort: poetry is not about comfort like a blanket. Poems that come under this heading are 'Mince Customer' and 'Fair Game' the latter about shotguns as ornaments. 'In the Pressure Cooker' has fatal usage 'appliances umbilically attached to the wall'. This is metaphor gone mad. No, not, even acceptable in the science fiction of eugenics. The bacon slicer school of Irish poetry and homage to rurality presents a fantasy about the Arcardian Idyll that is untrue.

There are less poeticisms in 'The Twisted Thread' and the diction does not drone. Droning is a million miles away from poetry. Irish poets should suffocate their speaking voice when writing. 'VW Polo 1990-2002' is subtle, purveying a lost love that lingers in her psyche. 'Lime Kiln Country' attempts a refrain 'I come from Limestone Country' and dangerously veers into rhetoric. Post-Catholic Ireland subsumes 'Living with St. Patrick' and 'His cloak is snooker-table green'. There is a calm satisfying eroticism and wit in 'The Worry Chest' and 'Cellulite Bandits': 'We are the cellulite bandits. We threaten with a flash of thigh.' 'A Good Rogeting' achieves the same

I can fall asleep over a phrase whose

meaning remains a stranger and wake

in the morning with Roget's Thesaurus

poking me urgently in the back.

Cotter's angelic expostulations do not always hit the poetry bullseye and he doles out some metaphors at their worst, such as 'but their wings kissed like fluttering eyelashes'—he lazily falls into this after the mention of butterflies. Similarly the lines: 'and we awaken to find ourselves/treading on our nightmares'. Ouch! Yeats gave license to writing 'tread on my dreams' but enough. The problem here is 'over the top' stylistics, cryptic language, and overt surrealism that makes for a queer mixture if not a concoction of language. At his Bleakean best, he just about gets away with it in 'Thoughts of the Rich Young Aristocrat After Meeting Jesus' who 'knows a girl of wealth with eyes of fire'

I think of her now in her patio of sunflowers,

Imagining the sapphire-laden casket I might bring to her,

Or the coolest purple silk from the shoulders of an oriental

princess

With her gold and her silver must she too tumble into fire,

While the whores with whom he cavorts can breathe forever

in his company?

The heavy irony in 'On Not Being Kavanagh' (title adapted from the movie 'Being John Malkovich'?) uses suffused language in marked contrast to Kavanagh's Byzantium of the Bog and Begorrah. The poetry scene is dealt with in "This Is Not A Metropolitan Press Poem"

These days too will pass, he mutters

as the Collected MacNeice tugs the threads

holding in place his duffle coat pocket.

MacNeice spent a lot of time treading on nightmares in his duffle coat! The long sequence 'Journal of a Failed Angel Whisperer' is a counterpoint to the angelic theme about motel life in lurid Las Vegas. Las Vegas is more disappointing that 42nd Street, worse still is the movie Leaving Las Vegas. Cotter doesn't manage to present American luridness. The sequence is too obscure and he presents privacy in poetry that is ultimately far too aloof. The more conventional 'Rumours' achieves something about unexplained deaths. There is some rightness of craft in 'Courthouse Steps', however his 'Pigeons waddle aimlessly, shitting everywhere/while amid the blindfold statuary of Justice/jackdaws consult.' The personification of jackdaws as legal eagles is obvious.

Cotter's closing departure is a bizarre Celtic mythology where the most successful poem is 'The Wedding Night of Aoife and Lir': 'Our bed was spread with swatches of red linen,/Silver-stitched with Newgrange spirals of sun and moon.' Cotter is not the worst with his zany surrealism merging into the exotic. Thankfully, he does not drone. Diction might yet come into his ken, if he can get a proper grip of it beyond the ghosts of Blake and Yeats. Still, these two over-towering influences serve him in good stead. His artwork 'Assemblage No 3' adorns the cover. Another clue to his method: found objects of no apparent connection with their red cloth background, from what one can make out in reproduction. Despite the jarring abstractions, one can admire his work that does not emerge on a single reading: a favourable portent. Mr Cotter is not derivative: just poetically disheveled at present.

Interesting collection that derives from art, poetry and life, getting the balance right while keeping the mystery. Runciman is personal without being cloying and breaks into a satisfactory narrative, painlessly admitting that he has lived with 'the stale joke' that 'my real parents were Marilyn and Elvis'. 'In the Blessed Absence of Television' he confronts his orphan past, 'As for secrets,/some we keep, and some keep us'. One of the stronger poems "My Father Is Telling Me The Story" has the telling irony of never knowing his father and mother. Place is celebrated alongside literary place such as Little Gidding that gave its title to one of T. S. Eliot's 'Four Quartets'. There is a poem of place in homage to Tintern Abbey. An Emily Dickinson parody mirrors his predecessor with strophes and dashes. More than anything, Runciman is a modern pantheist as evidenced in many poems, such as 'Broadmoor'. Nature is not given in nature-notes but rendered as central source:

One year snow fell taller than I was,

burying every bush: a squeaky white,

a cold, unfillable quiet

His language is self-assured, non-intrusive, and works though this quietude:

and in Ecuador a high, white-seared geography of cloud

slides over a hill of coffee flowering.—'How Dawn Begins'

American arcana abound, such as Chesterfields. The sense of the fleeting now, the burning moment at ease with the panoply of History is in 'At Castlerigg, Cumbria'. To him the world is to be found every place, as in 'What Was There Before and Is Still There'. He is very much at home in the world and this victory over self and incertitude rings through many of the poems, such as 'First Light': 'Who was it said the world is too much with us?/Who was it said we must risk delight?' His italics are quotes that make a paradox, linking Wordsworth and Jack Gilbert. Runciman can be classified as post-romantic. His titles come from writers' work that engulf his own lines, making him postmodernist also. He is sure of much as in 'If Ending Is Air, Then Why Not Happiness': 'The Book ends./It rests on the table, a planet, as Wallace/Stevens said.'

As you read his poems, you forget who wrote them. He loses himself amidst voices other than his own. A Protean poet who might well believe, like in the poem 'The World Has Never Been Described Anywhere': 'Viva la vida, says Frida Kahlo, and who'd say no?/I should read more, work and listen harder: time/is the class, earth the ripe impossible school.' It's alarmingly positive, isn't it? These poems validify this aesthetic. His front cover photograph of a used-books bookstore in a crumbling Georgian pile is defiant like Frida: live the dream!

—*Books Ireland* 2009

BEATNIKS, POST-ANGSTIANS, WITS AND NOSTALGICS

Elegies and Epiphanies: Selected Poems Hugh McFadden (Lagan Press)

North of Nowhere Gary Allen (Lagan Press)

The King of Suburbia Iggy McGovern (Dedalus)

Trapping a Ghost Nessa O'Mahony (Bluechrome Publishing)

The cover of McFadden's book, with Remington, sets the tone of the flaneur poet in Dublin's 1960s. His company is Kavanagh, Durcan, Jordan — McFadden is editor of the recent *Crystal Clear: The Selected Prose of John Jordan* (Lilliput Press, 2006). All these gallants feature in the poems with a soundtrack, as it were, from Bob Dylan, Buddy Holly, Billie Holiday, John Lennon, George Harrison and Luke Kelly. Typical of his generation, there is a decided preference for only half of the Beatles! Kavanagh, Jordan, Hartnett and even Christopher Marlowe have elegies thrust upon them.

Most of the work seeks epiphanies, particularly though the epigrammatic pieces, and also the haikus. With McFadden there is a dilemma: whether one is to admire the short or the more lengthy poems; distinct differences lie between the two: the shorts are often squibs or snippets, arresting as in 'Sudden Death', yet jettatura; overall there is a deeply personal shuddering reaction to poetry. He is stark in form; the respect for poetry reveals an intense introversion, as if poetry itself is rare, if not impossible. The effects of language alone are an eclipsing achievement, dispelling everything else in a method that recalls Robert Creeley *(vide* 'Poem' from 1964). The longer pieces just about allow more contact with the poet.

In the visionary poem 'Folk Lore' you are eyeball to eyeball with Blake, and God: two realities, the latter extremely pervasive in

272

McFadden. Meanwhile, in 'Demolition Dublin (1969)', 'Sixties politics rules okay?'

> someday the voices of the men
>
> of no property will be heard
>
> again: and then, my canine friend,
>
> it will be the long road for the old dog.

Dublin is given a cold eye in 'Bar Obscene'

> Take your pick—a wealthy
> lecher patting his corpulence
> as he eyes the scheming
> innocent with the thighs, or
> the boastful, fashionable
>
> murderer, red dye in his hair.

The entrancement of place is a rather successful string to his lyre —'Elegy for a City' centring on Rome might well be his best performance 'Rome of the small hills and large churches'). Otherwise, McFadden has what Joyce described as 'the deep unending ache of love' for family, in this case, his daughter Catherine, addressed as Kate elsewhere. It is difficult to 'use' the hearth for subject matter — 'Letter from the Hibernian Way' keeps it poise and perhaps avoids the mawkish...

> May you sip the sweet
> elation of love that has
> no reason:

like the dance that we used to do,
like the dance that we used to do.

In the end politics is healthily pervasive; he keeps faithful with the down and out, and shuns the rulers in the 1960s mode with a beatnik poem, 'Message To A Fearful America':

> Don't listen to
> Bush
>
> listen to Elvis...

And, from 'War Rhetoric & Rock 'n' Roll':

> No, I'm much too old now
> to listen to the same old lies
> about war.

Gary Allen's title makes one think of (closely) similar titles: *North of Boston* and *North* from Frost and Heaney, respectively. Here the title has a chill, due to its post-Angst pall which is where Allen's psyche seems to be pitched. His Northern Ireland cannot be the backward nightmare glance, yet he evokes some of this in 'On Walking Londonderry's Walls' where he can find no mainstay in the turmoil of the past, even if it was all very grim:

> These martyrs, noses and
> testicles seared off with hot
> iron,
> hearts exploding in the
> flames...

He is accurate in outlining Northern gore ('Eden'):

> What has failed moves quicker than a
> printing press from city, to country, to
> continent
>
> like the sudden surge of blood from a
> severed head, or the interpretation of
> the Bible.

The ghost of the troubles appear but none too regularly, and the references are usually from unconnected and other unrelated amorphous images, as in 'Interface' —

> You devoured a pregnant hare

caught on the wasteground between warring estates...

Otherwise, grandparents are quite prevalent in 'Beneath the Skin'—'making whistles from split grass stalks', which is a typical example of his use of the memorable line. This is grand for the isolated line but what it does for the entire poem, while arresting attention, may not fuse cumulatively. There is nothing 'wrong' generally with his performance. He seems committed to a certain deliberate intrigue, as in 'Standing Stones at Crebilly'. For Allen, the poem is a language machine. Strange to find French aesthetics in a man from Ballymena, but there you go: Ireland's hope has often been internationalism whether from within or from without.

Ultimately, what you discover in Allen, is the McGuckian obscure; and the enemy of understanding is implied to be reason. It is T S Eliot's old chestnut about poetry communicating before it is fully comprehended or understood. This is acceptable and has always been, except that language lost in knots of language with wild shifts of meaning asserts the irrational as sentient, but may not always make sense on the page, and any reader might well ask: what? And answer: *so what*. Poetry has also got a bad name from such poetry; however, poetry cannot afford to exclude this from its precipices since so many able practitioners fell, or fall into this fruitful labyrinth of bewildering detours from 'traditional poetry'; poetry coming from the opposite direction, its struggle with language's limitations in order to communicate the abstractions of complex experience, life and reality. But it is no secret that all poetry worth the name is a desperate struggle with language.

McGovern is another Ballymena poeticiser, but in a different vein than Allen; this is of the funny bone variety with leanings towards Durcan and Gavin Ewart. There is a fascination with Fifties and Sixties Ireland and Bally-go-backwards, as revealed by the cult status of *Father Ted;* the fad might pass since it is really a sort of indirect praise and nostalgia for the good old, bad old days. But might the jokes here not merit re-reading once the witticisms are registered? Octavio Paz in an interview 'outlawed' poets who were really closet-stand-up comedians, or words to that effect. Much of McGovern, to be frank, is corn.

I will open an Irish Pub

above in Tiananmen Square

inscrutably named *The Great Hunger*

"Get down this very instant on two knees

and say a God-Forgive-You, heartfelt *deckett!"*

(You'd found me reading 'thon black Protestant' Beckett.)

Long past the time of seaside rock

and schoolbook rhyme. Let us unlock

the graveyard, chime the old church clock.

The three extracts quoted above, from 'The View from Dundrum', 'A Rosary for a Sainted Aunt' and 'Time Up' respectively, sound wise, but when you examine them what they are saying is plainly untrue. Maybe it is better to be Lewis Carroll and make rhymes out of the ridiculous. Death might be ridiculous but such lines on death are ludicrous. No one has ever had to unlock the graveyard.

While this material might do well at a reading, audiences do vary, and poetry streamlined exclusively for laughter easily reveals the twee and the silly. It often ends up sounding like whimsy or aspiring to the Pam Ayres Hall of Fame. Even Betjeman, at his best, only 'leant on' humour, but often achieved a deeper layer. This is not to castigate McGovern; if he can make people laugh, he is the King of Suburbia; unfortunately, his line in satire at times reads like undergraduate literary jesting, the sort that makes fellow students classify you as a bit of a drole, as in 'From the Greek':

> ...but then again no man
> steps twice into the same
> flea-pit.

Well yea, if you know about Heraclitus's dictum this causes a very minor hee-haw. O Iggnominous bard whose varse might find McGovernance in *Private Eye* and Punch, perhaps?

Ghosts abide in Nessa O'Mahony's work. Great distances are travelled from Ireland to England, while the short sequence 'Venice Postcards' is by far the most satisfactory performance in the third and concluding section, which includes some translations. Of which, more in conclusion. Section 1 is haunted but tends towards the fatal nostalgic, where — among various elegies — the emotion does not quite fit the language (or is it the other way around?). Nothing utterly falls down in the execution, it is just that flaccidity occurs, marring the solemn matter of intention. However, Section 2 is a bold, adventurous, even experimental sequence with a keen title, 'Writing Slope'. It is epistolary verse with a narrative, avoiding even rudimentary sequential storyline, adding to the intrigue, yet at times made this reader yearn for an introductory note. Presumably, the base material is actual letters — if not, her achievement is all the greater. O'Mahony's lines manage to draw you into the dangerous revolutionary decade of the Irish twentieth century, amidst the courtship and marriage of Anne Flynn of Kiltimagh to Captain Patrick Breen, formerly of the Free State Army.

In the following lines a girl is handed a smoke by a fella after the hop; she fancies herself as Bette Davis in *Now Voyager,* which concludes with a couple lighting up looking out at the moon, except that for the speaker in the poem, it is the first cigarette:

I placed it between my lips and I took
a breath in, as I'd seen my brothers
do.

I felt my lungs close over like I was
deep in water and going under for the
third time.

I coughed and coughed and he laughed so hard

I thought he'd split himself. 'Take it slow,' he said...

- 'NOW VOYAGER'

The narrative sequence is a slice of life with various connected characters leaping through their lives from poem to poem. There is a real hint throughout of 'the still sad music of humanity'.

In the final section, she unleashes translations from Mhac an tSaoi, Eoghan Ó Tuairisc and Ó Direáin, plus a modernisation of Pushkin thrown in for good measure. Ó Direáin's 'An tEarrach Thiar' she gives as 'Spring in the west'

Stiff-buttocked
rowers oars
gently stroking,
the currach
loaded heading
for shore

slow over marigold neap tide
at the end of day;
spring in the west.

Because O'Mahony has various avenues to explore, the disparate strands of this collection can appear to come across from many directions and many disconnected occasions; but such is her work method, perhaps.

—*The Poetry Ireland Review* 2007

SIMPLE IS SACRED

Seamus Heaney in Conversation with Karl Miller
(Behind the Lines)

Writing Irish: Selected Interviews with Irish Writers from the "Irish Literary Supplement" ed. James P. Myers (Syracuse University Press)

Interpreting Synge: Essays from the Synge Summer School 1991-2000 Nicholas Grene (Lilliput)

A hundred and twelve pages in which only forty comprise the interview and some of the questions are longer than the answers. The bibliography is prodigious including citings of articles, essays, letters and dissertations on the Nobel poet; all of his published works have their review sources located in journals, periodicals and newspapers; there are even nine closely printed pages from critics who adore him and a few who do not.

Miller is certainly not the first to interview Heaney and is not very provocative. The lasting impression given by the interview is of a writer who is not punch-drunk by fame and unprecedented recognition but unsure of his worth, one might even attempt at parodying Harold Bloom's famous dictum about the anxiety of influence and suggest that Heaney suffers from influential anxiety? "I would say that the poets of Northern Ireland—not just me—became more visible and discussable than would otherwise have been the case because of the political conditions. But it's not right to say that these poets got attention only because of those conditions." He admits that "politics are a dangerous thing for a poet to be involved with". However, politics remain a millstone around his neck along with others among the Northern milieu of poets. It was their calling card.

Otherwise what is said is revealing as when he admits that "political poetry in Northern Ireland should not be a spectator sport". He wrote a song for Bloody Sunday, 'The Road to Derry' which missed its moment somehow through the ineptitudes of Luke Kelly. When commenting on the hunger strikes by Bobby Sands and his compatriots, he passionately states, "It was a moment for poetry to strike through social and political concerns, and to say that this was an awesome sacrifice. I regret that somehow I didn't make an intervention." His Nobel Prize address mentioned two victims from either side of the sectarian divide who squeezed each other by the hand facing imminent death before their killers; "the frailty of that gesture is all we have to go on". Heaney will not be bullied into propaganda and this alone means he is keeping faith with the office he holds.

Meanwhile he unashamedly glories in Mossbawn—the landscape of his childhood where Radio Eireann was the norm and not the BBC Third Programme. He admits to living "a kind of den life when I go home, among my brothers and sisters". However the lure of England is as strong as Harvard. He is working on a sequence about studying Shakespeare in school and jokingly refers to the TV dinosaur Clive James who coined the name 'Famous Seamus'. Harvard provided the oxygen of a "second living poetry environment, after the first one I'd known in Belfast". Miller doesn't ask him which was preferable or more beneficial. His favourite critic is Helen Vendler.

Finally, the unprecedented bestsellerdom of *Beowulf* with nothing Catholic, Celtic or Irish about it except the Northern Irish gloss in the language; yet the choice of epic somehow fits his purposes, albeit drenched in political undertones and a suspicious kind of fealty. However, Heaney is above the critic's lash and beyond criticism in what might well be a helpful isolation. Presumably he needs that much more than others outside his uniquely popular position.

This is in the same vein as the above except you get s i x t e e n well-known writers interviewed and in many cases there are revelations, personal, critical, biographical and even spiteful; it all makes for juicy dialogue teased out by the interviewers who are usually probing. Naturally every reader will have their favourites but are assured that the whole book is addictive and may become a minor classic. Each interview found its genesis in the pages of the *Irish Literary Supplement* and includes notes, index and further suggested critical works.

Perhaps the best performers are Kennelly, Mahon, Ní Dhomhnaill, Jennifer Johnston and Montague. Kennelly is marvellous and his dialogue might well be broadcast as a radio piece. He is self-deprecating, funny and Socratic. Random quotation can only lessen the impact, however "Violence runs through education, ambition, the dream of middle-class parents for their children, the moulding of personality." As a poet, he claims the ballad tradition: "I would like to write honestly. I don't think I've done it yet." John McGahern seems without stigma from early victimisation after publishing The *Dark* and recalls that his neighbours the Moroneys lent him many books as a growing boy.

Similarly Ní Dhomhnaill is in fighting form: "We female aborigines are beginning to get back to what we were going on about before we were interrupted by the male side of the psyche that caused Christianity and witch burning." She is utterly convincing about herself and the teanga. Jennifer Johnston thinks Ben Kiely's *Proxopera* "a dreadful book ... a load of romantic rubbish". McGuckian comes across as a metaphysical poet, "God is the true subject of all art." Her candour is everywhere. "Irish was imposed on me in such a parochial way I still have a horror of it." Similarly, Eavan Boland is pugnacious and feisty: "many of the younger writers who are best in poetry are women". Éilean Ní Chuilleanáin is majestically modest— "I wanted to be a chemist"—and considers her teaching job as nothing special but obviously has academia in her blood like her distinguished forebears.

Derek Mahon provides a lot of biographical information and a hilarious Kavanagh anecdote and is realistic about the North where "everyone's sectarian". He disliked the Hobsbaum clique in Belfast but admits that it might have been good for Heaney's development. What sounds prudish is that he has changed the word 'cunts' to 'twits' in the poem 'Afterlives' since its popularity.

One wonders why Hugh Leonard ever changed from John Keyes Byrne which sounds a better name for a writer? Leonard became a very successful adaptor for stage, screen and television while considering Da his best work, and his favourite playwrights, Beckett, Shakespeare and Lennox Robinson. He is down to earth after many triumphs as a writer and declares, "The Dun Laoghaire Carnegie Library was my university." He throws in a bit of gossip, "I once made a passing and uncritical comment about Brian Friel, and Heaney said, quite amicably: "We can talk about him: you can't." He also admits to the presence of cliques in Irish writing.

Tom Paulin is frank about his roots, "I'm concerned with the Unionist experience. I hope I understand the feelings of agony and displacement and not belonging . . ." He went to the same school as Peter Robinson of the DUP. Joyce was his adolescent hero. Paul Muldoon unbegrudgingly states, "I think Seamus is a brilliant poet but there are a few others." Ben Kiely evades no questions and is untroubled about his reading public and generally has the kitchen table full of letters to answer from admirers of his books. John Banville is tight-lipped and admits to a dislike of interviews; he is curt and to the point. The William Trevor interview suffers from brevity as well, but he prefers to listen than to talk. Michael Longley doesn't like William Carlos Williams and is full of wisdom on parenthood: "In a sense, it's a life sentence of course, but I would say that the profoundest thing that's happened to me in my life is being a father." Montague is elliptical at times, very entertaining and would like to see his love poem 'All Legendary Obstacles' in American anthologies. "I live in remote Cork, which is bad for my career, but good for my character."

A very satisfying collection of essays, not all of them generated by the Synge Summer School. The poems included are fillers and come from a gang of stalwarts including Heaney and Kennelly. However, one has to wait for Ann Saddlemyer's comments about Synge's soundscape near the close of the book before there is a complete basis accentuated for his aesthetics. She firmly roots him with Shaw and Joyce—artists whose musical background determined the form of their writing. Meanwhile, Synge's *The Well of the Saints* is shown as an inspiration to Yeats and Beckett; the two tramps in *Waiting for Godot* may well have come out of the first act of Synge's play. In Beckett's story 'Love and Lethe', the lovers abandon their suicide pact on arriving among the splendours of Wicklow, while evoking J. M. Synge.

Saddlemyer shows Synge's obsessional devotion to music especially Bach, Mozart, Beethoven and Schubert. He was able to forgo Shaw's *John Bull's Other Island* for the enchantments of an Esposito concert. Christopher Morash delves into the riots at the opening of The *Playboy of the Western World* on that famous day in Irish theatre, 26 January 1907. He makes it clear that the riot kept going throughout the best part of a week so the play was interrupted nightly. Synge ignored the critics with gusto since no review could equal a riot as the perfect reception for a new drama. When the police came to remove hecklers at the play, a member of the audience suggested they arrest Christy Mahon for the murder of his father. During a public debate on the controversy at the Abbey when John Butler Yeats spoke, the audience was further provoked into calling on W. B. Yeats to 'kill your father'. Synge enjoyed the debacle enormously and wrote to his beloved, "Now we'll be talked about. We're an event in the history of the Irish stage." . Frank McGuinness sources Synge's debt to Ibsen's *Peer Gynt*, finding Pegeen Mike shares with him "a snobbishness of extraordinary proportions". Similarly, Synge was obsessed by Ibsen's *Rosmersholm* with its double suicide and the great cry of pain that is at the heart of the play. Tom Paulin's brief piece tells of a love affair with Synge's The *Aran Islands*. He finds *Riders to the Sea* "reads like a verse play: 'Is the sea bad by the white rocks, Nora?'"

Meanwhile, Declan Kiberd brings in the longest essay on The *Aran Islands,* tracing Synge from when he took Yeats's advice to go west, bringing along a fiddle, box camera and alarm clock—the latter two items amazed the islanders who looked on photography as a fearful thing which they believed is merely a record of something to be forgotten. Kiberd shows that this prose work is chiefly anthropological and anxiety laden in the manner of Conrad's *Heart of Darkness* concerning colonialism. He doesn't delve too deeply into Synge's language and quotes Yeats, "The objectivity he derived from dialect was technical".

Martin Hilsky studies Synge's language and disagrees with St John Irvine that he was a 'faker of peasant speech'. He believes that Synge's language is, in Mallarmé's phrase 'the language of literature' and amplifies this by adding "Synge's idiolect is a translation from the Irish of Aran into English" in which he invented "one language for all the characters" in his plays. This specific interest derives from Hilsky translating The *Playboy of the Western World* for the Czech National Theatre.

Antoinette Quinn focuses on Maud Gonne's forgotten play *Dawn* based on experiences of 'famine and relief works in north Mayo'. There is reference to Gonne's disapproval of Synge's *The Shadow of the Glen*—*she* walked out at the premiere—it had struck home too close to her own experience of unhappy marriage. Synge's Nora from the same play owes something to Ibsen's *A Doll's House. The Shadow of the Glen* outraged nationalists such as Douglas Hyde, James Connolly and Arthur Griffith who disliked the exposure of real-life Ireland on the stage, preferring pageants that reflected their propagandist needs.

Angela Bourke is encyclopaedic in her discussion of keening. *Deirdre of the Sorrows* is explained as a keening soliloquy. Part of the ancient ritual of keening included drinking the blood of the victim; Emer drank Cú Chulainn's blood and Deirdre, according to the Irish sagas, demanded to kiss her dead beloved and set to sucking his blood; similarly 'The lament for Art Ó Laoghaire' includes the lines (in translation):

your blood was flowing from you: I didn't stop to wipe it

I drank it from my hands.

Another glitterato, R. F. Foster, examines the Yeats-Synge relationship. Yeats presumed that the younger man would become the perfect heir—there was only six years between them—whereas Synge had an intense artistic life in the following decade before his final illness. "The circumstances of Synge's death were reinterpreted by Yeats to put him in the category of Parnell, Wilde and Casement." Synge is seen as the emblematic figure behind Yeats's poem 'The Fisherman' which can be read in elegiac terms.

Anthony Roche is sparky in revealing Synge's lovelife—a fairly tortured affair—with Molly Allgood. Synge felt embarrassed by their age difference, he was thirty-five and she in her late teens. He loved her madly all right and was prone to jealousy. Sadly, he knew she could hardly be accepted into the straitlaced Synge family who looked on stage girls as coequal with harlots. One of her visits to Synge's home in Crosthwaite Park in Dun Laoghaire is reported as a stifling occasion. Their happier times were spent in Bray and Wicklow wandering around. However, poor John could only ever think of himself as her tramp, such was his lowly spirit.

This however is not to deflate the great playwright whose dedication to his last, an unfinished work *Deirdre of the Sorrows,* rent him between precious time with Molly and the solitude necessary for writing. Roche hints at the social struggle involved in Synge's major love affair. Neither of them could afford a small house and not even by pooling what little they had; besides his bad health required domicile with mother. Roche quotes classic bits of Synge: "In the middle classes the gifted son of a family is always the poorest—usually a writer or artist with no sense for speculation." What a painfully transparent swipe of autobiography. And the enigma of the artist: "It makes me rage when I think of the people who go on as if art and literature and writing were the first thing in the world. There is nothing so great and sacred as what is most simple in life."

—*Books Ireland* 2000

FRANKENSTEINS OR DRACULAS?

Translating Ireland : translation, languages, cultures Michael Cronin (Cork University Press)

Montale's "Mestiere Vile": The elective translations from English of the 1930s and 1940s

George Talbot (Irish Academic Press)

Lampion and His Bandits: literature of the cordel in Brazil Augustus Young (Menard Press)

Poems of a Wanderer Midang So Chong-Ju and Kevin O'Rourke (Dedalus Press)

The Distribution of Bodies Jacques Rancourt and John F. Deane (Dedalus Press)

No More Me and other poems Alain Bosquet (Dedalus Press)

The Word at Hand Lorand Gaspar and Roger Little (Dedalus Press)

Selected Poems Giacomo Leopardi and Eamon Grennan (Dedalus Press)

During the seventies and eighties a few Irish writers were at Iowa University in the Translation Workshop which was in part the brainchild of Paul Engle who had translated Kant—and rowed—at Oxford where his tutor was Edmund Blunden, a survivor from the trenches of the first World War. Daniel Weissbort, editor of Modern Poetry in Translation, also co-directed this workshop and explored such art treasures as the extraordinary sonnets of Giuseppe Belli and Artur Lundkvist's Agadir, a valid modern epic.

The author of Translating Ireland heralds an emerald era primarily of bilingualism which may even surpass the Iowan model. Many persons and events have set this in motion, namely Laurence Cassidy of the Arts Council; the founding of the *Irish Translators'*

Association (1986) chaired by Cormac Ó Cuilleanain and a quarterly bulletin *Translation Ireland*; Charles Pick, compiler of *Developing Publishing in Ireland* (1988); Michael Cronin, Liam Mac Coil and Jurgen Schneider whose report (1990) advanced the cause leading to Michael Ó Siadhail's *Ireland Literature Exchange* (1993).

There are visceral comments, such as Alan Titley's "Nobody must ever be allowed to say that Irish literature is written solely in English. They must never be free to ignore us in our own country," and Biddy Jenkinson's, "I prefer not to be translated into English," and Pol Ó Muiri with "we are simply witnessing poets while away the dark winter nights by translating Irish poetry . . . it is patronage and pity" and Barra O Seaghdha "the values of the English-language audience may become factors that penetrate and weaken the original impulse."

Concerning Gabriel Rosenstock's selections from Seamus Heaney *as gaeilge* and poems from Yeats, Cronin interprets the motive as "less the incorporation of the exotic or remote than a form of collusion moving, with the familiar which stresses Gaelic antecedents and contexts". There is the usual survey of Gaelic literature, headlining Nuala Ní Dhomhnaill: "We all have an emotional block about Irish. Right through the country; even I have it, everyone has it." There is scholarly display often from secondhand sources: Johannes Scotus Eriugena's general law for translative activity: "the internal value of the text is duly to be grasped; the bombast of words is often deceptive". Listed with the pride of a true Gael are "the oldest extant vernacular translations" from Homer, Lucan, Virgil and his gifted imitator Statius, respectively; Togdil Trot., In Cath Catharda, Imtheachta Aeniasa and Togdil na Tebe. After the Battle of Kinsale, Puritan Uilliam Ó Domhnaill's New Testament in Irish came on the scene, followed by the Book of Common Prayer. The Reformation arrived in Ireland despite the "perceived threat of translation to the successful completion of the colonisation process". The printing presses of the Franciscans in

Louvain maintained a balance, proliferating Catholic books from 1611.

Swift heard Carolan singing in the deanery and coined 'Splish splash in their pumps' for the latter 's 'glug glug i n-a mbrog'. Archbishop MacHale translated Moore's Melodies into Irish, "their native language" according to the Tuam cleric. George Sigerson's Bards of the Gael and Gall in its introduction, notes "every generation fuses with the great Past, in the adopted land they love". James Hardiman's Irish Minstrelsy, seen as a corrective to 'James Macpherson's pseudo-translations', was damned by Samuel Ferguson as "spurious, puerile, unclassical—lamentably bad". Cronin swiftly kicks him in the teeth: "Ferguson resembles Charlotte Brooke in that his Irish patriotism situates itself within the context of continued union with Britain." And in the same vein "The Nation was yet another incentive for Irish speakers to translate themselves into the English language." Wolfe Tone, the Fenians and Daniel O'Connell were indifferent to the teanga. O'Connell dismissed Peter O'Connell "as an old fool to have spent so much of his life on so useless a work [as an Irish-English dictionary]. Hiberno-English communes with the corpse of the dead language and draws a sustenance that nourishes: the translator becomes Dracula." Stoker was an Irishman, the reader is informed shortly afterwards.

Synge's worst fears about language revival, that the natives would become 'semiliterate in both languages' makes one postulate that Synge should have written his great plays as Gaeilge rather than in brogue Irish. Significantly, An Gúm organised translations from European classics within the period viewed by some revisionists as the Fascist era, 1923-1963.

Finally this book tends to be non-partisan and the yellow dust jacket covers occasional jaundiced opinion. Hands up who thinks Michael Cronin's text occasionally reads like a brochure with a dangerous long arm salute? Well, only during deeply felt lapses.

Strictly for intrepid enthusiasts, this polished-up and recycled thesis is a sombre and serious study and very readable, even when it enters the nuts and bolts of word shading for translation purposes, or the Practical Criticism approach still loved by professors and others. There is a feast of reference from Tom Corbishley's translation of Loyola's Spiritual Exercises to the insights of Borges ("Fears and Scruples by Browning foretells Kafka's work"). Dr Talbot is an interesting critic himself, "for Montale, Eliot was another link in a chain which stretched from Coleridge and Poe to the post-Surrealist French poets . . . the Futurist notion of originality in poetry, new words for every occasion, is an illusion." He doesn't have to convince this reader of Montale's gift for bringing "Animula" to bellezza and proving Eliot in Italian more Dantescan than expected.

Montale learned well from Benedetto Croce's aesthetics; translated many Shakespeare plays and daringly adhered to the sonnet schema for 'Full many a glorious morning have I seen' making a diffuse version beginning "Spesso, a lusingar vette, vidi splendere". The treatment of Emily Dickinson's poem 'The Tempest' brings in the "normalisation of cultural terms in translation"; so two lines, "the doom's electric moccasin/that very instant passed" become "e fu certo l'elettrico/segnale del Giudizio" making these lines central and the translation literally Biblical. Talbot doesn't imply that an act of translation is to tear the guts out of the original and construct a monster, thus making the translator Frankenstein. Hence the beautiful version of Hopkins' Pied Beauty' from Croce's prose translation.

Montale's vital collision with a novel Joseph Conrad loved, W. H. Hudson's Green Mansions, is linked to an influential essay by Carpi on Montale's "general belief in the dignity and superiority of the intellectual, whether in the context of popular religion, Fascism or consumer society—systems in which the individual is apt to be marginalised." Talbot labels Fascism "a nightmare in reason's slumber". Montale was destined to translate this novel, whose donna angelicata is Rima; the "name was an anagram of Irma, the first name of the real woman who became Clizia in his poetry". Clizia was based on the myth of Clytie and Leucothoe in Ovid's Metamorphoses. He collaborated with Lucia Rodocanachi under their title La vita della foresta.

Montale's work with Hardy's delicate lyric 'The Garden Seat' and Joyce's 'A Flower Given to My Daughter' prove the final stanza of the latter, a triumph in translation, projecting itself and the original to new life, "o mia azzurro-venata figlia" is a richer climax than "my blueveined child". With 'The Garden Seat' "Hardy's dead are there but Montale's dead make their presence felt". Talbot's integrity thumbs down Leonie Adams' poem 'Those Not Elect', and about Dylan Thomas quotes Montale, "Di lui fu detto the Hopkins lo aveva salvato da Swinburne," though perhaps Thomas wasn't always safe from Swinburne's influence.

Augustus Young treats the reader to a twenty-five-page introduction with as much as you wanted to know about the cordel but were afraid to ask. The cordel is a strict ballad form similar to Rap on matters of poverty and oppression. A few cordel writers enjoyed the monetary rewards of bestsellerdom. Cordel stalls are still on view and in 1989 Pinto Embolador's The Rich Man And The Poor Man "a hymn to the have-nots" hit the streets. The translator with Byronic gesture mailed a cheque from Iron, the magazine in which the translation had appeared and the letter was returned marked "address unknown" minus the cheque. These cordels are a study in irony. The perspective on economics would satisfy Silvio Gesell and Ezra Pound but not the average merchant banker. The cordel in English by James Hogan is perhaps Young's own work. The satirical swipes are lightweight with a brief biography of Brian Coffey. The book ends with lines written after a stay in North East Brazil, where the drought is so arduous that "when rain cascades down the rocks it looks like gold". The woodcuts add to the Brazilian atmosphere.

Kevin O'Rourke's versions give no parallel text either and are surely fine translations from the Korean So Chong-Ju who must be a true poet. Without boring this reader there is effective use of classicism, myth, history and folk but not fatally sweet folk all. The translator is an Irish priest living in Kyunghee. A lot of the book is enchanting. O'Rourke by implication must be some kind of poet also.

Jacques Rancourt, per the blurb, tours extensively reading from his oeuvre and is coincidentally an arts administrator with jurisdiction in France and Canada. There is a lyrical glaze in "L'Eau" which John F. Deane translates as "Water", less so with "L'Encre" where "comme une madeleine sur une tasse de the amere" is Englished "like Proust's sponge-cake over a bitter cup of tea". The use of 'sponge-cake' is heavy, especially when madeleine is only a bite-size bun.

The prolific Alain Bosquet has changed nationality a few times; born in Odessa, latterly Belgian, American and eventually French. Sam Beckett's translations are good but Bosquet wrote better poems such as "Une autre époque" which William Jay Smith translates. Roger Little translates "Un colloque" and lesser poems. He gives "What are you doing in your working clothes?—Repairing a sonnet" for a line from 'Poeme Poesie Poete Poetique'.

At first glance Lorand Gaspar belongs in pseuds' corner with persons who wear T-shirts declaring "poet, am I". However Gaspar might well join the Mallarmé, Paul Valery tradition. 'Iles' (Islands), on two readings still has something going for it. The quality of his poetics, here in huge bulk, makes them worth reading: "poetry threatens the Grand Catalogues of the Mental Museum of Humanity". He can also irritate with a few woolly sentences disproving himself that "what poets have to say about poetry is still poetry". He is convincing rather than self-conscious, quoting from Plato, St Paul or the Zen masters.

Finally to Grennan's Leopardi and an accomplished preface in fussy prose. The translator has 'lived' with Leopardi over ten years. Dante and Petrarch are not masters of despair compared to Leopardi, who is refreshing in an age when unrestrained *cri de coeur* is politically incorrect or else equated with the sphere of mental dysfunction rather than art. Leopardi does a lot of baying at the moon as in the 1819 "Alla Luna" and his lost lady is available only in dreams. He longingly craves isolation in "La Vita Solitaria" and is inconsolable facing la silente riva (the speechless shore), pen ch'esser beato Nega ai mortali e nega a' morti il fato (since fate forbids the state of bliss both to the living and the dead).

There is no Keatsian timor mortis here, just fear of old age but Leopardi died aged thirty-eight. The long piece with which Grennan closes is worthy of Leopardi's reputation, albeit a poet in the early nineteenth century of strict Romantic observance. Overuse of Vesuvius as a symbol doesnt ruin this major poem and is certainly not the usual metaphor-gone-mad which minor poets achieve so well. Otherwise "To Himself" shows Grennan ably doing the job. Leopardi is ever the symbolic persona of poethood, perpetually shocked, shocking, and a pain in the neck to everyone including himself.

—*Books Ireland* 1996

MAKING THINGS HAPPEN

Words Alone: Yeats & his inheritances R. F. Foster (Oxford University Press)

Poets and Partitions: confronting communal identities in Northern Ireland Jon Curley (Sussex Academic Press)

Colum McCann and the aesthetics of redemption Eóin Flannery (Irish Academic Press)

Professor Foster is entertaining and devoutly Anglo-Irish in his claims for Yeats's inheritances. Yeats saliently admitted in the Irish Senate that he was Anglo-Irish and the descendent of "no petty people." These are Foster's people and make his case convincing though not conclusive because since Richard de Clare (Strongbow) by arrangement married Aoife of Leinster (whose nuptials are among the illustrations) Ireland began its mad nightmarish history. Foster sources "the national tale" in the nineteenth century among his usual suspects: Edgeworth, Owenson, Maturin, Le Fanu and Lover. Yeats was brought up on readings from Sir Walter Scott who found his model in Edgeworth. There is however, no mention of Yeats's torch bearing for Balzac since Foster's case is based on his selected evidence. He calls up Isaac Butt, author of *The Gap of Barnesmore* who stated that "the Scotsman cultivates his thistle in his garden; the Irishman wears his shamrock till it withers on his bosom, or he drowns it…". Foster's castigations of native Irish on the bottle is Shavian. He is on solid ground stating that "Yeats's early work was made up of short stories and attempted novels" as well as the anthology *Representative Irish Tales* (1891) which parades Castle Rackrent as well as William Carleton and Gerald Griffin. A lively section discusses "the nationalists of the Nation and the nationally conscious Tories of the Dublin University Magazine" with incise reference to Carlyle as the vivid mentor to the DUM's founding editor, Charles Gavan Duffy. Thomas Davis is shown as cross-cultural in his poem 'Celt and Saxon.' The Act of

Union is not divisive. Daniel O'Connell and Repeal are sidelined. It all makes for good fun but does it advance towards logical cultural history?

Yeats wrote his first reviews on Ferguson. Foster also includes the Wildes: père and mère as oblique influences. Mangan receives less space except for mention of "his unhappy life" since he does not fit the master plan making Yeats the token cultural nationalist under the cloven hoof of Maud Gonne to whom "he was firmly in thrall." Surprisingly, Foster as Yeats's biographer is with F.R. Leavis, Auden and Eliot in decrying the poet's occult and supernatural beliefs which these three considerable figures found "so distasteful" and according to Leavis the poet's belief in reincarnation is not "necessary to the appreciation of Yeats's poetry." He makes slim claims for Le Fanu as an influence and also Bram Stoker's Dracula but naturally cannot deny Immanuel Swedenborg and Blake about whom Yeats wrote copiously. The key point is that the poet aged twenty-one noted in his diary: "Talent perceives difference, Genius Unity"—this becomes a mantra for Yeats. His work, not least the supernatural writings cannot be denied within the central structure of the oeuvre. Foster concedes this point by inference in these essays adapted from his Clark Lectures at Cambridge in 2009. Otherwise, Foster is the exponent of Protestant nationalism—a topic of major confusion and contradiction which needs him as its apostle. He neglects to praise Yeats as preserver of civilisation on the island and is generally dismissive of The Celtic Twilight and finds Kathleen Raine's introduction to the 1981 reprint too "reverent" and difficult "to read with a straight face."

Curley's study of poets from the North is lacking despite his fleeting familiarity with Ireland. He could well annoy readers and tends to hedge his bets: "Despite inevitable shortcomings, Troubles poetry has established itself as a valuable literature." He quotes Rushlight magazine condemning anyone who refers to the six counties as 'Northern Ireland' yet in his text designates the zone as Northern

Ireland. He is rather clueless in forgetting that nationalists insist one use North of Ireland exclusively. Such nomenclature is taken with high seriousness in Ireland. And whatever about quoting David Wheatley's "our morbid interest in self-definition" Curley does not categorically state anywhere that in the North of Ireland self-definition is starkly clear if never stated verbally in public except in confidential privacy. Curley seems incapable of grasping that 'the Troubles' is a typical NI diminutive for the sectarian war and bloodshed that spanned the closing decades of the twentieth century. What happened was in fact more tragic than the dictionary definition of the word troubles.

That said Curley's survey of poets and their poems is fairly rewarding because of his citing of limitations as in Hewitt's failure to artistically unify "a dichotomous Ulster" in his work. Hewitt's 'Once Alien Here' remains "a specious and desperate ploy for establishing a wished for reconciliation of opposites." Curley's implication is that Hewitt, Rodgers and MacNeice represent "a consistent viewpoint [that] is often compromised by the magnitude of conflict." In glossing MacNeice's 'Belfast' and 'Carrickfergus' he reveals the predominant tone of "dislike" of place. Hewitt's representation of place "is painfully confused" and this is also true of Mahon's 'Derry Morning.' MacNeice's 'Valediction' shows "a love-hate attitude toward their birthplace [Belfast]" which is easily proved in random quotation from the poem: "Your drums and your dolled-up Virgins and your ignorant/dead." Rodgers too in 'The Character of Ireland': "I am Ulster, my people an abrupt people/Who like the spiky consonants in speech." His best analysis in on Heaney and Muldoon in whose 'The Indians on Alcatraz' where actualities of Ulster are replaced "with inconsistent, enigmatic constructions." Heaney's 'The Grauballe Man' and 'The Tollund Man' in any direct NI context remain 'understated admonition, coming as a fleeting after-thought, is too little and too late." This is solid criticism. Similarly in 'Whatever You Say Say

Nothing' Heaney does little more than adopt "the cliché-ridden journalistic world he despises." In fact he outs Heaney using his own words in 'Exposure' as "neither internee nor informer" and as Curley says the "fugitive from sectarian strife." Curley is overloaded in hyperbole discussing Longley's flirtation with Homeric reference in 'Ceasefire' and 'The Butchers' whereas such poems hinting at the Siege of Troy make pretence to empathy with six counties horrors and tragedies: war may be universal in theory but it is painful, local and personal in fact. Muldoon is seen as an "irrepressible trickster" and Carson involved in "code-breaking linguistic antics"—useful labels. With regard to Muldoon's cynicism, he unwittingly dislodges a contradiction in that in '7, Middagh Street:' "For poetry can make things happen—/not only can, but must—." In this respect, between the lines Curley seems open if a bit tight lipped about admitting that 'Troubles poetry' is not only a misnomer but its practitioners were paradoxically elsewhere and provably unconcerned about their home counties in their careering verse.

McCann's readers may not enjoy this as much as his fiction since Flannery is pedestrian as a literary policeman on patrol plodding through the prose works. He cites Dermot Bolger locating McCann's position as "more modernized (but not modernist) and international." However, he is, like others dragged back to the island although an exile in New York which has provided a fertile backdrop compared to the two story collections: Fishing The Sloe-Black River and Everything in This Country Must. The latter has a story entitled 'Wood' with its I-narrator where the Orange Lodge is depicted through one family. Songdogs harks back to the old sod or as Flannery characteristically puts it: "loosely appropriates the structure and central drama of the bildungsroman, and its Irish contexts warrants its inclusion within discussions of the postcolonial bildungsroman." Claims are made for the novel's injection of photography as a "symbolic and representative device" as well as rivers "the most prominent symbol." The problem with his discussion of This Side of Brightness is that he overuses Mahon's poetry and Heaney's when dealing with Everything in This Country Must. Both poetries really do little to inform what is afterall fiction. He is quite deliberate in teasing out (to his own satisfaction) McCann's "urban netherworld in New York City" a landscape "wracked by the fears and indignities of its junked population." Dancer shows McCann fully out of Ireland in the arcane subject matter of Rudolf Nureyev that for Flannery "tantalizes the reader with the 'truth' value of biographical record." Such fiction is either superior to biography or it fails. McCann in Zoli tackles what he emphatically espouses as a writer "embracing empathy" in this case "a female member of a Roma community across the twentieth century." Flannery is always uncritical of his subject and tends toward much idolatry: there is not a line of critical impasse. The most promising of McCann's works Let the Great World Spin has the "embrace of criminality, destitution, addiction, and class division." It spans the Philippe Petit high-wire walk between the towers of the World Trade Centre and the 9/11 evil suicide bombings. The scope of the novel is beyond the terrorist attacks on New York to 2006 concluding "in post-Hurricane Katrina America." Flannery's central point is McCann's successful relocation to NY in terms of subject matter and self as novelist yet with hankerings back to the green and misty isle. It is ever thus.

—Books Ireland 2011

THAT SIMPLE?

Ciaran Carson: Space, Place, Writing Neal Alexander (Liverpool University Press)

Anne Enright eds. Claire Bracken and Susan Cahill (Irish Academic Press)

In the introduction Carson (b.1948) is located as son of a postman who in QUB meets the Hobsbaum Group, then works for the Arts Council up until 1998 and back to QUB in 2003 running the Heaney Centre for Poetry. Alexander never interrogates this poetry 'corporate' institutional backdrop which is the writer employed within the arts and/or academy, relevant too in the case of Michael Longley and other Northern poets. In these terms Alexander misses an opportunity in fully referencing Carson within his essential milieu. Instead, you get what the American professor and poet, Robert Wrigley presumed in introducing the present reviewer with some dread 'as visiting from the Euro Hermeneutics Zone'. Wrigley wittily admitted 'dreading' not only the word 'hermeneutics' but also most of its products!

Alexander brings in some of the dreaded hermeneutics such as Carson's Belfast is best understood 'as a compact literary collage, formally reflecting the mosaic of interdigitations that comprise the city's physical and social geography'. You get expert collisions with Foucault and Bergson on space and place while he admits that game playing is the centre of some poems such as "Alphabet City" where Carson 'conflates Belfast with a version of Virginia Woolf's London' and the use of 'alliteration becomes a means of orientation (or disorententation)'. Such postmodernist material pervades some academic analysis like imperfect ore. He seems to prefer Carson's prose books to the poetry. There is physically more to read, of course as in The Star Factory 'in which chapters are named after local streets or landmarks' deliberately resembling 'a jumbled street directory'. He alludes to Catríona O'Reilly's remark that the prose

Carson blends 'idiosyncratic associations and aleatory combinations with a countervailing concern for systems of classification and a pronounced "taxonomic bent". One can easily guess how Wrigley would react to the latter.

Still, Alexander makes this an expansive study as he deals on many levels with the 'poet, prose writer, and urban dinnseanchaí' as well as flâneur incongruously comparing his subject to European city-poets such as Baudelaire. Carson is ultimately engaged 'in revised versions of the city that disorient official cartographies and static figurations of the city'. Alexander sources the title for one collection from the ergot 'Belfast confetti' that is glossed as the 'miscellaneous rubble thrown during street riots'. This dim Belfast wit in excelsis reveals the sad street confetti, disharmony and carnage behind poems such as "Schoolboys and Idlers of Pompeii": 'Remember 1690. Remember 1916. Most of all, Remember me. I was here'. Carson's work articulates the apotheosis of lost identity using history, symbol and ceremony pasted onto good old divide and rule Belfast: it is that simple and complex. You are one or the other in Belfast: you cannot be both.

He uses Sontag on photography to examine the poet and at the other end of the spectrum assesses him as translator of Dante, Merriman and the *Táin* in a lively contrast with Kinsella's roadblock of a version that is far too canonical causing the sidelining of 'older' versions. Carson's Táin is fawned on by Alexander primarily because it hails from Belfast the more privileged location harnessed for hermeneutics by many academics in mainland Britain and Southern Ireland and such preference remains a great cultural imbalance of the latter half of 20th Century Ireland. Alexander fails to fully circumnavigate Carson's Gaelic and Traditional Irish music roots just as he neglects the poet's Englishness. Alexander scores best when locating the *Táin* as the greatest guidebook to Ulster with its storyline of two bulls, a man and a woman in mortal dispute, war and bloodshed. Carson's version is deemed better than Kinsella's sexless translation. The *Táin* more than *Ulysses* is the national epic with Maeve and Ailill in bed but not for long on John Bull's Other Island where everyone is as conversant about Cú Chulainn as they are about Vera Lynn, the Chieftains and Elgar.

A collocation and compendium that does not repel hermeneutically since it is not linguistically obtuse except for Gerardine Meaney's essay. Essayists abound: Elke D'hoker, Heidi Hansson, Anne Mulhall, Patricia Coughlan, Kristin Ewins, Matthew Ryan, Hedwig Schwall; Bracken's is the best essay. Cahill and Bracken interview Enright revealing her pre-Tiger, anti-Boom ethos: '[not] wildly enthusiastic about the boom'. In praising Richard Yates Revolutionary Road Enright states that 'the blandness of the suburbs was something to be desired' as she forgets the miserable wife in the story for whom suburbia is hell. These attitudes inform her fiction: she is anti-realist. She is a feminist in that 'my characters aren't very involved with the mirror'. D'Hoker locates Enright's short fiction with Sheridan Le Fanu, Bowen and 'the fantastic stories of Éilís Ní Dhuibhne'—vast parameters requiring a book length investigation that is not delivered. Heidi Hansson places Enright in Gerry Smyth's demarcation: 'despite new times, (Irish) novel and (Irish) nation still appear to be caught in a bind of mutual fascination'. Enright's staccato style promotes the cracked lip nail biting sentence that can irritate unless you are an admirer: 'I look at the photograph. My mother is beautiful. She is in love. She looks like etc' [The Wig My Father Wore] and Cahill finds repeated images of interconnection in the latter: 'Grace and her mother swimming while pregnant'. Bracken views this as 'late postmodernity' 'which is a subject of separation, as it struggles to place order on processes of cultural change'. All retrograde and redolent of the John Waters' longing for a return to the land of nostalgia, the schizoid Tir na n-Óg of De Valera's ideals. Hedwig Schwall also interrogates the incessant backward glimpse in Enright who roosts among characters who are not depicted in realism. In The Gathering, the suicider Liam from a family of twelve is 'the scapegoat of a culture that does not allow criticism'. Kristin Ewins insightfully sources Enright to Angela Carter's MA Creative Writing Course at the University of East Anglia where she subsumed the latter's 'feminist rewrites of traditional fairy tales, The Bloody Chamber, alongside Shakespeare's King Lear'. Lear does not fit Enright who is a quasi-magic realist. However such an early mentor as Carter can be pernicious since she was, along with Rushdie a notorious magic realist and this genre seems to locate Enright's fiction.

There is no dispute about Meaney's knowledge of Sophocles but linking the character Veronica in The Gathering with Antigone or even Ismene is invalid. The Theban plays from the dawn of western literature are the realist sublime influencing no less than Shakespeare, Nietzsche, Freud & Co. Julius Caesar and King Lear would not have been possible without Sophocles. You cannot locate a provincial folkloric fiction such as The Gathering with Antigone. It is absurd. You may as well link Batman to Hamlet or Fair City with War and Peace. Some academic exercises in comparative literature can deride all literature implying it is of one piece. Professor Wrigley may well be right about the academic Eurozone where discourse is squeezed into all kinds of analyse which even the French perversely practise in excess along the corridors of the Sorbonne on occasions. Plato, Aristotle and Kant would have sighed in disgust. Hermeneutics require careful realistic navigation like every flightpath. Realism is the greatest structure for fiction and realism in hermeneutics is essential for its logic and verbal integrity. Schwall sees Enright moving towards writing about a certain strata of Irish women and 'making them fall off their pedestals, to hit real life'—that's a progressive move for internal feminism.

—*Books Ireland* 2011

FREE THINKER SUPERTHINKER

The Complete Prefaces Vol. II: 1914-1929 Bernard Shaw eds. Dan H. Laurence and Daniel O' Leary (Allen Lane)

Language in History: Theories and Texts Tony Crowley (Routledge)

The joint editors bow out after a brief note and GBS takes centre stage. They prompt occasionally in useful footnotes, sometimes scolding him for misquoting from memory or for attributing wisdom to others which may be his own. The prefaces in this second volume are from the Great War to 1929. The year before the war, Shaw's mother died and he wrote an inspired letter about her death to Stella Campbell who played Eliza Doolittle in Pygmalion; its success was diminished for him because he'd fallen in love with her while still being the long-time husband of Charlotte Payne-Townshend; their marriage would survive his further infatuations with actresses.

Far more troublesome were his various condemnations of the war, printed in the New Statesman and The Times after the outbreak of hostilities, many of which were issued as pamphlets. He became public enemy number one and was declared pro-Kaiser by every jingoist, but went ahead seeking a performance of Heartbreak House, "my King Lear" with the 'sinking ship of society' metaphor and a Zeppelin air raid in the last act. The play was not staged during the war and the preface is a significant historical document, as was the icy preface to *The Quintessence of Ibsenism*, attacking inhumanity. Shaw, unrepentant, went on to publish Family Life in Germany under the Blockade, Peace Conference Hints, and How to Settle the Irish Question, all before the armistice.

James Joyce disapproved of Shaw's writing prefaces to the plays, and G. K. Chesterton found that after reading a lengthy preface he didn't want to read the play that followed. The prefaces still have validity, some on burning issues of the past that remain perennial, such as the important examination of society's motives for imprisoning law-breakers. Shaw never avoids the big questions and attacks with a scintillating imagination. He makes excellent common sense, is enigmatic without being cranky, and profoundly wise. Whatever about claiming Shaw as superman he is a superthinker. His scholarship is vast and applied with artistry, and the entire performance is intoxicating because of a lucid prose style.

The preface to The Dark Lady of the Sonnets is superior to the play, a commissioned oneacter. The preface reviews Frank Harris, who is flayed and praised. The Harris portrait of the bard is trenchantly cast aside and Shakespeare is given a very revealing exposure by Shaw who claims: "I am convinced that he was very like myself: in fact, if I had been born in 1556 instead of 1856, I should have taken to blank verse and given Shakespear a harder run for his money than all the other Elizabethans put together." Harris's bland book is refuted: "I cannot for the life of me see the broken heart in Shakespear's latest works. 'Hark, Hark! the lark at heaven's gate sings' is not the lyric of a broken man." He will not have any of Harris's cardboard cut-out Shakespeare. Harris is also shown as prophetic, about the imminent disaster of Oscar Wilde's refusing to catch the Dover train, and Shaw is dismayed at Wilde's naivety and public masochism. The preface also resurrects a mystery man, Thomas Tyler, whose edition of Shakespeare's sonnets named Mary Fitton as the dark lady who "reduced the great man to the common human denominator". GBS met Tyler in the reading room of the British Museum, one of many institutions endowed by the Shaw estate.

'How William Archer impressed Bernard Shaw' is a model of biographical memoir, deeply human, and judiciously revealing about Archer's private life. The observations on theatre-business corruption are brave and the premonitionary letter about Archer's death suitably funereal. The piece on T. E. Lawrence is less impressive. However Shaw would go on to write a play based on the soldier, Too True to be Good. The writings on education, parents and children maintain the usual standards: "Truth is a guilty secret, heavily punishable on discovery; and the parent who allows his child to be taught truth without leaving him an independent income must be prepared to hear his child curse him." "Public life is a paradise for windbags"—this is actually mild compared to mainstream home truths, and still leaves Shaw on Christianity, and on Saint Joan. The preface to Back to Methuselah is essential reading and has a brief digression on his aims and ideals as a playwright. He is always brilliant in digression and personal reminiscence, such as the revisit to Dublin's Molesworth Street where he worked as a clerk before running off to London, or as a young man meeting the Revd William Addis in South Kensington. After propounding Catholic theology, Addis said: "he should go mad if he lost his belief". Shaw in the prefaces is never cynical about religion. As he says himself: "these two anecdotes are superficial, trivial and even comic; but there is an abyss of horror beneath them." However the play Saint Joan seems at variance with its preface, which calls her "a Galtonic visualizer"; yet he discusses Jesus and the Gospels with piety devoid of mysticism and spiritualism ("life itself is the miracle of miracles"), and he attempts a unified vision combining diverse Christian thinkers. Earlier on in this huge book, he champions 'creative evolution', pragmatic socialism, humanitarian reform, political sanctity, moral perfection, and passionate truth-telling with the relief of comedy. He may not have been the agnostic freethinker that Michael Holroyd implied in his recent voluminous and excellent biography. Once upon a time, having to choose a twentieth-century writer to the exclusion of every other, Bernard Shaw was the considered choice. Choosing someone now is not that easy.

Professor Crowley's is a formidable textbook in pamphlet format. The references are dense and various, including linguistic scrutiny of Bernard Shaw, George Gissing, Defoe, Richardson and Patrick Pearse among many. It is somewhat unsatisfactory that he didn't proceed in a more specific manner. There are academic undertones in his joint focus on two great bellyaches for some undergraduates: Ferdinand de Saussure, founding father of linguistics, and Mikhail Bakhtin, another colossal bore for the apathetic student. However, these two are considerable fellows for lovers of linguistics. Saussure's only published book, *Memoire sur le systeme primitif des voyelles dans les longues indo-europeennes* is a study of 'language and race, language and the nation, the relations between language and political history, language and institutions, and the relationship between the literary language and the dialects'. Crowley makes him a Darwin of 'glossology' while "Bakhtin's assertion of linguistic democracy is similar to the proposition that all are equal before the law".

Idealistic quotations from Croce are linked to Fichte and Thomas Davis, who could write in The Nation of "the fiery, delicate organed Celt" who abandoned "this wild liquid speech [Gaelic] for the mongrel of a hundred breeds called English" and declared that "most if not all the names in Scripture will be found to be pure Irish"! Davis and Douglas Hyde are quoted minus the harp and shamrock, speaking sensibly: "If I had a friend in Ireland who did not know the English language, I would be the first to teach it to him". There is an unusually wacky line from AE (George Russell) worthy of De Valera: "the songs of London music halls may be heard in places where the music of the fairy enchanted the elder generation". R. C. Trench appears as a considerable linguist, searching for the original meaning of a word "by tracing it back to its root etymon". There is not enough space given to F. J. Furnivall, the mammoth lexicographer and founder of many societies devoted to Early English texts, Shakespeare, Browning, Wyclif and Shelley.

Jonathan Swift is proved to be for the abolishing of Gaelic, and Doctor Johnson against. The Sheridans father and son (the latter the playwright), are well exhibited. The father was a snob friend of Swift, but nonetheless a lax linguist who failed to realise the fluidity of language. Crowley is fruitfully discursive on language and class through many centuries, and the Irish scene isn't neglected up to the present day. Linguistic historians are open to fraud as much as other historians. For instance claiming Gaelic as Homer's native tongue: apparently Archbishop MacHale believed the Iliad was written in Gaelic first and then translated into Greek; and "druidism was not the established religion of the pagan Irish, but Buddhism" according to Charles Vallancey. Crowley says "antiquity signified credibility," and mentions the oft quoted scene between Stephen Dedalus and the English Dean of Studies; perhaps 'tundish' was the word for 'funnel' in Drumcondra in Joyce's day, but it is also in Shakespeare's Measure for Measure, which makes Joyce's claim fraudulent. Otherwise Crowley locates many linguistic oddities, and is diverting, especially if you are not facing an exam question on his text.

—*Books Ireland May 1996*

A SHAVIAN GUIDE FOR BEGINNERS

Judging Shaw: the radicalism of GBS Fintan O'Toole
(Prism/Royal Irish Academy)

This looks like a coffee table extravaganza but up close is more problematic with borrowed showmanship from GBS in the dedication: 'To my father Samuel O'Toole, Shavian, man and superman'. The 'path' to each chapter is a hodgepodge of so many illustrations, documents, press cuttings, book covers, photographs, handwriting, letters and stage notes, and in various colours. The promotional intent distracts from the text which is neither graphic-biography nor literary criticism. Amidst the random scrapbook of Shavian artefacts, the text proper begins after eleven pages of photos/illustrations. In a rare reference to one of the photographs: a self-portrait looking into a mirror, O'Toole states 'it is a kind of out-of-body experience: he is literally beside himself'. Actually the photograph is a blur. Out of context it might be anyone other than Shaw, except to an expert.

The book would be half its length of 358 without the glaring visuals that labour the 'novelty' of the family-album-feel. If this is all O'Toole has to say on Shaw, why not admit it rather than hiding behind a display of memorabilia. The chronology is 'pumped up' to eleven pages with hefty textboxes which could have been done in two pages. Pithy quotes are given separate pages. Reproducing the Éire stamp alongside auctioneer's brochures and prices for manuscripts is excessive. Ultimately, the mixed genre is a hilarious disaster, despite Fidelma Slattery's professional design. 'Christmas market' is the obvious ploy based on the ancillary events to the publication.

So after the blaze of colour what has he to say on GBS? Aye, there's the rub. Eight snappy chapters, really subdivisions for GBS on England, Ireland, theatre, poverty, and assorted themes but there must be a dozen PhD theses available instead of this slim commentary. Biographies and books on Shaw are legion including the voluminous Holroyd, widely heralded years ago and still to be seen in disparate units in second-hand bookshops with the one volume abridged edition, leaving O'Toole's effort close to prolix wiki.

His methodology adopts the infamous GBS preface with occasional headings but without the Shavian eminence. The text inside the multiple wrappings is occasionally cringe 'GBS was the invention of a single, obscure impoverished Irishman'. O'Toole hails 'all the actors and directors over many years who have illuminated Shaw's plays for me'. His list of local experts includes Caitriona Crowe and Gabriel Byrne who has made a short film on Shaw as part of the promotion for the book.

There is the continuous assertion of discovering GBS as if he were a literary phenomenon like George Gissing whose career missed out becoming notoriously popular. The hyperbole is awkward 'no-one ever wished that Shaw had been just a little more loquacious'. He wants to 'restore at least a little of that admiration for what Shaw did and what he got away with'. A little? Shaw is a global phenomenon. O'Toole just about admits tongue-in-cheek to not attempting a biography or critical study, and is intent on re-establishing GBS's fame: the 'quarter of a million letters and postcards' he wrote, and at the age of 87, among correspondents Margaret Wheeler seeking advice on infant identity. Shaw requires no rediscovery.

Holroyd is prime source material on the ménage-a-trois parentage: George Carr Shaw, the Dublin drunk with a 'genius for poverty' and the domestic triangle of Lucinda Elizabeth 'Bessie' (Gurly) Shaw, the mother (O'Toole introduces her as 'Lucida'), and George John Vandeleur Lee, the Dickensian trickster weirdo paramour of the mother. Bessie and Lee became an item, not merely the chaste Victorian lie that he was her singing teacher, and Lee became a member of the household eventually squeezing out Shaw the man of the house as the couple left for London, followed later by Shaw junior, aged 20. It is an easily solved mystery in official biography, O'Toole retells it badly in a plodding drawl; unfortunately, because it was the template for men-women relationships in some of the plays. Shaw's schooling from a Protestant to a Catholic one is rehashed from Holroyd, and the well-developed Oedipus complex dreaming of Bessie: 'she is my wife as well as my mother'.

Where O'Toole attempts to synthesise his subject as 'the child of a most unlikely imaginative marriage: between Oscar Wilde and Leo Tolstoy', and his clothes style 'a kind of anti-dandy' (89) the scholarly aspect registers zero; similarly in retelling Wilde, Douglas, (Frank) Harris, and Shaw at the Café Royal during the Queensberry libel trial. He is on safer ground locating GBS's thought 'from German romantic philosophy, his version of Schopenhaur's Will is moving towards the creation of a Nietzechean Superman' but the spellings should be Nietzschean and Schopenhauer. Analysis of the brief Movietone (1928) footage of GBS 'as Mussolini' in playful pose is gratuitous, and hinting that he was serious about being 'Fenian' in a letter to De Valera, misses the Shavian wit.

The politics are better reflected 'when it comes to nationalism, Shaw is anti-Marxist', however *St Joan* representing 'Casement's martyrdom' is well known. Damning Carson and wanting to 'make Ulster an autonomous political lunatic asylum' increases the wit content. Shaw's England before WWI is forced uncomfortably into trite parameters: 'Heartbreak House is a series of erotic parlour games—with cruelty, power and desire as the cards to be played. We should never be allowed to forget that above the drawing rooms of the Shavian stage there are bedrooms. Of course if Shaw is played sexlessly, the plays will seem sexless'. The latter is an obvious statement.

It gets convoluted with the 10 'distinguishing rules of Shavian theatre' coupled with the 'five kinds of laughter': 'hysteria, derision, mechanical laughter, the laughter of misery and the laughter of intellectual revelation' where 'GBS the didactic social critic' is 'radically different' from 'GBS the universal sage'. These lapses cannot be saved by 'Shaw's key insight that sexuality and economics are closely intertwined' and his plea for 'unconditional equality of income for everyone without regard to character, talent, age or sex' and that 'universal suffrage itself is a fraud'.

Shaw's best prefaces including the one to Heartbreak House as well as his 'attacks' on the so-called Great War for king and country, as well as his refusing a knighthood are essential elements of the astonishing reputation. Pirandello's lengthy criticism coheres in finding Saint Joan 'is a Puritan, like Shaw himself' whereas O'Toole's evaluation takes a hipster approach that appears catchy but not strong enough for assessing GBS. The following is weak 'Back to Methuselah is really Pilgrim's progress recast as evolutionary science fiction'. Similarly 'Back to Methuselah is the first of three early twentieth-century Irish attempts at a sweeping meta-history of humanity, to be followed by W. B. Yeats's A vision and James Joyce's Finnegans wake'. O'Toole's house style adopts an irritating mix of upper and lower case capital in titles.

The preface to Misalliance echoes Swiftian satire 'to introduce the shooting of children as a sport, as the children would then be preserved very carefully for ten months in the year'. The context as literary medium and rhetoric come into play importantly because such texts are deliberately provocative. O'Toole meets these stylistic contexts and takes to task Shaw's rights to citizenship which posited a seven year appeal for the citizen to 'defend his claim to live. If he could not, then he should be put into a lethal chamber'. Significantly and contextually, the follow-on line states that the citizen 'could, of course, be represented by counsel; and Death would be represented by an Attorney General'. Again context, wit, and satirical purposes must be emphasised.

GBS's imperial dictatorial tone is not always sanitised by *galgenhumor* and in Judging Shaw (a laboured title) Shaw is judged for what he wrote about Hitler, Stalin, and other dictators from the 1930s onwards. 'Shaw denounced Hitler's anti-semitic campaigns and laws' (Sp. Semitic) but was expressively dangerous and naïf on the Holocaust seeing the atrocities as occurring 'in every war when the troops get out of hand'. Such words are horrendously vile, despite being in his late 80s which was no excuse. O'Toole correctly has to out the old bird.

However, his summation cannot save the monograph trapped in lightweight phrases and cursory treatment on John Bull's other island (Shaw's published title is all in capitals), Man and Superman, Pygmalion, Major Barbara, Heartbreak House and Saint Joan: 'for all their lucidity, they remain enigmatic [...] Shaw is still thrillingly (and maddeningly) open-ended'. O'Toole's conclusion sounds confused as to ultimate meaning; it is true that Shaw was 'anti-Victorian' but the hallmark of Shavian drama is clarity like the prefaces. There is not enough emphasis on Shaw's comedy and the influence of music on his theatrical form. The real question besides the performance is why the RIA and the Department of Culture, Heritage and the Gaeltacht lashed out on a lavish production for a text which is haphazard, lazy, and a travesty of GBS, albeit projected at 'those who know Bernard Shaw perhaps as the author of Pygmalion'. Indeed, this can only claim to be a Shavian Guide for Beginners.

—*Books Ireland* 2018

LUNCH WITH SHAW

Denis Johnston: A Life Bernard Adams (Lilliput Press)

This has been a particular delight to read somewhat because the present reviewer met Johnston once in the 1980s in Dun Laoghaire Post Office and intrusively inveigled his way into a conversation that lasted more than an hour even walking the eminent playwright to his bus stop. He was a giant of a man in stature with a cautious speaking voice and half-squinting laser-looking eyes. If memory is accurate, he was frosty about Yeats, laughed at the mention of Lennox Robinson but revered Joyce and GBS. Revered might well be too mild a term. His only furtiveness seemed to be about *The Brazen Horn,* a book of esoteric speculation. He was delighted to discuss his play *The Scythe and the Sunset.*

Adams has a background that has something in common with Johnston making him a suitable biographer. He gives a good picture of the man with a deliberate inattention to the works since it is a life and not a critical biography. Johnston's life might well be set in a play by Shaw or himself in four acts: early theatrical successes; war correspondent during WW2; ten years in American universities followed by the bitter-sweet epilogue. Three women make up the strong cast: Shelagh Richards, the other half of their bad marriage, Nancy Horsbrugh-Porter and the central figure of Betty Chancellor, the enduring second wife. Walk-on parts include Churchill, Fieldmarshal Montgomery, Goering, Hilton and Micheal ('the Boys'), Bernard Shaw, Yeats, Wynford Vaughan Thomas, O'Faolain, O'Connor, W. H. Auden, Louis MacNeice and Behan, as well as his four children fathered with two women. But enough burlesque.

Adams does a lot well—scene setting the time of revolution and Johnston's parents William, a Northern Protestant who would become a noted Supreme Court judge in Dublin and Kathleen King whose father was a founder of the Elmwood Avenue Presbyterian church in Belfast where William and Kathleen married. Johnston's childhood was spent in middle-class Edwardian Ballsbridge giving him the same milieu and background as Synge, Shaw, Yeats and O'Casey. He spent two years as a boarder in Edinburgh's Merchiston's Castle that widened his sense of Irishness from a distance. When Denis was home for Easter 1916, the rebels occupied Judge Johnston's house believing that the owner might make a good hostage. Crown troops ousted the gunmen whom Mrs Johnston had fed and found to be 'very nice, civil boys'. Young Johnston was jeered back at school in Scotland when he talked about the incident.

Cambridge and the Liberal Club provided a challenge to the growing youth, who on one occasion spoke for the motion that Ireland be declared a Dominion of the Empire. He would become president of the Union in due course. Meanwhile he had fallen for a wild siren in Dublin, during his student holidays. She was Ethna McCarthy, who drank, smoked and generally held forth— a woman of strong personality who would become a distinguished medical doctor and whose personality also absorbed the young Sam Beckett until she plumped for Con Levanthal.

At Harvard Law School, Johnston completed his studies but never wanted to practise at the Bar. In his other reading he showed antipathy towards Freud but became enchanted with Shaw's plays and their argumentative, erudite and brilliant prefaces. Suddenly, however—one might easily pinpoint the moment—he became a playwright in intent. In Dublin the Drama League was more real and compelling than King's Inns. When Shelagh Richards stepped into the limelight his fate was sealed. Shelagh came from a law family with a mansion in Greystones and a handsome town house in Lower Fitzwilliam Street.

They took the leads in an amateur production of Shaw's *Major Barbara,* which was somewhat prophetic of their tempestuous relationship. Both were ambitious for a life in the theatre—she as actress, he as writer and both would later direct plays. They married in 1928 in what comes across as a human farce with elements of tragedy ('Judge's son marries actress' a local paper headlined it) and thereafter they flirted in and around their marriage of convenience. Adams shows how ill-advised it all was, but he naturally has to steer his narrative of the life around this disaster.

The Johnston-Richards marriage is a clear cue into the theatrical shenanigans about *The Old Lady says 'No!',* its rejection by the Abbey and successful adoption by the Gate. This in turn leads to a good old romp through the thirties artistic circles of Dublin and London with the emphasis on theatre. His next play *The Moon in the Yellow River* did well in both cities, Shaw asked him to lunch but had a collected volume of his own plays on the table as a buffer against any potential thunder-stealing young upstart.

Johnston began reading J. W. Dunne's *An Experiment with Time* for background to *A Bride for the Unicorn* and pursuing another actress, Betty Chancellor; it was a fatal attraction as regards his marriage. His hero GBS had warned about the allure of actresses but was hardly one to speak when it came to his raucous platonic affair with Mrs Pat Campbell.

Johnston worked for the BBC from 1936, first in Belfast and subsequently as war correspondent. In Belfast he got involved with another woman, Nancy, and for a while was a laconic polygamist as reported in his diaries, 'a wild man on the loose'. Adams does not moralise and keeps his distance as the reader can watch Johnston playing a deadly game of juggling three women somewhat like an ancient Pharaoh. Nancy would in time marry Barney Heron but that did not end things for her and Johnston, it just added to the complications. Johnston as father of two would soon have a child with Betty and incur the moral disfavour of his parents and the further vitriol of his estranged wife.

'Johnston's War' as Adams calls one of his chapters is a marked contrast to the roar of the crowd, the smell of the greasepaint, footlights, and curtains going up. His wartime reading was austere and ideal as he tested the classics in the heat of battle with *Ulysses* and Dante's *Inferno*. Just as the diaries gave a structure to the earlier chapters, Johnston's *Nine Rivers from Jordan* punctuate the flow throughout the war years. The book was made into an opera in 1969. Johnston wrote the libretto for music by Hugo Weisgall.

He found himself almost unafraid under shellfire. In North Africa encounters with Churchill and Monty are shown as memorable and often hilarious. Monty used his clout to get Johnston a jeep for his job. The playwright read *Mein Kampf* and hated Hitler, adopting a decidedly Allied war stance—give Jerry hell—that obviously suited the BBC. When the flak is flying and death is all around Johnston mentions praying to God for his own safety. He and his best buddy fellow broadcaster Vaughan Thomas formed a Welsh-Irish league of gentlemen outsiders among the rank and file.

Johnston's Italian campaign is just as exciting. When he is among the troops on the final battles with the Nazis and sees the remainders of the Jewish nation, his reaction is "This is an offence against the human race—an attempt to dehumanise the species—and those capable of such things will have to be killed themselves." Hitler's suicide in Berlin is greeted with amazing sang froid. When he joins his fellows at a press conference for the arrested Hermann Goering, the old Nazi admits ordering the bombing of Coventry and tells of his escape from death at the hands of the Gestapo having begged Hitler to surrender. As Goering was led out Johnston rose and saluted; the German Fieldmarshall stared a moment in perplexity and returned the salute. No-one knows what Johnson's peers felt about the solitary saluting Johnston, who had been to Buchenwald and according to Adams did not see through Goering's "shameless evasion of any responsibility for the camps".

One is hooked at this stage but the biography has reached its plateau and thereafter slopes to the close, including the three months in Massachusett's Amherst College, followed by ten years in nearby Mount Holyoke. These years allowed his passion for theatre to further blossom among students and he could often stage his own plays at will with a ready cast among the young. *The Scythe and the Sunset* had its premiere in Cambridge, Massachusetts. An old enemy, Gabriel Fallon, panned it in Ireland, finding it boring, while Elliott Norton was not entirely positive either. Johnston moved on for subject matter to Swift's love triangle with Stella and Vanessa coming up with *The Dreaming Dust* and stridently believing his own theory portrayed in the play about consanguinity ensuring that Swift and Stella were never lovers except in the platonic sense.

Meanwhile Johnston, who housed himself in a wide variety of countries and continents from La Prevost's Tower in Portmarnock in the thirties to a house on Alderney in the sixties, returned to Dublin in 1970 to live at 9 Sorrento Terrace, Dalkey. He lived another fourteen if less active years. He was buried in St Patrick's Close next to his second wife, Betty Chancellor. Shelagh Richards Johnston had placed a red rose on his coffin. Somewhat like Swift he had his two loving women through a long and fruitful life.

There must be no confusion about Johnston's work. One might applaud Adams' pleas for its merits. *The Old Lady says 'No!'* is as valid a work of literature as *At Swim Two Birds*. Both authors obviously found it daunting to have written a masterpiece—one a first play the other a first novel—so young, and in many ways they both then had to get beyond such a long shadow. Whatever about Flann O'Brien, Johnston moved on to fit out at least another six plays for theatre. Both also became fascinated by the work of J. W. Dunne mentioned above. Leaving aside Johnston's best-known international success *The Moon in the Yellow River, The Scythe and the Sunset* remains a progressive treatment of the Irish question. If O'Casey's *Plough* has kept its glister, Johnston's *Scythe* has not received the same accolades for who knows what reasons. Perhaps it is because of the elements of farce and absurdity in dealing with what we Irish prefer to be treated seriously—politics, nationalism and character. Similarly it deals with the so-called birth of the nation and such momentous events are the ultimate longest debate. Comedy may actually offend when closest to home and Johnston dealt with this medium expertly, as he showed early on in *The Old Lady Says 'No!'* that can still shock with its knockabout rousting Robert Emmett pantomime lead. Johnston's audience and enemies might well have been too serious for his satire. Even Yeats, who secretly admired him, was suspicious of showing Cathleen Ni Houlihan as a floozy mouthing in Moore Street parlance, in other words bringing the theatre of the street up on stage. Irish identity is complex and multi-layered from its historical legacy but also intensely brittle. A dumb floozy in a jacuzzi is often preferable to a walking talking living character who reflects things as they are through literature.

—*Books Ireland* 2002

BATTLER OF THE BOOKS

Jonathan Swift: a literary life Joseph McMinn (Gill & Macmillan)

Jonathan Swift: The Selected Poems A. Norman Jeffares (Roberts Rinehart)

Swift's Hospital: a history of St. Patrick's Hospital, Dublin, 1746-1989 Elizabeth Malcolm

The Quality of Mercer's: the story of Mercer's Hospital, 1734-1991 J. B. Lyons (Glendale)

"When I was a little boy, I felt a great fish at the end of my line which I drew up almost on the ground, but it dropt in, and the disappointment vexeth me to this day." Swift was fifty-one when he wrote these words to a friend. It is a good clue to his complex personality. Both Joseph McMinn's biography and A. Norman Jeffares in the introduction to his selection of Swift's poems quote the incident of the fish that got away.

But McMinn's biography skips over Swift's youth too quickly. When Jonathan Swift was born his father was already dead. His mother's servant took him into care. His Uncle Godwin bounced the six-year old off to a punitive boarding school at Kilkenny. Swift laboured at Trinity College before getting a degree. Through the uncle he became secretary to Sir William Temple of Moore Park in Surrey. He met the King of England through Sir William and, more important for his life, he tutored and began the lifelong relationship with Esther 'Stella' Johnson. Sir William Temple's son committed suicide and Swift saw this as an opportunity for gaining surrogate paternal attention. He left Sir William's service for the Church of England, but had to cool his heels later and beg a reference from Temple in order to get ordained. The library at Moore Park was Swift's actual university. From this decade came the first masterpiece, *A Tale of a Tub*. Printed anonymously, it denied the author any position as a clergyman in the Church of England when he was discovered as having written a satire on the Reformation or, in actual content, the tearing of the garments of Jesus.

Joseph McMinn's third chapter is the best. Through the Torys Henry St John (Secretary of State) and Robert Harley (Lord Treasurer), Swift was made the voice of The Examiner. McMinn says of his thirty-three contributions "Swift rarely displays a hint of partisan hysteria which could be used to dismiss the articles as the work of a bigoted hack." These were the London years of glory, 1711-14. The Scriblerus Club included poets Pope, Gay and Parnell along with Swift and Queen Anne's physician, Arbuthnot. "It is so laborious," Swift wrote of his History of the Last Four Years of Queen Anne, which was published posthumously. His longest poem (897 lines), about himself and a new lady friend of these London years, Esther 'Vanessa' van Homrigh, is in contrast to the Journal to Stella. "My library will be at least double when I come back," he wrote from London to Stella in Dublin. "Money spent on his library was a painful but vital indulgence," McMinn writes. There is rage against Sir William Temple in the Journal, but elsewhere its tender, personal language is an influence on Finnegans Wake, through which Swift stalks. Swift appears in Yeats' seance play *The Words Upon the Window-Pane;* in Beckett's *Malone Dies* a cousin-in-literature of Gulliver 'kills' everyone including the closing lines; and Shaw's pamphleteering is in a Swiftian vein. Who wrote more words during their life, Swift or Shaw?

The London years made Swift Dean of St Patrick's in Dublin, where he felt in exile. No mention of the friction between Stella and Vanessa by McMinn. Vanessa died in Celbridge in 1723. Swift rode around Ireland after she was buried. McMinn doesn't speculate on whether he was actually asexual or whether he married Stella in secret in 1716. Dr Johnson's 'Little Life' believes they did marry but continued living separately ever after.

McMinn is entertaining on the five Drapier's Letters, which made the Dean a national hero. With the pamphlets, they serve his fellow humans in a directly beneficial way. On 28 October 1726, Matte published Travels into Several Remote Nations of the World, the infamous 'Gulliver's Travels'. Swift's bestseller was negotiated with the London publisher characteristically through a pseudonym, Richard Sympson. An autobiographical poem written in the same year is in Jeffares' selection. So it was triumph in London and Dublin, while Swift fought with severe ailments, and Stella dying. His last birthday poem to her makes very good poetry; beloved Stella he had known for thirty years. After her death he wrote with Thomas Sheridan in The Intelligencer, a weekly. Sheridan, the author of The Art of Punning, had a son who was to write a life of Swift. By 1730 there were no more travels outside Dublin. A month after his death in 1745 *Directions to Servants* was published.

In this satisfactory biography, McMinn quotes Swift on his work: "It is finely written, I assure you, and, like a true author, I grow fond of it, because it does not sell: you know that is usual to writers, to condemn the judgement of the world."

John Dryden's doubts about Swift ever becoming a poet were based on six odes by the young man in his twenties. A. Norman Jeffares might have included one or more of the 'Political Poems' relating to Wood's halfpence. He has 'Cadenus and Vanessa', 'Verses on the Death of Dr Swift', 'On Poetry: a Rhapsody' and 'the Legion Club'. Swift's poems, generally, haven't got the range and formal accomplishment of vintage Dryden like 'The Hind and the Panther' or of Pope's 'The Dunciad' and 'The Rape of the Lock'. These last two extend Swift's method with subject matter of a satirical type, on women and dunces. Poetry is not created by subject matter alone. Swift's couplets are often equal to Pope and their elder, Dryden, but not always. Most of the poems would not have 'written themselves' that easily, even though they read like a first-draft success.

Is the best of Swift's poetry great light verse? No, it rises above that.

He wrote true poems to Stella. Jeffares has most of these in this well-produced Selection, which is in clearer modern type than the Oxford edition of all of Swift's poetical works (1967). He includes Yeats' version of Swift's epitaph; according to Yeats 'the greatest epitaph in history'.

A. Norman Jeffares is a much-capped player in the critical field. Many will want to see his choice of Swift's poems. Many will welcome it, and why not? Every selection has its whingers; every selection falls short of the complete collection. Selectors must not be blamed too vehemently.

Dr Elizabeth Malcolm, in the first chapter of her book, presents evidence against allegations of Swift's madness. "Swift was never insane; he did not die a raving madman in his own hospital; nor was his hospital the product of a maniacal joke." She has a list of symptoms explaining the Dean's bad health, including the apple eating incident at Moore Park. He ate over a hundred apples in one sitting. Dr Malcolm writes: "In fact Swift suffered from a disease of the inner ear known as Meniere's syndrome, which was not fully understood till 1861."

Dr Malcolm condemns Irvin Ehrenpreis (a respected three-volume biographer of Swift) who cites Walter Scott, Thackeray, Dr Johnson, Aldous Huxley and Father Prout. She writes: "According to such writers then, Swift was not only mad, but harboured a deep and violent hatred of his fellow human beings." She adds James Joyce to Ehrenpreis' list.

There are extracts from Swift's will and the hospital charters in an appendix; Dr Malcolm's elaborate history uses a lot of statistics and takes the reader from the earliest Director, William Dryden, to the present Director, Dr Anthony Clare. A notable medical superintendent was Dr Richard Leeper, whose portrait by Sean Ó Sullivan is reproduced. Dr Leeper and his milieu are ideal material for a novel. His was a record in terms of ability, achievement and service (1899 to 1941). In 1938 he recalled: "The hospital was just about 150 years old, and behind the times. Many of the patients were bedded on straw—just fancy that, in 1899! The wards were bereft of all decorations or suitable furniture. Rats ran along before me as I went round, and the patients ... glared at me out of their straw environment, in their cells. No lights, except stable lanterns in the hands of the night staff, enlightened the bedrooms, opened by a large deadshot lock key, as large as a small bunch of fire irons."

Dr Malcolm writes: "He compared St Patrick's in the 1890s to Hogarth's portrayal of Bethlem Hospital in London in the 1730s. 'Well, I have changed all this,' Leeper told the governors in 1938, and so he did." Dr Malcolm's book is surely the definitive history, with examples of long-term patients, the connections with St Edmundsbury in Lucan, the long-serving matron Marie Eynthoven, 1916, the Civil War, the North Strand bombing, the cinema in St Patrick's, Wittgenstein's close friendship with Dr Drury, and the concluding of the former's *Philosophical Investigations* from a room "in Ross's Hotel (now the Ashling) in Parkgate Street, just across the river from St Patrick's."

In 1984 the Royal College of Surgeons put up one and a quarter million pounds for Mercer's Hospital. Dr J. B. Lyons in this history says the price was in fact a good deal lower. The new library opened in 1991 and Mercer's Institute for Research on Aging was launched on 14 November 1990, when there was a performance of William Boyce's anthem 'Blessed is he that considereth the sick and needy', which had been part of a benefit concert attended by George Frederick Handel in 1741. Mercer's Hospital came into existence in 1734, when the Dublin Assembly Roll stated: "Mrs Mary Mercer with great charity given up a new building at the lower end of Stephen's street, facing William street . . ." and Dr Lyons tells us that the new building was completed by 1740.

"Grizel Steevens, Mary Mercer and Mary Aikenhead form a trinity of which any city might be proud," said Dr T. P. C. Kirkpatrick in 1934, the bicentenary of Mercer's and indeed, as Dr Lyons also remarks, three Dublin hospitals owed their existence to women. Mercer's had many blessed physicians who 'considered the sick and needy' in their day.

Dr Stephens was a student of the deeply Christian Hermann Boerhaave of Leyden; Dr Edward Hill "talked of the Greek and Arabian lights of medicine, Rhazes and Avicenna," and sold his library of more than 1,800 volumes fourteen years before his death in 1830. His favourite was *Paradise Lost*, of which he printed an edition using Milton's corrections. Dr Charles Lendrick, who witnessed the cholera epidemic of 1832 which killed 5,632 in Dublin, favoured cures using bleeding by the application of leeches. To him, diseases were "detrimental changes produced in the vital powers, involving the functions, organs or both", while Dr James Duncan's God in Disease. (1851) says disease is "due to the direct appointment of God Himself," and the purpose of serious disease on the sick "to make suitable preparation for the great change that awaits them."

Dr Jonathan Osborne, fluent in Latin and nearly so in Greek, wrote a book on dropsies. An enlarged edition was published in German in 1837. He became arthritic and used walking sticks until his decease when, according to his wishes, "the coffin was placed upright in the family vault in St Michan's church". Dr Richard Butcher, a brilliant surgeon, had "a modification of the bow-saw used by cabinet-makers" for his operations. His private life was unhappy. Dr Lister gave his name to listerism, an antiseptic treatment, and Dr Lyons brings his entertaining history into "the antibiotic age" with "the purchase of an ice-cabinet for the storage of penicillin" in 1942.

—*Books Ireland* 1992

IMMORTAL EXILES

Cadenus and Swift's Most Valuable Friend Sybil le Brocquy (Lilliput)

The Essential Samuel Beckett: an illustrated biography Enoch Brater (Thames & Hudson)

Images of Beckett John Haynes and James Knowlson (Cambridge University Press)

Writing Irishness in Nineteenth-Century British Culture Neil McCaw (Ashgate)

Did Jonathan Swift have a son named Bryan McLoughlin with Esther (Vanessa) Van Homrigh, and fostered by Esther (Stella) Johnson after Vanessa's and Swift's deaths? The son, allegedly conceived in London, is referred to as 'the little master' in letters, and mentioned in Monck Berkeley's Literary Relics (1789), "reported [wrongly] to be the Dean's son by Mrs Johnson [...] the boy strongly resembled the Dean in his complexion [...] he dined constantly at the Deanery on Sunday".

Le Brocquy mere makes this her central disclosure in Cadenus, and recreates the tempestuous relationship between Swift and Vanessa. Andrew Carpenter in the introduction does not accept her findings from the cryptic references in the Swift-Vanessa correspondence. If you give it half a chance it seems a plausible enough theory. Le Brocquy supported Denis Johnston's In Search of Swift (1959) concerning the patrimony of Swift and Stella; he had uncovered facts making Stella the niece of Swift—and thus legally unable to marry him. Carpenter is somewhat sympathetic to the literary detection of Le Brocquy and Johnston who produced work "to different standards from those of a university press".

Vanessa, one of the two great loves of Swift's life, was a solicitor when they met in London in 1711. They got engaged when he was forty-four, she twenty-three. Their romance set in London and

Dublin reads like a slim novelette of the eighteenth century, with duplicity on Swift's part as he flirts with Vanessa and constantly writes to Stella back in Dublin. When he and Vanessa are settled in Dublin (at different locations) he continues both relationships.

"I will see you in a day or two, and believe me, it goes to my soul not to see you oftener," (Swift to Vanessa). There are quarrels about Stella: "I have suffered since I saw you last; those killing, killing words of yours," (Vanessa to Swift). Swift refers to her 'huffs' and bad moods. She addresses him as 'Cad', referring to his poem 'Cadenus and Vanessa'. The letters have appropriate blanks and many secret phrases that remain coded to this day. Swift's paranoia about Dublin gossip was pervasive; hence the scanty reference to the boy. The relationship with Vanessa lasted over seventeen years.

The dramatic ending occurred with Vanessa's letter to either Stella or Swift (no scholar knows for certain), asking if they were married. Swift came to reply in person; this precipitated an argument, after which the Dean departed from Vanessa's life forever. She died soon after. Swift's own words on the occasion, as he fled from Dublin for a brief respite to the countryside, are preserved—"nothing more unqualifies a man to act with prudence than a misfortune that is attended with shame and guilt." The boy was left to Stella's guardianship and died eight years later, aged nineteen. The story does not end there.

Le Brocquy's companion piece, Swift's Most Valuable Friend, focuses exclusively on Stella, and of course the two-timing Dean. The central impetus for it comes from the Dean's brief note about Stella, written on the day of her death. "I cannot call to mind that I ever heard her make a wrong judgement of persons, books or affairs"—spoken like a lover, one might well add. This work is of less energy than Cadenus; it repeats itself without effective emphasis; for instance Bryan McLoughlin (Swift's son) is cited a few times as disliking Stella's dog Tyger.

Swift's position as Dean forbade attendance at the funeral of either of the women whom he loved. His demotion to Ireland rings through both works like a bell of doom. The reason given is his bad reputation in London. The long bitter exile in Dublin, away from the might-have-been of London and England, set a nigh immovable cloud over the life except for his later triumphs in literature which are not part of Le Brocquy's terrain. Details keep the interest—the greater part of Gulliver was written in the home of Swift's friend Thomas Sheridan on his Quilca estate in county Cavan. A township in Westmeath is called Lilliput with a small church named Laputa, both locations mentioned in Gulliver's Travels. Stella as poet is compared with Swift. Yeats thought her the better poet. Her poem 'On Jealousy' is quoted in full, and a poem looking to a time when Swift would no longer be alive:

To bear with dignity my sorrow,

One day alone, then die tomorrow.

Le Broquy emphasises that Stella's life of forty-six years, is little known "except what Swift has set down". She repeats the ultimate fate of the Dean many times; he was declared insane by a committee of nineteen set up to enquire into his state of mind, three years before he died at the age of seventy-eight.

Beckett is cast in immortality in two black-and-white pictorial mini-biographies. *The Essential Samuel Beckett* goes for the full life in over a hundred pages, or less than half covered by the biography and marvellous photographs, which concentrate on the years of *gloire* and public exposure, largely through the plays conquering the world stage. Some Irish critics relegate *Waiting for Godot* as a lesser work in the Beckett oeuvre. This is heresy to many Americans who are always crowning that play with evergreen laurels. There are oodles of photographs from productions of Godot here, from its opening on 5 January 1953 onwards. It was a grant-aided production secured through some favouritism among the selection committee and the money was only made available to a French director willing to produce the work of a foreigner.

Brater fits the other works into his account. Both prose trilogies are mentioned briefly: the early Molloy, Malone Dies and The Unnameable, and not least the later Company, Ill Seen Ill Said and Worstward Ho which was considered more of a unified trilogy by Beckett. Brater seems to miss the savage irony and depth of black humour in Beckett but laces the text with plenty of his comments. Perhaps only an Irish ear can see the wicked fun of Beckett walking in a sunny public park in London among friends, one of who remarks "Yes, on a day like this it's good to be alive," to which Sam replies "I wouldn't go as far as that."

Knowlson, the acclaimed Beckett biographer, with photographs by Haynes takes a different approach. Sam is revered as superstar in three essays, giving a portrait of the artist, his work as director and a discussion of the sources of the main images from his works for theatre. Any and every snippet of conversation or observation from the master is faithfully recorded: "People are not in touch with their spirit. What counts is the spirit." Again Godot takes centre stage in context, its chief impetus being Caspar David Friedrich's painting 'Zwei Manner betrachten den Mond' (Two Men Observing the Moon). Reference to paintings and Beckett is very informative, such as Ewald Dulberg's 'Abend mahl' (Last Supper). He is linked with many artists including Kandinsky, Klee, Rouault, Braque and Ballmer. Sport, from cricket to rugby to chess, and also music, is shown to be reflected in his work. Endgame in one photograph looks a claustrophobic family scenario with immobile Hamm, Cloy the servant, and the ageing parents ensconced in dustbins. Beckett at times looks like some of his own characters in the photographs, whether smoking, directing, in street-clothes as the isolata or looking enigmatic in sunglasses, a theatre set twice reflected in miniature in the lenses.

Swift and Beckett seem to conform rather well to being colonised voices, if you assume their creations are all Irish. Neil McCaw's collocation of essays are about how the dominant neighbour depicts Paddy and Mrs Pat, and how the natives write about their island that somehow always remains John Bull's Other Island. Michael de Nie is among the ten perceptive critics in this collection, where many writers are seen harnessed by their Irish birthright with the stigma of being colonial. De Nie skilfully portrays the cartoon presence of Irish stereotypes projected from the mainland. The Punch cartoons are consistently repulsive to the Irish. In one example, Doctor John Bull lists remedies for constraining the already chained and strait-jacketed Patrick, pinioned by two constables.

Trollope, commenting on his novel Phineas Finn, claimed that he was wrong to marry the hero "to a simple pretty Irish girl, who could only be felt as an encumbrance". The Bröntes had hidden Irishness way up there on the moors as they wrote their romances, according to Kathleen Constable. Charles Lever proved himself to be an adapter of Irish identity for a British market. The discussion enters the fiery centre of things through the editor, aided by Carla King, when land, tenancy, landlords and famine are examined in the works of Charles Kickham, George Moore, Letitia McClintock and Trollope.

Leon Litvack's discussion of Charles Dickens' three reading tours of Ireland ('65,'67 and '69), taking in Belfast, Dublin, Cork and Limerick, lightens much of what is sordid material to contemplate in the bulk of these essays, however expertly discussed. Dickens' fast friendships with some Irish in London, such as Thomas Moore (he was a big fan of the *Melodies*) and the artist Daniel Maclise is far happier stuff to read. He also made friends in Ireland. Dickens survived the Irish climate, the festivities, and even a rail disaster just as he had survived an uncannily similar one in Staplehurst. While the novelist remained antipathetic to Irish nationalism, both admiring and disliking Daniel O'Connell, his search for character essentials among the Irish made him a most welcome Englishman on Irish shores. He brought those aspects of the artist to his enterprise, with the ability to make his listeners and readers weep as well as laugh at their humanity.

—*Books Ireland* 2004

LITERARY CONSORTS

The Dolmen Press: A Celebration Maurice Harmon (Lilliput)

Dear Yeats, Dear Pound, Dear Ford: Jeanne Robert Foster and her circle of friends Richard Londraville and Janis Londraville (Syracuse University Press)

Liam Miller (1924-87) as shown by Jarlath Hayes, who is among the people who evaluate his life and work here, was a man of many parts: typesetter, printer, editor, writer, set designer, Yeatsian scholar and philatelist. Hayes, a formidable designer himself, saw Miller as heir apparent to the Cuala Press, inheriting the Yeatsian fire and indeed in the 'New Yeats Papers' producing such sterling work as Kathleen Raine's From Blake to a Vision and Hayes's favourite example of his typography, The Roman Missal.

Miller does not come across very well in interview; he is somewhat pedestrian and this must not be blamed on his interviewers, Andy O'Mahony and Kevin Casey—transcripts are given here. In the Casey interview, he does light up in telling about a favourite typeface—Caslon used in the early Dolmen books. To O'Mahony he revealed a personal favourite among the Dolmen editions, Denis Johnston's esoteric and somewhat bizarre work The Brazen Horn— "it is going to be discovered and become perhaps a cult book". Raymond and Nuala Gunn mention other favoured typefaces such as Garamond, Palatino and Pilgrim. They also talk about Kathleen Raine's communications with Yeats in the hereafter and beyond through her dreams, while Dillon Redshaw brings things back to earth discussing some influences on Dolmen design from the Golden Cockerel Press, Eric Gill and Rene Hague.

Liam Browne charts the earliest days of Miller as printer, undertaking commercial work including theatre programmes such as for Tennessee Williams' The Rose Tattoo staged at the Pike. He also fills in on Liam's homes and workshops—Glenageary, Baggot Street, Fitzwilliam and Mountrath. The likes of John Calder, Louis le Brocquy, Terence Brown and Maurice Harmon provide short but glowing tributes as might be expected. Bernard Share in a very personal narrative mentions his 'still-born poetic debut'; among their many jaunts together was one to Paris, to meet Beckett and get him to sign two hundred and fifty copies of his translation of Apollinaire's Zone. The meeting at Boulevard Montmartre is hilarious as recounted by Share. He well might make a one-act play out of their conversation from that occasion, when Beckett found it amusing that Miller and Share had to use an elevator with no light in it and could not find their way to his apartment easily, bearing a bottle of Jameson.

Besides Clarke, one most associates Montague and Kinsella with Miller's Dolmen Press. Both poets provide tributes here. Montague's is lengthy and comes from his recent memoir with marvellous pith from the Miller milieu—the great friendships with writers and poets and the version of Christianity that sustained him to the last. Kinsella comes in at the end in sombre tones giving his history of the Dolmen Press—'a kitchen industry'—from 1951 onwards and beginning with its precursors. Kinsella also unveils the situation at the end calling it "painful: the debtors [creditors?] hurt and blaming; his daughter in an impossible position, exposed finally to their questions". All tributes aside, this is the untold story and remains the subject of much gossip. Rory Brennan attempts to redeem the situation with laments for the shortage of state funding to nurture Miller's reign and, though he does not see him as the Robin Hood of Irish publishing, rather "if Penguin famously educated a generation, Dolmen—in Ireland—educated the taste of another."

As with other such commemorative essays there are no final balance sheets or audits here. The Miller of rumour and legend, the one remembered by this reviewer from the fringes of a book launch or two, is that of a bearded Byronic fellow flaunting his style and standards in the face of those rumours about debts. The epitaph of financial obloquy is often more trumpeted than his artistic excellence. Terence Brown at the launch made light of the financial scandal that hangs over Miller but many others do not. The unicorn and the dolmen might well be fitting symbols of the man—unique, deep, daring, aloof, of singular purpose and defiant in pursuit of his dreams beyond what innocent people would call the crass realism of the commercial.

JRF, as she is referred to by the Londravilles, her two able biographers who end with no mean assessment of her as a neglected poet close on the heels of Robert Frost and Kobayashi Issa. She produced five collections of poetry and a successful play, Marthe; this was enough to ensure whatever reputation remains which is further enhanced by her friendships with a considerable number of editors, patrons, writers, artists, diplomats and even President Masaryk of the Czech Republic.

Londraville and Londraville keep a fluid pace, avoiding the exhaustive laundry-list and passport details of fashionable biography. They discuss her involved relationships in isolated chapters rather than weaving many people in and out through the flow of the life. This method necessitates resurrecting people who have already been, as it were, disposed of and sometimes this gives a strange tone to the text.

Jeanne Oliver (1897-1970) was born in Johnsburg, New York state. Her father was a ne'er-do-well farmer and lumberjack, her mother basically an evangelical person. The bohemian daughter upped and married in her eighteenth year a man older than her father, Matt Foster (he was forty-six) and they settled in Rochester. Or almost. Jeanne's zest for visits to New York led to the chance of modelling work since she was a strikingly sensuous and intelligent woman far surpassing her husband's moderate temperament—proof of her physical beauty is shown in the nude photograph by J. J. Henner in the introduction. Soon she appeared in Vanity Fair, Cosmopolitan and on a popular brand of cigars. However, unhappy with being a mere spectacle as a public image she yearned for formal learning and education. Foster did not hold her back and put up the wherewithal too. For five years she resided in Boston taking college courses and doing occasional modelling.

Albert Shaw, editor of the American Review of Reviews literally snatched the well-known siren and opened up for her the world of journalism. As their love affair blossomed she established a firm reputation in literature and art criticism. From here on her life entered its most fiery and exciting period, 1910-28. Assignments brought her to London, Paris and Europe in general. Wartime reportage balanced the cultural content of her journalism— Zeppelins, U-boat attacks and soldiers alongside poetry and painting.

Café life in New York brought her in contact with that old rascal raconteur John Butler Yeats who adored her like many others. While she admired the likes of Kahlil Gibran, old Yeats found him "where art is concerned quite insincere". Meanwhile the wily old painter acted as a sounding board for her poetry, advising her to keep her work longer 'on the anvil'. The extracts from his letters to Jeanne are interesting on such matters. Their friendship occupies two exciting chapters.

Jeanne's theosophical leanings brought her into contact with Henry Steel Olcott, while she considered Annie Besant the finest woman orator she had ever heard. Her episode with Aleister Crowley is action-packed. After a night or two of passion, she absconded leaving the fiendish magician in pain. He must have cast a spell against her for she felt his presence for a long time, recalled his threats and recollected in her diaries the shame of casual sex. However, she was no prude. Crowley evoked her in his lines

O scarlet flower, smear honey

on the thigh

Of this shy bee, that sucks

thy sweetness dry.

Jeanne's studies in religion meant to her "the law of Karma, cause and effect, and the belief in reincarnation color all that I do, all that I think and feel".

In 1918 when her husband was sixty-four she fell in love again this time with John Quinn. Quinn's benevolent nature and patronage of so many writers and artists brought her further into the centre of modernism and its exponents. She would meet them all, including Juan Gris, Brancusi, Pound, Eliot and Joyce. Jeanne got to know Augustus John's sister, Gwen, gifted and indeed some believe more gifted than John himself as a painter. Gwen's confidences to Jeanne are reproduced from diaries, such as her affair with Rodin and a priest who apparently committed suicide over her. Paul Spencer Swan did a bust of her. Jeanne was made American editor of the Transatlantic Review by the ebullient Ford Maddox Ford.

Pound fancied her and there is a scenario of Jeanne and Pound undressed in the apartment of Georgette Christ with a rather chaste and true ending between all three? Jeanne was asked by Pound to act as agent for him in the US and their dealings with Quinn are fully fleshed out. Pound admired her elegy for John Butler Yeats more than other poems written for JBY. When the Transatlantic Review folded Jeanne used her influence to find new backers for a new magazine This Quarter which ran for seven years publishing many of the modernists. Pound in setting up his own magazine Exile in 1928 asked Jeanne for advice.

In a final brief chapter, Jeanne's later years from 1928 to 1970 are outlined. She became a tenant relations counsellor with the Schenectady Municipal Housing Authority in her fifty-ninth year and stayed with the MHA for sixteen years. Thereafter she was made Senior Citizen of the Year in 1959 and got involved with Zonta, an organisation of women promoting education and programs such as meals-on-wheels. As the literary history of her heyday was being written, she became a vital source of first contact with many of the leading figures and biographers such as Bernard J. Poll, Arthur Mizener and Michael Holroyd. Honours came her way such as an honorary degree from Union College, Schenectady. She was laid to rest in Chestertown Rural Cemetery alongside her old friend John Butler Yeats. By the sound of it she had a good old time as a bohemian; was happy to play second fiddle to her many men but was not averse to stealing some of their thunder as they were enchanted by her artistic talent, intellect and beauty.

—*Books Ireland* 2002

A COLD EYE

W. B. Yeats & George Yeats: the letters Ann Saddlemyer (Oxford University Press)

The Georgie Hyde Lees-Yeats letters have already informed the epistolary fabric of Saddlemyer's biography Becoming George—a triumph of its sort in a helter skelter of detail. The private arena of Mr and Mrs Yeats is never fully revealed while the letters begin with their marriage. Yeats addresses his wife as "Dear Dobbs" and "Dear George," however George was actually third on Yeats's list to Maud Gonne and her daughter, Iseult. He had proposed to all three women—George being the last and the one who accepted him. Yeats "brought" Iseult into his marriage and Iseult's marriage to Francis Stuart criss-crosses the correspondence for the first fifty pages through Yeats's vivid epistolary serial narration.

The older Yeats and younger Stuart were at loggerheads over Iseult; both obviously "in love" with her at differing levels of intensity. Yeats assesses Stuart: 'He is mad & I think a Sadist." However, Yeats's jealousy of Stuart alleviates: "I attained a much calmer view of the whole thing & felt very sorry for the young man." He eventually conveys a magnificence of humanity as ultimately the jealousy over Stuart ("Our Hero the Irish Gunman shaper of an Irish Ireland") abates but probably never ended.

Disappointingly there is little material on the occult, the banshee, astrology, mysticism as well as the ghostly instructors of George such as Dionertes who helped Yeats begin his greatest arcane prose work, *A Vision*. The correspondence has a wide constellation of poets, writers, statesmen, politicians and spiritualists among others as well as various figures who drop in and out. The biographical footnotes are of vital necessity and exemplary of their kind. While Yeats is much away from home his letters are full of news, opinion, speculation as well as cultural, political, social and literary commentary on his lectures, dinner companions, Abbey Theatre business, Cuala Press business, his agent Watt, his publisher Macmillan, and his editing The Oxford Book of Modern Verse amidst intermittent health problems and not forgetting ghosts, "enemy on the stair last night. May have been a warning..." There is also the supernatural in the form of a poltergeist "who has three times since four o'clock today thrown a brass ash-tray from my typewriting table." He ends the letter: "No further poltergeistery!"

George declares: "Dear Willy, You're a great letter writer." And so he is after a fashion but she is too. They make for enlivening correspondents. Yeats is "great" in his letters to others but not to his wife. His content in letters to George is also constantly shifting since he is preoccupied on many fronts. He is incessantly demanding. He moves from speculation to his needs for warm surroundings at clubs and hotels where he picks up colds easily.

"It is a miserable day cold & wet but there is a good fire here" [at the Saville] just as he enjoys the Athenaeum for the food and comfort. Occasionally there is a phrase befitting the poet: "Organizing is like a bumble-bee in a bottle. One tries all directions until one finds the neck."

As history unfolds, he comments on events. History is only one of his obsessions: "the Irish Republican Army is running short of ammunition *Loydd* George is getting stiffer in his attitude." In some letters incorrect spellings are conspicuous as with "Loydd" (above) which highlights Yeats's dyslexia. Saddlemyer in her transliteration from manuscripts faithfully reproduces Yeats's characteristic misspellings. Thus Gogarty is 'Gogorty'; Machiavelli 'Maccheavele'; Gauguin 'Gaugan' and more alarming 'here' instead of hear. In one letter, he writes "measles (or is it meazels or Meazles)" He was correct the first time! Metaphor he spells as "metephore." Noh plays are "No plays". Auden is spelt correctly only to be misspelt later as "Audin." Table cloth as "tabl cloth." Sleep [ing] pills as "sleap pills". One wonders whether Yeats who was suffused in mysticism, the occult, the Ouija board and Byzantine civilisation could spell these words. However, his printers sorted out the manuscripts along with George.

Pamela Mary Brown has stated that Yeats's feeling for language is based on sounds, vibrations and musical perception therefore spelling is not paramount for him. As a poet he is engaged not merely with language but with words as they are heard. He is in T.S. Eliot's phrase at the root poetic source primarily involved with music which though "inseparable from the meanings and associations of words" inherently come to the poet originally as pure sound regardless of how a word is spelt. Yeats is exalted amidst his dyslexia even if he cannot even spell "table" correctly.

Meanwhile, George is wife and particularly secretary, servant, as well as mother to Anne and Michael Yeats. Yeats as father is distant and caring yet immersed in his art: "I shall await with anxiety your next report about Michael" but in the same letter adds "From Swedenborg on that seems to have been the coming influence in the life of the soul…" He is attentive and sends his wife books by Wilhelm Wundt from London. His tone is slightly guilty as absentee parent: "Give Anne my love if you think she is old enough to understand & will not cry out 'Sacred Heart whats that.'" George "at home" in Dublin has stalwarts in Thomas MacGreevy and Lennox Robinson for consultation on aspects of the poet's steady stream of correspondence. The poet is highly dependent on his wife as presiding-all-purpose backup to the public Yeats. Yeats away from the hearth works hard but is socially active and culturally engaged: "went in the evening to the 'Chenci'—Today I shall see 'Medea.'" He means Shelley's The Cenci. His gossip is always ripe—Edmund Gosse speaking of Joyce: "Have you seen that disgraceful obscene book Ulysses? The author is a Sinn Feiner & a spy." Yeats defines Dev as "a theologian turned politician…' George can be witty as about the sign outside Robinson's house in Dalkey "'SHUT THE GATE' Lennox came home and saw it 'O if only we could write Hilton Edwards name on the back and send it through the post.'" The purchase of Thoor Ballylea coincides with Yeats as senator writing of renovation: "I cannot get that fine top room at Ballylea out of my head—fire-place & all magnifiscent." George is a home bird also: "green paint on Castle windows & shutters is fine." And as his constant helper she suggests: "I am sure you need a change of glasses—" since Yeats is reading Plato's Timaeus (and adds): "It seems the root of most mystical thought."

George's letters during the Civil War are fabulous documentary material while Yeats frolicks with Ottoline Morrell in England. George is opposed to the Cosgrave executions of November 1922 yet sounds unafraid of the war: "A stirring life." The Erskine Childers' execution provides her with further expert exposition of the Civil War. When Lady Gregory alerts Yeats to the fact that The Winding Stair is a novel by Alfred Woodley Mason subsequently made into a film, Yeats consults his wife since he wishes to use the title for his collection that became The Winding Stair and Other Poems. George is always on hand, bringing Swifts poetry to Coole Park as he is composing The Words upon the Window-Pane which Saddlemyer gives as The Words upon a Window-Pane. Yeats writes to George: "I have finished the play as completely as it can be finished without your criticism. Could you bring down your type-writer, & let me dictate a clean copy." Mrs Yeats is also social secretary: "For heaven's sake don't forget that you have GOT to be here on Thursday of next week for dinner..." In this case at the Governor-General's James McNeill.

Yeats is frequently ill and recuperates in Italy, Mallorca and Majorca with George arranging everything. His first will is witnessed by Pound and Bunting. Yeats's dalliances with Gwyneth Foden, Dorothy Wellesley, Ethel Mannin, Edith Shackleton Heald and Margot Ruddock could not be part of the letters here yet some of these figures are mentioned as "friends" since he resides with them and writes from their residences to his wife. Despite his sexual infidelity, he tells George "I miss you greatly". Yeats on his lecture tour of America writes vigorously from Ohio on reading D. H. Lawrence: "...there is passion as Shakespeare understood it." His nightmares about George being dead end happily: "I took you up & then bit by bit you came to life. I woke up very content." In 1938 with 175 subscribers for the Cuala Press edition of his New Poems 350 copies is only economically viable—a small edition considering his stature and reputation. Of these poems, he comments in an uncharacteristic off-guard manner: "Ezra [Pound]...writes that my recent poems are 'rather good' which for him is rapturous approval."

Among the final letters are some to his daughter Anne who had become a designer at the Abbey: "...you must not attack a man's faults. Coleridge lays the principle down in so many words, but the Dublin critics are cruel because ignorant men." His closing letter in the correspondence is also to Anne about proofs for "On the Boiler" and their passage through the Longford Printing Press. The final letters do not reach the sublime of the famous letter to Lady Pelham not in this collection ("You can refute Hegel, but not the Saint or the Song of Sixpence"). Yeats is masked and covert when writing to his wife except when expounding on literature, art, philosophy, mysticism and the supernatural. True to his epitaph, he casts a cold eye on life in these "Mr and Mrs" letters.

—*Books Ireland* 2011

KING OF THE CATS

The Collected Works of W. B. Yeats, Volume III: autobiographies eds. William H. O'Donnell and Douglas N. Archibald (Scribner)

The Collected Works of W. B. Yeats, Volume V: later essays ed. William H. O'Donnell (Scribner)

The Collected Works of W. B. Yeats, Volume XII: John Sherman and Dhoya by W. B. Yeats ed. Richard J. Finneran (Macmillan)

The Speckled Bird: an autobiographical novel with variant versions W. B. Yeats ed. William H. O'Donnell (Palgrave)

The Yeats Reader: a portable compendium of poetry, drama and prose ed. Richard J. Finneran (Palgrave)

Yeats's Collaborations: Yeats annual no. 15 eds. Wayne K. Chapman and Warwick Gould (Palgrave)

Yeats and the Visual Arts Elizabeth Bergmann Loizeaux (Syracuse University Press)

W. B. Yeats: Vain, Glorious, Lout: a maker of modern Ireland by Anthony J. Jordan (Westport Books)

He was spellbound by Wilde's conversation, referred to as 'an astonishment'. Many quotations are given. "Mr Bernard Shaw has no enemies but is intensely disliked by all of his friends"— which might well have applied to WB himself. AE (George Russell) once toyed with the idea of dedicating a book to him with the words 'To my oldest friend and enemy'. On the death of Swinburne in 1909, the thirty-eight-year-old WB declared to his sister, "I am king of the cats." He is barely represented on the Higher Level English Course in secondary schools, usurped by Heaney, Larkin, Emily Dickinson and Eavan Boland. Has his reign come to an end?

These autobiographical sketches are sparing on childhood details, almost silent about the mother but not on the well-off ancestors and the struggle with the father: "It was only when I began to study psychical research and mystical philosophy that I broke away from my father's influence." Accounts of contemporaries in Dublin, London and Paris are the real excitement here. The list of names includes Verlaine, and Ernest Dowson pining for the love of his earthly goddess reminds him of Maud Gonne: "Her complexion was luminous, like that of apple-blossom through which the light falls, and I remember her standing that first day by a great heap of such blossoms in the window."

WB does not sound as pompous as many seem to think. Henley revised his early lyrics (Pound would prompt him later) but Ibsen is given the *lash*— *Rosmersholm* has "a stale odour of spilt poetry", Shaw's plays have the consistency of a sewing machine, George Moore's face is described as like a turnip with eyes, his writing style laboured—this fusillade of invective is a howl—it is the apotheosis of Irish mud-slinging. Only Synge the surrogate son is hallowed. The passion really enters the prose, more for Synge than Gonne but she got it in the poems. There is fascinating commentary about the Cabbala, the afterlife, the Abbey Theatre—everything---one cannot but luxuriate in the sentences, a few melodramatic. He denies Sainte-Beuve's dictum, "there is nothing immortal in literature except style", yet the style is magisterial albeit delightfully self-conscious in places.

Style comes to mind here also. Diffuse, elliptical, rewarding because of the deep spiritual buoyancy. One could dwell on numerous instances of his ingenious use of adjectives. In certain respects the autobiographical mode can hamper WB's flow of the egotistical sublime and this finds a more fluid vein in the later essays on Swedenborg, Balzac's *Louis Lambert* and others—WB claims to have learnt about society from reading Balzac. There are many introductions to esoteric sacred books from India such as the *Upanishads*. New agers might well delight in his familiarity with Yoga, Buddhism, Hinduism, Shintoism and Eastern mysticism.

Introductions to his own works are suitably self-abnegating and ironic. The broadcast on modern poetry (1936) is absorbing for the comments on Pound,

Eliot, Auden, Spender and MacNeice. Further significant comments on poetry are in the introduction to *The Oxford Book of Modern Verse*. He mentions shortening *The Ballad of Reading Gaol* and the olympian reasons for doing so, "I have stood in judgement upon Wilde, bringing into light a great, or almost great poem, as he himself had done had he lived; my work gave me that privilege". Is WB the only anthologist who ever presumed to 'rewrite' the work of *a* poet? If he was short of space, as most anthologists must be, why not admit that he was merely presenting the poem in extract?

John Sherman, like its literary cousin *The Speckled Bird* (an earlier work) is a bit of a false start for W. B. and an artistic cul-de-sac. The treatment of the love lost is slightly hollow—Margaret Leland sneaks off with William Howard, a high church vicar and Sherman, whose name is as nauseating as his character, writes her a cheery note of congratulations. Sherman returns to his childhood sweetheart, another cardboard character, named Mary Carton, and they ascend to Queen Maeve's burial place outside Sligo to proclaim their undying love. In The *Speckled Bird,* the central female is Margaret Henderson adored by Michael Hearne. It is easy to recognise WB's friend MacGregor Mathers in the role of Maclagan, and other contemporaries thinly disguised. Margaret refuses to marry Hearne because she promised her mother to marry a Catholic. Oh Gawd, you might well squeal at the plot but it is revealing about the poet's early life. It took many drafts and outlines (they are given here) to transform the beloved into a myth. If WB spoke to Maud Gonne the way the hero in these two works of fiction speaks to the 'two Margarets', no wonder she lost interest in him. Reading between the lines, the wealthy Maud Gonne refused to marry WB not only because he was stilted—he was impoverished.

Dhoya is far more satisfactory and has the same mesmerism as stories in *The Tables of* the *Law.* Set in pre-history it allowed the poet's imagination to run wild and fashion a fitting love story.

What is wrong with the portable compendium is that it has gone for too much of the portability factor. You get selections from all his poetry collections but it depends on your taste to agree with what is here or cavil at what is left out. Too many works are given in brief extract —for instance, the essay on *Magic;* rendering it by the nature of the subject matter out of context. Thankfully, plays are given in full, including *Deirdre, The Words upon the Window-pane* and *Purgatory.* An added bonus is early versions of six poems including 'Leda and the Swan'.

The Yeats Annual is dedicated to Anne Yeats (1919-2001) and her brief memoir of Jack Yeats is a highlight among the cornucopia of contributions— A. Norman Jeffares and Ann Saddlemyer head the distinguished list— including some lengthy reviews pertinent to WB and Yeatsians. Essays are on the theme, the poet and collaboration. To single out two: Janis Haswell on *Calvary* and Laura O'Connor on WB and Frank O'Connor with quotes from the latter on WB's excellence, and deceit as a collaborator who often claimed to have located material which others had first brought to his attention. There are previously unpublished photographs of the poet and others.

Re-issued from the 1980s is a study referring to fifty works of visual art that WB found useful for his purposes. This is like an adult comic with text by Bergmann Loizeaux filling in where the visuals provide the pivotal departure for her discussion. WB is quickly identified as a Pre-Raphaelite enthusiast from birth almost, because of John Butler Yeats's influence. The young poet, according to Bergmann Loizeaux, saw Maud Gonne as "an Irish incarnation of Pre-Raphaelite beauty". WB is analysed as sculptural poet having a lifelong obsession with many paintings, such as Rossetti's 'The Annunciation', Palmer's 'The Lonely Tower' and Burne-Jones's 'The Golden Stairs'.

Bergmann Loizeaux gets critical mileage out of it all. Ezra Pound's taste in art is examined from the viewpoint of its effect on WB. When it comes to theatre, "Yeats's idea of drama as picture as it evolves into drama as sculptor" is discussed with examples from the work of scenic innovator Gordon Craig, and Edmund Dulac, the illustrator and stage designer, along with samples of his masks used in various plays. Bergmann Loizeaux does a lot here and is not to blame for finding a context for the anecdote about WB's rebuke to

Beardsley, "You have never done anything to equal your Salome with the head of John the Baptist". Beardsley replied, "Yes, yes; but beauty is so difficult."

Jordan turns the adjectives that denigrate Major John MacBride in 'September, 1916' on to their author. WB wrote a letter against his will to the self-important Edmund Gosse who had insulted Lady Gregory but toned it down so as not to lose favour—both were assisting the poet's petition for a Civil List Pension. According to Jordan, he was a bully to his sisters at the Cuala Press, especially Lollie; was opportunistic and two-faced in dealing with arts patron John Quinn, manipulated certain members of the Abbey theatre reading committee, hoodwinked the Fay brothers, dismissed Lady Gregory's dramatic works, yet 'nursed' J. M. Synge, saving his plays from detractors such as Maud Gonne and Douglas Hyde. His absence from the funeral of John O'Leary, the great Fenian, was unforgivable —WB did not care to be seen among those he despised.

Jordan is loud in defense of Major John MacBride, attacking WB and Roy Foster in the process. Cruise O'Brien and Barry Shorthall are shown as being fair to the galloping major. MacBride's alleged adultery with Eileen Wilson and indecent assault on Maud Gonne's daughter Iseult are found to be spurious, based on evidence from the Gonne-MacBride divorce case. WB's fascist tendencies are explored in the rousing final chapter—the poet fantasized about holding a position of power in the Free State such as Giovanni Gentile held under Mussolini. Poor WB is well and truly berated for his cultural elitism, for supporting selective breeding and eugenics, and for a Nietzschean obsession with the absolute power of the intellectual. Jordan finds him a vain, glorious lout especially for calling MacBride a fool elsewhere, and praising Hitler in the 1930s. The poet's reputation is monolithic and can survive such assaults but having been almost removed from the Leaving Certificate is another matter—to say the least it is a disgrace since in many respects WB is still king of the cats.

—*Books Ireland* 2003

WILLIE DESPAIRS

W. B. Yeats: the man and the milieu Keith Alldritt
(John Murray)

W. B. Yeats: a life Stephen Coote (Hodder & Stoughton)

Yeats's Nations: gender, class and Irishness Marjorie
Howes (Cambridge University Press)

Willie Yeats and the Gonne-MacBrides Anthony J.
Jordan (Westport Books)

Why two more biographies of Yeats? And why not, since Alldritt,
a novelist, has written a brief if appealing one, while for
readers who demand a bulky tome there is Coote. Alldritt
somewhat ingeniously compresses the main events of the life,
work, loves, friends and enemies. This is not to damn Stephen
Coote who uses compact and appropriately titled sections within
a six-part structure. His scholarship is first rate and primarily
rooted in Yeats's Celtic mysticism, membership of the Golden
Dawn, the pursuit of spirit mediums, Tarot predictions, the
supernatural and the occult. Alldritt concedes that a seance conducted by Elizabeth Radcliffe was momentous for Yeats, who
afterwards researched into the lives of the dead people the medium had contacted, and found her facts were uncannily true.
His scepticism ended and he wrote to Maud Gonne about this
experience which provided "the most irrefutable evidence of
the survival of the soul and the power of the soul".

Coote's preoccupation with the occult is intense. He is not vague
about the Order of the Golden Dawn, the Kabbala, or the rites of
Isis. The doings and undoings of MacGregor and Moina
Mathers, a couple of modern Magi, is extremely virulent and
readable stuff, with the added gloss on Robert Artesson and
Lady Kyteler who both had evil leanings.

Coote outlines Yeats's ancestry, including uncle George Pollexfen, a considerable psychic like his famous nephew. Uncle George predicted Arthur Symons' mental breakdown from which the latter would miraculously recover. Both biographers present the necessary dreamy childhood, bolstered by Yeats's magnificent *Autobiographies*. When it comes to the myth-maker, Coote observes that Thoor Ballylee became "a tower as central to Yeat's thought as Duino was to Rilke's or Bollingen to Jung's". And both equally plumb the main influences on Yeats, especially his father, the eccentric and laborious portraitist. Among the other influences were John O'Leary, William Morris, Oscar Wilde, Edwin Ellis, Walter Pater, W. E. Henley and Arthur Symons. George Moore mistook the young Yeats "for an Irish parody of a poet". Lady Gregory at first sight thought he "strove to look every inch a poet". J. M. Synge thought Yeats's play *The Shadowy Waters,* "cuchulainoid". O'Casey, recipient of his praise and rejection, thought he had "caught an everlasting cold" selecting poems for the *Oxford Book of Modern Verse.* Austin Clarke was dismayed to find him fishing near Coole. When the editor of *The Irish Times* phoned with high praise and news of the Nobel Prize for literature, Yeats asked, "How much, Smyllie? How much is it?"

Maud Gonne became a terrible beauty in Yeats's life. Yeats's glorification of her proved too much for her to endure. Persistent love poems elevated her to heights she felt unworthy of and this made him foolish in her estimation. Her continuous refusal to marry him increased the quality and quantity of his love poetry. She told him that "The world should thank me for not marrying you". Her sexual frigidity caused him incalculable distress. Coote traces Maud Gonne's sexual problems to 'Tommy' her 'army father'. "They roamed across Europe playing up to people's dangerous illusion that they were a honeymoon couple". Her sexuality was father-fixated to the degree of minor trauma so she retained an incestuous fear of sex. Yeats and Maud Gonne enjoyed intimacy on the astral plane through dreams and mutual psychic experience. There is reasonable evidence to suggest they had a physical relationship also.

Coote mentions Yeats finding sexual relief on his own in the woods of Coole. He found masturbation fascinating and exhausting. "The great event of a boy's life," he wrote, "is the awakening of sex." Coote discusses "the sexual torment that was to fill much of his life". In time he would have an affair with a married woman, Olivia Shakespear, whose daughter years later became the wife of Ezra Pound. In the nineteen eighties, John Harwood writing about the Yeats-Olivia-Shakespear situation, added some burlesque to the facts: "Oisin had never been required to unlace a corset in near-freezing temperatures, or wrestle with a nineteenth-century condom, and Yeats's knowledge of these subjects was very much the same as Oisin's." However in time Mabel Dickinson "delighted by her lithe, athletic figure and by her ready compliance in pleasuring him sexually". But he found "her sexuality coarse", according to Alldritt. Their friendship ended when he over-reacted due to a pregnancy scare.

Alldritt makes Pound's entrance into the Yeats story really significant and usually cuts to the chase, "between Yeats's thirty-fifth and forty-fifth birthdays were his least prolific decade as a lyric poet, when the greater part of his time and energy went into theatre". Coote charts the founding and rise of the Abbey Theatre and interweaves the contexts, the contents and inspiration for Yeats's plays such as *The Countess Cathleen,* his first success. *The Only Jealousy of Emer* is shown as a masterpiece with revelations about Cuchulain's betrayal of the three women in his life.

When it comes to family matters, both biographies give little quarter to Jack B. Yeats and sufficient to the sisters, Lily and Lolly. Yeats's mother remains a remote figure. "The coldness of his mother had betrayed him at the deepest psychological level".

Arthur Symons, author of *The Symbolist Movement in Literature,* mentor and flat-sharer with WB, would eventually be 'dumped' by him, and write to the American patron, John Quinn (who had an affair with Lady Gregory) "wish you had heard Maud laugh at Yeats's marriage—a good woman of 25—rich of course—who has to look after him; she might either become his slave or run away from him after a certain length of time." Incidentally Symons called Lady Gregory La Strega (the witch) and predicted that she would domineer and 'get' Yeats. Coote is rather brilliant showing her editings, forced on the poet's early versions of 'In Memory of Major Robert Gregory'.

Alldritt, reliably matter-of-fact, writes: "The 52-year-old Yeats married Georgie Hyde Lees three days after her twenty-fifth birthday, on 20 October 1917, in the Victorian Registry Office on the Harrow Road". Yeats's best man happened to be the founder of modernist poetry Ezra Pound, who wrote a telegram to Lady Gregory having been asked by the groom "not to use words that would be talked about in the post office at Gort for years to come." The bride was Bertha Georgina Hyde Lees. Yeats's decision to marry was as anxiety-ridden as it brought temporary bliss. Georgie "would nickname him William Tell" because of annoyance at his constant chattering. Prior to this, Mrs Tucker disapproved of her daughter's marriage. Lady Gregory endured Yeats's Maud Gonne obsession until she moved the poet towards marriage, after many rejections from Maud Gonne whose daughter, Iseult would later marry Francis Stuart. Initially, marriage gave Yeats a new lease of sexual activity after the deprivation of his early life. His marital infidelity was dismissed by his wife, "When you are dead people will talk about your love affairs, but I shall say nothing, for I will remember how proud you were". Sean Ó'Faolain said that Georgie was 'almost his procuress'. Yeats believed, "the tragedy of sexual intercourse is the perpetual virginity of the soul".

Alldritt makes full use of salacious innuendo when discussing Yeats's love-life; with Ethel Mannin (a four-year relationship), he told her "his poetry came out of rage and lust"; Dorothy Wellesley a bisexual poet, "encouraged him to enjoy thoughts, sensations, feelings and experiences of androgyny" at her grand house near Penns-in-the-Rocks; Margot Ruddock sought him out in Majorca after their affair and "talked wildly about killing herself". She almost managed it. Yeats and his wife had to "bear the costs of having her escorted back to England". Margot Ruddock, formerly an actress named Margot Collis, would enjoy some repute as a poet boosted by Yeats and die in a lunatic asylum, aged forty-four. Edith Shackleton Heald, also bi-sexual; at seventy two, he wrote to her, "O my dear I want to say all those foolish things which we sometimes read out in breach of promise cases."

Coote is useless when dealing with Yeats and other women after his marriage. He sounds rather prudish on these matters. Meanwhile the authorised biographer, Roy Foster, prowls the vaults of Yeatsiana having laid the ghost of Leland Lyons but not as yet "the Eagle" much awaited in the second volume, after the first, *The Apprentice Mage*.

The cover might have set Yeats dreaming—Countess Markievicz in military garb straddling a fallen pillar, gazing intently on a revolver, delicately supported in her hands. Seamus Deane quoted on the back cover, heavily puffs Marjorie Howes. And this is a rather good study of Yeats. The introduction promises analysis of gender and nationality. Her comment "that if Yeats had not met Maud Gonne, he would have invented her" is somewhat Wildean. Still she digs deeply enough in a short few pages and doesn't demand a politically correct WB because his "effeminacy and the lack of a genuine national and cultural identity" ended when he "rejected Celticism as effeminate". Matthew Arnold and Ernest Renan support her case. A contemporary of the younger Yeats, Lionel Johnson proves her thesis that *The Countess Cathleen* "makes, like Iphigenia, but in a loftier way, the sacrifice of herself a divine excess of charity." The play is put through the academic hoop.

She is compelling when relating the theories of Gustave le Bon derived from *The Crowd* (1895) to elaborate "the irrational and unconscious foundations of politics and society and the 'occult' technologies needed to manipulate them seriously". Yeats, she postulates, wrote by a credo that "the more unconscious the creation, the more powerful". The chapter titled "In the bedroom of the Big House" fleetingly explores sex in some of the major poems, such as 'Leda and the Swan'. Vintage Yeatsian quotations stud the text, "all noble things are the result of warfare; great nations and classes, of warfare in the visible world; great poetry and philosophy, of invisible warfare, the division of a mind within itself;" or the provocative Irish Free State senator, "If you show that this country Southern Ireland, is going to be governed by Catholic ideas and by Catholic ideas alone, you will never get the north." His antithetical side invoked St Thomas Aquinas's doctrine that "the soul is wholly present in the whole body and in all its parts".

He found, in the study of eugenics "an intellectual movement that seemed to gather together and confirm many important aspects of his race philosophy". She avoids making Yeats into too much of a mystery while presenting him as an acceptably profound poet who could claim that "my chief mystical authorities have been Boehme, Blake and Swedenborg". Thankfully, Yeats isn't deconstructed. There is the implication that he did not aspire to a common humanity while being able to observe in his contemporary, George 'AE' Russell, "you have the religious genius to which all souls are equal. In all work except salvation that spirit is a hindrance".

Anthony Jordan packs into his punchy, never-let-up, highly readable account, a lot more than any of the above biographers. He is partisan when it comes to John MacBride. The portrayal of Maud Gonne is refreshing about her liaison with Lucien Millevoye, who introduced her to guns which she liked and sex which she didn't. Despite sexual discomfort, she had two children with Millevoye: Iseult, and George who died in infancy. She became addicted to chloroform to endure the grief of George's death and kept his booties all her life and would die holding on to them at the age of eighty-six. The book has significant letters from Maud to Willie—Yeats throughout is referred to by the diminutive which he detested. Readers may well be divided between those who feel the use of Willie is amenable or not.

The chapter headings are like period-piece telegrams 'Maud Converts And Marries: Willie Despairs'. The book is not flippant and jokey at all about the Gonne MacBride relationship, subsequent marriage, speedy separation and bitter divorce. Research is used well, for instance Ezra Pound's comment cited by James Longenbach, that Yeats thought "Pearse was half-cracked and that he wouldn't be happy until he was hanged. He seemed to think that Pearse had Emmet mania, same as other lunatics think they are Napoleon or God". Yeats would make amends in the famous elegy 'Easter 1916'. The book comes up to the present day with Paul Durcan's grandmother Eileen Wilson, who married John MacBride's brother Joseph. The alleged sexual assault on Eileen by John MacBride caused grandson Durcan 'distress', since this differs with the happier memories "in which Eileen Wilson held John MacBride".

The photographs are well placed and if the quality of some of them is faded, this is more to do with the originals than their reproduction. Especially evocative, is the wedding photograph of Kevin O'Higgins with best man Rory O'Connor on one side and de Valera on the other. There is a photo of Maud Gonne's grave in Glasnevin and details of John Butler Yeats's death in New York in the presence of Jeanne Robert Foster. Foster ties up many loose ends, explaining how Maud Gonne's son Sean MacBride, as Minister for external Affairs, organized Yeats re-interment in Ireland.

—*Books Ireland* 1998

HORSEMAN GO SEEK

George's Ghosts: a new life of W. B. Yeats Brenda Maddox (Picador)

The Life of W. B. Yeats Terence Brown (Gill and Macmillan)

Despite a minor complaint or two this biography is something of a triumph. Here as in no other book before can you read about Mr and Mrs Yeats from the kitchen sink to the ouija board and on to the cocktail hour and other intimate occasions. Maddox, having rightly made the domestic scene a kernel of literary life, has already given the reading public books about Nora and Jim (the Joyces) and Frieda and Bertie (the Lawrences)—so it was perhaps a natural progression on to Willie and George. Incidentally, Yeats and Mrs Yeats hated their first names. William would not tolerate being called Willie and Georgie could not be called George and preferred the pet name Dobbs.

Georgie or Bertha George Hyde-Lees was destined to marry Yeats because of their previous association with the Order of the Golden Dawn of which both were Adepts Major. Yeats may well be said to have married in a state of crisis and had beaten a path to Maud Gonne and her daughter Iseult at various times which are part of this literary biography. Maud eventually married Major John MacBride while her daughter, Iseult married Francis Stuart—these characters make brief appearances in the book and often tantalisingly so. Stuart and MacBride are given an awful dressing down. Neither marriage would prove other than tragic and in Stuart's case Iseult would become as much a central myth in his life as Maud Gonne was for Yeats. However the fact that neither Maud nor Iseult wanted to marry Yeats was a blessing in the long run for him, in that the ethos of either woman might well have been the makings of a hopeless marriage for all parties concerned. If Yeats had married Maud

Gonne perhaps he might have been ruined as a poet since without her he soared.

When George and Yeats married in Harrow Road registry office in London they were seemingly compatible despite the age difference of twenty-seven years. While Yeats might be considered highly sexual, if not virulently so, his previous liaisons had been rather cursory if inexperienced with Maud Gonne, presumably Iseult but certainly Olivia Shakespeare. The book does not list George's previous sex life and actually omits the last thirty years of her life—she died in 1968. In many ways she became a springboard to Yeats's sexual adventure with other women later on in their marriage. Maddox deals with this obvious open-marital situation in an unprejudiced manner and wisely works with facts without engaging in any moralist, feminist or apologist mumbo-jumbo to explain what was an intriguing arrangement.

Yeats's high sex drive as a young man made him a constant masturbator but he was incapable of finding much joy in this practice. His premarital sex life even with the few affairs was a miserable existence for such a man. Happily with George all that changed except that as he grew older he was plagued with periodic impotence. George also found that his past loves especially Maud and Iseult Gonne were very much embedded in his soul, as it were, so from the very start she was more or less the third woman. Indeed, their first Christmas in Sussex was spent with Iseult Gonne as their guest. However when Mr and Mrs Yeats went between the sheets with communal intent they did get off to a shaky start and fortunately for both of them there was the bonus of George's Ghosts and of course Yeats's. Literally overnight George became for him a powerful medium clearly in tune with table turning and rapping. Her messages from the spirit world would in time be one of the chief sources for his mysterious book *A Vision*. She was also absorbed in the esoteric literature which he devoted years of study to and which quite obviously influenced the direction of his poetry from then on.

The early years of the marriage for Yeats certainly was an intensely happy period for a host of good reasons and not least as soon as they found common ground sexually. Critics and commentators have been divided about the reality of George's ghostly administers and sceptical when some of her instructors from the spirit world gave advice to Yeats on sexual matters. Similarly, Yeats did not want children at all as is obvious from his play about Swift *The Words Upon the Window Pane,* yet George's Ghosts persuaded him eventually.

Maddox has a very instructive digression on Yeats's mother "whom Willie seemed to resemble more than any of the rest" either Jack, Lilly or Lolly. His mother never knew about his writing poetry at all, such was her withdrawn state. The implication from the book is that Yeats's lack of sufficient mothering hampered his relations with women. As a theory it seems to have a certain Freudian triteness. However, Yeats was without grief at her death which may have been the result of their chilly if not loveless relationship. Writing to his then lover Mabel Dickinson some months later, he became quite emotional. "When a mother dies all things often go better with her children for she has gone where she can serve them better than she can here." Yeats's father was delighted with his son's new bride and got her to sit for a portrait, while Yeats himself went on a lecture tour to finance the refurbishing of the famous tower, Thoor Ballylee, a suitable gift for his beautiful wife. However as time went on George soon became dependent on literary friends of Yeats's such as Lennox Robinson and Thomas MacGreevy to act as an ear for her day-to-day problems because Yeats's self-absorption could not find the time to listen. She also drank steadily—according to chapter and verse quoted in the book, to excess—usually gin with dry Martini, but champagne was also to her liking. She smoked a lot, even more than her husband.

Despite the arrival of children the Yeatses managed foreign jaunts especially to the Ezra Pound circle at Rapallo. Yeats found in his life with George a complete new lease of inspiration or, as Maddox scatologically puts it, "his hard-won artistic creed told him that the spunk and shit of human existence are the wellsprings of creativity". Meanwhile he had to keep *pace* with her *sexual* appetite and sought the aid of Dr Norman Haire for a Steinach operation to have testosterone implanted where he most needed it. The operation gave Yeats an increased sex drive but he quickly sought out new partners. These were not all sexual liaisons as in the case of Gwyneth Foden, whose residence with Yeats and the Swami in Majorca is nothing short of hilarious as recounted by Maddox. The good that came out of his friendship with the Swami Shri Purohit was a translation of the *Upanishads*. His affair with Margot Ruddock was ill advised. She was an ambitious poet and needed a leg up careerwise. Her mental instability resulted in a public scene involving the press which unsettled Yeats terribly. Yet by Maddox's account, George took it all in her stride and remained almost unruffled.

Thereafter Yeats sought out more mature women, Dorothy Wellesley and the formidable Edith Shackleton Heald. Edith was well up to Willie's bedroom antics. When Yeats wanted to send her a naughty verse he consulted George. It is worth quoting for purposes of disclosure: A beating on the buttocks/Will warm your heart and mine/My lash is all good leathers/Yours a penny worth of twine. In less frivolous vein, he wrote to Edith, "We who create have to cultivate our wild beasts; most people have to subdue them."

As a father, Yeats was too old and too solipsistic to relate to his children but this may be an oversimplification. Anne did get involved with the design of sets for his play *Purgatory* however Michael, his son, never saw eye to eye with the father; politically they became sharply divided over de Valera. Maddox is quietly brilliant in her analysis of some of the poems and judiciously peppers her text with apposite lines from the great Irish genius. She embarks on a cool estimation of Yeats's demons who tortured him during his last months. He suffered mental anxiety and remorse, fearing that he had inspired the Easter Rising. She quotes critics who say he did or did not—the evidence would certainly make him a contributory agent. He was also tortured in his mind about Margot Ruddock whose life was a battle with insanity. The fate of Coole Park haunted him and his prophecy of its destruction came true. Can the emerald striped Tiger fling a pawful of gold and have it rebuilt stone by stone? In her scorching final chapter she really puts the cat among the pigeons and Yeats's remains are given prominence. Maddox calls for an exhumation of those remains, relocated from Roquebrune in France, where he was buried in 1939, to Drumcliffe in 1948 because along with a number of people including Nuala O'Faolain, she believes that his bones are not buried in Drumcliffe at all and that they are still resting in France. So whose bones are in Drumcliffe beneath the most famous epitaph in Irish literature since Jonathan Swift's? Perhaps they are the bones of Alfred George Hollis whose relatives discovered that his remains were missing at Roquebrune in 1947. Hollis, according to the funeral register, was buried next to Yeats. Maddox's solution to this mystery is that a DNA test be performed on the remains buried at Drumcliffe. Her outrageous closing remark is whether the situation bears enough gravitas to matter very much? It does matter. It matters a whole lot if the remains of Yeats are not at Drumcliffe. What country in the world would permit such a mystery which could easily be solved to remain unresolved? Immediate action needs to be taken—on that point she is correct. Surprisingly, so far, her book has not caused a single ripple with regard to the situation. Inaction in this case is a kind of infamy. Where is Yeats buried? One is inclined to read the consolation of W. H. Auden's tribute to him with great unease, 'Follow, poet, follow right/To the bottom of the night/With your unconstraining voice/Still persuade us to rejoice.'

To encompass *the life* of WBY in under four hundred pages is a tall order and perhaps Foster's awaited final volume may snatch the golden round. In the meantime Dr Brown holds the field. Early on, presented with a good pace is the lineage of mother Yeats and JB, respectively the miserable woman and the profligate bohemian painter. Close scrutiny is given to *Reveries over Childhood and Youth* and WBY's impermanent homes at Sandymount, Sligo, Howth and London where he fought to the knuckle with JBY asserting devotion to A. P. Sinnett's *The Occult World* "in revolt against his father's materialism". *The Wanderings of Oisin* is described as a formidable debut and analysis is provided with help from Harold Bloom and Richard Ellmann. Brown calls in a bunch of critics for analysis at every twist and turn of his narrative—the sonnet *No Second Troy* was inspired by *some* lines of Cowper's apparently. Long before he became an habitué of the Cheshire Cheese pub (London) along with Dowson, Lionel Johnson and others, WBY was a symbolist from absorbing Blake and by association with Arthur Symons who brought the French symbolists to English readers.

MacGregor Mathers led him into the ceremonial rituals of the Order of the Golden Dawn along with Maud Gonne. His second collection of poems *The Rose* evoked this esoteric experience and the milieu of AE 'the hairy fairy'. A distinction is made between WBY the occultist and the psychic researcher while spiritualist adventures always maintained domination in his life. The treatment of Gonne-WBY is well structured showing the latter's playing her off Olivia Shakespear whose novel *Rupert Armstrong* is a fictional account of their affair. WBY is presented as less of an unrequited, spurned lover simply because of Gonne's sexual revulsion derived from Catholic guilt. In other words, conscience makes for sexual cowardice. Besides, they later violently disagreed over politics, literature and religion which was the death knell for the flimsy romance worked into a myth by the poet. WBY, always full of contradictions, with a passionate love of country and a passionate hatred of Sinn Fein, "was trapped between the rising tide of Catholic national feeling and the obdurate cliff-face of his own caste's disapproval of his Fenian associations". The latter is typical of the style of the text which mixes hardcore academic passages of near mystification with others of perfect clarity and there is some use of arcane language such as eirenic, fissiparous, alterity, tetradic completion.

WBY is revealed in all his lust for any and every public controversy over Cathleen ni Houlihan, the Lane paintings and censorship, all of which breathed public life into his delicate isolation spent studying such dark luminaries as Friedrich Nietzsche. A respite from controversy came through John Quinn's arranging a lecture tour of the US; there would be many tours. In the Abbey Theatre he tended to view his ideal actors as puppets who didn't move around too much on stage or ask for too much pay. However, riots at the *Playboy* and *The Plough and the Stars* utterly changed the poet's attitude to Ireland. The loss of Synge went deep and he was then haunted by his fellow playwright's life lived "in the presence of death and childhood". With the publication of Moore's *Hail and Farewell,* he became furious at the portrayal of himself in the book which openly denigrates his onetime claims of peerage status when he was closer to steerage status. There wouldn't be another book so hostile to him until Francis Stuart's *Black List, Section H.*

The Easter Rising and its effect on the poet are illuminatingly exposed along with his holding back the elegy 'Easter 1916' until a marriage partner had been finalised—Georgie Hyde-Lees instead of Iseult Gonne. This elegy is analysed along with *Per arnica silentia lunae.* His friendship with Pound was of mutual benefit for both poets. Brown's scene setting of preWW1 London is reminiscent of Shaw's *Heartbreak House.* WBY's wife is quoted about her automatic writing, she was "seized by a superior power". Brown finds that *A Vision* "repels by its very oddity" but goes on to provide a synopsis including the firm belief in reincarnation. *Meditations in Time of Civil War* is fruitfully compared with *The Waste Laud*.

Leaving aside *The Second Corning,* WBY graduated to Norman Haire's *Rejuvenation* and pursued a flagrant sex life outside of marriage signalling a 'second puberty'. "This is delicate territory," according to Brown. He was sycophantic towards his extramarital lovers including one in the *Oxford Book of Modern Verse* (Dorothy Wellesley) and provided a sympathetic introduction to Margot Ruddock's poems *The Lemon Tree*. Brown finds the later work increasingly elegiac beginning with *The Municipal Gallery Revisited* and dislikes his adopting "the ravings of a mad ship's carpenter" in *On the Boiler* with its eugenics and politics close to Fascism and a yearning for restoration of the Protestant ascendancy. The last poems are interpreted in 'despairing cynicism' along with the play *Purgatory*—one might virulently disagree since WBY near the end wrote, "You can refute Hegel but not the Saint or the 'Song of Sixpence'". The book closes with reference to his influence especially on Beckett's plays and on the poetry of Auden, MacNeice, Allen Tate, John Berryman, Philip Larkin, Kavanagh, Kinsella, Montague, Kennelly and Heaney. With its speckled brown background to Lena Connell's fine photograph of the poet on the front cover and amongst the plates a pastel of Iseult Gonne by Maud Gonne, a dedication to Brendan Kennelly and a quote from Nietzsche this is an unashamedly critical biography.

—*Books Ireland* 1999

DOMESTICITY

Elizabeth Bowen's selected Irish writings ed. Eibhear Walshe
(Cork University Press)

Charles Maturin: authorship, authenticity and the nation Jim
Kelly (Four Courts Press)

Irish Women Artists 1800-2009: familiar but unknown ed. Éimear
O'Connor (Four Courts)

A delightful read: Bowen's miscellaneous writings in one volume.
A credit to Walshe's editing. He is light on source notes and could
have indulged himself more but the bibliography is complete. It may
be unfair to test this writing against Bowen's *oeuvre*, still
astonishing spurts of prose reach the lower slopes of the sublime
here. 'The Big House' does not shine as well as 'Bowen's Court'
(1958) and 'Bowen's Court: An Afterword' (1963). The latter
evokes neutral Ireland of the 1940s when "the wireless in the library
conducted the world's urgency to the place." As she ponders: "'Can
pain and danger exist?' But one did think that. Why? The scene was
a crystal in which, while one was looking, a shadow formed." The
WWII reportage is good social history also: "Lack of tea is more felt
than anything." Her respect for De Valera sounds mawkish yet her
grasp of neutrality is accurate: "Eire's first free self-assertion." She
is never platitudinous about Irish history: "we have everything to
dread from the dispossessed."

Bowen does not possess Maturin's (reviewed below) fear of the
native because she is native: "I regard myself as an Irish novelist."
Prejudice may reside upon her as Anglo-Irish and comments such as
"democratic Ireland no longer denounces the big house, but seems
to marvel at it." She revels gloriously in the Long Room, the banquet
and the house full of guests: Eudora Welty, Evelyn Waugh, David
Cecil, Isaiah Berlin, Cyril Connolly, and Virginia Woolf about
whom the cook said "I'd have known she was a lady by the stately

go of her!" In her complex identity, Bowen is Yeatsian, the "contribution the Anglo-Irish have made to Ireland is now recognized." Yet she can write of Ireland in the same piece 'Christmas, At Bowen's Court' (1950) "One is aware, for one thing, of the ancient Christianity inherent in her very rocks and earth."

Bowen's affair with Sean O'Faolain resulted in contributions to The Bell and a significant appraisal of "James Joyce" (1941) claiming that "Joyce, in writing Finnegans Wake, used the whole of his, by then, complete mastery not only of language but of its associations against the defences of mere intelligence." Of the book reviews included by Walshe, one regards them highly being Bowen-writing. Her editors singled her out to write on Ireland from an Anglo perspective yet this extends her position in explicating what is after all her birthright. She subconsciously or otherwise endured financial hardship and the demolition of Bowen Court, an idyllic "place to write in: as such it is happily ideal." In this respect, Bowen's complexity is Irish. And her dispossession solidifies the matter, hence passages like the following truly resonate: "Acceptances, do they not make up life? I wonder, looking out of the Long Room windows at the mountains behind, at the lawns in front and the lights through the veil of rain sifting softly, slowly over the lonely country."

As an academic study this is satisfying since he eschews jargon but is not clear of it, however, he is usually succinct: "Terror, not love, is the only true universal emotion according to Maturin." Kelly unwisely gives little space to Maturin (1780-1824) as successful playwright of Betram which Coleridge and Hazlitt responded in shock seeing it as "introverted sensibility" yet other critics found the play derivative of Byron's poetic persona with its damned Faustian hero. Maturin passively agreed with his audiences, "my muse I find it too atrocious for the stage."

Maturin was introverted, redolently Gothic and indeed pre-

Modernist in inverting Sydney Owenson's *The Wild Irish Girl* into his version of *The Wild Irish Boy* "beginning as an epistolary novel before moving on to a first-person narrative" in "revealing the true parentage of an orphan." The novel explores the author's pacifism and revilement of colonial violence. These themes can be said to permeate The Milesian Chief when Maturin turned his pen to the revolutionary United Irishmen movement. Kelly admits, albeit reluctantly that Connal, its tragic hero is Robert Emmett disguised. Maturin, unlike Thomas Moore, delved into politics and bloodshed showing that his villains "continually undermine idealized investments in national feeling." Maturin's Women, far from politics, is a love triangle featuring Charles, Eva, and ending with Zaira bereft and impoverished "unable to perform or employ her musical talents." One reads Maturin for the stirring style and story: "Paris, in May 1814, was, what no one now need be told, the metropolis of all Europe; all mankind were hurrying there, and astonished to find themselves there [...] all the riches of that dreadful harvest, that had been reaped in blood from one end of the earth to the other, were accumulated there."

Disappointingly when it comes to *Melmoth the Wanderer*, Kelly is lukewarm failing this masterpiece and dubbing its hero as "a deposed and problematically restored (crypto-Catholic) aristocrat." Kelly cannot enjoy Melmoth as a marvellous creation not least his longevity. In the novel his portrait was painted "in 1646, his absence from England during the English Interregnum, the Satanic pact in 1666, and his eventual death (or disappearance) in 1816, link him with moments of Revolution and Restoration."

Kelly sorts out Maturin's religious position in the closing chapter: "he is not against Catholics, but against Catholicism" Kelly goes for a mythic end, quoting James Clarence Mangan's sketch of stalking Maturin (unable to introduce himself) as the author somewhat like Melmoth "disappears" probably "into one of those bibliopolitan establishments" aka a Dublin bookshop. Is Shakespeare Hamlet? Is

Maturin Melmoth? Maturin's lack of self found selfhood in his Gothic fiction. His passive introverted life like Hamlet on stage creates a Gothic terrain of mostly, as Kelly suggests, terror.

O'Connor's introduction states the agenda as does the subtitle: the perception, achievement and reception of Irish women artists such as the 1960s when criticism "portrayed class in a negative manner." O'Connor champions Frances Isabella Battersby (nineteenth century) whose real identity remains uncertain while her watercolours of butterflies, birds and flowers are a botanist's delight or mere firescreen tapestry art. Catherine Marshall seems to forget that in trumpeting artists such as Kathy Prendergast, Alice Maher, and Dorothy Cross, art historian Anne Crookshank and art critic Dorothy Walker she is ignoring those who do not suit her agenda. Marshall parades (the unfortunately titled) NIWAAG (Northern Ireland Women Artists Action Group) consisting of Eithne Jordan, Pauline Cummins et alia and just about recognises shady academy dealings in proving the necessity for Sybil le Brocquy's anti-RHA group the "salon des refusés".

Myles Campbell makes a case for Louisa, marchioness of Waterford (1818-91) and John Ruskin who supported her "artistic reputation [which] did not survive beyond the Victorian period." Karen E. Brown's essay is an eloquent recounting of Evelyn Gleeson's ambient relationship with Dún Emer Industries. Carla Briggs writes a fabulous piece on Margaret Clarke whose Strindbergian (1927) remains a major work in oil. AE deemed the Ireland of the time swamped in "an anaemic art atmosphere" and disliked Strinbergian claiming that such a work "should explain itself."

Síghle Bhreathnach Lynch attempts to resuscitate the work of Lily Lynch (1874-1939) whose mosaics are crowd pleasing, easy going Celtic tracery, or in fact, pseudo Book of Kells design. Jane Eckett charts the glorious career of Moyra Barry beyond the Slade, and on her return to Ireland faced strong competition from "better-connected portrait artists such as Sarah Purser and Sarah Cecilia Harrison." Eckett does not develop her agenda and might have commented on the contemporary RHA clique in portraiture promoting the cosy cartel of Carey Clarke, James Hanley and Mick O'Dea and sidelining for instance, Maeve McCarthy. Riann Coulter only seems to half-believe Nano Reid's reputation in "abstract expressionism." Reid topples the book's agenda of women being sidelined since she is presented as being at "odds with her gender." Róisín Kennedy in praising Reid sidetracks into a panegyric for art critic Brian Fallon and abandons the agenda by over-rating Tony O'Malley!

Paula Murphy praises the sculpture, Gabriel Hayes (1909-1978) known for her panels on the former Industry and Commerce building in Kildare Street (Dublin) and The Three Graces. Hayes gained government commissions as a baroque artist whose heavy handed chiselling presents macabre figures. Jane Humphries is all theory in pursuing modernism as "culplable for the devaluation of the domestic in art theory" which she borrows from the theories of Christopher Reid. Modernism is many things in the eye of the beholder. Humphries is over the top praising Margaret O'Brien's installation "I live in the Cracks in the Wall." Irish installation/exstallation tends to exhibit post-Graduate eccentricity from its cradle. Una Walker rounds things off and admits that statistics are a "blunt instrument." Still, she wields facts, figures, and distribution charts about the ratios of male/female 3.5:1 for one-person exhibitions in Belfast between 1960-1995. Therefore, besides artists there were many half-artists exhibiting which certainly proves her point, unintentionally one presumes.

—*Books Ireland* 2012

'I HEAR AMERICA SINGING'

The Routledge Introduction to American Modernism Linda
Wagner-Martin (Routledge, 2016)

Wagner-Martin includes fellow critics to enable the vast structure
involved in establishing her central parameters, particularly
showcasing 'the African American achievement' (110). In this
respect, Jonathan W. Gray in highlighting a landmark The Book of
American Negro Poetry (1922) edited by James Weldon Johnson
which found ardent readers in the likes of Stein and Hemingway,
Paris-based and far from home who benefitted from 'the versatility
of black writing'. Her collectivism is a salient feature, and at its best
intoxicating as a theory of literature is engulfed in the zeitgeist.

However, it is not all plain sailing, Sheri Benstock is brought on
board for gender balance since 'the hegemony of masculine
heterosexual values [that] have for so long underwritten our
definitions of Modernism' (61). Yes and no, and certainly here there
is equal billing and readers not in the know, can discover some
brilliant females alongside the long established bulls.

Her writers are discussed as multi-genre and being involved with
'painting, sculpture, photography, and music' (3). Style becomes the
focus of this study where the image is central and based by many
writers on the impetus from journalism (5). Time is never linear as
she preferences fluidity and 'imaginative durée'(6) in many of the
referenced works. Content tends to be political with stark social
commentary, for example in Kate Chopin's The Awakening (1899)
influenced by Madame Bovary and Ibsen's Ghosts where the
heroine chose 'death by drowning' (fearlessly!) rather than domestic
life (12). Traditional lines and antecedents are thus noted. However,
Dreiser's gloom is hallmark 'American', and has to be 'tinged with
sufficient idealism' according to the author (14).

Larsen in The Sea Wolf (1903) is not an Ahab lookalike, he is more
educated which proves that modernism is didactic 'compelled to

better the lot of the average man' (Jack London) (17). Larden (London) spawned the American mystical hobo for subsequent decades from Nelson Algren's Somebody in Boots (1935) to Kerouac and beyond. She raves about Upton Sinclair's The Jungle (1906) foreshadowing The Grapes of Wrath (1939).

Social history underpins her engaging commentary as in 25m immigrants arriving in the US 'between 1880-1930' (27). Emma Lazarus is footnoted as 'ironic' with 'I lift my lamp beside the golden door!' (29) for some it may as well have been the colossal wreck of Ozymandias. Anzia Yezierska typifies life 'being much worse than expected' (28), hence her novels Salome of the Tenements (1922) and Arrogant Beggars (1927). Poets express realism, as in Lola Ridge's "The Ghetto" and Ruth Lechlitner's "Lines for an Abortionist's Office" (30). She quotes extensively, contrasts, develops and everything is strongly chronological, as if Modernism rolled along reflecting a coast to coast journey, decade by decade. At least that is the feel of it as some holdall had to be pushed onto the disparate material.

Standard modernist poetry is discussed as evolving through the 'mythic method' shadowed by 'Freud, Jung, Frazier' and significant others (49). Whitman is, of course, vital paternity setting off 'performance and choral' through Robinson, Sandburg, (Vachel) Lindsay, St. Vincent Millay (52). This is all agreeable and convincingly rooted, as Stein's aesthetics seem universally cross-genre derived from reading Sherwood Anderson who 'expresses life rather than describing or embroidering it' (54). Surprisingly, James and O'Neill are skimmed past while Hemingway is granted exciting pages In Our Time (1925) given as the apogee (65) of his method through 'Cubism' (66). She highlights the story "Now I Lay Me" (69). However, Dos Passos is elevated higher than Hem who set about 'creating a mirror image of (DP)' (71). A shameless letter of admiration from Hem to Dos is quoted.

Parallels abound as in Anderson's Wineburg, Ohio (1919) with Lewis's Main Street (1920) all referenced through Van Vechten's "The Revolt from the Village". Indeed, small town America and the flight from it, is a constituent of her theory. (82) Other nations fail in this regard, ultimately glamourising the 'village' as she presents the village shown up, seen through in hardcore literature. This is America at its most civilised, critical and incisive.

Faulkner is shown as self-serving, solipsistic in the best sense with 'that little patch up there in Mississippi where you started from. But that's all right too. It's America too' (93). His poems are shown as important to his novels 'having learned the essentials of writing good prose from his collecting poems into meaningful sequences' (96) 'to create the fiction that used every word' (97). Significantly, he is her champion of writing 'about racism unbridled' (102).

Back up North, the Harlem Renaissance is given full volume in Langston Hughes's "The Negro Mountain and the Racial Mountain". Clasping the nettle like this, gives her realpolitik not just literary smirch when Jean Toomer's short story collection Cane (1922) is hailed as it was in the beginning by Countee Cullen 'real race contribution, a classic portrayal of things as they are' (116). The chapter is a montage of fine stuff invoking Hughes's lines (115):

My old man died in a fine big house.

My ma died in a shack.

I wonder where I'm gonna die,

Being neither white nor black?

It rolls on like the American plains, as she sections the 1930s and 1940s into two neat chapters as closers. Theatre is shown as dialect authenticated, for instance Odets' Waiting for Lefty (1935) is social and political cutting edge 'subservice, even Red' like Hellman's The Children's Hour; Elmer Rice Street Scene; Dos Passos Airways Inc. (131)

And the catastrophic economic climate emerges in both fiction, Tom Kromer's devastating Waiting for Nothing (1935) and non-fiction like Louis Adamic's My America, 1928-1938 a statistical approach describing 'the ravages of the Depression' (141). James Agee's Let Us Now Praise Famous Men (1941) accentuates American prose always approaching the poetical with 'incremental sentences suggest the writing of both Thomas Wolfe and, more directly, Walt Whitman' (143). Her own irony enters with offside remarks as about FDR elected president in 1932 and 'beyond any doubt that America was in grave trouble' (153). Her patience will not abide the popular James T. Farrell's Young Lonigan (1932) 'ranked next to the scandalous novels of Henry Miller' (151). Hey, come on Miller is good. Wagner-Martin should accentuate Joyce's 'Aunt Josephine factor' in other words Ulysses was fit for his aunt to read.

Altogether Wagner-Martin brings you along without gasping in disbelief, however, close to incredulity occasionally, you are pushed from one theoretical framework to the next as in 'the literary progress of having the Joads leave the desiccation of the Dust Bowl (with its echoes of Eliot's The Waste Land)' (159). These parallels often make sense eventually, either by time or acceptance, and the same is often expressed of the road to Gatsby's as a waste land between West Egg and NY, where the Doctor T. J. Eckleburg billboard peers down in a kind of contemporary SpecSavers. She suggests that American Modernism evolved in part from the original frontier wasteland just as literature itself evolved from it, and through it. This is its appeal to the psyche, as in Carlos Williams's "These" (160):

The year plunges into night

and the heart plunges

lower than night

And Jeffers' "The Answer" addresses the questions of the twentieth century, both as backward glance and forward perspective through modernism: 'To know that great civilisations have broken down into violence, and their tyrants come, many times before' (160). She sobers up entering war literature, including Robert Penn Warren's All the King's Men (1946) 'a "war novel" only in the way state and national politics had the power to usurp the rights of private citizens' (164).

There is a parade of glorious literature surveyed here with perceptions, collisions and strange collusions. She is not prone to wallowing in these, as her closing salient remarks come from Elie Wiesel on the early reception of his Holocaust memoir Night 'the book sold poorly. The subject was considered morbid [...]'. (169). Her logic is that the age not so much demanded as bred the very modernist art, vitally from within the age, its era and evolving decades of modernism.

—*Make It New* 2017

DOWN THE MINE, UP AMONG THE STARS: [...] A CULT OF CELEBRITY

Wilde in America: Oscar Wilde and the invention of modern celebrity David M. Friedman (W. W. Norton)

Friedman, full of digressions, detours and narrative shortcuts focuses on Wilde's annus mirabilis when the 27 year old began his tour of America at the behest of Richard D'Oyly Carte who wanted to publicize Gilbert & Sullivan's operetta Patience. The Sporting Times of London had lampooned Wilde in advance of his departure as 'the sandwich man' for Carte. The character of Bunthorne in Patience was as much based on Wilde, as Swinburne and Rossetti in portraying a stage-version of a Victorian poet-aesthete who preaches beauty above all. Wilde's Poems already slated in Punch as 'a volume of echoes—it is Swinburne and water' was his sole prop because his lecture notes never got written on board the SS Arizona crossing the Atlantic; the lure of the champagne 'was too much to resist'.

Friedman's digression on Napoleon Sarony, the portrait photographer is vital. In the studio at 37 Union Square, Sarony and his staff 'captured' Wilde's image 'on specially treated glass plates' to be 'developed, printed, and reproduced for mass consumption across America'. Friedman gives Wilde's measurements: 'six feet tall, waist 38½ inches, neck 17 inches'. Decked out in his dandified best wearing a wool overcoat with 'massive fur collar' 'dark wool trousers' along with the cape, and 'a cane and a wide-brimmed black hat'. His manager continually replenished the wardrobe during the tour with items such as 'two pair of grey silk stockings to suit the grey mouse-coloured velvet. The sleeves are to be flowered—if not velvet then plush—stamped with large pattern'. When one of the photos appeared advertising men's hats for the Ehrich Brothers department store, Sarony sued and 'was granted copyright protection' in court as well as '$12,000 in damages—nearly

$300,000 today'. Wilde's clothes were just as important as his extempore lectures and bon-mots.

However, Friedman almost suffocates his book with material on clothes, such as Alice Cary Williams' memoir: 'patent leather shoes with silver buckles, then black stockings and above them green velvet knee breeches…a pale white hand which held a lily…and this deathly white face began to speak in a high chanting voice. On it went on and on, and when I thought it would never stop it gave a kind of shriek, lowered its eyes, and everyone clapped and shouted, "Bravo!" Then I heard Mrs Howe's voice, "I don't need to introduce Mr. Oscar Wilde"'.

Friedman can be praised for the use of newspaper cuttings reflecting on the whistle-stop tour. However, the Press were not enamoured with the shoulder length hair and the stagey voice. 'Questioned by more than a hundred reporters in fewer than three hundred days', the Chicago Daily News wrote on his departure 'Go, Mr. Wilde and may the sunflower wither at your gaze'. The Fort Wayne Gazette felt he was not much value for money either, 'he is not an elocutionist; his voice is as effeminate as a school girl's' while the Louisville Courier-Journal eugenically proclaimed 'he is neither a man nor a woman. He is between the two. He is not intellectual looking, but he has brains. He is an ass with brains', and furthermore picked up on 'an effeminacy of delivery best described as 'Sissy''.

Wilde pushed on undaunted, sneaking in readings from his poetry where possible but found much bitchiness as with Henry James who called him 'repulsive'. Lily Langtry described him as 'grotesque in appearance'. Ambrose Bierce thought him 'an imposter so hateful, a blockhead so stupid, a crank so variously and offensively daft'. Jefferson Davis, President of the Confederacy found something so 'indefinably objectionable' about Wilde that 'he excused himself early from the dinner table, pleading a slight illness'. There were happier occasions. Meeting Oliver Wendell Holmes, he borrowed his phrase 'when good Americans die they go to Paris'. Friedman points out that the phrase first appeared in Holmes's *Autocrat of the Breakfast Table*. Longfellow told an anecdote against himself. Queen Victoria had told the American poet, 'You are very well known. All my servants read you.'

The great meeting was with Whitman, author of *Leaves of Grass*, reported by one journalist incorrectly as Blades of Grass. 'He had the good sense to take a great fancy to me,' Whitman declared. Friedman quotes George Ives who had it from Wilde: 'the kiss of Walt Whitman is still on my lips'. He made two visits to Whitman and literary history records that American poetry literally kissed Irish poetry at these meetings. More could have been made of the Whitman-Wilde unity of being. It is, of course, fully present in the Letters edited by Holland & Hart Davis. Friedman's leitmotif discussing celebrity never materialises and might have developed into a more academic text. Quotes of Wildean aphorism dominate, such as one from George Gissing on those who 'no longer succeed in literature so that they may get into society but get into society so they may succeed in literature'. Not unsurprisingly, this still remains true of Celeb-Lit.

Wilde survived the ridicule of journalists through his wit. 'The story of George Washington and the cherry-tree has done more harm, in a shorter space of time, than any other moral tale in the whole of literature.' He told a reporter from the Chicago Tribune 'your city looks positively dreary', and described Salt Lake City's Tabernacle as 'a soup kettle' and 'the most purely dreadful building I ever saw with an interior suitable for a jail'.

He felt more at home in Leadville, Colorado that had 'eighty-two saloons, thirty-five houses of prostitution, twenty-one gambling rooms, and three very busy undertakers.' The lecture on aesthetics didn't go very well but a visit to the silver mine was an interlude in the night's drinking that resumed afterwards till dawn. In St Joseph,

Missouri he prepared for his lecture at Tootle's Opera House but the recent shooting of Jesse James stole the limelight. The St. Joseph Evening News called Wilde 'the fool who has cheek enough to run around among young women with breeches coming down only to his knees'. In Nebraska, he met the legendary poet, Edward Woodberry. They visited the state penitentiary foreshadowing Wilde's doing time in Pentonville, Wandsworth, and Reading which Friedman capitalises on.

Back in New York, and finally preparing to depart (he had taken in Canada's Maritime Provinces 'for nine talks in ten days') and waited on Lily Langtry's arrival to perform in a Tom Taylor play Our American Cousin. 'I would rather have discovered Mrs Langtry than discovered America', he told the New York Times. Taylor had gained fame because of an earlier play at which President Lincoln had been assassinated. Wilde's final undoing was through a gambler's hoax off Union Square, New York. He reported the incident to the police and identified one of the card sharks already wanted by the law known as 'Paper Dollar Joe' among other names. The New York Tribune reported that Wilde 'confessed before his departure that his mission to our barbaric shores had been substantially a failure. He came here to reform our taste and dress, and we paid little heed'.

Friedman launches into a toppling epilogue which fast-forwards the life and would have worked better as a Timeline. The life has baffled, intrigued and remains the greatest biography of any Irish writer along with Francis Stuart's. Friedman is not clear on monetary facts. Half-way through the American tour, Carte gave Wilde a cheque for $5,605 about '$129,000 today' and had 'before gambling losses earned £7,000 the equivalent of £700,000.' Therefore, did he lose $5,000 on gambling? Whereas, Friedman says he lost 'more than $1,000 in the rigged game.'

Then instead of consolidating the theme of celebrity and narcissism,

Friedman headlines ahead to nine years later as Wilde finds theatrical success, and married to Constance Lloyd, their two sons, and then the fatal meeting with Lord Alfred Douglas, his executioner if you like. The two years hard labour during which a fall in the prison chapel heralded festering cerebral meningitis, his fall from fame to poverty and absinthe-alcoholism.

Douglas, long after his family feuds, still inherited and literally became a millionaire twice over. Friedman wisely includes their final re-union giving Wilde's own words as he begged for money and Douglas 'went into paroxysms of rage, followed by satirical laughter...he did not recognise I had any claim of any kind on him.' Aged 46, Wilde died in debt amidst mythic scenes in the Hotel D'Alsace, Paris with a Catholic priest who 'received him into the (Catholic) church'. In part, it was an occult reflection of the demise of Dorian Gray, his fictional character.

Wilde was morally above others, without any touch of evil, unlike Douglas, therein lay only one of the tragedies of his life which yielded major works such as De Profundis and The Ballad of Reading Gaol. Friedman's conclusion attempts, as with all biographies, to explain Wilde's martyrdom caused by Victorian hypocrisy, the unjust Henry Labouchère Amendment (1885), and not least, his nasty 'lover'.

—*Books Ireland* 2015

MEN OF LETTERS

The Complete Letters of Oscar Wilde by Oscar Wilde eds. Merlin Holland and Rupert Hart-Davis (Fourth Estate)

The Wicked Wit of Oscar Wilde Maria Leach (Michael O'Mara)

Letters, Vol. I: Correspondence with Bernard Shaw and Charlotte Shaw 1922-1926 by T. E. Lawrence eds. Jeremy Wilson and Nicole Wilson (Castle Hill Press)

There have been many previous editions of Wilde's letters. Merlin Holland's introduction discusses the ups and downs of these getting into print and here, largely through the Herculean labours of his co-editor Rupert Hart-Davis who began the enterprise in 1954. Holland is famous for being the grandson of Oscar. When asked to comment on a window dedicated to his illustrious grandfather in Westminster Abbey, he said, "Well, he's neither in nor out and depending on where you stand, he's looking both ways".

This centenary edition might well be called a surrogate biography such is the scope of the notes, chronology and the pivotal sections in which the letters are presented. The early precocious young man often signed himself Oscar F. O'F. Wills Wilde to his Oxford friends. The FO'F being Fingal O'Flahertie. During his courtship of Florence Balcombe, he reverted to Oscar. She would eventually marry Bram Stoker and receive a copy of each of Wilde's published works as his career advanced.

When he sent copies of his poems to Browning and Swinburne there is the tone of respect coupled with supplication. He had to foot the bill for the publisher, Bogue. Reviews were awful. The *Saturday Review* said he was "marred everywhere by imitation, insincerity, and bad taste". He writes from the US to Whistler, " ...

they are 'considering me *seriously*. Isn't it dreadful? What would you do if it happened to you?" He visited Walt Whitman, Julia Ward Howe and the Irish Fenian exile, John Boyle O'Reilly, sometime editor of The *Pilot,* and a friend of Speranza Wilde, who published poems by her and Oscar. The last day of his American visit was spent gambling. He arrived back in London a celebrity but very broke, claiming he was cheated out of hundreds of dollars. He wasn't lying.

As Wilde conquered dinner tables, the London stage and the heart of Constance Lloyd-Holland who would bear him two sons, one winces at the familiar tragedy looming around the corner despite the high spirits of the letters. *The Picture of Dorian Gray* became a *succés de scandale.* He proudly sent copies to Walter Pater whom he idolised and also Mallarmé. The letter to Lord Alfred Douglas (Bosie) is florid, "Your slim gilt soul walks between passion and poetry. I know Hyacinthus, whom Apollo loved so madly, was you in Greek days." It is all too easy to trash Douglas as the brat and devilish footnote to Wilde's life yet he loomed far larger and more menacingly than that, but the story is too well known to rehash it here.

Meanwhile, one reads letters to theatre managers and actresses, and short notes of thanks for praise to his former mentor J. P Mahaffy, also William Archer and Edmund Gosse. He writes to Bernard Shaw thanking him for sending his book on Ibsen, " ... we are both Celtic, and I like to think that we are friends." Reading the letters to his solicitor about Douglas's father, the mad Marquis of Queensberry, is enough to make one fling the book across the room. He writes to Lady Queensberry explaining how to rehabilitate her wimp of a wastrel son. Telegrams flow thick and frequent on the eve of his arrest and weeks away from his subsequent sentence of two years hard labour.

The Prison section is the largest because of the long letter (actually over one hundred pages) to Douglas. What is remarkable about this letter as prison literature is not only the conditions under which it was written; there is a total lack of self-pity or castigation for Douglas, since Wilde had learned the hard way that he himself was blameworthy. He learned little in Oxford but learned everything in prison. However, the cost was beyond him physically, emotionally and financially.

There are many letters to the Home Secretary from prison begging for various mercies but all to no avail. However, the system did allow the poor poet at least a handful of books to keep him from the utter depths: Dante, Tennyson, Keats, Chaucer, Emerson and even Marlowe. The food played havoc with his digestion, the imposed labour shattered his nerves, the regime broke his spirit and a fall in chapel when he fainted would set in motion the symptoms that would lead to his death a few years later. He had faced the criminal judge; next he faced the bankruptcy judge and later the divorce judge.

The prison services transferred him to another jail to avoid too much publicity on his release. Ada Leverson's husband offered funds to tide him over. The Jesuits of Farm Street rejected his plea for a six-month retreat, he wept in front of his friends, composed himself and left for France, adopting the name Melmoth after Maturin's novelistic hero.

He wrote to Selwyn Image from Berneval, "I am thoroughly ashamed of having led a life quite unworthy of an artist." And to Carlos Blacker, "Why is it that one runs to ones ruin? Why has destruction such a fascination?" A brief reunion with Douglas ensured the final loss of ever seeing his sons again or his wife, and ultimately losing the small endowment she had levied for his needs, but she knew he was a spendthrift. That reunion with Douglas in Naples was a disaster both financially, romantically and companion wise; they loathed each other as never before.

He offered the advance rights on a play he hoped to write to anyone willing. The *Ballad of Reading* Gaol moved Leonard Smithers to publish his plays, the rights of which he bequeathed to his sons. The only great friend of his final years was Robert Ross whose devotion to Wilde was incredible; if anyone ever loved him besides his abandoned children and wife it was

Ross. The long poem did not appear under his name, instead under his prison number C 3 3. He claimed it was made out of skilly, the thin gruel he ate in prison, the source of vile dysentery. Constance, like everyone close to him, openly wept on reading the poem and Wilde remarked in a letter, "As art is the most intense mode of expression, so suffering is the most real mode of life."

His brother-in-law Otho wrote telling him of the death of Constance Wilde. Legally he could never visit his sons and between begging letters for money, kept good friends with Ross, Reginald Turner and Frank Harris when his health allowed such company. Debility was never far off and various doctors diagnosed neurasthenia; he often gave his address as 'In Bed, Paris'. He never wrote the promised play but saw the *Ballad of Reading Gaol* go into six editions and a first French edition. The last letter to Harris reads like a clerk trying to make an amount of petty cash go a long way. The owner of the Hotel d'Alsace accepted that he was a notable artist who was dying in poverty and never mentioned the accumulating bill.

The final letters here are from friends after his death informing others who were not present. A Dublin priest, Cuthbert Dunne, heard his confession and received him into the Catholic church while leeches were used to stem the bleeding as he died worrying about his sons, Cyril and Vyvyan, whose surname had been changed to Holland. They reached their teens in the guardianship of uncle Otho and were dispatched to boarding schools. The elder died in the trenches of the Great War, the younger survived to have a successful career as a writer.

Wilde's letters, even the grimmest, yield many laughs. Movies have tended to play up the tragic elements of his life, biographers know that his story is almost too good to be true. W. H. Auden could never understand why he married and had children. He was more than a husband and father, or less, depending on your moral opprobrium, but as a writer his poems are crowned with one of the greatest ballads since The *Rime of the Ancient Mariner;* four of the plays are always on stage and TV; his essays may not rank with Pater or Symons but live on as the epitome of that era; his stories for children are never out of print, his one novel has become a classic fairytale for adults—the hero's end with its hideous manifestation of the face deformed, was mysteriously enacted in Wilde's own death if you read Robert Ross's letter to More Adey written a few days after he witnessed the event.

The illustrations in *The Wicked Wit* of *Oscar Wilde* are pseudo-Beardsley by Mick Keates with sporadic plump-rumped and bare-breasted women looking comically erotic. The witticisms are grouped under ludicrous titles such as 'unsound art', 'blankets and coal' and 'second-rate sonnets'. However such misplaced headings can't damage the Wildean wit: "To love oneself is the beginning of a lifelong romance", "Most people are other people. Their thoughts are someone else's opinions, their life a mimicry, their passions a quotation", "Education is an admirable thing, but it is well to remember from time to time that nothing worth knowing can be taught."

One can open any page and find a laugh with a lot behind it and that is what makes one read on and on. "There are moments when Art almost attains to the dignity of manual labour"; "After playing Chopin, I feel as if I had been weeping over sins that I never committed, and mourning over tragedies that were not my own". In a review of Swinburne's poems, he wrote, "His song is nearly always too loud for his subject".

Three more should prove how enjoyable it is leafing though this book, "Morality is simply the attitude we adopt towards people whom we personally dislike"; "When people agree with me I always feel that I must be wrong"; and "When the gods wish to punish us they answer our prayers".

In the period covered by these letters, Lawrence didn't actually meet the Shaws very often. However such restraint is not evident in his regular correspondence. His father was Anglo-Irish, his mother English, and despite this lineage he was a strange mixture of a man.

After an early diffidence he finally sent his mammoth work *Seven Pillars of Wisdom* to the Shaws. GBS found it as long as the Bible but

Charlotte set to lovingly and read through it. Their conversion to Lawrence was instant: he was the man who had kept the Arabs fighting for the British instead of against them during the Great War and made Damascus 'ready' for his superior officer, General Allenby after the anarchy and pestilence of the retreating Turks—hence his heroic stature. However, when GBS wrote to Prime Minister Baldwin in 1923 seeking aid for the forgotten hero, Lawrence was in a peacetime Tank Corps in Devon glad of the routine but very restless and otherwise miserable. He befriended the novelist Thomas Hardy and his wife while GBS politely harassed the Prime Minister for a civil pension for the broken-down soldier. Shaw knew he had found a peculiar genius and advised him to set to and get his book ready for what seemed instant success, since the pension plan fell through after further requests to the establishment.

GBS was a busy playwright, pamphleteer and lecturer so he handed over the manuscript to his trusted wife while keeping a watchful eye on her progress, as the letters attest. Robert Graves included an extract in his shortlived journal *The Owl*. The Shaws found Lawrence confounding and diffident and deliberately snail-like in making progress towards publication. Impatiently, GBS sent him a copy of his play *Saint* Joan to the army barracks where Lawrence was a private, addressing it to his adopted name, 'To Private Shaw from Public Shaw'—the added irony was that GBS didn't understand why Lawrence had never gone ahead and courted the public reputation which he had already earned during the war. Lawrence got bogged down arranging expensive colour plates and maps for his book and GBS also found some of the paragraphs lacking in clarity—"You are no more to be trusted with a pen than a child with a torpedo"—and his letter explaining the rudiments of grammar is masterly and very funny.

Lawrence became the unofficial librarian to his army mates except on nights when they went to the brothels in Lincoln and Navenby while he took to his bunk and read the books regularly sent from Charlotte Shaw. He thus read many Irish writers: Darrell

Figgis, James Stephens, Joyce (preferring *Dubliners* to the novels) and O'Casey. D. H. Lawrence's presence in the literary firmament made him have second thoughts about publishing under the name Lawrence—he greatly admired The *Plumed Serpent*. On leave when he didn't visit the Shaws or meet them on their holidays, he went to concerts in London on his trusty motor cycle christened Boanerges; and once to Edinburgh complaining about the ham-and-eggs breakfasts along the way. The letters end with Lawrence making his way to India on board the SS *Derbyshire* in 1926 and one awaits the other two volumes with great expectation since the book reads like some vast Shavian drama with three intensely singular characters vigorously playing off each other. And what happened to his book—*Seven Pillars of Wisdom?* One simply has to wait in patience for those promised volumes.

—Books Ireland 2001

TO THE GALLERY OR TO THE GODS

Mother of Oscar: the life of Jane Francesca Wilde Joy Melville (Allison & Busby)

William Trevor: the writer and his work Dolores MacKenna (New Island)

The biography holds the germ of a further book. The fascinating thing is that the Wilde cult demands a complete biography spanning the lives of William and Jane, their offspring Oscar, Willie and Isola and thence to the grandchildren Cyril, Vyvyan and Dorothy. Melville's book naturally enough completes its own brief in giving a life of Jane Wilde who touched three generations and can hardly avoid a cameo of Oscar Wilde. Previous toilers in this field have included Montgomery Hyde who fully explores Oscar with extra emphasis on Alfred Douglas in three books. Terence de Vere White has a valuable exposition of William and Jane while the most recent biography of Oscar Wilde by Richard Ellmann has never satisfied the present reader but in passing neither has his book on Joyce though an established classic because of the spiteful tone to its subject in many places.

The book under consideration is haunted by the suggested biography above, of three generations of Wildes which is essential to explain the lives of certain family members. This approach to a literary dynasty is completely viable and has been developed to great effect for instance with the James's and the Sitwell's indeed something similar should be embarked on for the Yeats's to mention but one other example. Wisely enough a biography of Lady Jane Francesca Wilde is the imaginative hold all for Melville to deploy her book.

Lady Jane began as Jane Elgee, daughter of a Dublin solicitor; however on reading about her early life one is continually looking for prognostications of her future and the future of her progeny and also impatient to see William Wilde enter the picture and not least the famous sons.

Jane's prolific poetic output found its way into the Nation at first, through a rather good literary journeywoman's ruse by posing as a man, John Fanshawe Ellis and disputing the repute of James Clarence Mangan the poet of the Nation. It is a kind of infamy to be dismissive of 'Speranza' Lady Wilde's verse when one has only read the usual pieces in anthologies and the extra large helping of excerpts given here which rather support long held negative prejudices. One might safely add that she was obviously a very minor poet.

When Jane was twenty-nine her mother died and the house in Leeson Street was sold and the proceeds divided up. Then as she was unable to move in with pro-English relatives because of her public political persuasion, she opted for a speedy marriage to the surgeon oculist, William Wilde. Wilde was a notorious womaniser and had at least three children already, half acknowledged as nephews and a niece, when Jane first met him. They married and Jane soon had two sons at their home, 21 Westland Row, and after moving to a larger house, 1 Merrion Square, a daughter Isola was born.

The Wildes were leading socialites in Dublin and could count on invitations from the good and the great, following on their own talk-of-the-town at-homes on the windiest side of Merrion Square. Writers, poets and politicians were ten a penny on the guest list at the Wilde parties including Samuel Ferguson, Aubrey de Vere, Denis Florence MacCarthy, Charles Lever, Isaac Butt, Gavan Duffy and Sir William Rowan Hamilton who hugely enjoyed his liquor.

However, long before the birth of his daughter, Dr Wilde was again on a burgeoning adulterous affair and got into a lot of hot water with a mistress named Mary Travers. This did not occur until ten years later when Wilde had received a knighthood and Mary wanted a piece of the action. Mary Travers' slandering of the Wildes who were very much a literary Mafia of a family makes for highly readable stuff. Mary took to the pen herself or rather the poison pen: "Some sport I'll have or I am blest/I'll fry the Wilde breed in the west".

She hired town criers to mock the Wildes and publicly pamphleteered against them. When she began to publish libellous doggerel in various weeklies, signing many of them 'Speranza' the nom de plume of Lady Wilde, she had obviously gone too far for William and Jane. Travers gloried in the public revelations of her private liaison with William and his ill-treatment of her when she was a member of the Wilde household. Encouraged by her father, Mary Travers sent a writ to Lady Wilde after receiving a letter of complaint against her libellous placard campaign outside the Wilde household. The case went to court with the public gallery full and all of Dublin agog and a-gossip and even an old family friend of the Wilde's, Isaac Butt, defending Mary Travers. Butt's cross-examination of Mary easily unloosed the revelation that Dr Wilde had raped her while she was unconscious. In a second trial with Butt again defending, she lost her case and disappeared from the Dublin scene but lived on until 1919.

The case did nothing to dismantle the already much flawed marriage of Lady Jane and Sir William. Besides enduring the furore of the court cases, Wilde who had not gone into the witness box could not avoid a nervous breakdown soon afterwards. However, all these events were overshadowed by the death of their daughter aged nine. The family was devastated, especially Oscar experiencing the death of a family member for the first time and later wrote one of his best poems for her, 'Requiescat'. He had a lock of her hair among his possessions when he died.

When Sir William died, the funeral was attended by many dignitaries, and Victorian hypocrisy unleashed its utmost in virulent obituaries bolstering up his life without a hint of the scandals. Sir Samuel Ferguson wrote an elegy for his dead friend. Jane grieved and sold up their sizable holdings in Bray, Moytura and Merrion Square and moved to London.

Her residency in London was mainly at Oakley Street with a brief foray in Park Street. From both addresses she wielded total control of her sons and by then both were writers like their mother. They bore a striking resemblance to her, especially Willie with his equine facial features and Oscar who according to Max Beerbohm, was "a veritable tragedy of family likeness". Beerbohm found Willie, "very vulgar and unwashed and inferior" adding, "Scratch Oscar and you will find Willie." Melville easily proves her case that Oscar utterly worshipped his mother (according to Oscar, "All poets love their mothers") and remained unbroken in that love even after the rigours of prison life and wrote in De Profundis, that she "intellectually ranks with Elizabeth Barrett Browning, and historically with Madame Roland".

Jane began her salon life in London with an even more distinguished guest list than at Merrion Square inviting Oliver Wendell Holmes, Brett Harte, George Moore, Marie Corelli, Eleanor Marx and Bernard Shaw, not forgetting John Ruskin and Robert Browning. Poised in London, she used Oscar's growing success to prop up her own bygone reputation. When his poems came out with the publisher Roberts, she had Oscar arrange a collection of her poems and would eventually find a publisher in Richard Bentley for her Driftwood from Scandinavia. She was convinced that Oscar was unique, "I used to hope you would equal Pater, now I think you are far beyond and above Pater." Her high estimate of his prose is debatable and may be attributed to a mother's suffocating love for a son clouding her judgement. Meanwhile Willie was borrowing money, drinking to excess, writing for the Lady's World and attempting sculpture. Oscar said that "his brother's statues showed palpable signs of death but no hopes of living". When Oscar became editor of the Lady's World, he changed the title to the Woman's World and was soon petitioned by Jane objecting to a review which did not mention her writings. Oscar rectified the situation by puffing her when he reviewed a book by W. B. Yeats. Similarly Jane knew her ps and qs in the literary scene and quickly began greeting WB as 'My Irish Poet'! Otherwise she harassed Oscar about editorial policy and warned against rabid Bohemianism: "keep clear of suppers and late hours and champagne".

Joy Melville wisely reveals Jane's domineering influence over Oscar about his getting married but was emphatically and superstitiously against his marriage to Constance Lloyd. However Oscar won out and Willie was the best man at the wedding which was staged for publicity purposes with Jane in full regalia of frowsy Victorian fashion. Oscar played the role of devoted groom and had made a silver girdle for his bride which she wore on the wedding day. A rather unusual gesture for a husband! Like father, like son, Oscar was soon unfaithful but in a different manner to William Wilde's infidelities and became a fully fledged pursuer of young men, losing interest in Constance when he'd seen her as a pregnant woman.

Melville is very innocent, declaring her belief that neither Constance nor Lady Jane had an inkling of Wilde's overt sexual predilection which reflects poorly on the biographer's ability for in-depth psychological analysis. Wilde, despite this, was a good father when he was at home but far from an ideal husband. His absences seem more callous than if he had deserted the family and in particular, when Constance suffered her major fall downstairs he was away dining with some of the young men he called 'panthers'. Besides, his life would shroud Constance and their sons in awful tragedy, worse than if he had died at the time of his imprisonment or in the pursuit of his art. Imprisonment was a high price to pay for his sex life. However, the tragedy of every life is ultimately subsumed into the fabric of humanity where the pain is transcended either within the bounds of reason or the explications of some divine purpose.

There remains the incongruous situation of Wilde's defiant dash with the law and his unwise decision not to flee London and avoid imprisonment. It is Wilde's only perversion that he obviously desired to go to prison. He had visited a prison during his lecture tour in America which obviously kindled a desire for incarceration amongst the complexities of his psychological makeup.

Lady Jane died of bronchitis while Oscar masochistically languished in Reading Gaol. She had virtually become a prisoner in her own house in some kind of sympathetic reaction to his imprisonment. Obituaries appeared in both London and Dublin newspapers. Willie died the year before Oscar, leaving a daughter and a widow. He had also endured a previous bitter divorce in a life that by the family's standards might be uncharitably called a failure. The Wildes lived before the tabloid age, defiantly unaware of the pitfalls of courting publicity, and can be easily accused of playing up to or acting out a public image, neglecting to understand the actual depth of interest by the public which was actually less engaged than the Wildes' self-obsessiveness. In other words, they might have had what ever fame and glory they obviously craved without soaking up unnecessary private tragedy and then going public with it. Their enigma remains, not least in the city of their birth's recent erection of the bizarrely emerald and kitsch public monument in Merrion Square to Oscar which might easily be mistaken as the work of Willie Wilde junior.

The Anglo-Irish ancestry of William Trevor had long gone into decline when his father Bill Cox joined the Bank of Ireland staff and as manager of the Dundalk branch met another blow-in, Gertrude Davidson, who worked in the Ulster Bank. Gertrude Davidson came from County Armagh; Bill Cox hailed from Roscommon. They got married in Howth at the end of the War of Independence. The far-flung location from Dundalk reveals the nomadic life lived by bank people in the Ireland of those times. During the Civil War, the Trevors met General Michael Collins while they were stationed in Mountbellew. He was passing through with advice on security in the burgeoning Free State.

Trevor himself was born in Mitchelstown in a house adjoining the police station but his stay was brief and soon his father was booking the yellow removal vans of Nat Ross which moved the family and their belongings to Youghal. Not long after they did a stint in Skibbereen and then Tipperary but eventually wended their merry way to Portlaoise and even Galway.

After a mix of schools Trevor landed in Trinity College at the end of the war and happily found lodgings first in Blackrock but, prizing complete independence, as students will, rented a room in Terenure and learned to cook for himself. He soon made fast friends at the boisterous parties, aptly named 'blinds' often beginning in Ryan's of Anne Street and out to Goatstown 'on the bona fide' during holy hours. He found many friends, some for life such as Conor Farrington who would go on to become a well-known actor, David Hone, Patrick Pye and Michael Biggs who became established artists, Arnold Bradshaw, a Horatian scholar and Dr Paddy Hackett. Surprisingly or not, Trevor first made his name as a sculptor through regular entries in the annual Irish Exhibition of Living Art alongside Le Brocquy, Jellett and Norah McGuinness. He began a study of the art of the Book of Kells for a commission in England and met his future wife Jane Ryan, a student of modern languages. They married and found joint employment teaching in County Armagh.

Though Trevor was hailed as a major Irish artist in 1956, by the dawning of the 1960s London beckoned, he gave up teaching, went to work in advertising and published his first book A Standard of Behaviour thereafter changing his name from William Trevor Cox. As William Trevor, he settled in England and poured forth a prolific amount of writing including a successful play in the Beckettian mode, The Elephant's Foot. Though inherently Irish, if not puckishly so, he has been made an honorary Commander of the British Empire. By the time of completing a story collection The

Day We Got Drunk on Cake he embraced the dangerous contemplations of evil in the human condition in such novels as Mrs Eckdorf in O'Neill's Hotel in which one can detect a favourable influence in the dialogue from Flann O'Brien's The Dalkey Archive. No mean expert novelist, he can equally bring in a tour de force in the novella form such as Nights at the Alexandra and Reading Turgenev, praised by Francis Stuart who is also mentioned by Dolores MacKenna for praising the novel Elizabeth Alone.

Trevor would eventually break into film and television as well as writing radio plays. MacKenna is good on the transposition from the 1950s to the 1970s of the television version of Trevor's The Ballroom of Romance. The interview appended to the book is nothing short of marvellous. Trevor's many fans will find it spellbinding: "Writing is as much concerned with what you leave out as with what you put in. You write, the reader imagines: your task is to control the relationship." He also may scarify the creative writing industry by declaring, "There is no training for a fiction writer." He sees no connection between his previous life as a sculptor and his present life as a writer. "Writers don't really belong anywhere, and being midway between Ireland and the continent suits me geographically." When it comes to Irishness Trevor is well advanced on the evolutionary chain: "I don't mind where I go to church, whether it's a Catholic church or a Protestant church".

He remains highly readable and no bookcase in Ireland is without a few of his books. However, unlike other populist writers, he is not lacking in genuine depth.

—*Books Ireland* 1999

FLANELLESS FLANN *The Collected Letters of Flann O'Brien*
ed. Maebh Long (Dalkey Archive Press)

The standard biography and various commentaries are highly flawed
when compared with The Collected Letters of Flann O'Brien, author
of At Swim-Two-Birds (AS2B) among classic comic literature, and
not least as Myles na gCopaleen, infamous columnist the
'Aristophanic Sorcerer' of the Irish Times. This hefty volume at
600+ pages, fully refutes those who have failed the author in
misrepresentations of his life, character and writings. There is one
exception, Anne Clissmann's Critical Introduction while satisfying,
hardly qualifies as biography. Such an undertaking would require a
high five-figure commissioning fee. The future biographer will have
to be formidable, otherwise the only viable commentary is
Clissmann's despite being decades old. O'Brien's complexities as
comic writer involve his exposition of the tragic. Behind the
burlesque and fun, stark realities emerge. Women as characters are
absent, sex is non-existent, only hinted at in macabre horror. He was
stuck with Free State Ireland for subject matter, and then there is the
man who speaks freely in the letters.

O'Brien's relationship with the Irish Times was fraught and
conflicted as shown in the letters. This is never mentioned when IT
lay claim to him as their invention. Maebh Long's sensational
disclosure is that 'there is a sad dearth of letters to the Irish Times'
because most of this correspondence was destroyed 'when moving
offices to Tara Street in 2006.' (xv) Alarming in the era of digital
archives. Thus, forty years after O'Brien's passing, the author who
contributed largely to their provenance was casually 'deleted', or
perhaps not so casually.

The letters conclusively debunk the central myths & legends in
Anthony Cronin's No Laughing Matter: The Life and Times of
Flann O'Brien (1989) reducing it to the biography of blurb and gross
inaccuracy. Cronin marked O'Brien down as a deliberately Dublin-

bound provincial whereas he travelled, resided and worked in London on numerous occasions as Senior Civil Servant and latterly as author, made visits to Germany, and had numerous sojourns throughout Ireland.

Significantly revealing, is how he was subjected to a witch hunt and appalling discrimination within the Civil Service. Throughout this debacle he remained logical, reasonable, and shows none of the manic personality portrayed in No Laughing Matter whose commentary reflects Cronin's years as Cultural Commissar for the Haughey administration. What ironies, O'Brien as 'troublesome character' compared to Haughey and his henchmen.

There was only one 'major' incident during the seventeen year's up to his being appointed Assistant Principle (APO) in the Department of Local Government & Public Health. This exchange of letters involves the government's objecting that 'newspaper work adversely affects' (151) his job in the Civil Service. O'Brien cites the 'increment certificates' as proof of no deficiencies in his 'official work' year after year (151). He names C. E. Kelly of Dublin Opinion and Leon Ó Broin who had creative careers as well as Government jobs, and states that 'to treat me differently from other officials who engage in similar outside activities is unjust and indefensible' (151).

As author, his novel At Swim-Two-Birds travelled a tortuous path to publication because A. M. Heath literary agency found it had 'every possible defect from the commercial point of view' (7). Longmans eventually, if reluctantly wanted to publish it despite the 'obscure and rather hurried ending' (9). When they quibbled about the title, O'Brien was further harassed to admit 'I now like [it] less and less' and offered a weaker title 'Sweeny in the Trees' because the Gaelic epic poem Buile Suibhne is quoted with translations by the author in the novel.

Cronin's shameful version of O'Brien as moribund loner and drunk, cantankerously commuting in and out of the city is woefully untrue.

He had a circle of steadfast friends and admirers as the letters prove including Niall Montgomery, Cecil Scott, Niall Sheridan and not least Dorine Davin, UCD librarian and journalist which is revealed as more than a platonic relationship. His 'enemies' grew through his satirical letters to newspapers, especially a bagatelle of dubious angst between himself, Sean Ó'Faolain and Frank O'Connor over the latter's Abbey play Time's Pocket, unanimously panned by theatre critics. The 'controversy' over Time's Pocket (what a title!) is rollicking stuff including from the 'two Nialls': Montgomery & Sheridan, formidable creatives in their own right. O'Brien's comedy is never misanthropic and has lines of doggerel such as 'Picking Time's Pocket' '(or should it be, correctly, O'Faolawn/That shy and modest Munster lepracaun' (39). These personal targets of his were unable to laugh at themselves.

On publication of AS2B, O'Brien had ebulliently completed a far superior novel The Third Policeman which Longmans rejected in defiant ignorance 'we realise the Author's ability but think that he should become less fantastic and in this new book he is more so' (71). The reaction caused no diminution in output, as he unstintingly wrote columns for the Irish Times and contributed letters under various pen-names. Hilariously about Anton Chekov, pretending to have known him among other European writers in their milieu. This material could easily have been the beginnings of another novel.

Meanwhile The Third Policeman lay 'buried'. O'Brien lied about having lost the manuscript. This was his reaction to rejection but An Béal Bocht appeared to acclaim from such as Sean O'Casey saying it had 'Swift's scorn [and] the genial laughter of Mark Twain'. (115). He also began writing Faustus Kelly who 'sells his soul to the devil in order to become a TD' (117) the first of many plays.

Meanwhile the situation with the Irish Times was an occasionally hostile triangle of editor R. M. (Bertie) Smyllie, Tynan O'Mahony and O'Brien who after seventeen years simply wanted a pay increase. This coincided with the Civil Service career imploding when he found his name excluded from official notepaper. He complained logically and politely to his senior, John Garvin and a few months later sent a one liner of retirement. Finally, he wrote to Seán MacEntee (former boss) querying the superannuation allowance and left well alone.

These debacles bring O'Brien to the age of 42 afloat on seas of freelancing plus the fractured relationship with the Irish Times. He set about syndicating 'The Cruiskeen Lawn' column to provincial newspapers but needed board approval from guess who: the IT. To the poet, Sheila Wingfield he is forthright [the] 'mongrel Board' […] 'congregation of humbugs, twisters, ignoramuses and bastards' & 'The Editor, a dacent man in other ways, is a funk and—worse— married to a cookery expert'. (255) Writing to Brian Inglis, Editor of The Spectator 'I am most anxious to leave the dirty Irish Times' (254) 'a complete weakling as an editor, accepting instructions on petty matters from certain directors who make prams and who should properly be in them' (255).

La vie de lettres is leitmotif of the subsequent three quarters of the book. And a magnificent scramble too. He tried to begin a newspaper 'The Dublin Man', tried for Seanad Eireann with the manifesto 'Above all, I will speak my mind without regard to Whips and Big Brothers of Leinster House' (220). 389 votes meant that Senator Flann O'Brien never happened. He applied to Radio Eireann for various positions: Station Supervisor, Balance & Control Officer; to TCD for assistant lecturer in English. As 'manuscript pile' reader for Allen Figgis, he rejected six out of eight MSS in one year.

Tim O'Keeffe of MacGibbon & Kee is a seismic appearance in the life of O'Brien rekindling his career by offering to republish AS2B. O'Keeffe only gets a half-dozen mentions in the Cronin biography while another vital patron and friend, poet Leslie Daiken isn't mentioned at all. O'Brien discusses much literary exegesis with O'Keeffe, for instance revealing how Richard Ellmann ('canonised' Joycean biographer) plagiarised Niall Montgomery's essay 'The Pervigilium Phoenicis' on Finnegans Wake. The discussion of An Béal Bocht not being a mockery of Ó Criomhtain's An t-Oileánach is valuable in locating O'Brien bestriding Gaelic and English literature.

When AS2B was republished he declared 'the book is, of course, juvenile nonsense' (254) 'I detest AS2B so much'. Mac Gibbon & Kee published The Hard Life but both books were refused by Penguin 'a most remarkable writer [...] extremely hard to classify [...] would be too problematical'. (299). The Hard Life was delayed because Seán O'Sullivan preparing the cover, mistakenly titled it Hard Times after Dickens' novel.

Letters to public houses such as Galloping Green, Baker's Corner and JJ O'Rourkes over 'the slate' and carry-outs, paid or unpaid are logical, normal and sober. He is pugnacious once threatening to sue the RHA over the portrait "Myles na Gopaleen" by Harry Kernoff; he found it 'grossly offensive' 'shocking scrawl' 'atrocity' 'holds me up to public ridicule' (248/9).

Another myth debunked is O'Brien's presumed antipathy to Ulysses in that he began a campaign to have 'Joyce' re-interred in Ireland stating that 'a great many people would be happy to contribute to the cost' (305). He reviewed The Dublin Diary of Stanislaus Joyce (315) claiming it must be the work of Joyce himself. Writing to Tim Pat Coogan shows him opinionated (somewhat) about Irish Press social diarist 'Terry O'Sullivan' (real name Tomás O'Faolain, Nuala's Da) 'a pitiful poor bugger', and of Faber & Faber's T. S. Eliot 'I detest that firm and I believe T.S.E. is a homo' (323).

Letters to Hugh Leonard discuss the adaptation of The Dalkey Archive into a stage play. O'Brien's occult preoccupations that Saint Augustine 'punishing' him are revealed and also in an interview with the Guardian. The Cronin travesty-biography has only one mention of Leonard and never mentions Dorine Davin both hugely significant for O'Brien. There is the impression given that O'Brien never read anything other than Time magazine. Whereas the letters show him as pan-literary, theological, and much more. He reads Augustine of Hippo in Latin in the National Library, and Teilhard de Chardin while recuperating in hospital. His various hospital stays over many illnesses reveal sublime patience and wit. To judge him as the accident prone alcoholic is cruel just as to blame him for retiring early from the Civil Service.

Cronin debunks the central authors whom O'Brien expressly admired, particularly Aldous Huxley, and especially John William Dunne 'I am quite with you about Dunne. I bought his two books when they appeared'. (227) Dunne's *An Experiment with Time* and *The Serial Universe* were his introduction to Einstein's Time Space continuum and the quantum physics that permeate The Third Policeman where he reproduces one of Dunne's numerical tabulations. The novel is set in the abstract fifth dimension outside the laws of time and gravity. Cronin relegated Dunne's works as 'fairly classy hokum'. Similarly, Joyce & Aldous Huxley provided O'Brien with the technique of multi-narrators, time shifts, and points of view based on the latter's Point Counter Point. The letters absolutely confirm such aesthetic inclinations towards comic realism, fantasy, mysticism and SciFi.

Scholars and commentators proverbially search for the source of De Selby who appears in The Third Policeman and The Dalkey Archive part of a trilogy with The Hard Life. De Selby contemporaneously was 'seen' as James Joyce the central obsession of O'Brien's life. The narrator in The Third Policeman is author of a definitive work of secondhand exegetical literature 'The De Selby Index'. Such satirical parameters prove O'Brien's academia-bashing as well as creating the famous footnote character, De Selby. Cronin missed the inherent literary intention, finding the character merely a 'mordant amusement'.

The attempted 'lowering' of O'Brien's life and the reductionism of his work are laudably redeemed by this collection of letters edited by Long. However, the footnotes far too often enter Myles na Gopaleen satire, intentionally or not, such as 'Saint Peter was one of the Twelve Apostles and thought to be the first pope. He walks on the water to Jesus in Matthew 14:29' or incessantly giving full names as with 'Maria Philomena 'Maureen' Potter an actress and comedian […]' The Dalkey Archive Press are well-named, being in another dimension of real time and space with regard to not supplying the present writer with a review copy on request.

—*VILLAGE politics and culture* 2018

CAN A CATHOLIC BE A MODERNIST?

Flann O'Brien: a portrait of the artist as a young post-modernist Keith Hopper (Cork University Press)

Modernism and Ireland: the poetry of the 1930s Patricia Coughlan and Alex Davis (Cork University Press)

This book has a lot going for it as *cameo* biography, critical study and polemic.

However the ultimate thesis is suspect, and poking around in Flann O'Brien's novels for overt or invert sexual content is absurd. He was never in the same camp as de Sade or Anaïs Nin. His works are almost totally sexless. Furthermore, accusing the Anthony Cronin biography of collusion on some secret sexual life of the real Brian O'Nolan is nonsense. Hopper extends Wayne Koestenbaum's position in *Double-Talk,* outlining his subject's misogyny and male exclusivity from the perspective *of* today's political correctness. It is a mistake to exercise linguistic tests on a novel of one era in terms of the linguistic values of another.

Censure aside, he performs the job well, if a little slavishly filling in the background of formalism, post-modernism, metafiction and the anti-novel. This material may well be ideal for students. Hopper, a self-confessed formalist, in the long third chapter and beyond hails *The Third Policeman* as his best novel, with support from Rudiger Imhof, Mary A. O'Toole, Charles Kemnitz and Wim Tigges. He quotes from letters revealing the author's hopes of being banned; "Like *The Hard Life,* however *The Dalkey Archive's* hidden agenda failed to provoke the censorship mandarins, much to O'Brien's disappointment." There is an appendix to chapter four about An Tostal, a three-week festival in 1953 which Myles na Gopaleen in *The Irish Times* lambasted as cultural fascism and

"Titostalatinarianism".

Hopper's critical position is in opposition to the elegiac tone of the Cronin biography, which supports *At Swim-Two-Birds* as his masterpiece and this agrees with O'Brien's contemporaries, who lament a comic talent diminished, an artist losing his nerve in dear old dirty Dublin, an alcohol addict sunk in whimsical journalism.

Claiming *The Third Policeman* is "a murder-mystery of sorts", Hopper christens the narrator Noman. As the novel begins, the narrator is dead and gone to Hell; but postmodernism deconstructs, so O'Brien, aware of tradition, couldn't believe in fictional characters because of Descartes' probing about the existence of God. The ultimate joke of Noman, and also the solution to this whodunit is Descartes. Incidentally, this theory of Hopper's contradicts "the divine guarantee" of Cartesian certainty. Parallels with Synge's Christy Mahon are explored: "Noman is a reincarnated playboy of a post-modernist western world". With help from J. C. C. May's etymology, De Selby is decoded as "the self". Close scrutiny is given to De Selby, a footnote character who appears in footnotes in the novel.

Hopper's list of sources for *The Third Policeman* are somewhat incredible, with justifiable reference to Huysmans and particularly J. W. Dunne, who influenced Joyce (according to Eugene Jolas), also Borges and William Burroughs. The list might have included H. G. Wells, who promoted Dunne's work on serialism. In presenting every theory possible, he excludes none. Is this "literature's first 'serial' killing" perhaps? Are Divney and the narrator lovers? Such speculations can be endless critical fodder or useful peregrinations; does the book owe its circular framework to *Finnegans Wake?* Is Flann O'Brien the third policeman, with the fictional name of Fox, hitching a ride to eternity on a bicycle? The text is exhaustive without being exhausting and more detailed on this novel than even Anne Clissmann's pioneering study of the complete writings. Flann or Myles or Brian was 'the Aristophanic Sorcerer' but hardly the scholar and polymath some critics imply; for instance, the Huysmans connection is on the basis of *A Rebours,* yet J. K. Huysmans explored Catholicism in his last four novels, with detours through sex, decadence, vice and satanism; which is deeply profound compared to Flann O'Brien's nominal catholicism, and a few pints of plain to line the stomach for balls of malt.

These eleven essays explore the corner of Irish verse that is for ever modernist. Of course Beckett lumped Austin Clarke in a group of "antiquarians", while Devlin and MacGreevy are more metaphysical than modernist in the Poundian sense. Trevor Joyce's essay is about the New Writer's Press, which revived MacGreevy's poems in 1971 and showcased new names, as well as producing a gallant journal, *The Lace Curtain,* edited by the NWP founder Michael Smith, translator of many European poets. From one Smith to another—Stan Smith taps into Devlin's catholicism, mentions "Pascal's hidden God" and Lucien Goldmann's blend of Jansenism. Smith quotes well from the best of Devlin's carefully luxurious poems. Anne Fogarty's essay is gender-centred and protests about neglected poets of the era: Blanaid Salkeld who translated Blok and Akhmatova, Rhoda Coghill who translated Rilke, and Dorothy Large who was a Talbot poet, unlike the substantial Irene Haugh, whose only volume *The Valley of the Bells and other poems* ends with 'A Song of Defeat', "which may explain why she did not pursue her writing career". Fogarty adds that "the silences which affected the women writers were at once more hidden and more pernicious than those which also blighted the career of male poets". A quickfire contest between *The Bell* and *The Dublin Magazine* shows the latter more friendly to women contributors, and this leads her on to mirror Devlin's 'A Dream of Orpheus' with Coghill's 'To his Ghost, Seen after Delirium', "where Eurydice addresses Orpheus and asks for some sign of recognition of her identity".

Patricia Coughlan gives a fine study of *Echo's Bones,* linking the poems to Beckett's relationship with Peggy Sinclair. There are extracts from his letters: "Bronowski is using three turds from my central lavatory"—this to the "delicate reverential" MacGreevy concerning poems accepted for publication. She gives priority to Fritz Mauthner, the surrealists Crevel and Breton, who enabled Beckett to play around with language before making poetry. References to the intense sessions of psycho-analysis (1934-5) with Wilfrid Bion overlap into the essay by W. J. McCormack who writes, "Beckett and Clarke underwent treatment for mental disorders in their youth." Clarke was confined in St Patrick's, Dublin. Some of the experience is in a long poem 'Mnemosyne Lay in Dust' (1966), concentrating on fellow inmates and staff which fails to give a personal analysis of the trauma. McCormack companions it with the novel *Murphy* where Clarke is fictionalised as Austin Ticklepenny, pot poet, "the butt of Beckett's ill humour," and James Joyce's daughter as Celia the harpy. He complains about Yeats' exclusion of Clarke from *The Oxford Book of Modern Verse* (1936), "while cronies like Oliver Gogarty and Dorothy Wellesley were puffed"; yet McCormack's Penguin selection excludes 'In the Savile Club', a poem which is central to Clarke's problems with Yeats.

MacGreevy is well served by the expert biographical content of J. C. C. Mays, linking the poetry with its time. Mays gives plenty of scope and density; "this ex-British officer was a republican, this devout Catholic attended Trinity College and was the trusted friend of the agnostic Jack Yeats" and the friend of Joyce and W. B. Yeats. MacGreevy's poems "are masterpieces of pacing" but he is "a transitional figure" and an "amateur in the shaping of his career". The latter is cruel considering the circumstances of the life.

Susan Schreibman, editor of the excellent collected MacGreevy (1991), sifts through his papers for uncollected poems, and praises the wrong two out of three, because the third poem from which she reproduces eight lines seems the most promising. The title is 'Homage to Ruteboeuf'. Tim Armstrong compares a poem by MacGreevy with Shelley's 'Mont Blanc' and gives Coffey, Devlin and MacGreevy international stature, while discussing the contradiction of being both Catholic and modernist. Terence Brown's essay is a general rather than specific performance, though perhaps he strains a little to find revivalist parallels in the thirties modernity. He quotes Daniel Corkery "in Thurles at a hurling match . . . I first became acutely conscious that as a nation we were without self-expression in literary form". Corkery is obviously posing or perhaps the hurling was uniquely inspirational.

Thomas Dillon Redshaw presents a terrific display on George Reavey, the founder of the Europa Press who published Beckett, Coffey, Devlin and himself. Reavey by this account is a chronic bohemian, complete modernist and neglected poet. Here once more are the golden days of Paris between the wars, with Reavey enjoying the sort of contemporary career in writing the others must have envied. His legend is more as publisher than poet.

Alex Davis has written a brief, if very distinguished essay revealing Coffey as anti-surrealist and anti-romantic, and concerned over Yeats' elitism. 'The Missouri Sequence' is contrasted with Devlin's 'The Heavenly Foreigner' and without a cough or a blush Coffey believed poetry "becomes humankind". 'Advent' is his answer to Mallarmé's mighty poem, which he also translated under the title 'Dice Thrown Never Will Annul Chance'. The reply isn't a cushy number for humankind grappling with "earth's unfinished business". Davis cites the influence of Mallarmé who similarly endured poethood as a parent and breadwinner via teaching, with writing relegated to hobby status. Coffey would not permit himself the self-consciousness of making "the poem itself the subject of the poetry" and fully endorsed his Parisian mentor Jacques Maritain's essential "experience of the void". Davis accurately connects his "resistance to certain currents within modernism, as viewed through the prism of neo-Thomist aesthetics". There is the outline of a longer study here on unity between Coffey's philosophy and poetry, his distance from Mallarmé's "the only Reality is Beauty and its only perfect expression is Poetry" and the idealism of writing "truer than history all and everything".

—*Books Ireland* 1996

DISGRACING OURSELVES AGAIN

Ireland and the Vatican: the politics and diplomacy of church-state relations, 1922-1960 Dermot Keogh (Cork University Press)

Visual Politics: the representation of Ireland 1750-1930 Fintan Cullen (Cork University Press)

This book may become a standard text like John Whyte's *Church and State in Modern Ireland.* Here is proof of the grimness of diplomatic intrigue. Hopefully, he will not be burnt as a heretic for showing much of what lies behind the holy of holies. A companion volume is promised despite diminished access for the author to some Vatican archives. Still, vast material is presented from the founding of the Free State to the Peter Barry speech at Iveagh House in 1985. After the referendum of 1972 "the special position of the Catholic Church" was utterly transformed constitutionally.

Professor Keogh writes with restraint but some of the notes may make your blood boil when the Church of Rome is shown as all too human, profane, mundane. The first papal envoy on a peace mission in the troubled twenties implied that the Irish bishops behaved like "twenty-six popes". While an envoy to the Vatican, W. J. B. Macaulay, said "the bishops were nearly all old men who had supported the Redmondite party and then transferred allegiance to Cosgrave's government". As ever the "dread power of Rome" rankled among the majority in the six counties. The Catholic Emancipation centenary celebrations produced frenetic zeal for a Papal Nuncio for Ireland. Charles Bewley moved between the Irish College and the Vatican while informing the Department of External Affairs at Iveagh House. Bewley confronted a feisty Pius XI and told of the failure of the Anglo-Irish negotiations to end the 'economic war' and was curtly warned that "England had been patient with Ireland".

Pius XI disliked Jim Larkin's election to Dublin Corporation; "disgraceful that there could be communism in the city of Dublin".

Monsignor Paschal Robinson became the first Papal Nuncio, arriving to a regal reception. The state paid from his arrival in London to a private suite at the Shelbourne Hotel, and not least the house in the Phoenix Park. A Dubliner by birth, really an emigre—an outstanding Franciscan with academic roots after a New York childhood, a spell in journalism alongside Mark Twain and diplomatic experience as Vatican representative at the Versailles Peace Conference. Robinson was a late vocation who found himself "exiled" for the last twenty years of his life where "he did much to enliven the Dublin diplomatic circle."

The precedent of exalting Armagh over the Diocese of Dublin dates from this period—a politically convenient move for Church and state. Edward Byrne, Archbishop of Dublin "suffered a double disappointment in 1929 . . . the presence of a nuncio in his archdiocese and losing his only chance of being made a cardinal" when MacRory of Armagh was raised to the cardinalate. Coincidental with Mussolini's invasion of Abyssinia and the Spanish Civil War came de Valera's infamous 1937 Constitution. Rome controlled the final wording of the text which "helped remove any residual suspicion about de Valera at the Vatican". Later, Dev's initiative "to prevent the bombing of Rome strengthened the 'special relationship' between the Holy See and Ireland". There was some bombing with or without de Valera's dubious clout in the matter.

Cardinal Pacelli's part in Vatican affairs made him the next Pope, Pius XII, "the ascetical, suffering pope . . . enshrined on the living-room walls of many Irish houses during the 1940s and 1950s". The John Charles McQuaid era became public with the *Daily Telegraph's* headline "Eire and the Vatican". "McQuaid proved to be one of Mr de Valera's closest friends. All his sons were educated under Dr McQuaid at Blackrock . . ." In the postwar period Joseph Walshe became ambassador to the Holy See and the acquisition of the Villa Spada, Via Giacomo Medici 1 was purchased by the Department of Finance for a hundred and fifty thousand dollars.

Vatican hysteria over the spread of communism surfaced in the thirties and again before the Italian general election of 1948. Pius XII fearing "the Socialist-Communist bloc could very easily win plurality" considered moving the Holy See to Ireland but was also "ready to be martyred in Rome". There began fervorous funding by Irish clergy and Catholic institutions. £57,000 was lodged in the foreign account of the Istituto di Opere di Religione in the Munster & Leinster Bank, Dame Street, for the anti-Left campaign in Italy. Larger funds came from the US. This same year the long-serving Nuncio Paschal Robinson died. His funeral "was a moment of high ritual in a country where puritanical republicanism usually shunned the use of ostentatious ceremony". Robinson's death heralded a desperate scramble between Ireland and Rome who stubbornly opposed any "Irish-American or an American church dignitary" becoming the next Nuncio. Walshe negotiated through Pius XII's confidant, Monsignor Montini, later Pope Paul VI.

Walshe's private memos and dispatches at this time contain criticism: "Pius XII is being surrounded by men who only say flattering things to him", "The autocratic temperament of the Holy Father". Walshe perhaps wisely knew that "the heresies of today will be the doctrines of tomorrow". Whereas the true course of events was complete Irish filiality to papal authority and the appointment of the Pope's choice, Ettore Felici as Nuncio. Felici's fare was paid from Paris by the Irish Government. The Nuncio's arrival in Ireland nearly caused a constitutional crisis over presentation of credentials prior to the liturgical ceremony. Felici actually presented his credentials after the church ceremony at the Pro-Cathedral in Dublin where President Sean T. O'Kelly avoided a meeting until their official meeting at Áras an Uachtarain. Keogh makes O'Kelly a comical character because of his diminutive stature. The wife "towered over him—with or without his top hat". O'Kelly would later cause what Keogh calls "the Paris gaffe" when telling the press after a visit to Rome, "His Holiness assured us that Communism will be overcome and that this will happen during his Pontificate".

As it happened Felici's period as Papal Nuncio was less than two years and the appointment of an American, Bishop O'Hara, signalled a significant shift in Church-state balance of power, when the liturgical ceremony followed on the day after presentation of credentials to the Irish Head of State. O'Hara was lonely in the Phoenix Park. At a public meeting he made controversial headlines battling against Hubert Butler in the Archbishop Stepinac furore.

Walshe is the hero of the book—if hero is appropriate. He died in the fifties and was buried in Cairo having been papal chamberlain under the Order of the Sword and Cape for services rendered as Irish Ambassador to Rome. There is extensive presentation of his communiqués, letters and other official documents. His successor, Con Cremin, "extremely reluctant to give any character sketch of a former superior" described him as *fear ann fein i*—'he was peculiar'.

A maddeningly brief book commenting on representations of Ireland by visual artists over three centuries. Cullen presents Irish artists who fought prodigiously against the Royal Academy. Nathaniel Hone's 'The Pictorial Conjuror' is fully explicated without murderously dissecting the canvas. Hone painted a devastating satire on Sir Joshua Reynolds, President of the Academy. Reynolds's model "an aged pavior named George Wright" is the central figure of the painting, which was removed from exhibition after complaints by Angelica Kauffmann, who was rumoured to be involved romantically with Reynolds. The painting exposes Reynolds as a plagiarist, pilfering old masters to conceal the lack of imaginative composition. Hone was a victim of satire himself from Anthony Pasquin. James Barry was satirised by Francis Sylvester Mahony, 'Father Prout', who refused "to understand or acknowledge the artist's attempts to rekindle history painting".

Seamus Deane and other commentators are quoted on prejudice against the Irish, also a theme of Roy Foster's, *Paddy and Mr Punch,* cited by Cullen. Stage Irishism has always been a useful safety net for Irish artists and writers, especially in London. It was and is the road to advancement in the arts for many, who slag off their fellow countrymen when in London and return home to slag off the English; for example, Daniel Maclise. Little wonder that William Hazlitt commented on *Moore's Melodies:* he "converts the wild harp of Erin into a musical snuff-box".

Cullen explores James Barry's 'The Education of Achilles', and 'The Torso Belvedere'—its main inspiration and lifelong art source for Barry. Early recognition led to his appointment of Professor of Painting, a dubious role for a considerable artist. Later he reviled the Academy with public statements of financial corruption and was expelled to a life of neglect, dying in squalor. Cullen is disparaging of Barry who believed "that ultimate knowledge is only to be found in the transcendence of liberating death".

There are diverting pages on Daniel Maclise, William Mulready and Martin Archer Shee. These chaps did well in London. Shee became President of the Academy, received a knighthood and honorary membership of the Royal Hibernian Academy. Maclise's 'The Marriage of Strongbow and Eva' reveals "metropolitan interest in anthropological detail" and was "specifically commissioned to record the political union of Britain and Ireland". There is engaging treatment of Francis Wheatley's era—Grattan in the Irish House of Commons, the Irish Volunteers, the Regency Crisis—requiring him to juggle with art, national identity and colonial manipulation. Wheatley's painting of the Volunteers omits reference to the Free Trade controversy. Wheatley is contrasted with Vincent Waldre's work 'King Henry II receiving the submission of the Irish Chieftains' and George III supported by Liberty and Justice, both on the ceiling of Dublin castle.

Cullen reviews portraits of such notables as the Third Earl of Bellamont painted by Reynolds, among the scores of paintings illustrated in this deluxe book from the excellent Cork University Press. The Earl's ruling passion was women. Nicknamed "the Hibernian seducer" he was "wounded in the groin" while duelling. The comments on Daniel O'Connell are balanced and David Wilkie's portrait is contrasted with J. P. Haverty's depicting O'Connell "amidst the glens of Kerry, a huge mastiff by his side and a ruined castle in the background." O'Connell "found no difficulty in inhabiting both an English and an Irish world" and his pictorial representation seems at variance with designs on "mobilisation of Irish Catholicism and, later, the repeal of the Act of Union".

Cullen's digression on Richard Mansergh St George reaches a sublime tone. Hugh Douglas Hamilton's portrait captures the excessive morbidity of its subject and was also prophetic. Mansergh's life had fictional counterparts in the Gothic novels of Charles Maturin, Ann Radcliffe and William Godwin. The portrait shows Mansergh mourning at his wife's elaborate tomb, below an inscription "Non immemor" (not to forget). His wife died young leaving two children, and the pathologically unconsolable Mansergh, an Anglo-Irish landlord and hero of the American War of Independence, became reclusive, mentally unstable, and a laudanum addict. He locked the portrait in a room with a lengthy epistle sealed in a trunk for his children to read on their maturity. Mansergh St George came to a horrible end "a victim of the early stages of the 1798 rebellion. Hacked to death with a rusty scythe . . . his secret is history itself, the Anglo-Irish condition".

Cullen remarks that "there is little in Lavery's 1920s image of Ireland to distinguish Kathleen Ni Houlihan from her earlier incarnation as Hibernia with the proverbial harp". James Barry also lumbered Irish art with the harp. John Butler Yeats is trashed for making W. B. active, compared to the "introverted passivity" of his sister Lily.

Great fuss is made of Sean Keating's 'Allegory' and 'Night's Candles are Burnt Out'; "the paintings may almost read like essays in socialist realism, but they address the realities of 1920s Ireland". One wonders if these two works of Keating's wouldn't have found favour with Stalin, Hitler and Mussolini. Cullen may as well join George Russell, AE, who believed cubism came from "the reason rather than the imagination" and deplored Mainie Jellett whom Bruce Arnold calls "the single greatest force for change in art in Ireland between the two world wars".

Cullen says "The idea of nation has little to do with Jellett's vision and everything to do with Keating's who was preoccupied with forging a definitive view of Irishness". If so, the less Keating he. It is perhaps significant that Cullen's study ends in nineteen thirty, a golden decade for totalitarianism.

—*Books Ireland* 1997

RUSTIC BARDS

The Mystical Imagination of Patrick Kavanagh: 'a buttonhole in heaven?' Una Agnew (Columba Press)

Thomas Furlong, the Forgotten Wexford Poet: the life and work of Thomas Furlong (1794-1827) Sean Mythen (Clone Publications)

Una Agnew of the Sisters of Saint Louis has happily broken ranks with the more pugnacious Kavanaghtians, former habitueés of such hostelries as The Hill, Grogans, O'Neills and McDaid's. Many of them used to congregate (and may still do so) at his seat below Baggot Street bridge to offer homage yearly in early September. Peter Kavanagh, the high priest of the Kavanagh cult surpassed these ordinary acolytes in an often hostile supervisory manner, earnestly assured that his brother the poet was no less than William Shakespeare, William Wordsworth and Walt Whitman all rolled into one—at least that was the evident impression given to the present reviewer in little old New York in the 1980s. Patrick Kavanagh in the Pantheon of Irish Poets chuckles from Valhalla and Sister Una is in no doubt about such matters, in fact he chuckles a lot more securely in his eternal tenure next to WBY. This duumvirate seems likely to hold their tenancy well into two thousand unless the world ends on New Year's Eve. Even Kavanagh's begrudging contemporaries such as Austin Clarke, Francis MacManus and especially Robert Farren were in no doubt that he was just about as significant as John Clare or William Shenstone. However, while he stands wearing the green bays it is no secret that poetry lovers, to coin a phrase of Theo Dorgan's, are certain that Willie Yeats is top dog. Still, Kavanagh lived and died in the belief that he was the Ard Fhile incarnate and a minority within the majority of poetry users rests somewhat easier since he was after all a poet by vocation and not career.

Sister Una travels familiar ground for Kavanaghtians but hardly anyone of them will agree with a mystical Monaghan bard except perhaps James Liddy, "I take him to have been a Christian ... He was shy to speak of his belief in God except perhaps to his sister Celia." One might pause further after the opening preamble and relate that Sister Una's conveyance of things mystical is certainly not Dantesque as she doggedly pursues her thesis, "Is there a mystical dimension to Kavanagh's work?" she inquires of the reader and proceeds to adopt the legendary Evelyn Underhill's *Mysticism* which gives a structure which may or may not be successfully merged with Kavanagh's work. She finds in the latter, "the classic mystical pathway, outlined by Underhill, of Awakening, Purification and Illumination." Her research is a useful addition to Kavanagh scholarship usually written by devotees and heavily anecdotal. Hence she has clarified the birth date of the poet which remains somewhat confusing since the Liber baptizatorum at Iniskeen makes it 22 October, his father claimed it was the 21st while the Civil Register at Carrickmacross has 23rd.

Much store is set by Kavanagh being influenced by the PP Canon Bernard Maguire 'Salamanca Barney', an eclectic cleric who admired both Shaw and Chesterton, and was held in high esteem by the young poet who also had a grá for Father Pat McCannon, 'the silenced local priest' who introduced him to the writings of William Carleton. She does not say whether there is any significance in the fact that Paddy Maguire, the central persona of Kavanagh's *The Great Hunger* was suggested by the PP's surname. Sister Una may be too cloying about the fatherly influence of clerics on Kavanagh but mistakenly avoids mention of his disagreeable acquaintanceship with John Charles McQuaid who expected the wayward poet to apply himself to a pedestrian job. However, she is able to lambast those dark decades of the twentieth century in Ireland when dancing was supervised by clerical torchlight, having been banned at the crossroads.

Her presentation of his early love for school textbooks is all too human and accurate; thus he relished the Royal Readers, the Finlay Readers and the New School and College Literary Series, copies of which, usually without their covers, still live on in many Irish homes. From these books he learned poems by heart and in this safe school of his own making found much technical apparatus without ruining his talent for poetry. As it happened, Kavanagh was a bit of a dunce and seemingly quit or was asked to quit formal schooling in fifth class. None the less he could be seen skulking in the fields of a summer's day perusing Shelley's deeply tragic drama about Beatrice Cenci—incidentally a masterpiece of its kind.

AE and *The Irish Statesman* 'found' the poet and she recounts his famous journey, which now seems Whittingtonesque, to meet the mystical editor of that journal after the long trek from Monaghan. Her facts about Kavanagh's father are inherently gripping. He was a victim of the stigma of illegitimacy that inhuman aberration of bygone bureaucracy. So Kavanagh's grandfather was actually a Kevany who had a love-child with Nancy Callan from Mucker and the name became localised into Kavanagh. Apparently Patrick Kavanagh never knew these facts nor did his father tell him, and subconsciously it affected both their lives. It was a dark secret known to the father and shamefully concealed; a legacy to the son of a mystery never unravelled. Otherwise Kavanagh's father whipped him and disapproved of his introspective nature. Neither were useful on the small farm; the work was left to Mrs Kavanagh, Bridget Quinn. Sister Una avoids the heartrending squalor of the Kavanagh household at Mucker, the father drunkenly playing his melodeon, the wife struggling to keep the show on the road and Kavanagh himself almost the village idiot reading and writing nature poems, "Being made a fool is good for the soul ... it makes a man into something unusual, a saint or a poet or an imbecile." Kavanagh comes across as a strange mixture of all three.

In the early fifties he lived or actually relived a life like Mangan's from a century earlier. The libel action, foolhardily taken against *The Leader* made him famous in a week. Nowadays, it would have got him hackwork at least if not a celebrity CV viable for career purposes. However, the poor gom won no damages and was not the equal of the likes of Oscar Wilde before the Wigs and Bench. He ended as poor as before and by then with broken health. He lost a lung and miraculously recovered to write his best sonnets picking up on one of the better early ones 'Iniskeen Road: July Evening'. His writing of 'Prelude' dates from the year of his so-called disgrace and Sister Una marks its significance majestically. She is fervent in relating how he not only protected the wound wherein God entered but also shows how he was "one of the first Irish theologians to recognise the femininity of God".

Patriotic Wexfordians may claim Furlong as some kind of Irish John Keats; both poets lived roughly in the same period, Keats died in his mid-twenties while Furlong lived to the age of thirty-three. In his short life, Furlong's journey to Dublin kindled his writing career however he seems to have been one of that rare breed of writers who never see their writing in terms of any kind of career. He was born in Scarawalsh not far from Enniscorthy in 1794 and left his father's small farm to become a grocer's apprentice on the spur of the moment at age fifteen, having delivered a cartload of produce to a shopkeeper and publican named Hart of James Street in Dublin. Hart may well have become a surrogate father to the lad who precociously began to write, sending his efforts at first to Thomas Moore because he loved the latter's verse novel *Lalla Rookh* and penned a poem in praise of it. Walter Scott is said to have admired Furlong's poem 'The Love of Life'. It was probably brought his attention by Charles Maturin whose novel *Melmoth the Wanderer* enchanted the young man. When Hart died, Furlong found patronage with the Jameson whiskey distilling family on the strength of having published a slim volume *The Misanthrope with Other Poems* in 1821.

He had genius, not perhaps in the execution but in the ripe suggestion of the themes in his long poems. 'The Misanthrope' is grippingly dramatic as narrative poetry but does not always reach the sublime, nor perhaps has the real power to reach the egotistical sublime. His elegy for Hart is deeply felt but contains none of Keats' stoical paganism. His politics are clearly set out in 'The Plagues of Ireland' while his Catholicism in various notes sounds somewhat pugnacious; however he does not always convey the position of a profound believer. He is defiantly against the Act of Union and any Ascendency privilege, not least droit de seigneur. The latter, as obsessional subject matter, may reflect a personal family involvement since he had three sisters. Surprisingly or not, his translations in *The Irish Minstrelsy* contain some of his finest formal poetry. Metre, rhyme and diction merge into excellent translation such as with 'The Coolin'. The renderings of Carolan's poetry are fine also:

My voice is low

—my mood of mirth is o'er, I droop in sadness

like the widowed dove; Talk, talk of tortures!

—talk of pain no more—Nought strikes us like

the death of those we love.

The poems in praise of drinking suggest a fondness for the drop, but his early death may be no more than a statistical sign of the times he lived in. What brief accounts of his life have survived are full of conjecture; he may have been a rake in the way Shelley was presumed to be a rake. Some of Furlong's poems speak of something angelic and in one poem 'Fancy' the terrors of imagination convey convincingly his powers in that sphere. It is fanciful to suppose he met Shelley who made one infamous visit to Ireland taking in a tour of Killarney *en route*. Furlong's death heralded a large funeral and some of his meagre criticisms of contemporaries who are now forgotten must have meant that he had a coterie of enemies as well as admirers. Sadly or not his reputation has just about survived largely through his last and posthumous lengthy poem 'The Doom of Derenzie' which can almost be read in fit company with Coleridge's 'Christabel' and Keats's 'The Eve of St Agnes'. Here he finally achieved a vehicle for his apparent gloomy and Gothic imagination, involving horrible Whiteboy violence and an innocent man sent shaking to the gibbet. This poem reaches the spine-tingling sublime all right. Furlong refuses to relish the abomination of the gory details of a public hanging and leaves the reader with a great sense of shame and downfall. Whether the suspiration of the poem's close is either artistically valid or becomes a mere balladic cul de sac is a matter for everyone's individual sensibility. But Derenzie's doom is not a cause for the poet's despair and the power of the poem was prophetic in forecasting the ruin of the monolithic De Rinzy dynasty who were given a handout of vast landholdings in Clobemon under the Cromwellian settlement. Furlong's miltonic sense of triumph is Lycidasian and marks his commonality with fellow Irish poets who are a natural blend of the English and Celtic traditions.

—*Books Ireland* 1999

HEANEY AND OTHER NOBLEMEN

Seamus Heaney Helen Vendler (Harper Collins)

Transcultural Joyce Karen R. Lawrence (Cambridge University Press)

The Cambridge Companion to George Bernard Shaw Christopher Innes (Cambridge University Press)

A Yeats Dictionary: persons and places in the poetry of William Butler Yeats Lester I. Conner (Syracuse University Press)

The Heaney enigma really concerns his reputation rather than his poems. He may also be a victim of the unwritten cultural imperative that he must not receive negative criticism, especially in Ireland. However, adverse critics such as A. N. Wilson, Desmond Fennell and Eoghan Harris have not dented him. The latter, classified the Nobel prize winning poet as having the same content as Alice Taylor. Much of his poetry celebrates rural life and Harris presumes this is Alice Taylor's sole territorial interest. Wilson and Fennell think Heaney's stature is not as high as that in which his admirers hold him. Some believe that his leaving Ulster shortly after the Troubles began for the sequestered confines of a Wicklow cottage (even if it had connections with J. M. Synge) was a cop-out, especially for a poet.

Faber & Faber becoming his publisher in the 1960s showed that he had been loved in London; this meant adoption in Dublin and big-fellow status in Belfast. Northern poets since then have been able to expect wooing beyond the two islands, in America and further afield. The epithet Northern poet has been very lucrative, more so than being a Southern, Western or Eastern poet in Ireland. Heaney's London lauding was seen by many as a gesture out of British guilt to Ulster. With the publication of his fourth book, *North,* begrudgers said that it should have been called *South* because of the poet's self-arranged exile in the Republic in 1972 away from the troublesome six counties. In Ireland, he is accepted as inheritor of the Kavanagh line but without the Monaghan poet's satirical vein. In England, Heaney was accepted by, amongst others, Ted Hughes, whose death shocked the literary world last year; another pastoral celebrator but with the unenviable aura of having been the widower of Sylvia Plath. Since Heaney made a version of Sweeney, the mad poet, some expect him to be an Irish Robert Lowell (his sometime friend) whom myth has it was mad like Poe, Berryman and Plath.

Helen Vendler focuses on the poems from ten books over thirty years. Her chronology is partisan, listing events such as "1968-9: Catholic civil rights marches, countered by state police". The listing of Bloody Sunday, January 1972 might easily receive editorial veto from An *Phoblacht*. Throughout, her analysis is pedagogical. She gives the rhyming scheme for a sonnet pedantically: ababcdcdefefef. This nuts and bolts approach may frighten students of poetry and deprive beginners of its treasure. Heaney is also dismissive: "The efficacy of poetry is nil." This is bad tempered and may force the other extreme in saying that the efficacy of poetry is nil plus ineffable millions of infinite variety.

Poems such as 'Thatcher', 'The Forge', 'Rite of Spring', 'From the Frontier of Writing' and 'St Kevin and the Blackbird' are murdered by her dissections. The latter, she says, "is strung on seven 'and's". She tabulates words and phrases as a computer can with a document, but why should this be done to a poor helpless poem? Many of the poems, including 'Digging', reveal his obsession with the well-made lyric and can be read as solipsistic utterances embalmed in metaphors about poetry and its composition. In the latter, the pen is not mightier than the gun, which is a highly political statement. 'From the Frontier of Writing' has its quota of hefty metaphor which she validates: "Did the subjection of the writer at a real roadblock make him aware of an inner equivalent when writing?" In 'The Tollund Man', sparked off by reading P. V. Glob's *The Bog People* about murder victims from the Iron Age preserved in peat bogs in Denmark, she remarks, "their anonymity gave him [Heaney] an imaginative scope he would have been unwilling to assume in a literal retelling of local assassinations." If this is his reaction to sectarian murder why should it be thinly veiled in poetry, why not in prose?

She also implies that only an expert can unlock the mystery of a poem; with the further implication of an ultimate mystery which, once unlocked, renders the original poem redundant like some husk; and the dangerous suggestion that the poem never reached a *final* language if it has to be explained by someone who may not realise that poetry is not the preserve of Harvard, Harlem or Howth.

Helen Vendler's book does not compare Heaney with anyone; he remains a shrine, neither a Tom Moore nor a Tom Paulin. The role of an ambassador poet may be sneered at but he is one of the most distinguished that the world knows. Some natives dislike the lack of hatred in his poems and 'tis said that he doesn't hate himself enough. So, he can rest on his laurels but refuses to and the word is out that he writes on (despite the critics and their laptops) in the gloom and glory of the Celtic Tiger era—a tiger of no particular colour who still burns brightly.

Most of these essays stem from the fourteenth International Joyce Symposium in Seville. The editor writes about Brigid Brophy, author of the 1960s *In Transit: an Heroic-Cyclic Novel:* "a sitin' on the present tense" at an airport lounge where the androgynous narrator decides in favour of a journey through the stream of consciousness and against flying, after the death of relatives in plane crashes. Maria Dibatista hunts down Joyce's influence on McGahern's *Amongst Women*. Eavan Boland produces a tottering rhetoric as if inspired by Micheal Mac Liammoir. A pitfall for Irish writers is the assumption of personal biography with similarities to

Joyce's in Dublin. She obeys this time-honoured tradition

with cloying protestations about being an Irish woman poet. Cesar Augusto Salgado explores Borges' writings about Joyce. He is quoted, saying Joyce in writing *Ulysses* "lamentably wasted his undeniably verbal genius" and failed to construct characters in "baroque extremisms [...] which will never be communicated." Salgado claims that Stuart Gilbert's *James Joyce's Ulysses* (1930) is a fraudulent study of a novel of failed conceits especially regarding the Homeric parallels. Jose Lezama Lima caught the Joycean virus after writing an obituary in the Havana journal *Grafos* in March 1941. Twenty-five years later he published *Paradiso* which uses Havana as Dublin is used in *Ulysses*. Jacques Mailhos examines Georges Perec's *Life: a User's Manual* set in an instant (on 23 June around 8 p.m.). A postcard from *Ulysses* appears in Perec's novel. Literature is the slowest postal service. Intertextuality was brought further by Perec, who mentions a doll's house in his book which is a replica of Bloom's dream house in *Ulysses*.

Guillermo Cabrera Infanta is more Joycean than JJ. Michael Wood samples his puns which are Flann-O'Brienesque: "Everything happens in trees, says Tarzan", "As the crook flies." Polonius asks Hamlet what does he read, the Prince stutters "Wordswordsworth." Infanta has coined hybrid puns: "Nat King Kong and Shy lock Holmes."

His novel *Tres tristes tigres* has a central character who finds "more suspense in dictionaries than in Hitchcock." Srinivas Aravamudan ruthlessly pursues Joycean connections to G. V. Desani's *All About H. Hatterr* (1948) a critical success praised by T. S. Eliot and E. M. Forster. Aravamudan is the last word on Theosophy in Joyce and Desani. Helena Blavatsky, Henry Olcott, Annie Besant and A.P. Sinnett are called from the Astral plane and Isis is unveiled. Ronald Bush pits Joyce with Mary Shelley and Salman Rushdie. *The Satanic Verses* is concisely miniaturised; no mean feat when dealing with the magic realist novel which made a prisoner of its author under police protection which Flaubert might have enjoyed.

The closing section is multilingual. Fritz Senn is among the short-shrift writers about *Anna Livia Plurabelle* in translation into Italian, German, Romanian and Spanish. Di Jin, the Chinese translator of *Ulysses,* tackles the impossible with the Mr Breen/Mrs Breen and the putative lawsuit in the novel over the former's receiving an anonymous postcard with the message "U.P. : up,". This has confounded scholars and others. There are obvious slang explanations but none have been declared absolute.

In this large-format paperback some of the pages were uncut which meant chopping ahead at times. A host of contributors make up what might be subtitled "The Intelligent Bluffer's Guide to Bernard Shaw". They are Sally Peters, Kate Kelly, Charles Berst, Kerry Powell, Fred Marker, David Gordon, Fred Berg, Christopher Innes, Ron Bryden, Matthew Wikander, Tracy Davis, T. F. Evans, Jan Mc Donald, Jon Wisenthal, and Bob Everding. GBS is given a thorough grilling and roasting when accused of being the bedfellow of Harley Granville Barker because of jealousy over Helen Huntington with whom Barker ran off after divorcing Lillah McCarthy. Shaw the businessman is shown as shrewd on money matters, copyright, the Net Book Agreement (first proposed by Frederick Macmillan) and finding in Grant Richards a decent gent who helped produce first editions of the plays in book sets. The influence on Shaw of Ibsen, William Archer and Arthur Bingham Walkey are explored. Wilde's influence on Shaw's *You Never Can Tell* is sourced from *The Importance of Being Earnest* which he reviewed as a "really heartless play". Apparently, Shaw was jealous about Wilde's success in the theatre.

Shaw's use of contemporary playwrights, now forgotten, is

intriguing. Clo Graves's comedy *A Mother of Three* helped him accommodate his vision to the feminine perspective. As a drama critic he is also seen as having benefitted from Elizabeth Robin's *Alan's Wife,* Constance Fletcher's Mrs *Lessingharn* and Risden Home's *Nelson's Enchantress. Major Barbara* and *Man and Superman* are contrasted. The editor, Christopher Innes, expertly discusses the so-called experimental plays *Misalliance, Fanny' First Play* and *Getting Married,* showing how they influenced Brecht, Bond and Orton. *Heartbreak House* gets its just deserts; its source being found in the Russian genius about whom GBS wrote, "When I hear a play of Chekov's I want to tear my own up." Shaw's history plays are ably analysed by quoting him, "I never worry myself about historical details until the play is done; human nature is very much the same always and everywhere . All histories, all stories, all dramatic representations are only attempts to arrange the facts in a thinkable, intelligible, interesting form that is, when they are not more or less intentional efforts to hide the truth, as they often are."

Ramsay MacDonald's praise was high for *The Intelligent Woman's Guide to Social-Ism and Capitalism—after* the Bible . . . the most important book that humanity possesses. Has Tony Blair read it? After reading *Das Kapital,* Shaw remarked, "I was completely Marxed" perhaps for life. His vision of theatre as opera is proven easily by breaking the text of a speech from Don Juan in *Man and Superman* into aria-like lines; they "call out for musical treatment". The directives for casting the play stressed the need for actors with vocal contrast: "the four principals should be soprano, alto, tenor and bass." The Shaw legacy is global in impact. What about a 1999 production of *The Apple Cart* on RTE or at the Abbey which might provide public debate on local statesmen who seem to be a law unto themselves?

Professor Conner sounds like a genuinely warm fellow in his multi-dedication page. The list of books consulted is prestigious and reassuring. He presents Yeats's politics well, if one compares the entry on Pearse with *the* entry on Kevin O' Higgins. Yeats's changing views on De Valera, as noted by Conner, towards a more benign one in later years may have been a mask for the poet. The entry on Nietzsche is too sparse since Yeats found deeps in him. The Abbey Theatre gets a mention but only just. There is good clarifying scholarship since, bogus or otherwise, Thomas Mann is often credited but never wrote, "In our time the destiny of man presents its meanings in political terms." The phrase comes from a conversation Mann had with the American poet, Archibald MacLeish. Conner corrects Yeats's folklore about Queen Maeve and Ailell, who had seven sons and not nine according to Yeats. He suggests plagiarism on the poet's part with regard to the erotic poem 'Leda and the Swan' attributable to Thomas Sturge Moore's ode 'To Leda' published in 1904. The entries on Synge, Lady Gregory, Robert Emmet and Roger Casement contain fitting sentiment. Conner writes well on Maud Gonne perhaps the most difficult entry to fill, in such a dictionary.

He explains the use of 'George' by which name the poet called his wife simply because she hated being called Georgie. Cuchulainn is given an entry befitting his majesty. On 'Crazy Jane', Monk Gibbon is quoted with three stanzas from a poem of the same name which appeared in print before Yeats's sequence about Crazy Jane. This book has a complete list of placenames evoking the author's immediate reaction or l a s t i n g i m p r e s s i o n .

—*Books Ireland* 1999

THE HEAT OF THE DAY BEFORE

The Dubbalin Man Brendan Behan (A. & A. Farmar)

The Unappeasable Host: studies in Irish identities Robert Tracy (University College Dublin Press)

Reading Paul Muldoon Clair Wills (Bloodaxe Books)

The Present Lasts a Long Time: essays in cultural politics Francis Mulhern (Cork University Press)

Here is a selection from the rowdiest roisterer, or so legend has it. The articles are culled (the latter a word that might have made Behan sick) from his *Irish Press* contributions in the mid-fifties, some of which already appeared as *Hold Your Hour and Have Another.* The cover boasts about a first printing of a Behan story which is actually so so. Beatrice Behan is represented by some skilful cartoons featuring Brendan mostly and proving the inheritance of artistry from her father, Cecil Salkeld. Anthony Cronin is myth-makingly festive in an introduction which has none of the more insightful observations of his *Dead* as *Doornails* about Behan. Of the terrible trio that was Myles, Kavanagh and Behan, the latter was least able to find his voice. While all of them had output difficulties by today's standards when profligate writers abound; it might even be claimed that Behan never got to grips with literature at all, since his most famous play *The Quare Fella* comes directly from Wilde's *The Ballad of Reading* Gaol and *The Hostage* is a piece of plagiarism from Frank O'Connor's *Guests of the Nation* with Behan's love of ballad and song thrown in for bad measure. He called himself 'a Penguin educated citizen' with some exaggeration. The Gaelic fraternity believe that he should have gone completely over to their side and wrote strictly *as gaeilge.*

In these short journalistic pieces, he is not averse to parodying everything including the endangered teanga, 'came meal a vault yeh'. Elsewhere he admits "I am one of the compulsory Irish".

Borstal Boy, his account of Hollesley Bay Borstal avoids the stark realism that other prison literature has become famous for, such as that of Jean Genet who is misspelt as 'Jean Prevet' in the article 'From Dublin to les Champs Elysees'. One might be inclined to think that he knew little of Genet and name dropped, as one does in such situations and gets the name wrong. This is not snobbery on the present reviewer's part who can prove he is fiscally lower working class. Behan's claims of impoverishment were lies since he was not even upper working class. There is the quotidian myth of Behan's staunch working class roots while he was in fact grandson of a property rich granny. He was in fact about as working class as George Orwell or Ludwig Wittgenstein. And furthermore, Behan's father might have passed for something of an intellectual in any circle. Behan's own scanty reading can be attributed to a healthy disinterest in literature. Neither can it be a slander that like Myles and Kavanagh, each was a professional alcohol-addict which is no excuse for a small output though it may explain slim volumes. However Joyce who is also claimed by some as working class because of temporary residence north of the Liffey, wrote his big tomes on many's a hangover.

Behan's genius is a thing of hearsay; there are flashes of it here but strangely enough not in the humour. Cronin quotes a joke of Behan's about the Old Testament which is almost as old as Methusaleh and not a patch on New York Jewish jokes in the same vein. Behan's best bits from the *Irish Press* (a spookily partisan newspaper in its heyday) are the innocent anecdotes about himself as house painter cycling to Dun Laoghaire and instead of getting on with the job, reading the newspapers found under the carpets or killing a few hours along the Vico Road which did not bring out any criticism from him except some Shavian ecstasy about its beauty. In his comments about Ireland and elsewhere, especially when avoiding a summer's day in Co Down at Millisle in a public house, he appears as a cosmopolitan city slicker who might be at home in Paris, Miami or Istanbul. What is really startling is that the myth-makers, especially based on his Republican activities, are not accurate with regard to his politics either, since Behan was popularly well versed on England's history and Ireland's, and maintains that eminent tradition of Dubliners who have complex feelings about both. The colonial ethos is largely a creation of journalism and polemic. The picture of Behan as the scourge, blackguard and Ireland's Arthur Rimbaud, and a swine before the Pearl Bar is farfetched if judged by the naïve writing in these pieces. He was misunderstood, a victim of Republicanism, literature and publicity; somewhere along the line a genuine character was marred by himself and others. Some revisionism is needed to clarify the man and mock those sentimental enthusiasts who defame him.

What is immediately enthralling about the critic Robert Tracy is that he is not peddling the well trammelled list of references purveyed by various cliques. Thus there is mention of Maire MacNeill's *The Festival of Lughnasa,* Maria Edgeworth's *Ennui* and Lady Morgan's *The Wild Irish Girl.* In tracing the roots of Irish literature he logs from these two considerable ladies, on through the Banim brothers; however he may also be bogged down in the received polemical labels about Catholic siege, Protestant entrenchment, vice versa, and the literature of ascendancy decay. His book gains a new lease of life when discussing Joseph Sheridan Le Fanu who lived and worked in what is the present headquarters of the Arts Council. One wonders if Green Tea is drunk by the operatives and whether Le Fanu's ghost stalks their offices? There is an intriguing essay on Yeats's two dud novels; and the best essay 'Long Division in the Long Schoolroom' a lecture—many of the chapters were originally lectures. He cites Corkery and Seamus Deane; unable to cede to the Yeatses, Synges and Shaws any Hibernian identity: they are excluded from "the magic circle of Irishness". Yeats saw the Anglo-Irish as the true Irish. Edmund Burke wanted justice for

Ireland with the rights of all types of Christain on the island treated equally. Yeats insisted on the rights of Protestants a propos divorce in 1925. His Nobel Prize was described in the *Catholic Bulletin* as awarded to "a member of the English colony in Ireland".

Yeats's poem 'Among School Children' is given the full critical treatment. Tracy does not get any mileage out of the fact that Yeats wrote the poem after visiting a Catholic girl's school, St Otterans, in Waterford. The exploration of Yeats's fears for his own version of *Oedipus* at the Abbey after riots over Synge and O'Casey show the poet victimised by censorship and tempted to re-write Sophocles to suit Irish Catholic sensibilities—the play's theme of incest being too dangerous for the new Republic. Tracy has a fine lecture on Yeats and Cuchulainn whose image helped the poet prepare to die; "death is but a passing from one room to another". Synge is briefly sketched in, with a reference to his reading *Oedipus* while writing *The Playboy;* both plays include patricide. Synge's father is a bit of a mystery, dying when Synge was an infant. Yeats sent a wreath for Synge's coffin with the words, 'The lonely returns to the lonely'.

Tracy is good on Joyce, locating him in a Gaelic odyssey, the Tain. He quotes Joyce, "I'm at the end of English," and joins Ireland and Egypt together since Joyce used The Book of The Dead as a source for *Finnegans Wake.* Tracy writes, "the phallic pillar commemorating the Victor of the Nile" has been replaced with "the vaginal statue and fountain depicting a supine Anna Livia as an Irish Cleopatra, the irreverently named 'Floozy in the Jacuzzi'." Joyce began *Finnegans Wake* as the news of Tutankhamen's tomb made world headlines. Tracy quotes Beckett, *"Finnegans Wake* is not about resurrection. It is resurrection." Elizabeth Bowen is lavishly dealt with. The opening sentence from her novel *A World of Love* is indisputably classic, "The sun rose on a landscape still pale with the heat of the day before." Tracy might compare this with the opening sentence of Beckett's *Murphy,* "The sun shone, having no alternative, on the nothing new." Bowen considered her sense of nationality, "As long as I remember,

I've been extremely conscious of being Irish—even when I was writing about very un-Irish things." Roll up, roll up—are you Irish, half-Irish or quarter-Irish? obviously the professors are not the people to ask.

Clair has a formidable task to perform and quickly announces that Muldoon comes from Mael Duin 'bald head', a Gaelic euphemism for a seer. She tackles nine collections of his poetry in a tight space. One finds amongst his highly wrought stuff which tends to the epigrammatic in pitch, such as 'Why Brownlee Left'; 'I Remember Sir Alfred'; 'The More a Man Has the More a Man Wants'. The latter, written at the time of Bobby Sands death is seen as Muldoon's dirty protest, who true to Northern Irish myth keeps tightly lipped and almost unpartisan in a verse-play, *Six Honest Serving Men* about the IRA. He is more relaxed in literary territory such as '7 Middagh Street' and its ghostly voices from the W. H. Auden milieu including Kallman, Britten, Dali and MacNiece. His word play is often close to Joycean concoctions, or Flann O'Brien's "I pick up auden" (I beg your pardon). He is also a dangerous arouser of languages limitations when the mere shape of words by their spelling are close to other words of near similar spelling but in *this* tendency he might be the better for semantic abstention. Georges Perec is one of his heroes but hopefully will not flood his method with word games as the dominant mode. Perhaps there is also a Gavin Ewart influence on Muldoon? His happy exile in sequestered Princeton still holds him prey to the ghosts of Northern Ireland's victims of violence not always relieved by his wit: I'm not 'in exile',/though I can't deny/ that I've been twice in Fintona. Fintona had its share of dire sectarianism. Otherwise unforgotten landscape such as the Moy and local shops like Tohills, the seed merchants, are as evocative for him as the mountains of Mourne are for others, not least Percy French. In 'The Wire', American suburbia becomes enmeshed with Ulster and the reverie returns to nightmare.

It's to the credit of Cork University Press and Field Day for giving the author a publishing venue for this strange book. Most of the essays contained have already appeared in print in various journals, particularly *New Left Review* of which Mulhern has been editor. He is a valuable voice, well worth reading and no doubt a stimulating lecturer in the University of Middlesex and beyond. His work here is mainly the result of review commentary but is none the less for that. It might be taken as a substantial history of culture purveyed in polemics, though he states his agenda as 'Cultures of nationality [...] their general spirit is Marxist'. He might be put down as a Marxist once again but left Northern Ireland in 1969 for Dublin and academically made good and advanced to Cambridge five years later---what in hippy terms is known as the Led Zeppelin era. There are no shades of Denis Donoghue's arcane language though he is overfond of using the word 'taxonomy'.

He is no Marxolator in that he knows the bearded guru had no interest in art and found Greek drama merely had 'charm' which amounts to about the equivalent of Trotsky's love of literature in *Literature and Revolution*. Mulhern's text threatens a possible future tome on the brief life and works of Christopher Caudwell who fell in Spain with the anti-Fascists, short of his thirtieth birthday. Mulhern fills out the typical features amongst Irish intellectuals of those whose spiritual paradise is Paris, thus his passion for Louis Althusser and personal rebirth is dated to May 1968. Mulhern would grow up to believe Regis Debray's verdict on "the May explosion as a functional crisis of development for consumer capitalism in France", and attacked its intellectual notables for their "regression to irrationalism and political reaction". On Althusser, he is more than competent but all too brief because of the format: a critical essay. However the Francophile is well glyphed a propos his work on a play by Bertolazzi and some paintings by Cremonini, his disciple Pierre Macherey and devotion to Freud. Mulhern can be incisively educational on Julien Benda's depiction of spiritual treason but is gagged in an ideological snare in mentioning Michel Foucault's denial of 'the idea of society as an intelligible whole, the idea of a directed or directable historical process'.

When he comes to Raymond Williams the present is engaged: minority cultures, Arts Councils (a brainwave of John Maynard Keynes) and popular culture: tabloid journalism, pop videos, the movie and its predictable last resting place, the video. Williams is a realist stating that "there simply cannot be infinite production in a materially finite world". The massive problems of communities and their longing for identity based on media-recognition is highlighted. He provides a brief history of cultural theoreticians from T. S. Eliot through the Leavises (F. R. and Q. D.) and shamefully trounces them along the way up to Richard Hoggart's fashionable working class hero-intellectual, a by-product of Lenin, John Lennon and George Orwell. Hoggart embodies the confusions and contradictions inherent in locating class accurately, at once claiming to be a bread and treacle man while appearing almost colonial within national boundaries, in stating that his model institutions were; "adult education, the BBC and Penguin Books". The Leavises (already mentioned) are fairly well panned as cultural snobs and seen as somewhat anarchic because of their focus of adoration, mainly upon Henry James the Yankee and naturalised Englishman, Conrad, a Pole with a genius for using English, and George Eliot, one of the greatest women writers of all time. Mulhern's review of *The Field Day Anthology*, latterly dubbed 'the fealty anthology' caused its own furore not least his accurate location of its source being spiritually Derry but in fact University College Dublin and 'Deane's own faculty'. Deane is almost cleared of any nepotism because of his belief in rewriting everything, "un-blemished by Irishness but securely Irish". Mulhern raised the hackles of Field Day editor Luke Gibbons whom he deemed to be living in the past with a bad dose of post-colonial melancholy. Mulhern demands the negation of nationalism and proves himself an all-rounder, discussing the art of translation via Mangan, Ferguson, Eliot, Pound, Celan and

Louis Zukoksky. As a product of Northern Ireland he seems to be a different kind of exile from his fellow Irish men and women adopted by the British mainland.

—*Books Ireland* 1999

DONE YOUR THIRD HAIKU YET?

The Portable Creative Writing Workshop Pat Boran (Salmon)

The Truth about the Irish Terry Eagleton (New Island)

This manual for apprentice writers might well be displayed on the same shelf as books for weekend watercolourists which guarantee To Free The Artist Within. However, he may have anticipated such jeering and admits, albeit in a begrudging tone with regard to poems, that "the very idea that there might be ways of *teaching* (the italics are his) people how to write them seems ridiculous." Seamus Heaney is quoted to advantage near the end of the book: "Nobody can ever tell you how exactly they succeeded in writing the poems they believe in, so nobody can tell you how to write the ones you will have to believe in. My advice, therefore, is about reading rather than writing: keep reading those poets who bring you to life, the ones who excite you enough to make you want to write."

Philip Casey claims, "poetry is so rare and I'm not confident that I've written any myself, and therefore couldn't possibly teach how to 'do' it." Meanwhile Boran confidently exposes the creative methods of John F. Deane who told him that in order to find the quietness within himself to write, "sometimes I turn the sound on the television all the way up so I can't think". This seems ludicrous but if it works, why not?—once it's within the boundaries of noise pollution.

Boran alludes to writers and their bons mots about the art of writing. Robert Greacen believes that, "writing poetry is like trying to catch a black cat in a dark room". Might that just as well read a white cat in a snowstorm? If there is one great analogy for writing poems it would seriously debunk poetry since its accuracy would limit every poem. The text is littered with analogies, many of which are very old chestnuts also. Robert Graves is quoted: "a poem is an idea caught in the act of dawning" which is not much help compared to Michael Longley's Keatsian remark, "If I knew where poems came from, I'd go there."

His concept, that inside the poet lurks an Inner Figure who may be obstructing the process of writing, is bogus psychology. His suggestions for the use of symbols read like a lot of fakery and that about using dreams, to put it lamely, is very dreamy stuff and a long way from what Joyce called 'the dreamery creamery butter'. The introduction to metre goes on too long and turns his product into a tedious school-book. There is too much hectoring use of 'we' and an attitude that is often self-defeating; for example, "Another useful memory aid might be to note that the word dactyl is Greek for a finger (think of pterodactyl), and in the human finger the first, or base, joint is longer than the second and third." *One* might well ask him to explain how long is a piece of string? When the reader is treated to one *of* his compositions, 'Penknife' a tiny eight-line poem, the effect is disconcerting.

Furthermore, he has cobbled together a quasi-scientific textbook so that every *few* pages some indented lines are shaded in grey below an icon of a hand holding a pen. One of these grey areas suggests you, "write the first thing, and any subsequent thing, that comes into your head. Imagine you're drunk, imagine you're dreaming, imagine you're insane." He recommends the writing of "at least three haiku" per day. There's a prescription! Otherwise, he strongly advises "poetry related games you might play on your own or in a workshop proper". Who knows whether this advice will have the budding writer rolling on the floor with laughter or embarking on writing a first masterpiece? He incorrectly refers to Yeats's use of automatic writing where in fact his wife became an adept of automatic writing and influenced Willie. Mrs Yeats was obviously the closest the poet ever got to a portable creative writer's workshop.

Another of the grey areas alerts the novice to take "10-15 minutes, start right away and write your own 100-word autobiography," presumably while holding Boran's primer in one hand. He can be very irritating with general comments such as, "Kafka manages to do this remarkably well anyway" or "many of Beckett's characters, for instance, seem almost to have no past at all." The second-hand narration of the plot of Hamlet is so convoluted that one wonders if it is the well-known play he is talking about at all. Similarly he takes the opening of Roddy Doyle's *The Snapper* which begins "—You're wha'? said Jimmy Rabbitte Sr.," and goes off in a paean of praise as if it were the work of some extraordinary genius. Even when F. Scott Fitzgerald is cited, the remark somehow loses its power, "reporting the extreme things as if they were the average things will start you on the art of fiction". One would be far better off reading a critical biography of Fitzgerald or his final novel *The Last Tycoon*.

In the closing pages, he gives a brief list of living authors who offer helpful comments for beginners. His book may well assist writers since the process of writing is to say the least highly mysterious, but one reader was left feeling that it is a book by a Boran who neither loves nor hates writing with anything like a demented passion. The conveyance of what it might be to create literature is conspicuous by its absence. This is not too much to expect since there are such books, if not of the 'how to' variety. Neither can it claim to reach the dubious heights of *The Artist's Way* which also infuriated the present reviewer but has become a popular sourcebook for those who *experience* their creative discipline as a lonely, isolating affair and a miserable and often destructive vocation.

Eagleton's latest is not in the same league as his other polemical work, however there is no reason why he shouldn't soften his punches and dish up a whimsical A-Z undoubtedly aimed at the dedicated tourist who, while wandering through Celtic mists, hardly wants satirical invective about the natives? Perhaps his alphabetical entries should have come from the spleen rather than aspiring to the humour of Ireland's lonely fortnightly *The Phoenix*. Surprisingly, the entries hold the attention and had this reader skimming back and forth looking for laughs which are sometimes delivered and sometimes not.

His humour undercuts statements of fact and there are footnotes known as FIF's (Facts to Impress your Friends) which usually make the final undercut. His vision of the Celtic Tiger is trenchantly Marxist, revealing the present crisis behind the boom with the additional teaser in an FIF: "around 35% of the Irish are dependent on Social Welfare". The opening entry on Alcohol is not indicative of the fizzy brew to come. He defines Biffo in an Irish context as "big ignorant fucker from Offaly" and Buffalo is somewhat similar except it refers to physical looks and a neighbouring county. This should have the tourists racing to Laois and Offaly to see for themselves.

He portrays Craic as a very nauseating term from overuse but may overestimate Ireland's sexual ease. His belief that Dolmens house the dead who perished while waiting for ancient buses must be true. He gives Charlotte Despard, an activist friend of Maud Gonne, a terrible slandering and also George IV whose only interest in Dunleary was using it to hasten to the bed of his mistress.

The national characteristic of flakeyness he calls easy-goingness, in other words the Irish are subconsciously incapable of acting on their stated intentions. He doesn't give a damn about political correctness and is convinced that many of the fairies who attended the Conference of 1839 eventually ended up in San Francisco. The F-word can be indentified in class terms, he claims and thus to say 'fugghan bastard' renders the speaker lower-middle class and downwards. However, he knows that no

Irish person pronounces the word film except as 'filum'. Gay Byrne is glossed as "possibly the most important man in the country. See God". Does this require revision? He doesn't gloss that other RTE mogul Mike Murphy, the most important broadcaster on the arts? He also notes RTE's devotion to public prayer twice a day which hardly makes a Mecca of it but still not a bad effort. Seamus Heaney is ranked as a major Irish exporter and Joyce a leading industry (hardly big news) and the Irish buy more volumes of poetry than any other English-speaking people. This must exclude the Americans since they can't speak English. Some of the jokes are underGraduate: the difference between a joist and a girder? Joyce wrote *Ulysses* and Goethe wrote *Faust*.

His insistence on the Irish difficulty and confusion as to the meaning of Yes and No apparently comes from the fact that they are derived from Gaelic usage. Just as well to clear that up. He gives an address 'Northern Ireland: the Answer' care of his publisher for those with solutions to the Northern Ireland conflict. He believes that Dante began writing the Divine Comedy after a visit to Lough Derg but does not say which B&B he spent the night in or if Poetry Ireland arranged a reading for him in Galway. Finally, the Irish are not mad since Sigmund Freud declared them to be impervious to psychoanalysis. Eagleton finds the West of Ireland full of "New Age dropouts, artists *and Irish speakers.*"

Presumably he means the four corners of Ireland? He recommends that when you go West, call into the Yeats Country Shop which sells Innisfree Eggs laid in Drumcliffe Churchyard (while stocks last). He is otherwise deeply patriotic and insists that no Irish citizen real or imaginary ever uttered the word begorrah not even Oscar Wilde or GBS.

A likely story. Irish-Americans will be fully reassured by the book since the subtext is that John Bull is responsible for all that is not green in our valleys. Sean O'Casey said, "The Irish are always making a joke of serious things and turning serious things into jokes." Well now begorrah, sure God bless Us!

—*Books Ireland* 1999

SHADOWLANDS

Contemporary Irish Cinema: from the Quiet Man to Dancing at Lughnasa ed. James MacKillop (Syracuse University Press)

Media in Ireland: the search for diversity Damien Kiberd (Open Air)

Images, Icons and the Irish Nationalist Imagination Lawrence W. McBride (Four Courts Press)

Here's a stunning production with an impressive cast of contributors including two poets, Kathleen McCracken and Sanford Sternlicht. You've seen the movies, now read this book! Kathleen McCracken cites Orson Welles' dictum, "A film is what you write on the screen". Or what seems closer to a metaphor for filmmaking, Don Pennebaker's, "I take my images from reality, but the films are an imaginary dream of what really happened." That and a lot more.

In discussing the films of John T. Davis, McCracken understands the coded response to Northern Irish subject matter, as in Dust on the Bible. Brian McIlroy wildly declares that Michael Collins crosses the border and visualises the Unionist audience out of history. Maria Pramaggiore also gets her teeth into Neil Jordan, with a heavy-handed input from Freud, to tease out masochistic narcissism in *The Crying Game*. She quotes Judith Halberstam on the movie, "if sexual instincts often lead us astray, then how much less reliable are concepts such as national identity". The transvestism and gender bending in the movie have tended to downplay the gravity of the IRA kipnap and its grimmer scenario. Making the troubles kinky will not sanitise them. Kathleen Gallagher Winarski is less trivial while tracing Jordan's development to screenwriter-director but again there is some bland psycho-speak finding him guilty of an unresolved mother-conflict in Miracle.

Along with Pat Murphy, another leading figure of contemporary Irish cinema is Thaddeus O'Sullivan; his product has none of the

Hollywood genre that is Jordan's forte, and O'Sullivan's December Bride and Nothing Personal are concocted for cinema out of the Northern situation. The latter's depiction of Presbyterian humour is healthy for national understanding. O'Sullivan, his cohort Bruno de Keyzer and Pat Murphy have a distinctly European heritage behind them rather than a box-office obsession. The problem with many US films is the woeful common denominator of return on investment based on the tried and tested laws of entertainment as prescribed by Los Angeles since the days of silent pictures. The emphasis is on the dollar almighty and to hell with art.

Margot Gayle Backus finds British film roots in Sheridan's In the Name of the Father comparing it with Hanif Kureishi's Sammy and Rosie Get Laid. Treatment of colonial legacy and paternalism are highlighted as strengths of Sheridan's movie. Jennifer C. Cornell finds Stewart Parker's Lost Belongings a terrific depiction of the Northern miasma from the perspective of both sides of the Irish sea. Douglas Brode considers the critically acclaimed My Left Foot, however sourcing the movie in John Huston and John Ford does not seem reasonable. The Dead is given the once over by Moylan C. Mills with mention of its acclaim from critics Denis Donoghue, Richard A. Blake and Richard Shickel. Huston's "obvious love of Joyce's work prevented him from making radical and possibly damaging changes, especially in his re-creation of the final moments of the story". The closing scene between Gretta and Gabriel was shot to perfection over twenty-seven times, and when asked for an ultimate take, Anjelica Huston threw a wobbler and her father had to print what he finally got.

Jim Loter does credit to Cathal Black's incisive Pigs. The fact that he makes Heidegger a subtext to interpret the 'reality' of the film is a happy marriage of cinema and philosophy. Kerstin Ketteman tackles The Field and Hear My Song. Josef Locke, the subject of the latter, "is a master of escapes and elusiveness, thereby becoming an Irish people's hero". Her analysis of The Field is good, showing

'Bull' McCabe's descent into destruction and insanity beginning with obsessive greed leading to murder, the death of his son, ruination of his livestock and his ultimate suicide. However, as a movie it remains a typically Oirish melodrama which with a lot of artistry might have become a triumph of cinematic art. This was the challenge of both Brian Desmond Hurst and Alan Gibson in filming Synge's The Playboy of the Western World. Gibson, according to Sanford Sternlicht, advantageously does not go beyond the play, as Hurst did, in showing the race on the beach where Christy finally finds himself a hero and playboy.

MacKillop, the editor of this book, gives a strange performance on The Quiet Man, a movie that most people find a complete turkey. He admits that it is "the ultimate expression in a tourist's vision of Ireland". However, huge claims are made for the movie, since Grace Kelly saw it as her 'favourite film'. MacKillop found a plaque in the IFC honouring The Quiet Man and this for him justifies exalted criticism? In passing, top of this reviewer's film hate-list includes Gone With The Wind and The Sound of Music. To go even further: Darby O'Gill and the Little People is infinitely more watchable than The Quiet Man because it is so utterly over the top.

That said, MacKillop had edited a very valuable book and does a great service with his fifty page filmography, packed with everything from Knocknagow (1918) on through Return to Glennascaul (1951) right up to the present. Lastly, the index hosts the good, the great and the pioneering from Irish cinema history, including the late Liam O'Leary.

William Hunt provides a suitable introduction and Damien Kiberd in the preface announces that these papers come from the seventh Cleraun Media Conference held in the suburbs of south Dublin. Brendan Purcell's comparisons of media coverage in dealing with the Lewinsky-Clinton debacle are keen. He believes in the legacy of Socratic dialogue as conveyed by the Athenian's disciple, Plato, through the devastating excellence of truth analysed by two opposing speakers. He lists modern followers of this high tradition such as lgnazio Silone, Karl Kraus, Albert Camus, George Orwell, Pier Paolo Pasolini and someone who may not meet everyones standards of Socratic distinction, Gilbert Keith Chesterton.

Andy Pollak's anxieties about Lit-Irish racism are forcefully made about the imbalance between reporting, public opinion and the actual facts. We Irish are generally a nasty little bunch of racists. He has a strong riposte to the press baron A. J. F. O'Reilly which concludes his piece. Klaus Schonbach expertly parallels German racism with recent graphic examples from Der Spiegel. His theories of accountability draw on classical sources such as Max Weber whose concept *Verantwortungsethik* (the ethics of responsibility or accountability) are given due consideration. Mention of the Council of Europe's resolution on 'the ethics of journalism' makes one feel much comfort, yet realities enter Claude-Jean Bertrand's "journalists should be as autonomous as possible from the powers-that-be, economic and political". Bertrand maintains an unavoidable tone of scepticism about purity and the media: "politicians look upon media either as tools to be used for their own purposes—or as threats to their power that must be shackled". He chops up the lines of apparent confusion by segregating the six groups involved: consumers, professionals, media owners, advertisers, decision makers and regulators, and does not shirk incisive comment on the 'media accountability systems'.

Conor Brady is forthright in praise of the National Newspapers of Ireland and their efforts to get effective action from the government on the Law Reform commission, for the long overdue upgrading of publishing law. He seems at ease with the libel laws. Meanwhile he salutes the Dublin Institute of Technology and Dublin City University for providing good schools of journalism. Brady, a hardened professional, knows the ropes well, and off the cuff states that in journalistic practice, "one good source may be more reliable than half a dozen bad ones". He is also mindful of the character in Stoppard's play Night and Day who declares, "I'm all in favour of a free press. It's the bloody newspapers I can't stand."

Robert Pinker brings a systematised approach to the Press Complaints Commission and is suitably passionate about their onus and onerous requirements for code of practice and ethical self-regulation, dependent on the benchmarks of public interest, privacy, intrusions into grief and shock, children and harassment. With regard to the latter, his comments about the death of Princess Diana in Paris imply that she was killed by the paparazzi as it were, who pursued her speedily through traffic. Perhaps her fast lifestyle would have ensured some tragedy sooner or later anyway, in a life that was out of control by some standards.

The intrepid Sean Duignan, former spin doctor, provides a devilish concluding piece on press leaks both planned and unplanned and the worst sort, where "the source does not deny and actually confirms". He gives many examples, not least the one that ended the tenure of Albert Reynolds as Taoiseach over the appointment of Harry Whelehan as President of the High Court. Albert's cute-whoredom was his undoing in that case to the delight of many at the time. Duignan is merrily cynical about John Bruton's comment that "Goverment must be seen to be operating as if behind a pane of glass". Yea, sure. Ten foot thick opaque glass with a high spoof-proof factor!

This book is nothing short of lovely, both in its weight, format and with the added enhancement of plates and many illustrations which are a vital part of the text which needs the actual images under discussion to be on display. Gary Owens brings in spectacular work on the newspaper coverage of the Manchester Martyrs. The Martyrs would become famed in ballad, story and icon but on the day of their execution were casualties to the truth through journalistic melodrama. William Allen, aged nineteen, would surpass the other two in posthumous adoration as a darling lad with a sorrow-stricken sweetheart, Mary Ann Hickey.

Gerard Moran charts the development of Irish and English newspaper sketch-artists of the 1880s, especially Tom Merry's work. Thomas Fitzpatrick's lampoon of Parnell fording a waterfall on a tightrope carrying a woman on his back, shows the accuracy of cartoon reportage from 1891, when the leader was literally about to meet his fall.

The editor of the book, Lawrence W. McBride, traces the rise of literacy from the founding of the national schools which led to a sophisticated reading public. Again, Fitzpatrick is shown to good effect in a brilliantly effective cartoon of Parnell prior to his doom, whereas in earlier years his glory was heralded in sombre and majestic cartoonery such as in the Irish Times depicting him as the Irish Sphinx and the Weekly Freeman making him an ancient mariner steering 'The Home Rule' in sight of port.

Eileen Reilly investigates the book illustrations used in novels by George A. Birmingham, Emily Lawless, Miriam Alexander, B. M. Croker and Justin McCarthy to name a few. As the three-volume novel was replaced by the one-volume novel, book illustration increased in output. The Irish publisher James Duffy pioneered the introduction of nationalistic symbols on books such as the harp, shamrock, wolfhound and round tower.

Spurgeon Thompson leaps into the twentieth century with analysis of travel writing and photography based on J. M. Synge and William Bulfin. Synge is praised for avoiding stage Irishisms in reporting the natives he met on his travels and his use of photography is exalted above Bulfin's which are "standard tourist fare, much like the classic William Lawrence". Ben Novick quotes James Morgan Read "To persuade the masses to fight they must be led to hate". In a useful phrase, Novick discusses 'atrocity propaganda'. John Shuley & Co printed 7,500 copies of their massive recruitment poster,

'Irishmen Avenge the Lusitania'.

The tortuous saga of the delays in establishing the Edwin Lutyens Islandbridge Memorial to Irish soldiers who fell in the Great War is almost too painful to narrate here. Meanwhile, the Garden of Remembrance faced its own glitches and delays in coming to completion, designed by Daithi Hanley with the Children of Lir sculpture created by Oisin Kelly.

The Constance Markievicz monument caused a furore between Hannah Sheehy Skeffington who disputed Dev's interpretation of Markievicz's personality as too meek a representation, whereas the Countess "had challenged the capitalist system under which the poor were exploited". Sean Farrell Moran realises that the destruction of Nelson's Pillar was done by Irish nationalists in defiance of British imperial power. For many the action marked the destruction of a national treasure and in the event of no replacement for it, a further loss. However, Moran seems off the mark in saying that Sheppard's statue of the dying Cuchulainn pays little attention "to either Patrick Pearse's personal failure or the details of a military fiasco". Surely the statue is perfect in its encapsulation of Pearse's sacrifice and triumphant failure?

—*Books Ireland* 2000

IN CAMERA

Viewpoints: Theoretical Perspectives on Irish Visual Texts eds.
Claire Bracken and Emma Radley (Cork University Press)

Still-shots and photographs illustrate the textual discourse in this compendium of academic-analytic essays where the editors are among the fourteen contributors. 'Texts' refers to Irish film as well as TV serials with two exceptions: Justin Carville on Alfred Cort Haddon's lantern slide collection of Irish ethnology giving 'a window onto the world' of the late nineteenth century. The slides expose (no pun intended) the 'encounter between the photographer, the photographed subject and the technological apparatus of the camera'. Colin Graham chooses three contemporary photographic artists to discuss. Joe Duggan, Hannah Starkey, and John Gerrard whose work 'in computer-generated media is indicative' of the 'immersion in new forms'. Graham and Carville emphasise the concept of 'staged photography'.

Cheryl Herr contrasts Thaddeus O'Sullivan's short film *The Woman Who Married Clarke Gable* based on Seán Ó'Faoláin's story which recreates his fiction's 'incisive portrayals of individuals in conflict with one or another of the repressive forces that he attributed to Irish society'. Herr also merges the storyline with another movie of O'Sullivan's *December Bride* where 'a woman (who) defied her Protestant community to live with two men while married to neither'. Barry Monahan's essay is singular in defining what he terms 'film authorship' and particularly his formulation of a film's 'narrative beats' and 'cinematic silence'. These three tenets lead an audience through the visual storyline as in Lenny Abrahamson's *Adam & Paul* and *Garage* which Monahan dissects. His discussion certainly would top any post-cinema-visit remarks and is well rehearsed. Matthew Brown tackles Steve McQueen's *Hunger* and Peter Greengrass' *Bloody Sunday*. Both have NI subject matter which Brown states is 'a means to screen the more lurid pleasures of movie going.' This remark arrests the attention fully to his essay. He views *Hunger* as 'powerfully stylised': it is factually based on the Bobby Sands' sacrifice to the death in the Maze prison. Brown does not shirk from outlining, nor does the movie from filming the 'jarring images of the emaciated body of Sands' which he explains as 'formal experiments with screen fascination and its political content'. With regard to *Bloody Sunday*, Brown concludes that the Civil Rights movement as depicted in the movie could not 'escape the conclusion that non-violent protest ironically managed to rationalise violence'. Heather Macdoughall races through recent Irish Films *as Gaeilge* including the popular short by Daniel O'Hara's *Yu Ming is Ainm Dom*. Her plea is ultimately for 'international acceptance of Irish-language film'.

Emmie McFadden contrasts Stephen Frears *Liam* with Joseph Strick's *A Portrait of the Artist as a Young Man* showing basically that the latter was inspired 'via Strick's adaptation of Joyce'. Emma Radley discusses Paddy Breathnach's *Shrooms* and in the process (thankfully) lowers the repute of *The Commitments* to a Hollywood pastiche transposed to an Irish setting. Radley is keenly refreshing in exposing the frauds of local cinema who depict 'Ireland as rural idyll'. She happily champions *Shrooms* as a horror movie genre that exposes Ireland in the horror genre where industrial schools imprison child inmates who are in the hands of deadly Black Knights amidst 'beatings, torture and abuse'. This is the more nationally progressive genre as with Angela Walsh's *Song for a Raggy Boy* and Peter McMullen's essential *Magdalene Sisters*. Radley hails the cinema zombie genre in *Boy Eats Girl* where the students are tired of Joyce, Beckett and Yeats and recommend that (one) 'grow a brain, who reads them anymore' while the teacher asks: 'how does being Irish make you feel? Reply: suicidal!' Aintzane Legarreta Mentxaka is very good reading Kate O'Brien's involvement with cinematic techniques in her fiction as '*inverted imitation*'; for instance where 'the climactic scene in *Mary Lavelle* merges words and film'.

Anne Mulhall cavorts off to decipher various visual posters
advertising Lough Derg and Inis Rath as spiritual retreats and
investigates as to whom is their potential target audience. The
conclusion is that they are pitched as various genus of 'spiritual
seekers'. Claire Bracken unravels two TV series by the Fitzgibbon
and McElhatton team. Both were angry postfeminist Celtic Tigerish
disasters in terms of achievement, namely *Paths to Freedom* and
Fergus's Wedding. In the contemporary higher standards of the
series *Love/Hate* the latter two are fit for archival shredding whereas
Bracken cites them as pioneering in targeting 'phallogocentric
capitalism' and showing 'the feminine as object of support for a
neoliberal economy that continues to value masculinity as the
dominant maker of power'. This sounds about as intense as the
'troubles' of Alice in Wonderland in our era of capitalism-in-crisis
therefore her theory though well argued falls flat. Zélie Asava delves
into the Irish horror genre and merges two movies in her conclusion
stating that Steven Bradley's *Boy Eats Girl* 'explores class, sexual
and religious difference' while *Isolation* (dir. Billy O'Brien)
explores 'different forms of citizenship, class and cultural capital.'
Better stuff is Jenny O'Connor's treatment of the boy wonder of
Irish cinema, Neil Jordan as true Joycean where Patrick 'Kitten'
Braden in *Breakfast on Pluto* casts off 'the shackles of nation, of
gender and of sexuality'. O'Conner when exploring identity is
genuinely post-DH Lawrence as she utilizes that daring double act
of the French Academy, Deleuze and Guattari who claim that 'girls
and women do not belong to any sex, grouping or order'. *Ah les
intellectuels français!* Fintan Walsh, to euphemise his own usage,
really queers it up on sexuality in film and overuses the awful verb
foreground(s) a term verbally abused in academic faculties
throughout the nation. However, long nights over the lamp and
laptop have yielded him cinematic theoretical nuggets such as from
Jacques Ranciére concerning all filmic images which enable 'the

becoming-queer of *all* viewers'. You're telling me. Still, no sneering as Walsh who strongly steers by Patricia MacCormack's *Cinesexuality* and laments 'the erotic dearth in Irish film'. Here, here! Indeed many are to blame: politicians, censorious commentators and even the late great John Ford who came hither and manufactured that lamentable Irish turkey, *The Quiet Man* which set a mawkish standard when he should have known better.

—*Books Ireland* 2013

PRENTICE POETS

Company: a chosen life John Montague (Duckworth)

Yeats: the Irish literary revival and the politics of print Yug Mohit Chaudhry (Cork University Press)

Mrs Yeats in a cameo during the mid-1950s gives a glimpse of the later side of her life, the earlier times with WB being already well documented. She is depicted as one of the gang, almost, living *la vie litteraire irlandaise:* she excuses Austin Clarke for living through broadcasting and book-review journalism being a dry old stick because of his necessity of earning a living but as for Kavanagh, "At least he's lively." You get heaps of this kind of gossip here. Montague's own bi-polar fixations and confusions over Clarke and Kavanagh may owe something to the tutelary Mrs Yeats?

The memoir, strangely or otherwise, adopts a title used by Beckett for one of his short prose works or does it bend an early Montague title, A Chosen *Light?* Leaving such speculation aside, this is in a noble tradition since literary history as written by those who hung about and struggled and survived is often much more authentic than conventional biography. Hence this is easily in the same league as Frank O'Connor's My Father's Son, albeit in a highly conversational mode.

George (Mrs) Yeats comes across as an authoritative keeper of the flame. Montague admits that on first meeting her he had not read Yeats's *A Vision* and calls her a mystic but does not elaborate. Maud Gonne and her daughter Iseult never quite caught his fancy as they did that of John Jordan. Maud, he admits "was a subject of poetry: Mrs Yeats was a source." He gives the poet's *wife* a genuinely exalted tribute and shows her as the encouraging presence to his own early vocation as poet, "Forget about fame, envy, and competition".

He does not take up an omniscient position about his own doings with Madeleine de Brauer who would become his wife and who was the detonation for the poem 'All Legendary Obstacles'. His assimilation with her upper-class Norman French family is shown without any hitches, rather remarkable for the awkward persona of himself presented. The love of place and honouring of the dignity of the otherwise humble flat comes across well as they settle in Dublin in the basement of No 6 Herbert Street and later near the Gloucester Diamond. His 'steady' was with Bord Failte—neither praised nor damned as an employer. Doris Lessing's arrival in town brings in a loud-mouthed hungover Behan, who trashes her verbally and not long after hectors Montague about keeping the right company in France with "the writers, or the ordinary working class, *les ouvriers*". The impression of Behan's good knowledge of French is affirmed but this matter is often disputed if one asks other elders of the tribe.

Behan gets the most space and something of a reconstruction against previous infamy. Montague is comfortable with Flann O'Brien's laudatory and loving obituary for Behan from the *Telegraph* while a cautionary eye is thrown at Behan's appearances in Cronin's memoir *Dead as Doornails* and Aidan Higgins' novel *The Balcony of Europe:* "they lack both generosity and compassion".

Substantial claims are made for *Borstal Boy* and the travesty of its neglect as a brick-bat manuscript. Behan is presented as a poet, dying young not only because of diabetes, drink and excess but also from the severe beatings he received in Walton Gaol. His sex life is shown as having been unhappy, "but there is no rule that says an artist has to be sexually satisfied".

Liam Miller and Dolmen are pencilled in more deftly and more briefly with mention of his continual battles with insolvency. Montague's MacGibbon & Kee period and dealings with Timothy O'Keeffe and others is unfortunately too short. He recommended Heaney to O'Keeffe (Faber had just snapped him up) but turned down an early version of Francis Stuart's *Black List, Section H*. The portrait of Garech Browne is very welcome and leads onto discussion of Claddagh Records and music: O Riada, the Chieftains, the *fleadhanna,* as well as Robert Johnson and John Lee Hooker. Paris in the 1960s becomes a happier contrast to the continual blow-back from Catholic Ireland, and the relocation to a new beloved *pied à terre* at 11 Rue Daguerre is celebrated over breakfast: café au lait, croissants and tartines with Kafka, the Siamese cat.

The portrait of his friendship with Beckett is fabulous stuff, attesting to Sam's generosity, melancholy and hilarious mirth—a comic dialogue with Con 'Continental' Leventhal is reproduced. Beckett confided in Montague about the influence on his work from Calderon's *La Vida es Sueno*; when asked about suicide as an option, he replied "Out of the question" but agreed with Sophocles about preferring not to have been born. Montague's familiarity with living French poets is refreshing and ultimately fructifying for Irish letters. However, Ireland is placed above France because of an incident when *The Rough Field* was roughly turned down by Gallimard and Editions de Minuit, the latter's excuse being "Mais, c'est de la poesie! Ca vend pas." Moliere is quoted: "Poetry is a pastime."

He will not abide Olympianism or provincialism since his last episodes concern Berkeley, California (after cloudy skies in Dublin and Paris) among Kenneth Rexroth, Louis Simpson, Allen Ginsberg giving a first try-out to Howl and Kerouac drinking burgundy among the cast.

The author's infidelity is aired and Marianne Moore is met in Brooklyn. In Dublin, he takes Ted Roethke on a visit of homage to see Mrs Yeats and that brings the book full circle. Roethke buys a bottle, delighted to hear that she likes a drop and brings a bouquet of roses that end up on the carpet when the old lady opens the door to her guests. Roethke's *timor mortis* required a steady diet of alcohol but the hefty quotes from his work might lead anyone to believe that he is one of Montague's favourite poets. Plaintively, as you might expect, the volume ends with a reunion in Paris between Madeleine and Montague with a heavy heart for what he had done. The next volume has been expertly poised?

This is where you can re-discover Yeats "from the aspect of reading texts in the contexts for which they were first written". For instance, he sources 'September 1913' and its original sub-title

'On reading much of the correspondence against the Art Gallery'—the poem appeared in the *Irish Times*. Chaudhry challenges the work of recent critics—Ellmann, Jeffares, Bloom, Cullingford and Albright—as being incompatible with editors of the time in which the poem was published. This observation, however, seems obvious.

His main thesis throughout follows this somewhat tenuous position but he does extract interesting theories from his close scrutiny of the contemporary sources and how Yeats changed his tune as it were in subsequent re-printings of this and other works. Yeatsians will immediately recognize the reference to the sorry saga of Hugh Lane and his paintings and one of his enemies William Martin Murphy whom Yeats regarded "as one of O'Connell's heirs: Catholic, ill-mannered and philistine". The poet would pretty quickly amend his position in July 1916 when he wrote "'Romantic Ireland's dead and gone' sounds old-fashioned now. It seemed true in 1913, but I did not foresee 1916."

Chaudhry adds that the poem "was not responding merely to the art gallery controversy but to larger issues of Protestant marginalisation," however the poet also had "to produce work that would sell with publishers and editors". Rumours of Yeats's instant success are easily quelled when you read that his privately subscribed edition of The *Wanderings of Oisin* sold twenty-eight copies. His work for the *Dublin University* Review—eighteen pieces in total—embraced a wide scope, since Oldham, the editor, "had given the unionist and nationalist perspectives almost equal coverage." However "literature devoid of political leavening would not retain an Irish audience very long".

When writing for the *United Irishman* whose stock targets were Tennyson and Swinburne, both anti-Home Rulers for Ireland, Yeats found himself able to praise fellow Irish poet William

Allingham and also the English poet Wilfred Blunt.

Secretly becoming a devotee of Blake and Spenser, he made it his published viewpoint that he was against literature from across the water—this was merely the furtiveness of youth on Yeats's part. When he got other reviewing work with W. E. Henley's *Scots Observer* the situation became more complicated since he enjoyed his editor's social milieu but "Yeats's heroes—Pater, Morris, Blake and the Pre-Raphaelites—were Henley's aversions, and Yeats's associates—Arthur Symons, Oscar Wilde, Richard Le Gallienne and William Sharp—were Henley's pet hates". How Yeats and Henley got on among diverging literary tastes makes interesting reading.

Yeats's nationalist tendencies expanded on reading Carleton for review for the Scots *Observer,* making Joyce remark on the poet's "treacherous instinct of adaptability". The real excitement begins when it comes to his stance with Parnell—his letters of the period show no trace of grief at either his fall or death, in fact he was writing in praise of Davitt, the great Land Leaguer himself. John O'Leary, Yeats's mentor, finally supported Parnell as did Maud Gonne and the poet Katharine Tynan.

Whether Yeats was first moved by literary ambition rather than a desire to pay homage is still open to doubt. He was "the sole poet mourning the Chief in the Chief's own newspaper"—the *United Irishman* —but with a poem that remains one of his forgotten occasional effusions, 'Mourn—and then Onward'; the title reflecting a hasty youthful author.

Furthermore he was unsure whether "patriotism is more than an impure desire in an artist" and fleeting political upheaval may not always remain vital as the content of lasting poetry. Latterly, he considered such writing for the *United Irishman* as propaganda and looked back on Parnell as "a haughty Protestant aristocrat". He would further unify his thoughts on journalism in the *Bookman* four years after Parnell's demise and school himself to "love literature for her own sake and not as the scullery-maid of politics"—apparently Joyce may have read his review since he rebuked Roman Catholicism as a church that is the scullery-maid of Christendom?

Yeats for all his political to-ing and fro-ing revelled in a review of his Poems, not unsurprisingly in favour of them, by the *United Irishman,* because of his affiliations with the journal.

The reviewer found that it lifted poetry out of "the ruck of Young Ireland rhetoric" placing it with English and international literature. The poet was gratified by this and kept his sights set in that direction with a few detours thereafter.

—Books Ireland 2001

PUNISHMENT

The Governor: the life and times of the man who ran Mountjoy
John Lonergan (Penguin)

Catherine and Friends: inside the investigation into Ireland's most notorious murder Pat Flynn (Liberties Press)

Inside: Ireland's women's prisons past and present Christina M. Quinlan (Irish Academic Press)

Lonergan outlines the battles, some of which resulted in gaining rights for his clan—the prisoners. A lifelong fervent pursuit of reform rings through this account as his enemies lined up along the corridors of power. His job was often on the line: 'I always came down on the side of humanity, whereas the prison service at management level always came down on the side of security'. He stood alone during the infamous siege of Mountjoy against the department of justice, the army, the media, and the prisoners who had taken hostages. His actions resolved the situation though 'some officers believed that I was personally to blame for the siege because of my approach and philosophy as governor; they felt I should have been much tougher on the prisoners'.

He is defiantly outspoken: 'I never met any Minister for Justice for a formal one-to-one briefing or a private discussion.' Ray Burke's telling the staff in Mountjoy that prisoners were 'thugs and scumbags' was unacceptable to Lonergan. Pádraig Flynn 'never visited Mountjoy'. Minister McDowell 'turned back the clock fifty years or more in our approach to juvenile crime.' 'As a society we don't really care about our most troubled children.' His observations reveal national policy towards prisons. A senior official at the department of justice once informed him: 'We don't believe in planning ahead.'

Lonergan's expertise is based on forty-two years experience. He emphasises that punishment must not be taken further than detention. Overcrowding in prison provokes his jeremiad on Mountjoy that 'opened for business' in 1850 and remains a 'costly, destructive and brutal system.' He refused to perpetuate cruelty and inhumanity despite the overlords outside the prison walls.

His guides were a loving family background and good community values. His father had a few cows, grew vegetables, and was occasionally a butcher in the local parish of Bansha and Kilmoyler, County Tipperary. Sport and especially, running granted Lonergan lifelong fitness, good health and personal discipline. After vocational education the young Lonergan worked in the local sawmill, as a bus conductor in Dublin, and in 1967-1971 with the prison service in Limerick, Shanganagh and on to Mountjoy in 1984. He kept 'home and work life separate'. Always pitted between prisoners and prison staff, he began 'to open dialogue, but there could be no dialogue if I was going to act like a dictator or respond to people's contributions—however hostile—in a dismissive and arrogant way.' Lonergan challenged his own power for the higher purpose of those beneath him. His aim was 'to stop people regressing' simply because prisoners need 'the basics to support and sustain them as human beings.'

In 1988, he was transferred to Portlaoise 'the Calcutta of the prison service' where the issues of strip searching and demands for ordinary clothes instead of prison garb headed a long list. He highlighted the dangers of fire in the prison. Returning to the Joy in 1992, he inspected the new kitchen block with an auditorium where bungled plans on the part of the department of justice resulted in the stage area set too low for ideal audience viewing because of the ceiling height. The new woman's prison—the Dóchas Centre—literally, the Hope Centre 'officially opened in September 1999'. Sadly for Lonergan, it reverted to shared accommodation in direct opposition to his ideal of one person cells. Internal plumbing in cells is impossible, he laments due to the age of Mountjoy. He emphasises the cruelty of locking people in shared cells 'for seventeen hours on average every day'. He praises those 'who stand by the imprisoned, usually members of their immediate family.' 'They never give up, and that is really unconditional love'. He is intense on the plight 'of prisoner's children [who] suffer greatly.' His maxim states: 'our prisoners are us' and 'the public has ultimate responsibility' for the prison system which must include aftercare. He is unimpressed at the plans for Thornton Hall, expected to open in 2014: it is 'a disaster. Buildings have had to be redesigned two and three times often.'

He is not devoid of compassion for the victims of crime yet repeatedly enunciates the rights of prisoners. He may irk some at his 'acceptance' of illegal drugs in prison. Lonergan finally left Mountjoy in May 11, 2010 without regret and without any 'farewell functions'. Seventeen pages of acknowledgements has a roll of honour to those who helped him. Lonergan is an enigma as well as an astonishing man.

Former President of Ireland, Mary Robinson forewords this as 'not always a comfortable read' in fact it is a glimpse into a sea of troubles and concretizes Lonergan's lifelong findings. Quinlan's work stems from a PhD with statistical tables, photographs, as well as academic discourse on penology, criminology and sociology. Over seven chapters she has a vast reach: a research outline, a historical perspective, a contemporary perspective, a perspective from imprisoned women, a scholarly perspective, as well as a terrific chapter visually enhanced that explores space and identity in women's prisons. Quinlan reports on the women prisons which are 'patriarchal quasi-militaristic hierarchial regimes.' Her focus is mainly on the Dóchas Centre within Mountjoy and Limerick Prison where the current exercise yard might well have been inspired by the Gestapo as revealed in a photograph.

Quinlan's tour of history reaches heights of the Gothic in presenting Kilmainham, Lock hospitals and Magdalen homes (homes is quite the misnomer!) while a central fact of her thesis is that criminals are misrepresented in the press and media which adds to the cruel ways in which they are treated. Lonergan can be heard echoing through her book based on his dictate that detention is the punishment yet it comes with additional hardship meted out to the imprisoned by the system.

Some crimes are cultural, as in 1930 when a third of the prison population totalling a thousand souls were incarcerated for drunkenness while a mere handful were convicted of capital crimes. In 2008 of the 1,484 women committed to prison: 676 were under sentence, 552 on remand and 256 awaiting deportation. She is virulent that prison staff abuse power and are usually deviant, resulting in 'stigmatised identities of the women imprisoned'. 'The authorities in Ireland continue to regularly imprison destitute women, needlessly criminalising them.'

An imprisoned woman named Elena said of the prison staff: 'you should hear the way they talk to us. One day I heard one say, "oh, let's give the monkeys their medication, it will keep them quiet".' The Visiting Committee, according to Quinlan's interview reveals that they believe the Dóchas Centre is 'a holiday camp'. This sort of gossip and media fueled propaganda is shameful, cruel and inhuman. 'Two women spoke of women prisoners having relationships with male prison officers.'

Quinlan's psychological paradigms are compelling in defining the 'torture' of others imposed on the imprisoned in close confinement. Sartre's left bank angst is all too true of prison where 'hell is other people'. Or as Quinlan states: 'Women in prison space exist under a networked regime of constant surveillance, perpetual surveillance, the superpanopticon of the surveillant assemblage, the great pyramid of gazes.'

Her greatest service to justice is the reports on prison staff: 'The officers in Mountjoy call themselves "the jailors". They don't like working in the Dóchas Centre because, they say, it "is not a real prison".' She castigates 'the patriarchal nature of the bench' as well as 'middle to upper class male judges' sentencing 'women in difficult circumstances'. Prison work is rewarded for the most part by 'treats rather than recompense'. Kathleen McMahon who resigned as governor of the Dóchas Centre in 2010 stated that her role was 'undermined, [and] that there was a serious lack of consultation between the Irish Prison Service and key staff in prisons.'

Flynn as Garda Superintendent found himself at the crime scene in Jack White's pub in Arklow on 19 March 1996. He already knew both Catherine and Tom Flynn as a customer. He gives an investigator's version of the shooting dead of Tom and the imprisonment of Catherine after a sixty-one day trial on 11 April 2000—'the sixth woman in the history of the state to be convicted of murder'. The in-between events make for a lively thriller format built on suspects, the gathering of evidence and on towards the trial. Catherine was a suspect from the start. Her elder husband was murdered by 'a single discharge from a shotgun into the right side of the chest'. The Nevin family suspected Catherine who spoke of a break-in but there was no evidence and her jewellery was untouched. Tom and Catherine had married in Rome twenty years previously and bought White's pub a decade later.

As the plot thickens, two friends of Catherine turn out to be Detective Inspector Tom Kennedy and Judge Donnacha O'Buachalla. This is where, if it were the plot of a B-movie these two would provide necessary ancillary characters around Catherine who had lovers and which fact was known to Tom. Kennedy and O'Buachalla at the trial 'denied having a sexual relationship with Catherine'. Catherine was arrested in July 1996 and her motives for the crime are listed as wishing to inherit the pub and gain substantially from 'two insurance policies on Tom's life'. Flynn's real trajectory is naturally the trial. He sets this up in a sub-Raymond

Chandler fashion with Gerry Heapes, John Jones and William McClean providing the rogues gallery of those whom Catherine had solicited to murder her husband. Judge Mella Carroll in handing down a mandatory life sentence had this to say to the convicted woman: 'You had your husband assassinated not once but twice; once in life, and in death by assassinating his character.' The Press and Media grew fat on the Nevin trial dubbing her 'The Black Widow' and the Irish Independent called the debacle a 'sordid soap'. Flynn's snide tone of invective against Catherine Nevin never lets up in this sensational account of what is ultimately rather banal. Nevin 'entitled to apply for parole in 2007' did not do so since she 'has always maintained her innocence'.

—*Books Ireland* 2011

IN DEEP

Nostos: An Autobiography John Moriarty (Lilliput)

Eternal Echoes: exploring our hunger to belong John O'Donohue (Bantam)

Conamara Blues John O'Donohue (Bantam)

This is not conventional autobiography. It attempts to show the growth of a mind, if not of a soul. He eschews any attempts at narrative. The prevailing structure is one of myth, even creating myth from events that are simple, significant or otherwise from his own life. There is a fabulous presence of himself as a simpleton-pilgrim who progresses and regresses while steering clear of ego and super-ego. There are the bare bones of a life story and a few supreme spiritual guides. The style in places requires a lot of effort to read with full comprehension yet at its best is somewhat reminiscent of D. H. Lawrence without the explicitly sexual—here's a clear sample:

> a woman will talk about being horny. We talk about screwing and riding, about having a good shag, about having a good fuck or wanting a good fuck. Worst of all, surely is the awful word *screwing.*

There is otherwise no puritanism and the sensual as spiritual, in all its manifestations, is celebrated. Moriarty in his exhortations, shamelessly and sometimes playfully, delivers a bizarre and hortatory flow, paragraph after paragraph with repetitions, single-sentence paragraphs and a curious parade of poetry, songs, nursery rhymes, philosophy and mysticism. This, not unlike John O'Donohue (see below) is light years away from canon law and encyclicals. Nothing is dogmatic or prescriptive. No revered divine is other than a divine buddy close at hand. There is no fear and it is nearly all sweetness and light and revelation of a personal spirituality. In early youth, he heard the Jesus story or myth from a neighbour, Jameen Kissane. That version it seems was more true to him than any papal edict: "There were landlords out there at that time, John, and Jesus grew up and got too smart for 'em, and they did away

463

with him, the poor boy."

He will have none of the more ingrained institutional spirituality that claims to be of the one true church, and denigrates every other belief structure as a heresy. It seems that Moriarty had to unlearn the religion of his childhood finding fault with Genesis and finding terror in Darwin and Sir James Jeans' Lucretian nihilism. He gave a hollow laugh at Bishop Ussher's belief that God created the world in 4004 BC. Moriarty grew up on a farm that remains another mythic world for him. He quotes Dylan Thomas's *Fern Hill* as proof of the lyrical intensity of this farm outside Listowel. At Earlsfort Terrace a fellow student, Lydia Carlyle, captured his heart while the frothy philosophy of Nietzsche may well have gone deeper. For once in Irish autobiography the reader is spared rites of passage, estrangement from parents, the first taste of alcohol and the abominable dawning of the solipsist adolescent Irish male. He wrote Lydia a poem that he includes with others throughout the text. These owe a lot to William Blake but Moriarty makes no great claims for any of them. He explains, albeit elliptically, and explores so many of his beloved and revered guides such as Blake, Boehme, Whitman, Lawrence, Melville, Coleridge, Wordsworth and even Sylvia Plath but he is not averse to Bob Dylan, Joan Baez, Leonard Cohen or Lewis Carroll. Nor is he an intellectual snob and may well be an oracular shaman, an Irish sphinx?

The sanitised theological Christ of the Church he could not abide, and found more in Job and Melville's *Ishmael*. His love of the language of Job and Melville is utterly convincing, as are each source that he often repeats a page or so after their initial citing. Without giving any great detail at all of his college days, he travelled thereafter, through the kindness of his sister Babs, a British Airways hostess, and explored Greece and further afield. No country seems strange to him; he is a walker on earth and no more Irish than a seascape. Moriarty's global journeys are Janus-like, facing both ways but with the emphasis on the vast reaches of the past, as in the poetry of Henry Vaughan:

Some men a forward motion love, But I by backward steps would move.

Of his time teaching in a boarding school in North Staffordshire one hears little; instead you get myth piled on myth from Wales and beyond to Mallory. There is another ladylove, Marilyn Valalik, but no telltale stuff, instead beatitudes to Geoffrey Chaucer, the Mabinogion and Geoffrey Hill's poetry. He is whisked off to a university in Manitoba at a casual invitation, the details are scanty and mythic. It all happens as if by chance, destiny or miracle or the way a yarn turns naturally in its telling. The Canadian hinterlands of Manitoba immediately become another homeland with their therapeutic names: Yellow Knife, Moose Jaw and Medicine Hat. Moriarty can weave every myth from all the cultures of the world into one and unravel them afterwards to their original singularity or so it seems. "Revivify our myths . . . until they stand and live with us as aesthetic intelligences".

He travels to San Francisco in the psychedelic sixties: "even the Eucharistic tab of LSD consisted in yea and nay, in good trip and bum trip". He is none too explicit and does not bother to chart the lives of the hippies. From Haight-Ashbury, he takes himself off to Mexico City and thereafter to the Grand Canyon. His darker interior journey goes side by side from the Colorado river to the poetry of Emily Bronte:

There is not room for Death

Nor atom that his might could render void:

Thou—thou art Being and Breath

And what thou art may never be destroyed.

The deep crisis looms during his Manitoba times when he is thirty-three and what he calls the onset of spiritual puberty. "Fucking Irish Catholic," his colleague at the university calls him; "Stephen Dedalus all over again." This time he settles in Inisboffin with his savings from lecturing and sets out to find himself, remembering the words of his mother, "John doesn't even look like a fact of life". He proves the existence of God because of the fact that "infinite yearning does exist, and so, in the sense of being infinite satisfaction, in the sense of being infinite bliss, God exists." His logic being that "infinite yearnings require an infinite satisfaction". His God knows no wrath, revenge nor chastisement. Similarly when a neighbour and contemporary describes John Moriarty, it is in terms of "there is a little bit of a want in Him". This in itself shows the measure of his spiritual wealth, that his want is little and he is somewhat proud of being described so.

As he wends his journey onwards and upwards he comes to the conclusion that "Buddhism is pleasant to look at . . . whereas Christianity is horrible to look at," and the horrors of the dark depths within take him away from a dear friend Eileen to a Carmelite Priory. He experiences Pascal's sense of the infinite, "All this visible world is no more than an imperceptible speck in nature's ample bosom. No idea approaches it. We may extend our conceptions beyond a marginal space, yet produce only atoms in comparison with the reality of things. It is an infinite sphere the centre of which is everywhere, the circumference nowhere."

This spiritual agoraphobia leads him beyond Shakespeare's *Lear* and those blind ravings, to the mystical tradition of John of the Cross who recommends a walk in the dark, "in safety from his domestic foes, which are his own senses and faculties". Furthermore he adds, "What King Lear went through out of doors on a wild night was little compared to what St Teresa went through in her cell." His spiritual adviser at Chilswell near Oxford, states that "the rule of St Benedict was Europe's founding document". Suddenly his version of the pilgrim's progress has the ring of the Road to Damascus type of homecoming into the orthodoxy of Christianity but Moriarty does not make it all that sweet and simple and opaque. Chilswell, he feels can be another home or Nostos and is easily transformed into 'Childswell'.

This renewal of life in the Priory led him back to Connemara and afterwards a period as a gardener in Cashel. He had by then found some firm guides in Meister Eckhart, Marguerite Porete and others. The conclusion is as you might expect, blissfully peaceful. O'Donohue is not a voice crying in the wilderness if his success with the bestselling *Anam Cara* is examined. He is full of gentle advice—the tone not hectoring nor ever akin to a homily, otherwise might lose his audience which presumably comes from some Christian orthodoxy. He is not dogmatic, does not trade in planting guilt and sees it as belonging to a time when "god and the system were harsh and culture was more uniform, good and innocent people felt scrupulously guilty about nothing".

He comes across as utterly anti-institutional: "there are many places of power in the world: the Pentagon, the Kremlin, the Vatican . . . Most of our experience of religion happens within the walled frame of church or temple". TV, consumerism, fundamentalism ("most sinister forms of fundamentalism are practised in cults") and the banks are attacked: "There is the obscenity of banks buying Van Gogh paintings as products and storing them in their dark vaults where no eye can enjoy them." His weakness seems to be jingoistic opinions on so-called hard drugs and hard drug addicts in society. In this he seems prejudiced.

There is quite a touch of the pantheist about O'Donohue. He finds pantheism as far back as Aristotle, this "morphic affinity between us and nature" and even the latter's guru, Plato, who said, "All thought begins in wonder." And Merleau Ponty, "There is no thought to embrace all thought". When it comes to God, he is reminiscent of a sonnet by Coleridge on that subject—making nature his outdoor altar with the simple precept from the Bible, "Be still and know that I am God." And what will you do out in the great temple of nature? According to one of his spiritual teachers, St Bernard: "You wish to see? Listen."

Many other contrasting voices are quoted: the third century BC elegy by Callimachus for Heraclitus, Julian of Norwich, Hume, D. H. Lawrence, Camus, Sartre, Beckett and Kafka. O'Donohue also speaks about angels, "spirits of light and playfulness". They are musical and above all devoid "of the seriousness or narrowness that often accompanies dead religion." He declares that there is no other figure "in the Western tradition who has been so thoroughly domesticated" than Jesus. Quoting Dostoevsky's The *Brothers Karamazov,* he sees Jesus as having being pushed aside by the punitive theology of the Spanish Inquisition. He opts for Blake's 'Christ the Imagination'. Otherwise he quotes Meister Eckhart (considered theologically dangerous by the Roman Church): "The eye with which I see God is God's eye seeing me". Simone Weil goes further into this mysticism, "The apparent absence of God in this world is the actual reality of God".

He does not avoid discussion of human pain and suffering either. The key to O'Donohue's message is in evoking the ancient Celtic vision and imagination, combining nature and God. "We cannot live without some deity, whether it be Jesus, the Trinity, Allah, Mohamed or the Buddha." That said, Eckhart is the real presence here, "I pray to God that he may make me free of 'God', for my real being is above God if we take 'God' to be the beginning of created things." This is hard to grasp on one reading, it requires meditation like O'Donohue's book which is a spiritual boon almost throughout.

Conamara Blues is a confusing title for his book of poems. The fifteen sonnets based on the rosary are not the best work here. It is more of a duty to read them than a delight; they may claim to be devotional and hence difficult but the general obscurity does not reach much depth. Better, but not by much, are the simpler pieces 'Wings', 'The Pleading', 'The Night', 'The Angel of the Bog'. The message is: look to nature for everything and preserve it as ourselves. One poem is dedicated to the Burren Action Group that saved Mullach Mór. O'Donohue takes counsel with Keats's evocation, actually an embellished thought from a letter, "I am sure of nothing but the holiness of the heart's affections and the truth of the imagination". O'Donoghue joins the transcendentalists in going beyond the romantic poets, Keats, Shelley, Wordsworth and Coleridge by implying that whatever is planted in earth or on the wind including the dead somehow remains. In other words he is not just a believer, he is a profound one.

—*Books Ireland* 2002

WRITER TO WRITER: *The Republic of Elsewhere* Ciaran Carty (Lilliput)

Carty defines his method as interviewer who 'becomes an accomplice in a reconstructed version of what took place, a sort of fiction'. Forty-four writers are put through his 'impression of someone as they once were'—a quarter of them being Irish. He states where and when he met each writer, and how many times. The profiles are a blend of commentary and interview quotes.

Kazuo Ishiguro's remarks are stark 'I thought every city had a bomb. I still remember the peculiar sort of pride with which I discovered in an encyclopaedia at school that only two places in the world suffered an atomic attack and Nagasaki was one of them'. Ishiguro is more revelatory about the University of East Anglia's writing school and its networking connections with London's fiction publishers.

John Arden (reputedly descended from Shakespeare's mother) clearly states his politics 'things can't be settled in Ireland until people understand Connolly better than they do' and he says of the lugubrious Cruise O'Brien, 'he seems to see the IRA everywhere he goes in the world'. Arden's *Silence Among the Weapons* and *Books of Bale* are engagingly highlighted. 'Michael Billington dubbed Ayckbourn the 'Scarborough Ibsen' whose 'great obsession is cricket and this helped to break the ice.' Such an 'interview' reflects the coffee table status which predominates, however many of the photographs caught their subjects on bad hair, bad clothes and bad face days. One exception is Tom Lawlor's 'Edna O'Brien' by a window, one leg on the ledge, arms folded about the knee. An ingenious photograph 'showing' the long legs through the clothes.

J. G. Ballard explodes about English snobbery 'a friend of my parents [who] literally turned purple in the face at the thought of the National Health Service. People would sneer at the idea that a working-class woman was entitled to a washing-machine'. Interned by the Japanese as a child, Ballard 'met people my parents would never have allowed me to meet.' Carty can't pass any *bon-mot* such as Ballard quoting Somerset Maugham 'dialogue in plays is exactly what people would say in real life if they had two minutes to think about it first'. This shows Maugham's concept of drama more than anything. The glimpse of Saul Bellow is well done, if exposing how compression can be fatal to style and sense: 'In his masterpiece *Herzog* in 1954, partly a fictionalised account of the painful break up of his own brief disastrous marriage (the first of five), Bellow tried to poke fun at the preoccupation of contemporary literature with concepts at the expense of the reality they claim to represent.'

Kay Boyle demythologises Paris of the 1920s 'never saw it as a glamorous time' and emphasises that she did *not* have an affair with Ezra Pound who 'never wrote anything original [...] his *Cantos* were lifted from the classics'. Donleavy is the funniest about the tortured saga of his buying Maurice Girodias' Olympia Press 'for £5,000 at a bankruptcy auction' [...] I ended up suing myself'. Girodias' commented 'you may have your doubts about Donleavy as a writer but have no doubts about him as one of the great legal geniuses of all time'. The author of *The Ginger Man* said of Dublin 'if three people in the same room know who you are, you're famous'. He advised Carty to install a bed in his office 'Once you get up and move around your attention begins to get diverted'.

The Brian Moore interview is disappointing with only brief allusion to Hitchcock and the script of *Torn Curtain* 'I didn't like to contradict him'. Having written a film version of de Beauvoir's *The Blood of Others* he states that in occupied France during WWII 'the Germans didn't have to round up the Jews, the French did it for them'. The Irish interviews are not all as lively as this, compared with the 'darned' foreigners, especially 'his' poets. David Gascoyne's mental breakdown, life, and times is crushed effectively into two and a bit pages. His partner Judy Lewis says, 'when we first met he used to talk in the night [...] beautiful lyrical lines would come out in his sleep [...] But you don't do that anymore, darling'. Ginsberg is depicted hugging his Yeats 'who wrote with a tune in his head'. Pier Paolo Pasolini tells Carty that the consumer society represents the ultimate totalitarianism. Andrei Voznesensky wrote in disgust on a copy of his selected poems, translated by Herbert Marshall 'please don't read this terrible book of mine (not of mine at all)'. Carty adds ironically 'it seems he has fallen out with Marshall over the introduction and translation notes'. Voznesensky recalled Pasternak, Anna Akhmatova and Sviatoslav Richter. 'Pasternak was the purest person in the world, a very moral, idealistic man. And yet all the newspapers said he was a spy, he was an enemy, he was the desecrator of Russia. I could see this was not true'.

Meeting Houellebecq 'pronounced "Wellbeck"' author of *Atomised* brings up his mother Lucie Ceccaldi's memoir 'in which she calls him an "evil, stupid little bastard," [which] has upset him'. He discussed dealing with fame and notoriety through the movie *The Kidnapping of Michel Houllebecq* (2014) subverting 'the relationship between literature, art and the reimagining of reality'. Carty introduces personal reflection in the M. J. Farrell (Molly Keane) interview which enters the bazaar. She tells of her Anglo lifestyle 'a succession of terrible governesses'[...]'all that mattered in the family was the hunt ball' [...] 'Bobby Keane was the gentleman farmer Molly met at a hunt ball'. 'They were burned out by Sinn Feiners' to which Carty confesses 'as she says this, it occurs to me that my own father, who was a local commandant in that area at the time, might well have been one of the intruders, but I kept the thought to myself'.

Norman Mailer with as many wives as Henry VIII but no murders to his name, is encapsulated in a miniature biography, aged seventy-four in the Shelbourne with *Home Remedies for Common Ailments*. He sounds civilised after years of hellraising: 'more and more of the social life goes into dealing with the family [...] which is kind of agreeable, but a little tough on one's wife'. 'Each wife is a culture' […] 'you get a little slap-happy going through so many cultures'. This is qualified by Beverly Bentley, his fourth wife who framed the American novelist: 'His mother was the only Mrs Norman Mailer'. Hardboiled as ever, he admits to Carty that he was not bothered by the sensational memoir of his second wife, Adel Morales 'whom he stabbed at a drunken party'. 'Well I did stab her. It's the only thing that's accurate'. Mailer's moral history of America in books such as *The Armies of the Night* and *Harlot's Ghost* were based on moving beyond fiction, and into documentary, demanding that 'excitement without illumination is the broad road to pornogaphy'.

You have to hunt for the good snippets in Carty's interviews. For instance, V. S. Naipaul declares 'I couldn't understand English novels'. Edna O'Brien philosophically declares 'You cannot kill the inner parents'. Rushdie (Salman) 'There are no subjects that are sacred or off limits in fiction and that includes God'. Rushdie demands that 'writers, whether from India or Africa or, I am sure, from Ireland—[to] begin to excavate the supressed history'. D. M. Thomas catches the attention with his *Flying in to Love* including details such as that JFK 'stopped during the motorcade to shake hands with some nuns'. Significantly, Thomas gave up poetry 'poems had become too painful an emotional experience. I needed to fictionalize to escape'. The great Peruvian political writer, Mario Vargas Llosa evokes most interest about his private life: 'I married my political aunt, what you'd call an in-law. It's not quite the same thing'. He was 19, she 29 and after 'they divorced, he married his cousin'. Vargas Llosa, author of a novel about Casement, *The Dream of the Celt* (2011) is not much probed about the book.

There is a thesis statement in the introduction about writers not being from 'any country other than that of the imagination, a republic of elsewhere'. This assertion is largely ignored throughout the cramped spaces that forbids elaborate analysis in each interview. There is a general Mervyn Bragg artspeak which works best beyond his weakness for Noel Coward-Hugh Leonard-Lawrence Durrell *bon-mots* and witticisms. 'Durrell has his doubts about the imminent sperm bank civilization, what he calls "the taming of the screw"'. 'For old age, Yoga and Buddha are not a bad mixture' [...] 'Phase myself out agreeably in the lotus position'. To echo Carty's 'style' there is a lot of the bland leading the bland, hemmed in by Weekend Newspaper Magazine demands, but he manages to extract much entertainment, if not any major revelations from his pinioned interviewees.

—*Books Ireland* 2019

PSYCHE'S SWINGS

The Writings of Ivor Browne Steps Along the Road: the evolution of a slow learner Ivor Browne (Atrium)

Kicking the Black Mamba: life, alcohol and death Robert Anthony Welch (Darton, Longman and Todd)

Making Love Tom Inglis (New Island)

The hefty volume presents articles and talks from the 1950s onwards mainly containing his clinical observations on mental health and its institutions, society and not least the family. Each section is set in its context by a preamble. His text is non-academic and devoid of unexplained jargon without any fake connections section to section: forty one in all. He is some sort of modern Socrates (time will tell) in his relentless questioning methodology not merely of psychiatry but also spirituality, science, ecology and behaviourism. He is necessarily concise in the briefer sections such as 'Minorities', 'Psychotherapy: What is it?' and his key letter to the Irish Times in 2006 on 'Mental Illness'.

Although he discourses on LSD as a clinical tool in trauma-therapy in certain cases and the search for meaning, he is not an Irish Timothy Leary, Aldous Huxley or R. D. Laing. It is safer to place him (if one dare) as an Emersonian advocating self-reliance of the individual, especially the individual in crisis. Browne relentlessly blames society ('collapse of capitalism'); yet as for individuals ('we make each other sick'). A calm post-Shavian horse sense abounds in abhorrence of the necessity of medication but towards therapy 'where lasting positive change' involves 'pain and suffering'. Society at large is offered similar palliatives and Browne desires to see the group acting as functioning individuals. 'A living creature only functions satisfactorily when it has autonomy, that is when it takes responsibility, otherwise it becomes allopoietic or dependent, defined from without.' His ideal for the person, client and patient is that each one take control of their lives.

Therefore he has none of the imperious manner of the medical toff, and rebels against 'the elitist medical specialists' despite his earliest grounding in Dublin's Grangegorman and similar institutions ('a human warehouse...for all kinds of people rejected and unwanted by society'). 'Lobotomy of the 1950s was an accepted procedure by 'senior psychiatrists who ran Grangegorman'. Despite severe cases of the mentally ill which his professionalism had to administer to, he admits that 'a lot of mental illness is a dishonesty'. There is hardcore clinical practice outlined as with an early *Lancet* article on the treatment of alcohol withdrawal but he states that a 'paper of this standard would not be published nowadays'. This self-regulated tone is his stylistic couch-side manner with toughness as the hallmark. He dispenses openly with his 'philosophy' far beyond those who puff the book: Colm Tóibín, Catriona Crowe and Fintan O'Toole—all doyens of the Church of Liberalism. Browne is non-aligned, strictly non-ego and practical: in this respect he has collected from his papers for publication with supreme diffidence.

Browne's background in study and analysis naturally has roots in Freud, Jung and Adler, particularly the Adlerian concept of *gemeinshaftsgefühl*: the individual's relation to others, to work and community. This is a major realisation enabling his practice as psychiatrist. The usual suspects of unresolved experience, trauma, repression and fantasy levels are the central structure of Browne's search with his patients, rendering him a detective of the psyche's swings, roundabouts and labyrinths. His approach is not so much a patient's past as their potential future. To read him is to enter a hall of mirrors exposing one's own repressions, anxieties and neuroses with the imperative to keep alert and strive for mental health. His only reprimand as to procedures are those involving Cognitive Behaviour Therapy where persons suffering trauma hold 'negative attitudes...filled up with unresolved frozen experiences'. Browne therefore declares CBT 'ineffective' and shows that it 'can be actually damaging'.

Browne identifies 'love' as central, finding it in his predecessors such as Freud ('mental health is the ability to love and to work') and Marx ('humans are realised *made real* in their work'). His erstwhile masters were Babuji Maharaj as well as his onetime colleague in Harley Street, Joshua Bierer who was Browne's analyst. Bierer certainly influenced Browne's own practice and thought: 'self-organisation is the essence of what it is to be healthy and alive...to deprive a person of the very quality of being in control of him or herself is the worst thing that can be done to them'. There is a vast structure of thought and reference within the book which will benefit not only the medical practitioner but those who live unhappily close to Viktor Frankl's 'existential vacuum'. Swift realised, and Browne explores an Ireland ('not a well nation') full of madness and blossoming insanity from the six counties to the slippery slopes of the Republic. However, Dr Browne constantly reaffirms the reality that human beings 'have the ability to change and redirect their own destiny if they should so wish'.

Welch recounts a tortured existence interspersed within a family memoir. He is writing (mainly) in the year after his son Egan's death at the age of twenty-six. The narrative describes a metaphorical crucifixion of the son. Golgotha in this case being the Lower Bann, the general location of 'the Bann Scabbards'. While the setting is NI there are evocations of living in Leeds, Ballingeary and latterly, Coleraine. The title comes from Egan who referred to his cross in life, not as alcoholism but as 'something else': the black mamba a snake that eventually kills you. Behind the loss and tragedy is literature as life as well as Pauline Christianity. Other comfort is taken from Celtic-Druidic religion.

From early youth, Egan is both black sheep of the family (according to himself) yet highly sensitive while being the white-headed much beloved child. His siblings succeed in the real world and he is left behind, a benign character not unlike Hesse's *Knulp*. 'He felt himself to be the failure of the family.' Welch's career in academia takes off amidst many friendships including Derry Jeffares, the Heaneys, Seamus Deane, Patricia Noone of the George Moore Festival and others. His wife, Angela is a stalwart in various careers from the *Cork Examiner* to the Citizens Advice Service in the North of Ireland.

Egan lurks in the background of all this normality from the failed eleven-plus to business ventures including web designer and jobs such as renovating a pub against the odds for one who is present in the opening pages 'on the day of his third suicide attempt…'. Welch maintains architectonic layers within his search for the root cause to the death which was deemed not a suicide. 'I think it is the case that Egan sought out death as a means of coping with his failure to achieve the goals he had set himself.' The son had friends of misfortune. Guy Harper murdered outside Kelly's Nightclub in Portrush, and Joel who fell from a cliff to his death. Welch and Angela support their son's periods in treatment centres, north and south, from the Ross Thompson Psychiatric Unit to St John of God's, interspersed with Egan's efforts to stay alcohol free using Disulfiram (Antabuse). There are many scenes contrasted against more stable times when he undergoes a ceremony of divination against *malocchio*.

The concluding pages move from the flat in Ballymoney to his final drinking spree and descent to the river. The text ricochets emotionally. Wisdom literature occasionally grants Welch some light in the darkness as in Naoshige's saying: 'matters of great concern should be treated lightly.' However, the enigma of death by water remains. Welch witnessed his son after he was retrieved from the river Bann. The story superimposes the Christian, the Druidic and the Occult in its affirmation of his death as ultimate triumph beyond the conquering daemon who could only be outwitted in dying. Dreams and visions of the dead son follow the burial where he 'appears' to the author 'renewed, transformed' speaking in 'garbled language…it was alright, he said, but I had spilled drink on him. Which of course I had.'

'I watched Aileen die, and yet I have no real sense of what it is to die , what it was like for her'. Aileen McKeogh who died of cancer in 2005 is brought to life in these pages. Besides conventional drugs, Aileen used many anti-cancer regimes in 'reflexology, reiki, shiatsu and metamorphosis'. Inglis's self-questioning almost impedes his flow for he has a deadly story to tell especially their last three years together. Aileen's final effort to paint a watercolour and her last game of bridge are where Inglis is the perpetual tragic spectator: 'She looked beautiful. Her face showed no signs of the disease…she looked more ready to be married than to die.' Paralleled to the finality of her departure is the saga of their lives. Inglis opens the family closet to his grandfather's gambling, syphilis and court marshal. His Uncle Frank's perversion. His father's alcoholism and death on the 14 bus.

Ancestry on both sides of the family is a dim background since in a memoir such as this where the battle is with cancer the clock ticks loudest for Aileen whose presence and plight overwhelmingly dominates. The narrative evokes the days of wine and roses as she remains the central focus: 'rugby songs and crude jokes were not for her…she disliked that bikes were always black, so she painted hers green'. 'We were still young in the summer of 1970'.'We met up with Tom Hobson, my best man…on the morning of our wedding. We smoked a couple of joints and drank a couple of gin and tonics. Aileen did not want a white wedding…she made her own wedding dress, in her favourite colour: purple.' The honeymoon is in a lock house on the barrow at Graiguenamanagh. 'She introduced me to pornography, bringing back copies of *Hustler* from London.' The Paris Metro, 1974—'she had taken me to the erotic film *Histoire d'O*…the carriage was empty…she waited until the next stop and calmly removed her knickers and sat on top of me.' Later the University of Carbondale also provides sexual romping. Inglis's *a la recherche du temps perdu* exudes the happier times underscored by juxtapositions of his grief. Aileen's diary entries and excerpts from letters imprint her voice in the text. 'I think I might probably have had many relationships if I hadn't met you so young'.

They had a son and daughter, Arron and Olwen and lost a son, Luke. Their careers blossomed and then the cancer struck. It becomes gothic when 'Aileen wanted to confront her frailty and mortality...part of the confrontation would be to take a photo of herself in a coffin.' She was 'taking her 200 pills a day...her liver had swelled up and was pushing against her stomach.' 'She continued working up to four days before she died'. 'Most of all, I miss that we never really got to talk about what it was like to die'. Inglis's bereavement involved a legacy of nightmares with Aileen in grotesque reappearances yet hardly equalling her death from cancer. His courage in the telling is everywhere. Telling in that nothing is concealed or glossed over. Inglis chooses an ethical response through his writing proving that stark realism is cathartic in terms of complete presentation.

—*Books Ireland* 2013

BROADCASTING

Inside RTÉ: a memoir Betty Purcell (New Island Books)

Purcell's journey to RTE begins on the fringes of the Women's Movement in Gaj's Restaurant, with fellow activists Joe Little, Mary Raftery, Fintan O'Toole, Julian Vignoles and Alex White, all bound for media glory. There follow eighteen years at the Radio Centre, first on *Women Today* under Marian Finucane, who made 'the most intimate conversations happen over the airwaves' through her 'mischievous sense of humour, a warm sympathy with ordinary women, and a passion for change'. Purcell's commentary on RTE personalities is on this friendly level, except for one notable exception: Eoghan Harris. *Women Today* became *Liveline* in 1988, adopting the trusted formula of listeners providing content. Reading Purcell makes one realise that TV and radio programmes are generally perishable, such as *Side by Side, Day by Day, The Way We Were* and *Bodywise*. The book is laden with such forgotten titles.

Her best pages are on the Section 31 censorship instigated under Gerry Collins and perfected by Conor Cruise O'Brien. Unfortunately, she is not Orwellian enough and loses the opportunity to become a major whistle-blower. Between the lines are hints as to how RTÉ packaged the troublesome North by filtering news during the Guildford Four and Maguire Seven campaigns. She does voice concerns over Section 31 causing Jenny McGeever's sacking and the coverage of the Gibraltar Three funerals that 'included the voice of Martin McGuinness'. There are intriguing glimpses of Mary McAleese's isolation on the *Today Tonight* team because of her Belfast background.

Purcell delves into the power lobbies: 'Workers' Party people, led by John Cadden and Tish Barry, had dominated the Section Committee of the union during the late 1970s'. The *Today Tonight* team held 'views very similar to the positions of the

Workers' Party'. The *bete noire* is Eoghan Harris and 'his Workers' Party comrades'. 'Harris prevented legitimate debate about issues in his heyday in RTE.' She could have made more of this compelling material. Perhaps fears of libel demanded the airbrushing out of this aspect of RTÉ's political reportage.

There is a soft focus on John Bowman as she says that *Questions Answers* facilitated 'open dialogue between the public and office-holders in the exercise of democratic accountability'. She regards as 'a particular skill' Bowman's ability 'to spot where a person was coming from by the wording of their questions'. The RTÉ Broadcasting Authority is covertly discussed. Her treatment of Garret Fitzgerald is excessively 'luvvy', especially for his role on the Authority. Purcell later organised a four-programme special on Fitzgerald at 80.

There are no revelations about directors-general Bob Collins, Joe Barry, Noel Curran and Cathal Goan. When Joe Mulholland and Liam Miller pushed to become assistant directors-general, Purcell voted against them because, she admits, of in-house politics. Comments on salaries or pay cuts are veiled.

Purcell inadvertently reveals RTÉ's cosy *realpolitik* when Bob Quinn proposed 'an outright ban' on advertising and sponsorship during children's programmes. She was quick to put him right: 'Bob's principled but extreme position could not win the day'. Later she was instrumental in *The Late Late Toy Show,* which is surely the longest Christmas advert on RTÉ.

There is some grappling with RTÉ's demagogy, which results in the wasting of public monies. Wilful RTÉ spending is palpable in her comments on this topic. She effectively highlights that, despite a licence fee and copious advertising revenue picking up the tab, budget deficits have visited RTÉ-land in the 21st century.

Her move to *The Late Late Show* resulted in a personality clash with Pat Kenny, who became one of RTE's overpaid, his salary reaching 1m per annum in 2007. Her reasons for leaving the show are commendable: over Kenny's interview about a child sexual abuse case. Despite this, she lauds *The Late Late* for dealing with 'universal truths through the medium of human interest stories'. She fondly recalls unwinding after each broadcast in the hospitality suite, where 'a comforting glass of wine would take the edge off the pain on those nights'.

Her description of working on *Would You Believe* shows a producer under pressure, while her comments on *The View* reveal the programme's rigid agenda. There is one illustrative example when Mannix Flynn criticised an actress (unnamed) on *The View*. The fallout was considerable, which gives the distinct impression that adverse criticism of any RTÉ programming is not tolerated. She spends many pages highlighting *Prime Time's* 'Mission to Prey' documentary, which failed to produce evidence of paternity and child abuse by an Irish priest in Kenya. In contrast, her treatment of the programmes about Irish female slavery and paedophilia receives brief space.

Purcell signs off in characteristic RTÉ fashion after 33 years under the mast that gave her life 'a profound meaning', working with 'a strong public national broadcaster'. In typical RTÉ speak, she maintains that 'as an individual, I sometimes rose to the challenge; at other times not'. She is guarded and cautious throughout on RTÉ's inner machinations. Glimpses she gives left this reader wishing for more and must be regarded as an opportunity lost. In contrast, Bob Quinn's memoir, *Maverick* (2001), gets inside RTÉ to a greater extent, which makes Purcell's product more of a celebrity one.

—*Books Ireland* 2014

SAME STORY

A History of the Media in Ireland Christopher Morash (Cambridge University Press)

Cultural Perspectives on Globalisation and Ireland ed. Eamon Maher (Peter Lang)

The time-span—sixteenth century to the present—is too lengthy for this one-volume history in order to deal sufficiently with the substantial agenda. Morash admits (in the introduction) that this is a materialist history: 'history of things' and adheres to this precept but at the fatal cost of an expansive overall connective discussion. His method is not far off Diarmaid Ferriter's work presenting post-enclopedic, media-genic, sound-bite tabloid sections. Morash's trajectory begins with the real life bestseller of 1641; Temple's (illustrated with woodcuts) The Irish Rebellion. News of the rebellion was relatively old by the time it got into print. Belfast's Northern Star edition of 30 January 1793 being far quicker reporting the execution of Louis XVI in Paris from eight days earlier. United Irishman, Arthur O'Connor noted the potential for propaganda in his first editorial of 28 September 1797 in The Press: 'That no Liberty can survive the Liberty of the Press'. They don't give us editorials like that anymore!

Morash, enamored by technology, loses sight of his content in extolling the first railways hefting newspapers from the printer's to far-off destinations. Similarly, he shunts through the early nineteenth century concerning advances from wood to iron to metal printing, and in illustrating print from Daguerrotype to the first magazine of its sort, The Dublin Photographic Journal (1855).

The Nation is under discussion when the first trans-Atlantic telegraph ousts any brooding on Nationalism. Soon, it is time for Parnell and the infamous bad press he got from The Times. Kitty O'Shea announced to Mr Parnell: 'The Times is unusually stodgy. Do eat your breakfast first.' Queue the Phoenix Park Murders, then

Pigott's forged letter, and you are up to the invention of the telephone, and another magazine launched in 1893: The Phonogram about early recording culture. Not forgetting the typewriter, magic lantern, and kinetoscope as Morash leaps forward to the first Irish film of any length, Kathleen Mavourneen (1906) based on William Taver's play. Indeed, such paradigms and content are unchanging in the history of Irish media and film when he points out that The Lad from Old Ireland (1910), The Quiet Man (1952), and Far and Away (1992) 'more or less tell the same story.'

Morash romps through the founding of 'TÉ', or 'Telly Éireann' to viewers in the East of the country, and 'Jellyfish Hair-On' to discerning Dublin kids. Classic Irish plays were televised in the 1960s but soon dropped by 'ARR TEE HEE' for its usual stir-a-bout programming which Morash fails to comment on, as he recycles much over-used material in other polemics about the censorship of books as well as Gaybo, the Bishop and the Honeymoon Nightdress. Reception for the BBC must have been bad in Enniscorthy since Colm Tóibín is quoted praising the lugubrious Late Late Show: 'nobody ever turned it off [...] you just never knew what you might miss'. Generally, East Coast viewers (as Morash admits) had other options from up North and cross-channel, or happily socialized on Saturday nights taking a break from the box. Morash has little time for academic asides and analysis as the satellite era begins, followed by the digital revolution; having skirmished into modern Irish Film where he rounds up the usual suspects and concludes with a predictable quote from McLuhan. 'Struth! There is a definite lack of engagement of the more serious issues concerning the mid-twentieth century Irish media here. This is a history for the likes of Larry Gogan, Mícheál Ó Muircheartaigh, Jimmy Magee, and even Gaybo: still guest stars on 'ARR TEE HEE's' talk-shows all these years later.

Well not exactly; this comes from the Humanities Institute of Ireland based on workshops at UCD and IT, Tallaght. Participants' papers are strictly from connected academics, no novices are included. The line out is: Michael Cronin, Catherine Maignant, Grace Neville, Eugene O'Brien, Peadar Kirby, Tom Inglis, Anne Fogarty, Alison O'Malley-Younger, Tom Herron, Patrick Lonergan, Willy Maley, and the editor, Eamon Maher who enlisted Sir Fintan O'T to foreword it. There is as one anticipates from the foreword much Irish Times citation; however this is trumped by Neville's essay gleaned from Le Monde criticizing Ireland, and asserting that the cute little Island has lost its glitter since someone made off with the le grand wherewithal (3 October 2008): 'In the financial crisis enveloping Europe, Ireland is doing its own thing' or 'l'Irlande joue en solo)'. Government intervention in underwriting Irish banks (Anglo and otherwise) that already are suspect in their internal dealings, the property soap bubble, and what is an external based economy are part of Le Monde's realistic thrust. The journal also predicted the impasse (19 September 2000): 'L'Irlande, bientôt victim de son success?' Certainment, ooh la la!

One way out of this current debacle might be a seasonal spiritual holiday (hardly, possibly?) as Maignant recounts new movements attracting visitors such as the Temple of Danaan, the Fellowship of Isis as well as Celtic pilgrimages and Celtic Christianity, especially Brigidine spirituality. Her figures are impressive for membership to such cults and Mary Condren is quoted, as well as Bev Richardson's Irish school of witchcraft. Eugene O'Brien holds the interest and puts his faith in SMS and mobile phones using deconstruction theory espoused by the tedious French philosopher of chic and deconstruction, Jacques Derrida whose works read like a Parisian academic on too much Beaujolais. Yes, a mobile phone allows you to be in contact with the world is the gist of this essay! Peadar Kirby assesses contemporary religious culture mainly guided by the stealth of Irish Times journalists and uses the infamous journalistic sign-off to the ying-yang debate on the subject as to whether we are more or less holy: 'Only time will tell.' Indeedy.

Tom Inglis samples life in Ballivor, no, not a town in Pakistan: it is actually a village in County Meath. One of his main sources is a native GAA hero complaining about the population quadrupling during the Tiger era and finding himself surrounded by 'blow-ins'. This essay is more accurate of some natives stating that globalisation is taking things too far altogether. Lit takes up half of the book, and be japers it is the usual suspects: Heaney, Friel, McGahern and Roddy Doyle, basically one Dub and three culchies with a smattering of others who do not get the same billing. Anne Fogarty and others strut their stuff. Much is made of Faith Healer, Friel's play of soliloquizing that is really a series of yarns or one long yarn as long as a night in a deserted pub when company is in short supply. The analysis arabesques and summersaults with all kinds of theories.

'Seamus Heaney: The Poet Unhoming' follows well-worn territory in locating the Irish poet and finding the universal in the local as case proven in the final paragraphs. Heaney's backyard becomes the whole world! Quite a theory. McGahern is given the same sort of treatment by Maher, who actually if one reads him closely enough, is damned in the novels, except for the erstwhile Amongst Women which may haunt the nation a while longer. McGahern's fiction does not compare with his real work in the Memoir of the brutal Garda father, the meek mother and the psychical casuality of it all, little Johnny McG. This implication is understated and may be the more lasting legacy since his last novel That They May Face the Rising Sun sparks Maher into lame appreciation that teeters close to fake reverence.

Patrick Lonergan presents the only piece of dangerous territory, asking: 'when is an Irish play a global success, and ipso facto, then a "great" play?' Answer, though it takes him pages to reach it, is when it is first aired in London or New York, otherwise it is only 'a fairly good play' when premiered at home. This has held true since the golden age of the Abbey Theatre. Unfortunately, he chooses the contemporary hodger-podger, Conor McPherson's The Seafarer that passed the global lithmus test, airing foist in New Yoik where it gained a Tony award for best performance by Jim Norton. Lonergan lets slip however that this Christmas Eve bachelors' saga of drink, cards and the devil knows what, actually revolts against the Celtic Tiger, and furthermore McPherson cannot represent his dominant Faustian theme in 'terms of the epic grandeur of an overreaching hero like Marlowe's Doctor Faustus'. In other words, the playwright stoops to folkloric caricature rather than engage in any soul-searching in this dramatic swagger-swagger version of look back in strictly repressed Irish anger. McPherson himself gives the game away too in a comment on his play: 'Ireland is going to get back to what it knows now-hardship.' Oh here we go again: mother will you bring in the tea with a good few spoons of misery!

—*Books Ireland* 2010

SLIPPERY SLOPES OF PARNASSUS

Hopkins in Ireland Norman White (University College Dublin Press)

Light Years Augustus Young (London Magazine Editions)

Hopkins comes across as a vassal at Newman's University in White's critical *Hopkins in Ireland*. Dr William Walsh, Archbishop of Dublin, virulently opposed the appointment of the English priest, otherwise seen as eccentric and disparaged for his appearance—five-foot-two with dropped shoulders and a seemingly much larger head than his body. There is a good chapter on Newman's own struggles with the Irish Roman Catholic hierarchy.

White is the definitive biographer of GMH but one would have liked louder articulation here on the abuse of Hopkins—this of course does not take from the biographer's treatment of similar material elsewhere. There is a savage infamy hanging over the life of Gerard Manley Hopkins and some of it can be blamed upon the Jesuits.

After giving a brief of the life of the Roman Catholic convert and troubled priest prior to his posting into exile in Dublin in 1884, White gets into top gear analysing the poetry written during this period, particularly the sonnets of despair. Hopkins' conversion from Anglicanism made him guilty about his family, who thought him disloyal and found the conversion distressing, especially his father.

Hopkins in Dublin is presented as an utterly miserable fellow. He was obliged to perform the *Spiritual Exercises* of St Ignatius Loyola which opened his imagination to needless mortifactory horrors. There were endless examination papers for correction as part of his duties and otherwise he suffered continual loneliness, "To seem the stranger lies my lot, my life /Among strangers". The priest and the poet fought a destructive battle within him resulting in the poems but also perhaps in his early death, aged forty-five.

John Butler Yeats is quoted remarking with regret that Hopkins ever put on the collar since his faith was too heavy and puritanical, if not ultimately self-negating. Yet, as a poet he had good friends in England such as Robert Bridges and Coventry Patmore but not, one must emphasise, Newman.

The *Month* and the *Stonyhurst Magazine* can be accused of a certain ignominy. It was a Father Coleridge who rejected Hopkins' longest poem, The *Wreck of the Deutschland,* that was never published in his lifetime. Even the *Irish Monthly* edited by Matthew Russell SJ never invited him to contribute poems; instead, the lowly poet sent in two translations into Latin of Shakespeare's songs. Shame on the jebbies!

White speedily notes the mark of pessimism that entered the poems, "Selfyeast of spirit a dull dough sours". The news of suicide of friends from his Oxford days added to his drooping spirits. Temptations of 'the unreasonable deed' harassed him and it may be bland to suppose that the sonnets which he wrote cushioned him against taking his own life. White ranks the sonnets of despair alongside *King Lear*—a very high rating. His letters are a masterpiece of prose writing—those from this period attest to the depths of despair.

Not even a visit to a monster meeting at the Phoenix Park could lift his spirits. His politics were 'imperialistically pro-British' and thus strongly anti-Home-Rule while he is shown as snobbish towards Irish tenants. White condemns him for his attitude towards the English working class. Somewhat happier occasions were the brief visits to the Patmores in Hastings. Other short holidays included retreats at Clongowes, Dromore in County Down and, most relaxing of all, short stays in Monasterevin. Here he stayed with families loyal to the Jesuits who resided in Monasterevin House and Togher House. When he missed a meeting with the poet Aubrey de Vere his disappointment was assuaged on hearing that de Vere did not rate John Dryden, the English Catholic poet and playwright, at all. Otherwise, in Dublin he had a few social occasions with John Butler Yeats and the poet Katherine Tynan but for a man of cultural refinement and poetic sensibility it was paltry as an outlet for his temperament.

It was apparently during the rained-out summer of 1888 that Hopkins wrote "That Nature is a Heraclitean Fire and of the comfort of the Resurrection" using the Bywater edition of Heraclitus as part of the impetus. White's comparison of Hopkins' sources is a delight but his gloss is appalling—that after writing the poem "there were no convincing signs that his deep problems had been solved".

"Five wasted years almost have passed in Ireland," he confided to his diary in 1889 ending with the comment, "I wish then for death." Six months later he contacted typhoid from the water system at 86 St Stephen's Green. First he manifested sleeplessness and rheumatic pain but massive complications of paralysis of the digestive system were followed by peritonitis which medically put him beyond hope of survival, as he worried about stacks of uncorrected examination papers. His parents were summoned.

White's close in his biography is more stirring but he does go on to conclude with Hopkins' revenge and ultimate championing by his friend Robert Bridges who fought against the early posthumous disinterest in the poems. Bridges persevered with a resolute vengeance based on his confidence in their obvious merits. Eliot, Pound, even Yeats and William Carlos Williams amongst the moderns, saw nothing in them, but Hopkins would gain footing from critics and poets such as Leavis, Richards, Empson and Graves. 'Rabbit Britches', as Pound called Bridges, got the poems into print in 1918 since he was Poet Laureate and an influential *litterateur* and had avoided the approaches of the literary tycoon Edmund Gosse and the Jesuits who also had developed an interest in the poet by then.

When a new edition was called for in 1930, Hopkins was, in modern parlance, 'made'. He had, as the old song says, gone though hell for a heavenly cause to reach the unreachable stars in poetry. Then, of course, in fashion, everyone could claim him including the Jesuits. There is one great irony, however: while Hopkins is never out of print and continually studied, and one of the greatest poets of his time—how many of Newman's doorstop of a collected poems have survived? Well, if you consider a few that became hymns and the dubious colossus *The Dream of Gerontius*—*largely* because of its being the inspiration for a choral work—very few.

White manages to make otherwise morbid subject matter into a magisterial book and is unafraid to praise the poems which are often still derided for being too confessional and metrically obsessed. One is inclined not to feel too sorry for poor Hopkins, whose poetry ultimately worked *ad maioerem Hopkinsensi gloriam.*

If you have read Beckett's *Murphy* and Burgess's *Enderby* this is somewhere in between but strictly a memoir and easier to place with the latter title, since the hero is a poet-drudge who finds some solace in the science laboratory. James Hogan, twenty-something son of a history professor from UCC reflects on his past while flying out from Cork in a Viscount. He is London bound for a spell in a purgatorial Bohemia and scoops of childhood pour from his memory as he sips his drink high in the clouds.

His passive resistance renders him a shadowman armed with fifteen English pounds, at first sponging off the Kennys as he invites himself into their household. The anxious unwelcome guest is well sent up with bursting luggage on arrival and finds everything in London as baffling as the tube map. Independence is asserted when he slots into the digs system with the Beveridges for five pounds all in, including the gut-wrenching suet pudding, Mr and Mrs B, and the daughter sulking inside the serving hatch. Life is portrayed as quirky and eccentric. The array and manner of his fellow lodgers are denigrated for the fun of it. The attic room in Romford is all very fine for jotting down his neat little verses and reading Pascal, Camus and Sartre but he is situated in the homeland of his idols and soon yearns to meet them.

The drudgery for him of being a poet is balanced by work in Romford hospital, in the lab, where his unrequited passion for Elizabeth makes him her confidant and money-lender—she eventually leaves her boyfriend, a married man, and returns to New Zealand. He changes lodgings in the pursuit of the muse. All an aspiring poet can do is tramp out to poetry readings in search of like-minded spirits. A visit to Ayot St Lawrence and Shaw's habitat inspires a leap into the unknown and total devotion to his art as eventually he becomes runner-up in the Cork Gin Poetry Prize. Ah, the slopes of Parnassus in sight at last!

Hogan took his name, Augustus Young, from Dryden's MacFlecknoe, King of Fools. He sends himself up as a self-conscious poet deliberately basing his own efforts on the greats—if you must steal, steal from the best such as Holub and Popa—"Flattery sustains vanity in a literary youth".

At a party in Putney wearing his French beret, he meets Alma who works for Hutchinsons. She provides a curious history and half likes his work. Tickets for Hair the musical seal their bizarre unromantic romance. There is neither kiss nor tell about any of it. Slowly he meets the members of the living pantheon starting with the egomaniacal George Barker, "Who are you to reduce my work to two poems?" inquires the elder on being praised by the aspirant. John Heath-Stubbs is less bruising on the ego than Barker's bark and bite. Only with the arrival of his landlord and confidant, McFee, does he find a fitting confrere. There are no more London patrons, only the rather odd but kind landlord. Young mocks himself for trying to feel like Dante in exile having written a review in a small Irish poetry magazine, "Seamus Heaney's spawn have hatched into tadpoles". Jeff Squires is portrayed in a decent light—the text is peppered with poets but he pours plenty of salt on their tails usually, except for David Marcus, and Basil Bunting who explains Yeats's obsessional friendship with Pound, "He needed an injection of Ezra's energy" in order to knock out the Last Poems. Even Kierkegaard cannot keep London pure for him so he abandons it for Dundee. Celtic longings, perhaps.

The last section almost sinks but if you have got that far you may well see it through. Ancestry and family loom large and top billing must go to Aunt Hanna. Her antidote to the nightly rosary was a few pages read out loud from *Les Miserables*. The suggested light years of youth of the title suddenly can be seen in terms of the light years of cosmology if not eternity and mortality as the elegiac strain enters the tableaux when he recalls people who drowned during his youth, a school friend who died, and lastly "I was twenty-one and my father was dying"—the year 1963 and what a father, revered in an unsentimental and model account. There is a terrific swipe at Dev attending the father's funeral: "Started a civil war because of a symbolic oath".

Young is a restrained memoirist: there is no cloying ego, not much solipsism considering the subject is pretty much himself and his poetry; there are even lengthy quotes but there is nothing rhetorical or shabbily embarrassing, "Is the past falsified or fossilised?" "My memories of my father's memories, my father's memories of my grandfather's memories". No false flourishes at all hardly.

—*Books Ireland* 2002

KENNELLY: FATHER AND DAUGHTER Brendan Kennelly: Behind the Smile Sandrine Brisset (Raglan Books)

A media saga that turned nasty and developed into a full blown scandal continues in the ongoing interpersonal feud over Sandrine Brisset's *Brendan Kennelly: Behind the Smile* (Raglan Books). Published in April, it has been withdrawn from Eason's and major retailers, including the TCD Bookshop because of the angered Kennelly clan. The biography was hailed by Minister for Arts, Heritage and the Gaeltacht, Jimmy Deenihan at a glittering launch event in the Shelbourne Hotel, Dublin. An all-smiles-night with David Norris chiming in, Mary Black singing, Frankie Gavin fiddling, the wine flowing and glasses chinking under the chandeliers. The launch coincided with celebrations for the poet's 77th birthday. The party atmosphere has long since palled. Brisset is effectively banned and in literary limbo without supporters despite extensive acknowledgements in the biography from academics and legal experts such as William Binchy.

Behind the Smile turned into a nightmare for the author who has lost her 'ten years of friendship' with Kennelly, quoted on the cover: 'I feel she knows more about me than I do myself.' This renders the publication authorised. The cover photo of Kennelly is by Brisset. The real crisis is the poet's daughter, Kristen Kennelly-Murphy aka Doodle (born 1970) part of the generation of siblings of Irish divorces. Her adolescence and early youth is already a media circus mainly through appearances on RTÉ chat shows and in *Sunday Independent* profiles and articles in their *Life* magazine. The headlines speak for themselves. 'Doodle Kennelly Cuts and Pastes her Nipples.' 'Fat Cow, Skinny Bitch.' 'My Drugs Hell' where she is photographed in a padded cell. 'Doodle Does Depression.' 'Scarred Doodle Kennelly Comes Back from the Edge.'

There is no question of Doodle Kennelly being a victim of salacious material in the biography which substantiates her already widely exposed traumatic past. Brisset is sceptical over 'harrowing sexual experiences' in her adolescence and doubts 'whether the authorities were informed of these alleged crimes'. She wonders whether Doodle Kennelly's 'aggressive self-promotion can be reconciled with the fragility of true mental illness.' Unfortunately, the woes and tragedies of the daughter have to be part of the biography since they are part of her father's poetry. Doodle Kennelly has been replete in her public announcements of pain. On the *Late Late Show* in 2005, she admitted that 'each of her pregnancies was marked by guilt and anxiety that the baby would not live.' The biography fulfils its brief in exploring this 'public image as celebrity' based on Kennelly and Kristen Kennelly who is completing a memoir.

Her major brachioplasty at the Blackrock Clinic—no mere nip and tuck plastic surgery—as well as other highly personal details does not make for easy reading. This is a father-daughter contest 'unravelled in the media' where 'the features of Kennelly's public mask were taken over by his daughter who became an accusatory mirror.' Brisset states that 'trauma created a close bond' between Kennelly and his daughter 'but according to their testimonies, emotional blackmail was a decisive component in the relationship.' Publicly and privately a 'complex blame-game' has been turned into biographical fodder. Kennelly is, however, almost lost as poet-subject matter occasionally in the text where the presence of his daughter overshadows him. However, without the complex, distressing and sensitive issues there would be evasion in *Kennelly Behind the Smile* on the part of the author.

Kennelly himself has a surgical history at the Blackrock Clinic which restored his health and also resulted in the anaesthesia-induced hallucinatory poem 'The Man Made of Rain' (1998). Brisset fawns over Kennelly with epithets such as 'superstar poet' while castigating the era of his adoration of C. J. Haughey whose life's work the poet declared was 'a fine quality poem—delightful in fact.' Kennelly is shown 'no less elitist than Haughey' when giving the funeral oration for CJH where he praised the disgraced former Taoiseach as an Ard-Rí. The declaration contained the inference that Kerry-born Kennelly was the Ard-fhile. Many of the Aosdána collective of writers such as Anthony Cronin, Paul Durcan and Theo Dorgan would have given their eye-teeth to send off the Fianna Fáil demagogue and wallow in some of the dubious glory which rendered Kennelly more a 'king's jester' than bard.

There is a commendable assessment of Kennelly's poetry now overshadowed by his public denouncing of the biography. Kennelly via Patrick Kavanagh claims that his poems come from 'self-critical laughter.' In 'The Man Made of Rain' he states 'more men die of caution/than excess'. Brisset outlandishly locates him alongside the Jewish American Beat poet, Allen Ginsberg and tortured confessionalist poets Anne Sexton, John Berryman and Sylvia Plath. These comparisons are misguided.

Kennelly as distinguished TCD Emeritus-Professor is rightfully lauded. Meanwhile his public neurosis as scapegoat of *Late Late Show* fame during the period 1995-2005 guaranteed him a wide audience for his poetry *Cromwell* and *The Book of Judas*. The public mask of the happy bard with 'the dancing dimples' is proved as simply not true behind the soft-focus newspaper profiles that 'managed' his past as alcoholic, ladies' man, wayward academic and divorcee. His contemporaries shunned a poet who advertised Toyotas, promoted AIB, Kerry Gold and *The Sunday Independent*. This public persona has enabled ego-deflating-lines cutely tucked into the poems: 'Sure even that fat little bollox/Out in Ballylongford, Kennelly,/Is half-able to write.' 'A machine smile on his face/Plus a lust for gusty acclaim/No applauding gods can satisfy.' The prolific poet admits to over-producing because of public demand where 'the cult of personality can supercede the quality of the writing' but otherwise his work reflects an inherent sense of personal failings.

He is summed up as 'an Irish version of Balzac's *Old Goriot*, a paternal scapegoat sacrificing himself for his adult progeny' and suffering from long-drawn out divorce guilt. Kennelly separated from his wife, the American poet and academic Peggy O'Brien after twenty years. Doodle Kennelly 'held him responsible for the marital break-up…a responsibility that he seemed to accept and from which he publicly blamed himself.' *Behind the Smile* proves that public truths which emerge from private lives can shock and horrify. In this case, a father and daughter are the walking wounded whose traumata were made public by themselves, largely. Publicity demands revelations in order to exist as living publicity. Therefore in actuality behind the smiles on launch night was the vicious cycle of a father-daughter struggle that has slowly emerged and like never before is unembroidered beyond Sunday afternoon journalism. It is the incomplete portrait of Doodle Kennelly that eclipses this painful family biography.

—*VILLAGE: politics and culture* 2013-14

OF MONEY, SEX AND POLITICS

The Economy of "Ulysses": Making Both Ends Meet Mark Osteen Syracuse University Press.

James Joyce and the Problem of Justice: Negotiating Sexual and Colonial Difference Joseph Valente Cambridge University Press.

Joyce, Race, and Empire Vincent J. Cheng Cambridge University Press

Joyce for Beginners David Norris and Carl Flint Icon Books

Martin Steen's book may well become influential. The early chapters were seen by the eminent Joycean, Richard Ellmann. It attempts a "synthesizing of the economic motifs" in *Ulysses:* "a counterfeit classic, a copy of an epic . . . it claims that all narratives are genuine and counterfeit". He is slightly hysterical about James Joyce's squandermania, financed by Edith McCormack, Harriet Weaver, Sylvia Beach and others, but mentions the hospital bills of JJ's daughter, costing three-fourths of the artist's income. Is it unfair to cite the sabbatical, two research grants, two fellowships and a publishing subsidy which Professor Osteen acknowledges for his book?

There are graphics of the House of Keys advert and Leopold Bloom's proposed poster for the Trinity College bicycle race: "Advertising is thus an appropriate occupation for the reincarnation of Homer's man of many turns," and he refers to an advert of the Pope drinking a cup of beef tea with the caption: "Two infallible powers. The Pope and Bovril". Much analysis of minutiae traces the philosophy of Heraclitus in the Proteus episode and the use of two plays by Shakespeare in the novel; and the footnotes are entertaining, for instance about J. S. G. Boggs, artist and counterfeiter, the scandal of the evangelical Dr Dowie and a digression on the master forger James Saward.

Half way through things change, when two chapters, entitled

'Erotic Commerce' give a full explication of Bloom's masochism, "linked by operations of filthy lucre" in the brothel. He estimates that Stephen Dedalus spends $200 in current exchange rates "for a single day and night's debauches" and by then has threepence less than Bloom.

The Eumaeus episode is pleasantly dissected, "a verbal Trojan horse . . . where clichés encircle each other in uneasy mutual orbits," and the narrator is "hopelessly rent, *Gulliver's Travels, Dracula* and *Ulysses* lame" and "inconsistent". Bloom's hermaphroditism in Circe is superseded by Mrs Bloom's soliloquy, which makes the reader into a hermaphodite according to Osteen, who writes that "in presenting the economy of Dublin, Joyce also participates in it by offering the text itself as both commodity and gift. If one may master a text, such mastery might displace the mastery imposed by Church and State."

This book adheres to a colossal monetary agenda. He doesn't overglorify *Ulysses* nor idolise the author. There is plenty of discursive reference to fellow critics, enabling future debate. Of its sort, it is a very fine piece of writing.

Joseph Valente sets out to locate 'the trial scenario' in JJ's works. At first his grasp seems outside his reach. The Anita/Honophurious trial in *Finnegans Wake* and 'the double trial of Leopold Bloom' in 'the Walpurgisnacht of Circe' are studied at length. Using an article JJ wrote for an Italian newspaper, he implies narrow nationalism and Sinn Feinism. The article concerns a convicted murderer, Myles Joyce, who spoke Gaelic only, which the prosecutor ridiculed, and the hangman added to the brutality of the public execution. Valente's opening chapter is referentially staggering, a crucible of jurisprudence, beginning with Aristotle's concept of a social contract, phronesis. Besides the social theorist Edward Said and the feminists Helene Cixous and Catherine MacKinnon, he includes Pascal, Rousseau, Swift, Thomas

Paine, Mary Shelley, Wilde, Gandhi and even JJ's Whiteboy grandfather. He concocts a theory of Ireland "the Sister Isle . . imaged in wifely terms" and Matthew Arnold's "feminine idiosyncracy of the Celts", not forgetting JJ's "anxiety over colonial feminisation and *the* loss of male entitle-merit it implied". The story 'A Mother' from *Dubliners* is explained at length through the 'code of gender justice', 'ill will among women' and the 'internecine enmity of the Irish'. JJ is labelled an emergent feminist opposed to 'a specifically Irish brand of phallogocentrism'.

Moving on, he scrutinises the very brief diary which Ellmann made into a publishing coup in the late sixties, titled *Giacomo Joyce,* concerning a chaste affair between JJ and Amalia Popper, a Jewess whose father became the model for Bloom. The diary, which Valente calls 'sexist' and 'masochist' provides him with a mineshaft for extraction of dubious critical ore. He compares JJ's only play, *Exiles,* with Ibsen: "a cross-gender pastiche of *A Doll's House"*. In *Exiles "the* masculine romance is mediated from start to finish by a figure of feminine otherness that it excludes". Women are "the long haired, short legged sex" according to JJ. Valente's detective work finds colonial-nationalist politics in JJ's notes, which are not in the final version of *Exiles.*

He throws in the psychoanalytic perspectives on literature of Felix Guattari and Gilles Deleuze who was the keynote speaker at the 1994 Joyce Symposium. Jacques Lacan the postFreudian is applied also. Occasionally the book requires extra attention as it tends towards hokum and jargon; still the meaning connects with the message, "paternal identification in *Ulysses* seems a pathway of deliverance from the labyrinth of maternal abjection", while Bloom in the Circe episode "undergoes feminisation, infantilisation, and bestialisation". Vincent J. Cheng never deviates from his title. It's quite a book, all things considered. The promises of the foreword and introduction are not broken. He's a much-travelled Asian of Catholic upbringing with a high opinion of Irish critics and of social theorists Frantz

Fanon, Edward Said and Antonio Gramsci. Lavish use is made of JJ's critical writings; Sartre and Fanon are utilised to look into Parnell's downfall. He refers to an intriguing study by Ruth Bauerle titled *Date Rape, Mate Rape: a liturgical interpretation of 'The Dead'.* Another story from *Dubliners*, 'Araby', evokes for Cheng Edward Said's "every European, in what he could say about the Orient, was consequently a racist, an imperialist, and almost totally ethnocentric"; and Robert Young's *White Mythologies:* "Orientalism represents the West's own internal dislocation, misrepresented as an external dualism between East and West". It is no bother to him reading into *Ulysses* cultural imperialism, Hellenism, Hebraism and Anglo-Saxon racism, Arthur Griffith and Douglas Hyde as racial purists, xenophobia in the novel's characters, and A. C. Swinburne's concentration-camp sonnet, 'On the Death of Colonel Benson'. Bloom is described as "a Jew and rank outsider suffering at the hands of white Aryan male authoritarian domination". JJ is re-invented as a deeply political, colonial author, "a renegade from the Nationalist ranks and a professed cosmopolist" who rejects "the ideological foundation behind the *Citizen's,* the Gaelic League's and the Literary Revival's motivations" and in "sympathy with Buddhist methods of non-aggression and pacifism".

Cheng quotes English authors from Mrs Gaskell to D. H. Lawrence, revealing their Celtophobia. Even Disraeli in mid-nineteenth century: "The wild, reckless, indolent, uncertain and superstitious [Irish] race have no sympathy with the English character"; Sidney and Beatrice Webb visiting Dublin: "The people are charming but we detest them"; and Mahaffy of Trinity College with his "corner boys who spit in the Liffey".

Cheng contrasts the satire in Cyclops and Aeolus against "the nationalist tendency to nostalgise and sentimentalise . . . death, martyrdom, capital punishment". His sources are usually interesting: "It is the magic of nationalism to turn chance into destiny" *[Imagined*

Communities. Benedict Anderson. Verso 1991]. The book has apposite illustrations including Throwaway, winner of the Ascot Gold Cup, R. B. Haydon's painting of Wellington's chestnut charger at Waterloo, and *Punch* cartoons of the period. He declares: *"Finnegans Wake* is a primer for a failed revolution that would have allied Ireland to Europe rather than simply separating twenty-six counties from Britain". The notes are good stuff: "Both Stannie (JJ's brother) and Gogarty had referred to *Finnegans Wake* as 'literary bolshevism'," and David Pierce: "could the time understanding *Finnegans Wake* be better spent changing the world? Is there not a tyranny on Joyce's part in requiring so much time and attention from the reader?" Certainly if JJ's writings were completely destroyed, they could probably be reproduced from the numerous critical studies of which these three are further additions.

Presumably David Norris could have written this book in his sleep. The accompanying cartoons by Carl Flint make the enterprise not quite a comic book but a funny comic. It is inaccurate to say 'cartoons', because JJ is always depicted as middle-aged in every drawing, whether a babe, a student or a Daedalus with wings; the Joyce face used is a photo-montage. Flint is capable of rendering definite atmospherics, with dense gloom on inspection breaking into fun. A double-page depicting elements of *Finnegans Wake* might make a good poster. Elsewhere the Cyclops eye between the nose and forehead of the Citizen holding court in the pub with his dog is great gas. One necessary quibble: the version of 'Ecce Puer' is incorrect; a word in the first verse is different from the original poem.

The text doesn't shirk on the details of JJ's life; his alcoholic father, the years of struggle for recognition and a Dublin publisher's savagery, which very possibly ensured his permanent exile from the city of central inspiration. Some believe his ghost haunts the city. There is also a considerable financial aspect; and while the Joyce industry does not imply a one-writer literature, there are among Joyceans lapsed Joyceans, Joyceans in embryo and non-Joyceans, those who put him on a pedestal.

—*Books Ireland* 1995

CENTENNIAL CASH-IN

The Scandal of Ulysses: the life and afterlife of a twentieth century masterpiece Bruce Arnold *Liffey Press*

The Joyce We Knew: memoirs of Joyce Ulick O'Connor (Mercier)

Joyce in Art: visual art inspired by James Joyce Christa-Maria Lerm Hayes (Lilliput)

The Cambridge Companion to James Joyce Derek Attridge (Cambridge University Press)

Faithful Departed: the Dublin of James Joyce's Ulysses Kieran Hickey (Lilliput)

For Your Enjoycement: the removal of Paddy Dignam Sean Lennon (Fingal County Libraries)

A Bloomsday Postcard Niall Murphy (Lilliput)

Arnold returns to the fray over a decade later with a revised version, less about art and more about finance, copyright law, and scholars as feuding warlords. Grandson Stephen Joyce hoped for a book such as this that would recount "the turbulent history of *Ulysses* and of its various editions".

The prophetic element of the novel is revealed in Arnold's facts as in the struggle between Mulligan and Dedalus, little Jacky and Tommy on Sandymount Strand in *Nausikaa* and all the warring twins in *Finnegans Wake* from Mutt and Jute to the Mookse and Gripes. In Arnold's context there are John Kidd and Hans Walter Gabler with a swaggering pugilistic punch-up not short of occasional laughs. Kidd's fall from academic grace renders the poor fellow a good candidate for Macintosh, the mystery man in the *Hades* episode of *Ulysses*. No academic strives to be anonymous; Kidd as reported here, is on a one way ticket in that direction.

Arnold knows that the publications of the Joyce industry could pave a path from the tower in Sandycove to Howth Castle and environs: a not too inaccurate hyperbole. He delicately chooses his morsels of remaining Joyceana to leaven the details of the internecine situation of Kidd vs Gabler. There is a host of academics mentioned, including the bête noire to many, Stephen Joyce, and his bagman Seán Sweeney, the estate's trustee.

Some of the enchanting detail concerns the cover of the first edition and Joyce's pronunciation—Oolissays as opposed to the various Irish and American accents *Youllissees*. He rehashes the early reception of the novel, its disparagement and banishment. *The Sporting Times* provides the title and cover picture, with Joyce and Sylvia Beach below a poster. While there is some mention of Irish writers O'Faolain, Denis Johnston, Niall Montgomery and Kavanagh who did not idolise Joyce, the narrative never moves far from the academicians and institutions vying with each other as to who is the reigning monarch among Joyceans. Arnold has mingled with the Joycean royalty and remains human. He has interviewed some of them in Monte Carlo on film (RTE 2 February 1991).

The great achievement here besides the staggering detail, is the unmoving scales with Gabler and Kidd balanced fairly. Jack Dalton and Anthony Burgess are shown as decent people among the furies, as it were. Burgess eventually repudiated the Gabler *Ulysses* ("Leave it alone ... I think it's time to leave it alone"), and Fritz Senn agreed but seemingly not many more of his ilk.

There is a kind of impudence on the part of the editors, as if any jumped-up academic can correct *Ulysses* in the absence of the original author. Arnold pours scorn on the modern interfering in-laws of editorial process in direct opposition to the original autonomous artist with pen and paper or laptop and disc. Gabler is quoted, "a critical edition of *Ulysses* resides in Joyce's autograph notations." Yes, fine, but he makes claims for a "text of highest overall authority" and a "continuous manuscript text ... the intention of the text [rather] than the intention of the author". Perhaps his 1984 edition should appear with Hans Walter Gabler on cover and title page and a brief mention of James Joyce in the acknowledgements at the back? Gabler worked off a list of over 5,000 alterations to the editions of the 1926 backed up by Hugh Kenner and other academic luminaries and putting Kidd in the position of a mere noisy antagonist eventually to be squeezed out, even though-or perhaps because?-Kidd had caught his senior changing the names of real persons in *Ulysses,* Captain Buller and H. Thrift to Captain Culler and H. Shrift and so had scored many points. Conspiracy is not beyond the bounds of possibility, but Arnold presents the hostilities with masterly restraint.

This is a superbly entertaining polemic based on conferences, articles and book reviews from such as *The New York Review of Books,* the *TLS* and exclusive Joycean publications. Arnold accepts the continuous carnival of Bloomsday with a shrug and demands that the unread read our national epic that overflows with great fun and comedy as well as being a fitting monument to its author. These personal memoirs by five of Joyce's friends and acquaintances were first published in 1967 and are here expanded with introduction, brief biographies of the memoirists and engaging asides such as on meeting Joyce's son and other first-hand commentary.

The overall impression is the importance of Dublin to Joyce. The sadder subtext concerns his exile in Europe and the fact that Dublin never left his psyche. It would be found written on his heart, according to one anecdote. The material is first-hand from fellow students at Belvedere and UCD Eugene Sheehy and William Fallon, and closer friends Padraic Colum and Arthur Power. In Sean Lester's case the contact was brief. Lester's list of press coverage (in a diary) of Joyce's passing, noted in newspapers, reveals the revilement of the author in both England and Ireland: Sir Edmund Gosse contra-Joyce, AE undecided on his talent, the *Irish Times* recalling him as "self-opinionated and vain".

O'Connor tells of Colum's stature in the Irish Renaissance, praised by Yeats, Pound and others. His bulky anthology of Modern Irish Verse is forgotten. *Our Friend James Joyce* (1959) by himself and wife Mary is a terrific account of the Joyces in both Dublin and Paris-only a tantalising excerpt is here. Similarly, Arthur Power's illuminating account that was ultimately incorporated into *Conversations with James Joyce* (1999).

The five personal accounts build to a portrait of the man without spurious academic analysis. Instead, you encounter Joyce's impoverished youth, the tragedy of his father's decline into poverty, his daughter's insanity, fame and exile, his passion for Irish music and sport, a love of the English language over French, and into his fifties astonishment at Newman's prose style. The ultimate abandonment of his father, that O'Connor finds lamentable, is also highlighted by Colum, the old man became a down-and-out on sufferance in a boarding house in Drumcondra.

Fritz Senn rubberstamps this critical extravaganza in a brief foreword: "Critics who explain Joyce or put him in context had better understand what they write about (not that they always do), but artists are under no such compulsion." Lerm Hayes relishes her critical commentary of the Royal Hibernian Academy exhibition marking the Bloomsday centenary.

This mammoth catalogue is both engaging and annoying, as it spans the frivolous to the conceptual in various mediums-a spool of thread to a tin of *merda d'artista*, and lots of other items that might be found in a museum or a household. Joyce can be praised or blamed for affecting so many people on so many different levels. Lerm Hayes finds him "the artists' writer". James Elkins concludes that he was "repeatedly blind to visual experience and visual art." He feels more comfortable with Joyce's influence on verbal artists-Nabokov and William Gass. He wonders where "will modernism's most troublesome inheritance finally come to rest?"

Irish artists are not neglected from Sean Scully to Eamonn O'Doherty who seem modest next to installations such as Jeffrey Shaw's 'The Legible City' or aural-visual works such as John Cage's *Roaratorio*. Shaw's work invites the viewer to pedal a stationary bicycle in order to read a diffuse sentence across a cityscape made up of building-sized text-"Matter so shaken to its core to lead to a change in inherent form to the extent of bringing about a change in the destiny of the material." Now you know.

The catalogue has a life beyond the exhibition and achieves this largely through reproductions at every turn from Wyndham Lewis to Joseph Beuys-who found *Finnegans Wake* "a dynamic medicine" for a depressive crisis. Some might find the opposite is true? The immensely satisfying photographic exhibition at the Towers Hotel in Ballsbridge of nine portraits of Joyce taken by Josef Breitenbach was also part of the Bloomsday centenary, but Breitenbach is not mentioned by Lerm Hayes.

Attridge hails "the massive heap of books", "the metatextual mountain" about Joyce and debunks those alarmed in terms of shelf-space, natural resources or time, since Joyce is in effect being read even through critical essays in which he is quoted. These are pithy essays from eleven academics including Seamus Deane in which the maestro is shown as never less than intentionally brilliant, hence the academic is on a just aesthetic cause that is at times slightly unnerving. Very little negative criticism but for mention of Wyndham Lewis and Andre Suares and a rebuke from Paul Claudel (quoted by Jean-Michel Rabate)—"a man who separates himself from the source of life and who only lives on himself, as they say, is autophagous." All the material is edifying; it would be arrogance to deny this. The canonical veneer, the pomp and circumstance of notes and the academic trimmings tend to blur some ineffable essential of the art of Joyce, despite the critical slopes and the flock of critics nibbling away as they ascend to expound with assurance.

Seventy-three black-and-white photographs of Dublin taken by Robert French about the turn of the century, at first familiar, but on closer examination showing the changes to streetscapes, as well as the costumes, hats, trams, bicycles, horse-drawn vehicles—the reality of the city that young Joyce adored.

Sean Lennon juggles the macabre and the comic in dealing (mainly) with Paddy Dignam's funeral in cartoons. Horses and people have bizarre facial expressions while Lennon does not deaden his art with slavish Joycean detail. Whenever he wants to add in his own details, he does—Molly Bloom seems to have only three fingers on her right hand—there's one for the scholars to dissect—and a young Joyce appears in some of the illustrations holding a bunch of flowers. This is merrily irreverent.

Niall Murphy has produced what can be subtitled 'Everyone's Picture Book *Ulysses*.' Those of us who have read the original can buy this for our non-Ulysses-friendly friends. This will end the arcane *Ulysses* Reader's Club mentality by letting the Joyce out of his novel into a plain account an "O, rocks! she said. Tell us in plain words" *(Ulysses* Bodley Head, 960 p. 66) with the added spice of two hundred and fifty-two period picture postcards (colour and b&w). There is a discussion of the pictorial postcard and a brief biography of Joyce. The homeric background and schema of *Ulysses* is set out in six pages—a triumph of jargon-free, waffle-free exposition. Leading character sketches are given (he can't be expected to tackle the whole of 1904 Dublin, as Joyce attempted) and outlined events such as they are where action is subordinate to significant detail and style.

Anyone who can concisely synopsize the complications and artistic fireworks of Stephen Dedalus in discourse over Shakespeare deserves praise. Murphy, if you don't count the four colour postcards from the chapter, gives Scylla and Charybdis in five and half pages—it took Joyce dose on thirty-six! Scylla and Charybdis in *Ulysses* presents. Joyce's recurrent father and son theme transposed from Hamlet, the ghost of Hamlet's father and the life of the bard of Avon. Incidentally for the postcards alone this is a rare auld romp around Jubbelin.

—Books Ireland 2004

ALL ABOUT EVERYTHING

Irish Writing in the Twentieth Century David Pierce (Cork University Press)

A Tour of the Darkling Plain: the Finnegans Wake letters of Thornton Wilder and Adaline Glasheen eds. Edward M. Burns, Joshua A. Gaylord, Thornton Wilder and Adaline Glasheen (University College Dublin Press)

This bulky anthology presents an overtly political statement by the editor about literature and politics, if not literature and history. Pierce locates the century in the ten years of stirrings preceding it since for his purposes he begins in the 1890s when the seeds of the intellectual and cultural revolution were sown to become the Irish Literary Revival. He is quite certain and history bears him out that this revolution was instigated by those Irish who were also Protestant and Anglo-Irish. Douglas Hyde's call for de-anglicising is the opening gambit of this anthology of appeasement. Hyde was loud in calling for the restoration of Gaelic names and everything else that is rightly the domain of the Gael and already enshrined in his document are the early drafts of post-civil-war party policy as adopted by Fianna Fáil. Hyde followed the flow of history from the Young Irelanders and Thomas Davis—the younger Yeats would, soon after in The Rose, cite his poetic masters as Davis, Mangan and Ferguson.

This call for Gaelicisation echoes through all of Pierce's selections at the beginning of the book and no wonder when one discovers his background—a Sussex lad with a County Clare grandmother. Once upon a time this gallant lady hoisted the local priest out of her cottage when he came to halt a night of music and dancing with the neighbours, but she returned his collar to the presbytery door next day. Hence it is no surprise to see William Trevor's The Ballroom of Romance included. Pierce is home to roost with this manifesto of an anthology, counting himself among what Brendan Behan called 'the compulsory Irish', all seventy million of them. When he includes Shaw and Synge, one quickly sees that the minority Irish sect from which they come has defined Ireland and not least by their humour—thus in John Bull's Other Island when the valet asks Tom Broadbent, "Is it a dangerous part you're going to, sir? Should I be expected to carry a revolver, sir?" Tom's mythic reply goes, "Perhaps it might be as well. I'm going to Ireland."

Shaws's play prophesies Ireland with the gun in the century ahead and makes the Englishman highly efficient since he will build a hotel locally and tap into the potential for Irish tourism. Meanwhile, Larry Doyle is bitter with his Irish past and the defrocked cleric, Father Keegan, is still present on the landscape a hundred years on with the native Doyles doing very nicely in the boom. Three years later in 1907 The Playboy of the Western World brought the callow youth Christy away from his father's influence after a violent row and into a common Mayo locality. Synge's penetrating realism offended both Gaels and Anglo-Irish in the first week of its reception as world class theatre, but that mixed audience would line-out for the years of conflict.

When Shaw is quoted writing to the Daily News as the executions of the 1916 leaders were being mercilessly carried out, he is passionate in disparaging England for slaughtering prisoners of war, albeit in some cases minor poets, immediately making them into major patriots. George Russell's essay in the New Nation quotes his elegy for the dead, a lesser poem if compared with Yeats's 'Easter 1916'.

However, in terms of the turmoil of Irish history, Russell is begging for pluralistic peace among the tribes, hence his poem commemorates Pearse and Connolly, and also Tom Kettle and John Redmond. He is writing in the crucial period prior to the civil war, declaring himself Anglo-Irish with the rider that "partition is no settlement" and furthermore sets the conflict in terms of nationalist and imperialist ideals. Russell's essay is a key document and Pierce makes it so, since the Anglo-Irish if not always Anglo-Irish unionist minority of Ireland is carefully given voice in this anthology. Yeats on divorce is prefaced from the Senate's proceedings and is shown not to be an extempore speech, though one in which the senator-poet quickly and trenchantly asserts his ancestral background. Otherwise the nationalist perspective is never neglected either in prison literature or in poetry. Jim Phelan, Darrell Figgis and Frank Gallagher provide the necessary accounts of incarceration. One might cavil that Tom Clarke, the first signatory of the proclamation of 1916, is omitted but who's in and who's out is unhelpful, when what is here complies with Pierce's agenda.

When it comes to the 1930s there is a double irony in that Ernest Boyd's comment about 'the Anglo-Irish writer' James Joyce's refusal to be elected to the Irish Academy of Letters is echoed in his exclusion from this anthology due to a dispute with the Joyce estate. Of the bigger picture—and everything became bigger in Irish literature because of Joyce—Ulysses, far more than his own claims for Dubliners, has a strictly anti-nationalist and pro-European liberal Ireland in mind. Nothing in the selections here is as anti-nationalist in this vein except perhaps Eimar O'Duffy's The Wasted Land. In poetry the strong voice of MacNeice is presented sounding out from Autumn Journal as Yeats was penning his last poems in 1938. Kavanagh's The Great Hunger and its sterile solitary sexuality might be said to have made the countryman poet a martyr and pariah among Dublin's rurally minded settlers of the 1940s and 50s.

Joyce too would find circumspect followers in O'Connor and O'Faolain, both influenced by the master, yet O'Connor would find delight in translation from Gaelic in the Hyde tradition. O'Faolain's modern Irish folk, like his lovers in the story Lovers of the Lake, end up united in sceptical prayer, but once away from Lough Derg remain unfree to vent their passion in sexual embrace and are booked into separate rooms at a stuffy hotel. The Lough Derg austerity and its Catholic dominance would continue through Denis Devlin and reach as far as the 1980s in modern Ireland and in the interim many would remain faithful to the Catholic mode if not always in their work. Even the Abbey Theatre, with its take-over by Ernest Blythe, might be said to have reverted to Irish Catholic kitchen drama. The only contemporary of O'Connor and O'Faolain with modern libertine couples depicted in his fiction of the period was Francis Stuart. His pugnacious essay The Soft Centre of Irish Writing (1976) attacks O'Connor and O'Faolain while praising Beckett and remains valid in the new century with the different versions of Ireland, from the lying and sugary to the sharp and true. But for all Pierce's selections, represented in these strivings to make literature out of real Irish life and people, the minority is consistently presented here. Such as and including Hubert Butler and Brian Inglis sounding the lonely Anglo-Irish voice so that the triumph of Beckett with a literature free of Irish history and politics could and did mount the world stage as a universal statement of not only his people but all people.

The Northern Troubles would never render the backward-looking gaze on to the birth of the Free State as redundant, and the emergence of dissenting women's voices, the first of which being Edna O'Brien in the wake of Kate O'Brien, would finally show up the viciousness of Irish paternalism. The Deane-Heaney interview from the Crane Bag in 1977, two years after North established Heaney in Belfast, Dublin, London and beyond, immediately gets political and mentions Cruise O'Brien's giving voice to the Northern Protestant. Heaney justifies his own straddling of non-English origins as well as admitting to Anglo-Saxon roots. Thus the Irish can claim Englishness—and the real Irish are perhaps all closet English? By the time he would write Station Island, safely beyond the Catholic jurisdiction of Lough Derg his real gods would be Carleton, Joyce and Kavanagh, with Carleton being one of the first to give voice to the national capacity for violence. Thomas Kinsella amongst others of the 1970s, and long before the brainwave for Gaelic preservation and promotion and the glories of T na G, would sound the clarion of the Irish poet as iceberg, floating in a Gaelic ocean with English as the spoken and written language at the top. Kinsella noted "the traumatic exchange of one vernacular for another".

Hence when Pierce reaches the 1980s—his critical and documentary section for each decade has one heading of the latter followed by an imaginative writing section—one finds Mary Holland commenting on the IRA Brighton bombing and polemics concerning Van Morrison and U2. The crop of northern material is strong as ever with Padraic Fiacc, Ciaran Carson, Friel's Translations alongside the southerner Kennelly's Cromwell. Facing the 1990s one can easily see his conclusions by the inclusion of Martin Mooney's kitchen drama which revisits terrain much better achieved by Synge and Lady Gregory, and Sebastian Barry's Anglo-Irish paranoia about marginalisation in the Steward of Christendom. But there is mature work in Mahon's The Hudson Letter in the MacNeice tradition, Seamus Deane's Reading in the Dark, Ní Dhomhnaill's clantaí translated into English by Muldoon, and you even get Ó Tuama's dissertation on poetry in Irish—while there are other entries about anxiety and/or glory over Gaelic.

The two squealing pups in the litter at this point are Tóibín and O'Toole, what one might call the double act of contemporary commentary and risk being sued or vilified by Kevin Myers for exclusion. Tóibín's 'piece' to give it popular in-house journalistic parlance, fires a few shots across the bows of Kiberd who is in turn part of another duo, known in the trade as the Kiberd twins. Cunningly enough, Pierce includes this piece of heresy which will not accept a cosy reading of history such as his anthology tends to lean rather heavily upon; whereas Toibin, a screaming liberal ("I hate the Rising") will have none of Kiberd's super-saturated fatty Irish heritage vision of reality and cult of the 1916 Rising, as espoused in Inventing Ireland (1995).

The other whippet is Fintan O'Toole and his piece on A. J. F. O'Reilly which is actually a notoriously nationalist *cri de coeur* against the branding of Ireland—this may be the new struggle for the Irish soul between the very oldest polarities God, Caesar and the shamrock. One wonders if O'Toole would provide such an unveiling of C. J. Haughey. Tony O'Reilly's sleight of hand may in fact be typical of the Irish businessman joking about flirting with Marx as a youth, glad that the civil war is long over, modern poverty marginalised, culture colourfully packaged and the boom set to continue. He too might be comfortable with Pierce's selections and a glimpse of ourselves through literature almost as intoxicating as the glory and splendour of being alive. The implication is that the war in the North is over; tribal Ireland will sit down to talk, eat and maybe even to pray together and that includes the Anglo-Irish who might well claim to have set the whole thing in motion through such innocent-sounding groups as The Irish Literary Society of 1892. Whether this anthology would please modern day Sinn Fein or the DUP remains part of the ongoing Irish question.

Their correspondence begins in 1950 when Glasheen was thirty and Wilder fifty-three. He was the successful workhorse of a writer, twice Pulitzer prize-winner and professor at Harvard. He had caught the Joyce bug as a young man and campaigned in the hope that his hero might get a Nobel prize for financial reasons; and eventually joined the league of persons, mostly Americans, who became fundraisers at one time or another. Joyce's ability at finding patrons annoys people to this day.

Glasheen (1920-1993) was a humbler drudge into Joyceana than Wilder but one who would thrive over twenty years with two revised and expanded versions of *A Census of Finnegans Wake* and a belated celebrity as a high priestess of the cult. The two hundred plus letters over twenty-five years show two critics investigating and in the process unravelling the guts of that bedazzling and infuriating novel, *Finnegans Wake*. Whether one can 'translate' or explain the large bulk of obscurity within the Wake is highly debatable. The difference between agony and enjoyment over the text is apparent on every page, however, unless one has done the ecstatic and pleasurable hard labour reading the novel, these letters will be even more of a mystery.

Wilder constantly exhibits his frustration with the novel as he swears never to open it again and goes off to pursue his writing career, but one feels with a desultory hopelessness at times that he will never reach the literary pinnacle that Joyce achieved. There is something vulgar and naive about Wilder's implication through his obsession that Joyce's book contains the riddle of the universe and that patient study in defiance of frustration and fatigue will unlock it. He almost converted Robert Lowell and Cleanth Brooks to the quest but didn't have to in the case of Hugh Kenner, Fritz Senn and many others.

Glasheen is stolid in persistence and one can see how she unearthed her first nuts of knowledge, such as Joyce's use of The Book of the Dead and other sources all fully fleshed out here with copious notes by the editors. But their mutual need to know the mystery persisted; Wilder comments that one of its many named persons, Finn "dreams the book"; furthermore, he asserts the importance of Mallarmé and De Sade but since Joyce lists a veritable phonebook of names from all history who knows the precedence of anyone over anyone else? Suddenly after years of digging like the hen mentioned in the novel, Glasheen announces: "FW is a book about Shakespeare. He is the dreamer." Her theory is, however, compelling. Wilder asserts that the Joyce family is "in the forefront of the book". Twenty-four years into their combined excavations, Wilder exclaims: "we're still picking up pieces of lint, not mapping the book!" Wilder goes back to reading it and later declares, "Resurrection is the theme of the book". He naturally begins to loathe Joyce, finding in the text that "he sneers at Goethe, sneers at Shakespeare". Similarly Glasheen pronounces, "Ulysses scares me rather. It is at heart a very very cold book. FW (excuse me mentioning it) is lots warmer".

However they are no warmer in solving its supposed riddle but wait . . . In Appendix III, Wilder exclaims, "The entire book is based upon—or accorded to—the Service of the Mass." Glasheen decides that: "Finnegans Wake poses an overall uncertainty—are the characters acting in a divine or a human Mystery play? Is the author God? Shakespeare?" Meanwhile her opinions change over the years, latterly she comments, "Ulysses moreover, is an encyclopaedic collection of elegant technical demonstrations of precisely How To Do It." Joyce is rightfully registered as a classic to be read and considered and contemplated. The appendices about the Joyce descendants and their appendages make spicy family gossip; Stephen Joyce, the grandson, is shown to be allergic to academics. His mother Helen Kastor-Joyce, divorced from Giorgio Joyce, the son, is shown as a painful case. Her brother, Al Kastor is a boor, but a truth-teller about his sister, and hater of her father-in-law; he is worth quoting with the proviso that such familial wrangling is already contained in Finnegans Wake, "James Joyce was an alcoholic, a sponger and a son of a bitch. I told Helen so. She was in love with him, not with Giorgio." And Joyce himself had such faith in the family notwithstanding all those statements to the contrary in his early works.

—*Books Ireland* 2001

STREET ANGEL

John Stanislaus Joyce: The Voluminous Life and Genius of James Joyce's Father John Wyse Jackson and Peter Costello (Fourth Estate)

James Joyce's Ireland David Pierce (Yale University Press)

James Joyce: Reflections of Ireland by Bernard McCabe and Alain Le Garsmeur (Little, Brown)

James Joyce never found better fictional characters than himself and his father, John Stanislaus Joyce. Joyce boasted about the portrayal of the ordinary man in *Ulysses*. This is very much a biography of an ordinary man who fathered a famous writer. John Stanislaus Joyce may well have been the main inspiration for Leopold Bloom, Simon Dedalus and H. C. Earwicker. In *Finnegans Wake* the recurring story of the Cad and Earwicker is derived from an incident which happened to John Joyce crossing the Phoenix Park. He was jostled, mugged and robbed of a week's takings as a rates collector. It is also believed that he invented the incident to account for the missing cash. That was his story, and like a thief or a novelist, he was sticking to it.

This hefty book which is full of Irish history has a genealogy of Joyce ancestry; including not least the author of *The Boys of Wexford,* Robert Dwyer Joyce and Patrick Weston Joyce, author of *Irish Names and Places*. John Joyce was the only son of an only son, James Augustine, who married Ellen O'Connell, a distant relative of Daniel O'Connell. John Joyce was born on the fourth of July, eighteen forty-nine. His earliest school cannot be located accurately but he did attend St Colman's, Fermoy—a long way for an only child from his native Cork city. Presiding over St Colman's Diocesan College was none other than the famous Dr Croke. They sat beside each other in the refectory apparently.

His father died aged forty, and shortly afterwards John abandoned his vocation. He went to study medicine at Queen's College, Cork. He never qualified and got syphilis. The biography digresses on Bassereau's distinction between hard and soft chancre in syphilis. John Joyce cured his soft chancre with carbolic acid. Elementary medical studies had stood him in good stead. He acted with the college dramatic society, playing a stage Irishman and the lead role in another farce earning plaudits from the local press, who said he was a considerable actor. He ran off from college to join the French in the Franco-Prussian War. His mother set out in pursuit and brought him back from London.

John Joyce began wooing Hanna Sullivan, a Miss Justice from Youghal and later on, Annie Lee. His repertoire included the popular song 'Tim Finnegan's Wake'. During his life he worshipped the great singers of the period: Campanini, Therese Caroline Tietjens, Joseph Maas, Sims Reeves, John McCormack, and would claim that Barton McGuckin, on hearing him sing, said he'd the best voice in Ireland. Through his prosperous relatives, the O'Connells, he gained experience which got him a job as secretary to a distilling company in Chapelizod. He lost the job and his share capital which was half of his inherited fortune. The Liberal Club at 54 Dawson Street made him secretary. He claimed "I won the election in Dublin". Sure enough the Liberal and Home Rule candidates defeated the Conservatives in the election of 1880, with John Joyce an ardent campaigner. He would constantly recall the night of the election when he drank champagne and received huge cash handouts. By then he had begun courting May Murray, whose mother along with his own mother disapproved. In Rathmines Church the groom was ten years older than his twenty-year-old bride. John Joyce's mother returned to Cork shortly after the wedding. The first born, a son, lived eight days. When John Joyce's mother died, he found himself rich and so James Joyce was born in fashionable Rathgar at 41 Brighton

Square. May Joyce's third pregnancy ended in a still birth. Though never in regular employment, he would father six children by the age of forty and become 'a street angel and house devil'. May Joyce wanted no more of their marriage by then, due to his excessive drinking and his vanity. He kept photographs of old flames on top of the piano until the maid threw them into the fire.

Jack B. Yeats remembered the incident at a public meeting in Leinster Hall, when John Joyce shouted at Tim Healy, "You're an impostor! You're only waiting for the moment to betray him!" John Joyce was at one of the scuffles between Parnellites and Anti-Parnellites in Dublin, after the London vote which began Parnell's downfall. A few weeks after the funeral of Charles Stewart Parnell, May Joyce gave birth to her ninth child and the family had to abandon their house, Leoville in Blackrock, for less salubrious surroundings in Hardwicke Street. There followed many changes of address, often unbeknowst to the landlord. In a drunken fit, he attempted to strangle his wife. After a police warning, he was never physically violent towards her again, but continued the verbal abuse, usually while drunk. Her mainstay was her sister Josephine Murray whom John Joyce hated but not as much as he hated her husband, Willie Murray. Losing his job as rent-collector but luckily not his pension rights, he found employment with *Thom's Directory*—a badly paid job. Then their son Georgie, aged fifteen, died of peritonitis. John Joyce had given up drink for days and stayed by the boy's bedside.

His wife died, aged forty-four at St Peter's Terrace, Phibsboro. After yet another harrowing move the widower rented a house in Cabra. There were ten children. He was fifty-four. His oldest son, James, was twenty-one and the youngest, who suffered extreme grief reactions which only James could sooth, was nine. When the young daughter saw the ghost of their dead mother, James also began to see it and was plagued with nightmares involving 'the skull'. The father and his oldest sons, James and Stanislaus, took to the drink and there were terrible drunken arguments at the house. It was little wonder that James left Ireland with Nora Barnacle. Stanislaus soon followed them. Meanwhile John Joyce drank with anyone who could pay, including detractors of James such as Oliver Gogarty and Vincent Cosgrave. Around this time another son, Charlie, kept a diary which is a horror of drunken misconduct and excess by the alcoholic father, listing his improvidence, the awful ructions and near-fatal disasters. His catch-cries drunk or sober were, 'Shite and onions'; 'Jesus wept, and no wonder by Christ'; and 'Agonising Christ, wouldn't it give you a heartburn on your arse.'

When James returned from Europe briefly, a father himself of two children, he was reconciled with John Joyce in a pub in Rathfarnham, the Yellow House. They drank and enjoyed a singsong in an anteroom which had two pianos. James went back to Trieste and brought his sister Eva to help mind the children. John Joyce's youngest daughter, Mabel, died aged seventeen. Nora Barnacle came on a visit home to Ireland and gave George Roberts a tongue-lashing for delaying the publication of *Dubliners* with Maunsel & Co. "The episode did not endear John to Nora."

James Joyce arrived on the scene with his son Giorgio and the results were even worse; "The unbound sheets were beheaded [and] the 125,000 odd pages" used as wrapping around other books. So much for the first Irish edition of *Dubliners* in 1912. When James, Nora and both children left for Europe, father and son would never meet again.

Willie Murray, aunt Josephine's husband, died of GPI "the third dreadful stage of syphilis" and John Joyce made a will referring to himself as "Retired Rate Collector". He was never a great admirer of his son's works; *Dubliners* he thought was mis-titled, it should have been 'Dublinmen' and was otherwise "a blackguard production"; *Ulysses* was the work of "a nice sort of blackguard". James Joyce craved the approval of his father but didn't criticise him publicly. "The humour of *Ulysses* is his; its people are his friends." "Hundreds of pages and scores of characters in my books came from him". John Joyce separated from his children and they married or fended for themselves while he "may briefly have sampled complete destitution". Ever a feckless survivor, he became a lodger with the Medcalfs in Drumcondra, his final abode after so many peregrinations and changes of house, over and back across the Liffey. His son Charlie carried on the Joycean fecundity, fathering eight children by 1920 and at that time living in rooms in North Great Georges Street.

James Joyce sent a surrogate son in the person of Patrick J Tuohy, the artist with a withered arm, who painted a portrait of John Joyce, which won a bronze medal in the Tailteann Games. Sir John Lavery made the award. The portrait was reproduced in *The Dublin Magazine* and *The Irish Times.* Tuohy, a perfectionist, required endless sittings which suited his subject who was al-most bedridden. They shared a great interest in music. The portrait was exhibited at the Royal Academy in London and afterwards went on tour to America. John Joyce was sought out by many others during his retirement at Medcalf's in Claude Road—Robert McAlmon, Flann O'Brien and Niall Sheridan.

James Joyce never broke the final vow of exile which forbade his ever visiting Dublin again. Instead, he periodically sent the pub-lished writings and a gramophone record of his voice reading pages 136-7 of *Ulysses* for John Joyce, whose last known remark was, "Tell Jim he was born at six in the morning." James's sister Eileen sent a telegram to the famous writer in Paris, "Pappie dying". James sent telegrams and made phone calls to doctors requesting the fullest medical help for his father. Years earlier when John Joyce had sent a telegram to him as a young man in Paris with a misprint of the word 'mother', 'NOTHER DYING COME HOME FATHER', James had rushed home. In the nineteen thirties, Joyce had a myth to maintain. He shared a taxi in Paris with Thomas McGreevy on the day he got news of John Joyce's death. McGreevy reports, "When we reached the entrance to the Metro at the Trocadero, however, Joyce said, 'Don't go just yet.' I waited. He began to talk but suddenly he broke down. He cried and cried and cried for several minutes . . ."

John Joyce was eighty-two when he died. He was survived by eight offspring. James sent a wreath of ivy. John Joyce's belongings included signed copies of his son's works which were stolen by journalists from the Medcalfs in Drumcondra—all except a copy of *Exiles,* covered in candlewax. His favourite son, James, was the sole beneficiary under the estate which came to a round total of £36.12s.1 d. It cost about half of that to bury him and erect a headstone in Glasnevin. Joyce "told Eugene Jolas that he could hear his father talking to him. 'I wonder where he is,' he said." Among the closing lines of his last book, *Finnegans Wake,* are, "it's sad and weary I go back to you, my cold father, my cold mad father, my cold mad faery father".

Without making any odious comparison, Pierce's book is far better than the McCabe and Le Garsmeur one. Alain Le Garsmeur's photographs are good without being too arty. He is equally expert in colour and black-and-white. *Finnegans Wake* is so all inconclusively referential, that almost any Irish scene can fit as a photographic image from the text or for the text. Sometimes the photos disregard their format of being a visual for a textual reference, so any café in contemporary Dublin represents the Burton restaurant. Most textual references are still available for photography such as Sandymount Strand, the National Library, Trinity College, Clongowes Wood College, the Phoenix Park, Mulligans Pub and St Stephen's Green. McCabe's textual extracts aren't lengthy enough to put a voracious reader to sleep. You may find that both of your arms are flexed when opening the book full length—so it is exacting bedtime browsing, unless you are a very slow reader who needs a lot of exercise.

If you are ever stopped in any part of Ireland and questioned about James Joyce by someone who has never read him and who desperately wants to read about him, you could recommend Pierce's giant-sized paperback. Good value, hard wearing and scholarly, without revealing a life spent reading Joyce. His text is engaging, almost stunning. The approach seems eccentric, even digressive on Thomas Moore and Joyce, Parnell and Joyce but take another look. This is not to detract from Pierce as a legitimate critic, except he does tend to treat *Ulysses* as a roman-a-clef. Still, his interpretations generally sound plausible and he probably doesn't imply that Joyce can be explained and exposed, found out and that's that as it were. Pierce's text obviously gave the lead to Dan Harper's few photographs and the proliferation of illustrations and photographic reproductions—not all of James Joyce, but including good ones of Nora Barnacle; the clairvoyant and unstable daughter, Lucia; Harriet Shaw Weaver, an English patroness; Davy Stephens, the legendary newspaper-seller who figures in 'Circe'; Michael Cusack, Italo Svevo, Erskine Childers, plus Samuel Beckett and Thomas MacGreevy photographed together. The combination of words and pictures is the secret ingredient of the book. Otherwise, it has two valuable appendices. A chronology of the life and times in I, and II with brief biographies of family members, friends and contemporaries. And the book passes the bedtime reading test which its companion narrowly failed.

—*Books Ireland* 1998

PROSPECTOR'S LUCK

Talking of Joyce Umberto Eco and Liberato Santoro-Brienza (University College Dublin Press)

Reading Joyce Politically Trevor L. Williams (University Press of Florida)

Irish Poetry after Joyce Dillon Johnston (Syracuse University Press)

Joycean Cultures / Culturing Joyces Vincent J. Cheng (University of Delaware Press)

Samuel Beckett's hidden drives: structural uses of depth psychology J. D. O'Hara (University Press of Florida)

The introduction is by J. C. C. Mays to the texts of two lectures on 'the Dante of Dublin' (Gogarty's nickname for Joyce). Umberto Eco's *The Aesthetics of Chaosmos* (1982) is a forerunner of his lecture 'A Portrait of the Artist as a Bachelor' of Arts. Joyce's exam results were not great in academic terms! Eco traces his "quest for a perfect language . . . the lost perfection of the language of Ailam" with Dante Alighieri's 'noble vernacular' *in* mind which the Florentine poet favoured over Latin. Eco refers to the seventh century *Auraicept* composed in Gaelic by the seventy-two wise men of the school of Fenius Farrsaid, a precursor of Esperanto inspired by Isaiah, "I shall come, that I will gather all nations and tongues." Eco finds Joyce lacking with regard to medieval philosophy. He claims that *Finnegan Wake* was in defiance of St Jerome's tirade on the 'witchcraft of words' and is the verbal equivalent of the Book of Kells. The decision "to start *Ulysses* from the top of a tower was an unconscious prefigurement of Joyce's final purpose of forging a *polygluttural* and *multilingual instrument* of communication". When everyone begins speaking like the characters in the *Wake,* will the Joyceans inherit the earth?

If Liberato Santoro-Brienza's lecture Joyce's Dialogue with Aquinas,

Dante, Bruno, Vico, Svevo was the starting point for a critical book he would have his work well and truly cut out for the forseeable future. He recounts Joyce's hostility to Rome where there is a plaque to the Irish writer at No. 52 Via Frattina, "Rome reminds me of a man who lives by exhibiting to travellers his grandmother's corpse." Professor Santoro-Brienza finds Joyce *antipatico*. Joyce's prose is contrasted with the Neapolitan philosopher Vico and his concept of 'visual thinking'. The Joyce-Svevo relationship is convivially discussed. Joyce discovered the Italian writer utterly neglected and became his tutor in English. In time Joyce made Svevo's novels famous. Stanislaus Joyce introduced Svevo's *Senilita:* "it may not be too far-fetched to see in the person of Bloom Svevo's maturer, objective, peaceable temper reacting upon the young man's fiery mettle." Svevo's wife Livia had "long and reddish blond" hair which reminded Joyce of the Liffey. She picked a bunch of flowers for Joyce after he read out his story 'The Dead'. Joyce lived in Trieste at Piazza Giambattista Vico but the Vico Road in Dalkey is not named after the author of *Scienza Nuova* (Joyce thought it was). The beautiful Dalkey highroad takes its name from a town near Sorrento called Vico Equense.

Williams has an anecdote about lecturing with the Gabler Penguin *Ulysses* during *the* Gulf War when a student asked why bother with Joyce? This book might well be his full reply. Williams is worth reading for his political viewpoint, "In my war alerted classroom it was the easiest of tasks to point out the extent to which the media, in accepting the Pentagon's binary *view* of reality, were prepared to censor themselves." His epilogue says that the Joyce industry reflects the market competition of capitalism with many competing versions of *Ulysses* on sale. He is rightly concerned, in Marcuse's phrase about forces in society that "close down the universe of discourse". He is self-*critical* about critics like himself who use "a literary text to put across personal views, but are not willing to perform in public this ideological undressing, this unmasking of one's agenda: there is rarely any kudos to be obtained in any walk of life by pointing out that the emperor's new suit of clothes is not quite as advertised."

There is a *fine* chapter on the history of Joyce criticism from Georg Lukács and Karl Radek on through R. D. Charques who thought *Ulysses* was "a sustained onslaught on bourgeois aesthetic values delivered by a method which is itself the logical culmination of bourgeois culture". Sergei Eisenstein like Alick West admired the use of interior monologue to "hypnotise the reader into feeling that this kind of consciousness is the only thing that is real". Ilya Ehrenbourg called Joyce "un ecrivain pour ecrivains" (a writer's writer). Philippe Sollers said he "opposed the fascism of his era with the powerful vehicle of humour". This was scoffed at by a panelist at the 1975 Joyce Symposium: "Perhaps the people of Auschwitz didn't have enough humour." Hugh Kenner claimed, "Joyce published hardly a sentence that does not offer some word to be aware of." Unfortunately there is glancing reference to Wyndham Lewis, a considerable novelist himself who wrote the earliest anti-Joycean critique in *Time and Western Man* (1927).

Williams mentions Irish critics on Joyce: Seamus Deane's "myth of defeat" and "cultural inferiority"; W. J. McCormack's "displacement of Gaelic by English as the vernacular language" and Terry Eagleton's "unepiphanic non-event" concerning the meeting of Stephen and Bloom. Williams usually makes good sense, "the Homeric correspondences usually require pedantic demonstration". *Dubliners* is "a gallery of human wrecks". "Bloom's contention that the 'hungry man is an angry man' unites Joyce and Marx to expose 'religion's complicity with the state in producing an inverted sense of reality". "He also finds that Stephen's phrase about trying to wake up from the nightmare of history, is from Marx who called history a nightmare on the brain of the living and also finds a chunk of Walter Benjamin similar to Bloom's thoughts. The references to Sydney Olivier's *White Capital and Coloured Labour* (1906) which uses the title of

Kipling's poem "White Man's Burden" is dubiously thrown in to add more fuel to the controversy about Conrad's *Heart of Darkness* highlighted by Edward Said and Chinua Achebe.

First published in 1985 the second edition offers a new preface and an afterword. The chapters couple-off poets such as Clarke & Kinsella; Kavanagh & Heaney; Devlin & Montague; MacNeice and Mahon which seem like marriages made in heaven except that the living spouses may not be able to report blissful unions in terms of finding themselves paired off because of assumed similarities. Johnston shows Clarke's use of sexual fantasy in *Tiresias* but shirks on lengthy discussion of *Mnemosyne Lay in Dust*. He is convincing about sexual guilt in Clarke's work and interesting on Kinsella's sequence "The Messenger". Heaney's praise of Kinsella is quoted: "his treatment of psychic material which is utterly Irish Catholic." Johnston praises and damns Heaney but likes *Station Island* and the translation from Dante about Count Ugolino in the tower from *Field Work*. Devlin is linked to John Donne—a marvellous comparison in the light of Donne's 'Ecstasy'. Montague is hailed for a lyric such as 'The Well Dreams' or a love poem 'Tracks'. Montague claims, "The real position for a poet is to be a global-regionalist."

MacNeice is seen as a master of the political poem based on Yeats's influence. *Autumn Journal* in quotation is always impressive. Mahon, called another searcher of the otherworld which Johnston labels *Tír na Mna* in his case, with the implication that Mahon's Byzantium makes the poet "an atom to a Universe". Mahon who can turn it on in a poem 'The Sea in Winter' is back in form with recent collections much in the MacNeice *Autumn Journal, Autumn Sequel* line. Johnston's book left this reader pigeonholing poets but sent him back to many such as Richard Murphy's 'Seals at High Island' and Paul Muldoon's 'Gathering Mushrooms'. The afterword attempts the impossible, giving a survey of the contemporary scene including poetry in English versus poetry as Gaeilge. Overall it fails miserably to address the actual politics of the Public Poetry Scene still prevailing long after Cyril Connolly detected its enduring atmosphere "as warm and friendly as an alligator tank". The best quotes are usually from Kavanagh, "There is something of the prospector's luck about a great poet's success."

Fourteen essays sounds like too many but each is brief and compacted. This reader absorbed them randomly but it may be less confusing to comment on them successively if generally. Christine van Boheemen's is about sexuality in Joyce and getting beyond the body. She does not label him a phallocrat. Clara D. McLean in an excellent essay finds Bloom "sexually paralyzed by his fear of his own bodily interiors". Harly Ramsey digs deeper using *Ulysses,* Freud and Julia Kristeva to study the connection between melancholy, depression and sexuality: "Bloom assumes a position culturally identified as 'feminine'." The conclusions are based on Bloom in Circe. Bonnie Kime Scott is almost as steamy as her colleagues when discussing the Jane Heap letters to Florence Reynolds published in the *Little Review* when Joyce's novel was on trial in the US. The essay speculates on the quality of orgasm between Gerty and Bloom during the latter's voyeurism on Sandymount Strand. Carol Loeb Shloss gets this reader's first prize. She is currently completing *Lucia : to Dance in the Wake,* the biography of Lucia Joyce's 'Madness in Progress'. Her essay augurs well for what may be a magnificent book because of the prose of conveyance. The excerpts from psychiatric literature are essential for the subject. Alison Leslie Gold wrote an experimental novel *The Clairvoyant* about Lucia who wrote to Joyce, "If I should ever go away, it would be to a country which belongs in a way to you, isn't that true father?" Naturally, Carl Jung, one of Lucia's doctors, is quoted, "To say that insanity is a dream which has become real is no metaphor." Susan Stanford Friedman, (her name puns!) pursues Joyce as loyal feminist or not? John Whittier-Ferguson tackles Joyce's reactions to the Irish Rebellion of 1916, World War I and politics in general. R. B. Kershner's excellent essay flagellates Denis Donoghue in the notes and brings together Kenner, Sacher Masoch, (Circe is based broadly on the latter's *Venus in Furs)* Horkheimer and Adorno who both claim that Culture is a paradoxical commodity. So completely is it subject to the law of exchange that it is no longer exchanged; it is so blindly consumed in use that it can no longer be used. Therefore it amalgamates with advertising.

Catherine Whitley gives a nod to Declan Kiberd to help her dissect the Ballad in chapter two of *Finnegans Wake*. Erika Anne Flesher examines the work of illustrators for Joyce: Cober, Hamilton and Motherwell. Samples from the artists are reproduced. Irene A. Martyniuk beats a similar path but may get more attention with samples from Joyce's buddy Frank Budgen, courtesy of Indiana University Press. The example of Joyce's own sketch for Bloom ranks him about as good as Bernard Shaw at drawing. Cheryl Temple Herr develops a tough political theme with the use of Allen Feldman's study of terrorism in Northern Ireland. However to be critical, it all becomes gorblimey including David Seymour's paintings. This is no reflection on Seymour's art but let's face it, if Joyce relates to everything and everything to Joyce, is criticism entering the shadowlands of Lucia Joyce? Benjamin Harder might well be accused of accentuating the sexual in a discussion of Stephen's ashplant. Topping off this collection is Mark Osteen who contemplates hats from Joyce's life, contacts and works. The illustrations are good fun. Bloom's hat "radiates both the resilient dignity of Charlie Chaplin and the self-aware wit of Oscar Wilde."

As literary detective James Donald O'Hara is ably assisted by Freud ("Love is homesickness"), Jung ("the mother is the first world of the child and the last world of the adult"), Rank ("the experience of being born causes our first anxiety") and especially Beckett's *Molloy*—"*an* inadvertent satire of Jungian mythology?" Molloy "wants to resuscitate the torpid bliss and effortlessness of childhood." Molloy is like Leopardi saying, "I don't know why and I don't want to." Molloy, and Moran the character in part two of the novel, are analysed in terms of narcissism and neurosis. Surprisingly there is no mention of Wilfred Rupert Bion with whom Beckett had two years of therapy, while good use is made of Beckett's comments in interviews and otherwise. "In the quarrel between Freud and Jung, I sided with Freud." On art: "form will be of such a type that it admits the chaos and does not try to say that the chaos is really something else." To Gabriel D'Aubarede he talked of his anti-intellectual and anti-philosophical stance. Israel Shenker found him moody in saying, "The kind of work I do is one in which I'm not the master of my material, I'm working with ignorance."

Emphasis is placed on Beckett's *Proust,* "the heart of the cauliflower or the ideal core of the onion would represent a more appropriate tribute to the labours of poetical excavation than the crown of bay." O'Hara finds this comic and adds, "The core of the onion may evoke tears, but it certainly does not suggest hidden knowledge." Beckett according to O'Hara equated the psyche to an onion and rejected "the position of the writer who knows all about his characters and about life." O'Hara writes well about Beckett's *oeuvre* which is still a breath of fresh art when a lot of fiction seems to be so easily explained in some quarters that it is a wonder it had to be written at *all* in the first place. O'Hara's 'conclusion' recalls a meeting with Beckett and after attempts to lighten the atmosphere by remarking that many "found positive value in his writings. He was not mollified. 'They find in them something that I do not,' he said."

—*Books Ireland* 1998

SHEMITE

Conversations with James Joyce Arthur Power
(Lilliput)

James Joyce's Judaic Other Marilyn Reizbaum
(Stanford University Press)

The Supreme Fictions of John Banville Joseph
McMinn (Manchester University Press)

This book (originally published in 1974) can be read
pleasurably at a sitting and if there was a sequel you would
want to rush out in search of it but alas you cannot. The book
is highly studied and mannered, and benefits greatly from this
when one thinks of Ellmann's much praised tome on Joyce
which is in fact a lesser product than the slim volume under
review. Power knew his Plutarch and there is no better source
model for constructing a short biography, not least since
Shakespeare rifled the same Roman to infamous effect for
Julius Caesar, Coriolanus and other historical personages.

Lilliput have swelled out the format with the original
foreword from Clive Hart and a new one from David Norris
who provides his usual cheery performance—it may as well
be said that the Senator is one of the legion of Joyceans who in
part owe their livelihood to James Joyce. Power, like the few
genuine Irish friends of Joyce, when repatriated to Ireland from
Paris kept a very low profile about his friendship with the
master and not at all for reasons of their estrangement. On
their final meeting in London he made two fatal errors:
inviting Joyce to a restaurant where the food was pretty bland
and afterwards refusing to acknowledge that the birth of
a Joyce grandson was a momentous event.

Power's details are artfully delineated and *serve* the higher purpose
of his structure. Since he basked in the presence of the Irish genius

he obviously learned respect for prose composition as a mysterious discipline though it is usually touted around in terms of a pastime which engages like an average day's work. Joyce is shown as a drinker of Saint Patrice wine but "not a conversationalist". The impression wrongly given by Ellmann is one of a drunken speechmaker but of course Ellmann never met his subject. Similarly Joyce is presented as vehemently against making a show of himself and scorning notoriety in the manner which Beckett adopted much later in the twentieth century. Joyce was artistically opposed to Chekov and Synge. He castigated the latter, whose plays were 'romantic fantasy' where the "characters only exist on the Abbey stage". His favourite dramatists as one might expect were Shakespeare and Ibsen.

He is described as being largely indifferent to his adopted Paris, haunted by Dublin and explicit philosophically: "I don't think much of this life." He hardly rated any of his contemporaries including George Moore and highly ranked *The Brothers Karamazov* and Hemingway's story 'A Clean Well Lighted Place' as pinnacles of literary achievement. He admired Eliot, Proust and Gide but totally disregarded Picasso, Matisse and Braque. Ballet bored him.

Power's studio was in the rue de la Grande Chaumiere, next door to where Modigliani worked and died. When he invited Joyce to a party there, the Irish writer was miffed by Patrick Tuohy, the painter who clapped and mocked as he entered. Joyce never forgot the occasion and kept a stony silence during the event such as it was. Jo (spelt Jo by Power) Davidson another painter also heckled Joyce by implying that his silence meant he was burnt out, "It has all gone into his book" *(Ulysses)*. Power is excellent in conveying the subterranean unpleasantness of literary gatherings, their actual undercurrent of nastiness masquerading in some assumed moral high ground of discussion with exalted contents. Joyce is seen as survivor and 'literary conspirator' through his life and writings and though destined by chance rather than contacts to achieve fame he clung to family and a few friends as sufficient human intercourse when he could have wined and dined with virtually anyone and everyone.

Naturally one pounces on his utterances about *Ulysses,* "fundamentally a humorous work", "smells of the Dublin of my day ... its degradations and its exaltations"; "I suppose my work is middle class." Power presents a writer whose original genius "lies in his scribblings" and at the close of endless struggles remained certain of the influence of his art. Only a fool would dismiss this dense cogent study from an insider, examining Joyce's assumed Jewishness in creating the character of Leopold Bloom. First off Reizbaum is not longwinded: her book is brief and yet covers a very wide area with immense erudition and not a hint of pedantry.

The fact that her subject is highly serious about Jew and Gentile in major portions of *Ulysses* makes it all the more intriguing. En passant she refers to her Joycean credentials which date from the convivial and communal seminar in Zurich twenty years ago with the more sombre addition that the book is dedicated to her parents, Rose Grynshpan Reizbaum and Max Reizbaum, holocaust survivors.

With the myriad-minded author of the voluminous *Ulysses* she has to plump for a thesis tag and finds it in Bloom's 'ostensible defense of his Jewishness' and at the same time his denial of it to Stephen Dedalus. Otherwise the book pivots around two confrontational scenes from *Ulysses:* Stephen with Deasy and Bloom with the Citizen. She leaves aside the easy reference to noble Jews in literature: Daniel Deronda and Scott's Rebecca in *Ivanhoe* and ignoble Jews such as Shylock and Fagin in order to explore some precursors for Joyce such as Nietzsche, Freud and Otto Weininger, who is presented as hugely scared of his feminine side as shown by quotes from his *Sex and Character.*

A good list of sources for Joyce's knowledge about Jewish lifestyles is given, such as Carlo Cattaneo and naturally Italo Svevo and not least Irish antisemitism involving a certain Father John Creagh against the Jews of Limerick. What is wonderful is her

535

exposition of Nietzsche with many quotations absolving him from antisemitism, "The Jews, however, are beyond any doubt the strongest, toughest and purest race . . ." Meanwhile she cites critics of Joyce such as Steven Conor who finds him "not Jewish enough".

She is self-deprecating about interpreting the Circe episode but goes on to provide her best chapter. After all it is one of the funniest pieces of twentieth-century theatre surprisingly rammed into a lengthy novel; so when she quotes Dr Dixon reading Bloom's bill of health it's quite easy to shake with noisy laughter. Her use of Freud is calm and avoids being doctrinaire; however she manages to insert the Schreber case which fascinated both himself and Jung. Then she applies this case history to the feminisation and perversion of Bloom. Her conclusions about the closing three chapters of *Ulysses are* the quietest parts of her text. On reflection they sound lax except for the crucial understanding by her that Stephen and Bloom only meet for a brief encounter and that there is no promise of a triangular future for them and Molly Bloom as some interpreters posit, post-textually, such as William Empson. In this, one can wholeheartedly approve of Reizbaum's summation.

This will go nicely beside your collection of Banville and also, if you own it, Imhof's critical study. McMinn delivers the goods with a fulsome treatment of all the fiction and in many respects it can be read as a reductive analysis of his subject. The book might well be subtitled 'Banville Bottled or Bottled Banville'. Mr B is sourced in Beckett and Arthur Koestler, in fact he pilfered the essence of Koestler's *The Sleepwalkers* for much of the tetralogy about Copernicus, Kepler, Newton and Mefisto. There is no case law for plagiarists, of course. Steal from the best is the only law. But when it comes to his novels they seem to be an implied codicil to Beckett's monumental trilogy with its unsettling narration and inherent denial of the truth potential of fiction albeit an announcement of the death of the novel, if such were credible. Citations from Wallace Stevens and Nabokov rest uneasily on

Banville but not necessarily certain affinities with Fowles and Eco. Post-modernism and parody are never far off his method and all this is highlighted by McMinn; for instance the opening of *Nightspawn* echoes Keats and Dostoevsky. For some readers these may be blatantly heavy antecedents for beginning a novel but it is all grist to the postmodernist mill, or millstone depending on one's taste in fiction.

Banville is not always quoted to good effect by McMinn and there is nothing Beckettian in the novelist's announcing that in the writing of *Birchwood,* 'I took stock characters', like the end of *Birchwood.* Whether one writer can easily bask in another's aesthetic credo is also the big problem with his continual shadowing of Beckett. McMinn helpfully admits, 'Writing about the futility of writing is, or may become, a tricky business.'

The character who is scared of women is another feature of his fiction and may well be a rehash of a particular Romantic school, 'To try to tell her what he felt would be as superfluous as talking to a picture'. Also yearning for lost childhood and the pastoral landscape of early youth are abiding obsessions. This vision comes across as sickly and unclassical. McMinn faults *Mephisto* as 'difficult and not wholly satisfying' but obviously enjoys Freddie Montgomery who features in a trilogy of novels, best known of which is *The Book of Evidence* because of its Booker listing. As a novel depicting in part the terrain of prison it remains unauthentic to readers who have actually spent time inside. With it Banville entered a profitable phase of plucking much hyped news material for his fiction, in this case the murderer Malcolm Macarthur. Meanwhile the saga of 'the General', Martin Cahill's theft of eleven paintings from Russborough house fuelled the core of *Athena.* Latterly, *The Untouchable* is based on the life and contacts of the spy, Anthony Blunt. *The Untouchable,* according to McMinn can be read as a tale about Oscar Wilde with its evolving melodramatic revelations at the end.

McMinn has four fleeting pages about Banville's plays, a translation from Kleist, entitled *The Broken Jug* which the author humbly calls 'an Ealing comedy' and the self-consciously Beckettian *Seachange* written for RTE. While mentioning Beckett one might as well add Sister Wendy Beckett whose public persona involves books and TV lectures based on paintings of the old masters comparable to Banville's use of visual art in his fiction. McMinn's book reproduces some gems including 'Dürer's Mother' and van der Weyden's 'Portrait of a Lady' on the cover.

Much is made of George Steiner's critique of *The Untouchable* from The *Observer* in which Steiner craved acknowledgement of his own work by Banville; and also the critic with the infamous initials, J. C. C. Mays, who gets on the Banville wagon believing that he is 'Beckett's true inheritor'. However, one is safe in saying that the next monolith of Irish fiction has not been discovered yet or else remains unpublished or largely unknown. While it is possible to admire Banville's method somewhat, he is alas, a practitioner of post-modernism with all its labyrinthine paraphernalia of narrative structure and delving into the encylopaedist's manner with added irony placed on irony and faux naïf all over the text, which may in the end be a launching pad for the imagination but is often a crutch or at its weakest a failure of imagination. That said, McMinn's study is nigh flawless.

—*Books Ireland* 2000

A BIZARRE THEORY THAT MAPS AND LETTERS FROM THE 1830s–40s MIGHT HAVE INSPIRED Joyce, Beckett, Synge and Mangan

The Ordnance Survey and Modern Irish Literature
Cóilín Parsons (Oxford University Press)

Quite extraordinary claims are made that (to put it in actual perspective) the British Board of Ordnance Survey, which began in 1824, 'found creative expression and also opposition' in 'John O'Donovan's capacious antiquarian letters, James Clarence Mangan's dematerializing forms, John Millington Synge's overlapping scales, James Joyce's encyclopedism, and Samuel Beckett's abstract landscapes'.

The book is concerned with examining 'scale' and 'archive', and tells the reader that 'we cannot think scale without thinking archive, for questions of scale were the impetus for creation of archive'. Think 'scale' as on a vast scale and you will sort of grasp what is being discussed. Yes, it's bizarre to theorise that maps, notes and letters from the 1830s and 1840s might have inspired Joyce, Beckett, Synge and Mangan. The definitive primary source is the voluminous OS Letters, which run to 43 volumes. The obtuse argument (invariably given in hectoring tones) is that the Survey 'sets an agenda for representations of landscape and space well into the twentieth century'. While O'Donovan is highlighted and dominates each chapter, Mangan, Synge, Joyce and Beckett are granted a look-in, if forced into tenuous parallelism with the Survey as points of departure for their writings. Bizarre, yes.

The enterprise might have comic potential for a Flann O'Brien/Myles na Gopaleen—he is quoted in the opening, but the book is engaged in LitCrit that is eternally short on laughs. The wodge of wordscape involved is not all agony in the reading and there are the additional pitiable facts about poor old Ireland. The Ordnance Survey remains as one of the disturbing aspects of British imperialism laughed off in Friel's *Translations*.

To cut to the chase: Parsons's thesis committed to book form cannot logically reflect *pari passu* literature and map-making, but of course the book swaggers in the attempt, which is equally disturbing as regards the Academy's credibility in assigning such subject-matter as the world collapses in post-capitalist fallout. However, the Survey's cruel and cold machinations are hinted at if not decisively elaborated. The maps of Ireland by John Speed, William Petty and D.A. Beaufort— barbarous seventeenth- and eighteenth-century cartographers— represent an infamy that cannot ever be sweet. Edward Said's wisdom (quoted) states that 'imperialism after all is an act of geographical violence'. Said is unmuzzled in saying that the goal of the Ordnance Survey included the Anglicisation of names, the redrawing of boundaries, land valuation and to 'permanently subjugate the population'.

The secondary welter of sources has much work to do in the opening chapter, not least discussing the depopulation caused by the Great Famine, with genocide halving the native Irish to 'four million by the close of the decade'. An acceptable historical stance is shown through some consulted sources that disestablish the Survey as primal infamy, such as in Stiofán Ó Cadhla's stating that more is 'to be learned about the surveyor than the surveyed, more about the mammoth metropolis of London than the humble hovels of Galbally'. George Petrie and John O'Donovan understood their limitations as ultimately flawed map-makers. O'Donovan's enthusiasm was tempered with realism 'one hundred years too late' 'to recover the correct names of places' pertaining to 60,000 townlands and, not least, other localities.

Cadhla rightly shows how O'Donovan is also suspect, 'putting in i for e as Bin for Ben', or as in County Down (1834), where Carcullion was desecrated to Kirk-Ullen from the original Gaelic *Carr an Chuillin* ('rugged place of holly'). Ireland still holds thousands of such desecrations. O'Donovan had little cultural conscience and few ethics in dispensing 'a state nomadology' and was remunerated for it all, but according to Parsons was 'an itinerant scholar gathering information' (more accurately called controlled misinformation). For officialdom, as Parsons honestly states, 'the study of history was a dangerous pursuit for a state sanctioned project'. Thus the conniving Chancellor of the Exchequer, Thomas Spring Rice, objected to Larcom's and Colby's local histories that would 'open all the debatable questions in Irish party division'. Pierre Nora is quoted on history, which is defined as 'reconstruction, always problematic and incomplete, of what is no longer'.

The Mangan section is flawed in reading his poetry 'addressed to ruins' as 'a commentary on the Survey's archive'. He was derided by his biographer O'Donoghue, who deemed him 'of slight use', and also, Parsons chimes in, 'not a model employee'. She pursues a well-hallowed list of Mangan's poems that use 'placename lore'. O'Donovan, writing in 1839, is slotted within her argument for using Mangan's 'Lamentation of Mac Liag for Kincora', 'not a trace of it is now visible'. Synge's letter to Spencer Brodney is identified as spawning 'an industry of mining [Synge's] memoir *The Aran Islands* for source material for the plays', which is re-mined rather than new-minted while being contrasted with O'Donovan's lengthy letter about the Aran Islands for the Survey's purposes. Synge's memoir is juvenilia, but of course Parsons files it alongside *A Portrait of the Artist as a Young Man*, quoting P.J.

Mathews with its 'reverse trajectory from Paris to the west of Ireland', which is laughable academic diatribe. Establishing that Synge read O'Donovan's letter is one thing, but implying that Synge found the islands exotic is also laughable, because his dramatic characters are not Atlantic-shelf rustic simpletons.

Parsons goes on to drown in obfuscation, finding modernity alien among island folks who are rather premodern: 'modernity as an experience that is both proleptic and analeptic, disturbing…anticipatory and restorative'. Obfuscation is prevalent as literary terms are placed on parade. Thus Synge's parataxis (not a form of island transport) is defined via Theodor Adorno as 'a cubism of language'—close to Parsons's usage. The link between Joyce and the Survey is based not so much on *Ulysses*, which is described as largely 'maniacal', as on a sole claim that his first biographer, Frank Budgen, felt that Joyce was 'surveying and mapping Ireland'. *Ulysses* is stolidly disliked with its 'virtuosic excesses', the Cyclops chapter for its 'quantity of detail'. Frederic Jameson is quoted on Cyclops and Eumaeus as 'the two most boring chapters'. The novel is dismissed as encyclopaedic and aligned with Diderot and D'Alembert, whose *Encyclopédie* was 'a kind of world map'. Joyce's boast of *Ulysses* being a potential reconstruction map for Dublin is seen as 'disingenuous', since the Ordnance Survey map alone could 'rebuild the fallen city'.

Beckett is consigned to her epilogue. Dealing with a few stories from *More Pricks than Kicks* makes for brief mention of landscapes not requiring any knowledge of any map. Eoin O'Brien's *The Beckett Country* displays photographs of places 'alluded to, and often erased in Beckett's works'. Parsons has to grapple with reality. Therefore Petrie's letter to Larcom is cited in full, and how O'Donovan and Curry toured the Dublin mountains, finding 'a grand example of a cromleac in its original state concealed beneath a tumulus of earth'. In as much as she quotes the surveyors, she eventually sounds like Flann O'Brien's 'Keats and Chapman' trying to find a work of literature on a map. Beckett as literary quantity surveyor is postulated thus: 'even before the famine, which Joseph Roach identifies as haunting the world of *Godot*, the landscape of Ireland is seen by its cartographers as crosshatched with the markings of modernity'. The whole argument really breaks down at this point because *Waiting for Godot*, as the world knows, is set in no recognisable location. The text of the play specifically states: 'A country road. A tree. Evening.' Estragon is quoted rebuking Vladimir: 'You and your landscapes! Tell me about the worms!' Indeed.

Still, Beckett in *More Pricks* has 'a cartographic view', with Wicklow 'full of breasts and pimples', which according to Parsons 'is unspeakable'. The comic element is of course lost in pursuit of the argument of the Ordnance Survey as precursor for literature. Maps generally evoke no comedy. Beckett's Molloy is not involved in any sort of Ordnance Survey. Parsons is closer to the mark in quoting Molloy as devoid of any mapping propensities, 'and don't come talking at me of the stars, they look all the same to me, yes, I cannot read the stars, in spite of my astronomical studies'. Therefore, to protest for Molloy's cartography in the novel is spurious and ridiculous, as in 'when you mean Bally plus its domains and Ballyba when you mean the domains exclusive of Bally itself' demonstrating that 'there are clearly echoes here of the Ordnance Survey'. Her argument, of course, is that the Survey's 'maps were not just modern but modernist'. The book demands 'a new furrow in the field of space and place-based studies of Irish literature' and for 'the longer-term cultural impact of mapping projects', as well as for 'the rich tradition of topographic poetry and political critique'. LitCrit's wobbly post-Joycean departure: 'A Portrait of the Artist as an Ordnance Survey Map', perhaps?

—*Books Ireland* 2016

UNCROWNED

Parnell Reconsidered eds. Pauric Travers & Donal McCartney (University College Dublin Press)

Parnell—a novel Brian Cregan (Blackwell's)

Travers (two essays) & McCartney (three essays) amidst the other six contributors present Charles Stewart Parnell through polemical discussions that investigate major events in his life. McCartney sets Home Rule as the Irish El Dorado against the following background of 'the three Home Rule Bills of 1886, 1893 and 1912 proposed to confer on Ireland considerably less autonomy than that attained by the independent colonies of Canada, Australia, New Zealand or South Africa'. He establishes 'what Parnell meant by Home Rule'—it being akin to Repeal: 'I have been looking through a mental microscope but I can find none [different] between them' His assessment of the sexual scandal avoids the Victorian ethos, and instead highlights two other sexual dalliances prior to the liaison with (Mrs) Katharine O'Shea. McCartney concludes echoing Yeats: 'The bishops and the Party/That tragic story made'. Parnell is pitted against fate to please 'the Liberals, preserve the unity of the Party, ensure victory at the elections and make Home Rule certain.' Parnell was daunted by ambition like a tragic Shakespearean hero.

Travers delivers clear cut analysis avoiding 'what-if history' in examining some of the major Parnell speeches such as in the Cork Opera House on the *Ne Plus Ultra* of Irish Nationalism. His portrayal of Parnell is in close focus from his election to the House of Commons in 1875 as Irish land movement leader, the epoch making Kilmainham Treaty, his release from prison and the quest for Home Rule; in contrast with Daniel O'Connell who was able to foil Peel, Parnell was incapable of foiling Gladstone. In Dublin, the Augustus Saint-Gaudens monument to Parnell remains far off from the Liffey in comparison to John Henry Foley's Daniel O'Connell monument as if position in posterity elevates the latter at the expense of the other's reputation and legacy. Travers is haunted by Parnell *almost* winning 'an Irish Legislature' for Ireland and also discourses on the man and his religious beliefs amidst courting the Irish clergy as well as the native Irish. Significantly, Parnell (in his own words) felt the necessity of 'tranquillising the fears of the Protestant section'. Travers disagrees with F. S. L. Lyons that Parnell 'lacked any real understanding of Ulster Unionism'. Paul Bew is quoted finding in Parnell a post-Tone figure pleading for national 'religious toleration'.

D. G. Boyce grasps the nettle of the life story pitted against fate particularly the various manifestations of the Land League and the presence of agrarian upheaval. His key point is the Gladstone-factor that potentially held out some concept of Home Rule for Ireland but who 'felt deeply deceived by Parnell's assurances that there was no possibility of his emerging from the (Mrs O'Shea) affair with any stain on his character'. Gladstone preternaturally mistrusted a private man in love who could not clearly read the political landscape while enmeshed in the road to Home Rule via Irish Land 'wars'. John Morley decisively notes that Parnell's fall occurred when 'platform-men united with pulpit-men in swelling the whirlwind.' Margaret Ward writes on Anna Parnell, sister and poet whose 'Tale of a Great Sham,' posthumously edited by Helena Moloney remains the singular contemporary riposte to Michael Davitt's masterpiece 'Fall of Feudalism in Ireland'. Felix Larkin and Myles Dungan explore Parnell and the Press. The depiction of editors being offered to resign or be thrown into the street after the Parnell split is keenly told. Newspapers loyalties are dramatically exposed as when the Parnellite and staunchly nationalist *Irish Daily Independent* by 1916 was calling for the executions of Connolly and MacDermott in 'two notorious editorials published on 10 and 12 May' of that year. Dungan proves how a publication like *United Ireland* achieved the 'mythologizing [of] Parnell...as the radical leader of a quasi-revolutionary movement. He was anything but. He simply required the services of a skilful propagandist'. Fionnuala Waldron discusses Parnellites after the split who were Dublin vintners. Parnell was partial to a glass himself yet publicly supported the temperance movement calling drink 'a very great evil' but was pitched between the two factions during the Intoxicating Liquors (Ireland) Bill of 1891. Pat Power shows the links between Parnell's ancestors with Paris as well as his Fund used for various political purposes that by 1886 reached an estimated £45,000. There is scanty information about the Parnell liaison with an American Mary Woods which remains mysterious.

James Harrison is private secretary to the great man and narrator in this historical blockbuster. It is unfair to classify Cregan in the Leon Uris, Walter Macken, Francis McManus school despite occasional slap dash stylistics. Gladstone in the prologue pronounces to Harrison: 'A marvellous man, a terrible fall.' 'Mrs Delia Stewart Parnell, as she always introduced herself, was a formidable and loquacious woman of American birth'. 'Davitt was thirty-one years old, coincidentally the same age as Parnell'. Harrison is hardly Nick Carraway of the *Great Gatsby* but in plodding pace evokes suspense since Parnell's life is a novelist's dream. The Parnell saga could easily sustain a grand opera. There is the marvellous cast list from Joseph Gillis Biggar, Isaac Butt, John Dillon, the Parnell sisters, and of course, Justin McCarthy correspondent for the *Daily News*. The research is bursting to the seams while the Mrs O'Shea debacle is far too mutely handled and strictly asexual. Instead, Cregan trenchantly moves behind the scenes of the Irish Party in the House of Commons as well as courtrooms in London rather than elaborate on scenes in Ireland except for occasional background. Mrs O'Shea abruptly enters the text when the narrator informs Joseph Biggar: 'That O'Shea and his wife have been estranged for years; that he lives in London and she lives in Kent; and that he has mistresses in London and in Madrid' As fast reported badinage this weakens the novel. A pity he footnotes the love story for the hard core politics but in chastely hinting at the lovers, rolls out the cliff hanging events which destroy Parnell.

The Irish Party on the Commons floor battling with Disraeli is typical of what Cregan does well but he might have benefitted from a diary format or at least headline dates. Parnell is given his stature as David in London taking on the Goliath parliament, fighting landlords in Ireland and preaching to Irish tenants: 'you must go to your landlord and offer to pay a fair rent.' The Lough Mask House-Captain Boycott episode where the Ulster Expedition of soldier-farm labourers under Captain Somerset Maxwell arrive in Mayo is one of many apposite digressions. Boycott's final flight through Dublin under police protection reveals the times.

Tim Healy and John Dillon emerge as Brutus and Cassius to Parnell's Caesar. Cregan's intent is soon revealed as he opts for the traditional storyline in presenting Parnell as naïve in his presumption of holding the leadership of the Irish Party, maintaining Gladstone's support and bringing the Irish voters with him while conquering the Catholic clergy. Cregan unfortunately misses out in unravelling the man as foolishly or otherwise 'in love,' embarking on an affair that was so mishandled at the expense of his career. In this respect, Parnell as emotional weakling plays no part in the novel. Cregan in pursuing this leader's deflection from the Irish Question for a romance instead of pursuing his real dream remains the enigma. There is no sight of the Parnell of legend portrayed in Katharine O'Shea's memoir as potentially Ireland's first Prime Minister of an Irish Parliament or in popular culture as uncrowned King of Ireland.

Parnell's fatherhood in gaol hearing of the death of his daughter Sophie with Mrs O'Shea lacks decisive drama. Captain O'Shea is a far more vivid character than his wife in Cregan's telling. O'Shea as potential duellist with Parnell and blackmailer using the infamous letters alongside the public response to the adultery makes for good reading. Parnell and the London *Times* grant Cregan full scope. The Parnell Commission yields melodrama. Pigott's evidence which runs to several chapters achieves keen serial pace. There are so many rascals at Parnell's feet even the revelations of Pigott's forgery and suicide can never redeem the Chief. Press jingoism falsely linking Parnell to an approval of the Phoenix Park killings of Cavendish and Burke is sharply established. The briefing of Parnell and Mrs O'Shea by Sir Frank Lockwood QC prior to the public divorce case is very well done. Lockwood ironically tells Harrison: 'The Divorce Court is no place for a lady like Mrs O'Shea.' Gladstone's famous letter about Parnell (quoted in full) is a masterpiece of understatement during the crisis as the Irish leader loses all support which provides vivid pages. The fall like all falls is accurately shown as painful. Davitt says: 'I will have nothing more whatsoever to do with him [CSP] as long as he lives'. The Manifesto of Parnell in the *Freeman's Journal* is the pathetic panegyric over the ruins of the career. Cregan bodes onwards through the sad voting out of Parnell in Room 15. The incident at Castlecomer when a voter flings a bag of lime nearly blinding him in one eye is symbolically the beginning of the end. Cregan's book should find popular readers and in any event is an excellent students' guide to this haunting story.

—*Books Ireland* 2013

CULTURAL CHATTELS

Transforming 1916: meaning, memory and the fiftieth anniversary of the Easter Rising Roisín Higgins (Cork University Press)

For God and Ireland: the fight for moral superiority in Ireland 1922-1932 M. P. McCabe (Irish Academic Press)

Lord Nelson was an Englishman

A man of great renown

But when Ireland gets her freedom

We shall pull his Pillar down

Higgins is circumscribed by the Pillar (quotes the above) and stands by her agenda of deliberating on how the fiftieth anniversary of 1916 was 'handled' in Ireland. Close to 2016, she notes that the re-establishment of official commemorative military parades in O'Connell Street, Dublin resumed in 2006 having been suspended in 1972. The failure of 1916 commemorations to achieve more than a 'stylized annual ritual' and the reactions of officialdom to Easter Week are her central thesis. The Rising beyond its military engagement, caused looting, civil disturbance and civilian casualties. The first anniversary 'was commemorated in a riot' of 20,000 people and the tenth anniversary saw O'Casey's *The Plough and the Stars* enable theatre riots.

Higgins never mocks but outlines the absurdity of many cantankerous committees involved in the 1966 commemoration: basically, cushy jobs for insiders with much fall-out as over the Garden of Remembrance designed by Daithí Hanly and it's commissioned sculpture by Oisín Kelly which was not unveiled until the 1970s. The Garden's opening had a comic mishap when the key to the intricate electronic gate failed to perform. 1966 commemorations were foreshadowed with far more absurd problems. The Fianna Fáil National Executive 'fought' among themselves as to the appropriate date to commence the pageantry based on April 24 1916: should it be April 24, 1966 or Easter Monday April 11, 1966? Absurd alright! Dissention among cultural committees is a long standing Irish sport and inhabits the book.

The 1960s seemed prophetically propitious for the Rising anniversary with the Princess Grace visit and the founding of Telefís Eireann in 1961, the Kennedy visit in 1963 and the seismic fall out of Nelson's Pillar in March 1966. The Pillar bomb of 8 March, reputedly placed by Liam Sutcliffe, and its brother bomb by the Irish Army became a street party to finish the job on 14 March. One onlooker was wise among the multitude: 'they'll go wild about this in America.' The Pillar was a 1916 re-enactment using real scenery and real explosives.

At committee level it seemed fitting to highlight the leading patriots Pearse, Plunkett and MacDonagh as poets while James Stephens 'Green Branches' officially favoured as literature over Yeats's 'Easter 1916' deemed controversial, and O'Casey's *The Plough and the Stars*—a forbidden text. The Abbey theatre was duly advised against the play being performed during 1966! Otherwise, Joyce Kilmer's 'Easter Week' was pushed with its pedantic opening: "Romantic Ireland never dies!' Relatives of the patriot Sean Mac Diarmada declined to take part in official celebrations in Kiltyclogher because of the 'ban on the historic Easter Lily.' *Aiséirí* devised by Tomás MacAnna at Croke Park, lost out in public support to the Telefís Eireann's production of *Insurrection* which lies in the vaults in the Montrose Studios under some ban 'too explosive to be seen again.' *Insurrection* devised by Hugh Leonard, who always had problems with Pearse as a character, foregrounds Connolly in this serial programme that owed much to the American Western crossed with News reportage, yet it lost out to a documentary *On Behalf of the Provisional Government* at the Jacobs Awards later that year. TÉ daringly broadcast *The Plough and the*

Stars which won an award. Yet another pageant at Croke Park, written and staged by Bryan MacMahon, *Seactar Fear, Seacht Lá* was more successful with a cast of close to 400—excerpts from the dialogue here makes one yawn. Louis Marcus's short film *An Tine Bheo* circulated in cinemas dwarfed by George Morrison's *Mise Éire*.

De Valera's speeches of 1966 predictably wallowed in the patriotic: language, nationhood and the shame of partition while poverty, emigration and stagnation were brushed over. Commemoration expenses were often lavish as with Taoiseach Lemass's party at Dublin Castle: '414 bottles of ale and stouts; 7 gallons of wine; 346.25 bottles of spirits' were drunk. The Official IRA boycotted public events and held their own, highlighted by the arrest in May 1966 of Seán Garland making him part of the government's surveillance on 'republicans, socialists and communists who shared an unhappiness with the status quo.' Higgins fully explores 1916 ownership, invoking the Tim Pat Coogan article in the *Sunday Telegraph* 'The I. R. A. Fights On' April 6, 1966. Coogan was reprimanded by External Affairs for untoward remarks in 'an influential British publication' that might be 'greatly distorted abroad'. Beyond official publications, speeches, books and brochures, dissent was silenced from IRA veterans, and Labour's Brendan Corish damned the Taoiseach for taking over 1916 'for the electoral purposes of Fianna Fáil.' Official republican publications such as the *United Irishman* decried 'the fallacy of the Jubilee celebrations' and the empty 'rhetoric of the Fianna Fáil "patriots."'

In the North, Paisley and Terence O'Neill moved to curtail 1916 commemorations with parade restrictions, tricolour flag restrictions, and co-operation with Lemass over prohibiting Dublin-Belfast trains on 16-17 April 1966. However, only one parade was banned in NI in County Derry. Higgins cites many who believe that the commemoration 'contributed to the outbreak of the conflict in Northern Ireland.' Higgins projects towards 2016, acknowledging that in 1966 history remained dangerous and was therefore censored. 'A sense of the nation's lack of completion was present in the statue of the Children of Lir, in the inability of the Kilmainham Museum to deal with the civil war and in Emmett, who was memorialised but not epitaphed.' 1916 was all about a United Ireland while commemorations usually achieve the status of St Patrick's Day celebrations. She preordains that 2016 will culturally and commemoratively reflect 1966, which seems accurate as the issues remain, if less well highlighted in the cultural media, schools or public pulpits, while economic hardship, emigration and emotive flag waving are as explosive as ever. Between the lines, one laughs bitterly with this book which exposes public manipulation of 1916 as a cultural chattel. Higgins is always neutral and without inhibition parades many sources including outsiders who viewed the 1966 pageantry such as the *Daily Express*: "awash with a fortnight of ceremonies dedicated to that merry and sad abortion, the Easter rebellion of 1916."

Behind McCabe's study is the vast panoply of revolutionary suffering, sacrifice, dying and vitriolic political division while the bloody rags of Irish history in this extraordinary decade determined the birth pangs of the Republic. This is really about a propaganda conflict surrounding the Irish struggle with activists taking on the Church as well as various enemies, not least the Crown. Catholic publications and their scope informs the study but always in attrition are republican voices, particularly used well here are those of the infamous 'MacSwiney sisters, Mary, Eithne and Annie.' A typical example of the propagandizing of the era is Archbishop Mannix, a native of Charleville, Co. Cork and his controversial 1925 Irish visit. The complexity of the Church as anti-republican and anti-partition is obvious.

McCabe finds key predecessors pitted against the Church's hatred of Irish patriotism which stole their thunder and parishioners, especially the Fenians who denied 'subversion of faith and morals' by the Irish Revolutionary Brotherhood. Irish revolutionaries since Catholic Emancipation were avowed secularists including Charles J. Kickham and John O'Leary who ignored Pope Pius IX's ban on Fenianism at the behest of Cardinal Cullen. Fenians and their rebel descendants in any event can be classified according to Tomas O'Suilleobain's phrase as rigorous adherents to the 'Republican Gospel.' Mary MacSwiney articulated it thus: 'If our fight is wrong to-day then every fight ever carried on for freedom in Ireland was wrong.'

The bête noir is Bishop Cohalan who stalks these pages as an Irish Richelieu. Coholan's 'moral outrage' deemed MacSwiney's hunger strike to the death a suicide. However, Republicans like the MacSwiney sisters, Ernie O'Malley and Frank Gallagher held that 'it cannot be wrong to die to profess liberty.' Dissenting clerics inform the conflicted decade such as Fr. Patrick Browne of Maynooth and staunch Sinn Feiner, Fr. Michael O'Flanagan. Surprisingly, some bishops disobeyed Canon law and McCabe fills out an extensive cast of characters, including 'feverently nationalist' bishops: Fogarty, Hoare, and Hallinan. O'Flanagan's republican profile in America resulted in his being prohibited from entering the Six Counties 'from September 1925 to October 1938'; the order was subsequently re-enforced once more from January 1939 onwards. Cardinal O'Donnell speaking in 1926 stated that 'Northern Ireland was a fixed entity and its inhabitants had to take this into account.' Fr. Browne demanded that bishops preach peace yet 'they have no right to require unto that end the acceptance of their views' and 'we do not take our politics from Rome.' Eithne MacSwiney concurred that bishops had no such rights over citizens, no more than Italian bishops could order its flock 'to swear allegiance to the Kaiser.'

Count George Noble Plunkett's claimed Benedict XV had given his blessing 'to the men of the Rising' which inflamed controversy in London. In 1921, Benedict XV had to endure a backlash from Ireland over his pro-British sentiments amidst the Treaty

Negotiations. On the signing of the Treaty in London, the Pope was careful to send congratulatory telegrams to both King George and De Valera. The Monsignor Luzio Irish visit was another debacle, and his contemporary report on a peace mission is a conclusive appendix. Luzio's stand-off in the Shelbourne Hotel veils his paranoia about the visit: 'they kept watch over me around the clock.' He favoured lifting the ban on the refusal of sacraments to Republicans and that clergy be 'completely prohibited from taking part in political affairs.' Luzio's final statements on the visit concerns Papal non-interference in 'the political affairs of Ireland'. All of his efforts went unheeded. Mary MacSwiney 'attacked' Archbishop Gilmartin for his silence over the General Mulcahy executions of the Four Courts leaders in the Civil War: 'no word of protest passed your lips when the revolting crime was committed.' She also deplored the death of hunger striker, Denis Barry who was refused a Christian Mass by Bishop Coholan. McCabe concludes that if Cumann na nGaedheal 'moved towards secularism…Fianna Fáil displayed an almost deferential attitude towards the Irish bishops.' He always keeps a keen edge of delicacy on his material within the highly fractious skirmishes between Church, revolutionaries and laity.

—*Books Ireland* 2013

BENEFACTOR

John Hunt: the man, the medievalist, the connoisseur Brian O'Connell (O'Brien Press)

With its lavish appearance this deluxe production has high value and a fantastic illustrative selection of the Hunt treasures. Otherwise, it is a fairly traditional biography of John Hunt and soon involves his wife a German Catholic (Mrs) 'Putzel' Hunt, formerly Gertrude Hartmann of Schloss-Mannheim. 'Jack' Hunt though born in Watford of well-to-lineage—indeed a family with strong credentials as architects, 'ended' up in Ireland. He attended the King's School, Canterbury and later read medicine at St Bartholomew's but strayed towards the British Museum. He apprenticed himself to various art dealers, moved amidst enclaves close to the likes of William Randolph Hearst, befriended Sir William Burrell and converted to Catholicism at Farm Street. The Hunts lived exotically at Poyle Manor, Buckinghamshire for ten years from 1936: the beginning of many residences as both engaged in their passion of 'art sleuting'. However, as far back as 1934 Hunt was an established dealer who 'collected for himself in the very field in which he traded'. He worked out of Bury Street, Mayfair with a keen eye for magnificence such as the twelfth century Temple Pyx (copper alloy) which he sold to Burrell. Hunt and Putzel were invited to witness the Sutton Hoo excavation in Suffolk in 1939.

In a remarkable *volte face* the Hunts 'arrived' in Ireland in 1939 and became immersed in ancient Irish art as well as becoming friendly with Adolf Mahr who was De Valera's controversial appointee as director of the National Museum. Hunt's Irish passport was issued on the critical date: August 30, 1939 while his British exit permit facilitated the move. Their house at Poyle was taken over as a war hospital. Putzel tried desperately to aid a Jewish family the Markuses who became victims of the Nazi evil. Philip Markus was murdered by the Gestapo in 1944. The Hunts settled near Lough Gur having been involved in an archaeological dig nearby. Jack pursued his M. Arch. at UCC. In 1945, he presented Taoiseach De Valera with a crucifix in homage of Ireland's neutrality during the war. Jack's innate brilliance at locating and finding public space for artefacts such as The O'Dea crozier and mitre lends his life a national philanthropic legacy to his adopted country. He had the patron's disposition as in his granting the Mary Queen of Scots Triptych to the infamous Father D'Arcy S.J. for Stonyhurst college despite a potentially legal debacle from which Jack withdrew which showed immense panache on his part. Another treasure had a less happier conclusion that of the Emly Shrine an 'illegal export dated from the 1950s' from Ireland to the US.

O'Connell is hectic, vibrant and engaging in detailing the life. The restoration of Bunratty Castle and its opening in 1960 is a great example of Hunt as cunning and wily when he had found in Lord Gort the perfect philanthropist for such a vast undertaking. Hunt went on to establish the Bunratty folk village which proves that his obsessive persistence was among the vital elements in achieving his vision of heritage and the past.

Friendship was also part of the Hunts' abundance as with Sybil Connolly, Peter Wilson of Sotheby's and Sandy Martin among many others. Hospitality was another major facet of Jack and Putzel and shows how they weaved their path through life finally locating to Drumleck House in Howth which they restored magnificently. A notable visitor was Jacqueline Kennedy who mistakenly believed that the Victorian bell-pull in her rooms meant house servants. Hunt collected her shoes left outside her door and 'polished them himself with some ceremony.' Like Chester Beatty, Jack Hunt was a keeper of national treasures and his legacy is immense as in the restored crannog and island castle at Craggaunowen in County Clare. He wrote many articles notably contributing for *Connoisseur* while *Irish Medieval Figure Sculpture 1200-1600* is singular and the Hunt Museum (former Custom House Limerick) displays to the public a collection of close to 2000 artefacts. O'Connell signs off in exposing the speculative journalism of Arthur Beesley and Judith Hill in the *Irish Times* and Erin Gibbons in *The Irish Arts Review* suggesting that Hunt was involved with 'art looted by the Nazis' and Gibbons's claim of the Hunts and 'pre-war Nazi connections'. This makes for the stirring final chapter where research into various archives at MI5 and G2 (Irish Intelligence) as well as the Garda Síochána, refutes such allegations backed up by experts from the art world and not least the Jewish international community such as Harry Frank Guggenheim of New York as well as the fact that the Hunts had many Jewish friends in Germany such as Wolf Donndorf (Putzel was godmother to his son, Michael) during the war which proved their anti-Nazi position. President Mary McAleese publicly refuted allegations of Nazism concerning the Hunts in the Hunt Museum in 2008.

—*Books Ireland* 2013

FADÓ

Prodigals and Geniuses : the writers and artists of Dublin's Baggotonia Brendan Lynch (Liffey Press)

Behind the Green Curtain: Ireland's phoney neutrality during world war II T. Ryle Dwyer (Macmillan)

The main title comes from sculptor Des MacNamara. Photographs are prevalent, especially Baggot Street Bridge (circa 1900) and on to McDaid's, the writers and artists of Davy Byrne's with Cecil Salkeld's mural 'The Triumph of Bacchus', and the backroom of the Palace Bar which Alan Reeves depicted in his drawing of its bohemian customers in *Dublin Culture* (1940). This book does exactly what it says on the tin (as it were) after a choppy introduction from J. P. Donleavy and his first involvement with John Ryan's *Envoy*. Baggotonia is an unusual coinage in terms of geography. Lynch (could be clearer) places its existence long before Parson's Bookshop however, further downtown Ely Place, Fitzwilliam Street, and Merrion Square must be part of its locale if it is to include George Moore, John Butler Yeats, and The United Arts Club with Shaw and W. B. Yeats.

Overall, Lynch has an agenda and makes a wide sweep in a gossipy style within twenty chapters that highlight in excelsis Kavanagh, Behan and Flann O'Brien while designating later figures as peripheral acolytes and sidekick prodigals including Leland Bardwell, Anthony Cronin, Paul Durcan, John Montague, Michael Longley and Thomas Kinsella with the accurate inference of them as being very minor poets. Beatrice Salkeld Behan is rendered in a fine portrait. Robert 'Bertie' Smyllie receives top billing as *Irish Times* helmsman up to 1954, last of the legends in terms of contemporary broadsheets, and whose motto proclaimed: "The best newspapers are run by a committee. A committee of one. The Editor." Smyllie's precedents for the *Irish Times* are still adhered to in part but with modern differences. He notably framed the front page for 8 May 1945 with a V of photographs of allied leaders which was both tongue in cheek and obvious. He had Yeats fully assessed by newspaper standards, showcased *Under Ben Bulben*. *Finnegan Wake* was lavishly reviewed in 6,000 words, O'Casey had an occasional soapbox and Archbishop McQuaid was scrutinised with his cloak held up by a cleric when on public and private parade. Smyllie never read unsolicited copy, lived for opera and his gramophone, his bicycle and portable typewriter while cultivating one overgrown finger nail, donning a green sombrero and often roaring in pubs: "Pissmires and warlocks, stand aside!".

Lynch never wanders much beyond his big three (Kavanagh, Behan and O'Brien) while O'Connor and O'Faolain are sidelined - untrue in terms of O'Connor's works most recently in *Everyman*. Keeping with the agenda: Parsons Bookshop and May O'Flaherty become the target for further big three exaltation while ignoring May's feisty censoriousness. He focuses exclusively on Alan Simpson who with Tennessee Williams' *The Rose Tattoo*, Beckett's *Waiting for Godot* and Behan's *The Quare Fella* became the three *succés de scandale at* the Pike theatre which shows up the Abbey's plunge into mediocrity. Lynch neglects the Gate and on the trail of scandal features the lugubrious Kavanagh versus *The Leader* libel action. He skips over Francis Bacon and makes Harry Kernoff the great artist, which places Jack B. Yeats in the shadows, and he revives (Cecil) Salkeld and ignores Sean Keating (thankfully). The Gallery owner he champions is Victor Waddington.

His attempts to ingest life into Gainor Crist (the inspiration for Donleavy's *The Ginger Man)* and Ernie Gebler (once married to Edna O'Brien) reach descriptive rigor mortis. Lynch becomes rhetorical: "Ernie Who? The winners write the histories". He means the survivors. The final chapter has a list of posterity's missing-in-action. There are many, including George Desmond, 'Hoddy' Hodnett, Eoin 'the Pope' O'Mahony and Owen Walsh. Posterity is the toughest judge with only two possible verdicts: oblivion or posthumous fame. Lynch has produced a tourist guide to an Atlantean world of writers, a suitable companion to the literary pub crawl and a bluffer's guide to Kavanagh, Behan and O'Brien.

Ryle Dwyer as a leading commentator and historian, the author of *Fallen Idol* (1997), an exposé of the crimes of Charles J. Haughey, presents a valuable work of analysis that avoids the pitfalls of going for the entertainment factor, as in Joseph T. Carroll's *Ireland in the War Years, 1939-1945*. A serious subject explored through vast resources between De Valera, Churchill and Roosevelt with David Gray, Sir John Maffey and Edouard Hempel based in Dublin as ambassadors for the United States, Britain and Germany. Ryle Dwyer interrogates the diplomatic battles between Dublin, London, Washington, Berlin and all power centres among a vivid cast of ancillary officials including John Cudahy and Joseph P. Kennedy in this evolving kaleidoscope of classic reportage. The historical perspective includes the Irish twentieth century by proxy with Anglo-Irish and Anglo-American relationships examined in the breakpoint years of world war.

The portrait of Churchill is not the usual strident one in Irish histories, nor the portrait of De Valera: this is no cartoon version of the bulldog and the Irish terrier snapping at each other. Britain's wartime leader, intent on defending his island, needs Ireland as potential ally and military base but to no avail. Dev skilfully achieves his mission to maintain neutrality for many reasons based on his traumatic experiences of 1916, the war of independence and the civil war. When Churchill tells Gray "he was sick of the Irish" Dev rebounds, blaming Churchill for "pushing Michael Collins into firing on the Four Courts in June 1922". Dev was anti-Germany and feared the Nazi war machine "would try to implement the IRA's Plan Kathleen" and invade Donegal proclaiming themselves Ireland's liberator.

The hellfire summer of July 1940 is deftly discussed as the central cauldron for Ireland's wartime distress. Roosevelt indirectly armed the South of Ireland through Canada, however 20,000 rifles would never have been a safeguard against a Nazi invasion. Ryle-Dwyer scotches the ports saga in citing Colonel William J. Donovan, adviser to Roosevelt, as early as 1941, saying: "Lough Swilly would be scarcely any improvement over Lough Foyle." Thus the importance of a few Irish ports to the world war is debunked. Bombings by the Luftwaffe of Belfast and Dublin are placed beyond any

561

conspiracy theory involving Britain as *agent provocateur.* Quite the contrary, since De Valera covertly assisted Britain in various actions such as granting *Robert Hastie,* the air-sea rescue vessel a secret berth in Killybegs, the fueling and salvaging of RAF planes in the Free State and where possible turning a blind eye to RAF pilots wishing to escape back to Britain. Luftwaffe pilots who crash landed in Ireland were strictly under lock and key for the duration of the war. The RAF's decisive victory in the battle of Britain and the Nazi defeat at Stalingrad marked the beginning of the end for Nazism by which time Ireland was a staunch neutral quagmire.

Ryle Dwyer does not court sensationalism yet cannot avoid it. Ambassador Gray was an occultist and used the services of medium Geraldine Cummins throughout the war. Dev interpreted Churchill's famous telegram after Pearl Harbour as a drunken missive, "Now is your chance. Now or never. 'A Nation Once Again.' Am ready to meet you at any time." The Dev-Churchill cat and mouse game over the six counties is also debunked as mere diplomatic phoney currency and ultimately as phoney as Dev's total vision of neutrality. Maffey depicted Dev as having a 'martyr complex'. Gray wished the US to seize the German legation in Dublin early in 1945 but Dev resisted. Dev's condolence ceremony with Ambassador Hempel on the death of Hitler was radically criticised by *The New York Times* in outrage along with the world press. The only riposte to this public scandal is the 160,000 men and women from Southern Ireland who served with the Allies including a total of six VCs.

Gray's memoir *Behind the Green Curtain* remains unfinished; however Ryle Dwyer presumably has raided the largesse of the manuscript. Gray had the real insider's story of the era and what you have here is from the same mould.

—*Books Ireland* 2012

JOURNEYS INTO A BALKAN HEART OF DARKNESS

Balkan Essays Hubert Butler (Irish Pages)

These essays maintain high seriousness because of their content, which shades fully into the Holocaust. One of them, 'The Final Solution', should be on the Leaving Certificate and college history curricula. Butler's depiction of Eichmann is chilling; the language provokes in the mode of Swift's *A Modest Proposal*, while the tenor of discourse is Shavian. This is no exhibition of *belles lettres*: language conveys the matter. Ireland is indebted to Anglo-Irish stylists over many centuries and Butler represents this line.

His essential gravitas is embedded in the subject of 'where race or region is roughly identified with religion (as in Ireland), behaviour takes second place. Different views of the message of Jesus Christ attract bombs from different quarters.' Butler is mute on 'The Irish Question', but it subconsciously permeates the essays on imperial wars with land-grabbing and massacres, while he accepts nationalism because 'small nations have been less likely to be corrupt than large ones'. His republicanism is cultural and nonmilitary, with the aspiration for 'a great conciliation of Protestant and Catholic'. The use of 'conciliation' is typically Anglo-Irish despite his good intentions. Butler's controversies with the Catholic Church in Ireland proved scandalous, not least as it also strained the plight of Anglo-Irish identity in the Free State, latterly the Republic of Ireland. He emphasised that 'there is no trade union of the oppressed'.

The writing on Eichmann stems from these contexts: 'If we accept that he was genuinely attached to his Jewish "helpers" we get closer to the horrible complexities of human life'. 'Like all genteel Nazis he strongly disapproved of the coarse Jew-baiting in which vulgarians like Julius Streicher, editor of Der Stürmer, indulged.' 'Eichmann always called his Nazi employers by their formal titles even after they had been hanged.' Butler's history of human behaviour is contrasted with ethics and the now-unfashionable genre of morals.

Hubert Marshal Butler, educated in privilege at Charterhouse and Oxford during the 1916 Rising, War of Independence and Civil War, had a rector grandfather in Kilkenny who fled during the Tithe War. Butler's moral plea involves a philosophy and theory of history based on 'the First World War [that] began because Austro-Hungary wished to impose its Germanic culture on the Southern Slavs'.

The infamous assassination of Archduke Franz Ferdinand by nationalists in annexed Sarajevo (Bosnia) prefigured Butler's coming of age. 'The new nations born in 1919 out of the three dissolved empires lasted till Adolf Hitler shattered them twenty-one years later.' Austria-Hungary, whose fate was sealed at Sarajevo, had been 'like a well organised household: the Austrians had been the landlords; the Hungarians the stewards; the Czechs had been the butlers and housekeepers; Croats, Serbs and Wallachians were the outdoor staff'. 'In Czechoslovakia the Czechs were pledged to give a measure of independence to the two million Sudeten Germans on its western frontiers. The Czechs failed to do this, so Hitler was able to appear as a deliverer when he invaded.'

Butler's moment of 'conversion' in becoming a Socrates in carpet slippers is recognisable when he alludes to François Mauriac at the Gare d'Austerlitz (Paris) in 1942 seeing 'the crowds of children packed into cattle wagons at the station. There were 4051 of them between the ages of two and fifteen.' Butler's 'The Children of Drancy' (not included in Balkan Essays) addressed this material more emotionally, including reference to one of Hitler's industrial patrons, Karl von Siemens, 'whose firm installed the electricity at Auschwitz'. Russian poet Joseph Brodsky is quoted on 'the loss of life owing to political violence' of the twentieth century exceeding 'a hundred million in Europe alone', bearing on Butler's vision of 'the post-war world's ethics as "dirty-grey"'.

Varieties of totalitarianism are discussed, particularly the bureaucracies where death on a large scale begins with typewriters, official documents and secret files on thousands and thousands of innocent people. He proves that bureaucracy in dictatorship is the bookkeeping of large-scale deathdealing. 'It was first d'Annunzio, and then [Mussolini], who introduced the new passionate racism—the disease of the twentieth century—to Italy.' Yes, ultimately, despite being a poet, d'Annunzio was a scoundrel. Butler brings you on a tour of passionate racisms at home and abroad, particularly where 'Czech despised Slovak, Croat despised Serb, Germans despised almost everybody'. The wide lens involves even Maria Pasquinelli, who assassinated General de Winton at Pola in 1947, believing that 'Dalmatia, Croat or not, must be annexed to Italy'.

Butler arrived in Yugoslavia on 9 October 1934, when King Alexander, a Serb, had 'been assassinated in Marseilles by agents of the Croat leader, Pavelitch. The shadow of the assassination hung over the whole country. Hitler had come to power in Germany and Jewish refugees were flocking to the Dalmatian coast. In Italy and Hungary, Pavelitch and his helper, Artukovitch, were training the army of the Croat rebels, who were, in 1941, to sweep into Yugoslavia with the Nazis and proclaim the Independent State of Croatia.' Out of this convergence, Butler as linguist and teacher in Zagreb found himself immersed in world history.

Enter Alojzije Stepinac, a Satanic being 'who had stood beside the coffin of his murdered king, [and] reappeared before his countrymen as Archbishop at the right hand of his king's assassin'. Butler constantly reiterates his mission, quoting Slavko Goldstein on the Croatian massacre of 1941, 'one of the ten largest genocides of the twentieth century', when '500,000 Orthodox Christians were slaughtered. It was accompanied by a Conversion campaign in which 250,000 Orthodox Christians were forced into the Catholic Church.' And under Monsignor Stepinac, primate of the Church in Yugoslavia, the Croat troops 'all passed over to the Nazis'.

When Stepinac was arrested as a war criminal in 1949, 'a crowd of 150,000 ... assembled in O'Connell Street to protest against the imprisonment'. In America there 'were even greater demonstrations'. 'The war ended, the communists came to power and the inevitable Orthodox revenge was stayed by the suppression of both churches ... the Vatican was grateful for this at first and permitted and encouraged its clerics to take posts in the communist government.' Butler, daringly for his era and status in the Irish Republic, stated that the 'Communists saved Yugoslavia from a bloody civil war on racial lines, which would have been inevitable'.

During WWII Archbishop Sharitch had even penned an 'Ode to Pavelitch' whose lines are translated by Butler: 'May He, the King of Heaven / Always accompany thee / Our golden leader!' When Monsignor, later Archbishop, Stepinac went on trial in Zagreb during September–October 1946, he 'pleaded "not guilty", declared his conscience was clear and announced that he would not reply to any questions put by the prosecution'. He was imprisoned and released a few years later.

Butler is passionately clear: 'those who live through a time of terror and suffering seldom minimize what they have endured or seen others enduring. We get different accounts of the same event. And those who inflicted the suffering will give a diametrically opposite account of what happened.'

He encountered the Catholic rightwing backlash that became national news in Ireland when he was 'attacked' by such notables as the foreign editor of The Catholic Standard, Count O'Brien of Thomond. The Minister for Agriculture, James Dillon, praised the Catholic hierarchy, Stepinac and the former Führer Pavelitch, who had 'so gallantly defended freedom of thought and freedom of conscience'. Butler is credited with bringing to Ireland the reality that Pavelitch was the 'counterpart of Himmler', under whose rule 'the gas chamber and the concentration camp were introduced into

Yugoslavia'. Chris Agee in the Introduction elevates Butler's contribution to human rights and historical truth-telling in exhibiting the disbelieved news that 'Catholic Croat confronted Orthodox Serb and Hitler's war had triggered off a massacre of the Orthodox by the Catholics'.

Butler's dramatis personae are memorably shocking, including Andrija Artukovitch, Pavelitch's Minister of the Interior, who is profiled as an evader of post-war justice. Pavelitch had 'fled to Rome, disguised as a Spanish priest called Gomez', and Artukovitch arrived in Ireland in 1947. Butler's narrative unleashes a withering and punishing wit, outlining his zany pursuit of Artukovitch throughout Catholic institutions in Ireland. The essays become Chandleresque, locating the fiend, comfortably domiciled in Rathgar, Dublin, with his daughters at the Sacred Heart Convent in Drumcondra. Then, a year later, the family coolly moved to California, no less.

There is balance rather than vilification concerning the Vatican, which cannot but appear as complicit, whatever about Cardinal Tisserant's stating in 1942 that 'I know for sure that even the Franciscans of Bosnia Herzegovina behaved atrociously'. By 1952 Yugoslavia's 'Tito appealed to the USA for the extradition of Artukovich', which was blocked by a US–Serbia Treaty of 1901.

Butler's Balkan Essays have a Heart of Darkness 'narrator' who locates evil demagogues comparable to Kurtz in Conrad's novel. The final analysis reveals genocide, cover-up, denial, propaganda and otherwise public lies, conflicting histories, victims, victors, vanquished. 'The horror! The horror!'

—*Books Ireland* 2017

BLACKLISTED

Francis Stuart: Face to Face Anne McCartney (Institute of Irish Studies)

The Wartime Broadcasts of Francis Stuart 1942-1944 Brendan Barrington Review (Lilliput)

"In a cell meant for one or at most two, we were ten and twelve and we were starving. I remembered that I'd been a writer, and was no longer a writer but felt that I would never again be a writer. It was a despairing experience, but looking back, I see that the kind of writer I am probably had to reach that complete giving up of his vocation." This book is teeming with such vivid extracts as well as attempts to explain how such experiences led "to the brink of illumination" for Francis Stuart.

There are many extraordinary facets here, not least that McCartney takes up a feminist agenda a la Kristeva, Cixous and Irigaray and finds Stuart PC simply because his work "parallels many of the strategies of contemporary feminist criticism; a fact which perhaps is most clearly demonstrated in the way he depicts women." His women characters are "beyond victim status . . . which shows women in control". She even accords him higher accolades as novelist because he "upsets the hierarchical order of the phallocentric value system and thereby leaves the way open for the women reader to turn to her own experience and begin to read as a woman." However she is also aware that in some of the novels "women characters are imaginative realisations of his fantasies and obsessions, not attempts to represent or define women in any realistic way"—yet "he owns up to the fictionality of all such constructs". One can agree with McCartney that in his later work, "he moves away from the fallen angel stereotype in order to create characters who are at once sexual and spiritual".

She first discovered his work in 1987 while on a bus to Dublin—two passengers were lambasting Stuart. Having reached her destination, by chance she found *Black List, Section H* in a secondhand bookshop. She considers that the novel is autographical—'a writing of the self'—and it may well have forced her to "question and reassess the whole system of values which forms the basis of self-identity ... For Stuart the difference between the psychotic and the writer is merely one of degree, since both inhabit a world of fantasy."

She finds his work permeated by religion, "as subject, form and consequence, but primarily ... as a paradigm for his fiction, with the Gospels providing a blueprint for his novels." She quotes from *The Abandoned Snail Shell,* "For truth is very difficult to receive. The chasm between knowledge of the world and the sensation of truth is deep." She admits that for Stuart, "redemption is the acceptance of desolation and suffering" and enforces this point by quoting Ivor Browne, "It is generally suffering which most acutely claims our attention and focuses our being, more than comfort, joy or even passion." Basically her thesis is that for Stuart, "the human mind is incapable of contemplating suffering on a vast scale" hence his work can be read as a "convincing account of the struggle to survive."

McCartney is not remiss in quoting Plato, Kant, Blake, Shelley and other greats to develop her theories. Not all of Stuart's novels are given the full treatment and some are just about mentioned but that is no fault since what she does she does very well indeed. And her intent is certainly passionate if not personal since she mentions a broken marriage in which she tried to impose a Stuartian model of human relationships involving her ex-partner and her new partner living under the one roof. There is a fine statement about the significance of Saint Therese of Lisieux as someone who may have implicitly inspired Stuart's method of writing. She also admits to having found a copy of *The Story of a Soul* by Saint Therese in extremely bizarre if not overtly occult cir-cumstances.

McCartney is convinced that his decision to go to Germany "was driven by a subconscious desire to experience the conditions about which he had been writing for so long." She felt that "conventional criticism would fail to get to the heart of his work" so she has written a unique text which includes the personal and believes that along with Joyce and Beckett he is "one of the leading Irish novelists of the twentieth century".

As a critical work naturally enough there is little truck with assembling a huge biographical structure, and this is very satisfying since pretty quickly the reader may well be immersed in her obsession with his major novels.

Here for the first time are the majority of Francis Stuart's radio talks, broadcast from Berlin during Hitler's Third Reich. Their publication with an introduction by Brendan Barrington of the Lilliput Press continues the controversial polemics surrounding Stuart's odyssey to Germany which forever compounded his image of being a dissident writer along with Pound, Celine, Wyndham Lewis and others. The contents of the broadcasts are somewhat disappointing by literary standards, leaving aside their continuing sensational influence, compared to Stuart's other writings especially his greatest novels.

However, they are trenchantly anti-British within a staunch nationalist if not militant Irish Republican tradition, "It is because of the dynamiters of the last century and not because of the men who condemned them, that we survive." He repeatedly affirms his devotion to Pearse claiming that, "As soon as I had written a talk I asked myself if there was anything in it contrary to Pearse's outlook; if there was, I tore it up and wrote another." And not only Pearse: he is equally devoted to the other leaders of the 1916 Rising, and not least the War of Independence heroes: Cathal Brugha, Liam Lynch and Michael Collins. His obsession with the unfinished business of unifying Ireland, referred to in the broadcasts, was as intense as

De Valera's credo on that subject, except that Stuart supported the bombing campaign by the IRA in England during World War II. Neither is De Valera beyond his praise, nor the Catholic Primate of all Ireland, Cardinal MacRory.

His appeals for a United Ireland might well have been quoted in leading articles in *An Phoblacht,* "Ulster will once again be free Irish soil". He looks forward to a great sporting event to be held "outside Belfast to celebrate the return of the six counties .. . Ulster is Irish as much as Connaught or Munster". While he does not support coercion of the Northern Unionists, he dares to suggest, "It is of no importance that the Tricolour should fly from the City Hall in Belfast instead of the Union Jack ..." There are pro-German statements in support of the city of Danzig being reclaimed by the Reich. In praising the German Sixth Army outside Stalingrad, he singles out the bravery of the ordinary soldier: "I am glad to be living among such people". However, he states that he is not casting disparagement on the average British soldier. He also broadcast that the inspiration for all German soldiers is "rooted in one man, Hitler" of whom he adds, that he was "completely fired by enthusiasm" when he first heard about the German leader before coming to Berlin.

Stuart's vociferous anti-democratic diatribe can be understood along with his pre-World War II utterances against both Communism and Fascism; still the broadcasts may sound somewhat contradictory. "The Axis leaders do not shout about the Commandments or religion or humanity." His overall viewpoint can best be summed up in his hatred of the Allies' statements that the war was a "crusade for liberty, humanity and idealism against the forces of aggression and barbarism". He is most virulent in detesting "this heresy of commercial Christianity from the United States .. . which gives successful businessmen a solid respectability." Repeatedly, he condemns Churchill and Roosevelt. His vituperative attacks on the socio-economic realities of life would remain an abiding concern of his fiction, in novels such as *The Chariot* and his last work of fiction, *King David* Dances.

The editor provides a useful if lengthy introduction with a potted biography of Stuart, stating that he went to Germany first on a lecture tour before war was declared. Then with the outbreak of war, and some luck with visas, he managed to get back into Berlin from neutral Ireland to take up a job offer. This, at first seemed a heady adventure for a writer in his late thirties whose career was going off the boil and whose marriage had sadly foundered. In this context, a lecturing job in Berlin was the only available solution to his problems. When the offer of broadcasting came his way, the extra money was attractive for four talks a month.

Barrington attempts to find evidence of Stuart's antisemitism in some of his pre-war books, *Try the Sky*, *In Search of Love*, *Julie* and *The Great Squire*. He points the reader in the direction of Raymond Patrick Burke's thesis which claims to expose antisemitism in some of the novels; a letter from Stuart to the *Irish Times* in the 1930s opposing Irish aid to victims of Kristallnacht because according to Stuart 'charity begins at home'. Barrington, implies that there is a case against him as Nazi collaborator, if not some kind of antisemitic slur attached to his name. He also finds the persona of H in his most famous novel *Black List, Section H* 'a literary construct' alien to the evolution of his political ideology. He will not accept the notion of a neutral writer broadcasting to a neutral country.

Barrington also debunks the concept of his being an outsider as illusory, by quoting Thomas Kilroy who believes it is "consoling to the society of liberal aspirations". He implies that Stuart's association with Aosdána has removed for ever the idea of the outsider. He may well be right, except that hopefully there are a handful of mavericks outside the fold who cannot or don't wish to gain entry. Stuart's Aosdána membership like much else in his public life met with rancorous controversy. Barrington does not mention that the libel case taken by Stuart against Kevin Myers and the *Irish Times* in the 1990s was settled in Stuart's favour thus exonerating him and the contents of his writings as being devoid of antisemitism.

On the other hand, he also claims that "antisemitism was not at the core of Stuart's enthusiasm for Hitler and the National Socialist project". He cannot abide the championing of Stuart by fellow writers who praise the Berlin period in the novels, *Victors and Vanquished* and *Black List, Section H* are for Barrington no less than a transforming of the years of collaboration into fiction. Barrington's ultimate implication is that Stuart's involvement with the Reich was a natural progression from an evolving ideological position. In this ongoing controversy there will remain for perhaps a long time two opposing camps—those who defend and those who attack and denounce Stuart.

The present reviewer is completing a biography of Francis Stuart, including much more detail than can be expected from Barrington's introduction, but he does achieve a certain balance.

—*Irish Examiner* 2001

HUSH HUSH

Irish Secrets: German espionage in wartime Ireland 1939-1945 Mark M. Hull (*Irish Academic Press*)

MI5 and Ireland, 1939-1945: The Official History Eunan O'Halpin (*Irish Academic Press*)

British Intelligence in Ireland, 1920-1921: The Final Reports Peter Hart (Cork University Press)

When Gunther Schutz landed by parachute in Ireland before dawn on 13 March 1941, he was way off his planned dropping zone, like other German agents before and after him. Instead of county Kildare he was not far from New Ross in county Wexford. The Gardaí arrested and frogmarched him into Taghmon. He was carrying his suitcase that contained the essential equipment of every spy—a radio transmitter crudely disguised inside an attaché suitcase. When he asked what would happen to him, a Garda remarked, "Don't worry, we'll hang you, that's all."

Schutz got an Irish breakfast at the pub: a pint and a sandwich before being taken to Dublin for interrogation by Dr Richard Hayes and Colonel Dan Bryan of G2. There were no German agents hanged, in fact they were treated 'rather well' in jail, whether at Sligo, Athlone or Dublin, by any international standards.

Hull has a huge cast of characters, mainly spies and also the German Ambassador Hempel who was based at the German Legation in Northumberland Road, Dublin, and the ever-vigilant head of Irish Intelligence (G2) Colonel Bryan in the Phoenix Park. In Berlin, the chief of Intelligence operations at Abwehr, Admiral Wilhelm Canaris—who would eventually fall foul of the Nazi hierarchy and end up on the gallows—was responsible for the influx of German agents to Ireland including O'Reilly and Kenny, both citizens of Eire.

Hitler with the advance in planning for operation Sealion—a

proposed invasion of England—sought many proposals for German espionage directly relating to Ireland. The IRA found credibility with Berlin because of their bombing campaign in England, the successful raid on the Irish Army arsenal at the Phoenix Park and the largely fictional accounts of their strength to German sources before and after the outbreak of war. Over a dozen agents arrived at various times in Ireland, though one threesome, OW, Tributh and Gartner, landed together in July 1940. They were all easily apprehended following an MI5 tip-off to G2, and received substantial sentences under the Emergency Powers Act and Explosive Substances Act.

G2, like MI5, did have the edge on the Germans just as the staff at Bletchley Park in England monitored the German war covertly. Intelligence staff of G2 tapped the phone line 61986—at Hempel's headquarters, read his mail and kept twenty-four watch on the premises. Behind the scenes, at a meeting with MI5 in London, as early as 1938, Colonel Liam Archer (G2) set up what would be known throughout the war as the 'Dublin link'. This co-operation was shrouded under a blanket of Irish neutrality and meant that the British Isles were effectively contra Hitler, and had the upper hand in dealing with the largely ineffective IRA. The IRA had complicit dealings with Germany and Hull fully outlines the main protagonists: Helmut Clissmann of the German Academic Exchange Service, Sean Russell, Stephen Held, Joseph McGarrity and Sean MacBride. MacBride's phone was tapped and his letters were opened during the emergency but he never ended up in custody.

Frank Ryan and his abortive mission to Ireland with Sean Russell is presented in fascinating detail. This was organised by the German Foreign Ministry and the Abwehr under consultation with Admiral Canaris, and the hideous Edmund Veesenmayer, later appointed as German Minister to Hungary where he oversaw the deportation of thousands of Jews to the extermination camps.

When it comes to one of the most successful of German agents, Hermann Goertz, the novelist Francis Stuart enters the picture since he befriended the spy in Berlin prior to Goertz' mission to Ireland. Goertz is given the most coverage here of all the spies. He is shown to be a desperate man, something of a degenerate, ultimately befuddled by the suspicious, secretive and disorganised IRA members that he linked up with, as well as having love affairs with Irish women while evading capture in Ireland for a year and a half. After the war, on his release, he became paranoid and made use of the cyanide capsule, part of his kit, safely stored for years through *numerous* searches and different prisons. Goertz' funeral in post-war Dublin was an event equivalent to state honours, reported in the press, attended by a large crowd of eight hundred, the coffin draped in the swastika flag.

Hull becomes fully intriguing in outlining de Valera's man in Spain, the Irish minister Leopold Kerney, a buddy of Dev's and conduit for German-Irish communications. Kerney had assisted in the shady deal whereby Frank Ryan was released from Spanish custody and royally installed in Berlin by high-ranking Reich personnel.

Hull's conclusion echoes his introduction concerning the limitations on the Abwehr's success as an intelligence-gathering service in both Britain and Ireland, since its head, Canaris, was always at odds with the Nazi leaders. The Abwehr was disbanded in July 1944, following the assassination attempt on Hitler, but up to then was an adjunct of the overall intelligence services, including the Geheime Staatspolizei (the Gestapo) and the Kriminalepolizei (the Kripo) along with other Nazi organisations. In terms of espionage and counter espionage, G2 outwitted their German counterparts thanks to Colonels Liam Archer and Dan Bryan, Dr Richard Hayes alias 'Captain Grey', Commandant Eamon de Buitlear and Douglas Gageby later of the *Irish Times*. Hull manages to keep a potentially bizarre narration from slipping into comedy or farce as one peers behind the scenes at what was a truly frightening time in Irish and international affairs.

Colonel Dan Bryan and Dr Richard Hayes feature on the cover of this book, looking suitably menacing. German agents, after their arrest, faced these two stolid fellows and a barrage of questions before they were incarcerated.

There is a full note on the Irish section of the Security Service (SIS) followed by the documents from a project supervised by J. G. 'Jock' Curry, written by Cecil Liddell of MI5 for the purpose of providing a clear record for future guidance in the post-war period. The documents, in précis form, cover a timespan from pre-war information about Ireland, through the activities of Germans in Ireland before and during the war, mainly agents who were dropped in by parachute. There is mention of the breaking of Hermann Goertz' code and of most of the people dealt with in Hull's book above.

What is very obvious from the documents is that the Dublin link was "established at the request of the Éire Government and operated with the full knowledge and approval of the British and Eire Governments". Bearing this in mind, the number of times that Sir John Maffey, the British representative to Ireland, appears in the text reveals the close bonds between the two countries. Maffey is cited as demanding the withdrawal of all diplomatic wireless telegraphy sets in Dublin after secret meetings in April 1943, in order to ensure minimum leakage of intelligence to the German legation with the approach of Operation Overlord, the invasion of France planned for June 1944.

There are many accounts of anti-allied activities, not least from enemy ships on the high seas. The *Irish Pine* landed 10,000 rounds of ammunition in canned food cases at Limerick in 1942 for IRA units. There was intense surveillance of U-boat activity as the 'battle of the Atlantic' was slowly turned from German to British domination. Among the many high-profile names is naturally Dev. "In March 1945 there has been ample evidence of de Valera's intention to revive the Partition question ... he even referred to the possibility of the use of force".

In just over a hundred pages you are given a behind-the scenes look at the world of secret police, spies and undercover surveillance, showing how important a role 'Emergency Ireland' played in the scheme of things. Every detail in O'Halpin's text is deadly serious compared to Hull's occasional picaresque digressions. The official tone adds to the gravity. One is amazed at how much the intelligence services knew. What is even more chilling is that they had a handle on everything. Clearly the outcome of the war depended on many factors, and the Dublin link was by no means an insignificant one.

Two reports in fact: the author(s) of the first unknown while Ormonde de Winter wrote the second with his inimitable comments, of which more in a moment. The War of Independence can be fully felt from the British Intelligence perspective in both reports. The main strongholds of Dublin and Cork are described in terms of IRA units aided by intelligence and communication from the local populace—one gets the feeling of British Intelligence living in chaos. Cork is listed as having a thousand gunmen lurking for the kill while the number in Dublin is not given. The officer class of the IRA is praised as being highly efficient at their business. By the time of Collins' purge of British agents up to and including the infamous day, 27 November, there is a faltering tone in the report about those killings that "paralysed the special branch".

The only breakthroughs for British Intelligence came through seizure of IRA documents and papers in raids, and through anonymous letters from the populace. However, these letters could not be fully trusted and following them up was often costly, when they turned out to be bogus or deliberate decoys. Similarly, "Sinn Fein realised the danger of men who drank too much". Information gathering from Protestants of the north was deemed unreliable due to their negative feelings about nationalists. In contrast, Protestants in Bandon were particularly of use in what was an IRA hotspot. The secret movement of British agents in towns and villages was nigh impossible. Ford cars and plain-clothes personnel were often deployed in raids instead of military men and armoured vehicles to ensure the element of surprise.

Ormonde Winter (really looking the part on the cover with monocle and unlit cigarette) is notable for his asides. "The Irishman is of an intensely inquisitive nature," and "No Englishman can fully grasp the inner psychology of the Irish rebel character." Concerning the bugging of prison cells, "the microphone of English manufacture seems ill adapted to the Irish brogue." His tone shifts to rage decrying Augustine Birrell, chief secretary of Ireland (1907-18) for underfunding Intelligence operations and, in particular, having been tipped off prior to the Rising of 1916 and foolishly choosing to disregard his informants.

Winter's frustrations abound, concerning the huge rewards offered to informers. Peter Hart notes inaccuracies on Winter's part about Sean Hales being an informer and Ernie O'Malley as the leader of the notable Macroom ambush, whereas in fact it was Tom Barry. Collins, the Scarlet Pimpernel of the War of Independence, is the ultimate sticking point—his photograph everywhere and yet the guerrilla leader was untouchable. The report is not beyond a compliment, referring to "the indefatigable Collins".

Winter at times sounds like a proto-Thatcherite, recommending martial law with intense curfew restrictions and population control through ID cards. He understood the ruthlessness of Collins and his unceasing desire for a Republic through physical force, the intractability of the Irish situation, and he understood Protestant and Catholic in metaphorical terms—"oil will not mix with water". There is something prophetic in his statement that the Treaty "will bring the semblance of peace to this distracted nation of born agitators". Winter subsequently escaped the Irish, worked as settlement director for ex-policemen, did some anti-Soviet duty in Finland in 1940 and wrote his memoirs, *Winter's Tale (1955)* which includes an account of his unhappy times in the nation of born agitators.

—*Books Ireland* 2003

DEVIL ÉIRE

De Valera: the man and the myths T. Ryle Dwyer (Poolbeg Press)

De Gaulle and Ireland Pierre Joannon (Institute of Public Administration)

The Haughey File Stephen Collins (O'Brien Press)

The Long Goodbye: a cartoon tribute to a Taoiseach Martyn Turner (Irish Times Books)

De Valera was very much part of the twentieth century Zeitgeist, with Stalin, Hitler, Mussolini and Franco, though certainly with more affinities with Franco than with the other three grim titans.

T. Ryle Dwyer smartly covers the life but includes strict censures. He attacks the Longford-O'Neill biography as a whitewash job. This biographer says de Valera was a bad parent, a bad orator, and while he doesn't say it almost implies that his childhood was as traumatic as Edgar Allen Poe's.

"My father and mother were married in a Catholic church on September 19th, 1881. I was born in October 1882." He was christened George Edward in New York, his birthplace. His Spanish father died and his mother remarried, having sent him home to the half-acre farm in Bruree, County Limerick. "He was left in Bruree to be reared in loveless surroundings, amid lurid speculation about his legitimacy," Dwyer writes. At the local school he was registered under his Uncle Pat's surname, Edward Coll. As a boy, he begged his mother to come and take him to America but she would not.

A scholarship got him to Blackrock College in Dublin at fifteen. "On his first night, he later recalled, he lay in bed thanking God for his deliverance from Bruree." A Royal University degree led him to teaching. Learning Irish at the Gaelic League, he met Sinead Flanagan. They married in 1910. During the Rising, in Boland's Mill, "de Valera did not actually surrender with his men," Dwyer writes—and "with a pregnant wife and three young children, it seemed the height of irresponsibility to become involved in the rebellion of 1916." His wife obtained a reprieve of her husband's death sentence on the grounds that he was an American.

De Valera's credentials as a patriot and hero are evident even from his exploits during 1918-32. His vision of an independent, Gaelic, Catholic Ireland led him into dealing with US President Wilson and the Paris Peace Conference, the League of Nations, and to jail in Dartmoor, followed by a farcical escape from Lincoln jail, becoming Priomh Aire in the first Dail of 1919, the fundraising tour of the US, battling with Daniel Coholan and the Friends of Irish Freedom, and the futility of pleading his cause with President Harding who would not dictate to Britain. There followed the talks with Lloyd George, the treaty signed without Dev's presence in London, the treaty approved in the historic Dail vote of sixty-four to fifty-seven, the civil war which took the lives of the cream of the country's eligible leaders, Dev's arrest by Free State troops in Ennis and then, after six months in solitary confinement, his return to the same Ennis platform, laughing the event off. Then his arrest in Derry and month in Crumlin Road jail; the founding of Fianna Fail in 1926, a financially successful tour of the US in 1930 and the setting up of the Irish Press newspaper ("Any government that desires to hold power in Ireland should put publicity before all," were de Valera's words). With the defeat of W. T. Cosgrave, he came to power in 1932, while the land annuities and the economic war with Britain dominated the political agenda.

De Valera's republican ideology included the aim of coercing the Northern Unionists in 'Carsonia' as he called it. He believed that "those Unionists who were not willing to accept the 1937 constitution should be transferred to Britain and replaced by Roman Catholics of Irish extraction from Britain."

Churchill played on de Valera's dreams of a United Ireland and an end to partition. His cable to Dev in 1941 was menacing. The two men executed in Ireland in 1940 for de Valera "marked an irrevocable step in his break with the IRA".

There remains savage criticism of Dev's totalitarian censorship, the Westport Protestant librarian incident, the sacking of Eoin O'Duffy, the six-month teachers' strike in the forties and the Fethard-on-Sea mixed marriage crisis of the fifties. Sean Lemass succeeded him as Taoiseach in '59, and Childers succeeded his presidential years in 1973. This biographer has not exorcised the spirit of de Valera, even after eight books on Irish history. His closing chapter is reminiscent of a dinner guest who pontificates under an idee fixe.

De Valera's messianic actions, realised in political power, did in his time create another brand of Irish schizophrenia. His reply to the British PM's VE Day speech was a moment of unity of spirit in Éire. According to T. Ryle Dwyer, Churchill in his speech made him the personification of the devil and evil in Éire by pronouncing the name as 'Devil Éire'. "Nothing could erase his share of guilt for the events leading to the civil war," Dwyer writes.

De Valera's own hero was Lincoln, whose great civil war speech was an impassioned plea for the idealism of democracy, while understanding the high price paid by union soldiers in its pursuit. Hearing the recording of de Valera's reply to Churchill can strike the Republican soul. He heard the shots executing the 1916 leaders. Or is it the dictatorial voice of puritanism in Dev's speech that strikes the pluralist liberal soul.

At first sight this book looks like a very well produced brochure. It is almost a biography. Pierre Joannon's essay makes convincing parallels between De Gaulle and de Valera: "Neither of them was a bourgeois . . . Both were devout catholics." The two leaders met on 17 June 1969 at Aras an Uachtarain. De Valera said "The European nations are too old; they have too deeply ingrained a personality to be capable of dissolving one day into a vaster European whole." "It is exactly what I think," said General de Gaulle.

Dermot Keogh writes about the diplomatic situation during the war years between neutral Ireland, de Gaulle's Free French in exile and Vichy France. From Keogh's analysis it is not heretical to assume that the de Valera government was more pro-Petain. Ronan Fanning tackles the de Gaulle wilderness years, from the end of the war until his election as President in 1958. Her refers to the diplomatic work of Sean Murphy, Con Cremin, Conor Cruise O'Brien and Ambassador (William) Fay. Joseph T. Carroll's pages on Ireland's EEC application are informative on the number of years and the Irish delegations who made our chances of membership become real.

Former aide-de-camp Admiral Francois Flohic has an atmospheric, evocative piece on the General and Mme de Gaulle's Irish visit (10 May to 19 June 1969). Claud Cockburn writes of his friendship with de Gaulle during the war. It is a colourful article, outlining Cockburn's hardships and the General's. Patrick Campbell's contribution is about his failure to get an interview with de Gaulle during the Irish visit. It is a witty understatement titled 'The General in a Green Silence'.

The book also has a foreword by Charles J. Haughey, two letters from de Gaulle to de Valera, the Irish Times obituary on de Gaulle, a chronology of his life, notes, an index and illustrations.

The Castlebar-born son of a Free State officer, his father-in-law was Sean Lemass, who appointed him Minister for Justice in 1961. He stepped into the Finance Ministry, allowing Jack Lynch to become Taoiseach in 1966. This biographer has no revelations about the Arms crisis of 1970: "the real surprise was that Haughey should be so centrally involved."

1981, the year of the Stardust fire and of the H-Block hunger strikes to the death, also saw the first of five general elections of the decade, when the number of Fianna Fail seats held fell and rose, fell and rose, and fell again. Stephen Collins writes "Haughey helped to cripple the national economy for the next decade," referring to the eighties. "Economics is a dismal science," according to Haughey; economists are 'dismal scientists' and there is a 'Doheny & Nesbitt School of Economics'.

The year after becoming Taoiseach, he was verbally attacked by Margaret Fail and founded the Progressive Democrats. Less than four years on, Haughey's hold on power depended on O'Malley's new party. The Sunday Press headlined the Eirfreeze Larry Goodman fraud. "Goodman's private jet was being parked at Casement military aerodrome at Baldonnell," Collins writes.

Haughey was in hospital in 1988. The following year he proposed Brian Lenihan for President. Garret FitzGerald on RTE's 'Questions and Answers' confronted Lenihan about phone calls to Áras an Uachtarain by senior Fianna Fail members "in an effort to persuade President Hillery . . . to ask them to form a government" in January 1982. A UCD post-grad student had tapes with admissions about the phone calls. When these were made public, Lenihan refused to resign as Tanaiste. Haughey sent Bertie Ahern and Padraig Flynn after him as he campaigned with his sister, Mary O'Rourke, Minister for Education, through Longford-Westmeath. One morning "a helicopter piloted by the Taoiseach's son Ciaran Haughey came into view over Athlone and circled ominously above the house" where Lenihan had spent the night. He resigned reluctantly. Padraig Flynn, Environment Minister, verbally attacked Mary Robinson, then Presidential candidate, in a sexist way on RTE's 'Saturday View'. Fianna Fail advertised in newspapers prior to the election against Robinson, asking "Is the left right for the Park?"

On 15 January 1992 an RTE 'Nighthawks' interview with Sean Doherty led to a press conference at which he confirmed Haughey's part in the phone tapping of two political journalists in 1982. The Taoiseach resigned on 30 January 1992.

Stephen Collins has completed a task of some detail in this book which is at best a journalistic filofax. There are many mysteries still to be revealed. Perhaps the man himself will write an autobiography, memoirs, or—even better—the True Confessions of Charles J. Haughey?

Here are Charles J. Haughey's years as Taoiseach in sixty-six Turner cartoons, taken from the Irish Times. Sixty-six portraits of Charlie as a pair of eyebrows? In the absence of a national TV programme similar to England's 'Spitting Image', Martyn Turner's cartoonery is good stuff. Some of the cartoons are more chuckleful than others. It would be difficult to pick a winner out of them all. The former Taoiseach is facially conspicuous for his hooded eyes which severe critics have called reptilian. "It is part of the magic of caricature that someone can be identified by features that he doesn't possess," writes Martyn Turner in a brief memorable introduction. Elsewhere he continues: "The survival of Mr Haughey became a political issue in itself. The cartoonist's response was to create a political symbol for this political issue. In my case the symbol was a tiny man with a vast red nose, hair than ascended to heaven and thick dark eyebrows."

—*Books Ireland* 1992

THE LIFE AND CRIMES OF CJH: Haughey Prince of Power
Conor Lenihan (Blackwater Press)

A contradictory biography praising CJH while its real narrative only appears sporadically and is about the sacking of the author's father, Lenihan Snr as Tánaiste and Minister for Defence in 1990 and losing his bid for Áras an Uachtaráin weeks later. The official letter from the Office of the Taoiseach requesting his resignation, signed by Haughey is the sole appendix to the book. Lenihan Snr was pushing forward his candidacy for President against Mary Robinson until being foiled by the anti-woman remarks of Padraig Flynn. There are various anecdotes such as at the top table in the Burlington when Haughey demanded homage on his tenth year as party leader from the sycophants (literally), Richard Harris, Brendan Kennelly, Chris de Burgh, and RTÉ royalty Gay and Kathleen. At the same event, Lenihan Snr was excluded from the top table, and instead seated near Seán Doherty who vowed 'to even things up with Haughey' calling him 'a tramp'. Doherty spilt the beans on the Arnold/Kennedy phone-tapping in 1992.

The author, Lenihan Jnr has a pedigree that includes 'Political Correspondent at the Palace of Westminster', 'dealing with P. J. Mara on a daily basis', 'helping Ahern in his bid to become Taoiseach', and he is nephew of Mary O'Rourke. He quotes from O'Malley's memoir *Conduct Unbecoming* but personally never avoids adulation for CJH. 'Enormous personal appeal' possessing 'a more radical nationalism in the republican tradition', and bizarrely views him as 'a Walt Disney cartoon classic' without specifying which title. The use of biographers, Ryle Dwyer and Arnold, otherwise provide the main texture of the book. Arnold's depiction of Haughey as 'essentially cold and suspicious; the stare is reptilian' may prove definitive along with Fitzgerald's capstone appraisal 'a flawed pedigree...a wish to dominate, even own the state' and Dick Spring's speech about his 'greed for office...disregard for the truth...contempt for political standards'.

Lenihan Jnr includes the Moriarty Tribunal and its disclosures about CJH's illegal money dealings reaching €45m. Nor does he avoid a lacklustre recitation of the wellknown facts about the personality of the demagogue, son of a Free Stater, Lieutenant in the FCA, North Dublin ward boss, and the marriage to Lemass's daughter. And consistent hypocrite supporting Archbishop McQuaid's banning of Edna O'Brien's *The Country Girls*, the man from TACA, the 1960s post-Christian Brothers' Boy in mohair-suits doing the social rounds in The Shelbourne, The Hibernian, Jamet's, The Russell and Groome's. Vote-catching for Dev's retirement in the Áras by utilising the 1916 semicentennial as emotive iconography merely.

O'Malley, early on, spotted the Haughey mafia and the 'Donegal Mafia' behind which was the Fort Dunree Camp as training centre for 'members of the IRA'. Lenihan Jnr explains the power-challenge forcing Lemass to offer Haughey the Finance Ministry and Blaney the Agriculture Ministry leaving Lynch to see off Colley (59 votes to 19) and become Taoiseach. Peter Berry at the Department of Justice is described as 'a sort of J. Edgar Hoover of Irish life' and the brisk narrative on the Arms Crisis foreshadows CJH's rise and fall, as well as his public cover-ups. Lenihan Snr 'rarely spoke his mind on the phone' during this period was 'under suspicion as well as under surveillance' which proves that phone-tapping was deemed acceptable. The version of the Arms Crisis given is that Lynch 'knew much earlier than he insisted that weapons were to be purchased' and 'backed off and decided to blame the entire fiasco on those ministers, and Captain Kelly'. Haughey, Blaney and Gibbons were 'briefed at every step of the way, if not by Captain Kelly, then by the Army's Head of Intelligence Colonel Michael Hefferon'. Still, Lenihan Jnr is perplexed as to why 'Lynch opted to put those involved on trial in the courts' and adds 'my father always said that the main person pushing for a prosecution was George Colley.'

The return of CJH is well done, and his enlisting Reynolds with the country and western caucus. 'Some preferred the Mercedes but Haughey felt the Jaguar cut a greater dash, with its leather seats and inlay'. Good choice for rural vote-catching in the 70s. Meanwhile back in the city, 'Haughey's constituency machinery' cranked out cheques and Christmas turkeys. In summer, the charity gymkhana with marquee and CJH in riding gear with silver trays and matching teapots on the lawns of Kinsealy. Glasses were raised in The West County Arms as FF rode into power, seeing off Conor Cruise O'Brien on Election night in '77. Lynch's token peace-profile flopped as Mountbatten at Mullaghmore and 18 British Paras in Warrenpoint were killed on the same day. Haughey's 1980 Ard Fhéis was 'like a Baptist revival meeting rather than a political conference'.

The tone is bizarre as he states that CJH was 'the first person to compliment Mrs Thatcher on her legs'. Such commentary takes from the gravity of the 1980s, the Anglo-Irish summit with its catchcry coined by Lenihan Snr 'the totality of relationships'. McCreevy and O'Malley contesting CJH's leadership is plonked into a chapter entitled 'Dissidents'.'My father was not too happy with the Gregory deal either', he claims and never questions his subject's ruthless quest which the blurb hails as 'a career richly defined by corruption, scandal and the pursuit of power'. 'Richly' is historically accurate.

The pace is steady with the phone-tapping scandal, the P. J. Mara era, the axing of O'Malley, and Fitzgerald's failed Divorce Referendum of 1986 when 'Haughey issued a personal statement expressing his belief in the importance of the family. Years later it was revealed that he had just returned from holidaying with Terry Keane'. Lenihan Jnr tries one arch bluff stating that Keane 'did not seek to cash in further by turning her serialised articles on the affair into a published book'.

The real scandals fit Lenihan Jnr's 'Let-us-now-praise Haughey' syndrome. He is also self-censored by his own adage: 'when you grow up in a political household you learn to bite your tongue'. With Dermot Desmond as 'patron', CJH becomes financial saviour (!) and the IFSC's contribution 'to economic recovery and investment was enormous'. Apparently, the legacy of this Napoleon of Crime is that he created Temple Bar, Ryanair, IMMA, and harnessed the OPW to kit out the Merrion Street Department of the Taoiseach. Tom Garvin as CJH admirer is quoted 'historians will give credit to Haughey for starting the Irish economic miracle that took root in the late 1990s'. Patrick Maume's *Dictionary of Irish Biography* is also acquiescent, defining him as 'essentially a technician of power rather than an ideologue and his inconsistencies must be seen in this light'. Inconsistencies indeed.

CJH and the liver transplant for Lenihan Snr in the Mayo Clinic is narrated truthfully with Haughey ordering Paul Kavanagh who fundraised €270,000 but 'no more than €70,000 was spent' on the medicare? Lenihan Snr and the 1982 Duffy MA thesis with its revelations in 1987 on *Nighthawks* through Shay Healy activated the beginning of the end and leads to Lenihan Jnr's outrageous summing up. 'Haughey was not guilty in all of these business or financial transactions'. And he lists them. Bernie Cahill and the Irish Sugar Company/Greencore with Dermot Desmond as advisor through National City Brokers. Michael Smurfit and Desmond purchasing the J. M. and O'B site in Ballsbridge. The UCD/Carysfort site purchased by Pino Harris. Nora Owen and the sewage pipe for Kinsealy. The ESB's generator for Inishvickillane. Ciarán Haughey (the son) and Celtic Helicopters. And Ben Dunne's €1.3m bank drafts to bury CJH's AIB overdraft.

Lenihan Jnr feebly suggests that CJH should not have used 'the description of Desmond as a "business friend" [which] invited people to ridicule Haughey on the basis of how he categorised friendship'. Media 'oppressors' such as Damien Kiberd and *The Sunday Business Post* are criticised. And there is palpable pleasure in his recounting how CJH survived the 1991 challenge from Reynolds (55 votes to 22) who considered Haughey 'a very fair leader'. He 'will probably be remembered as being good for the country but bad for politics'. Having retold this at the RHA among the Gallagher 'property developer family' they 'fell around the place laughing at the cleverness of it all'. Surprisingly, Lenihan Jnr believes that Haughey spent his life 'trying to keep up with the bills and keep the banks and the creditors at bay'. Easons display the biography in 'Just Published' and 'Irish History'. It should be on the 'True Crime' shelves.

—*VILLAGE: politics and culture* 2016

HISTORY HURTS

The Transformation of Ireland 1900-2000 Diarmaid Ferriter (Profile)

Do Penance or Perish: Magdalen asylums in Ireland Frances Finnegan (Oxford University Press)

Ferriter does not give as much analysis as his title suggests but there is a staggering parade of facts. This is history for the informed and space is always a problem: Michael Davitt (too brief), William O'Brien (United Irish League) well outlined. Michael Collins takes second place to Dev; the 1916 rising is barely mentioned compared to the lockout of 1913. The War of Independence comes to life while the Civil War is neglected. O'Duffy's fascists get more space than the International Brigade. Two inaccuracies—Lady Gregory's Poets and Dreams should be Poets and Dreamers and Francis Stuart's collection of poems *We Have Kept the Faith* is treated as a prose work, but this is quibbling in comparison to the mass of material that is presumably accurate.

Ferriter, perhaps for balance, over-praises de Valera: his diminution of the IRA, and the ingenious rise of Fianna Fail largely though the establishment of cumainn in the 26 counties. "De Valera believed in State control of all areas of Irish life." Dev's constitution, hand in glove with the Church of Rome, is put in context by giving the electoral vote: 685,000 in favour, 527,000 opposed. Ferriter's detailing of the Catholic Church as 'the effective government of Ireland' in the early decades of the Free State is immensely satisfying to read; even Noel Browne wrote an obsequious letter, out of terror, to McQuaid, 'ruler of Catholic Ireland'.

Strong quotations crop up everywhere: from Pearse in 1913 heralding the revolution, "There will be in Ireland of the next few years a multitudinous activity of freedom clubs, young republican parties, labour organisations, socialist groups and what not." Bernard Shaw to Michael Collins' sister, "Let us all praise God that he did not die in a snuffy bed of a trumpery cough, weakened by age and saddened by disappointment that would have attended his work had he lived." Minister Brian Lenihan's comment on a visit to Artane Industrial School in 1968, "get me out of this fucking place"—many of the inmates must often have uttered the same.

The use of statistics breaks the relentless flow of personalities and gives a glimpse of the people: "Between 1869 and 1913, 48,664 children were admitted to industrial schools in Ireland, and 2,623 died while in custody." Wartime emigration is shown in realistic terms; many Irish just wanted to work in Britain and some served with distinction for the allies. By 1961 there were 130,000 Irish-born in London. In 1999, Ireland's population was 3.72 million with 8% of the workforce in agriculture.

Modern historians and commentators Joseph Lee, Dermot Keogh, Tom Garvin and Terence Brown are, as it were, at Ferriter's elbow. Much valuable use is made of many other commentators such as Sean Ó Faolain, Austin Clarke and later on Nuala Ó Faolain, Colm Tóibín, Nell McCafferty, Eamonn McCann and (not too much) Fintan O'Toole. Extracts from poems by various poets are quoted including Montague and Hewitt. Many key texts are cited: Alan Bestic's The Importance of Being Irish. John Whyte's Church and State in Modern Ireland. Mike Milotte's Banished Babies.

The election of Mary Robinson to the senate in 1969 marks a shift from the dominant male patriarchy. The arms crisis is outlined without emphasizing its scapegoat, Captain Kelly. Haughey is not shown in a good light; Reynolds is, while the emergence of bungalow blight in the countryside heralds the 1990s and the mixed blessings of the Celtic Tiger era.

Ferriter ably asserts Irish class differences and pinpoints the first revelations of the hidden Ireland with the Granard grotto death in 1984 of a fifteen-old in childbirth. Thereafter, Bishop Casey and his son; the priest found dead in the gay Dublin sauna, the paedophile priest Brendan Smyth and media-priest Michael Cleary, preacher of Catholic morality and priestly celibacy, who also had a secret son. Church and political scandal and corruption are contrasted with the martyred Veronica Guerin.

There are derogatory remarks about the "petty-minded Sean MacBride" and Cruise O'Brien calling Pearse "a maniac, mystic nationalist with a cult of blood sacrifice and a strong personal motivation towards death. A nation which takes a personality of that type as its mentor is headed towards disaster." This is refuted by quotation from Terence Brown on the essential uniqueness of the 1916 rising; in other words without the revolution there would have been no transformation. Foster is quoted, "We are all revisionists," along with F. S. L. Lyons' Culture and Anarchy stressing the multiplicity within each Irish person.

W. H. Auden wrote of Yeats, "Mad Ireland hurt you into poetry." To read Ferriter is to engage with the madness and the hurt of our history and to acknowledge that one Irish historian's version may be another's diatribe. What about a new history of Ireland by a total outsider or foreigner, perhaps, one of our closest neighbours?

Finnegan's value lies in her twenty-plus years of research into the origins of this regime for fallen' women, administered principally by other women beginning with the penitentiary or 'Magdalen' system in the British Isles from 1835 onwards. It was do-gooders, especially evangelicals, and even Gladstone, full of kind wishes and concern, that fostered this system. Behind the scenes, Victorian prudery and money dictated.

Ireland saw a flourishing of these houses of inflicted pain, up and running by the close of the nineteenth century in Limerick, Waterford, New Ross, Belfast and the notorious Lock Hospital in Cork. The shipping magnate Richard Devereux added to his prestige by becoming a substantial benefactor of such institutions. Finnegan's detail builds into what seems incredible, as she introduces what one might call the mini-Hitler of the system, Mother Mary of St Euphrasia Pelletier, foundress of the ironically titled Our Lady of Charity of the Good Shepherd of Angels whose nuns were her henchwomen. Pelletier wrote the rules for the Magdalen asylums that were universally applied to inmates; some were mothers and prostitutes suffering from various illnesses including venereal disease and syphilis. If they were pregnant their offspring were literally confiscated and passed on to rich families.

The facts are bleak. 'Fallen' women had been pushed into prostitution by poverty. Some victims of rape and incest were rejected by their families or were destitute from birth and became prime fodder for the Magdalen Asylums. Snippets of personal stories with the names of their young victims give substance to the harshness of a system that stripped them of dignity, including their names in many cases. In the nineteenth century inmates who proved too difficult to control, pacify and ultimately dehumanise, were dumped back on the streets. In twentieth-century Ireland, the system held on to its victims who were gainfully employed in various aspects of what became a nation-wide laundry service providing substantial profits from their slave labour.

The average day began at five a. m. and ended at eight-thirty p. m. Within this schedule the actual working day was twelve hours, food was measly and periods of silence on a par with enclosed orders of medieval monasteries. Sometimes, instead of conversation, prayers and hymns were said or sung out loud. Mortification was encouraged; carved pious mottoes adorned the drab quarters: "Unless Ye Do Penance, Ye Shall All Perish". Some of the inmates brought religious zeal into the dormitories—their beds had "bundles of nettles, branches of thorns and pillows filled with stones" while in the Limerick asylum they "mixed soot and soap with drinking water to punish themselves for past intemperance". Lesbianism, known as 'particular friendships', was punished and in fact any of kind of friendship was stamped out by the nuns who spoke of the inmates as 'the children', irrespective of their age.

It gets worse. Finnegan evokes the internal tensions of the average Magdalen whose 'children' were "depressed, pining for their babies, or frantic to escape—resorted to tantrums, window smashing and refusal to work". Cruel institutions find little problem with those in their charge, by increasing the level of cruelty to break down the individual. It may sound dramatic but these places were concentration camps without the gas chambers.

Many of her statistics relate to the nineteenth century but a figure for 1958 is revealing. The number of 'children' held at Magdalen asylums in Europe and as far as Ceylon, numbered close on 50,000. And what happened to Mother Mary of St Euphrasia Pelletier? She was beatified by the Church of Rome. Her sisters are seen in a Corpus Christi procession in Dublin, wearing veils and cloaks, and flanked by Gardaí. Church and State had dealt savagely with some of the 'comely maidens dancing at the crossroads'.

—*Books Ireland* 2005

HOMO HERO

Roger Casement in Death or Haunting the Free State W. J. McCormack (University College Dublin Press)

Roger Casement: the black diaries with a study of his background, sexuality, and Irish political life Jeffrey Dudgeon

The Crime against Europe Roger Casement (Athol Books)

Sir Roger Casement's Heart of Darkness: the 1911 Documents Angus Mitchell (Irish Manuscripts Commission)

Casement Angus Mitchell (Haus Publishing)

When I was boy during the fiftieth anniversary of the 1916 Rising, my history class often singled out Casement the hero. One turned in a Roger Casement essay based on the school text about the patriot, gunrunner and co-organiser of the Irish rebellion, oblivious of the fact that Roger was, to use a phrase of the period, as queer as a three-handled brush.

Casement the martyr-patriot who tried and failed as a Republican gunrunner still seems far more palatable in some quarters—as he is too in the light of Ed Maloney's recent book on the IRA and their successful gun-running in the latter half of the twentieth century. The older generation has little time for revisionists such as McCormack, shamelessly reducing legends and myths to the facts.

McCormack's dramatic title makes no secret that he wants to out those in denial about Casement's life. The book has a cast of hundreds, with footnotes to explain who was who. He makes them all fit his grand design in the time-honoured manner of the academic—that if you propound a literary-historical theory it had better hold everything together, however tenuous at times the threads might seem.

McCormack's study is only about Casement by proxy, and might well be subtitled 'a biography of Casement biographers'. Of particular concern is the apologist and hagiographer (W. J. Maloney 1882-1952), the Edinburgh-born neurologist who served in the Royal Army Medical Corps during the Great War. His propagandist book The Forged Casement Diaries (1936) from the Talbot Press revealed that twenty years after Casement had faced the hangman, his profile in Irish history was subject to a conspiratorial cover-up. By the thirties many who had dished the dirt on Casement were dead and Irish minds rested easy that their Dublin-born patriot's reputation was intact. He had gone to the gallows with such prayerful serenity according to John Ellis, the executioner, that it had haunted him for life.

Casement might not have hung but for the allegations of sexual perversity, and more so for the fact that his infamous diaries contained accounts of imperialist brutality in Africa. Casement had a glittering array of enemies and McCormack gets legalistic in outlining their origins, political background and so forth, including John Redmond. Casement supporters included a group of literary luminaries: Bernard Shaw, Sir Arthur Conan Doyle, Chesterton, Galsworthy, Masefield, Yeats but notably not Joseph Conrad.

McCormack revels in his scholarship, unravelling the major cover-up by Denis Gwynn who wrote the first biography, The Life and Death of Roger Casement (1930). Dr Patrick MacCartan, friend of Casement's and avowed Dev supporter, went along with the accepted cover-up as did Maloney who had never met Casement, "The greatest weakness of Maloney's argument is his inability to articulate—even in this very basic sense—the charge laid against his hero."

The irony and hypocrisy of Gwynn was that Augustine Birrell, essayist, lawyer and Chief Secretary for Ireland 1907-16, told him that Casement's incriminating diary was genuine—while the Irish government in the 1930s did not want an independent examination of any Casement documents or diaries.

Maloney would be elevated to an Academician in Yeats's Irish Academy of Letters in 1937 while Yeats's poem 'The Ghost of Roger Casement' supported the forgery theory. The poem did reach wide public notice through the Irish Press. Yeats's stance in private is interesting; in correspondence with one of his lovers, Dorothy Wellesley, he writes "If Casement were a homo-sexual what matter!" Much controversy followed the serialisation of Maloney's book in the Irish Press. The poet Alfred Noyes claimed that the Casement diaries were not the work of British forgers, still Maloney identified Noyes as "the principal forgery trafficker in America" alongside Cecil Spring-Rice. Meanwhile in the Irish Press many voices approved of Maloney—in other words supported the forgery theory. The opinions and beliefs of Peadar O'Donnell, Francis Stuart and a host of writers from that period are fully explored. McCormack does not hold back from deriding these misguided Casement enthusiasts who, failing facts, became the foolish faithful—Casementalists, he calls them. Joseph Bigger, TCD professor and friend of the Casements, admitted at the time "the family knew perfectly well that Casement was a homo". Meanwhile De Valera in 1937 cautiously avoided any inflammatory statements on Maloney's book with the comment, "Roger Casement's reputation is safe in the affections of the Irish people."

Maloney disregarded Casement's sexual proclivities, tracing the case for and against his mental instability. Along with Gwynn, he expounded the "horrors of his experience in Putumayo" that caused such disturbance to the Irish patriot on witnessing colonial abuse of power and excess—McCormack does not spare the reader the outer limits of depravity, much of it disturbing to read a century later. One of Maloney's major sources was George Gavan Duffy, Casement's solicitor at the trial, who later carefully "avoided a real repudiation of the diaries". Maloney, the misguided biographer, cobbled together a flawed book in the light of evidence from the diaries of Casement's own sexual exploits in far-off Africa and thereby became a trader in received opinions about Casement that were false. He soon lost interest in Casement after publication, pursuing medical matters more in keeping with a doctor than sexual politics in an era when its hour had not come. Besides, his ailing wife who had endured a twenty-five-year illness, died in 1946, and Maloney died six years later.

McCormack is not too insistent about his own tests on the diaries in the 1990s as proving that they are one hundred per cent in the handwriting of Casement. What is certain though is that his rage is not against the British establishment that dispatched the Irish patriot but rather against those politicians, commentators and writers who jumped in on the wrong side of the argument. No wonder that Conrad did not sign any petition for leniency in order to save Casement's neck, lumping him in with his central character in *Heart of Darkness*, the evil Mister Kurtz. McCormack shows that Casement's colleague Armando Normand, an active sadist who managed a rubber company on the banks of the Amazon, had more affinity with Mister Kurtz. Casement, taking him all in all, comes across in this meticulous and exactingly detailed text, as a pawn in the African colonies that were being raped and enslaved by empires other than the British.

Dudgeon deserves nothing but praise despite his various repetitions and jumping back and the forth in the text, not to mention the longueurs in introducing of his background, Casement's antecedents. His study of the sexual life is given much space alongside the infamous diaries, or to be accurate, betwixt entries. Once the Black Diaries were published in 1959 Casement's private life was public but had been mentioned and gossiped about ever since his second and final trial in 1916.

Commenting on Wilde, Joyce lamented not his life but that he had never written about his sexuality. Casement's diaries are stark and explicit, but Dudgeon fills out and explains details that might easily escape the heterosexual reader. In a euphemism of the time, Casement was 'musical' and allowed his girl cousins to dress him up in their clothes. His alcoholic mother, Annie née Jephson died when he was nine, while his father, a former army Captain, left the boy, one of four children, an orphan at the age of twelve. Casement quit school in Ballymena and before reaching twenty was a clerk in Liverpool and thereafter went to sea. The diaries reveal a vigorous sexual appetite, finding partners at random on board ship, at hotels and everywhere and anywhere in Africa, Europe and the US. Sexual expenditure for the year 1911 was £35, spent on forty-nine different partners.

Casement is credited with two fairly successful relationships: from his earlier years with Joseph Millar Gordon, and in later life with Adler Christensen who betrayed him. Dudgeon has a list of those disgusted at his sex life including Eamonn Duggan, plenipotentiary to the Treaty of 1921. Bulmer Hobson refused to believe in the revelations because he was a friend and confidant of Casement's. Dudgeon also deals well with the authentication of the diaries.

The real story here is Casement advancing the cause of British Imperialism in Africa, working at various trading stations, as transport manager, surveyor, customs officer, consul, spy, consul-general and on various investigation expeditions which resulted in official reports that were published in his lifetime. With his knighthood and retirement on pension the scene shifts to his burgeoning Irish nationalist persona. 'Congo Casement' of Protestant persuasion was on his way to becoming an Irish Republican hero and Roman Catholic from early in his life, according to some commentators. Dudgeon shifts a gear and the contrasting narrative to the diaries is enthralling with Casement in the US, Ireland, Britain and Germany—suddenly a knight of the realm is a leading Irish revolutionary organiser. One of the strange elements about Casement the gunrunner is that he is shown as being squeamish about firearms, and there is the occasional witticism comparable to Wilde: "I attribute my good looks to quinine and think of recommending that drug to all ladies in search of new complexions".

Casement is explained as a great talker but not a master of pornography nor are the snatches of his poetry up to much. Yet he can be seen as a genuine heroic figure in the energy of his life and the level of achievement both for and against the British Empire. His experience beyond the British Isles formed him and thence he turned vehemently against John Bull, "I could understand fully their whole scheme of wrongdoing at work in the Congo".

Alice Stopford Green felt he had an obsession with Wolfe Tone but similarly he was obsessed with John Mitchel and at the same time could enjoy Somerville and Ross. He was a man of destiny. Someone whose self-reliance emerged in early youth, he was at home with himself everywhere and apparently without sexual hang-up in an age of unease about almost every sexual preference. Casement was a tall man, elegant, a gentleman, and one whom the ladies would have seen as eligible. However, a glance at the photographs of his fantasy-males accompanying the diaries are revealing—these were not just examples of the natives from the far-away places he worked in—they were, in modern parlance, what he was into. One might well hazard a guess that, when we are safely beyond the old order of Ireland by 2016, he will be seen as a far more intriguing patriot even in movie-makers' terms than the other men and women of the Rising.

If you are not familiar with their writings, here's a chance to read some of Casement's 'The Crime Against Europe' is expectedly pro-German, written six weeks after the Great War began and published later that year. The contents reveal no startling political commentary in their analysis of the alliance of England, France and Russia against Germany. There are no predictions of how Europe would change dramatically in the ensuing decades. However, there is perspicacity in observing the role that control of the seas would play in the war and the inkling that Germany would be defeated, as well as showing Casement's prose style.

Maloney's 'Casement as Traitor-Patriot' is actually the preface to his The Forged Casement Diaries. It is trenchantly defensive of its biographical subject, setting him up in a good light as saint, martyr and patriot against the propaganda that arose over his trial, and Maloney asks, "which was true—the image propaganda imprinted, or the image it obliterated?"

The greater bulk of this short brochure is taken up by the fulminating of Douglas Clifford, a polemicist in the bare-knuckle tradition. Everything can be swiped at and is, in his introduction: from Britain and Alfred Noyes to the Great War, Irish Fascism, Margaret Thatcher, and particularly W. J. Mc Cormack and his Roger Casement in Death. He finds Mc Cormack inaccurate and cites where, so he is no shadow-boxer. However, Athol badly need a rich peer of the realm or other grant aid to dress their pamphlets up better.

This is a mammoth and utterly fascinating work of scholarship using photographs, including one of a Huitoto woman, hauntingly beautiful. Coloured maps inside front and back cover are marked to show Casement's voyages when he was sent by the Foreign Office to report on the atrocities. His consular and nationalist sides are fully rendered; his sexual exploits ignored. There are far more letters here than other documents. Each chapter covers a month of a hectic year with details of meetings with George Moore, Havelock Ellis—these are fleeting social contacts compared to people from the industrial, political and foreign office arenas: Sir Edward Grey, William Cadbury, Woodrow Wilson, Theodore Roosevelt, and US President William Taft.

The material was gathered from various collections on both sides of the Atlantic and every jot is significant, from footnote to extracts from House of Commons parliamentary debates. The energy of

Casement comes across, his humanitarian passion and workaholic zest. Some of the more intimate letters from his London domicile in Philbeach Gardens show the many facets of this complex man who signs himself, 'Ruaidhri Mac Asmund' to nationalists, 'Scodgie' to his favourite cousin, Gertrude (Gee) Bannister and quotes all of Yeats's 'The Lover Tells of the Rose in his Heart' to Alice Stopford Green. There is a hilarious letter to Bulmer Hobson on how to market a book, with a libellous sideswipe at Easons for inefficient distribution methods. The book was Alice Stopford Green's Irish Nationality that became a favourite of Casement's. Arthur Conan Doyle got the germ for The Lost World from Casement's vigorous conversations. Doyle wanted Casement to write a novel about his experiences.

Casement's generosity with money comes up again and again. His brother Tom writes with gratitude for various cheques but annoyed about being humbled with handouts. Patrick Pearse sends details about placing an Indian student at St Enda's in Rathfarnham—the yearly fee was £39.17s 5d.

The real dark centre is Casement's investigation of the crimes of the London Rubber Company known as the Peruvian Amazon Company, and his reports to the Foreign Office, some of which were reported in the newspapers. Casement describes slaughter, torture and inhumanity. He demands that the slave drivers be brought to justice. When he mentions the dead from one region in excess of 30,000 his rage is palpable. This gives the real grit to Mitchell's work. It is harrowing stuff, reminiscent of holocaust literature from the 1940s. Otherwise, Casement cuts an eccentric figure, as in an appendix by a fellow traveller Dr Dickey who found him comical in a three-piece tweed suit in the equatorial regions walking with his dog and knobbly stick as if he was in the Glens of Antrim. At the end of this voyage of discovery into the heart of Casement one cannot but believe the emotive comment of Father James McCarroll who attended the condemned patriot in his final moments: "Roger

Casement was a saint. We should be praying to him rather than for him."

Mitchell with both *The Amazon Journal of Roger Casement* and the 1911 Documents noticed above to his credit brings in a good performance in this pocket biography. Haus's series includes Churchill, Dostoevsky, Gershwin and Marguerite Yourcenar. There are plenty of photographs and other facsimile material with brief notes on persons and events in Casement's life, providing a pictorial fast-forward approach for the busy skimmer and mugger-up. At a glance the text looks like a bygone missal, except the footnote numbers are for some reason in red.

Casement's life lends itself to this brevity and the cliffhanger chapter endings. The heights he reached in public life bear the first intimations of his fall from grace as a knight of the realm as he confronts his destiny with nationalists in Ireland and America and begins driving a spike into the heart of the empire. Meanwhile there are apt key quotations—that after living on and off for sixteen years in Africa, "I had come to look upon myself as an African;" and about his being happy "to die a thousand times for the sake of Ireland". The message from Mitchell is that the age of Irish patriots has passed and Casement was a creature of extraordinary courage and transcendence. Such a moral hero is a staggering challenge to our goals of materialist security and more awesome for having given up his life on the gallows for the cause of nationalism.

—*Books Ireland* 2003

A VIVID, PACY ACCOUNT OF A BLOODY EPISODE IN IRISH HISTORY

The Twelve Apostles: Michael Collins, the Squad and Ireland's fight for freedom Tim Pat Coogan (Head of Zeus)

Michael operated a war policy whereby 'shooting was a disagreeable necessity to be used with discrimination' but the 'Squad', his élite unit, did not 'always conform to a doctrine of minimum force'. As a kind of Scarlet Pimpernel, Collins fits graphic history or a True Life Drama series, yet he remains a legend and enigma beyond understanding. He cannot be unravelled by research or contemporary accounts: such is the myth, the man, the escapades and the tragedy. Academic analysis is useless in trying to 'explain' the life.

Coogan accepts that Collins and the Squad fought a war, and without war there would have been no Republic. The promises of Home Rule were a British political manoeuvre to gain enlistment. Statistically, there were far more Irish Nationalists than Unionists in the trenches of World War I. He begins by highlighting the background in a highly accessible manner.

Randolf Churchill's 'Orange Card' speech of 23 February 1886 is fired into the fast-moving narrative, along with Carson's anti-Home Rule 'Don't be afraid of illegalities' speech of 7 December 1913 that legitimated the Ulster Volunteer Force. Balance is added to the narrative about 1913 by using A.T.Q. Stewart's The Ulster Crisis. Carson took delight in organising the import of German guns for paramilitary Unionists, making them 'the Kaiser's Irish friends'. Westminster and the British monarchy were linked through blood ties to Kaiser Wilhelm II, who believed that Britain 'would surely not dare to fight a European war when a civil war was apparently threatening'. Coogan's history presents what is not visible in any mural or any printed jingoism.

The Irish Volunteers, the 1916 Rising and the aftermath are speedily outlined. Collins emerges as a traumatised hard drinker, gunman and natural-born leader. His actions are traced to the executions of the leaders of 1916. Coogan assumes that the reading of Chesterton's novel of anarchy, The Man Who Was Thursday, provided a template for the success of his methods.

The story is propelled forward contextually in asides such as Kathleen Clarke's visiting of the condemned Thomas Clarke in his cell. Collins was critical of Pearse, inflamed by Connolly and driven to progressive vengeance after the execution of Kevin Barry (whom he had been prepared to spring from Mountjoy Gaol until Barry's family objected). Upholding his forebears' principles, Collins's few words at Thomas Ashe's funeral in 1917 were indicative of his war: 'The volley which we have just heard is the only speech which it is proper to make above the grave of a dead Fenian', although he became a demagogue after the land slide election victory for Sinn Féin (73) against the Irish Parliamentary Party (6) in 1919.

His genius was in his ability to recruit gunmen. 'Ruthless' and 'autonomous' hardly describe him as he brought the war face to face with his enemies, often drinking in the same pub as them. Squad members, including Vinnie Byrne, armed themselves by stealing the enemies' weapons. Those weapons are described, as are the methods of killing. The business of assassination was devised by Collins, who supervised from his High Nelly bicycle between drinking sessions, rooftop escapes and journeys from one safe house to another. The Squad audaciously socialised while planning everything (all city centre locations),which adds to this outlandish, daring, fantastical account.

Extreme incidents made Collins legendary, such as breaking into the RIC headquarters in Brunswick (now Pearse) Street on the night of 7 April 1919, arranged by 'the confidential clerk' Ned Broy (who went on to become commissioner of An Garda Síochána). Collins's pilfering of British Intelligence photographs and documentation meant accurate profiling, backed up by RIC informants loyal to him and the Squad. James McNamara, Joe Kavanagh, Seán Noonan and especially David Nelligan could almost be fictional characters. Seán Lemass (later Taoiseach) as Squad member receives little mention.

The Squad had female members too: 'Lily Mernin, Ireland's Mata Hari', Susan Mason, Nancy O'Brien (Collins's cousin), Eileen McGrane and Dilly Dicker. These women had jobs with the British military and police, making them vital informants; Dicker in the postal system intercepted 'letters destined for the British Secret Service [that]would find their way into her handbag or her bosom or inside her elastic-legged knickers', according to Meda Ryan.

Hugh Martin, writing in the London Daily News in the summer of 1919, recorded the tension as British military personnel and equipment showed 'the infamy of stamping on freedom in Ireland. The issue may be delayed but it is in no doubt.' Collins's methods were deliberately different from those of the 1916 Rising. The Squad 'were salaried personnel', all younger than him, and, like Broy, expert at choosing key targets, including RIC Detective Sergeant Patrick Smyth (known as 'the Dog') and Daniel Hoey. The Squad's killing of Hoey was an emergency plan in order to protect Collins from capture. Most hits were in daylight, requiring more than two operatives who delivered the fatal shots. Headshots were the modus operandi. No target could be allowed to survive for many reasons, not least since witnesses could threaten the Squad's anonymity. Squad members usually emptied 'the entire contents of their revolvers' for a sure kill.

Planning also involved the getaway: an example of this was the hit on Frank Bourke, chairman of the Dublin and South Eastern Railways at Westland Row, where David Nelligan fired the first shots 'masked by the noise made by the trains'. Getting in and out of railway buildings added to the logistics of the hit. The Alan Bell shooting required disconnecting a tram in commandeered Simmonscourt Road for Tobin and McDonnell, who later reported back to Collins that inner-city hits amidst crowded streets offered the safer getaway.

The intense exactitude of planning using insiders explains how Britain's top spy, John Charles Byrnes, believed himself to be en route to trapping Collins when he was heading towards Squad members lying in wait. Coogan adds ironically that, 'though he did not succeed in capturing Collins, he did at least have the distinction of meeting him and sitting down with him (briefly)'.When the assistant commissioner, William Redmond, mounted a plan to capture Collins, it also led to a double-cross. Redmond, wearing a bullet proof vest, proved to be an easy target outside the Standard Hotel rather than having to be followed inside. On hearing the news Collins remarked, 'Redmond had not been up to the Standard'.

Nevertheless, the Squad failed on numerous occasions to kill the viceroy, Lord French. Their rampage by the end of 1920 meant that the Daily Chronicle (controlled by Lloyd George) admitted that 'revenge politics' would 'become the norm', such was the British outrage at the Squad's success. The shootings of Tomás Mac Curtain and the Barry execution had escalated the war, already exacerbated by the bringing in of the notorious Black and Tans by General Macready and Hugh Tudor. The Squad recruited a teenager, Seán Culhane, who shot DI Oswald Swanzy in a daylight ambush in Lisburn, Co. Antrim, which resulted in 'a pogrom directed against Catholics ... thirty-one were killed' in the aftermath, and 'two hundred injuries were reported in Lisburn, Banbridge and Belfast'.

The commissioner of the RIC in Munster, Lieutenant Colonel Bruce Smyth, killed in his country club in Cork, was told by the assassin: 'Your orders were to shoot on sight: you are in sight now!' Squad humour was always of this nature. Passing a church on the way to a hit, two gunmen were asked 'Are you going to the funeral?', to which they replied 'No, we're going to arrange one'.

Coogan sets up the Bloody Sunday hits of 'nineteen British operatives' in his inimitable style, and gallops through the return of de Valera from America, the Dev–Collins power struggle, the Anglo-Irish Treaty, Sir Henry Wilson's assassination in London and the Civil War. It was Dev's order to burn the Custom House (25 May 1921) that 'marked the end of the Twelve Apostles as an elite unit' which had effectively defeated the British Empire.

There is a terrific distillation and overview of Partition, as well as 'the dangerous summer of 1922'. The Squad continued under Collins into the Civil War as the book gets bloodier and darker, not least because Desmond Fitzgerald, Free State minister for defence, burned police reports of the era. Free State judicial executions and the Anti-Treaty soldiers' reactions resulted in grim Civil War atrocities, particularly in County Kerry. Coogan is unremitting in the details. He cites Vinnie Byrne, who said that after Collins's death most soldiers 'would have shot de Valera if they could have got near him'. De Valera is quoted as telling his son, Vivian, many decades later: 'If it weren't for the executions, the Civil War would still be going on'. Coogan's concluding page is simply that the Civil War centenary will be impossible to stage as a merely cultural commemoration.

—*Books Ireland* 2017

AN UNEVEN WORK, MISSING OUT ITS SUBJECTS' COMPLEXITIES

Revolutionary Lives: Constance and Casimir Markievicz Lauren Arrington (Princeton University Press)

Arrington sleepwalks (I will explain) in this double biography setting up Constance Markievicz (hereafter Markievicz) 'born to a sense of adventure' simply because her father Sir Henry Gore-Booth of Lissadell was an Arctic explorer. Sir Henry's philanthropic attitude towards 'tenants laid the foundations' for her social activism. Lissadell's festive atmosphere induced her bohemianism since the demesne flowed seasonally with 'whiskey and wine. Port and Madeira, champagne of the best vintage'. At twenty-four she moved back to London (her birthplace) living in Sloane Terrace, becoming an accomplished painter at the Slade with high society friends including Prince George, the future king. She wrote in her diary 'what Vulgar people the Royalties'.

Arrington rarely gets to grips with her complexity, her boredom, her ennui, her resemblance to Ibsen's and Shaw's theatrical heroines as privileged debutante in aristocratic circles, pursuing her art, the troubled relationship with her family and poet-sister Eva Gore-Booth, her spiritualism with William Morris and Madame Blavatsky. Markievicz as woman of destiny emerged onto the Irish revolutionary national stage becoming president aged twenty-eight of the Irishwoman's Suffrage and Local Government Association in Sligo. The biography states 'Yeats would turn to Fascism, Constance to Bolshevism' 'demanding something to live for, something to die for' whereas it was the lifetime commitment 'to aggressive reform [that] sprang from her study of James Connolly's writings, her interpretation of the Bolshevik Revolution, and her familiarity with the landscape and tenants in the west of Ireland' should have been more central in the book. Otherwise the analysis is merely academic and dismissive: 'socialist, Christian, and Irish republican tropes in her (Markievicz's) writing for the Irish Worker illustrates the various components of her political thought and the way that she was able to manipulate different discourses in her propaganda' (98).

Casimir Markievicz (the husband) was an artist, 'bit of a cad' and Catholic. They 'married three times' with one of the ceremonies at St Mary's Marylebone (London) officiated by 'Lissadell clergyman Frederick Sheridan Le Fanu' nephew of the Gothic novelist. 'Con and Casi' had met at the École des Beaux-Arts and moved into an apartment in Montparnasse with his son Stanislaus and their daughter Maeve Alyss as well as 'a servant named Josephine'. Both part-time parents indulged in travel with visits to Casimir's family estate in Zywotowka 'nominally Poland but also considered a part of Russia' and seasonally Lissadell for long pastoral and social holidays.

Markievicz absconded from idle aristocrat to radicalized revolutionary after meeting Belfast stalwart, Bulmer Hobson of the IRB, Máire nic Shuibhlaigh of Inghinidhe na hÉireann and Helena Molony for whom she designed the masthead of Bean na hÉireann later used in The Irish Worker. She began writing under the pen name 'Maca' desiring to 'organise a woman's movement on Sinn Féin lines'; 'if we must contend let it be in seeing who'll be the most Irish'. Her true brainchild was Na Fianna Éireann in the spirit of James Fintan Lalor and Wolfe Tone rallying youthful recruits: 'learn to shoot, learn to march, learn to scout, learn to give up all for Ireland'. 'Keep your last bullet for yourself, and don't whine about men protecting you'. Casimir contributed to Bean na hÉireann and wrote The Memory of the Dead based on the 1798 Rising inspired by Yeats's Cathleen ni Houlihan which Markievicz 'credited with keeping her spirits up during imprisonment after the 1916 Rising'. She took part in public demonstrations with John MacBride and others 'burning of the Unon Jack'; and especially with Jim Larkin during the infamous Lockout strike when she was assaulted by the

DMP 'several of them kicking and hitting me as they passed' (91). The nomenclature of Casimir's 1913 letter to the Irish Times echoed through the century beginning with 'these acts of uncalled for and inhuman cruelty' were 'indeed, a Bloody Sunday for Ireland'. As Markievicz waited with Connolly on the day of Larkin's release from Mountjoy Jail she claimed it was 'the proudest of my life, to be associated with the workers of Dublin' and 'their great and noble leader'. Casimir went off to the First World War (history should have placed him with Markievicz in the Rising) and was 'decorated with the St. George Cross for bravery' fighting for 'the Russian imperial army on the eastern front'.

Sources recounting the Rising display some incorrect facts, for instance on Darrell Figgis who committed suicide. He wasn't 'murdered in Bloomsbury'. There are attempts to deny and ameliorate Markievicz and the shooting of Lahiff. However a contemporary witness, Nurse Geraldine Fitzgerald is cited accurately and 'in his recent history of the Rising, McGarry cites Max Caulfield's history, which reports that Lahiff was shot three times in the head'. You can't pussy foot about regarding Markievicz who was a professional soldier and had even threatened to shoot Eoin MacNeill for abandoning the Rising. Depicting Markievicz 'stretched out in Kathleen Lynn's car, while the men hunkered down in their trenches' is deflating to the Citizen Army Major. More true to her character is refusing 'a lift to the barracks' after the surrender. Her arrest was world news from New York to London to Moscow.

Arrington doesn't flinch on her conversion to Catholicism and clinging to a crucifix during the executions hearing 'the English murdering our leaders'. The book picks up post-Rising at the Sinn Féin Conference when against De Valera's advice, she outed MacNeill as the coward of Easter 1916 stating what others 'did not have the courage to say in public'. Further terms of imprisonment followed. In 1918 with 'Maud Gonne, Hanna Sheehy Skeffington, and Kathleen Clarke'—all transported to Holloway. On being elected 'Madame Markievicz, M. P.' she signed her letters 'Constance Markievicz, I.R.A.' and 'took her seat in Dáil Éireann' becoming 'one of its most radical members'.

She was arrested in Cork in 1919 followed by Britain's efforts to 'deport her' delayed 'by questions regarding Markievicz's nationality'. Threats on her life including a 'Death notice from the Black Hand gang in the Police' coincided with the Michael Collins operation shooting 'twelve British intelligence agents and two auxiliary policemen'. On trial in 1920 she 'refused to acknowledge the authority of the court' and conducted her own defence. Christmas Eve, 1920 she was sentenced to two years hard labour in Mountjoy where she read Yeats's The Celtic Twilight and was 'surprised to find it so bad'.

Arrington has no sense of the ongoing unresolved Irish Question and refers to the War of Independence as 'the Anglo-Irish War'. Markievicz was clear on how Lloyd George, Churchill and Chamberlain politically engineered a strategy 'to divide us' and the Treaty as 'a sugarcoated Home Rule bill, which would disestablish the democratically elected Dáil'. She opposed the 'Cheap State Army', 'nobody likes the Freak State' and demanded the 'worker's republic' 'proclaimed at Easter 1916' and established 'by the democratically elected First Dáil'. Fundraising in America, the New York Evening World described her as 'emotion like a flame' where she called Griffith and Collins traitors explaining that the Treaty was 'accepting the subordinate position of a British dominion'. On the deaths of Collins and Griffith she felt 'two pawns...had been swept from the board'.

Her estrangement from family, and loss of inheritance meant she was 'taken in by the Coughlan family' at 1 Frankfort Terrace (Rathgar). She was hospitalized two weeks after going forward for Fianna Fáil in the 1927 elections. Her funeral became 'a political commodity for Fianna Fáil' who wanted to outdo the Kevin

O'Higgins' funeral 'for political reasons'. Hence our toxic Civil War—much of it ignored by Arrington who goes on to discuss the Markievicz' legacy in biographies, including O'Faolain's as well as the statues in her honour including Arthur Power's in Stephen's Green 'defaced in 1945 and 1947'.

Liam O'Flaherty felt she had the 'voice of a spoilt child'. De Valera said she had stepped 'down from her own class to which she belonged into the life of the plain people of Ireland'. Yeats includes her in 'Easter, 1916' with MacDonagh, MacBride, Connolly and Pearse but she in not named. O'Casey evokes her when the Citizen Army soldiers saluted the flag of the Starry Plough: she did not salute but instead 'returned to the oiling of her automatic with the remark that the flag bears no republican message to anyone'. Despite Arrington's blunders historical, ideological and otherwise, she renders Markievicz's powerful words in many quotations from letters and speeches which are parallel to her heroic actions against British imperialism and against those who wanted to compromise Irish Republicanism. Markievicz was a complex revolutionary and what goes with the job—a crack shot.

—*Books Ireland* 2016

REJECTED, DISOWNED AND BANNED

A History of the Irish Working Class Writing ed. Michael Pierse
(Cambridge University Press)

Declan Kiberd's Foreword sets up various contexts from 'the minority community in Northern Ireland after 1922' who took 'Wolfe Tone's appeal to "the men of no property", repeated by Parnell, as a rallying cry' and up to the crash of 2008 with 'a wholly new kind of underclass—youth.' Pierse as editor from a household where 'Joe Hill' was part of the repertoire, provides the introduction to this labyrinthine compendium of essays—twenty-three contributors—the overall approach encyclopaedic. Each essay usually merges its thesis with vast points of reference, at times an overwhelming welter of references from the genre of 'working class writing' (WCW) about class divisions, poverty, survivors and victims as in The Silver Tassie 'Shells for us and pianos for them'. The largely unexplored feature is the contradiction of art and life, as in Lee Dunne's Goodbye to the Hill staged in 1990s where many of the audience had never 'been to a play before'.

Pierse, author of Writing Ireland's Working Class (2011) obviously pushed his team into 'the policing of social inequality, through epistemic and judicial violence' amongst many parameters. However, Northwards 'the more recognisable conflict between orange and green as one between rich and poor' is accurately debunked. The timeline is from the XVII century to the present reflecting his exigencies ultimately for a work modelled on the The Intellectual Life of the British Working Classes (Jonathan Rose). Pierse's demands may not have been met in these essays and his commendable pragmatism is based on Michael Zweig's definition that 'the poor are typically working class people who don't make much money'. Join the club.

Pierse suggests that 'necropolitics is repeatedly the site of a radical contestation that refuses silence'. He finds the necropolitical in

Robert Tressell, Seán O'Casey, Patrick MacGill, Frank O'Connor, Thomas Carnduff, James Plunkett and Brendan Behan all of whom observed 'in their families or immediate communities, the dispensability of working-class lives.' H Gustav Klaus articulates the marginalisation of WCW beside 'women's writing, race and ethnicity theory or ecocriticism' and the expulsion of the genre from QUB's Humanities unit. Klaus lifts the lid demanding that beyond 'caution, indifference or denigration' WCW is excluded by the arbiters of taste who find it 'uninspiring, unexciting, uninteresting, unprofitable, unaesthetic'. Klaus demands nothing less than the genre being supported extensively to reflect 'full participatory democratic culture'. He illustrates this referencing Borstal Boy direct contemporary of Alan Sillitoe's Saturday Night and Sunday Morning which should have 'become the great Irish working-class classic of its time' but Ireland 'rejected it, disowned it, banned it'. (Klaus mistitles the Sillitoe novel).

Andrew Carpenter explores colonial-capitalist structures in Henry Jones whose patron was Lord Chesterfield, Ellen Taylor a Kilkenny housemaid, poet and playwright, and Swift's fun with working-class secondhand usage "Mary the Cook-Maid's Letter to Dr Sheridan" that rhymes ditch, bitch, sluts, guts. Carpenter, stalwart scholar of the Hibernian Tudor to Georgian, highlights the impoverished Murrough O'Connor, Patrick O'Kelly's Killarney, an Epic Poem and John Burns' Remembrancer (1775) 'an extraordinary book' 'the most intellectually energetic of Ireland's eighteenth-century working class'.

The levity of Carpenter does not avoid the unfortunates while John Moulden emphasises the tragic in the Denis Hagan-Fanny Blair affair (1785). An anonymous ballad based on the events in Armagh became better known than "De nite afore Larry was stretch'd" in England and 'it spread too to the United States'. It is ranked greater than the work of the 'Rhyming Weavers' even surpassing James Orr's "Donegore Hill" discussed by Frank Ferguson. Mouldon also unearths Alexander Crawford, Antrim's songster 'one of the most prominent leaders of local labour'. Crawford is a precursor of Woody Guthrie and protest songs.

Christopher J. V. Loughlin classifies the Whiteboys as vast 'trades' union for the protection of the Irish peasantry' and correctly heralds the main crises in history including defeat of the 'Gaelic social order', Grattan as 'elite Irish Whig' against arming 'the poverty of the Kingdom', and John Mitchell's 'genocide thesis' when An Gorta Mór 1845-51 was London's failure to effect the plan. Davitt and Connolly are portrayed as the monoliths they were for agrarian justice and national revolution. Marx stated the facts that the Irish were 'forced to contribute cheap labour and cheap capital to building up "the great works of Britain"'. Engels despicably in The Condition of the Working Class in England (1845) is anti-Irish.

Paul Murphy classifies Yeats and Gregory supporting the genre writing about the wretched where their audiences, according to F. S. L. Lyons 'rated each new play by PQ—peasant quality'. Synge provided a shift of class downwards from his landed background writing about tinkers and peasants. John Brannigan stays definitionally close to Pierre Bourdieu's working class-aesthetics as 'dominant aesthetic' and definitively shows class difference between Behan and the likes of F. S. L. Lyons. O'Casey perceived literature as jarring 'incongruously against the working-class economy of necessity'.

Twentieth century drama, stage to screen from Terence MacSwiney's The Holocaust (1910) to Strumpet City (adapted), Hatchet, and later works adhere to working class themes. Heather Laird and Elizabeth Mannion pursue this agenda from St John Ervine's Mixed Marriage (1911) and The Orangeman (1914) depicting the protagonist as 'a sober, industrious, decent bigot, with a mind like concrete'. O'Flaherty's story 'The Sniper' (1923) unfolds a Civil War plot of brother killing brother. James Moran focuses on Connolly and Jack White, both former British soldiers, making up a trio of friends with O'Casey that resulted in a political 'parting of the ways' before 1916. The Plough and the Stars presents on stage 'an exploitative system in which working-class men are positioned to kill the family members of fellow working-class men'.

Ledwidge's 'a soldier's heart, is greater than a poet's art' is contrasted with Kettle's anti-Redmond stance 'died not for flag, nor King, nor Emperor'. Paul Delaney locates Connolly's genius in attacking 'Irish apologists' and 'the apostate patriotism of the Irish capitalist class' as worse than 'English slanderers of the Irishman'. Robert Tressel's principle of inventing nothing about 'lives on the verge of starvation' extends from Jim Phelan who wrote Lifer and other felonious WCW up to Mannix Flynn's *James X.*

Tony Murray referencing Maeve Kelly's Florrie's Girls and Mary Hazard's Sixty Years a Nurse discusses the self-starting 'lesser mortals [who] had to sacrifice ourselves on the altar of duty'. There is no difference in the sublimes of hardship between the latter memoirs/autobiographies compared to Walter Macken I am Alone and Donal Mac Amhlaigh's Dialann Deoraí proving that tears are a luxury for the poor.

Mary M. McGlynn happily 'outs' John Wilson Foster's essay 'Irish Fiction 1965-1990' which 'does not mention any working-class writers or, indeed, refer to the working class at all'. Let them eat cake, John. Adam Hanna produces sterling stuff placing the shadow men Heaney, Longley and Mahon where education 'separated their lives from those of Northern Ireland's working class' in opposition to Bobby Sands who 'valued poetry for its capacity as a political vehicle, and that he disdained poets who did not share these views'.

Mark Phelan discusses contemporary WCW playwrights from the North of Ireland. Stewart Parker's Iceberg set on the divide 'from a shared poverty, a deprivation both fuelling sectarianism' and Graham Reid's Hidden Curriculum where the teacher 'cossetted from the conflict by his middle-class status' is ignorant of students' war-zone lives. Rosemary Jenkinson's Bonefire (2006) depicts 'working-class loyalists [...] as little more than violent drug-taking "chavs"' and Christina Reid's The Belle of Belfast City (1989) presents 'how the sectarian politics of hard-line loyalism are hardwired with far-right National Front'. This cutting-edge realism joins with Marie Jones and Martin Lynch whose Wedding Community Play (1999) 'transported audiences to terraced homes in an interface area' to eavesdrop on the dialogue but it was 'mainly middle-class audiences entering the mean streets of east Belfast'.

Claire Lynch singles out O'Casey's Proustian length autobiography with 'his commitment to the working class' while Eamonn Jordan's scholarly exegesis raises the ideological standard. He quotes Paul Murphy on class not as identity but 'a practice and performance of disparities' and pushes the envelope questioning if 'the circumstances of poverty are for the comfort of bourgeois audiences'. He criticises the lack of 'conflict of classes' exposing the solidarities and the homogeneity of working-class drama and its avoidance of prejudice 'within their own class ranks' against those who are 'more marginalised than themselves'.

Patrick MacGill in Children of the Dead End believed that the worker killed by a falling rock was a pioneer of civilisation giving 'up his life for the sake of society'. Niall Carson's essay on working class poets quotes MacGill: 'The Great Unwashed—of them I sing' 'I write of the ills which society inflicts on individuals like myself'. Behan after Larkin's funeral wrote bhíomar sa tsráid ag máirseáil/Beo buíoch don mharbh we were on the street marching/Alive and grateful for the dead. This book provocatively attacks the silence of the establishment while proclaiming that practitioners of the genre make do, hopefully survive, and work on. Working class writers of the world, unite!

—Books Ireland 2018

FROM MARCHING TO MILITARISM

Northern Ireland's '68: civil rights, global revolt and the origins of the Troubles Simon Prince (Irish Academic Press)

Originally published in 2007, Paul Bew writes the foreword to the new edition, admitting the counterfeit of projecting the Six Counties in unified communal terms: 'we are socialists. We are progressive. Trying to stop us marching through your villages is ridiculous because we are carrying a banner of enlightenment'. Prince traces this 'enlightenment' but is clear on internecine division up North while realistically probing the (Northern Ireland Civil Rights Association) NICRA's origins, precursors and leaders. There is tacit acknowledging of 'the Troubles' as war, preceded by attempts at gaining civil rights. According to Prince, evidence can show that the NICRA marches which were banned in the late sixties became the casus belli.

Prince's version of history is acceptable on the actualities of NICRA against rigorous opposition. Along with this is the theoretical aspect of revolution finding its genesis in the individual and small groups but within alliances that were conflicted as to manifestos, intended actions and overall planning. As it happened the marchers in 1969 from City Hall, Belfast to Guildhall Square, Derry were ambushed and attacked at Burntollet by the 'Paisleyite group led by Ronald Bunting' while the RUC stood aside.

Unfortunately, the discussion of Media coverage is partial but vital 'the publicity for the march was aimed as much at inducing the BBC, Ulster Television and Telefís Eireann [CX: Teilifís Éireann] to send camera crews as at bringing out the citizens of Derry'. 'Telly' Éireann got the scoop of the bludgeoned marchers at Burntollet and Derry and sold the footage to the BBC and the world.

While activists, including Eamonn McCann are not denigrated, the 'naivety' of their peace-marching adds to the heroic factor. McCann easily saw through Terence O'Neill's 'liberal mask' hiding 'the old

Unionist background of open suppression'. Grappling with entrenched Unionism is Prince's major exposé of Nordpolitik. From Basil Brooke's 'illegal vigilante force' of the 1920s 'men wearing Special Constabulary uniforms [who] did murder Catholics' to his speeches, exemplified by July 12, 1933 openly demanding bigotry and sectarianism 'employ protestant lads and lassies'. Unionism despised the post-WWII welfare state, anxious as to whether 'Catholics as well as Protestants would receive benefits' and were able to carefully manipulate the administration of the NIHT (Northern Ireland Housing Trust). Brooke's Flags and Emblems Act (1954) ensured 'display of the Union flag in all circumstances and to remove the Irish tricolour'.

Prince presents the major events including Brian Faulkner's instigation of 'two days of rioting [...] predictably, followed' when the 10,000 Orangemen paraded 'through the Catholic village of Dungiven' in 1960. The Matthew Report (1963) to the Wilson government asserted that nationalists could be compared to 'the Negro in the United States' which sets an international perspective. The Lemass-O'Neill Stormont meeting (1965) shows Paisley propagandising an 'IRA-Vatican plot'. The Easter Rising Commemorations heralded UVF killings of Catholics in June 1966 which were 'part of the wider Paisleyite Movement' and prefigured decades of victims, the majority civilians.

The book follows a tinder box narrative of inevitability as he sets out the agenda for the isolated minority, the Six Counties as Europe's anachronism and begins a hymn to Eddie McAteer & Cahir Healy as Nationalist mice among Orangemen whose politics slowly added to the emerging conflict. McAteer's attempts to engage with the Republic's Lemass, Aiken and Co meant that 'the Northern Irish were very much on their own'. The IRA's Operation Harvest beginning in 1956, and EEC membership in 1963 were part of the domino effect bringing NICRA to pass.

The momentum had already increased by the time Dungannon housewives Dunlop, Dinsmore and McCrystal claimed discrimination from the NIHT. They gained much support through the Dungannon Observer's correspondents who 'advocated a Northern Ireland version of the March on Washington'. A year later, Conn and Patricia McCluskey launched the Campaign for Social Justice (CSJ) movement. One of their pamphlets, The Plain Truth reached a circulation of 100,000. Newsprint with statistics matched social realities and were influential on radicalizing the minority. For instance, in many locations including Omagh, Catholics were 61.2% of the 'population but Protestants had the majority of the houses and jobs'. The CSJ's coverage in the Sunday Times (1966) under 'John Bull's Political Slum' (80) added further kudos.

The squatting of 9 Kinnaird Park, Caledon County Tyrone (1968) is seen as pivotal in triggering 'more activism and action' to highlight Ellen McDonnell and her three children in Derry 'on the housing waiting list for eighteen years'. Their squatting in Harvey Street provided focal points for revolutionary forces since Derry ranked as 'one of the most overcrowded cities in the whole of Britain and Ireland'.

Prince's detours unavoidably slow up the narrative by necessity to introduce left wing ideologues. The biographer of Connolly and Mellows, Desmond Greaves in contrast with 'Red Roy' Johnston became opposed within the legendary Camus versus Sartre split over 'Communism and revolutionary violence'. Anthony Coughlin is given more space than Betty Sinclair 'godmother of the civil rights campaign and the chair of NICRA'. Prince states that the activist leaders were steeped in Lessing's The Golden Notebook, Fanon's The Wretched of the Earth, and, even Kerouac's On the Road but especially George Breitman's 'How a Minority Can Change Society'. Kerouac's road trips espousing Bohemian 'sex, drugs and rock and roll' seems peripheral to American radicals Tom Hayden and his cohort Sandra Cason of the NSA (National Student

Association) as ideational backdrop for NICRA's marchers understanding Che Guevara's 'the duty of a revolutionary is to make a revolution'.

Meanwhile, the zeitgeist brought Eichmann's trial for mass murder, Herbert Marcuse lecturing in Berlin, protests against the Vietnam War, and Rudi Dutschke adopting Sartre's revolutionary position. Splits and breakups were part of the struggle: 'Séan Mac Stíofáin's Catholicism and ['Red Roy'] Johnston's Marxism could not be reconciled in the Republican movement'.

McCann's statement, inherently revolutionary is conclusive: 'to provoke the police into overreaction and thus spark off a mass reaction' goes hand in hand with Stokely Carmichael's 'once your enemy hits back then your revolution starts'. The aftermath that became the sectarian war is outside the present book's scope, the post-NICRA period that led to The Battle of the Bogside, Bloody Sunday, and Operation Motorman; both latter actions by the British Army and London accelerating 'Republicanism versus Loyalism'. NICRA's peaceful good faith in public demonstration breaking through to social justice meant that marchers were easy pickings for loyalist gangs and for police violence and arrests. This is the emotional and moral core of Prince's thesis.

The four significant marches in succession escalated towards the war from their beginnings in 7 October 1968 when QUB students at City Hall heralded 'Student Power had come to Belfast' and Bernadette Devlin found her voice as leader. The more seismic marches were 2 November 1968 and 16 November 1968, both making the Craigavon Bridge in Derry famous in history. The ban on these marches fueled further successes for the civil rights movement under mixed leadership with McCann, Michael Farrell, Gerry Fitt, Ivan Cooper, Eamon Melaugh, Paddy Doherty and Finbar Doherty. Events prove that the Bogside could also provide the evolutionary militant citizenry. McAteer fearing the worst removed himself when NICRA spread to Armagh on 30 November with the expected Paisleyite loyalist violent reactions.

The 'big march' of January 1, 1969 meant war was imminent. On the 6 January along Rossville Street the gable of a house announced to the world media 'You are now entering Free Derry' and would become as historically redolent as the GPO in Dublin. The situation reached its crisis point as marchers became citizen-military during the Battle of the Bogside, August 1969 which had definite roots as 'part [of] the global revolt' where 'foreign activists arrived at the then centre of revolutionary Europe to learn at first hand'.

McCann and Devlin were invited to the Sorbonne as leading 'la lute Populaire Irlandaises' with 'backing of the Palestine Liberation Organisation, the African National Congress, and America's Black Panther Party'. The revolutionary geniuses were realistic, however as Ramparts, Derry's Labour Party news-sheet proclaimed: 'Come Back Mrs Pankhurst, We Have Not Yet Overcome'. Many revolutionary groups sent observers and activists to learn from the Irish methodology. 'The Black Panthers were enormously popular in the Bogside', McCann recalled.

Devlin and McCann remained committed to working class social justice. Their position amidst right wing Catholic nationalists was like Marxists protesting to the College of Cardinals. McCann admitted that 'the left failed in Ireland [...]' without 'a coherent class analysis of the situation and a clear programme based upon it'. Prince as subtext celebrates their lifelong commitment born during the grim black and white era of 1968 which lit the fuse. The text reads like a DIY Revolutionist's Handbook on how to march, raise barricades and enlist a militarised army behind them. Prince addresses the polarities of political manoeuvres that advance towards extreme politicization and into militarism.

—*Books Ireland* 2019

TRUE NORTH

The Boundary Commission and its Origins 1886-1925 Paul Murray (University College Dublin Press)

When God Took Sides: religion and identity in Ireland Marianne Elliott (Oxford University Press)

Belfast and Derry in Revolt: a new history of the start of the troubles Simon Prince and Geoffrey Warner (Irish Academic Press)

Forgiving and Remembering in Northern Ireland ed. Graham Spencer (Continuum Books)

A welter of politicians, power brokers and others are quoted in this examination of territory and boundary. The 1914 Buckingham Palace Conference in discussing Home Rule concluded in favour of an Ulster loyally steered by the duumvirate of Carson and Craig. The BPC's conclusions were largely adhered to by the Government of Ireland Act (1920) whose chairperson Walter Long was Carson's predecessor and involved with supplying arms to the UVF in 1914. Murray in the appendix cites articles 11, 12, 13 and 14 of the Anglo-Irish Treaty of 6 December 1921. Article 12 "[...] in accordance with the wishes of the inhabitants, so far as may be compatible with economic conditions and geographic conditions, the boundaries between Northern Ireland and the rest of Ireland[...]" predicated the Boundary Commission. Murray's central thesis is that article 12 was "the Magna Carta of border Nationalism" and "proved a major liability to the Nationalist cause."

Padraic Colum knew Arthur Griffith's blind spot with regard to Article 12 since he was "preoccupied with the oath [of allegiance], the crown and the Empire... [and failed to note] the unsatisfactory formulation of the boundary clause." Like Griffith, Ernest Blythe and Collins presumed that the (present day) six counties would be far less geographically with huge areas surrounding Derry and

Newry to remain in the Southern jurisdiction. Tensions mounted: "given that both Carson and Redmond wanted Tyrone in its entirety for his own side." Carson's and Craig's Orangeism and Unionism amassed Loyalist support in England through many notable figures such as Kipling, Elgar and Earl Roberts of Kandahar. Churchill gave £1.4 million to the Special Constabulary in collusion with Lionel Curtis, Adviser on Irish Affairs and agreed on the necessity "to protect Ulster from extravagant claims on her territory."

Murray shows partition as imminent well before 1921. Thomas Babbington Macaulay had foretold the fate of the North to Daniel O'Connell in 1833: that there would ensure "a separation of the legislatures of the North and South of Ireland." The Anglo-Irish Treaty had significant bait within its structure for Nationalists: Ulster and potential Irish unity. The final six counties shape was defined from London never Dublin while Craig and Carson are depicted as unsure of their ultimate claims.

Murray's fascinating account lays bare the nuts and bolts of The Boundary Commission that came into being in 1925 headed by Mr Justice Richard Feetham, former South African judge with Eoin MacNeill as Irish Free State assessor. While MacNeill asserted the denied franchise of Nationalists in the North to decide their future boundary and territory, Feetham directed policy from the stance of making "economic considerations dominant." T. M. Healy coined the catch cry: "Feetham-cheat 'em!" MacNeill 'demanded' Derry for the Free State while Feetham wished to consolidate Lough Foyle "from predation by Donegal fisherman." Gerrymandering ensured that the political constituencies favoured the Unionists. MacNeill wanted PR while Craig found it alien to his sensibility. Curtiss perceived that a plebiscite on the border would meet with "the armed resistance of the Protestant majority." For De Valera "geography was the final arbiter in determining the Irish nation." John St Loe Strachey defended a two Irelands territory. The commission made its final decisions on 17 October 1925. The rest is the holocaust history of the six counties.

Elliott's agenda focuses on religion and identity in Ireland with occasional truisms: "Irishness has not been a broad church; its characteristics, defined by hostile outsiders and embittered insiders, have been narrow and sectarian." In exploring the theology behind antipopery she exposes the dangerous game of sectarian tennis across a forty shades of green net using many sources. Her impetus was the Oxford University Ford Lectures as she rages through the centuries with many's a zany comment such as: "prehistoric Ireland would have been quite a racial mix, sharing populations with Britain as well as continental Europe and Asia."

Elliott's polarizations are obvious and well trodden: Dolly's Brae contra A Nation Once Again but she quotes prolifically giving sharp contrasts. Canon Sheehan the bizarre novelist 'used' Protestant characters who are "converted, reformed and eventually nationalised" while in his The Intellectuals (1911) Catholicism is depicted as "the religion of the kitchen, the poorhouse." J. C. Beckett regarded the ascendency as primates among the Irish Nation while being "self-consciously English in tradition and culture." Art MacCooey's "Tagra an dá Theampall" depicts the rich church of Ireland and the poor Catholic church. Swift's Holyhead is pointedly schizoid in being subservient to England while loathing the native Irish. Grattan, Berkeley and Tone are pigeon-holed by Elliott into this category. D. P. Moran's *The Philosophy of Irish Ireland* is fascism tending towards *Mein Kampf*.

She fuels the book with discussion of fiery pamphlets such as Foxe's Martyrs, Maria Monk and the Advance of Popery. Her history of religious divide reflects the hysterical works of Protestant and Catholic polemicists and their "vivid martyrologies" while her strongest material includes the Loyalist from 2007 who says: "As a young teenager I thought God was Protestant." Thomas Moore's An Irish Gentleman in Search of Religion (1833) culminates in a key insight about Catholics' lack of self-criticism when their culture is under attack. Berkeley's "A Word to the Wise" is prejudiced against Catholics while Kickham's Knocknagow is a classic of "peasantry in their victimhood." The Fenian ethos is an earlier prototype of Davis's "The Penal Days." Elliott somewhat cosily avoids any close commentary on sectarian bloodshed, house-burnings and carnage except through second-hand polemics. Only Hubert Butler and Brian Inglis permit her to inform a ghostly outline of the horrors of Ulster.

Prince and Warner apologise for daring to attempt such a history as well as the exigencies of historians yet still plunge ahead with their version. Their best line is a somewhat mixed metaphor "like a shard from a broken mirror, a group narrative puts into the hand both a distorted reflection and a potential weapon." In the North heads are continually shaken if not rolled despite centuries of polemics. There is nothing more real than the Falls and Shankill uncomfortably bordering on each other in Belfast. Prince and Warner tread 'safe ground' discussing John Hume's Derry Housing Association and the Credit Union in 1966. The 145 Divis Street Tricolour crisis and Billy McMillen (atypical name for an IRA commander) is fitfully highlighted amidst the riots of September 1964. The authors miss their chance in not underlining flags in Ulster as perennially provocative.

The "Captain Johnston" statement in the Belfast Telegraph 21 May 1966 is redolent of sectarian tensions and again the authors neglect to discuss a newspaper that prints exhortation to violence in its pages such as: "Known IRA men will be executed mercilessly and without hesitation." Prince and Warner seem too cool to emphasise the internecine plight of Belfast divided in murderous breakdown and 'proceed' to the riot on 5 October 1968 at Derry Railway Station in the Waterside organised mainly by Eamonn McCann. The authors render this riot as the genesis of (their favourite appellation) "the Troubles."

The People's Democracy in 1969 that resulted in the attack on Civil Rights marchers at Burntollet Bridge is well outlined as with their rendition of the Battle of the Bogside but they relegate Bloody Sunday to a mere footnote. Significantly, they explain how non-Nationalist Left and Labour were always sectarian. The riots and shootings of 27-28 June 1970 provide the authors with a formidable scenario where they instance the Hugh McAteer funeral as resulting in "the Protestants [were] outgunned by the IRA in east Belfast." Despite their caveat about historians, Prince and Warner too often handle NI history as if it were playdough semtex. It isn't.

There is the feeling that it is impossible to review this book since who is capable of estimating heroism as espoused in these testimonies. Robin Eames states that "reconciliation can never be imposed by legislation or by political working arrangements." Spencer discusses the CGP (Consultative Group on the Past) exploring the why of the victim and the why of the perpetrator. Brian Lennon is disturbing on present policing and the Orange parades as well as the future stability of the six counties. He daringly classifies Protestant fears as opposed to Catholic resentment. Michael Jackson unfortunately gives his background away in blaming the Easter Rising's fiftieth anniversary for beginning the Troubles. Ruth Patterson enunciates new beginnings as vital amidst the Restoration House project. Timothy Kanahan calls for fresh starts as the safest road ahead, quoting Dr Martin Luther King.

Most contributors raise the clarion call for forgiveness. David Stevens begs for ethical responsibility from writers since there "can be no 'official' interpretation of the Troubles." Aidan Troy brings the reader to the boundary interfaces. His concerns are for the interface peace walls—over eighty in Belfast. Johnston McMaster prescribes Paul's Letters to the Romans as a blueprint for forgiveness amidst the complex politics. Glenn Jordan explores shared spaces and highlights the victories in peace for the EBM (the East Belfast Mission). David McMillan calls for uniting children beyond "contested pseudo-Christian identities." Michael C. Paterson, a former RUC constable disabled by a bomb blast presents his testimony of reconciliation and recounts meeting the IRA man who caused him such suffering. David Bolton avoids any tincture of preaching in evolving the necessity of reconciliation and cites Isaiah 61:3: "To bestow beauty instead of ashes and praise instead of despair."

The interviews include Jo Berry and Patrick Magee who says: "suddenly you know you've killed this man, you've met his daughter [Berry]...over time you get to appreciate him as an individual." David Clements publicly forgave those who murdered his father and appealed to the killers, making himself available to offer pastoral support. He states: "a forgiving spirit is better than a bitter one." Duncan Morrow, former Sentence Review. Commissioner lucidly explains his theory of the victim's power to forgive which is "the only power the victim has." Chris Hudson investigates the Protestant-Catholic nexus. He mediated between Steven Travers and a member of the UVF to aid the writing of the book Miami Showband Massacre. Richard Moore's interview recounts his being blinded by a plastic bullet as a young boy and meeting the soldier responsible, named Charles years later. Moore's declaration of unconditional forgiveness is startling. All of these testimonies reflect an indefinable pinnacle of humanity to achieve supreme spiritual heights beyond evil.

—*Books Ireland* 2012

GAEL FORCE

Irish Nationalist Writings 1895- 1946 Maud Gonne and Karen Steele (Irish Academic Press)

Pearse's Patriots: St. Enda's and the cult of boyhood Elaine Sisson (Cork University Press)

Gaelic Prose in the Irish Free State, 1922-1939 Philip O'Leary (University College Dublin Press)

Surrey-born upper class society belle, her mother from the Cook Empire, father a British Army captain transforms herself into a fire-eating rabid Irish Nationalist Republican; has two children with French activist Lucien Millevoye, one of whom, Iseult, marries the reviled writer Francis Stuart. Maud Gonne becomes a Catholic convert, marries Major John MacBride, divorces within a year, their son becomes the distinguished Sean MacBride. This is only some of her pedigree that might well have furnished Bernard Shaw with a more complex Eliza, instead of the poor flower seller in *Pygmalion.*

Steele protects her subject in the tight-lipped introduction and brief commentary before each of the seven sections. Otherwise she follows the canonical Foster-Jeffares-Ward line. On the positive side, the soul of Gonne is laid bare, if not her heart in the writings. Her true love is the bewitching woman "*Hibernia,* Mother Ireland, ... never to rest until Tara of the Kings shall be free once more and Kathleen Ni Houlihan be a Queen among the Nations."

Her speeches and articles plus some letters to various publications unleash a doctrinaire green avalanche of invective against so many targets. The British Empire, the Orange Order, De Valera's constitution, Kevin O'Higgins, Cosgrave's Free State and the execution, on his orders, of Generals Rory O'Connor, Liam Mellows, Dick Barrett and

Joe McKelvey on the infamous 8 December 1922. Her political colours are proudly and loudly on display. *Dawn* a brief drama is primarily Nationalist and secondarily Celtic Twilight, "The river of blood must flow, but there is freedom on the other side of it." Steele accurately confirms Gonne's disapproval of the writings of Synge, O'Casey and Joyce but Yeats as adoring poet was acceptable.

What makes one fall in love with her, besides the obvious attributes, is her passion for justice and liberty. Hence the pieces Political Prisoners *(Voice of Ireland,* 1924); The Famine Queen *(United Irishman,* 1900)—her outburst against Victoria's Royal Visit to Ireland, seen as a covert recruitment ploy:

> Taking the shamrock in her withered hand she dares to ask Ireland for soldiers - for soldiers to protect the exterminators of their race.

And elsewhere, "How long will England be allowed to astound the world by her crimes?" When she writes of starvation in Ireland, eviction and children, she tugs at the heartstrings albeit in a melodramatic manner. One thinks of the plaintive voice of Edna O'Brien. "Countless fathoms of grey water, ridges of waves innumerable, and the vast, dense curtain of rolling mist lie between Ireland and Ireland's children far away in America." Her certainty of war in July 1938 may not be singularly prophetic but the allegiance in the same year with Hitler, fascism and anti-semitism is hugely revealing. Maud Gonne's crank status as mere Muse to Yeats requires a lot of adjustment and this publication will clarify the all too familiar portrait. There are lots of photos of the young beauty and ageing activist.

Sisson attributes Pearse's central place among the leaders of 1916 to "the needlessness of Willie's execution, and also to the publicity surrounding Mrs Pearse". This is rather contentious. Pearse by all accounts was an astonishing man; he even startled General Blackadder who sentenced him to death.

Sisson leans heavily on the biography by Ruth Dudley Edwards, establishing, tentatively at times, theories about Pearse's amalgamation of "Christian Celticism and Gaelic warrior pagan culture"— St Enda's motto from the Fianna translates, "strength in our hands, truth in our tongues, and purity in our hearts". He annexed a summer retreat for St Enda's at Rosmuc to further fructify the Gaelic dimension of the curriculum.

She explores the implications of the school's dramatic output, the staging of a Passion play at the Abbey (1911) with Pearse playing the unrepentant thief and William as Pontius Pilate. Other actors included future wives of Padraic Colum and Sean MacBride, Mary Maguire and Mary Bulfin respectively. St Enda's produced five Christian plays between 1908 and 1915. Pearse's stories for children such as *Iosagán,* also adapted for the stage, had a strong Gaeltacht setting with Gaelic speaking children merged with the Christ Child—a potent blend of revolutionary fervour drawing on the rural Irish family. Pearse's (short-lived) magazines *An Claidheamh Soluis* (sword of light) and St Enda's *An Macaomb* (the child) presented versions of the same. Among associates of Pearse were Colum, Joseph Campbell and Standish O'Grady who wrote material forming a nexus of cultural consensus. The *Ioin* provided an epic primer and inspiration for open-air pageants gearing up a disparate body of potential insurgents into a cohesive force emblematic of Cuchulainn, Flom and the Fianna. For Pearse's purposes, religious martyrdom and pagan warriorship merged in youth as a catalyst for change. Sisson usefully reveals Pearse's love of opera and visits to Germany for Wagner's *The Ring* cycle.

St Enda's had the moral support of O'Casey, Casement, Hyde, Markievicz, Gonne, Yeats (WB & Jack), Beatrice Elvery, Baden-Powell and Wilde's sometime partner, the abominable Lord Alfred Douglas. Pearse wrote further plays, *The Master* and *The King,* the latter finding a production in far-off Bengal. By then he had been inducted into the IRB through Bulmer Hobson leading to the ultimate nemesis: revolution. Five of the staff (three poets amongst them) of St Enda's—Joseph Plunkett, Thomas MacDonagh, Con Colbert, Pearse and his brother, were executed for their part in the Rising.

Sisson discusses Pearse and sexuality, the "highly sexualised love poem to a young boy" entitled "Little Lad of the Tricks" and whether he was "homoerotic, homosexual and paedophile". The brief troubled platonic relationship with Mary Hayden, hinted at here, adds a further dimension. The only conclusive comments concern St Enda's, its locations in the twenty-first century: the Hemitage, a museum dedicated to the life and educational work of the patriot and fittingly, Cullenswood House now *a gaelscoil*.

O'Leary outlines the setting up of an Gúm, the Irish Folklore Commission, an Coiste Tarmaiochta (the terminology committee) in the Department of Education and unravels scholarly faction-fighting among Gaels, Gaeilgeoiri and others. Seamus Grianna referred to "the people from An Mug" and Ó Cadhain said "Most of the work done by An Gúm ... was translation, preponderantly from English. Many have commented on the futility of it." Ó Conaire is less censorious: "True literature will never be created to order," but he was not opposed to the translation agenda.

O'Leary lists the translations, with commentary on a high percentage of them. This makes the whole enterprise and his work more awesome. Swift, Carlton, Stoker, Conan Doyle, *Inis Atlaint* (Plato's Critias). Biographies of historical figures: Emmet, Mitchel and notably Ó Brain's *Parnell: Beathaisneis*. By 1937, An Gúm's 300 publications had sold a quarter of a million copies.

The Gaelic League's opposition to the Roman alphabet, the infamous cló rómhánach, an edict of Dev's, is fabulous material to read about and O'Leary exposes every source. This debacle meant that the days of *an cló gaelach* were numbered. Further rancour and rumbling entered the fray as to which dialect would achieve supremacy. The Western seaboard feared the Munster dialect gaining supremacy because of Dineen, Padraig Úi Laoghaire and members of the translation department of the Free State Dáil, Liam Ó Rinn and Colm Ó Murchu.

The core of the study is the hunt for the new Gaelic literature against the circulation of English literature that would imply anglicising the twenty-six counties. *An tOileanach, Peig* and *Fiche Blian ag fas* along with Eamonn Mac Giolla Iasachta's *Corsai Thomeris* and Liam Ó Rinn's *Mo Chara Stiofin,* a memoir of Stephen McKenna, are among the masterpieces discussed with their critical reception. A *Dublin Opinion* cartoon of 1933 shows every nook, cranny and cave of the Great Blasket filled with people scribbling or typing while a currach is being rowed to the mainland, laden with manuscripts—this catches the flavour of the times.

When it comes to film in Irish there is less detail: Béaslaí's *An Danar,* was first performed at the Abbey (1928). Mac Liammoir is given much space; his *Diarmuid agus Grainne* opened Taibhdhearc na Gaillimhe. His squib 'To Certain Anglo Irish Writers' catches the prevalent isolationist mentality plus the phenomenon of an Englishman converting to Celtic Gaeilgeoir:

> Your vaunted 'culture' still we spurn
>
> Whose home on British ground is set.
>
> For still the Gaelic flame will burn—
>
> We are not all West Britons yet!
>
> Your alien culture take elsewhere
>
> Ye little gods of Merrion Square!

S. O'Hegarty was able to admit "English has become, in the course of time, a mother language here." Yeats, Joyce, Synge came in for infamous derision but O'Leary also shows the admiration of their achievement by many Gaelic authors. O'Flaherty, praised for his play *An Dorchadas* (1926) was lamented for defecting to English, and replied, "I don't write for the money ... I'll start a religious paper in the Irish language and make a fortune on it".

O'Faolain's conflicts with former mentor Corkery are affecting to read. Sean Ciosain's "An Bheirt Intleachtoiri" (1935) sends up O'Faolain and O'Connor as Joyceans and *poseurs*. Seosamh Mac Grianna fell foul of An Gúm, worked for them for three and a half years, and damned them. His novel *An Druma Mór,* submitted in 1930, was eventually published in 1969. Mac Grianna as *enfant terrible,* felt there was "no literature in Irish worth reading ... no Gaeilic writer worthy of being called a writer. Everything of any value is across the Irish Sea."

O'Leary does not shirk from exposing the gold and the dross from this troubled and intriguing period of literary history.

—*Books Ireland* 2004

RAGING AGAINST THE DYING NATION'S LIGHT

The Selected Essays of Seán O'Faolain ed. Brad Kent (McGill-Queen's UniversityPress)

The 55 essays/reviews (most of them) from The Bell, spanning 1928–76, are best assessed through copious quotations to authenticate O'Faolain raging in hellish internal exile. 'The class that came to power and influence was not a labouring class; the more able among them were petit bourgeois, middle-men, importers, small manufacturers'—in other words, 'the middle class mentality' of 'reaction, conservatism, sentimentality, and intellectual cowardice' which he deplores in 'The Stuffed Shirts'.

Pity streaks through many of the essays, as he asks: what will 'shatter the ice that binds the Children of Lir' in a country which is 'politically, culturally and psychologically just not there'? His targets remain clear and constant: 'the final stage of the revolution around 1922 became—as it is to this day—a middle-class putsch'. 'The loss of the North is depriving Ireland of half its vitality. For the case for Irish unity is not merely legal, or merely rational, or merely constitutional. It is purely and simply a human necessity. Our Irishism is only half-Irish without the Northern strain, just as the North is only an artificial half-alive thing without the blood of Ireland running through its veins.'

Kent's introduction discusses how the Free State 'had become a stagnant backwater that had failed to be caught up in the current of world events and the stream of intellectual developments'. He does not include O'Faolain's 'Virginia Woolf and James Joyce, or Narcissa and Lucifer'. The footnotes are occasionally pure Myles na Gopaleen: Keats, 'a major English Romantic poet'; Gethsemane, 'where Jesus is said to have prayed before being taken into custody to be crucified'; 'The Gresham is, to this day, one of Dublin's poshest hotels'.

O'Faolain is assailed by church, state, censorship, 'Gaelic

Revivalists and Catholic Actionists', commencing in 1929 with the banning of Crime and Punishment and Anna Karenina. The Land of Spices and The Tailor and Ansty, among many homespun works, were also banned, because 'books must be what is called "safe" books. There must be no come back from the convents or the clergy.' On the banning of the last two volumes of À la recherche du temps perdue he wails: 'I sup-pose, about .02% of the population ever heard of Proust, and where the rest (in the old joke) think Sodom has something to do with Begorrah'.

He wrote biographies of Hugh O'Neill, Tone, O'Connell, and two of de Valera. As a failed activist Republican among the Free Staters, his indignation is articulated with comedy: 'there is a lot of Hans Anderson still left in men like De Valera'. He 'split Sinn Féin, split the I.R.A., split Cumann na mBan, split Clan na Gael, double-split Sinn Féin, double-split the I.R.A., split the whole country and spends the rest of his time splitting words'. 'Those searchlights which he turns on his heart have some very well-timed blackouts'; 'nobody can now say whether Mr de Valera has written ÉIRE on his coffin or his cenotaph'. There are mood swings and reappraisals: Markievicz's lecture on the Brehon Laws is 'an extraordinary medley of Marx, Republicanism, and Gaeldom'.

His rancour explodes in discussing Orange Terror: The Partition of Ireland(1943), and elsewhere states that 'the English middle and upper classes have always known that war is part of the price of power'. The essay on Eoin MacNeill and the Boundary Commission requires wit as antidote to his lamentations: 'Ah,well! MacNeill may have lost the North—but he has found the birth-place of Saint Patrick'. MacNeill's 'no possible foundation for a national culture except the national language' is rebutted by O'Faolain's plea that 'the shanachie by the fire, and Shaw in his study, are moved by the same vital urge'. Historical figures are raised above his contemporary writers, who are levelled. As people, Joyce, Yeats, O'Casey and Shaw are criticised, but not Æ (George Russell), who is elevated.

He embodies the repressed Free State ego: 'You read Martin Chuzzlewit...you wish you could do anything even a hundredth part as good', and yet attacks Dickens, who successfully 'presented his whores and fences and sharks and pimps' and 'would not as much as look at the light of hell in human beings or the impenetrable darkness of their souls'. He praises O'Flaherty, who 'pulses with genuine hate', and demolishes Daniel Corkery's 'submerged Celt theory'. Corkery is a 'type of exclusivist for whom the essential test of literature is a political, racial, or religious test'. The Hidden Ireland is 'tendentious', with 'so many elaborate generalisations' lacking solid accurate history and a 'nationalisation of culture'. Corkery wants 'to slobber over' the people, whereas 'the genuine writer writes for no audience but himself. That is the rock on which the self-conscious Nationalist has broken.'

Writers are judged on their grasp of history, which dominates his thought. Henry VIII with his fat guts burnt the Irish monasteries, and 'Dublin rotted on the stalk of the eighteenth century'. Yeats 'never, I saw, had studied anything deeply'. 'The Marxist critic will never be able to do anything with Yeats.' Jack B. Yeats and 'his later more "queer" style in painting' is given a thumbs down.

'Irish literature still carries an honourable prestige; but nobody would care to maintain that it has as much prestige as it had around 1915.' Writing in 1962 in Studies, O'Faolain rejects the novel after Joyce and O'Flaherty; 'plenty of honourable efforts (perhaps, I might suggest, like my own efforts)' but the 'best product of our period' is the short story. Otherwise Joyce, abhorred by conservatives and clergy, is deflated by O'Faolain for the 'maltreatment of language'. *Ulysses* is the 'gesture of no meaning and of every meaning' and *Finnegans Wake* is decried.

Politicians such as Senator Liam Ó Buachalla are outed: he will wipe out 'the whole fraternity of gypsies, tinkers, and travelling-folk in general in a typical totalitarian lust for absolute State control over the individual'. 'The Murder Machine known as the Department of Education... the Radio, where nobody is allowed to discuss anything frankly'; the University class where 'no student knew the love-story of Deirdre'. O'Faolain opposed compulsory Irish based on Pearse's The Murder Machine(1916): 'Irish should be made the language of instruction in districts where it is the home language ...where English is the home language it must of necessity be the first language in the schools'. He fulminates that 'our so-called Nationalism is the shadow' and his longing for exile manifests every where, and in 'Literary Provincialism' with denial: 'it does not really matter much where a writer lives' since 'to the modern novelist life is evil and it is, apparently, his self-chosen task to prove it'.

Portrait-essays include 'Roger Casement' and achieve the sublime: 'we Irish revere him because, quite simply, he was that rare thing—an integrated man'. Casement's arrest posing as the author of 'A Life of St Brendan' reaches absurdity and tragedy after the disastrous voyage from Germany with guns and ammunition that becomes legendary. Casement's brother enters folk history for suing the Daily Express over his hat that gave him the appearance of being 'dissolute, debauched, and incapable of managing his affairs'.

The essay on Tone is reverential, with asides on O'Connell and Davitt. Tone is seen as magnificently paradoxical, wishing for a bloodless revolution through the supremacy of ideology; yet the Irish Question can never avoid the 'most furious and sanguinary contest'—in other words, retaliation and conflict. O'Faolain marks the birth of the modern nation from 1759 and notes that the vitality of Tone would initiate 'Jacobin ideas spreading, at whatever highly simplified remove from their original form, among a Gaelic speaking peasantry'.

O'Faolain's credo is 'I have no love for national literature as nationalists understand it'; and 'every artist becomes, thus, the critic of his times, which, though merged into him, may as easily evoke hate as love'. He aims to rise above 'the efforts of small groups to impose their narrow-minded definitions on the rest of us', but 'all intelligent men can do is to cast scorn on the fake thing when it shows itself, and to try to save, in every small way, the unspoiled living People'.

Ulysses charts the last day(s) of 'British' Dublin, while this volume of essays vividly evokes the Free State more than Frank O'Connor's work. O'Faolain provides a vigorous counter-flow to the 'Dreary Eden' of McQuaid and de Valera with a lot of iron in his soul: '25% marry before the age of 34'; women are described from the pulpit as 'the unclean vessel'; waltzing is outlawed as 'belly to belly dancing'. Cathleen Ni Houlihan 'after giving birth to the Free State ... has ever since been locked up in the sacristy lest she should do anything worse', and 'a despotism disguised as a democracy' reigns. O'Faolain's veracity is the isolated voice of integrity under immense pressure.

—*Books Ireland* 2017

CRITIC AND CELT

Celtic Studies in Europe and other Essays Séan Ó Lúing
(Geography Publications)

Kingfishers: essays on Irish and English poetry Giuseppe Serpillo
(Goldsmith Press)

Critical Ireland : new essays in literature and culture ed. Aaron
Kelly and Alan A. Gillis (Four Courts Press)

Outcast weeds by a desolate sea—

Fallen leaves of humanity.

Lady Wilde's lament for the ravages of the famine and unprecedented
emigration can easily be applied to Ó Lúing's involvement with Gaelic
literature, culture and civilisation. The survival of Gaelic despite the
Elizabethan and Cromwellian wars of conquest submission of native
Irish is well explored. He contrasts Hugh O'Neill with
Vercingetorix, both defeated by ruthless imperial powers, England and
Rome. Beyond the nightmare of history visited on Ireland and its native
language, he praises the band of scholars not always native who saved a
language as vital and ancient as Sanskrit—German Celtologists "reaching
from Zeuss, through Windisch, Zimmer, Meyer and Thurneysen up to
Pokorny himself". Ó Lúing has essays on these and more in his easy all-
embracing style, almost throwaway were it not for his evident passion in
every rough line. He makes his subject fascinating whether it is the
assertion of Gaelic's rightful place as an ancient and classical language
within a world class literature via the writings of Adolphe Pictet in the
Paris of 1837 or Myles Dillon finding patterns between Celt and Aryan.
Zeuss's *Grammatica Celtica* published in Leipzig in 1853 would further
stem the possible extinction of a great language by offering the world a
canon of Irish grammar and further the international study of it. Classics of
literature would follow such as Ernst Windisch's edition of the *Tain Bó
Cuailgne* (1905). Windisch's brightest disciples were Kuno Meyer and

Heinrich Zimmer. The flow was not only of European scholars into Ireland to study the native speakers in their own land; the Irish also left to fructify and commingle in Europe and beyond.

Naturally, Douglas Hyde is commemorated as love poet and literary historian, someone who was a linguist before becoming inflamed with a love of Gaelic and its revival. Robin Flower found Gaelic in the dusty purlieus of the British Museum manuscript department and began his lifelong attachment to the Blaskets and its inhabitants. Marie-Louise Sjoestedt from France also became fascinated with the Blaskets and Dunquin in the thirties making the trek as often as possible from Paris via Cherbourg to Ireland. In time she would become an able critic of the literature. Carl Marstrander aided by the National Library staff members who appear in Joyce's *Ulysses* John Eglinton and Richard Best—would carry on work left over by earlier scholars, John O'Donovan and Eugene O'Curry, which culminated in his Dictionary of the *Irish Language* (1913). Marstrander's task was awesome and, in conjunction with the Royal Irish Academy, benefited from two bequests, from Alice Stopford Green and Maxwell Henry Close. Frank O'Connor commenting in 1964 on Marstrander's ongoing work called it, "a project comparable in scale and possible importance to the Shannon Scheme".

Keeping Gaelic from solipsism were the likes of George Thompson who would become friends of a fellow Hellenist, Stephen MacKenna, and translate Plato's three dialogues about the last days of Socrates as *Breith Bhais ar Eagnuidhe* (1920). Thompson's Gaelic version of Homer's Odyssey remains a lost treasure of Irish scholarship. He will always be celebrated as the Svengali of Muiris Suileabhain who wanted to dedicate *Fiche Bhlian ag Fas* to him. When it comes to an essay on Tim Enright, the Oxford University Press comes in for high praise for keeping the 'Blasket books' in print down the years "giving the island's literature and the island itself recognition throughout the world". Mention of the Blaskets is not complete without referring to Edward Meyerstein, friend and colleague of Robin Flower. For such as these scholars, the island was the equal of any Greek isle steeped in culture and history. When Ó Lúing writes about Meyer he is not a slavish patriot wallowing in the fact that a foreigner found such worth in Ireland; rather he remains amazed at his subject's love of learning reaching as far as studying Shelta and beyond to selections from early Irish poetry.

His great joy is that people such as Meyer, had they lived, would have triumphed in the establishment in 1940 of the School of Celtic Studies in Dublin. And Ó Lúing was not a provincial, and far beyond culchie-consciousness—a Kerryman at ease in Dublin professionally, as he was in the Oireachtas Translation Office or equally happy reading a Dictionary of Irish or Baudelaire, praising the fuschia-lined road out of Tralee through the Dingle peninsula or the glories of Gothic Cologne. The obsession with his native language is inspiring and people, like him will always ensure its survival and healthy flourishing. No wonder he quotes Meyer in full flight:

> It should not be forgotten that the Irish, being the first western nation to cultivate learning long ago, developed expressive native terms of its own for every scientific term of Greek or Latin. In mathematics and medicine, in astronomy and grammar, they had a perfect native terminology.

Professor Serpillo is a Sard. That raises expectations of his being a refreshing commentator on Hopkins whom he has also translated into Italian, and, Patrick Kavanagh—the latter more easily rendered of the two, presumably. From the outset, it is disappointing that he avoids full discussion of his subject as mystic seeker after silence and God, which identity was surely central to Hopkins. He is far more comfortable dissecting the poems in terms of "sounds, words, phrases, sentences, idioms, some never expressed before, some worn out by too much slovenly usage, [that] refuse to be ruled, like magma from a volcano." His exegesis is never exhausting and comes in short spurting chapters liberally peppered with quotes from previous critics on

Hopkins and other experts such as Sapir, Whorl, Carroll and Ong. This is not to suggest that Serpillo cannot speak for himself and he is almost inoffensive when he implies the motivation, the impulses, drives and the inspiration in attempting to explain Hopkins where others might not be so brave or so innocent, perhaps.

He does spend rather a lot of energy and somewhat slavishly on picking out Hopkins' similes and metaphors; the former prevalent and often over-abundant in his earlier and less brilliant poetry. Similarly, he is not averse to going on about his use of parentheses and accuses him of jingoism. He makes a final wild sweep thus:

> He had frequent glimpses of truth but some part of his soul was charged to the end with some weight (intellectual, social, psychological) which kept dragging him away from permanent bliss.

All very well as a comment and one prefers a critic to express full conviction; however Hopkins comes out of this practical criticism unresolved. As a poet he doesn't respond very well to dissection. Such is the delicate linguistic and loud diction of his poems that are stressed to the limit of perfection by the use of each word. Hence to pull the poetry apart and paste up extracts, reads at times as if in a complete vacuum, especially where there is no reference to his awfully difficult life as a poet and priest. Hopkins was abominably mistreated by the religious order that dominated him—a fact that is only being slowly revealed in modern biography.

Professor Serpillo goes on in the final four chapters to consider many aspects, political and elegiac, of Irish poetry from Yeats to the present time. These pages are subject to fewer lesions of whole poems and with variety and contrast in interesting quotations from Kinsella and Montague, Heaney and O'Grady among others. He manages to keep the discussion lively but is not well served by the all too human typos and omissions and text gaps that are ever the dreaded printer's devil but may have been avoidable.

Here's something you may not want to miss arising from two academic conferences in Dublin (1999) and Belfast (2000). The essays are bite-size compressions for happy casual browsing. It might be a good test of these writers that in a small space they have had to engage you, get on with it and quickly have their say. David Cotter cries out from apartment-dwellers' Dublin in which he sets an incomplete scene of a Friday night hashish party among non-nationals discussing such topics as "our market-driven academies teach nobody to speak the truth and draw the bow". Cotter's manifesto might well be the concrete quality lacking in such symposia. Two other tigers snarl and deliver feisty contributions on literary reviewing: Stephen Hull dares to air the embarrassing interview with a humanities graduate (anonymous) who resents the unmentionable "saturation of the market with people with non-professional degrees". John Kenny discusses 'The Critic in Pieces' but is never cynical or bitter and espouses the theory that reviewers might well be chastened if there was a quick response in print from the author they have carved up. Kenny's wide range of sources on literary reviewing make the piece a mirror image of his ideals for what might be called the reviewer's art.

Hanne Tange's offering could be taken as a dominant theme reflecting the non-solipsistic nature of the material here, though it is difficult to fit every essay into the reviewer's hold-all. Tange points out contrasts between "Joyce's experimental English and MacDiarmuid's literary Scots". There are three other pieces on Joyce but one need not yawn: they are enjoyable. It is also refreshing to see neglected books considered such as Nicholas Allen's treatment of AE's overtly political novel The *Interpreters* (1922). Stephanie Bachorz becomes even more political, jousting with coloniser and colonised with a lot of help from Theodore Adorno. What might ultimately grab you about this is the number of literary figures discussed and ingeniously compared, including Wilde, Parnell, Yeats, Daniel Corkery, and Maurice Leitch. In some cases an essay on a writer by differing academics accidentally or otherwise complements the other. Literature, take it or leave it, has always involved commentary from various sources and this keeps the entertaining, even the conversational, to the fore. And why not?

—*Books Ireland* 2001

COSMOMICRON

The Cosmic Game: explorations of the frontiers of human consciousness Stanislav Grof (Newleaf)

Turtle Was Gone a Long Time III: anaconda canoe John Moriarty (Lilliput Press)

Honey from Stone Chet Raymo (Brandon)

His list of acknowledgements instills a high interest from the start. He is very respectful to many fellow workers in the vineyard, as it were, such as David Bohm, Joseph Campbell, Fritjof Capra, Rupert Sheldrake and Albert Hofmann among others. He has an ease and humility that is reflected in the huge level of communication on every page however one might quibble with the book's classification in psychology/science when it might be spirituality/mysticism. He provides vast evidence from himself and others about holotropic experience. There is an e-mail address for those interested in Holotropic Breathwork, gtt@dnai.com. 'Holotropic' is derived from the greek holos (whole) and tropos (turning). Arthur Koestler coined the term holon but was orthodox in his scientific worldview and not as open to cleansing the doors of perception as Grof, whose agenda is vigorously in contention with scientific explanations of life's origin and meaning. He uses a holographic model of the universe and dares to imply a holographic brain in humans: one that can encompass the totality of the universe.

He is a follower of Abraham Maslow who studied "peak experiences" in peoples' lives. Maslow wondered as to why if so many people are having peak experiences, is the world not getting better? Grof is not a pessimist, but is in danger of looking over his shoulder to see how he has scored with those scientists who refute all things spiritual as bogus wish-fulfilment. However, undaunted like David with Goliath, he fires slingshot after slingshot at the self-proclaimed infallible Church of Science. He is a Jungian contra

Freud and a convincing voice for the actuality of transcendental experience. It might be said that he believes in a lot more than the conventional God formally evoked in the court rooms and the institutions of Democracy. One feels that he has had mystical experience: "it is essential to complement everyday practical activities with some form of systematic spiritual practice that provides experiential access to the transcendental realms".

He might also be described as an Eleusinian—if one may coin a word for those who support the use of psychedelic drugs to induce transcendental states. At Eleusis in ancient Greece, a psychospiritual ceremony was a regular occurrence at which participants in a hermetically sealed environment such as a cave or temple drank a sacred potion, kykeon, which contained alkaloids of ergot similar to LSD. Plato, Aristotle, Epictetus, Alcibiades, Euripides and Sophocles were some of the neophytes at Eleusis and Cicero's *De legibus* is an ecstatic account of the impact and effects of the ceremony. Grof supports the setting up of "centres offering supervised psychedelic sessions". It maybe a long time away before students can take Honours Psychedelia as a subject for the Leaving Certificate?

His story about peyote and the Patawatome Indians in a Kansas prairie is part of his journey in pschedelia which began with experiments in the sixties on a training programme for LSD at the Maryland Psychiatric Research Center. He is obviously hated, will be, by the hard-liquor ethyl-alcohol lobby in the US and worldwide, who always want their drug to sell well. This is why they support the bad publicity or outright banning of mind-altering substances such as those used by the ancient Aztecs, Mayans Olmecs, and Mazatecs including hashish, mescaline, the mushroom Psilocybe mexicana, ololiuqui, ayahuasca and the bark of the eboga shrub.

He is formidable on the largely unsung history of persecution of yet another minority up to modern times: "People who have direct experiences of spiritual realities are in our culture seen as mentally ill." The psychiatric confraternity in the US concede that "mysticism might be a phenomenon that lies between normalcy and psychosis" while Buddhist meditation is described as "artificial catatonia". He manages to reach heights of indifference when bothering "to reconcile such concepts as cosmic consciousness, reincarnation or spiritual enlightenment with the basic tenets of materialistic science."

Institutional religion actively discourages direct spiritual experiences while their revelations are based on visionary experiences. He gives many examples, including Origen (AD 186-253) who was declared a heretic by the Second Council of Constantinople for supporting reincarnation. In the Gnostic gospel found in Nag Hammadi in 1945, Jesus is reported as speaking about reincarnation in the Pistis Sophia. Grof's vision still has a scientific itch for more actual contact with the divine. He quotes Freeman Dyson, "the universe must in some sense have known we were coming". This reflects the average scientific utterance when it comes to the mystical. More profound is Jack Kornfield, a friend of the author's whose probing question to the Tibetan Kalu Rinpoche about the essence of Buddhist teachings, received the answer, "You do not really exist." Also quoted is Fritjof Schuon's Shakespearian sounding phrase, "The universe is a dream woven of dreams: the self alone is awake." Grof mentions the Cabala's inference that "one of the reasons God created the universe was to overcome boredom".

This book does not reveal any belief in the fierce God of fundamentalism and deals with OOBEs (out-of-body experiences) and near-death experiences which help to eradicate fear of death. He also evokes the essential dogma for anyone who wants a new life by "dying to our identity as a skin-encapsulated ego" and thereby undergoing "psychospiritual death and rebirth". Grof should not be dismissed as a hippy guru because he is aware that humans are inherently evil and destructive, and they find "great difficulties in accepting it". He is compelling about the dangers of world over-population, global poverty and the impending crisis of hyper-rich versus hyper-poor. "Our planet is in great trouble and if we keep carrying old grudges and do not work together, we will all die"—he quotes Chief Seattle's words to the European colonisers of the last century with even more urgency. Grof has touched and been touched by the global mystical tradition and finds organised religion too tame and too dangerous: "The fact that, on a higher level, we have a free choice whether or not we enter the cosmic game creates a metaframework that redefines everything that occurs within it."

This is the third volume of a trilogy. Previous titles for those, who, like the present reviewer have not yet read them, are: Crossing the Kedron (1996) and Horsehead Nebula Neighing (1997). Moriarty is hailed by many, such as Mark Patrick Hederman, Fintan O'Toole and Alice Taylor as the mystic of Mangerton Mountain, a sage and a philosopher. The three volumes have been consistently rushed into print over three consecutive years. Anaconda Canoe has a lengthy introduction which is "both prologue and epilogue". The glossary might well be more extensive. The question and answer format of the introduction is pitched between mystical meanderings mumbo jumbo?—and meaningful text. Moriarty has a diffuse style. He is prone to hyperbole and often writes headlines instead of sentences. The text is chock-full of fine quotations (without acknowledgement, bibliography or source!) from Lao Tzu, Meister Eckhart, Gautama Buddha, The Bhagavad Gita, the Upanishads, the Tibetan Book of the Dead, the Egyptian Book of the Dead, St John of the Cross, Teresa of Avila, St Kieran, St Patrick, Julian of Norwich, Job, Jonah, Joseph Conrad, D. H. Lawrence, Coleridge and Wordsworth, Sir Thomas Browne, Dante Alighieri, Jacob Boehme, Sir Walter Scott, Sylvia Plath, Emily Bronte, Kant, Nietzsche, Rilke, Hölderlin and various myths taken from the Blackfoot Indians, Innuit and Aztecs.

The quotations are edifying, but in the context of the interlinking commentary—is it meant to be a commentary?—they read like a very arbitrarily chosen anthology. The list of references is far too wide for the good of his thesis and almost impossible to synthesise. Readers who have not read extensively in these areas of thought may get lost amongst the dense verbal forest and the muddy torrent of language which makes Moriarty somewhat like Casaubon in George Eliot's Middlemarch attempting to write a Key to All Mythologies.

He chants and exhorts in a very pally manner with the poets, mystics and saints in his text and why not, one might say? The following is fairly typical; having answered his own question as to his awareness of being a naive realist or not, he mentions Jesus in Gethsemane and Emerson's poem about a raped women (the entire poem is quoted) and then this:

'If Longinus thinks that he has speared Jesus, and if Jesus thinks that he has been speared, then look at me, Ralph Waldo, transcendently wise, emerging unperturbed and refreshed from a siesta which, Brahma be praised, continued from the sixth to the ninth hour. Good Heavens! All this Good Friday turbulence! It is so uncivil. No need at all, I say, for a Lamb of God who takes upon him-the sin of the world. Do but climb to the summit of the nearest hill and you will see that the shame of child abuse is in no way different from the fame of St Francis of Assisi's sanctity. 'No. I'm not a Docetist.'

The word 'fame' is an associative echo of the word 'shame' and no real meaning is conveyed to this reader.

Is this an apocryphal Gospel according to John Moriarty? Is he striving to give coherence to an immense body of thought? The vision is obscure, the mysticism is suspiciously invalid. It is difficult to engage with his sense of the divine or the abyss but it might be wonderful to walk up into the hills with him and hear him explain his explanation.

Chet Raymo presents a curious mix: meditations on astrology, cosmology and mysticism with many interesting digressions. Thankfully he has adopted a pre-ordained structure from medieval monasticism where "the day was divided into eight canonical 'hours'—Matins, Lauds, Prime, Terce, Sext, Nones, Vespers and Compline". The eight essays are based on experiences which occurred approximately during these periods. The title Honey from Stone is from Saint Bernard of Clairvaux. The book is also a travelogue around the landscape of the Dingle Peninsula and happily flouts the convention of travel books which pursue the exotic, the faraway and create a heroic narrator who is constantly denying such status. Raymo travels light and finds the world in Dingle and close by the vast cosmos. His companions are the astronomers Aristarchus, Galileo Galilei, Johannes Kepler, Camille Flammarion, Lewis Swift and a few mystics: Meister Eckhart, "Put on your jumping shoes which are intellect and love"; Richard Rolle the fourteenth-century Yorkshireman who today might be uncharitably called a drop-out, "What is God? I say that you shall never have an answer to this question." Rolle could be heard on the moors chanting the name of Jesus continuously on his life-long spiritual quest. Julian of Norwich to whom Christ appeared holding a hazel nut and said, "It is all that is made." Juan de Yepes (John of the Cross) imprisoned by his fellow Carmelite friars at Toledo in 1577 for eight months because he supported reforms in the order. His tiny cell in perpetual darkness became the source of mystical experience.

Raymo brings things down to bedrock and celebrates the first geologists who surveyed Ireland, including Joseph Beete Jukes, James Flanagan and George Victor du Noyer who did not know that Dingle was the same distance from Dublin as Dingle had been from Newfoundland millions of years ago. Raymo explores ULOs (un-identified luminous objects), comets, star clusters, meteors and the like. He is awestruck by a place called Christ's Saddle on the Great Skellig and worships the splendour of the sun and Vega. "We are falling toward Vega at twelve miles per second, spiralling down on to that blue star out of the black backdrop of the universe. We will be there in half a million years." He revels in Vega's distance "twenty-seven light years away, 160 trillion miles ... I have sipped 10,000 stars. I have tasted the universe."

—*Books Ireland* 1998

THE LIES THAT LAST

Conversing with Angels and Ancients: literary myths of medieval Ireland Joseph Falaky Nagy (Four Courts Press)

Law and Disorder in Thirteenth-Century Ireland: the Dublin parliament of 1297 James Lydon (Four Courts Press)

From Author to Audience: John Capgrave and medieval publication Peter J. Lucas (University College Dublin Press)

The First Chapter Act Book of Christ Church Cathedral, Dublin, 1574-1634 Raymond Gillespie (Four Courts Press)

Professor Nagy is an expert in his field and possesses in abundance a conviction that the medieval world is just as valid as the modern world. This is not to imply that he is an antiquarian. Reading his book moves the imagination closer to the ancient Celt's desire to read the glass book. Columba, during a life fraught with turmoil, was privileged to read the glass book for three nights, however "Columba will bear the scars of his encounter with the angel till his death." Columba had his work cut out for him when, at the Convention of Druim Cet, "he limits the number of poets and the size of poetic retinues, so as to reduce the burden of maintaining poets for the population at large." By doing so he "persuades the men of Ireland not to banish poets altogether." The taming of the poets doesn't preclude the appearance of the likes of Geilt Suibne, who is cursed by Ronan but 'adopted' by Moling, whose swineherd slays the poet for an alleged sexual assault on his wife.

Druim Cet came about because of a cultural crisis. Columba was recalled from exile to address the *aes ditna* (what would he think of the present members?). Columba finds value in poetry: "Christ himself purchased three fifties of poems [that is the psalms] from David." Columba was always profound: "If every poem is a lie, then clothing and food are lies too, as are the whole world and even clayey man. To obtain the lie that is more lasting, I will give the lie that is more transient; for I am not taking anything blue, red, or fair green with me to the grave."

Nagy's use of the Táin (the translations are from the beautiful version by C. O'Rahilly) and other pre-Christian Irish mythology, is to achieve an illumination of "less explicitly Christian branches of the literary tradition". His dealings with the Táin are various, including "Who is more virile, the young Cu Chulainn or Fergus, his senior? Cu Chulainn or his coeval, Etarcomol? What is the status of the soul and cult of Patrick's sister as a 'fallen woman', and what is the ecclesiastical status of her lover and the offspring of the illicit union? Can a child born of a dead woman become Patrick's bishop, and "can the besmirched Mac Nisse fill the gap created by the cursing of Olean?" Only Nagy's book will tell you, if you haven't heard already.

The Táin was the cause of great ructions in the medieval world. First off, it went missing and no-one could recite it from memory. Eventually Ciaran of Clonmacnois having been contacted in his dreams "directs Senchan to Fergus's grave in Connaght." Fergus is eventually revived and recites to Muirgein, the son of Senchan. This is another instance of the glass book in mythology. The glass book must not be explained away as some kind of ancient video, nor should it be equated with some ancient form of teletext. The medieval world embraced wider social parameters and the imagination was freer whereas in the modern techno-era imagination is secondary if not taboo.

Nagy's Saint Patrick is a mystic in his *Confessio* by divine authority and evokes the Pauline "nescio, Deus scit" of 2 Corinthians 12:2,3 ("I do not know, but God knows"). The explication of Muirchti's biography is masterly, indicating the layers of metaphor, linking pagan with Christian, Irish oral tradition with literature in Latin. Nagy shows Patrick as a valid spiritual guide, because of his resemblance to biblical figures such as Moses, Daniel, Peter, and Christ. Daniel "challenges the authority of kings and becomes even more authoritative". The reference is to Patrick's ordeal with King Laoghaire on the hill of Tara. Also, Patrick's "duel with the Druids" is analagous in Muirchies biography with "Peter's contest with Simon Magus". Nagy avoids conjecture about Patrick. Moses, the Hebrew prophet, was buried on top of Mount Sinai, which has led to speculation in the absence of facts about Patrick's place of burial. He may have been laid to rest on Cruachan Aigli (Croagh Patrick) where he received his major revelations and where his favourite charioteer Totmael died.

There are fitting digressions about charioteers and heroes and gods, Krishna and Arjuna, Cu Chulainn and Loeg, Patrick and Odran, who gives his life to save the saint as they drive through the territory of Failge. Patrick had destroyed Failge's idols. In revenge, Failge throws a spear at the passenger in the chariot thinking it is Patrick, except on that occasion Odran was being driven around by the saint. When Brendan arrived at the Isle of Ravenous Mice, he literally fed one of his hangers-on to the four legged creatures—his crosán, a lowly type of poet-entertainer (perhaps the equivalent of the modern stand-up comedian). When the mice have nibbled the poor unfortunate to death, Saint Brendan and his crew watch his soul ascending to heaven. When Brendan returns, his foster mother, Ita rebukes him for going to sea in a coracle made of animal skin, instead of wood. Her words are metaphorical, as is the incident of the death of the crosán. Ita herself is later eaten by a beetle and manages to write a poem about it as she dies. Professor Nagy's work is literally a magical device for priming the imagination, it is not just a book.

This is dedicated to the late Jocelyn Otway Ruthven. Professor Lydon contributes two essays and a preface in this book with shock value about Irish history. His opening essay gives a sense of the rancorous state of Ireland in the reign of Edward I. The native Irish attacked the settlers' castles with intent to exterminate. Among the list were Sir Richard Harold and John de Courcy, whose murderer escaped and "was not to be found, but is among the Irish in waste land, where no serjeant or bailiff dared to go to attach him". Lydon's other essay refers to the justiciar of Ireland, John Wogan, appointed in 1195. Lydon looks ahead to the mid-fifteenth century when "the authority of parliament was well established in Ireland". The road to stability is charted in part by Cormac Ó Cleirigh who gives examples of the doings and undoings of settlers defending themselves in Northern Kildare and in Offaly "against the hostile Irish dynasties of the midlands". He outlines the conquests led by Maurice fitz Maurice and Gerald fitz Maurice, who died after a period of captivity, aged twenty-two. He deliberates on the 'divide-and-rule' strategy and its complexities, when native Irish adopted an "amenable stance towards the colonists", sometimes changing their names for protection. Ireland was pervaded by "a murky, perilous environment, where war alternated easily with peace, temporary alliances were formed and dissolved, and where the joint celebration of a religious feast-day could act as the trigger for mass murder". Piers de Bermingham carried out a massacre on leading members of the O'Connor Faly dynasty at Carbury castle. However, siege and counter-siege were prevalent, such as at Ballymore Eustace and Geashill.

Brendan Smith is graphic about frontier life where there was no rule of law between settler lords and native felons. "In Ireland there was much more official hostility to march law than in

Scotland or Wales." Katharine Simms expertly outlines some Irish dynasties, O'Donnell, Mac Mahon, O'Brien and Mac Carthy, who were regulated by "political overlordship ... regardless of territorial ownership, resulting in one baron supporting 'his' Irish chief in rebellion against another, who was legal landlord .. ." Sean Duffy shows the levels of degeneracy (quasi degeneres) which the parliament of 1297 found intolerable. Yet, degeneracy was the norm thereafter as invader and native commingled. But not before the shiring of Ireland, which Gerard McGrath explores during the reign of Henry II. Shiring created new geographic areas such as Meath which had been annexed to Dublin before 1297. Shiring meant the appointing of more county sheriffs. By 1306 the number of shires had increased to twelve. Philomena Connolly introduces the text and a translation of the historic document enacted by the Parliament of 1297, preserved in the Black Book. Her details become pointed with mention that the White Book was destroyed by fire in 1610, and the Red Book perished in the Four Courts fire of 1922.

Lucas has produced a very accessible if highly specialised book on the fifteenth-century John Capgrave "an author in search of his public". Born after the Chaucer era, he entered the Augustinian Order in adolescence; was ordained in due course and spent most of his life writing at the friary at Lynn, modern-day King's Lynn. In contrast, his fellow scribe William Gybbe at nearby Wisbech is used to explain authentication difficulties until a third manuscript of any work is perused, to identify the singularities of individual authors. Capgrave's work is still extant, thanks to sixteenth-century antiquaries John Leland and John Bale. It comprises twelve books, sometimes appended with a triquetramark, which is a cipher on Capgrave's initials, JC. His earliest work *Life of St Norbert* is in verse. *Solace of Pilgrimes* comes from his middle period. His latest prose work was *Abbreviacion of Cronicles.*

Capgrave sought patronage from Duke Humfrey of Gloucester. Furnivill wrote, "Capgrave, being an Englishman, was of course by race and nature a flunkey, and had an inordinate reverence for kings and rank." Thus Capgrave, in a preface to *In Genesim* addressed Duke Humfrey, "Permit me among the most worthless, O most generous Prince, to increase this your greatness in accordance with my ability so that, be cause you favour writers, you may win the praise of writers."

Capgrave would meet the disappointments which embittered Dr Johnson, who famously referred to a patron as "a wretch who supports with insolence, and is paid with flattery". Capgrave soon gave up on Humfrey and found Sir Thomas Tuddenham to finance his Italian travels. Lucas's finest chapter is a worthy digression on patrons, packed with marvellous matter, "Maecenas, Patron of Horace, Augustus, patron of Virgil, and Titus, patron of Josephus". Reference to Jean Froissart proves how "most later medieval English authors were so only on a part-time basis". Capgrave tried to run a scriptorium and have his manuscripts copied, which was publication for him, as such. There is intriguing mention of Beryl Smalley's work on Richard de Bury, a medieval patron who wrote about patronage in *Philobiblon.*

Lucas provides an extensive in-depth source for Capgrave's spelling and punctuation, especially, with regard to the latter; whether it is for reading aloud or not, since he often divided his texts into convenient units for speech-delivery, using punctuation for pauses and intonation. There is extensive line and page reference given, and computer facilities at UCD have been brought to bear on Capgrave's orthographic usage. "A modern grammatical function is not necessarily to be assumed for medieval punctuation." Lucas can instruct without mystifying, if the reader stays with him, on through Chambers and Daunt's *Book of London English* amongst others, seeking a basis for Capgrave's passion for consistency and continuity. Lucas implies approval of J. H. Fisher's dictum, that "historians of the English language are agreed that the genesis of the standard language is not literary."

Four Courts Press make public access to much valuable and intriguing material through this book which at first sight looks archaic. However far from it. First off, the reproduction on the case of the book and on the half-title page of an early sketch by William Wright (1658) is a unique graphic of Christ Church Cathedral. This volume is the third in the Christ Church document series, Gillespie writes in the preface. Three plates are reproduced: the seal of the dean and chapter and facsimiles of handwriting by two chapter clerks, John Durning and Thomas Howell. Gillespie's introduction should not remain unsung; without it what follows would be labyrinthine. How simply extraordinary in many ways, what unfolds, like some wildly experimental novel with a host of personages and events, over seventy years, radiating from the ecclesiastical focal point of the Cathedral to localities like Clondalkin, Clonkeen, Winetaverne street and Lucan. The Cathedral comes to life, its orders and regulations, not least the form of oath for every vicar including "no strange woman or of ill fame shall attend to the vicars chambers at undue times under penalty before noted."

Many notable people are fleetingly glossed in the notes: Arland Ussher whose son James Ussher became archbishop of Armagh; Thomas Bateson the first music graduate from Trinity College whose madrigals were published in London in 1604 and 1618. The bulk of the text is more profane than sacred and reads like a text from the Registry of Deeds and Leases. No wonder that the following is from 19 December 1604 "A lease made unto Sir Henry Harrington, knight, of an old castell, and xviii acres of land in the parish of Kilcullen" at twenty pound sterling, payable twice yearly. Many of these contracts were officially signed in the presence of witnesses upon Strongbow's tomb in the Church.

Otherwise there is the sense of private conscience subject to public admonishment. This from 8 March 1615: "Tho. Cooper was called before the Deane and Chapter and convicted of contumacie and unreverend behaviore both in Chapter and Quiere." On 26 August 1630 "The Organist was admonished not to walke the body of the Church in tyme of divine service." And bigamy on 25 April 1633 when Richard Brookes, shooemaker "for living in open and notorious Adultery to the great dishonor of God Almighty and scandall of the Church and hurt to his owne Soule being married to a woman with whome he nowe liveth, haveing another wife yet liveing."

The domain of the historian, in an age of print and technology, has the benefit of greater information and storage facilities, but this book was made possible by the diligent chapter clerks, whose handwriting is vastly superior to present-day illegibility. In a time of mass attendance at computer courses, handwriting classes might be s o c i a l l y d e s i r a b l e a l s o .

—*Books Ireland* 1998

TELLERS OF TALES

The Stones and Other Stories Daniel Corkery (Mercier)

The Sea's Revenge and other stories Seamus Ó Grianna (Mercier)

The Stealing Steps John Arden (Methuen)

No atmospheric details are too incongruous for his pen, whether they are landscape, weather, exact location (Munster), dialect or dialogue. Corkery should not be dubbed a purveyor of folksy shallowness, a regional writer, because of the influence of his native city, a purveyor of mere 'Corkery'. In 'The Priest', Father Reen despairs of his people—a subtle story, as with all of the stories selected by Delaney from the four collections. Corkery will not in the artist's manner, in the classic Irish phrase, explain things away to death. He will not produce a plodding plot and an easy solution. He will not desecrate the mystery.

Paul Delaney sounds almost apologetic in the introduction but concludes: "His best stories rank among the finest in the history of Irish literature," and this collection bears testimony to that. Corkery (1878-1964) is above Maugham, O'Henry and the like, and with stories neatly set up, albeit ingeniously entertaining, trick endings. He must be included in the modern canon along with Joyce, Mary Lavin, Benedict Kiely, Mary Beckett and Maeve Brennan—to give a few names off the top of the head.

To digress a moment—there is negative polemic contra Joyce (hardly Anglo-Irish?) in Corkery's *Synge and Anglo-Irish Literature*; is the title racist? Contorting it to 'Corkery and Free State Literature' one tends to think of passion and sexuality excluded by Free State writers but it is portrayed, if not overtly, in 'The Ruining of Dromacurrig' and especially in 'The Spancelled'. One depicts a man grieving for the love of his life who takes it out on his horse, the other portrays a woman almost missing a second chance at marriage after a bad first.

'The Stones' and 'Vision' are both praised by Delaney and others—the former on mortality, set up in a fabulous myth, the latter showing the heartbreak of a boy's growing up and seeing for the first time his real home life.

Corkery manages that rare thing: shock, frisson, the terror of life, if you like. It may well come from his tragic vision. There is no humour, no rollicking Irish laughter and carousing. His openings are devoid of tenseness as you are brought into his own peculiar Munster twilight. He has the qualities that Conrad insisted a writer must have. Corkery may not have them in abundance but he has them enough to bring you to the end of his stories, to make you see and your senses reel because of the fabric of the words and the magic they have performed.

It would be cultural snobbery to demote Ó Grianna (1889-1969) below Corkery in some canonical game of literary classification. Ó Grianna revels in his Rannafast and the wider borders of his universe, barely stretching beyond Donegal. This is of course his strength. He can find the universe in a single village. Like Corkery, one hears the dialect above literary dialogue. There is ample evidence of this debate in Mac Congail's introduction and appendices, made up of Ó Grianna's letters in which he boasts of the superiority of 'the Irish of the people' above book Irish.

This is highly acceptable since oral literature is far younger to civilisation than print. The whole original purpose of the dithyramb and almost every rhyming scheme was a preserve of the poet-storyteller prior to wax tablets and latterly the laptop. Hence Ó Grianna's work has been transposed from the Gaelic by his own hand into a form that echoes the bare bones of the seanchai, even one dares say the sean-nós singer. There is this desperate striving after a lost civilisation, that for Ó Grianna meant chiefly the native language. It is the same plea that sears through the pages of Fenimore Cooper's The Last of the Mohicans and Ó Criomhthain's

An tOileonach. There is nothing unnatural in this; one reads works in any event in English, that were written before the language was out of its swaddling. Ó Grianna might be said to be something of a master of the digression. It serves him well. Very often his central character has gone away to America; he will change and events will also change before his return. It is also an opportunity for the writer to outline characters who will play a lot more than an ancillary role in his life.

His characters are given through their full life story, rather than the more traditional form of the genre, in which a life is represented by some salient incident or a series of significant events. When he reveals how politics mark and mar people, he is the complete recorder, the truly picaresque historian bringing you through the time tunnel of his story-telling to the time, place and events that shaped the thinking. 'Home Rule' shows lovers star-crossed in a Romeo and Juliet manner whose forebears are from different political persuasions. The 1916 Rising in 'Manus Mac Award, Smoker and Storyteller' provides the backdrop for sorting out some marital disharmony. 'Edward Devaney' is inherently political in its treatment of pro and anti-Treaty persuasions.

He is awfully good at the depiction of men and woman, and undoubtedly the best stuff is in this vein, 'Fair-Haired Mary' and 'Denis the Dreamer'. He is philosophical in 'At Sunset' about the passing of time. The title story, 'The Sea's Revenge' concerns fate and destiny. 'The Best Laid Schemes' deals with a man who plays with the affections of a woman while holding an ulterior motive. If you are tired of the over wrought short story, perhaps you might get together with Ó Grianna.

Arden is a stalwart on the scene, a Yorkshireman who has entrusted himself long since to Galway pudding, and serves it up particularly well in two stories, in which Molly Concannon features. 'The Hag out of Legend, originally entitled 'The

Stealing Steps, comes from Mr Shakespeare's *Hamlet* and is a worthy tale of the demise of a writer into drink and oblivion while on the trail of material for placating the muse but alas to no avail.

Let you not be put off by a melancholy tale, for Arden will have none of it in the other eight stories. He takes on a kind of jousting-mockery along the lines of Anthony Burgess in *The Devil's Mode,* a story collection mixing literary history and fiction. 'Breach of Trust' (Pritchett Memorial Prize winner) recounts the plight of two competitive playwrights (fictional) in 1820s London, Tom Longshank and Erasmus Grail. Their moribund lives get even more complicated when Roseanna Twigger becomes a mutual fascination. Rivalry is not in it, when Longshank dies abruptly and Grail's passion cools in travelling, or does it?

'A Grim All-Purpose Hall' has another voluptuous central attraction, Miss Clemency O'Raw (Arden is refreshingly non-PC). She is a player, tackling Webster's *The White Devil,* a play further empowered with superstition, and in this story the fabricator of mayhem and murders off-stage. 'Molly Concannon & the State-of-the-Art Development' makes for good satire where Molly settles into a bungalow, and Greenview, a proposed factory development is soon sited on her doorstep. The characters comprise Eugene Gilmartin TD, Brid from the Refugee Support Group, Fatima, a fugitive Kurd and her daughter, Balkis. Molly easily finds a weapon in Fermanagh, Fatima seems well versed in guns and the Gardai appear. Here Arden manages some topical comment while filling a short story with far more engaging content than your run-of the-mill.

His afterword sets the background to the stories and their central theme—old age—a bad admission, since he manages to keep them in the main youthful. Spike Oldroyd takes up four stories and might well lean on personal material. Oldroyd in 'The Dissident' lives near a small pub-owning IRA loudmouth, Martin de Porres McGranaghan who is eventually charged with killing a member of the Garda Siochana. There are three subsequent adventures with Oldroyd; one follows him to a university in Oregon.

Arden's, for all his covert ribaldry is a healthy mind; there is nothing that will make you break into hysterical laughter but there is a satirical sting in some of the tales. The women characters, Ute and Zelda among others, get a bit of a roasting and why not? He proudly displays—beyond the movies, tv, videos, talking books and CD roms—a far older art form: storytelling on the printed page. Can anything be more peaceful to ingest?

—*Books Ireland* 2004

HOT PROPERTY

The Letters of Liam O'Flaherty ed. A. A. Kelly (Wolfhound Press)

Liam O'Faherty's Ireland Peter Costello (Wolfhound Press)

The Black Soul Liam O'Flaherty (Wolfhound Press)

The Wilderness Liam O'Flaherty (Wolfhound Press)

Short Stories: the pedlar's revenge Liam O'Flaherty (Wolfhound Press)

The first letter in this book, to Edward Garnett, is one of the most important in O'Flaherty's life, because it was the beginning of a beautiful friendship. A. A. Kelly the distinguished editor of these letters, calls Garnett 'literary godfather' and how fitting an epithet. Garnett whose mother was Irish, a necessary attribute for dealing with O'Flaherty perhaps, was working at the time for Jonathan Cape. He took an awful pounding by way of having to manage everything for O'Flaherty: advice artistic, financial, medical; endless encouragement, editing sessions, a grant from the Literary Fund, manoeuvring to get him the James Tait Black Memorial Prize for a novel, making endless introductions for him—indeed everything except organising his laundry, about which O'Flaherty was obsessive.

However, he had just about got through an early life, that might have sunk many another budding writer. Having been born on Aran was a large part of his destiny. A. A. Kelly says that his father's "terrible bouts of melancholia" affected him. He was bright enough to win a scholarship to Rockwell, but never really had a vocation to become a priest. After a year of Classics at UCD he found himself in the trenches of Flanders, not only because of the influence of Redmondite politics but also his avid need for adventure—a lifelong need. As a witness to the extremes of watching young people marched off as gun fodder in the third battle of Ypres, and the unholy slaughter of close to a quarter of a million in order to capture the tiny village of Passchendaele, he became a casualty with shell shock and neurasthenia. He was discharged from the Irish Guards a wreck with his nerve fibre weakened for life. The noise of the typewriter was an assault on his nerves, until many years later he found some tranquillity using a Smith-Corona.

Though he wrote, as others would, a disturbing account of these experiences in *The Return of the Brute*, the war would remain a subject which he was physically and mentally unable to discuss with anyone.

The letters to Garnett have an obviously guarded tone in places, because the relationship is one of author to publisher's editor. Still, Garnett must have been a latter-day saint. He even had to provide interesting books for the perky and promising O'Flaherty to read: Turgenev's *Fathers and Sons*, Borrow's *The Romany Rye*; short stories by Maupassant and Tchekov; but O'Flaherty, after many attempts, couldn't read Flaubert's historical novel *Salammbô*; and the books he begged in London from literary editors were rarely if ever reviewed by him. When he left Cape the relationship with Garnett naturally changed; O'Flaherty, by then of some repute, could afford to swashbuckle in a noisier manner with his agent, A. D. Peters.

In many ways the letters are a barrel of laughs since O'Flaherty gives the impression, that he is not allowing the writing career to dominate him. However this conviction has its doubtful moments, "If a thousand lies are necessary to write a book five thousand are necessary to advertise it and telling lies is a game at which only very clever men can play with any hope of success." Or in even grimmer mood he feels that, "no literary individual is a whit of use to the world except as a tolerated ornament." He wasn't quite a master of despair but had sufficient audacity to avoid whinging. His bravura is wonderfully mixed with clear self-knowledge and real humility. Dissatisfied with his second novel, *The Black Soul*, dedicated to

Garnett, he complains, "Reading Conrad did the damage." He is very self-deprecating about the limitations of his talent, while it seems he needed very long hours for solitary and constant rewriting, and even then was unsure of perfection.

On a good day, "When I have a writing mood I forget everything and every unpleasant person and thing than can meet with me . . . It stirs one up and one is better for it afterwards. The thing in life is to feel and go on feeling more and more acutely. Thus one gets a wider comprehension of reality".

The business asides in the letters, are essential wisdom about the eternal truths concerning literary life; with the added bite, that this is the howling of a writer who was a steady success in every way. Often, his humanity rolls out with endless humour, prefixed with a lot of 'by jove's' —a favourite remark. The literary gossip is priceless, to Garnett amongst others: "Shaw's abortion on Saint Joan did not cause your digestion a permanent ill?"; J. B. Priestley "a most unbearable ruffian, one of Lynd's gang"; O'Casey "a dramatist in overalls"; Yeats, "a man who rose to fame on the shoulders of those men who stirred this country to fervent enthusiasm for ideals in the last generation"; George Russell (AE), "a profound realist and sceptic in his editorial pages—elsewhere he is a mystic, a bounder and a fool ... As AE controls a newspaper we shall probably drive Yeats out of the country"; "An odious woman called Marianne Moore is now editing The Dial"; "It turns out that Malraux, in spite of having been a revolutionary writer for years, is a worse censor than most"; "I saw Behan but didn't quote Shakespeare to him"; Kavanagh: "I've been told he now has a cheque book, which he takes out solemnly now and again, in the bars he frequents, but without making any attempt to draw money. Just stares with pen in hand absent-mindedly and then puts everything away once more untouched"; "Brian Hurst is filming The Playboy in Kerry, using Siobhan McKenna as the female lure and God knows how many pansies as the male ones"; "They go on calling Scott Fitzgerald a genius, I mean Time magazine" and a big swipe at an old friend: "Francis Stuart has now given up both horse racing and Jesus. What on earth has he got left apart from Gertruda whom he brought back from Germany as apologia pro vita situ, in other words a living proof that he had put away his love for Adolf Hitler and turned his face towards Israel". O'Flaherty found a great ally in John Ford, who would film his infamous novel *The Informer* after the earlier uncommercial version by Arthur Robinson.

When his marriage to Margaret Barrington broke up, he happily found the central woman of his life, Kitty Tailer 'Kitty Pie'.

His wanderlust may account for the brief marriage to Margaret Barrington, who wrote a novel about their relationship. O'Flaherty's travels must be the most extensive of any twentieth-century writer, making it impossible for any biographer to be totally accurate, because of incomplete information. So, ever cantankerous, he would finally settle in Dublin, despite Good Friday, "the most hateful day of the Christian year in a Roman Catholic country like this". He would renew, the more-hate than-love relationship with the city, while fully enjoying the football finals and rugby internationals; and, when he was able, walk to Leopardstown races or get to the Curragh and Baldoyle with friends; and solitary film-going, such as two visits to see *The Secret Life of Walter Mitty*. His criticisms of Dublin are inherently refreshing but equally savage and politically revealing, "This cursed town is like a desert for a man interested in things of the mind solely. A cursed blasted desert, a rotting corpse that was once part of a dying empire." These years were marked by persistent letters to Kitty Tailer; often walking over a mile to the GPO rather than use the local post office. As 'the woman in his life', she was not always with him, until the closing years; and would eventually become his ideal agent and business manager, since he was a hot literary property in actual terms from the publication of the *The Informer* onwards. His stories appeared 'everywhere', such as in T. S. Eliot's Criterion and would have been in Transition, the magazine surrounding James Joyce in Paris, except the editors apparently lost his submission. Seamus Cashman of the Wolfhound Press resurrected O'Flaherty's reputation in the seventies and remains keeper of the flame. And later on, Garech de Brun of Claddagh Records issued sound recordings of O'Flaherty's works: The Mermaid, Red Barbara, The Stolen Ass, Dill and The Ecstasy of Angus. Indomitable to the end, O'Flaherty refused to write a foreword to the Folio edition of The Informer in the sixties, and by then was a living Irish writer whose books had been translated into many languages, including Hindi and Vietnamese. The letters to Kitty reveal the real man, or at least as much as he would disclose to his true love, and for this reason they are rather remarkable.

This book deserves an award on many counts: it's a very brief anthology of his work; the photographs, illustrations and design are exemplary; and Peter Costello provides a linking biography, which is effective in highlighting the diversity of the life and times of its subject. The layout gives a documentary feel to the whole production, especially the Civil War photographs and those of Dublin in the troublesome twenties. The pastoral scenes from Ireland, including the islands, avoid obvious clichés; while the stills from O'Flaherty's novels turned into films are a good extra. The photographs of O'Flaherty himself show a very Irish face yet a singular one, and in his eighties he still looks irascible, feisty and full of fight as ever. The illustrations from The Ecstasy of Angus, and some of Harry Clarke's nudes based on the novel Mr Gilhooley add to O'Flaherty's celebration of sexuality, making him a sort of Irish D. H. Lawrence, crossed with the macho of Ernest Hemingway. Critically, he's closer to Hemingway's writing and far more elemental and affirmative.

His high achievement as novelist and short story writer is obvious; for example chapter IX of The Wilderness and many many stories, the best of which are extraordinary, for the originality of their primitive naturalistic writing, which presents an authentic and lifelike quality. The nature sketches are only one strand of his talent. Late in life, when he read a review of a book in the Daily Telegraph, mentioning himself as a neglected writer, he seemed delighted to tell Kitty the news. The solitude gave him the ideal conditions to proceed with his last novel, *The Gambler*. O'Flaherty had spent more time alone voluntarily than in Bohemian circles world-wide. Yet somehow he was still writing for the money right up to the end; and told Kitty, that if, "I die in humiliating debt to my beloved, I die trying to reach the moon, or Mars, or Venus, or trying to uncover the unique and unfathomable gift that shines with divine splendour in the naked beauty of her omniscient eyes". Well, he never finished *The Gambler* but he was faithful to his Kitty and his art, and has left rich treasure in his writings.

Costello's text is full of surprise: mentioning James Joyce and O'Flaherty visiting Stonehenge—a wonderful scene to imagine. Joyce, who would evoke the Druidic shrine in *Finnegans Wake*, walking Salisbury Plain with the young O'Flaherty, who had written a book on Tim Healy, one of the calumniators and ultimate destroyers of Parnell, whom Joyce revered this side of idolatry.

—*Books Ireland* 1997

TINSELTOWN

Liam O'Flaherty *Hollywood Cemetery* (Nuascéalta)

O'Flaherty's *Hollywood Cemetery* (1935) as exploitative hell-hole is a precursor of *The Last Tycoon* (F. Scott Fitzgerald), *The Day of the Locust* (Nathanael West) and *The Disenchanted* (Budd Schulberg). He does not possess the overarching mythology of these American novelists, and the style is like a drunken fiddler, however, his tycoon Jack Mortimer 'Flesh Peddling King' is a Harvey Weinstein prototype with hints of sexploitation, alongside his 'second in command' Myron Luther who 'picked brains […] instead of pockets'.

Celluloid City produces artificial gods where 'beauty is all boloney unless it's a valid signature to a cheque'. The novel's scenario is vaguely reminiscent of David Lynch's *Mulholland Drive* 'the most beautiful creatures imaginable, women gathered into Hollywood from all the corners of the earth by the lure of a screen career'.

The plot moves jerkily from Ireland to England, across the Atlantic reaching Celluloid City half-way through with a cast of walk on caricatures. Mortimer hires a successful novelist Carey having 'picked up' Angela Devlin of Ballymorguttery in a small hotel in Cork. She is 'sold to Mr Jack Mortimer, for the term of one year' to be moulded into a screen goddess. He tells cameraman Schultz, her 'eyes could set fire to an Eskimo's igloo'. Carey's novel 'The Emigrant' will unveil the goddess, meanwhile her veiled face is a publicity ploy.

Carey is foiled by Mortimer in Tinsel Town when his novel is 'shelved'. Devlin will appear in a new movie *The Veiled Goddess* written by Sam Gunn, assisted by Lee Donlin. Carey seeks revenge through publicity wizard Puff Green, author of the scandalous exposé *I Strip the Stars*. Green becomes Batman to Carey's Robin in pursuit of Mortimer, reversing publicity as malevolent weapon: 'the life and soul of this industry'. Carey begins serialising 'I Love

Angela Devlin' in the *Pacific Eagle* showing how Mortimer 'trafficked in human souls' and is holding her hostage in a 'Santa Monica medieval fortress'.

Carey hosted by Claude Wiley Washington Bryant is given a brief glimpse inside Hollywood's illuminati. The plot unravels with the 'Irish-American Brotherhood', the love affair between Carey and Devlin, and a plane crash in Mexico.

O'Flaherty is no Horace McCoy or Raymond Chandler but ultimately parodies the movies with his chewing gum plot while stolidly impounding that 'Hollywood is but a manifestation of the modern hatred of the human intellect'. As his mouthpiece Carey, states 'I am definitely realist of the school of necessity.' The public spectacle with a banner that says 'welcome to the cemetery of the living dead' caps O'Flaherty's satirical exit from Celluloid City in real life, and fiction.

Tomás Mac Síomóin's afterword unveils O'Flaherty, pissed off with John Ford's 'whimsical paddy-whackery of *The Quiet Man* rather than the bleak naked truth of his own (novel) *Famine*.' Jenny Farrell amplifies the O'Flaherty-Ford artistic fall-out that did not end their friendship. He hoped Ford might shoot *Famine* as epic movie instead of shooting it down. This highlights our industry split between two genres: 'Quiet Man' or something less stage Irish.

—*Books Ireland* 2019

SUFFICIENT UNTO THE DAY

The Storyman Bryan MacMahon (Poolbeg)

Priestly Fictions: popular Irish novelists of the early 20th Century
Catherine Candy (Wolfhound Press)

The Feminization of Famine: expressions of the inexpressible?
Margaret Kelleher (Cork University Press)

Here is MacMahon's life from the perspective of the university of the marketplace. The terrain of this autobiography is essentially bygone but engagingly in the mode of Synge's "popular imagination that is fiery". He doesn't give much detail from his later life while comfortably performing the task he knows best—being the storyman. Still, there are other features which raise it above a memoir.

There are good set pieces such as his collection of answers from diverse people to the question, "How are you?". His Johnsonian definition of humour is marvellous but too long to quote. The stories and anecdotes are mainly from his beloved Listowel, that princely town in the kingdom of Kerry. Some of the material is historical and has added pith for all that. For instance, he believes the civil war was a continuance of the Parnell split in horrendous form and recalls that "As a boy I stood aside and watched petrol being poured on the piled up record books of our local workhouse".

He is ripe when evoking "the musical clamour of the public house, the din of the marketplace and the clack of the printer's office". There is a vivid account dealing with Printer Bob in the days when printing played a very different role in a town. His first sight of an early edition of *Ulysses* "looked like a fat swatch of newsprint cut into squares holed and corded at one corner—reading for hanging up in an outhouse of a rural privy". The meeting between himself and the playwright George Fitzmaurice is one of the finest things in the book.

MacMahon recalls the publication of his first story in The Bell.

Naturally, he slots in recollections of O'Connor and O'Faolain. Elsewhere, he analyses his method of story writing, referring to 'The Breadmaker' and others, including his well-known 'The Windows of Wonder' and his play, *The Honey Spike*.

The book's pivotal advance is through a cornucopia of stories and is also gilded with rhymes, jingles and poems such as 'Sonnet to a Chamber Pot'. MacMahon has the knack of being able to flit from one yarn to another, whether it's lecturing on Peig Sayers in Canada or explaining effectively the central muse of his life, Joanna Caughlin, his mother. In the exemplary last chapter he lists his refuge as "Silence, intimacy and the lamp". There follows a meditation on death, referring to many writers. MacMahon's engagement with his people is as valid as any of the writers he quotes, not least AE's poem 'When' and Donn Byrne's "elusive, almost unbearable ache that lies at the heart of humanity".

What a good book! Without getting on her polemical horse and trashing the clergy, here is a calm and well planned study of three priests who took to novel writing. However that is only half the story because she is neither quaintly congratulatory nor anticlerical. Instead she sets about her business with complete engagement. Without heavy handed scoopfuls of history she presents the historical era of 'the Catholic Truth Society of Ireland, the Catholic magazines, the Catholic organisations'. This is only the background to her three Roman-collared novelists, with crucifix in one hand and pen in the other. They were Canon Patrick Augustine Sheehan, Canon Joseph Guinan and Father Gerald O'Donovan. All three were born after the middle of the nineteenth century and lived into the twentieth, the last of them until 1940.

O'Donovan was the most rebellious and eventually left the priesthood for a marriage which produced three children. Thereafter he found a mistress, Rose Macaulay, whose satire *Potterisin* became a bestseller in 1920. O'Donovan's literary career began in the purlieus of London after his flight from the priesthood. In London he received a fairly good reception, getting huge support from George Moore who valued him as a literary artist. It many ways Moore's novel about a priest, The Lake, was inspired by O'Donovan's best novel Father Ralph. There is clear evidence if you compare the two books. Happily, Father Ralph was re-issued in 1993 thanks to Steve MacDonogh's Brandon imprint.

O'Donovan became a big noise as a publisher's reader with Collins, signing up among others Henry James. The malcontent characters of Father Ralph reveal O'Donovan's disillusionment with the church of his time. The novel maintains its original bravery of conception and is still highly relevant in the atmosphere of the present crisis in the Catholic Church.

Candy's study works well because of the contrast inherent between O'Donovan and the two canons. One doesn't have to use any heavy irony in noting that Guinan and Sheehan were made canons in cosy parishes once their literary talent proved useful to the Church. Indeed, one easily winces at the devious careers of these two best-selling turn-of-the-century canons, puffing themselves up, puffed up by their bishops, the Catholic press in general and their obedient flock. This is not of course to take any laurels from the more famous of the trio, Canon Sheehan, whom Tolstoy hailed and whose friendship Oliver Wendell Holmes considered an honour.

It is only fair to say that Sheehan, though a bit of a phenomenon in his day, was largely a promoted icon writing for people of his own mind set. Candy gives a good picture of a man much divided in himself producing a formula type novel after the success of his third book, My New Curate. There are still sets of his novels in second-hand shops in clerical black covers. He's not much called for in re-issue but who knows, the Canon Sheehan Summer School in Don-eraile may be a thing of the future.

As revealed in Candy's study, his work is backward looking and with the added complication that the simple faith propounded in his novels may actually reveal a priest who was not of the same simple faith, since Sheehan's own library was like that of an ardent searcher after an allusive rather than a revealed truth.

Canon Joseph Guinan comes across in the same mould as Sheehan, except more strident and party political, making no secret of being pro-treaty during the civil war. Almost any passage at random from his novels, shows a smug despotism by the Church over the State. One is inclined to recoil from puffing or damning this rather incendiary author. However The Soggarth Aroon was a huge popular success going into four editions in the year of publication, 1905.

Candy's book is highly readable. It may even cause inner turmoil for some readers, due to her restraint when dealing with the huge liberties taken by power-wielding clerics such as the two canons and their backslapping hierarchies. With the hammer swing of history, it is alarming to see how the revolutionary programme of the Free State became divisively catholicised. It is even more confounding that these canons were good priests for their communities after a fashion. However, a host of hardworking curates had to back them up, while they lived the successful life of writing bestsellers by the Irish and American standards of the time.

The main flaw in Candy's book is its format which is that of cross cutting continually when discussing her three novelists instead of dealing with each separately. She has a good introduction and a better final chapter which might have gone on more in its closing comments. The first appendix is very interesting and relevant with its table of sales figures on the three novelists.

In retrospect this book leaves an unwieldy overall impression. It comes close to being a hysterical feminist tract. There is a vast display of scholarship and reference. In many respects Margaret Kelleher cannot be blamed for her inability to make the text cohere.

It is admirable that there is no evasion of her deep and serious subject. She is no metaphysical coward. So in the higher interests of valid polemics, it might be dangerous to dismiss the book on academic grounds since the subject matter is grave and in need of treatment. One hopes the book will be much read and discussed The main thesis centres on "women's resistance to demoralization and apathy .. in relation to the Irish 1840s famine". One of her various sources is the nineteenth-century philanthropist Sidney Godolphin Osborne: "Men and boys sink sooner under famine than the other sex." There is much evidence proving that women are tougher than men. Naturally this is not a gratuitous contest, especially with the experience of James Mahony, an artist for the Illustrated London News of 1847 who witnessed "a woman carrying in her arms the corpse of a fine child, and making the most distressing appeal to the passengers for aid to enable her to purchase a coffin and bury her dear little baby".

There is a proliferation of descriptions of famine deaths and of course there was a lot of death which realistically justifies many similar quotations. Most great famine novels are discussed, with some exceptions, such as Lever's The Eve of St Patrick. Well to the fore is Carleton's The Black Prophet which was prophetic about the "fearful visitation" of potato blight. There is exposure of Carletonesque ambivalence in the death of one of his characters, Margaret Murtagh, but otherwise he is given his laurels as a writer of diverse neutral viewpoint. Trollope's Castle Richmond gets off less lightly and is considered from the angle of "famine as female spectacle". Kelleher balances her study with other famine writers, Louise Field's Denis and Annie Keary's Castle Daly. These authors dealt with the real necessity of famine relief and also Maria Luddy, a historian who is effectively quoted throughout.

On into the twentieth century with wonderful use of Maud Gonne's play Dawn and a lecture which she delivered in Luxembourg in 1892: "Whole families, when they had eaten their last crust, and understood they had to die, looked once upon the sun and then closed up the doors of their cabins with stones, that no one might look upon their last agony". Yeats is decried for deriving his play The Countess Cathleen from Rosa Mulholland's The Hunger Death. And so to analysis of O'Flaherty's masterpiece *Famine*, Tom Murphy's play of the same name, Mairtin Ó Cadhain's *Gorta* and Banville's *Birchwood*.

The book makes an innovative change of direction near the end, examining Bengali famine literature with extracts from Bhabani Bhattacharya's So Many Hungers! which doesn't shirk dealing with the plight of women and girls forced into prostitution because of famine. The voyeuristic male is attacked here, as earlier on in the book when considering the Irish famine. Finally and somewhat neatly, President Mary Robinson's visit to Somalia in 1992 is seen through the President's diary A Voice for Somalia. The book finds a new theme near its close with interesting quotes from Fergal Keane's Season of Blood revealing media exploitation and the media's "famine fatigue" as a story loses mediagenic content. In the words of the journalist Ian Stephens, "Death by famine lacks drama".

—*Books Ireland* 1997

Printed in Great Britain
by Amazon